DAVID REMNICK

LENIN'S TOMB

THE LAST DAYS
OF THE
SOVIET EMPIRE

VINTAGE BOOKS

A DIVISION OF RANDOM HOUSE, INC.

NEW YORK

FIRST VINTAGE BOOKS EDITION, MAY 1994

Grateful acknowledgment is made to the following for permission to
reprint previously published material: Martin Secker & Warburg Ltd:
Thirty-two lines from "Requiem" from *You Will Hear Thunder* by Anna
Akhmatova, translated by D. M. Thomas. Copyright © 1976, 1979, 1985
by D. M. Thomas. Reprinted by permission.

Library of Congress Cataloging-in-Publication Data
Remnick, David.
Lenin's tomb: the last days of the Soviet Empire / David Remnick.
—1st Vintage Books ed.
p. cm.
Originally published: New York: Random House, 1993.
Includes bibliographical references and index.
ISBN 0-679-75125-4
1. Soviet Union—Politics and government—1985–1991.   I. Title.
[DK288.R46   1994]
947.085'4–dc20   93-42199
CIP

Book design by J. K. Lambert

Author photograph © Gasper Tringale

Manufactured in the United States of America

10   9   8   7   6   5   4   3   2

DAVID REMNICK

LENIN'S TOMB

David Remnick is a staff writer for *The New Yorker* and a frequent contributor to *The New York Review of Books* and other publications. He was a reporter for *The Washington Post* for ten years, including four years as Moscow correspondent. A graduate of Princeton University, he is a visiting fellow at the Council on Foreign Relations. Mr. Remnick lives in New York City with his wife and two sons.

Acclaim for

DAVID REMNICK'S

LENIN'S TOMB

"An eloquent and riveting oral history of an epochal moment of change."
—Michael Ignatieff, *Los Angeles Times*

"Remnick is an observer of great scope. . . . He writes with enormous ease, and the humor and honesty of a modern de Tocqueville."
—*Christian Science Monitor*

"A superbly reported account of the fall of the Soviet Empire."
—*U.S. News and World Report*

"Remnick has written what may be the definitive narrative of the last days of the Soviet Union. . . . [*Lenin's Tomb*] is a history that combines old-fashioned narrative of great events with the more fashionable approach of describing common lives. It succeeds smashingly." —*Birmingham News*

"Always vivid, often funny, sometimes moving." —*USA Today*

"David Remnick has written one hell of a book." —*Baltimore Sun*

"A riveting account of the unraveling of the Soviet Union . . . *Lenin's Tomb* . . . reads like a novel. Mr. Remnick develops with artistry and compassion a handful of characters who best reflect the themes of the waning years of Soviet rule." —*Atlanta Journal-Constitution*

"David Remnick has produced a prodigious and fascinating account of what it was like to witness the collapse of both an empire and its imperial history. . . . It is difficult to imagine anyone writing about the disintegration of the USSR more graphically, more intimately or more comprehensively."
—*Wisconsin State Journal*

"Remnick's gripping and valuable first reading of events is destined to achieve a permanent place in the literature of Russian history."—*Kansas City Star*

"*Lenin's Tomb* is touching, witty, and informative."
—*Raleigh News & Observer*

"Remnick has given us a book that is essential reading for anyone interested in the final years of the Soviet Union. It should not be missed."
—*Wichita Eagle*

to my parents
and to Esther

CONTENTS

PREFACE

Long before anyone had a reason to predict the decline and fall of the Soviet Union, Nadezhda Mandelstam filled her notebooks with the accents of hope. She was neither sentimental nor naive. She had seen her husband, the great poet Osip Mandelstam, swept off to the camps during the terror of the 1930s; she described in ruthlessly clear terms how the regime left its subjects in a permanent state of fear. The people of the Soviet Union had been made, as she put it, "slightly unbalanced mentally—not exactly ill, but not normal either." But Mandelstam, unlike so many scholars and politicians, saw the signs of the Soviet system's inherent weakness and believed in the resiliency of the people.

On August 20, 1991, a rainy, miserable afternoon, I walked among the crowds protecting the Russian parliament from a potential invasion by the leaders of a military coup. We all saw that day what so few could have predicted: Soviet citizens—workers, teachers, hustlers, children, mothers, grandparents, even soldiers—all standing up to a group of ignorant men who believed themselves yet another improved version of the Bolshevik regime and possessed of a power to freeze, even turn back, time. In their hurried calculations, the conspirators assumed "the masses" were too exhausted and indifferent to fight back. But tens of thousands of ordinary Muscovites were ready to die for democratic principles. It was said then and is said even now that the Russians know little or nothing of civil society. How strange, then, that so many were willing to give up their lives to defend it.

I do not usually have a great memory for the things I have read, but that afternoon of the coup, hours before it came clear that there would be no attack and the putsch would fail, I thought of a short passage, bracketed in black, in my paperback copy of Nadezhda Mandelstam's *Hope Against Hope:* "This terror could return, but it would mean sending several million people to the camps. If this were to happen now, they would all scream—and so would their families, friends and neighbors. This is something to be reckoned with." The leaders of the August coup had not reckoned with the development of their own people. They understood nothing. They were jailed for the miscalculation, and the struts of the old regime collapsed.

———

As I write, the euphoria of those August days is past and Russian democracy is a delicate thing. There are days when it seems that little has changed, that the fate of Russia hinges, once more, on the skills, inclinations, and heartbeat of one man. This time it is Boris Yeltsin: heroic during the coup, flexible, clever, but also, at times, reckless with language, careless with the bottle. No one knows what would happen should Yeltsin fall from power, the result of a stroke or an uprising of the hardline nationalists, neofacists, and nostalgic Communists who dominate parliament. As this book goes to press in April 1993, the power struggle between Yeltsin and parliament is unresolved and has underscored the lack of a clear and workable constitution, legal system, and system of authority. The institutions of this new society are embryonic, infinitely fragile.

In January 1993, Yeltsin's program of economic shock therapy has resulted in only fitful progress, much pain, and, everywhere, anxiety. Food and other supplies are in some places more plentiful, but prices are out of control. The inflation rate is beginning to look Latin American. The heads of the vast military plants show little interest in converting to a peacetime economy, and the absurd subsidies they receive make a mess of Russia's finances. A brash new class of young hustlers and even some honest businesspeople are thriving, but the old, the weak, and the poor are despondent. The crime rate is out of control. And everywhere there is a new demagogue—Communist, nationalist, or simply mad—ready to exploit the failures, vanities, and misfortunes of the elected government. The danger of the authoritarian temptation still lurks in Russia. So far, nearly all the potential successors to Yeltsin promise to be less inclined to radical economic reform and more likely to carry out an aggressive anti-Western foreign policy.

Elsewhere in the former Soviet Union, the situation is at least as worrisome. There are unlovely little wars in the Caucasus, coups d'état in Central Asia. Moldova, Latvia, Estonia, and Lithuania charge Russia with imperialism for leaving behind its troops. The Russians, for their part, complain that the leaders of the Baltic governments treat non-Balts as second-class citizens. Armenia is broke and on the edge of breakdown, Georgia is consumed in civil war. Despite a series of historic treaties with the United States, the unresolved conflicts over arms stockpiles between Russia, Ukraine, Belarus, and Kazakhstan trouble our sleep with dreams of what James Baker once called "Yugoslavia with nukes."

Despite it all, I am partial to Mandelstam's brand of hardheaded optimism. This book, after all, chronicles the last days of one of the cruelest regimes in human history. And having lived through those final days, having lived in Moscow and traveled throughout the republics of the last empire, I am convinced that for all the difficulties ahead, there will be no return to the past. In the West, we cannot afford to look away from this process. To refuse help will endanger Russia, the former Soviet Union, and the security of the globe.

It will take many books and records to understand the history of the Soviet Union and its final collapse. We are, after all, still debating the events of 1917. To write history takes time. When asked what he thought of the French Revolution, Zhou Enlai said, "It's too soon to tell." To understand the Gorbachev period will require a new library covering an immense range of subjects: U.S.-Soviet relations, economic history, the uprisings in the Baltic states, the Caucasus, Ukraine, and Central Asia, the "prehistory" of perestroika, the psychological and sociological effects of a long-standing totalitarian regime.

I went to Moscow in January 1988 as a reporter for *The Washington Post* and saw the revolution from that peculiar angle. Like a lot of reporters in Moscow, I was filing three and four hundred stories a year to editors who would certainly have taken more. Even then, in the midst of that feverish work, it seemed that the multiple events of the Gorbachev-Sakharov-Yeltsin era followed a certain logic, a pattern: once the regime eased up enough to permit a full-scale examination of the Soviet past, radical change was inevitable. Once the System showed itself for what it was and had been, it was doomed. I begin in Part I with that essential moment—the return of history in the Soviet Union—and then move on in Part II to the beginnings of democracy and in Part III to the confrontation between the old regime and the new political forces. Part IV is an attempt to describe, from multiple points of view, the August putsch—that most bizarre and climactic of episodes—and its aftermath. In Part V, we see the final attempt of the Communist Party to justify itself while, all around, a new country is being born. Throughout, I tell the story largely through the eyes of a few representative men and women, some well known, others not.

I am sure if Nadezhda Mandelstam were alive today she would not dwell long on celebration. She would be ruthlessly critical of the inequities and absurdities of politics in post-totalitarian Russia. She would warn of the problem of expecting an injured and isolated people to make a rapid transfer to a way of life that no longer promises cradle-to-grave paternalism. She would, despite her own love of Agatha Christie novels, warn against the new tide of junk culture—the sudden infatuation with Mexican soap operas and American sneakers. She would not ignore the difficulties, even disasters, ahead. But she would, I think, remain optimistic. Optimism is a belief in a gradual and painful rise from the wreckage of Communism, a confidence that the former subjects of the Soviet experiment are too historically experienced to return to dictatorship and isolation. Already there are signs all over Russia and the rest of the former Soviet Union of new generations of artists, teachers, businesspeople, even politicians on the rise. People "free of the old complexes," as Russians say. A day may even come soon when getting from one day to the next in Russia will no longer require the sort of miracles we witnessed in the last several years of the old regime. Perhaps one day Russia might even become somehow ordinary, a country of problems rather than catastrophes, a place that develops rather than explodes. That would be something to see.

PART I

BY RIGHT OF MEMORY

The struggle of man against power
is the struggle of memory against forgetting.

MILAN KUNDERA

CHAPTER 1

THE FOREST COUP

O n a dreary summer's day, Colonel Aleksandr Tretetsky of the Soviet Military Prosecutor's Office arrived at his latest work site: a series of mass graves in a birch forest twenty miles outside of the city of Kalinin. He and his assistants began the morning digging, searching the earth for artifacts of the totalitarian regime—bullet-shattered skulls, worm-eaten boots, scraps of Polish military uniforms.

They had heard the alarming news from Moscow on television and radio before coming to work that morning: Mikhail Gorbachev had "stepped down" for "reasons of health." The GKChP—the "State Committee for the State of Emergency"—had assumed power, promising stability and order. But what to make of it? Kalinin was several hours north of Moscow by train and a long way off the trail of rumor and information. And so like almost everyone else in the Soviet Union on the morning of August 19, 1991, Tretetsky set to work, an almost ordinary day.

The digging in the woods outside Kalinin was a merciless project. A half-century before, at Stalin's direct order, NKVD executioners slaughtered fifteen thousand Polish military officers and threw the bodies into rows of mass graves. The month-long operation in Kalinin, Katyn, and Starobelsk was part of Stalin's attempt to begin the domination of Poland. The young

officers had been among the best-educated men in Poland, and Stalin saw
them as a potential danger, as enemies-in-advance. For decades after, Moscow put the blame for the killings on the Nazis, saying the Germans had
carried out the massacres in 1941, not the NKVD in 1940. The Kremlin
propaganda machine sustained the fiction in speeches, diplomatic negotiations, and textbooks, weaving it into the vast fabric of ideology and official
history that sustained the regime and its empire. The Kremlin took history
so seriously that it created a massive bureaucracy to control it, to fabricate
its language and content, so that murderous and arbitrary purges became a
"triumph over enemies and foreign spies," the reigning tyrant a "Friend to
All Children, the Great Mountain Eagle." The regime created an empire that
was a vast room, its doors locked, its windows shuttered. All books and
newspapers allowed in the room carried the Official Version of Events, and
the radio and television blared the general line day and night. Those who
were loyal servants of the Official Version were rewarded and pronounced
"professors" and "journalists." In the Communist Party citadels of the
Marxist-Leninist Institute, the Central Committee, and the Higher Party
School, the priests of ideology swerved from the dogma at their peril. There
were secrets everywhere. The KGB was so keen to keep its secrets that it built
its vacation houses in the village of Mednoye near Kalinin, where the Polish
officers had been executed and buried in mass graves, the better to keep watch
over the bones.

But now something had changed—changed radically. After some initial
hesitation at the beginning of his time in power, Gorbachev had decreed that
the time had come to fill in the "blank spots" of history. There could be no
more "rose-colored glasses," he said. At first, his rhetoric was guarded. He
spoke of "thousands" instead of tens of millions of victims. He did not dare
criticize Lenin, the demigod of the state. But despite Gorbachev's hesitation,
the return of historical memory would be his most important decision, one
that preceded all others, for without a full and ruthless assessment of the
past—an admission of murder, repression, and bankruptcy—real change,
much less democratic revolution, was impossible. The return of history to
personal, intellectual, and political life was the start of the great reform of the
twentieth century and, whether Gorbachev liked it or not, the collapse of the
last empire on earth.

For decades, the massacres at Kalinin, Starobelsk, and Katyn had been a
symbol for the Poles of Moscow's cruelty and imperial grip. For a Pole
merely to hint that the Soviet Union was responsible for the massacres was
a radical, even suicidal act, for it made clear the speaker's point of view: the
"friendship of peoples," the relationship between Moscow and Warsaw, was
one based on violence, an occupier's reign over its satellite. Even Gorbachev

knew that to admit the massacres would be to undermine the Polish Communists. But by 1990, with Solidarity in power, Gorbachev saw little to lose. While General Wojciech Jaruzelski was visiting Moscow, Gorbachev finally conceded Moscow's guilt and turned over to the Polish government a huge packet of files on the massacres at Katyn, Starobelsk, and Kalinin.

Soon after the Kremlin's admission of guilt, the excavations began. Working with Soviet army soldiers and Polish volunteers, Colonel Tretetsky started work in Mednoye on August 15, 1991. Tretetsky, a career officer in his mid-forties with a thin mustache and sunken cheeks, had spent several months uncovering graves in Starobelsk. With every new grave, he felt himself more deceived. He had believed deeply in Communism and the Soviet Union. He served first in the navy and then, after studying law in Ukraine, signed on in the military for life. He served nearly four years in East Germany and even volunteered to be sent to Czechoslovakia in 1968, the year the Soviet Union crushed the "Prague Spring."

"I was dumb," Tretetsky said. "I believed in it all. I would have given my life for the Motherland on a moment's notice."

He petitioned the military for a commission to Afghanistan and served there from 1987 to 1989. Tretetsky came home to Moscow only to get a bitter taste of the real history of the country he knew so little about. He was assigned to the Military Prosecutor's Office, which was conducting massive investigations into the rehabilitations of people who had been repressed over the past seventy years. Slowly, he began to learn about some of the ugliest incidents in Soviet history: the purges, the massacre of the Polish officers, the army's bloody attack on peaceful demonstrators in 1961 at Novocherkassk.

Put in charge of the excavations, first in Starobelsk and now in Mednoye, Tretetsky attacked his work with passion and precision. In Mednoye, he knew perfectly well where to dig and what to look for. He had already interrogated a local man, a retired officer of the secret police, who had helped carry out the orders from Moscow in 1940. Vladimir Tokaryev was blind and eighty-nine years old by the time history caught up with him, but his memory was clear. Sitting with Tretetsky and a videocamera, he described how in April 1940 his unit of the secret police shot Polish officers in the woods outside Kalinin—two hundred and fifty a night, for a month.

The executioners, Tokaryev said, "brought with them a whole suitcase full of German revolvers, the Walther 2 type. Our Soviet TT weapons were thought not to be reliable enough. They were liable to overheat with heavy use. . . . I was there the first night they did the shooting. Blokhin was the main killer, with about thirty others, mainly NKVD drivers and guards. My driver, Sukharev, for instance, was one of them. I remember Blokhin saying: 'Come on, let's go.' And then he put on his special uniform for the job: brown leather hat, brown leather apron, long brown leather gloves reaching above the elbows. They were his terrible trademark. I was face to face with a true executioner.

"They took the Poles along the corridor one by one, turned left, and took them into the Red Corner, the rest room for the prison staff. Each man was asked his surname, first name, and place of birth—just enough to identify him. Then he was taken to the room next door, which was soundproofed, and shot in the back of the head. Nothing was read to them, no decision of any court or special commission.

"There were three hundred shot that first night. I remember Sukharev, my driver, boasting about what a hard night's work it had been. But it was too many, because it was light by the time they had finished and they had a rule that everything must be done in the darkness. So they reduced the number to two hundred and fifty a night. How many nights did it last? Work it out for yourself: six thousand men at two hundred and fifty a night. Allowing for holidays, that makes about a month, the whole of April 1940.

"I took no part in the killings. I never went into the execution room. But I was obliged to help them by putting my men at their disposal. I remember a few individual Poles. For instance, a young man. I asked him his age. He smiled like a young boy. I asked him how long he had been in the frontier police. He counted on his fingers. Six months. What had he done there? He had been a telephone operator.

"Blokhin made sure that everyone in the execution team got a supply of vodka after each night's work. Every evening he brought it into the prison in boxes. They drank nothing before the shooting or during the shooting, but afterward they all had a few glasses before going home to bed.

"I asked Blokhin and the other two: 'Won't it take a lot of men to dig six thousand graves?' They laughed at me. Blokhin said that he had brought a bulldozer from Moscow and two NKVD men to work it. So the dead Poles were taken out through the far door of the execution room, loaded onto covered trucks, and taken to the burial place. [The site] was chosen by Blokhin himself. It was near where the NKVD officers had their country homes, near my own dacha, near the village of Mednoye, about twenty miles from Kalinin. The ditches they dug were between eight and ten meters long, each one being enough to hold two hundred and fifty bodies. When it was all over, the three men from Moscow organized a big banquet to celebrate. They kept pestering me, insisting that I should attend. But I refused."

On and on the blind man droned, pointing his finger at "the others," denying the importance of his own role, no less a cruel, bland beast than Eichmann in Jerusalem. But Tokaryev was hardly the issue now. Nor were the executioners themselves. Blokhin and three of the others had long ago gone mad and committed suicide. The point was that nearly everywhere they went, historians, prosecutors, archivists, and journalists discovered that the legacy of Soviet power was at least as tragic as everything they had heard from "forbidden voices": Solzhenitsyn's *The Gulag Archipelago,* Varlam Shalamov's *Kolyma Tales.* Now no book, no voice, was forbidden. To regain the past, to see plain the nightmares of seventy years, was a nearly unbearable shock. As the return of history accelerated, television routinely showed documentary films about the slaughter of the Romanovs, the forced collectivization of the countryside, the purge trials. The monthly literary journals, the weeklies, and even the daily newspapers were crammed with the latest historical damage reports: how many shot and imprisoned; how many churches, mosques, and synagogues destroyed; how much plunder and waste. Under this avalanche of remembering, people protested weariness, even boredom, after a while. But, really, it was the pain of remembering, the shock of recognition, that persecuted them. "Imagine being an adult and nearly all the truth you know about the world around you and outside your own country has to be absorbed in a matter of a year or two or three," the philosopher Grigori Pomerants told me. "The entire country is still in a state of mass disorientation."

The men of the Communist Party, the leaders of the KGB and the military and the millions of provincial functionaries who had grown up on a falsified history, could not bear the truth. Not because they didn't believe it. They knew the facts of the past better than anyone else. But the truth challenged their existence, their comfort and privileges. Their right to a decent office, a cut of meat, the month of vacation in the Crimea—it all depended on a colossal social deception, on the forced ignorance of 280 million people. Yegor Ligachev, a conservative figure in the Politburo until his forced retirement in 1990, told me ruefully that when history was taken out of the hands of the Communist Party, when scholars, journalists, and witnesses began publishing and broadcasting their own version of the past, "it created a gloomy atmosphere in the country. It affected the emotions of the people, their mood, their work efficiency. From morning to night, everything negative from the past is being dumped on them. Patriotic topics have been squeezed out, shunted aside. People are longing for something positive, something shining, and yet our own cultural figures have published more lies and anti-Soviet things than our Western enemies ever did in the last seventy years combined."

When history was no longer an instrument of the Party, the Party was doomed to failure. For history proved precisely that: the Party was rotten at its core. The ministers, generals, and apparatchiks who organized the August coup of 1991 met secretly at KGB safe houses outside Moscow many times to discuss the ruin of their state. They talked of the need for order, the need, somehow, to reverse the decline of the Party. They were so deluded about their own country that they even believed they could put a halt to the return of history. They would shut it down with a decree and a couple of tank divisions. The excavations at Mednoye and the other sites of the Polish massacre were no exception. The putschists would try to undermine the work as well as they could. Long before the coup, Valery Boldin, Gorbachev's chief of staff and one of the key plotters in the August coup, tried to control the damage by secretly transferring many key documents on the case from Division Six of the Central Committee archives to the "presidential archive," which he controlled. But that small step did very little. Boldin and the rest of the plotters were now prepared to eliminate everything that aggrieved them. They would end the return of history. They would turn back time. Once more, fear would be the essence of the state.

On the day of the putsch, Tretetsky's men, both the Soviets and the Poles, tried to keep their minds on their work. They dug up old graves and washed the bones and skull fragments in battered bowls. But as the news of the coup reached them, piece by piece, it became harder to concentrate. The soldiers under Tretetsky even heard that the troops deployed on the streets of Moscow were from their own division: the Kantemirovskaya Division. They turned on a television in one of the tents near the work site and saw familiar faces, friends sitting on armored personnel carriers near the Kremlin, outside the Russian parliament, and on the main streets of the capital.

"The weather was wretched," Tretetsky remembered. "It rained nearly all the time, and so to dry the fragments of uniforms, we had to put them in tents, fire up a furnace, and keep the tent open to circulate the air." The team worked until late in the afternoon, when Tretetsky told them all, "The work for today is over." He told them nothing more.

All day long, Tretetsky had been getting calls from the headquarters of the KGB command in Kalinin. The KGB general there, Viktor Lakontsev, warned Tretetsky that the excavation "was no longer necessary," that work should stop and that he must come immediately to headquarters. Tretetsky refused, saying work would go on as planned. He said he would come to KGB headquarters only at the end of the working day. Despite his brave front, Tretetsky was frightened. "I knew there was trouble," he said.

That evening Tretetsky was driven under KGB guard to Lakontsev's office in Kalinin.

The work must stop, Lakontsev insisted. "If it does not," he said, "we cannot guarantee your safety or the safety of the Polish workers."

Tretetsky had to laugh. Throughout his work in Starobelsk and Mednoye there had always been KGB men at the sites—"observers," they called themselves. "Our United Nations observers," the workers called them.

Tretetsky would not back down. "Over my dead body," he thought to himself. To Lakontsev, he put the refusal more subtly. He told the KGB general that if it was a question of the Poles, he would take responsibility for their safety. The Poles could live together in the tents with the Soviet army troops instead of in the city.

"The investigation cannot stop," Tretetsky said. "What would I tell the Poles? I need to talk to my own chief. This is not an easy question." All the same, Tretetsky thought, "Lakontsev is a big boss, and who am I?"

When he returned to his camp, Tretetsky called Moscow and was told that there had been no stop-work order. He was relieved. Exhausted, he went to sleep in his tent. But not long after, the commander of the army troops woke him saying that an order had come from Moscow: the soldiers had to return to the Kantemirovskaya base in the town of Naro-Fominsk outside Moscow.

"Listen, Viktor," Tretetsky told the commander, "this is an oral order, isn't it?"

"That's right."

"And to bring your men here, you had a written order."

"Yes, I did."

"So why should you obey?"

The troops stayed where they were. The KGB had tried to trick Tretetsky and they had failed. There never had been an order from the Military Prosecutor's Office in Moscow.

At nine the next morning, Tretetsky went before the men and said, "The work goes on. Let's begin now. Everyone is to work intensively, with enthusiasm. And that's it!"

The KGB sabotaged the tractor the men had been using for the excavation. But by now Tretetsky had connections with people in the area, and a collective farm lent him one of its tractors. The Polish workers were especially grateful and pounded Tretetsky on the back. For two more days, the Soviets and the Poles worked at the graves and listened to the radio reports coming from Moscow. Slowly, the news improved. When the men heard that the coup was on the verge of collapse, they seemed to work even harder. Finally, on the morning of August 21, after the plot had failed and troops had returned in relief and triumph from Moscow to their bases, Tretetsky went before his men. He would not live the lie any longer. He refused to return to the past, except to study its bones.

"The criminal investigation ordered by the president of the Union of Soviet Socialist Republics, Mikhail Sergeyevich Gorbachev, goes on!" he cried out. Then the colonel gave the order and his men began to dig.

CHAPTER 2

A STALINIST CHILDHOOD

Not long after my wife, Esther, and I moved to Moscow in January 1988, I was having tea and cake with Flora and Misha Litvinov at their apartment on the Frunzenskaya Embankment, where many families of Communist Party officials, active and retired, lived. The Litvinovs were a dazzling couple in their seventies, dazzling in their kindnesses and the unassuming way they seemed to know everyone and everything going on in Moscow. Misha was the quieter of the two. His reserve, I supposed, was the result of a lifetime sandwiched between a father, Maksim, who served in Stalin's inner court as foreign minister and a son, Pavel, who helped strike one of the first blows against the regime as a dissident. Surrounded by history and its actors, Misha made an art of listening. He listened patiently, with nearly imperceptible amusement. There was not much that would surprise a man whose father slept with a Browning automatic under his pillow in case of attack and a son who flipped the bird to the men of the Politburo. In a room of friends or strangers, however, it was Flora who took the lead, provided the family positions, made the polite inquiry.

She asked what I'd be writing about in Moscow.

"I'm looking for Kaganovich," I said.

Flora's face tightened. She and Misha had known more than one American reporter in the past, and they had undoubtedly heard more reasonable journalistic ambitions: a mastery of arms control, human rights, Kremlin politics. Strange boy, she must have thought, but she was too kind to say so.

At the time, Lazar Moiseyevich Kaganovich was in his mid-nineties and the last living member of Stalin's inner circle. As the people's commissar, he was once as close to Stalin as Goering was to Hitler. He helped direct the collectivization program of the 1920s and early 1930s, a brutal campaign that annihilated the peasantry and left the villages of Ukraine strewn with an endless field of human husks. As the leader of the Moscow Party organization, Kaganovich built the city subway system and, briefly, had it named for himself. He was responsible as well for the destruction of dozens of churches and synagogues. He dynamited Christ the Savior, a magnificent cathedral in one of the oldest quarters of Moscow. It was said at the time that Stalin could see the cathedral belltower from his window and wanted it eliminated.

Did Kaganovich still believe? I wanted to know. Did he feel any guilt, any shame? And what did he think of Gorbachev, the current general secretary? But that wasn't it, really. Mostly I wanted just to sit in the same room with Kaganovich, to see what an evil man looked like, to know what he did, what books he kept around.

Misha listened, but with a certain ethereal inattention. As I talked, he was twisting and folding a napkin into . . . something. He had lately become a master of origami, the Japanese art of paper folding. He had filled an entire room with his paper menagerie: octagons, tetrahedrons, storks, bugs.

"You know," he said, mashing out a crease with the butt of his palm, "Kaganovich lives downstairs."

Downstairs? I already knew that he lived on the Embankment, probably in one of the better buildings still stocked with the descendants of Old Bolsheviks and the Stalinist guard. But here, downstairs? In old photographs, Kaganovich was a huge man with a Prussian mustache and onyx eyes. In retirement, he had been the champion of dominoes in the Frunzenskaya Embankment neighborhood. He would play all comers in the courtyards. Once, when Brezhnev was still in power, Kaganovich made a call to the local Party committee and demanded that his courtyard be equipped with spot-lights so he could play dominoes on summer nights. He still had the right to use the plush Kremlin hospitals—the "fourth administration"—and he was very much alive. Here, downstairs.

"It's apartment 384," Misha said. "We used to see him once in a while in the elevator or in the courtyard. The thing is, we never see him anymore. He never goes out, they say. He never answers the door. Maybe he has a nurse. I'm not sure he can walk. He is completely blind."

With that, Misha took a pair of scissors and made the slightest incision in his napkin. Slowly, he unfolded the paper. A turkey ruffled its feathers in his palm.

———

Afternoons in Moscow, when I had a spare hour or two, I would visit Misha and Flora's building—50 Frunzenskaya Embankment, entrance 9—looking for Kaganovich. Over many months, I rang the bell at apartment 384 hundreds of times, sometimes for a half hour or more. I slipped notes under the door and into his mailbox. I rang and knocked and listened, my ear pressed against the door. Sometimes I could hear a kind of mumbling inside, other times a shuffling sound, slippers padding along the floor.

Kaganovich's daughter, Maya, an old woman herself, came evenings to check on her father and prepare his dinner. She would not talk to me, and whenever I called her at home she passed the phone to someone else. "Look, he is too old to see anyone," one relative told me. "We don't want people coming here and bothering him with unpleasant questions about the past. It might upset him."

I'd hang around in the courtyard mostly talking to people about Kaganovich. "He doesn't let anyone near him," one of the neighbors, a young engineer, told me as we sat on one of the benches in the courtyard. "I think he's afraid of the world now. One of these days, he'll just die, and he'll be lucky if they mention his name in *Pravda*. The bastard once had the power to kill every one of us."

Another day in the courtyard, one of Kaganovich's oldest neighbors, a woman with a Byelorussian accent and eyes as blue as cornflowers, was taking her daily walk. Children were jumping rope and playing hopscotch, and the old men and women watched them. "Not long ago," she said, "you'd see Kaganovich out here all day, playing dominoes or sitting off by himself with his daughter. Everyone knew who he was, what he'd done under Stalin. There are a lot of people in these buildings along the embankment who were big shots in the Party, but nobody like Kaganovich, no one still alive. Me, I always stayed away from him. Where I come from they have a saying: 'The farther away you keep from the czar, the longer you stay alive.' "

I had Kaganovich's phone number—242-6751—but he never answered. A Russian journalist who had spent years trying to talk to Kaganovich later explained to me there was a code: dial the number, let it ring twice, hang up, and dial again. I tried, and an old man came on the line.

"Hello?"

"Hello, Lazar Moiseyevich?"

"Yes?"

"Lazar Moiseyevich, my name is Remnick. I am a reporter for an American newspaper, *The Washington Post,* and I would like to come visit you, if possible."

"It is not necessary."

"I've heard your health is not very good, but I—"

"It is not necessary. I feel awful. I can't see anything. I feel awful."

"Perhaps, on a day you are feeling a bit better, we could—"

"I always feel awful. No interviews. I don't do interviews. Why should I do interviews?"

His voice, weak at first, was beginning to pick up a little, as if just the use of it was a kind of exercise.

"Lazar Moiseyevich—"

"I said no interviews. That's it!"

"Well—"

The line went dead. In the months ahead, he must have changed the code. The old one no longer worked, and playing with new codes of the same sort didn't work either. Doorstepping was again the only hope. Reporting is often foolish work, but there was something especially shaming about knocking endlessly on a tyrant's door. It raised insane questions of etiquette, such as what the rules of harassment are where a mass murderer is concerned. One afternoon I went up the elevator to see Flora, and with a motherly smile she listened to my complaints about the closed door downstairs.

"Well, what if he does open it, what would you learn?" Flora said. "Do you think he'd break down and apologize?"

"Well, not exactly."

"He's an old man," she said. "What does it matter?"

———

Then Flora told me a story.

On a winter's night in the time of Stalin—1951 or 1952—Flora opened the door to her son's room and bent low to kiss him good night. Pavel rolled toward her, the bedclothes rustling. In the dark, there was a shine to his face. He'd been crying, and his breathing had a wheezy jump to it. Pavel was a big child, self-assured and smart, but now it seemed that he was lost, scared even to speak.

"What's wrong?" Flora said. "What is it?"

Pavel was quiet a long time and turned away, turned into himself somehow.

"Please, tell me. What's wrong?"

"They said I can't tell you," the boy said. "I gave my word."

"Why not?"

"It's a secret."

"A secret?"

"Yes," he said. "A secret."

"You can tell me," Flora said. "It's right that you keep your word, but you can always tell your parents everything."

Pavel's grandfather Maksim Litvinov was Stalin's foreign minister in the first years of the regime. He'd died just a few months before, but the family still lived, by the standards of the time, in privileged circumstances. Their legacy included an apartment in the House on the Embankment, a magnificent outpost for the Communist Party elite overlooking the Moscow River with huge rooms and special cafeterias and theaters. For the families of the elite there were foreign books, competent doctors, marmalade for the toast, tomatoes in wintertime. The Litvinovs even had their own cleaning woman—a lieutenant in the KGB. In the summer they spent much of their time at a dacha in the town of Khimki outside Moscow. Surrounded by birches and pines, the house had originally been built for Stalin's family. Many of Pavel's schoolmates were the sons and daughters of the Communist Party hierarchy, or what was left of it after the first wave of purges. At school, they all joined the Timur Society, a band of zealous young patriots, the Bolshevik Cub Scouts.

"Tell me. Please," Flora said once more to her son. "What is it? What could be so secret?"

Pavel was frightened. He had sworn his silence to the Timur Society, and he knew enough to be afraid. But, still, he could not deny his mother.

There was a new hunt on for "enemies of the people," he said. One of his best friends had told him so. Flora recognized the boy's name. He was the son of an officer in the KGB.

"He said there can be enemies of the people anywhere," Pavel went on. "Anywhere. Even in our own homes!"

Flora felt a rage gather inside her. She knew the adults who supervised these groups were doing nothing less than training children to work as informers, as traitors against their own families. She was terrified—for her son most of all—but not completely surprised. These were children, after all, who were taught to revere Pavlik Morozov, the twelve-year-old Young Pioneer who was made a national hero and icon for all Soviet children when he served his collective by ratting on his own father for trying to hide grain from the police. These were children raised in schools designed according to the "socialist family" theories of Anton Makarenko, an ideology officer of the KGB. Makarenko insisted that children learn the supremacy of the collective over the individual, the political unit over the family. The schools, he said, must employ an iron discipline modeled on that of the Red Army and Siberian labor camps.

Now the story was pouring out of Pavel. He said that two strange men had told him that soon he would have a "special task." Flora knew pretty well what that meant. They wanted the boy to report on the family.

Stalin and his circle had always been wary of Maksim Litvinov and his odd family. Although Maksim had served the regime impeccably as foreign minister and as ambassador to the United States, he was nothing at all like the most loyal of Stalin's gray henchmen. He was a man of the world. He spoke foreign languages. He had foreign friends. Maksim had also married a foreigner, an eccentric Englishwoman named Ivy who wrote fiction, had heterosexual and lesbian affairs, and preached C. K. Ogden's gospel of Basic English, an 850-word system for learning the rudiments of the language. When her husband gave her George Bernard Shaw's *Intelligent Woman's Guide to Socialism* to read, she gave him volumes of Austen, Lawrence, and Trollope.

Especially after his forced removal from the Central Committee in 1941, Maksim Litvinov was possessed of a certain sympathy for the political interests of foreigners. In 1944, he told reporters that Stalin had imperial designs on Eastern Europe and wondered aloud why the West did not intervene. In an article for *Foreign Affairs* in 1977, the historian Vojtech Mastny described Litvinov as the "Cassandra in the Foreign Commissariat," a diplomat unafraid to complain about the "rigidity of the whole Soviet system." Stalin, of course, was listening. Khrushchev wrote in his memoirs that the secret police drew up an elaborate plan to "ambush" Litvinov while he was on the road to the dacha in Khimki. Litvinov, however, was a lucky man. For years he slept with his revolver close at hand, but in the end he escaped arrest. Miraculously, he died of old age. "They didn't get him," Ivy remarked to her daughter just after Maksim's death. The family and historians could only guess why. Stalin undoubtedly valued Litvinov's contacts in the West, and he may have thought the foul publicity abroad was not worth the execution.

But even after Litvinov died on December 31, 1951, his family still lived in fear of Stalin's whim, of a knock on the door. Pavel's parents, Misha and Flora, and his aunt Tanya were more subtle characters than Ivy, more attuned to the risks of their time and country. But they, too, behaved in a way that could have landed them in jail or in front of a firing squad. Misha was a celebrated young engineer at the Aviation Engines Institute and a self-made Hero of Soviet Recreation: a mountain climber, a jogger, a dabbler in game theory. Surely this was suspiciously eccentric behavior. Pavel's aunt Tanya was thrown out of an art institute for an "excessive interest" in "decadent Western art." At home, at least, they all spoke their minds. Once Pavel brought a book home from the library about the derring-do of Pavlik Morozov. He was entranced by the boy's great service to the Bolshevik state, his heroic betrayal of his father. Flora spun off into a rage. She tore out the pages and said that Pavel should never, never betray his parents. No child should, no matter what such foolish books said.

"Even if the parents are bad?" Pavel said.

"Yes. Even if they are bad."

Now Flora had to decide what to do about her boy and his "special task." She would not allow Pavel to become another Pavlik Morozov. In the morning, Flora put on her finest dress and went to the apartment of Pavel's friend, the son of the KGB man. She would try to bluff the officer, scare him into thinking that someone "on high" supported the Litvinov family. She tried to dress the part of a powerful Bolshevik matron and wore an elegant scarf and a pompous hat.

"You have no right to carry on negotiations with my son!" she told him. "You will stop at once!" She left immediately, still shaking with anger and a giddy sense of her own daring. Only a little later would she begin thinking about what she had risked.

In the next few weeks, Misha and Flora talked long about what they should do about their children. They decided they could no longer hold back as much as they had. It was not enough to tear up a book once in a while and then retreat again into a baffling silence. If they were to prevent Pavel and Nina from becoming the sort of young Stalinists that the schools were so eager to create, then they had to speak the truth whenever possible. They had to describe what had happened to so many of the parents and grandparents of Pavel's friends at school, how they had been thrown into the vans known as Black Marias and shipped off to camps in Kolyma, Vorkuta, and Kazakhstan, where they had vanished. They had to begin to impress upon their children that Stalin, the Mountain Eagle, was a lowly beast. Pavel must learn somehow to think outside of a system that engulfed him all day long.

Flora and Misha could not afford to be too direct too often. Such were the times and the dangers. Nor could they compete very well with the immensity of the Stalin cult in all its forms: the parades celebrating Stalin as a god on earth, the newspapers describing his heroic deeds, the radio addresses, the history books written by the Kremlin ideologists, the rallies and paramilitary drills of the Young Pioneers. Pavel had learned to love Stalin the way other children in other places learn to love God. Stalin was a kindly deity, omniscient, a gentle father. He rarely appeared in public. Instead his image was painted on banners, zeppelins, billboards, and icons. His words filled the schoolbooks, the newspapers, the airwaves. "It's not easy to compete with that," Flora thought. "Perhaps it is impossible."

On the day Stalin died, in March 1953, Pavel was thirteen years old and inconsolable. He cried for days. In the schoolyard, he got into fights with the children who failed to mourn Stalin as deeply as he did. At home, he was furious when he discovered his parents and their friends laughing and joking about Comrade Stalin. He saw them in the kitchen, not mourning but celebrating. Pavel reddened, stormed out of the kitchen, and went off to bed, angry and confused.

It was not easy for any of the Litvinovs in those years after Stalin's death. Misha and Flora were young parents, and they were often at a loss in dealing with Pavel. He struggled in school. He married at seventeen and quickly divorced. He drank a bit, played in marathon card games, and gambled on the horses at the Hippodrome. "The horses were an obsession with him," Flora said. "We were scared that Pavel would end his life a broken-down gambler."

But Pavel was growing up, and he was in no way immune to the "thaw," the wave of anti-Stalinist sentiment, history, and ideology encouraged by Khrushchev in the middle and late 1950s. Hundreds of thousands of prisoners returned home from the labor camps, and all of them had stories to tell. The Litvinovs knew many intellectuals who had been in the camps: writers, artists, scientists, even Party officials. It was a time of revelation for Pavel. He sat at the kitchen table and heard for the first time the real history of the years under Stalin. One of his parents' closest friends, a physicist named Mikhail Levin, came home from prison in 1955 and described the conditions there, the senseless deaths of countless innocents. "It was the experience of waking up after years and years of sleep," Pavel would say a long time after. "All the fantasies of childhood and Stalin were suddenly painful and ridiculous."

In the early 1960s, Pavel got a job teaching physics at the Lomonosov Institute and eventually became friendly with a group of intellectuals who monitored the first celebrated dissident trial—the trial of the "anti-Soviet" writers Andrei Sinyavsky and Yuli Daniel. Among the older writers and scientists, Pavel was a kind of pet: a charming young man of intelligence and curious pedigree. He immersed himself in this new world, reading the underground manuscripts known as samizdat, taking part in the endless kitchen-table discussions that were the center of all intellectual life. Pavel read Solzhenitsyn, the camp stories of Varlam Shalamov, Robert Conquest's *The Great Terror*. He helped draft letters in support of political prisoners and released them, at great peril to himself, to Western journalists. He also married into one of the best-known intellectual families of Moscow. He married Maya, the daughter of the literary scholars Lev Kopelev and Raisa Orlova. Kopelev, who had been one of Solzhenitsyn's cellmates and the model for one of the characters in his novel *The First Circle*, was also a model for Pavel Litvinov. Kopelev had grown up a committed Communist, a true believer, and then "got an education." Kopelev's life, for Pavel, was living proof of a man's ability to see and think clearly, to act honestly, even in the conditions of a nightmare.

———

On August 21, 1968, Pavel and six of his friends reacted with horror to the shortwave reports coming out of Czechoslovakia. For months they had been listening for every detail of the Prague Spring, cheering on Alexander Dubček's attempt to create a "socialism with a human face." They waited to see how Khrushchev's conqueror and successor, Leonid Brezhnev, would deal with the rebellion of a satellite state. Would he show the same ruthlessness Khrushchev showed Hungary in 1956, or would there be a new sense of tolerance? Now the answer was clear. The voice on the underground Czechoslovak station was brittle and choked: "Russian brothers, go away, we have not asked you to come," the voice said. Pavel's close friend among the early dissidents, Larisa Bogoraz, was crushed. Her husband, Anatoly Marchenko, was in jail for his political activities, and now she saw that the regime itself was prepared to stamp out large-scale dissidence with soldiers and tanks.

"We need a bold act, a movement," she thought. "We need it now."

Pavel, Bogoraz, and five others met to talk it through. They planned a brief noontime demonstration for August 25 against the invasion of Czechoslovakia. They knew well the consequences for such an "anti-Soviet" activity: a prison term, internal exile, or a long stay in a psychiatric hospital. They prepared themselves for nothing less than that. Pavel began to gather his possessions and give his books away to friends. His fate was inescapable.

On the night before the demonstration, Pavel went to the Kopelevs' apartment for a party where the famous bard Aleksandr Galich was singing. The mood was funereal, and the vodka did nothing to lighten it. The Prague invasion was surely the end of the "thaw" and all hopes of a "socialism with a human face"; Brezhnev had begun a movement of blatantly neo-Stalinist politics. For all its hesitations and half-measures, the Khrushchev era would soon seem like a paradise lost. The invasion, the novelist Vasily Aksyonov said, "was a nervous breakdown for the whole generation." At the party, they spoke of their anger, how they were ashamed before the Czechs, the Hungarians, and the Poles—before the entire world—to be a Soviet citizen. They were not citizens at all, they felt; they were subjects.

Then Galich began to sing a song of the Decembrists, the rebels during the reign of Nicholas I:

Can you come to the square?
Dare you come to the square
When that hour strikes?

Pavel felt Galich's eyes on him as he sang. The double meaning of the lyrics, their reference to the dissent of another century and the clarion call to a new generation—it was lost on no one, least of all on Pavel. When Galich put down his guitar, Pavel was tempted to announce the plans for the demonstration, but he decided against it. He was afraid that the older people in the room would feel compelled to come. For them, years in internal exile or prison could mean death.

The next day, at a few minutes before noon, Pavel, Larisa Bogoraz, and their friends gathered at Lobnoye Mesto, the spot on Red Square where the czar's executioners once chopped off the heads of heretics against the state and the church. At the sound of the noon bell on Spassky Tower, they unfurled a series of banners. In Czech: "Long Live a Free and Independent Czechoslovakia." In Russian: "Free Dubček" and "Hands off Czechoslovakia" and "Shame on the Invaders." The poet Natalya Gorbanevskaya brought her three-month-old son to the square. When the others showed their signs, she reached into the baby carriage and pulled out from under her sleeping son the flag of Czechoslovakia.

The demonstration would not have lasted long under any circumstances. KGB men had followed Litvinov and the others to the Kremlin. But a special contingent of KGB officers was also stationed on Red Square that day. They were there waiting for the end of a meeting inside the Kremlin between Brezhnev and the leaders of the Prague Spring, who had been brought to Moscow in handcuffs on the night of the invasion. When the officers saw the banners, the guards pounced on the demonstrators, shouting, "These are all dirty Jews!" and "Beat the anti-Soviets!" Pavel's face was badly bruised, and the art critic Viktor Fainberg lost a few teeth. The officers packed the protesters into unmarked cars and headed for the police station.

After a few moments, the square was quiet once more. The summer tourists went back to watching the changing of the guard at the Lenin Mausoleum. They gaped at the candy-striped whirl of St. Basil's Cathedral. The old women peddled vanilla ice-cream bars and the old men sold snapshots to the visiting comrades from Sofia, Budapest, and Hanoi. Suddenly, guards blew their whistles and ordered people to clear the lane coming out of the Spassky Gate from the Kremlin. A line of official black cars drove through at terrific speed. Then the guards blew another signal. The coast was clear. No one

knew it then, but one of the men in the caravan was probably Alexander
Dubček, the leader of the Prague Spring and now a prisoner of Moscow.

"It would have been wonderful if Dubček and the others had seen the
demonstration of support for what they had been doing. They didn't,"
Andrei Sakharov told me later. "But most important was that somewhere in
this country there were some people who were willing to uphold its dignity."

The trial of the Red Square protesters, of course, was a sham, a totalitarian
theater piece. On October 11, 1968, Pavel was given the chance for a last
statement before the sentencing:

"I will not take your time by going into legal details; the attorneys have
done this. Our innocence of the charges is self-evident, and I do not consider
myself guilty. At the same time, that the verdict against me will be 'guilty' is
just as evident to me. I knew this beforehand when I made up my mind to
go to Red Square. Nothing has shaken these convictions, because I was
positive that the employees of the KGB would stage a provocation against
me. I know that what happened to me is the result of provocation.

"I knew that from the person that followed me. I read my verdict in his
eyes when he followed me to the metro. The man who beat me up in Red
Square was one I had seen many times before. Nevertheless, I went out into
Red Square. I shall not speak of my motives. There was never any question
for me whether I should go to Red Square or not. As a Soviet citizen, I
deemed it necessary to voice my disagreement with the action of my government, which filled me with indignation. . . .

" 'You fool,' said the policeman, 'if you had kept your mouth shut, you
could have lived peacefully.' He had no doubt that I was doomed to lose my
liberty. Well, perhaps he is right, and I am a fool. . . .

"Who is to judge what is in the interest of socialism and what is not?
Perhaps the prosecutor, who spoke with admiration, almost with tenderness,
of those who beat us up and insulted us. . . . This is what I find menacing.
Evidently, it is such people who are supposed to know what is socialism and
what is counterrevolution. This is what I find terrible, and that is why I went
to Red Square. This is what I have fought against and what I shall continue
to fight against for the rest of my life."

No one escaped punishment. Pavel Litvinov was sentenced to five years in
internal exile. He was sent to live in a remote village in Siberia—not far from
where the rebel Decembrists had been imprisoned more than a century
before.

After he returned home to Moscow, Pavel saw that he faced an unavoidable choice: jail or exile abroad. If he continued his human rights work—and
he could not do otherwise—he would be sentenced this time to a prison
camp, a far more severe fate than he had known in Siberia. An application

for emigration, a KGB officer suggested to him, would likely meet with a "positive response." Pavel said his farewells to his friends and family at a bleak party in 1973.

"I thought that when I left the country it was forever and that I would never see my parents again," Pavel said. "This was a typical experience for many people. You left, and for you the people you were leaving behind were as good as dead. They were alive, but you lost them the way you lose people when they die."

———

Pavel and Maya Litvinov began a new life in the United States. Pavel found a job teaching at the Hackley School, a small private school in Tarrytown, New York. They traveled, they met new friends. But for years they lived in a painful limbo. Pavel Litvinov had gone through a transformation, from obedience to independence, that had cost him his family, his home. Most of those he had left behind did not have the means or the chance to win their independence. The Soviet Union was no longer what it was under Stalin. But even with the prison camps in ruins, the system survived. The fear remained, and no one was free.

In nearly four years of living and traveling in what was once the Soviet Union, I often found myself wandering accidentally into old prison camps. During the first strikes in the Siberian coalfields in 1989, some miners in the Siberian city of Kemerovo told me to look over a fence and into a field—that low set of buildings to the left of the cows. Barracks. In a working prison outside the city of Perm in the Urals, I had tea and cookies with the commandant. He had buried a few dissidents in his time and now he was thinking about his pension. At one time the entire country was part of the camp system—the gulag archipelago, as Solzhenitsyn called it—and you did not have to travel far from home to see it. One evening I was drinking tea and visiting an old man in an apartment house on Leninsky Prospekt just down the street from where I lived in Moscow.

"I've always felt honored to live here," the man said.

The apartment was just one room, and the heat was off and the plumbing was rotting.

Why? What honor can there be in living here? I asked him.

"Solzhenitsyn helped build this dump," he said, his gold incisors flashing. "He was on the prisoners' crew when they put this place up."

At every one of these meetings, it was not hard for me to feel at once connected to the place, and lucky to have escaped it. Both my grandfathers, Alex and Ben, were born around the same time and in the same sort of place. They lived in muddy villages around the turn of the century: Alex outside

Vilna (now Vilnius), Ben outside Kiev. Neither village, so far as I have been able to determine, still exists. Neither of my grandfathers knew much, or wanted to know much, of his boyhood in the Russian empire. They were bewildered in old age by the craze for "roots." There was no nostalgia in them. They were lucky to have escaped. Upon hearing the rumors of pogroms they fled Russia on foot, on horseback, on wagon, and finally on a ship. They came to Castle Garden and Ellis Island. Alex sold "notions" in New York: girdle snaps, nylons, hairpins at a corner store on Prince Street and Broadway. Ben worked as a salesman in clothing stores in Paterson, New Jersey. When I began learning Russian in high school, my grandfathers smiled with curiosity and let it go at that. If they knew seven or eight words of Russian, it was a lot. For them, Russia was a burning house they had fled in the middle of the night. Just before I left for Russia, I flew to Miami Beach. Ben had managed to trade in his house in Paterson for a small room with a view of the Atlantic Ocean and an ambulance in the basement garage. He was one hundred years old. When I told him I was planning to live in Moscow for three or four years, he said, "You must be crazy. We almost got killed going out and you, meshuggah, you want to go back in."

My wife's family was even more suspicious of our going to Moscow. And with good reason. They were less successful at escape. Esther's grandfather Simon was a renowned rabbi, born in Byelorussia. After taking a pulpit in Poland, he married Nechama, the descendant of seven generations of rabbis. Robinson was her maiden name: son of rabbis. Eventually he moved back to Byelorussia, where he was both a rabbi and a teacher of philosophy in the local gymnasium. In 1939, an officer of the NKVD secret police came through the town of Diesna looking for Simon. The townspeople and congregants refused to give him up. But when Simon found out about the agent, he sought him out and invited him to his home. When the agent arrived at the door, he said something strange. "If you don't mind," he said to the terrified family, "I'd like to pray with you first."

When they were finished praying, it became clear that the NKVD man was a kind of double agent, or at least an agent with a hint of mercy. He told Simon that the police were after him. "You must leave," he said. "Leave now with just the clothes on your back."

Simon fled to independent Lithuania, and his wife and children soon followed. But in June 1940, just days after the Soviet occupation of Lithuania, he was arrested and jailed for six months in Vilna. Then he was deported to a labor camp in the town of Sukhobezvodnoye—meaning "Dry, Without Water"—in the Urals. He was never heard from again.

As relatives of an "enemy of the people," Nechama and her children, Murray, Rita, and the baby, Esther's mother, Miriam, were all deported to

Siberia. Nechama was put to work on a collective farm. When she refused to let her son go into the army—she claimed Polish citizenship—the two of them were arrested and jailed. Rita, at fourteen, was left to fend for herself, and Miriam was put into a children's camp in western Siberia. After the war, Miriam and her sister, brother, and mother fled Russia.

For the longest time, Esther's grandmother refused to speak of the past. By the time Esther began to insist that she needed to know what had happened, Nechama could no longer think clearly. Her mind moved in and out of time, from one language to another. Three months after we were married, Esther and I moved to Moscow. "I hope you come home once in a while," Miriam said, "because I don't think I could visit you there."

CHAPTER 3

TO BE PRESERVED, FOREVER

In the years after Stalin's death, the state was an old tyrant slouched in the corner with cataracts and gallstones, his muscles gone slack. He wore plastic shoes and a shiny suit that stank of sweat. He hogged all the food and fouled his pants. Mornings, his tongue was coated with the ash-taste of age. He mumbled and didn't care. His thoughts drifted like storm clouds and came clear only a few times a year to recite the old legends of Great October and the Great Patriotic War. Sometimes, in the gathering dark of his office, he would set out on the green baize table all the gifts that foreigners had given him: the gold cigarette dispenser, the silver Eiffel Tower, the colored pens, the crystal paperweights. The state was nearly senile, but still dangerous enough. He still kept the key to the border gate in his pocket and ruled every function of public life. Now and then he had fits and the world trembled.

But how the state kept alive, how it got from day to day, was a mystery. History was a fairy tale and the mechanisms of daily life a vast Rube Goldberg machine that somehow, if just barely, kept moving. If not for the plundering of Soviet oil fields and the worldwide energy crisis, the economy might have collapsed even before it did; and by the early 1980s, KGB reports declared that the cushion of oil profits was all but gone. The abyss awaits us, the most trenchant of the secret police reports declared. The economy was doomed. Nothing, and no one, worked in any recognized sense of the word. I saw the serfs of a collective farm outside Vologda in northern Russia herded onto buses to buy their food in the city. Their own harvest had rotted in the rain. In the steel town of Magnitogorsk, I saw miners spending their breaks at a local clinic sucking on "oxygen cocktails," a liquid concoction infused with oxygen and vitamins. On Sakhalin Island north of Japan, I saw a few hundred thousand salmon, fish that could have sold on the Ginza or Broadway for a fortune, writhe and rot in the shoreline nets while the trawlers sat rusting in port. Sakhalin is closer on the map to Hollywood Boulevard than Red Square, but the fishermen couldn't "make a move until they get the telegram from Moscow," a local politician told me. The order from the ministry came a week after the salmon had gone white and belly up.

But somehow the state never completely collapsed. There was bread, at least, and parades marked the triumph of the state's persistence. Even the May Day parade of 1988 was not much different from those before them. I stood in the reporters' section just to the right of the Lenin Mausoleum and watched the leaders come out looking faintly embarrassed, but pleased as well that it was all hanging together: Lenin's edgy portrait still hung on the side wall of GUM, the state department store; strongmen heaved dumbbells and gymnasts skipped through hoops in a show of "physical culture"; the workers of the Moscow automobile plants carried the banners they received in the morning and drank down the vodka they got at parade's end. Only the music changed: Pete Seeger songs boomed out of the Kremlin loudspeakers as the workers of the ZIL automobile factory marched by the reviewing stand. As Sergei Ivanov, a Soviet scholar of the Byzantine period, wrote, the rites of Communism had their roots in Constantinople, when the leader's rare appearances "before the people were accompanied by thoroughly rehearsed outbursts of delight, specially selected crowds who chanted the officially approved songs."

It was Oz, the world's longest-running and most colossal mistake, and the only way to endure it all was the perfection of irony. There was no other way to live. Even the sweetest-seeming grandmother, her hair in a babushka and her bulk packed into a housecoat, even she was possessed of a sense of irony that would chill the spine of any absurdiste at the Café Flore. One morning I was sitting in a courtyard in Moscow talking with an ancient of the city, a sweet wreck of a man. He needed help desperately, and it was still a time when a foreigner seemed the last recourse for everything from KGB harassment to this man's problem: his wife was dying of leukemia. How could he get to the Mayo Clinic? He'd heard the doctors there were "beautiful." They could save his wife. As he talked, I happened to glance up over his shoulder and saw a woman on the tenth floor hurl a cat out her kitchen window.

"Animal!" she screamed. "No room for you here! Be gone!"

The cat hit the pavement, and it sounded like the soft pop of an exploding water balloon. Now the two of us, the old man and I, were watching: the woman at the window, her face twisted into an angry knot, the cat struggling to get up on its broken legs.

"Ach," the old man said, turning away, "our Russian life!"

His smile was like the smile on a skull. He went on talking.

In an era of rot, the laureate was a genius of irony and part-time drunk named Venedikt ("Benny") Yerofeyev. In the seventies, Yerofeyev's friends circulated his masterpiece, a modern *Dead Souls* called *Moskva-Petushki,* the name of a train route between the capital and a town where many people lived after they returned from the camps. Yerofeyev's book, published in English as *Moscow Circles,* is a novel of wandering that goes nowhere except down, deep into the soul of man under socialism. His greatest relief is in the mastery of the binge. He is an artful mixologist. When there is no real vodka at hand, he conjures, with nail varnish and lavender water, the "Tears of the Komsomol Girl": "After one glass your memory is as strong as ever, but your mind just goes blank. After the second glass the brightness of your mind amazes you, but your memory goes blank." His best recipe, the "Finis coronat opus," is Cat Gut: 100 grams of Zhigulev beer, 30 grams of "Sadko the Rich Merchant" brand shampoo, 70 grams of anti-dandruff shampoo, and 20 grams of insect repellent. And now, "your Cat Gut is ready. Drink it from early evening in large gulps. After two glasses of this, men become so inspired you can spit at them from five feet for half an hour and they won't take the blindest bit of notice."

Yerofeyev made his living at any job he could keep. He didn't keep them long, generally, but he did rise to the post of foreman. He commanded a small brigade of men who were laying cable, or pretending to, in the town of Sheremetyevo outside Moscow. "This is what we would do. One day we would play poker, the next day we would drink vermouth, on the third day we'd play poker, and on the fourth day it was back to vermouth. . . . For a while everything was perfect. We'd send off our socialist pledges once a month and we'd get our pay twice a month. We'd write, for example: 'On the occasion of the coming centenary we pledge ourselves to end production traumatization.' Or: 'In honor of the glorious anniversary we will struggle to ensure that every sixth worker takes a correspondence course in a higher educational institution.' Traumatization! Institutions! . . . Oh, what freedom and equality! What fraternity and freeloading! Oh, the joy of nonaccountability! Oh, blessed hours in the life of my people—the hours which stretch from opening to closing time! Free of shame and idle care we lived a life that was purely spiritual."

The state, of course, did not allow this sort of thing. *Moskva-Petushki* was published only in 1988, and then only by a temperance journal. But the state never got the joke with Yerofeyev; otherwise he would have been jailed or exiled. Let him laugh. What it could not tolerate was a challenge uncomplicated by irony. When Brezhnev shoved Khrushchev out of power, the state still had the means to squash what little freedom it had allowed. The censors went through the libraries with razor blades and slashed from the bound copies of *Novy Mir* Solzhenitsyn's *One Day in the Life of Ivan Denisovich*. Then they slashed Solzhenitsyn from Russia, hustling him from a prison cell to a jet and finally to his exile. It could not tolerate Solzhenitsyn's sneer, Brodsky's impudence, or Sakharov's superiority. The regime would rather kill its brightest children than give way. A magnificent life-support system, with millions of agents, informers, police, wardens, lawyers, and judges all working at its bedside, kept the old tyrant breathing. Their watchfulness was admirable.

"Every life has a file, if you will," Brodsky told me in his basement apartment, his New York exile. "The moment you get a little bit well known, they open a file on you. The file begins to get filled up with this and that, and if you write your file grows in size all the faster. It's sort of a Neanderthal form of computerization. Gradually, your file occupies too much space on the shelf and, quite simply, a man walks into the office and says, 'This is a big file. Let's get him.'"

They got him. At his trial in Leningrad, Brodsky encountered the soul of the regime, its peculiar language.

JUDGE: What is your profession?

BRODSKY: Translator and poet.

JUDGE: Who recognized you as a poet? Who has enrolled you in the ranks of poets?

BRODSKY: No one. Who enrolled me in the ranks of human beings?

JUDGE: Did you study for it?

BRODSKY: What?

JUDGE: To be a poet. Didn't you try to take courses in school where one prepares for life, where one learns?

BRODSKY: I didn't believe it was a matter of education.

JUDGE: How is that?

BRODSKY: I thought that it came from God.

Just before he left the country in 1972, Brodsky adopted an old Russian tradition and wrote a letter to the czar.

"Dear Leonid Ilyich: A language is a much more ancient and inevitable thing than a state. I belong to the Russian language. As for the state, from my point of view, the measure of a writer's patriotism is not oaths from a high platform, but how he writes in the language of the people among whom he lives. . . . Although I am losing my Soviet citizenship, I do not cease to be a Russian poet. I believe that I will return. Poets always return in the flesh or on paper."

Brodsky's letter, Sakharov's manifestos, all the broadsides and master-works of the dissidents carried with them the air of futility. The idea of change, of the resiliency of the word against the state, seemed a kind of dream, a conceit to live out the day and get to the next one. Just before his exile, Solzhenitsyn wrote his "Letter to the Soviet Leaders." "Your dearest wish," he informed them, "is for our state structure and our ideological system never to change, to remain as they are for centuries. But history is not like that. Every system either finds a way to develop or else it collapses." And with that, Solzhenitsyn was gone.

Lydia Chukovskaya, who wrote a novel about the purges while she waited in vain for her husband to return from a prison camp, got up at a meeting of the Writers' Union at the height of the anti-dissident campaign and said:

"I can prophesy that in the capital city of our homeland there will inevitably be an Aleksandr Solzhenitsyn Square and an Academician Andrei Sakharov Avenue."

Inevitably! Who believed it? Even the bravest of the brave—and Chukovskaya was among them—had their doubts. When I met her she was in her nineties and living with her daughter Yelena on Gorky Street. Yelena greeted me at the door and asked me to wait a moment until Lydia Korneievna was ready to receive me. There was nothing royal about this, nothing vain, but rather a woman gathering herself. Yelena led me into the room and Lydia Korneievna was seated at a small table. There was a teapot and two cups with chipped saucers and a plate of cookies. Her hand was already on the handle of the pot.

Lydia Korneievna had not been well. Her wide, light eyes were glazed with rheum. The skin of her face was fine, a kind of papery white, as if it would burn if you touched it. Like all Moscow intellectuals of a certain kind and class, she had photographs of well-known poets and writers stuck behind the glass of her bookshelves. In many apartments this is both a vanity and a connection, a way of announcing one's sense of quality and aspiration. Lydia Korneievna had no vanity and no one deserved the portraits of Solzhenitsyn and Sakharov more than she did. She had risked all to defend them. She had lost the right to publish. Probably all that kept her safe in her bed was her age and the fact that she was the daughter of Kornei Chukovsky, a children's writer as revered in Russia as Dr. Seuss is in America.

For a while, she talked about her friends, her walks with Anna Akhmatova in Leningrad, her love for Sakharov. Her sentences were formal and clear, and her voice, though weakened with age, had a liquid sound. Then the lights went out in the entire apartment block. It was night and there was no moon and the room was black. Lydia Korneievna could hardly tell. To her it was like the slight change of light in a room when the fire settles into itself. And not noticing, she kept talking. After a while she did sense some difference, a change in the air, a certain coolness and quiet. Her mood changed. For a moment she paused, as if she were finally going to mention the darkness. Then she said, "You know, when we talk about all these people, I know now that they are all gone. It is horrible to say, but you must imagine a state that used every means to kill the best among us. All dead or all gone."

After a while, Lydia Korneievna said, "The lights. They're out. How strange!"

Yelena came in with candles and we continued talking until Lydia Korneievna announced, "I suppose I'm tired."

On the way out, I told Yelena a little of what her mother had said. She nodded. She had heard this many times before.

"But you must remember," she said, "even Lydia Korneievna has hope. She adores that young boy. Dmitri Yurasov. She adores him. You should meet him if you can."

———

While the world spent 1987 and 1988 waiting for Gorbachev's newest initiatives, his shifts in ideology, the boldest ideas for the creation of a civil society were debated on Saturday mornings in Moscow. At first small groups of young intellectuals—the "informals"—met at home and even typed out their declarations on onionskin paper. But after a while, the older voices gathered. Sakharov had returned from exile, and Moscow Tribune, a loose amalgamation of scholars and writers who all had lived through the promise of the thaw, was one of his regular platforms.

The first time I saw Dmitri Yurasov was at a Saturday-morning session of Moscow Tribune at Dom Kino, the headquarters of the Filmmakers' Union near the Peking Hotel. The scene was nearly always the same. Moscow Tribune's sessions would begin at ten or eleven with speeches by the best-known of the group: Yuri Afanasyev, a bearish-looking historian of the French Annales school, who had been put in charge of the Historical Archives Institute; Yuri Karyakin, a journalist and Dostoevsky scholar who nearly drank himself to death during the Brezhnev years; Nikolai Shmelyov, an economist and short-story writer who had once been a member of the Khrushchev family by marriage; Leonid Batkin, a scholar of the Italian

Renaissance whose slight heresies and refusal to join the Party prevented him from teaching in Moscow; Galina Starovoitova, a demographer, an expert on Armenia; Len Karpinsky, the son of revolutionaries, a journalist who had once been blessed by the Kremlin as "our great hope" and later betrayed it by becoming what he called a "half-dissident." And always, there was Sakharov, off to the side, sleeping through the speeches at times, clearly weakened by his years of forced exile in Gorky but ready to perform when it came his turn.

Yurasov was sitting in the back rows. He was twenty-four years old and the youngest person in the hall. He was a tough-looking kid in ratty jeans and a bleached jacket. His hair was cropped close; he looked like an army recruit on leave. When one of the speakers said something not to his liking, he sneered, as if rehearsing to be James Dean. Dmitri, or Dima as everyone called him, was known as the young kid who collected information on people who had been imprisoned or executed under Soviet power. He kept the names on index cards, and he had about 200,000 of them—that is, 200,000 out of tens of millions.

Moscow Tribune meetings never really ended. Instead, after a few hours, they sort of trailed off like smoke. The first-string speakers had left for home and even Afanasyev, who was the radical left's master of ceremonies, was getting ready to leave.

I offered Yurasov a ride home.

"Wait here, just a second," he said when we got to his apartment.

I heard him inside, frantically throwing papers into order. This was a futile effort. He led me to his room, a tiny place with journals and magazines in five-foot stacks on the floor. On the wall there were a few posters of rock stars and a calendar with a photograph of a sexy girl from Brazil who looked as though she had just had three drinks and a bad meal.

"Before we start," Dima said, "you should read this."

He handed me a short stack of letters.

"Respected Dmitri Gennadiyevich!

"My father Afonin, Timofei Stepanovich, lived in the town of Tolmachevo in the Novosibirsk region. As I remember it, he was a member of the local military party committee and was chairman of the farm council. In 1930 he was arrested by the NKVD together with other residents of the village and taken to Novosibirsk. In the court documents of the military intelligence he was judged guilty of Article 58-8-10 and 73-1 of the Russian criminal code and sentenced to be shot. On February 13, 1930, the sentence was carried out. . . ."

There were many such letters in his files: people now in their forties, fifties, and sixties telling the stories of their parents who had disappeared, the sketchy details of their arrests, the open questions.

Finally, Dima handed me a short note, a testimonial from a woman who had written to him asking if he knew anything at all about her dead father:

"In his catalog, Dima found my father's name. He named the place of his imprisonment and, evidently, his death. Dima showed me that one of the investigators into my father's rehabilitation had said my father was a librarian. Was this some arbitrary thing he did in his camps or his real profession, I don't know. But something changed inside me. From the anonymous gray mass of pea jackets, my father had emerged as a particular man, a special man. Not all were called librarians! A father! I have a father!"

"Now maybe you can see what I do," Dima said, taking back the letters.

———

Dmitri Yurasov was born in 1964, the year that hard-line forces and Stalinist revivalists in the Kremlin toppled Khrushchev for the heresy of "voluntarism." Next to the Litvinovs, the Yurasovs were an unremarkable family. They lived in a cramped apartment on Leninski Prospekt and worked as midlevel engineers. They read no samizdat and did not care to. Dima's mother, Ludmila, grew up singing paeans to Stalin ("I'm a little girl, I dance and sing,/I've never seen Stalin but I love him so"). She joined the Communist Party, not so much out of an overwhelming sense of conviction but rather as a mark of distinction, a way to advance at work.

Like every other Soviet schoolboy, like Pavel Litvinov, Dima grew up outside of history and deep within the mythologies of his time. He was trained from the earliest age to become a "Soviet man." This was a matter of policy, one that had altered very little since Stalin's death. "The Communist Party of the Soviet Union proceeds, and has always proceeded, from the premise that the formation of the New Man is the most important component of the entire task of Communist construction," said Mikhail Suslov, one of the leaders of the plot to overthrow Khrushchev and Brezhnev's ideologist. In their first year of medical school, students were informed that there were two species of human beings: *Homo sapiens* and *Homo sovieticus.* As a schoolboy, Dima sat through his lessons in the latter. He learned to read using primers that substituted "Grandpa Ilyich" Lenin for Dick and Jane. His history lessons were a litany of garlanded triumphs beginning with the revolution and ending with record harvests in the Black Earth Zone. Summers, Dima went to Young Pioneers camp, outposts that taught the virtues of military discipline and the supremacy of the group over the individual.

But Dima Yurasov also had a young mind that was somehow, innocently, subversive. Even in the fifth and sixth grade, he read constantly in the sixteen-volume *Soviet Historical Encyclopedia,* books written by Party historians and ideologists and approved by a hierarchy of censors. There were approved articles on the Revolution, the Civil War, the Great Patriotic War—each one an instruction in the pseudo-theology that the study of history had become decades before. On rare occasions, evidence of the thaw under Khrushchev washed up on the page. The censors, it turned out, could not catch everything. One day when he was eleven years old, Dima was reading about a scholar who had been, the encyclopedia said, "illegally repressed and rehabilitated after his death." Dima had never seen such a phrase. It was as strange to him as a sentence of Burmese.

Dima asked his mother for an explanation. She brushed it off. This was nearly two decades after Khrushchev's secret speech denouncing the crimes of the Stalin era, and yet the atmosphere of neo-Stalinism was so pervasive that ordinary people, even in the relatively sophisticated city of Moscow, were not prepared to talk to their children about the nightmares of the past. They themselves knew so little about it. Khrushchev's speech, after all, had never been published in the Soviet Union, and much of the literature that came out during the thaw period had been pulled from library shelves.

And so Dima set out to learn history on his own. He went slowly through the volumes of the *Great Soviet Encyclopedia* and wrote down the names of all those generals and politicians and artists who had died in 1937, 1938, 1939, 1940, the years of the Great Terror. The cause of death was almost never listed. For each name, Dima set up an index card and filled out the most rudimentary information. It was a game, a mystery. "A little like stamp collecting," he said. "Like the way kids imagine they've gone to Yemen or the Sudan when they've found the stamp. It was a sense of connection to something I had only the vaguest ideas about. And what was strangest, I couldn't really talk to anyone about it."

During the day, Dima was a good enough student and excelled in history as it was taught. He could recite with ease the mythology of the country he lived in. He was obedient and enjoyed the teachers' praise that his good memory won for him. In the evenings and weekends, Dima filled out his cards with the names of the disappeared. He had little idea what to make of this strange phenomenon, but his catalog of the disappeared continued to grow.

"Then there was this breakthrough," he said. "While I was in the eighth grade, I read in the papers the minutes of the Twenty-second Party Congress," where Khrushchev gave more body and detail to his denunciation of the Stalinist terror. "When that happened, the game changed. It wasn't a game. At first it was just these strange names that seemed to disappear at a certain point in history. Then it became a matter of their fates. It was becoming more obvious to me what had happened to these people."

In high school, Dima signed up for the history Olympiad, an academic contest sponsored by the Young Communist League. "A lot of the questions were on the order of 'Who was the first boy to join the YCL?' and 'How many medals and honors did he win?' Stuff like that. But there were questions that went a little deeper. I decided to win." He went to study at the Central State Archive of the October Revolution. Dima met one of the directors there and asked about a few issues related to the contest. He had also brought along his stack of index cards, a stack that was growing by the hundreds as he made his way through the encyclopedias. He was hoping for more information.

"What do you want to know?" asked the director.

"I want to know whether these people were 'repressed' or killed," Dima said.

The woman lowered her eyes. Her voice dropped nearly to a whisper. "We'll answer questions about the Komsomol," she said, "but we needn't talk of these people you are talking about. It is unnecessary."

The woman was in her mid-forties and not at all cruel in what she said or how she said it. Instead, it seemed to Dima that she knew only that these were forbidden things and must not be spoken of. She was terrified.

When Dima was seventeen, he decided to apply for both work and study at the Historical Archives Institute. His mother was baffled and wondered why he didn't try for a more prestigious place. Dima said very little. He kept his passion well hidden, not so much because he enjoyed the secret but rather because he was no longer a boy; he knew how dangerous his interest could be for those around him.

To win a post at the institute, Dima had to take an entrance exam. Around that time he had read in samizdat Solzhenitsyn's essay "Live Not by the Lie." The essay recognized the difficulty, even the impossibility, of outright rebellion in a totalitarian state; instead, it implored the reader at least to refuse cooperation in the lies of the state. Better not to be a journalist than to write the lies of *Pravda.* Better not to teach history at all than to read *The Short Course* to young minds. Preserve yourself even if you cannot save the world.

But at his entrance exam, Dima found himself writing an essay that extolled the sham autobiography of Leonid Brezhnev, *The Little Land,* which was filled with heroic exploits that had never actually taken place. Brezhnev never even wrote the book, and yet he rewarded himself with the year's top literary prize, a spectacle not unlike Ronald Reagan awarding himself the Pulitzer Prize for his own ghost-written book. "What can I say? I was one more Soviet person who faced a choice and humiliated himself," Dima said. "And you know what? I got a top grade. How wonderful."

Dima's job at the institute was mainly clerical: organizing boxes of documents, counting pages, sorting files. But it was paradise. Alone in a closed room, he had enough time to comb through secret documents and copy out as much information as time allowed on his file cards. Once, when all his fellow workers in the department went out to cash their weekly paychecks, he stayed behind and scanned the files of the NKVD for 1935. He shuddered remembering the stark sight of those papers: one execution after another.

"Sometimes they would send me to the basement to find a file and I'd take five minutes to find it and twenty to copy it out. I tried to copy at least one hundred files every day. It all proved to me very soon that the *Great Soviet Encyclopedia* was a multivolume lie. The documents testified that people were tortured, that their tongues were burned with cigarettes, people were forced to stand sixty hours in a row just facing a wall. Prisoners were beaten so badly that they had to be carried to the firing squad. There were descriptions of the theater director Meyerhold, how he was forced to drink his own urine, how his interrogators broke his left arm and forced him to sign his 'confession' with his right. I remember being in shock when I read about how 208 people were shot down in the Dmitrov Camp for an alleged attempt on the life of Yezhov, who was on an inspection trip to the camp. There were women, old people. The information was like a nightmare, like being caught in a huge avalanche and it goes on and never stops. But I didn't make the connections. I couldn't hook it all up with ideology, policy. It was all on the level of the raw accumulation of data about this person and that and not much more."

Dima lost paradise when he was drafted into the army. But even during his two years of service, he continued his explorations. He even began writing a novel, "The Brothers Kaganovich." The book was based on a well-known incident in Lazar Kaganovich's life. One day Stalin told Kaganovich that there was evidence against Mikhail, Kaganovich's older brother and the head of the defense industry. Lazar Moiseyevich did not hesitate. "What has to be done must be done," he said. Mikhail Kaganovich was arrested. He killed himself in his jail cell.

Late at night, Dima read parts of his manuscript of "The Brothers Kaganovich" to his buddies. A few days later, he discovered the manuscript was missing from his drawer. His officers had confiscated the papers. The next morning he was accused of "insulting Soviet power," a charge, the officers said, that could lead to a trial and a prison term. Never mind that it had been more than a decade since Kaganovich had been thrown out of the leadership by Khrushchev and reduced to running a concrete factory in the provinces. Never mind that the story of the two brothers was based on fact. These were facts that a young soldier like Private Yurasov had no business knowing. They were, for him, nonfacts. The only way out, the officers said, was to write a letter admitting guilt and begging forgiveness. The Soviet system's lust for confession had not changed much since the days of the Terror. Dima wrote the letter and considered himself lucky that the incident ended there.

Back in Moscow, it was not easy at first finding a job once more in the archives. The officials at the Historical Archives Institute never actually accused Dima of a crime or wrongdoing, but they had their suspicions. Dima knew he could not go back there and be allowed access to the *spetskhran*—the restricted archives. But friends tipped him off to an opening at the archive of the Supreme Court. Somehow, because the secret police apparatus was never quite as efficient as it seemed, he got the job. It was a trove of information that only the highest officials—and the archive workers—could see. In the basements of the Supreme Court were files on two and a half million criminal cases after 1924. Most of the files had not been touched since the moment they had first been shelved.

"This was it!" Dima said. "These documents were the only proof that a man or a woman had died or lived!"

Dima worked mainly in a room designed to prevent just the sort of research he had in mind. There were four desks crammed into a tiny office all facing one another; that way no one could do anything without three other people seeing. But still, Dima tried. He accumulated names, facts, the fates of thousands of the lost. After eighteen months he had accumulated 100,000 cards and established a standardized form:

1. Last name
2. First name
3. Middle name
4. Year of birth
5. Year of death
6. Nationality
7. Party status
8. Social background
9. Education
10. Last place of work and
    status before arrest
11. Facts of arrest, repression
12. Facts of rehabilitation

But the workplace system of *stukachi*—informers—finally caught up to Dima. One of the bosses found a book of lists in his desk, and there was a search. Once more, Yurasov's quest to recover the lost names of history was over. He was fired.

CHAPTER 4

THE RETURN OF
HISTORY

Dima had good reason to worry. The new Soviet leadership did not come into power with much public daring.

Two months after Mikhail Gorbachev took office in March 1985, he delivered a speech celebrating the fortieth anniversary of the victory over Nazi Germany. There he proclaimed that "the gigantic work at the front and in the rear was led by the Party, its Central Committee, and the State Defense Committee headed by the General Secretary . . . Iosif Vissarionovich Stalin." This passage inspired ringing applause from the members of the Central Committee. In February 1986, Gorbachev told the French newspaper *L'Humanité* that "Stalinism is a concept made up by opponents of Communism and used on a large scale to smear the Soviet Union and socialism as a whole." The Party, Gorbachev assured *L'Humanité,* "had already drawn the proper conclusions from the past." And finally, in a meeting with Soviet writers in June 1986, Gorbachev said, "If we start trying to deal with the past, we'll lose all our energy. It would be like hitting people over the head. And we have to go forward. We'll sort out the past. We'll put everything in its place. But right now we have to direct our energy forward."

Communist Party officials across the country were simply in no mood for full disclosure, even if Gorbachev was. In mid-1987, the local Communist

Party boss in Magadan, a city that was once the gateway to the notorious Kolyma labor camps in the far east, told a group of visiting Western reporters that the issue of the Stalinist purges "does not exist here for us. There is no such question."

"We lived through that period, and this page in history has been turned," the official, Aleksandr Bogdanov, said. "It's not necessary to speak constantly about that." Nearly three million people were killed in Kolyma alone.

Gorbachev, who grew up inside the Party bureaucracy, knew well that to lose completely the support of such dinosaurs as Bogdanov—to say nothing of the dinosaurs of the Central Committee, the KGB, the military, and the police—would have meant an immediate end to his leadership. Years later, the liberal mayor of St. Petersburg, Anatoly Sobchak, wrote, "A totalitarian system leaves behind it a minefield built into both the country's social structure and the individual psychology of its citizens. And mines explode each time the system faces the danger of being dismantled and the country sees the prospect of genuine renewal."

Whether he relished the task or not, Gorbachev was acting as the keeper of the secrets, the chief curator of the Party's criminal history. Just as the Soviet regime combined brutality and the technology of the totalitarian state to leave behind tens of millions of corpses and a perverse social order, it also used the completeness of the state, the pervasiveness of every institution from the kindergartens to the secret police, to put an end to historical inquiry. Stalin was not the first leader to enforce a myth of history, only the most successful. As the scholar Walter Laqueur points out, modern historiography, with its demands of integrity and evidence, is less than two hundred years old. Pariscop Villas of the Incan Empire was perhaps the first of many to assemble an official state history on the order of his dictator. In Russia, Nicholas I not only crushed the uprising of the Decembrists, he also tried, with some success, to expunge the threat to his authority from the history books.

Stalin inherited the tradition of manipulating human memory, and came closest to perfecting it. For the first ten years after the Bolshevik Revolution, there had been a degree of coexistence among historians, a debate between orthodox Marxists and their "bourgeois" opponents. That all came to an end at the first—and last—All-Union Conference of Marxist Historians held in 1928, the same year that Stalin became the unchallenged leader of the Bolshevik state. As the conference made clear, Stalin's consolidation of power gave him absolute control over history. In 1934, the Communist Party Central Committee issued a decree calling for a strict ideological version of history to become doctrine in all textbooks, schools, universities, and institutes. Stalin himself supervised the writing and publication in a run of fifty million copies of the famous *Short Course,* an angry ideological tract that was, in the words of historian Genrikh Joffe, "like a hammer pounding nails of falsehood into every schoolboy's and schoolgirl's brain." *The Short Course* was a textbook of determinist history with all events leading, necessarily, inexorably, to a glorious conclusion: the rightness and might of the present regime. In such a text, history is free of inner struggles, of ambiguity and choice, of absurdity and tragedy. The Big Lie always has an unfailing internal logic. Opponents are revealed as enemies of the state, slaughter as necessity. All is clear, all is expressed in the language of myth and epithet. Stalin's rivals for power—Bukharin, Trotsky, and the rest—were "White Guard pygmies whose strength was no more than that of a gnat." This was how history—the only history—of the regime was handed down to its subjects. An entire people's understanding of themselves was meant to dwell within this text. To question or defy the dogma was to admit guilt before the criminal code.

After Stalin's death in 1953 and the start of Khrushchev's attacks on the "personality cult," *The Short Course* was no longer the catechism. There was a new text, the revised *History of the Communist Party,* which made sure to play down the titanic role Stalin had assigned himself. A few historians even seized on the thaw as an opportunity to write more open appraisals of the crimes that Khrushchev had only touched upon. Viktor Danilov, for one, went ahead with work on a pioneering study of the collectivization campaign.

But when Brezhnev overthrew Khrushchev in 1964 and slowly began to institute a neo-Stalinist movement, the "gray cardinal" of ideology, Mikhail Suslov, turned his attention to history. The pendulum swung hard once more to dogma. Brezhnev and Suslov appointed Sergei Trapeznikov, a Party historian-apparatchik, as the head of the Central Committee's Department of Science and Educational Establishments, putting him in charge, in effect, of every history textbook and school lesson from Estonia to Sakhalin Island. To make sure the "thaw" had been thoroughly eliminated from historical studies, Trapeznikov banned Danilov's study of collectivization from publication. In the true Stalinist tradition, Trapeznikov saw collectivization as necessary and just. Trapeznikov decided that the glory of collectivization required a responsible historian. He appointed himself.

So complete was the Communist Party's hold over the study of history that nearly all the historical works of any value written in the Soviet Union were by dissidents: Roy Medvedev's Marxist study of Stalin, *Let History Judge;* Mikhail Gefter's essays on Stalinism; and, far greater, Aleksandr Solzhenitsyn's "literary investigation" of the camps in *The Gulag Archipelago.* Medvedev and Gefter, despite their devotion to the Revolution and Lenin, were cast to the margins of Soviet society and put under constant watch by the KGB. Brezhnev's attempt to return to Stalin a measure of his former stature would not tolerate apostasy. Solzhenitsyn's trespasses were far greater. He exposed the inherent illegitimacy of the regime and every Soviet leader including Lenin. This could not be tolerated. In 1974, Solzhenitsyn became the first man forcibly exiled from the country since Trotsky.

The repression of dissident writing and study was but a small part of the state apparatus that controlled history. Trapeznikov made sure that the Academy of Sciences, the Institute of History, the Institute of Marxism-Leninism, the universities, the journals, and the schools were all free of "other-thinking people." Balts or Uzbeks or Ukrainians could not dare suggest that their histories or cultures were somehow different from Russian and Soviet history. That would undermine the myth of a common Soviet fate and Soviet man. All potentially explosive issues, from Lenin's dissolution of the popularly elected Constituent Assembly just after the Revolution to the invasion of Czechoslovakia in 1968, required a stock fairy tale and a neutralized nonlanguage to prevent even the hint of debate or "other thinking." When it came to the invasion of Afghanistan, for instance, historians wrote of "internationalist duty" and the "invitation" from "socialist brethren"—or they did not write at all.

"Only a fool or an ideologue would even think about making the study of Soviet history his profession," said Sergei Ivanov, the Byzantine scholar. "Anyone with a genuine interest in history and a sense of honesty made sure to stay as far away from the Soviet period as possible. That's why the only hints of criticism you could read in our scholarship were analogies or metaphors, historians writing about the fall of Constantinople or the French Revolution or the rise of fascism and at the same time providing a subtle undertone that maybe a few people would understand. But if you really made Soviet history your field, you were sure to lose—one way or another." Small wonder then that the most effective spokesman, later on, for a radical reform in the study of Soviet history would be Yuri Afanasyev, who had been schooled almost too well in Party politics but whose specialty had been the history of France.

Moscow was home to many scholars of the Soviet period—not only Medvedev and Gefter and Afanasyev, but also professional ideologues, cynics, and liars. I spent an astonishing evening at Moscow State University with the head of the history department, Yuri Kukushkin. For hours, Kukushkin, one of the most celebrated time-servers in his profession, a man with close connections to the Central Committee and unusual access to Western books and Soviet archives, went on about how he had had "absolutely no idea" that Stalin's collectivization campaign had been so "costly." Everything in his voice and manner appealed for sympathy, as if he, too, had somehow been a closet dissident.

"I am afraid if I try to speak about what I feel inside, I will fail," Kukushkin said. "Bitterness prevails. If only one man could do it all. If we had access to the documents. We worked in a situation that was like a chemist assigned to make a discovery, cure a disease, but he is only allowed to use the chemicals assigned to him by the keeper of the laboratory. The truth is, I didn't know anyone who knew the real facts and consciously twisted them."

But for all his righteous desire to do the right thing, Kukushkin still wanted controls, he wanted the "right people" to do the scholarly work. "Of course we need balance in our studies, but now we are pouring nothing but sewage on Lenin's bald head," he said. "I am sure our state will survive this. I'm sure Lenin will, too. But if a people no longer believe in the future, if they can only see darkness in their common past, then they will go into a state of spiritual dystrophy, and I am not sure we can cure this. In order to inspire faith, we have to show not only the filth and the crime and the blood in our history, but also what there was to be proud of. We are a great and mighty state. We repelled foreign assailants. We must be proud of this. As a man and as a historian, I am concerned that we do not annihilate ourselves spiritually."

Courtesy of Trapeznikov, the academies and universities had been stocked with countless Kukushkins. But there were also men and women like Genrikh Joffe, who saw themselves somehow as honest though they knew all too well that the system was too strong, that it mocked their petty attempts to undermine or fool it. Joffe, the author of many books about the February Revolution and the Romanov dynasty, was in his early sixties, "so I was too young to have suffered through the worst, deadly assaults on historians under Stalin." But he did receive the standard Stalinist education, the endless drilling in *The Short Course* by scared and ignorant teachers.

"That was our world, the structure we lived in," he said one afternoon. "There was a slight euphoria in the postwar years, a slight thaw, but in 1949, 1950, they accused me of being a 'preacher of bourgeois ideology.' Whatever that meant. It turned out that two friends of mine—friends!—had stolen a couple of my notebooks. And in my notes on some lecture, I had written in the margin saying, 'They must think we are idiots to believe all this.' Nothing more. Just a private moment of frustration and doubt. Later on, I couldn't find my notebooks and thought I'd probably lost them somewhere. I didn't pay it much mind. But the next time I saw them was when I had to appear at a public meeting in front of one hundred people, students and friends at the university, the Komsomol committee people and all the rest. All my so-called friends were suddenly avoiding me as we walked into the hall. And then, from the podium, the Communist Party secretary pointed at me and cried out, 'Look who sits here before us! Joffe! He thinks you are all idiots!' "

For his sin, Joffe paid a relatively small price. He was sent to teach in the provincial city of Kostroma until after Stalin's death.

Back in Moscow, Joffe worked at the Lenin Library and began working on his books. "There were certain small things you could do to make yourself feel at least a little honest," he said. "One technique was to introduce foreign sources and then make sure you criticized the 'bourgeois falsifiers.' I am not sure now that I am ashamed of that. I did manage to amass a lot of material on the February Revolution. Maybe, if I'm very lucky, some readers might have gotten the sense that there was more to the February Revolution than just being an opening act for the October Revolution. Maybe they got the sense that it was the moment that overthrew the monarchy and flirted with a kind of democracy, however weak. But I doubt it.

"Unfortunately, I compromised too much, and this is hard to bear now. Truthfully, I don't know if the way I negotiated my way through life was a completely conscious choice. I think it was just my nature. By nature I am a man of compromise, not an extremist. I am not a young man, and to live through these changes, this flood of information, is not easy. I sometimes feel guilty for changing my view of history so quickly. But how can it be otherwise? How can one fail to see what's what? Should I ignore it all for some sort of foolish consistency? I remember the historian Eduard Burdzhalov, who had been perhaps the most important historian on the liberal side of things when Khrushchev made his revelations about Stalin in 1956. Before that, Burdzhalov had been an inveterate Stalinist, the editor of *Culture and Life,* which had attacked the Jews, the so-called cosmopolitans. I asked him, 'How was it possible for a Stalinist, a party careerist, to turn around and change so abruptly?' He couldn't answer at first. But then he said, 'If someone has the chance finally to express himself, to speak the truth, why should he miss the opportunity?' "

The return of history first began with Khrushchev's "secret speech" denouncing Stalin in 1956. But the "thaw" was extremely limited and, as it turned out, reversible. Without a full and careful assessment of the past, one that could not be crammed back into the genie's bottle, real reform, much less democratic revolution, was impossible. Dmitri Yurasov and the democrats knew it, and Gorbachev knew it, too. The return of history to the intellectual and political life of the people of the Soviet Union was the foundation of the great changes ahead.

After two years of hesitation and the language of avoidance, Gorbachev used 1987 as his moment to begin what Khrushchev had started. He opened the door to history, and he did it first with a movie, then with a speech on the seventieth anniversary of the October Revolution.

———

Tengiz Abuladze, a small and elegant man with piercing eyes, lived and made his films in the Georgian capital, Tbilisi. By 1980, he had established his reputation as a filmmaker of extraordinary intelligence with two allegorical works: *Supplication,* which appeared in 1968, and *The Wishing Tree,* in 1977. Meticulous in manner and in his style of work, he spent years thinking and writing, letting his ideas mature, before he shot a single frame.

Unlike the musty cave-apartments of most Moscow intellectuals, Abuladze's airy house in Tbilisi was a fine place "to live and breathe," he said. Over a lunch of Georgian red wine—"Stalin's favorite"—and the local variation of pizza called *khachapuri,* Abuladze talked of how he came to make *Repentance,* a film about the legacy of evil and the moral need—for both nation and individual—to confront the past. Although television and newspapers were the principal means of the glasnost explosion, Abuladze's film was the bridge to the recovery of historical memory. More than any other work of the period—Mikhail Shatrov's historical plays, Anatoly Rybakov's and Vladimir Dudintsev's novels—*Repentance* stunned a people into a state of awareness. The national screenings of *Repentance* in 1987 and 1988 had such a powerful effect that they can be compared to Lenin's "agit-prop" trains that traveled throughout the provinces, bringing with them portable theaters to show propaganda films on the glory of the Bolshevik Revolution. As an artist or theorist, Abuladze might not be on the same level as the greatest of the early Soviet directors, Sergei Eisenstein, Dziga Vertov, and Aleksandr Dovzhenko. But because of its political resonance, *Repentance* was the most important work of subversive art in the country since the publication of *One Day in the Life of Ivan Denisovich* during Khrushchev's "thaw."

Abuladze did not have to travel far to get the spark for *Repentance.* "I got the inspiration from a true story, an incident that took place in a village in western Georgia," he said. "A man who had been sent unjustly to prison was finally released. His entire life had been broken, destroyed. And when he came home, he found the grave of the man who had sent him to jail. One night he went into the graveyard and dug up the coffin. He opened the coffin, took out the corpse, and leaned it up against the wall. This was his act of revenge. He would not let the dead man rest. This awful fact showed us that we could show the tragedy of an entire epoch by using this device. That was the spark for the treatment and then the script."

With his daughter-in-law, Nana Dzhanselidze, Abuladze wrote an eighteen-page treatment and then a script in 1981 about a kind of Every-Dictator, a tyrant named Varlam who destroys one life after another in a time mirroring the late 1930s under Stalin. Varlam, a provincial mayor, promises to build a "paradise on earth" for his people. Instead he ravages them in fits of paranoia and sheer indifference. As an old man, he even tries to shoot down the sun with a pistol.

"The people need a great reality!" Varlam says, echoing the twisted paternalism of Lenin and Stalin. Later, he defends his own paranoia, saying, "Of every three people, four are our enemies! Yes, do not be shocked. One enemy is greater in quantity than one friend!"

Varlam is so ruthless that in one scene he befriends an artist named Sandro and then sends him off to die in the camps, declaring him guilty of "individualism" and friendship with "anarchist poets." Sandro's daughter, haunted for decades by the memory of the martyrdom of her Christlike father, eventually digs up the grave of Varlam and leans the corpse against the wall. She will not forget, and she will not let those around her forget.

The film, which is filled with the sort of allegorical devices and local grotesques common in Fellini, is about the necessity of memory, the need not only to battle tyranny of the present, but also to deal with the insanities of the past. Varlam's son Abel is little better than the father. He temporizes; he repeats the sins of the father. He has no conscience, no memory. And he prosecutes Keti, the daughter of Sandro, the woman who has repeatedly dug up the grave of the tyrant.

Tornike, Abel's son, cannot comprehend the life he has inherited. He rages against his father. In perhaps the most important scene in the film, Tornike confronts Abel, a battle that can be read not only as the conflict of generations, but as the singular struggle of man against power, the struggle of memory against forgetting.

"Did you know all that?" Tornike asks his father.

"All what?" Abel says.

"About Grandpa."

"Grandpa never did anything wrong. Those were complicated times. It is difficult to explain now."

"What do the 'times' have to do with it?"

"Plenty," Abel says, getting angrier. "The situation then was different. It was a question of national survival. We were surrounded by enemies who wanted to crush us. Should we have just patted their heads?"

"Was the artist Sandro Barateli an enemy?" the boy asks.

"He was. Perhaps he was a good artist. But he failed to understand many things. I'm not saying we didn't make any mistakes, but what are a few lives when the well-being of millions is at stake? We had so much to accomplish. Look at it from that perspective."

"So you applied mathematics to human lives, with proportions paramount?" the boy says in disgust.

"Don't be sarcastic," Abel says. "It's time you understood that a public official places the public interest above private considerations."

Tornike's contempt for his father has deepened. "A person is born human," he says, "then he becomes an official."

"Your head is in the clouds," Abel says. "Reality is different. Varlam was guided by the interests of society, and sometimes what happened was not his doing."

"Tell me," says the son, "would he have destroyed the entire world if so ordered?"

At the end of the film, Tornike shoots himself in despair.

———

The year was 1981 and Leonid Brezhnev was general secretary and Eduard Shevardnadze was the most powerful man in Georgia. Abuladze brought the script to Shevardnadze. "Shevardnadze read the script and said we must find a way to do this," Abuladze said. "He told me, 'The year 1937 was in my home, too.' He was a witness to all that happened. His own father was among those arrested. I remember it all, too. I was a child, and though I cannot remember all the specifics, I remember the emotion, the fear. My father was a doctor, and he always had a suitcase ready with some clothes in it. He had nothing to do with politics, but he knew there could be a knock at the door at any time. They made the arrest and you never returned.

"So Shevardnadze told us we must find a way to do something on this topic, by all means. But he said it had to go through Moscow. We went to Rezo Chkheidze, the manager of the film studios, and he told Shevardnadze that there were film programs for the republics and for the entire Soviet Union. For the republican program all we had to do was specify the topic of the film and the name of the director. So we sent a telegram saying, 'Director Tengiz Abuladze wants to make a film on a moral and ethical problem.' That was all. Moscow gave its permission, saying only that the film sounded 'interesting.' Then Shevardnadze had a good piece of advice. He told us, 'The more general you keep it, the better.' And so in a way he was an extra author to the film."

Abuladze made sure that Varlam was not simply a direct analog for Stalin. Varlam, as played by the brilliant Georgian actor Avtandil Makharadze, had a Hitlerian mustache and wore a pince-nez that immediately evoked the image of Stalin's secret police chief, Lavrenty Beria. Abuladze dressed Varlam's guards in medieval armor to deepen the sense of time. Finally, he gave Varlam the last name Aravidze, which is a bit like Kafka's semi-anonymous

K. In Georgian, there is no name Aravidze, but the root of the word, *aravin,* means "no one."

"We wanted even the name to hint at Varlam's being the very image of the totalitarian, the dictator, anywhere or at any time," Abuladze said. "They are all in there: Stalin, of course, but also Khrushchev and Lenin, too. A friend of mine met Molotov before his death and he told Molotov, 'You know, it's a pity that Lenin died so early. If he had lived longer, everything would have been normal.' But Molotov said, 'Why do you say that?' My friend said, 'Because Stalin was a bloodsucker and Lenin was a noble person.' Molotov smiled, and then he said, 'Compared to Lenin, Stalin was a mere lamb.' "

Abuladze shot the film in five months in 1984. But Konstantin Chernenko, a protégé of Brezhnev, was still in power, and so the film simply remained "on the shelf," along with the works of dozens of other filmmakers.

Soon after Chernenko died and Gorbachev came to power in March 1985, Abuladze's old friend Shevardnadze was appointed to a position on the Politburo. The prospects for *Repentance* brightened. In the spring of 1986, Abuladze called Shevardnadze in Moscow and asked him if he could use his influence with Gorbachev to get the film shown in May at a big film festival in the capital. Shevardnadze felt a certain pang of guilt or obligation and met with Gorbachev.

"I owe a lot of people back home and I can't repay them all now," Shevardnadze told Gorbachev. "But there is one debt I must pay no matter what happens, and you can help me."

Shevardnadze arranged a screening of *Repentance* for Gorbachev. When the film was over, Gorbachev, whose grandfathers had both been imprisoned during the Stalin era, gave his approval to release the film.

But a crisis intervened: the nuclear disaster at Chernobyl. The decision had to be put off.

At around the same time, Elem Klimov, a director and the new head of the Filmmakers' Union, set up a "conflict commission" as a way to move some of those many films that had been banned under previous Soviet leaders off the shelf and onto the screen. Klimov realized that the themes of Abuladze's *Repentance* were so explosive that it would require a decision at the highest level. He went to the liberal ideologist of reforms Aleksandr Yakovlev. Yakovlev was astonished by *Repentance* and called Abuladze into his office and revealed his plan. They would "leak" the film, showing it first to limited audiences in carefully selected venues. Then they would slowly increase the number of screenings, creating a certain inevitability about *Repentance*.

As it turned out, the interplay between the screenings of *Repentance* and the timing of major political events was uncanny. In October 1986 there were several showings of the film, mainly for audiences of well-connected intellectuals in Moscow, Tbilisi, and other major cities. Then in January 1987, Gorbachev presided over a breakthrough plenum of the Central Committee at which he gave the clearest indication yet that he was preparing a radical reform of the political and economic systems. Filled with self-confidence now, Gorbachev returned to the public stage a month later, this time telling a gathering of journalists and writers at the Kremlin that the "blank spots" of history must be filled in. "We must not forget names," Gorbachev said. "And it is all the more immoral to forget or pass over in silence large periods in the life of the people. History must be seen for what it is."

Repentance played in thousands of theaters. Millions saw it—including the young man named Dima Yurasov.

———

After he'd been fired from his job in the archives of the Supreme Court, Yurasov had been working as a laborer, unloading trucks at a printing plant. The film helped raise his spirits. Now it seemed to him that change was no longer an empty promise. Yurasov discovered that he was not alone in his quest to learn more about the past. Groups of Moscow intellectuals, most of them old enough to remember the promise and the collapse of the thaw, began organizing discussion groups and public forums. With the sponsorship of Aleksandr Yakovlev, Yuri Afanasyev was appointed rector of the Historical Archives Institute. Afanasyev quickly launched a public campaign arguing for a radical revision of Soviet history and organized a series of lectures on the Stalin era. He invited scholars and the survivors of the purges to come forward at last and speak.

Yurasov, for his part, began thinking that he might "legalize" the work he had begun long ago in the stacks of the archives. He wanted to show people what he had done so far; he wanted their help to expand his collection of the names of the lost. He started going to these lectures and discussion groups, if only to be closer to people who had lived the life he had been reading about in the archives.

On April 13, 1987, Yurasov went to an "evening of remembrance" at the Central House of Writers. The first few speakers gave guarded talks about the crimes of the past. This was an older generation, one accustomed to using a language that hinted at truth, then retreated. They were trained in the art of euphemism and allegory. Their most direct complaint was about the lack of information.

Dima felt frustrated, stifled. Just before people got ready to leave, he asked for the floor and got it. With the angry, put-upon look of a petulant rock-and-roller, Yurasov described his work. He said he had collected 123,000 file cards of information from his own subterranean research. He said he knew from experience that there were at least sixteen million files in the archives covering arrests and executions. When he was rummaging in the files, Yurasov told the audience, he had discovered a confidential letter from the chairman of the Supreme Court of the USSR to Khrushchev reporting that between 1953 and 1957, 600,000 people, who had been executed during the Stalin era, had been rehabilitated posthumously. Another 612,500, Yurasov said, were rehabilitated between 1963 and 1967. He described how from 1929 on, all "anti-Soviet" crimes—the general term used during the purges and after—were recorded on a huge index card file in the archives of the Interior Ministry.

"I have statistical material," Yurasov said. "Not complete, of course, but it gives a general idea."

The crowd was astonished, not only by the numbers but by Yurasov's access to them and his precision. One of the evening's main speakers, an older historian, took the microphone after Dima sat down and said the young man clearly "knows much more than I do and, I expect, more than anyone else in the hall. I am very grateful to him."

As the crowd was leaving the hall, one member of the audience asked Yurasov if he really thought his "sincerity" would lead to anything.

"Well," he said, "it will soon become clear whether a perestroika has begun, or whether it's merely words again."

———

In the summer of 1987, Gorbachev and Aleksandr Yakovlev began drafting a speech on history that would be delivered at a jubilee celebrating the seventieth anniversary of the October Revolution.

This speech would involve one of the most difficult rounds of political and rhetorical maneuvering in Gorbachev's career. To begin with, Gorbachev himself was still convinced of what he called the "rightness of the socialist choice." He continued to see Lenin as his guiding intellectual and historical model. There is absolutely no evidence to suggest that Gorbachev was out to undermine, much less destroy, the basic tenets of ideology or statehood of the Soviet Union. Certainly not in 1987. He also knew well that the Central Committee, the Politburo, and regional Party committees were dominated by men whose careers and very being were based on the persistence of a fossilized view of the world, one that did not challenge too hard the official version of Soviet history: the "necessity" of the brutal collectivization and industrialization campaigns, the "glory" of Stalin's leadership in the war. To keep his hold on power, Gorbachev could begin with only small doses of truth.

In the summer and fall of 1987, the Politburo held numerous sessions on how best to approach the Revolution Day speech. Gorbachev had little choice but to play a game of strategy and euphemism. The Communist Party was not only the most powerful political constituency in the country, it was the only one. What later became known as the democratic opposition hardly existed. The broad range of pro-reform forces, from the former dissidents like Andrei Sakharov to the early "informal" groups like Democratic Perestroika, all put their hopes in Gorbachev. That was where the power was, and they wanted to keep it that way. Gorbachev faced a Politburo in which the committed reformers were a minority of four: Gorbachev, Yeltsin, Yakovlev, and Eduard Shevardnadze. Hard-liners like Yegor Ligachev and moderate conservatives like Nikolai Ryzhkov were in the clear majority. "It would be foolish to think that the conservatives then were any less conservative than the people who led the August coup," Shevardnadze told me. Every word of the history speech was a potential battle, a political war. Yakovlev told me that when Gorbachev passed around a proposed draft, a majority of the members of the Politburo insisted that Gorbachev not call Stalin "criminal." On that question, Gorbachev exercised his option and overruled his colleagues.

In October, Gorbachev went before the entire Central Committee in a closed plenary session for a trial run of the November speech. Like Khrushchev in 1956, Gorbachev gave specific figures to describe the Stalinist terror: how ten of the thirteen Old Bolshevik revolutionaries who survived until 1937 were purged; how 1,108 of the 1,966 delegates to the 1934 Party Congress and 70 percent of the Central Committee were "eliminated"; how "thousands of Red Army commanders, the flower of the army on the eve of Hitler's aggression," were killed; how the triumphs of the war came in spite of—and not because of—Stalin's leadership. As he recited this bloody litany, Gorbachev noticed a kind of disturbed murmuring in the crowd. Breaking off from his text, he retreated slightly.

"Comrades," he said, "please bear in mind that not everything I have stated here will go into the jubilee speech in detailed form. It will include only general, overall assessments of the complex periods in our history."

Some time before the anniversary and the public speech, Ligachev rang Gorbachev on the phone. Ligachev told me that his and his wife's families had been "wounded" by the Stalinist purges, and, yes, he, too, supported the screenings of *Repentance*. But now he was beginning to fear that a strong speech from the general secretary would "blacken" Soviet history.

"This would mean canceling our entire lives!" Ligachev told Gorbachev in a rage. "We are opening the way for people to spit on our history."

Gorbachev knew his prerogatives, but he also recognized the delicate balance of power. At the end of the Central Committee plenum one of the strongest supporters of reform, Boris Yeltsin, resigned in a fury, accusing

Ligachev of "bullying" and even Gorbachev of creating a "cult of personality" that permitted too little disagreement within the Politburo. Yeltsin's resignation, and the furious, ritual denunciations that followed, made it clear that Gorbachev was operating in a political environment that he would one day compare to a "lake of gasoline." In the coming months, as minutes of the plenum became public, people would learn just how volatile, even vicious, the atmosphere in the Party leadership could be. Even Yakovlev and Shevardnadze felt compelled to join the hard-liners in heaping abuse on Yeltsin. Gorbachev, too, showed little mercy. One day, Yeltsin's bravado would be made to order for the historical moment. One day, the hard-liners would refuse to be manipulated and would launch a counterattack, first political, then military. That would be Yeltsin's moment. But now as Gorbachev tried to manipulate the historical debate, subtlety and compromise were required. Yes, Gorbachev would spit on Stalin—but carefully.

———

On November 2, 1987, at the Kremlin's Palace of Congresses, Gorbachev delivered his speech to a national television audience and the great relics of the Communist world. Erich Honecker of East Germany, Wojciech Jaruzelski of Poland, Fidel Castro of Cuba, Daniel Ortega of Nicaragua, Milos Jakes of Czechoslovakia, Nicolae Ceauşescu of Romania, Gorbachev's own Central Committee: they were all there to hear what would, and would not, be said about the history of the regime. Soon, all of them would fall to revolution and election—all but Castro—and in large part, the reason was this speech. Bland, hedged, filled with the Communist Party Newspeak imagined by George Orwell and perfected by committees of cowardly men, Gorbachev's speech nevertheless opened the gate. And the lion of history came roaring in.

To read it now, just a few years later, the speech seems like a relic from another world, an ideological incantation in which the descendants of the tyrant pay annual tribute to the past and the rightness of the Party's course.

"Dear Comrades! Esteemed foreign guests! Seven decades separate us from the unforgettable days of October 1917, from those legendary days that became the starting point of a new epoch of human progress and the true history of mankind. October is truly mankind's hour of genius and its morning dawn. . . .

"The year 1917 showed that the choice between socialism and capitalism is the main social alternative of our age and that there is no way to advance in the twentieth century without moving toward a higher form of social organization, to socialism."

Only many paragraphs and rounds of applause later came the hint of real purpose, an almost apologetic break with the tone of ritual celebration.

"If today we look into our history with an occasionally critical gaze," Gorbachev said, "it is only because we want to get a better, a fuller idea of our path into the future."

Gorbachev was in a pathetic patch here, and when he turned explicitly to Stalin, he promised even-handedness, a balanced view. "To stay faithful to historical truth, we have to see both Stalin's indisputable contribution to the struggle for socialism, to the defense of its gains, and the gross political mistakes and the abuses committed by him and his circle, for which our people paid a heavy price and which had grave consequences for society." Gorbachev even paid tribute to the notion of a determinist course of history and the very kind of historical thinking in *The Short Course*. "Looking at history through sober eyes and taking into account the totality of domestic and international realities, there is no avoiding the question: Could a course have been chosen in those conditions other than that put forward by the Party? If we wish to remain true to historic method and to life itself, there can be only one answer: No, it could not."

Only one answer possible! The applause was deafening.

But then came the reason for all this bilge, a moment of candor that Khrushchev in 1956 could only venture in secret. Finally, a Soviet leader had come before the public, before millions watching on television, to speak a few paragraphs of truth:

"It is perfectly obvious that the lack of the proper level of democratization of Soviet society was precisely what made possible both the cult of personality and the violations of the law, arbitrariness, and repressions of the thirties—to be blunt, real crimes based on the abuse of power. Many thousands of members of the Party and nonmembers were subjected to mass repressions. That, comrades, is the bitter truth. Serious damage was done to the cause of socialism and the authority of the Party, and we must speak bluntly about this. This is essential for the final and irreversible assertion of Lenin's ideal of socialism.

"The guilt of Stalin and those close to him before the Party and the people for the mass repressions and lawlessness that were permitted are immense and unforgivable. . . . even now we still encounter attempts to ignore sensitive questions of our history, to hush them up, to pretend that nothing special happened. We cannot agree with this. It would be a neglect of historical truth, disrespect for the memory of those who found themselves innocent victims of lawlessness and arbitrariness."

A few paragraphs submerged in this great stew. As if to save himself, to avoid going too far, Gorbachev quickly retreated to the tone of celebration and absolute self-confidence.

"Neither the grossest errors nor the deviations from the principles of socialism that were committed could turn our people and our country from the path they embarked upon in 1917. . . .

"The socialist system and the quest and experience which it has tested in practice are of universal human significance. It has offered to the world its answers to the fundamental questions of human life and appropriated its humanist and collectivist values, at the center of which stands the working-man. . . . In October 1917 we departed the old world and irreversibly rejected it. We are traveling to a new world, the world of Communism. We shall never deviate from this path."

And, the transcript tells us, "[prolonged and stormy applause]."

At the time, many historians in the West called the speech a huge disappointment, if not a sellout. But for all the glaring insufficiencies of the speech—its unwillingness to criticize Lenin, its praise of the brutal collectivization campaign—Gorbachev opened the most important discussion of all. Intellectually, politically, and morally, the speech would play a critical role in undermining the Stalinist system of coercion and empire. The Kremlin's reluctant "discovery" in 1989 of the secret protocols to the Molotov-Ribbentrop Pact, which signed over control of the independent Baltic states from Nazi Germany to Moscow, accelerated the liberation of Latvia, Lithuania, and Estonia. A roundtable discussion published in *Pravda* simply arguing the merits of the 1968 invasion of Prague came just as hundreds of thousands of Czechoslovaks were demonstrating in Wenceslas Square. The *Pravda* article confirmed the Kremlin's shifting attitude toward its own past and helped rob the Czech Communist Party of its last shred of "legitimacy." The Polish people would learn the truth about the massacres in the forests of Kalinin, Katyn, and Starobelsk and the origins of their country's subjugation to Moscow. There were dozens of other examples. History, when it returned, was unforgiving.

CHAPTER 5

WIDOWS OF REVOLUTION

Two months after Gorbachev's history speech, my wife, Esther, and I moved from Washington to a two-room apartment on October Square in central Moscow. No. 7 Dobryninskaya Street was a titanic L and had the hulking gravity of Co-op City in the Bronx, but little of its charm. Except for the foreign cars in the parking lot and the armed guards protecting them, the building looked like most others in the city. It was a ruin the day it went up and it was always threatening to come down. Concrete fell away from the walls in chalky little chunks. The elevator slammed shut like a cattle-car door. At $1,200 a month, my masters at *The Washington Post* were paying hundreds of times more in rent than the average Muscovite did for a similar place. This may be counted as the last vestige of state socialism. The Communist Party bureaucracy that ran the building—an agency of harpies and spooks called UPDK—gouged foreigners for hard currency whenever they could. I once asked if I might have a phone line capable of calling abroad, a maneuver that should cost about $15. This would cost $20,000, UPDK replied. So you had to love them for that.

Across the street from us was the city's biggest statue of Lenin, a bronze behemoth that had run the workers' state more than $6 million. It was a glorious thing to see. A mythic wind bulged Lenin's bronze coattails and billowed his trouser legs as he pointed toward the "shining future."

The city was littered with horrific monuments, and each had its own nickname and local following. The husky statue of the poet Mayakovsky was known as "Mr. Big Pants," and the soaring, silver phallus paying tribute to the Soviet space program was known as "The Impotent Man's Dream." But Lenin was ours, our rendezvous, as in "Let's meet near Lenin's left shoe." He was irresistible. Tourists were forever coming to stare up the great man's skirts and take a picture. Nearly four years after we arrived, local engineers were measuring Lenin for destruction. The best strategy, they felt, was to saw him off at the ankles and bring him down with a crane. But that's getting ahead of the story.

The weather when we arrived was filthy: a drizzly cotton-wool sky, muddy snow humped along the curbs. The ancient cars slogged like hippos along the swampy streets, their movement barely perceptible through the fog. The world of Russia moved in slow motion. A light snow or rain would fall and the sidewalks would be iced for days. Just to stay upright, you had to walk with a certain slide and push, your feet never quite leaving the ground. Here and there you would see someone—invariably a block-sized babushka, knees sore and numbed from hours waiting on lines, her nerves frayed with the rub and bump of shopping in stores with nothing in them—suddenly slip fiercely, flipping a couple of feet in the air and landing square on her hip. A fall like that could kill you. Usually it just left black-and-green bruises the size of dessert plates. Soon I had two myself, one for each side, the insignias of arrival.

I had imagined a winter out of David Lean's (not Pasternak's) *Doctor Zhivago,* a CinemaScope vista of whiteness and cold. But real winter was endless and foul, a gray slog that began in late September and ended with the even uglier spectacle of late April, known euphemistically as spring. The melting snow, the dun-colored landscape, the buses so caked in mud that you could not see out the windows, the sudden appearance of defeated-looking weeds, all reminded one Russian friend of "an old whore disrobing." If the sky was blue over Moscow ten or fifteen days between September and May it was a lot. Living without light was like living on another planet, another realm, and by the time we'd been there a year, we both felt like mushrooms, mushy and beige. I once asked a painter I knew why he did not emigrate when his work was starting to sell for thousands of dollars in Europe and America. "For the light," he said.

The rooms were bugged, of course. Not that we ever saw the mikes. But doubting their existence was both stupid and bad form. Stupid, because I didn't want to say anything that would get a Soviet friend in trouble; bad form, because I felt that if our offices did not think we were under "psychological pressure" we might lose the cost-of-living allowance. No successor would forgive me that. In the bad old days, a foreigner's apartment was pretty much off-limits to ordinary Soviets. Our predecessors, "pre-Gorbachev," would never have dreamed of having Soviet friends over for dinner. The only Soviets you had as guests were people you couldn't stand: low-level officials, shady instituteniks, and hack journalists, all of whom were spooks, or at least extremely cooperative with "the organs." They were safe. But the prospect of having a real friend show his documents to the militiaman stationed at the compound gate was too grim. Now, under Gorbachev, that was gradually changing. Friends now pointed to the chandelier and said, "I hope the microphone is on, because I have something very important I want to say. Gorbachev sucks." Or doesn't suck. Whatever. Fear was slowly on the way out.

———

As a resident of the October Region—a cigar-shaped ward running south along the length of Leninsky Prospekt—I thought it wise to visit the men who ran the place. This was something no reporter would ever have dreamed of doing before. But glasnost, this curious striptease of ideology and language, was now at center stage. With each week another taboo fell to the floor. It hardly mattered that Gorbachev's committee-written speech on history had been an exercise more in evasion than revelation. One day it was all right to know that Stalin was "rude," as Lenin put it in his last testament; then it was all right to know he had slaughtered millions during the collectivization of Ukraine. Gorbachev was also making political performance a form of glasnost. In foreign capitals and Soviet cities, he ordered his limousine to stop, got out on the streets, and worked the crowds. No one had ever seen such a thing: a modern Soviet leader who walked without an aide at each elbow.

"Who is Gorbachev's chief supporter?" the joke went.

"No one. He can stand up all by himself."

The puffy gray men in the lower ranks of the Communist Party, men who had run the cities and towns like feudal princes, were beginning to get the idea that a little contact with the serfs they commanded just might prolong their dominion. And so it was that I was extended a warm welcome to the Regional Communist Party Committee of the October Region.

"Please come by," Mikhail Kubrin, the Party secretary, said over the phone in that extra-casual tone so in vogue in 1988. It was a tone, at once nervous and flip, that wanted you to get the idea that these fellows had been doing nothing but chatting up the constituents since the days of Lenin. Then, as a flourish of confidence, Kubrin said, "Bring a notebook."

I arrived at the October Regional Party Committee, a gray concrete hulk. In the lobby, an old woman with legs wrapped in elastic bandages mopped the floor with filthy water. She kept missing the same spot, over and over. There was the overpowering smell of disinfectant, bad tobacco, and wet wool. This was the winter smell of Russia indoors, the smell of the woman in front of you on line, the smell of every elevator. Near an abandoned newsstand, dozens of overcoats hung on long rows of pegs, somber and dark, lightly steaming, like nags in a stable.

Suddenly, Kubrin appeared, all smiles and handshakes, a real glasnost man.

"Welcome, Comrade Resident!" he said.

Kubrin led me up a flight of stairs to his office. He was a New Age sort of Soviet leader with a European tie and a good haircut. He was at that middle rank in Moscow where loyal service to the state might bring a trip to the Bulgarian coast in summer. And there, too, was Yuri Laryonov, the head of the municipal government apparatus, a meaty fellow with Gorbachevian rhetoric and a Brezhnevian brow. Laryonov spoke sweetly enough, but his handshake made it clear that he was capable of crushing a Volga sedan or at least a petty bureaucrat when and if the occasion demanded. His face was as worn and gray as steel wool.

We sat down at a huge table of polished blond wood. A secretary, jittery and quick, served tea and cookies all around. She set down a chipped amber bowl filled with the wrapped candies produced down the road by the Red October chocolate factory.

"Well, what is it you would like to know?" Laryonov said, smiling and rolling his candy wrapper into a tight little spear.

"To tell you the truth," I said, "I come as a resident as well as a reporter. I'd love to know why every year you shut off the hot water in the district for a month. A whole month at least. The heat is nothing to write home about, either."

This tack was known at the time as "exploring the limits of glasnost."

Laryonov leaned forward in his chair and smiled the smile of a hungry cheetah spotting a gazelle with a sprained ankle. "I'm glad some of our foreign friends live in our district," he began, "but, sir, if you write a lousy article, we'll not only turn off your hot water, we'll turn off your lights and turn your sewage pipes around."

We all laughed, but it was clearly time to change the subject. The talk turned to the trials of running a city district of 230,000 people, forty-four schools, eleven technical colleges, the Academy of Sciences, the Gubkin Institute of Oil and Gas, the Red Proletariat machine-tool factory. To say nothing of the chocolate plant. Like every politician I have ever known, the men of the October Region wanted you to feel sorry for them, to feel for a moment their terrible burden. And for the next hour or so, the two of them,

Laryonov and Kuprin, whined about their common plight. For the first time, people were calling them on the phone and complaining about the garbage pickups that never came, the ten-year waiting lists for a phone, the fifteen-year waiting list for an apartment. There was a couple, divorced for more than five years, calling to say that they were forced to live together in a one-room apartment and if the Party couldn't find them another room somewhere the Party would have "blood on its hands, as if it needs more of it. You pigs. Goodbye."

The two of them, Laryonov and Kubrin, sighed magnificently. I mentioned that there had been a great many articles in the press about the privileges of the party apparatus—the cars, the apartments, the vacation retreats.

This was not the right thing to say, apparently.

"The only privilege we have," Laryonov said angrily, "is working weekends. And the privilege of people calling us on the phone and telling us we are petty bureaucrats. And that is not the worst thing they say!"

"Not the worst," Kubrin said, his head in his hands. "Not the worst thing at all."

———

It was not easy getting the feel for Moscow that winter of our arrival. One freezing morning, Esther and I decided to visit the Kremlin churches. We took the metro to the Lenin Library. As we were coming out of the train, I saw a man with no legs pushing himself along on a dolly cart. What hell it was to live disabled in Moscow: no ramps, elevators that gave out every other day. You hardly saw anyone on crutches or in a wheelchair, though. The state packed most of them off from childhood and stuck them in "internats," dismal homes outside of town. And now this man was wrist-deep in slush, the commuters rushing around him or bumping him with their knees and net shopping bags stuffed with potatoes and beets. His face, angular with a slight gray beard, seemed familiar. I thought I remembered his picture from an old book about the dissident movement.

I badly wanted to write something about the disabled and began to introduce myself. But before I could go on much further, he said, "Help me up these stairs, would you? There is a demonstration in fifteen minutes." As Esther and I helped him, he said he was in fact the man in the book: Yuri Kiselyov, the founder of the Initiative Group for the Defense of the Rights of Invalids.

When we got to the top of the stairs, Kiselyov pointed to the front of the library and a small crowd milling around. "Well, there they are," he said. "The demonstrators. And the rest of them. This should be something to see."

I had no idea what he was talking about. All I could see was some students and passersby, a few buses parked on the street.

"What demonstration?" I said.

Yuri rolled over to a slight young man with a black beard who was passing out a mimeographed newspaper.

"This is Sasha Podrabinek," Yuri said. Podrabinek had been jailed twice for his protests against the regime's use of psychiatric hospitals as prisons. Now he was editing a unique newspaper called *Express-Khronika,* a mimeographed weekly paper filled with short news items: a taxi drivers' strike in Chekhov, an emigration case in Kharkov, a mass rally in Yerevan. It was as if Podrabinek had developed an underground Associated Press in a country that had never had such a thing. All week long, he and his staff took dictation from their far-flung correspondents. On Saturday mornings, when the police were not too much in evidence, Podrabinek passed out his paper on the Arbat and in Pushkin Square.

"You see those people on the top step?" Podrabinek said now. "They're Crimean Tatars. At noon they're going to unroll a banner." It was a strange feeling, as if we had wandered onto a backlot at Universal or MosFilm and we were waiting for the crew to fix the lights before the big scene.

Podrabinek turned to the street.

"Now. See those yellow buses?" he said. "With the tough guys sitting in them? They're all KGB and hired goons. Just before noon they'll come out and try and stop the whole thing."

We were all standing on the library plaza, glancing from one side to the other. I checked my watch. It was 11:58.

The KGB made the first move. An officer in an enormous blue overcoat and black felt boots climbed out of the first bus, three others trailing behind him.

Surrounded now by KGB men, Podrabinek lowered his voice and continued narrating for my education this sidewalk guerrilla theater: "Watch how they circle behind the Tatars. . . . Notice the cameras. . . ."

The lead officer tried to dip his head closer to listen. One of the other agents lifted his lapel to his mouth and started muttering.

"Would you like me to talk a little louder for your microphone?" Podrabinek said.

The agent did not smile. He looked down and spotted Kiselyov on his cart.

"You are anti-Soviet, aren't you?" he said. We all waited for Yuri's answer.

"It's you who are anti-Soviet," he said.

Then the officer pointed to the Tatars waiting for the noon bell on the library steps. They were just a few of the many thousands who had been deported during the Stalin era, all under the pretense that they had supported Hitler during the war. Stalin wanted to destroy any sort of national movement or feeling in the Soviet Union in his quest to create a "Soviet man." He was prepared to kill him to do it. Gorbachev, for his part, told his comrades on Revolution Day that all this had been a triumph. Multinational harmony had been achieved.

"Why do you bother with them?" the officer asked me, this time using a confiding between-us sort of tone. "It's their problem, not yours."

At noon, the KGB plainclothesmen, goonish young men with strips of orange cloth tied around their sleeves, poured out of the buses. A few started snapping pictures with Instamatics, and one guy panned the scene with a Sony videocamera.

Now the protesters took their cue as well, unfurling a banner that read: "Let Us Go Back to Our Homeland." The officer told them they were in violation of a recent order of the Moscow Communist Party banning demonstrations without authorization.

"They denied us permission," one of the Tatars said.

"Then that's it," the officer said, throwing up his hands and signaling to his charges. The KGB men ripped the banner to shreds. The Tatars did not put up much of a fight as they were led away to the buses.

Meanwhile, another officer demanded our passports and documents and wrote it all down. Then the officers with the cameras took our pictures.

The whole demonstration lasted no more than three minutes. Esther and I tried to flag down a cab with Podrabinek and Kiselyov. We waited a long time and no taxi. After a while one of the KGB officers came up behind us and, sweet as could be, said, "You might have better luck getting a cab on the other side of the street." Then he walked away.

Kiselyov laughed and said, "The KGB want us to think they're just people with a job to do."

The protesters were kicked out of Moscow. Most of them went back to Tashkent, the capital of Uzbekistan, where their families had been shipped in railroad cars in 1944. They were planning another series of demonstrations for the spring.

———

But for all the demonstrations and local politics in those early days of glasnost, the greatest changes so far were not on the streets, but on the pages of the weeklies *Moscow News* and *Ogonyok,* the thick journals *Novy Mir* and *Znamya,* and in those tentative but startling speeches of Mikhail S. Gorbachev. Reading was the thing. Every day, the papers were filled with the ghoulish and the heartbreaking; novels were serialized in the monthly journals after a wait of decades; history and literature were now breaking news. It would be a mistake to think that the outpouring of articles, the publication of long-banned books and poems, was a phenomenon limited to the Moscow and Leningrad intelligentsia. "The truth was that by the time *Zhivago* and Brodsky and all the rest came out, the intellectuals had already read them in samizdat editions," the fiction writer Tatyana Tolstaya told me. For Tolstaya, glasnost meant that she no longer had to hide her foreign books in her ground-floor flat in central Moscow. "Glasnost," she said, "is wonderful for the intelligentsia, but, first and foremost, it is a revolution for the proletariat." What was really incredible in 1988 and 1989 was to ride the subways and see ordinary people reading Pasternak in their sky-blue copies of *Novy Mir* or the latest historical essays in the red-and-white *Znamya.* For a couple of years, stokers, drivers, students, everyone consumed this material with an animal hunger. They read all the time, riding up escalators, walking down the streets, reading as if scared that this would all disappear once more into the censor's black box. A people that had been deprived for so long of all that was best in their language consumed classics on the installment plan: Anna Akhmatova's *Requiem* one week, Andrei Platonov's *Chevengur* the next. So many people would read one copy of *Novy Mir* that they would have to wrap it in a makeshift bookcover to protect it from fraying. Often they used *Pravda,* giving it, at last, a worthy purpose. A few foreigners also had places in that early pantheon, especially the British historian Robert Conquest for his work on the purges and, most of all, George Orwell for his uncanny description of the totalitarian state. "People read *Nineteen Eighty-four* for the first time and they discovered that Orwell, who got his education at Eton and on the streets of colonial Burma, understood the soul, or soullessness, of our society better than anyone else," the philosopher Grigori Pomerants told me.

In the dailies, there were articles on prostitutes, drug addicts, KGB informers, hippies, motorcycle gangs, nudists, mass murderers, rock stars, faith healers, and beauty queens, and all of it was new. No one had ever read anything like it. The weekly *Ogonyok* was publishing startling stuff on the war in Afghanistan by Artyom Borovik, a journalist in his late twenties who used his connections to get to the front. His father, Genrikh, had a more than passing relationship with both the KGB and Gorbachev himself. While his father was working as a "journalist" in New York, Artyom was prepping at the Dalton School. Artyom's English was as good as it gets. He said his models for his reports on the troops in Afghanistan were Michael Herr's book on Vietnam, *Dispatches,* and Hemingway's journalism from the front. Eventually, he wound up with free-lance assignments from *Life* and an on-air job with *60 Minutes.*

———

For a reader, the hardest business was dealing with political prose. Until the very end, the prose of the Communist Party and its journalistic organs was clogged with the "Novoyaz"—the Newspeak—formed over dozens of years, great clots of language that had no purpose other than meaninglessness, the putting off of meaning, the softening of meaning. Gorbachev had given his crucial speech on history showing an uncanny ability to go on and on, for paragraphs, in the language of ritual: ". . . unforgettable days of October . . . a new epoch of human progress and the true history of mankind . . . mankind's hour of genius and its morning dawn . . . the rightness of the socialist choice made by October . . . a higher form of social organization . . ." This was language from the Newspeak appendix of Orwell's novel, gobs of pseudo-elevated language that expressed the sentiments of almost no one. Gorbachev was still operating in the hermetic culture of the Communist Party, a world in which the Leader had only to communicate to the members of the Party and, especially, its leaders. To speak directly and honestly to the people about the true state of deterioration in the Soviet Union would have been to risk the fury and revenge of the nomenklatura. The people hardly listened anymore to the old clichés. Who, after all, still believed that a new "epoch of human progress" began in October 1917? Certainly not the farmers of southern Russia humping hay on their backs while their tractors lay rusting in the mud. Who believed this was a "higher form of social organization"? Certainly not the workers and patients at the hospital in Krasnoyarsk, where the head physician said that the only way to get needles was to "scrape the rust" off the old ones and use them again. No, this was the old ritual in which the leadership spoke a dead language—a colorless, lying Latin—and the people spoke the vulgar tongue. The Party language had a ruinous effect on Russian, so much so that when people heard a speech by Sakharov, one of the first things they would comment on—even before the inevitable wisdom of it—was the purity of his Russian. Orwell would have loved that.

In the history speech, Gorbachev was also capable of self-deception. "Comrades," he said, "we justly say that the nationalities issue has been resolved for our country." That sentence alone reflected the Party's most suicidal illusion, that it had truly created a Soviet man, a multinational state in which dozens of nationalisms had all dissolved. Within a year, events in Yerevan, Vilnius, Tallinn, and beyond would prove otherwise. At least in public, Gorbachev seemed to have no idea of where events would lead, no idea, even, what the general movement of history was. "In October 1917 we departed the old world and irreversibly rejected it," he said. "We are traveling to a new world, the world of Communism. We shall never deviate from this path. [prolonged and stormy applause]"

In retrospect, it appears that the speech was a crucial moment in the intellectual and political history of the empire's decline and fall. But at the time, Gorbachev seemed intent on replacing a clearly odious, untenable official history with a more liberal one, a model that proposed revised catchwords and icons for his stated goal: reforming socialism. Looking at the period after Lenin's death, Gorbachev saw an opportunity lost, a dream betrayed. His rejection of Stalinism and embrace of socialist "alternatives" was the basis of his original vision as well as the long-held hope of an entire generation of party officials and intellectuals who became idealists during the Khrushchev thaw.

These *shestidesyatniki*—"men of the sixties"—were half-brave, half-cynical careerists, living a life-in-waiting for the great reformer to come along and bring Prague Spring to Moscow. While they took few of the risks of the dissidents, the best of them refused to live the lie and found subtle ways of declaring at least a measure of independence from the regime. Some hurt their careers by refusing to join the party. Others joined research institutes or publications in the provinces or Eastern Europe where they could express themselves a bit more freely. They kept something alive within themselves. When Gorbachev took power, he put members of this thaw generation in positions of power. They edited key newspapers and magazines, led influential academic institutes, and even made policy recommendations to the leadership.

For about a year after the speech, Gorbachev was the country's principal historian, and he wanted to control the flow of revelations, keep them within certain bounds. Yuri Afanasyev, the rector of the Historical Archives Institute, soon discovered that while archives on the Stalin era were forthcoming, papers critical of Lenin and other first-generation leaders were not. A popular documentary released in early 1988, *More Light,* made a demon of Stalin but trod lightly around Lenin and the Red Terror. Later, Gorbachev's Party ideologist, a dense character named Vadim Medvedev, told reporters there was no way the Politburo could allow publication of Solzhenitsyn, especially considering the anti-Leninist heresies in *The Gulag Archipelago* and *Lenin in Zurich.*

In its way, Gorbachev's schematic view of the Soviet past was as ideologically driven—though not nearly as pernicious—as the old Party version. To legitimize his plans for a liberalized socialism, Gorbachev and his generation in the Party intelligentsia even created a new set of icons. They emphasized the "late Lenin" of the less draconian New Economic Policy of the early 1920s; Khrushchev, as the initiator of the anti-Stalinist thaw; Yuri Andropov, as a general secretary of the Party and technocratic reformer who "died too soon"; and, perhaps most of all, Nikolai Bukharin, the relatively flexible Bolshevik ideologist who was executed by Stalin in the purges.

Gorbachev, as general secretary of the Party, had no choice but to find a Lenin of his own. But if Gorbachev intended to appear the humanist Party man, a Soviet Dubček, he could not look to the fury of Lenin's *State and Revolution* or his bloody-minded letters and cables ("We must kill more professors!") after the Bolshevik coup. To highlight a slightly more forgiving spirit in the Leninist canon, Gorbachev's circle leaned on a few late essays such as "On Cooperation" and "Better Fewer, but Better," in which Lenin seemed willing to endorse a less centralized, coercive economic and political system. Gorbachev's Lenin was represented perfectly in the historical plays of Mikhail Shatrov, *Dictator of Conscience* and *Onward, Onward, Onward.* In those plays, Lenin was the infinitely wise and patient revolutionary, humane, willing to change; Lenin as both *Mensch* and *Ubermensch.*

Khrushchev represented good intentions betrayed by political stupidity. He was the bumptious peasant who dared to undercut the Stalin cult but then lost his way in the 1960s with a series of capricious decisions that so upset the conservatives in the Politburo that they overthrew him. Until the moment of the August coup, Gorbachev remained obsessed with the example of Khrushchev, repeating to his aides, as if it were a mantra, that "the most expensive mistakes are political mistakes." He would try to balance forces, stay in the middle, and survive. He would be wiser than Khrushchev and finish the vague, improvisational reform he had begun.

Andropov, the KGB chief before he became general secretary, was important to Gorbachev for two reasons. First, Andropov believed that the first step toward an efficient, working socialism was to eliminate cheating, loafing, and double-dealing in the workplace and the bureaucracy. As a KGB man, he knew just how deep the problem was, and he was prepared to do something about it. In his short reign, Andropov upset the hard-core Brezhnevites by firing the lazy and arresting a few of the corrupt. The second reason was Andropov's unstinting promotion of the career of Mikhail Gorbachev. Andropov greased Gorbachev's graduation from provincial secretary to the Central Committee, and he never stopped campaigning on Gorbachev's behalf. As he was dying of kidney disease at a hospital for the Kremlin elites, Andropov even dictated a testament to be read to the Central Committee asking that his protégé assume his powers in his absence. But, as Andropov's aide Arkady Volsky told me, the party elders made sure that the testament was never revealed at the Central Committee plenum, and another Party mummy, Konstantin Chernenko, won the post instead. "Kostya will be easier to control than Misha," one of the Politburo members said as he left the room where they had settled the issue.

For Gorbachev, the most meaningful new icon of all was Nikolai Bukharin. While Gorbachev was on vacation and writing his history speech, one of his aides sent him a copy of a biography of Bukharin written by a historian at Princeton University, Stephen Cohen. (There was no Soviet biography of Bukharin at the time; his name was mentioned officially only as a criminal, a backslider.) Cohen's book takes the view that Bukharin represented the road not taken—a more liberal alternative to Stalinist socialism. Such a figure could only be attractive, even an inspiration, to Gorbachev and many other reformers of his age in the party and among the intellectuals. The Bukharin alternative showed that all was not lost, that the line from Marx to Lenin did not lead necessarily to economic failure and genocide—to Stalin. Bukharin had forcefully rejected Stalin's "Genghis Khan" plans and endorsed a far less brutal collectivization, a more mixed economy, and a limited pluralism. He was no democrat, but no butcher, either. His ascent (unlikely as it was) would not have led to a civilized state, necessarily, but it might have saved countless lives. Although he spoke of mass-producing "standardized" socialist intellectuals "as if in a factory," Bukharin was also remembered as the one Party leader willing to protect the poet Osip Mandelstam from the secret police.

In his Revolution Day speech, Gorbachev broadcast what seemed to be a series of mixed signals on Bukharin: "Bukharin and his supporters, in their calculations and theoretical attitudes, effectively underestimated the significance of the time factor in the construction of socialism in the thirties. . . ." Meaning that Stalin was right to enforce an accelerated push to collectivize the farms and build gargantuan industrial plants in the Urals, northern Kazakhstan, and elsewhere.

But then, later in the speech, Gorbachev said, "In this connection it is worth recalling the description of Bukharin given by Lenin: Bukharin is not just a most valuable and major theoretician of the party. He is also legitimately considered to be the favorite of the whole party. But his theoretical outlook can only be regarded with very great doubt as being fully Marxist, for in him there is something of the scholasticist. He has never learned dialectics, and I don't think he has ever fully understood it."

There it was: the breakthrough compliment, appropriately outfitted in Leninist language, and then the ridiculous modification. As if there were more than a dozen men in the Palace of Congresses who had an idea—or gave a damn—what "dialectics" meant.

———

In a cramped apartment in south Moscow, a woman in her seventies watched the history speech on television. She listened carefully to Gorbachev's every word, and when she heard the word "Bukharin," she edged closer to the set. Anna Larina, who was Bukharin's young wife when he was sentenced to death at the 1938 Moscow show trials, had been waiting a half century for this moment. She hoped for justice. When Gorbachev finished, Larina leaned back, exhausted and feeling let down. Would Bukharin be rehabilitated? There was no clear signal at all.

"I felt like I was back in limbo again," she said.

When I first met her that year, Anna Larina seemed improbably young for a woman whose life spanned nearly all of Soviet history. Her face was deeply lined, her hair a gray nimbus, but she moved easily and her eyes had the shine of polished stone. In pictures from the 1930s, she was stunning. She poured out the tea and served a plate of biscuits as she ruffled through the old photographs.

"I grew up among professional revolutionaries," she said, showing me a picture of her father, Yuri Larin, a close comrade of all the Old Bolsheviks. "Life was very intense and they all believed in their own saintly ideals. I'd even say they were fanatics. That's what brought them to their deaths." When she was a child, Larina's father was sick, so weak he could not lift a phone receiver, and so the old revolutionary received Lenin, Bukharin, Stalin, and other Bolshevik leaders in his rooms at the Metropole Hotel. Little Anna met them all.

"Of course, I saw Lenin when I was a little girl," she said. "There was one episode when Bukharin and Lenin were both in my father's room. After Nikolai Ivanovich left the room, Lenin said that Bukharin was the golden boy of the Revolution. I didn't know what this meant and said, 'No, no, he's not made of gold, he's alive!' "

What seemed so strange to me was how Larina remembered those years as an intimate arrangement, the way one might remember childhood Thanksgivings. When Larina was ten, she watched Bukharin and the rest weeping at Lenin's funeral. She remembered standing in the Hall of Columns, near the coffin and Lenin's sisters, across from all the makers of the Revolution. Outside it was incredibly cold. There were fires burning on the streets, funeral marches everywhere, huge crowds coming to see Lenin.

Larina and her family lived in room 205 of the Metropole. Bukharin lived just upstairs. By the time she was sixteen and Bukharin was forty-two, she had a terrific crush on him. One day she wrote Bukharin a love letter finally confessing her feelings. As she climbed the stairs to slip the letter under

Bukharin's door, she saw Stalin's boots ahead of her. He was clearly headed for Bukharin's room. She gave Stalin the letter and asked him to deliver it; for a moment, at least, one of the great murderers of the twentieth century played mailman for a young girl in love.

For three years, Bukharin saw Anna all the time but worried that she was too young, that to marry her would ruin her life. Anna had her father's blessing: "Ten years with Nikolai Ivanovich would be more interesting than a lifetime with anyone else."

Anna never got ten years. She married Bukharin, and they lived in the Kremlin in an apartment that Stalin had abandoned after his wife committed suicide. Bukharin soon admitted to his bride that for the past few years he had considered Stalin a monster bent on destroying the Party of Lenin and ruling through sheer force of terror and personality. Though she had grown up around Stalin, Anna now tried to keep her distance from him. She remembered hearing how one day Bukharin had taken a stroll with Stalin's wife and Stalin hid in the bushes, watching the two of them. Suddenly, he darted into the clear, screaming, "I'll kill you!"

For years, Stalin kept Bukharin off-balance, as he did everyone else in the Party hierarchy. Many of the major Bolsheviks opposed Stalin, but never quite at the same time. At a Party meeting in the late 1920s, Stalin said, "You demand the blood of Bukharin? Well, you shall not get it." Then, in 1935, Stalin once more pledged his friendship to Bukharin at a banquet. Raising a glass, he said, "Let's all drink to Nikolai Ivanovich."

"It was strange," Larina said. "As late as 1936, it looked as if Bukharin's position was more stable. He was appointed editor of *Izvestia,* he was on the constitutional commission, and it even looked as if there could be a democratization process going on in the country. But Stalin played his chess game very cleverly. Bukharin figured that Stalin might kill him politically—that was fine, but Nikolai Ivanovich figured he was a talented man and he would survive. Or so he thought. He thought he could work as a biologist. It didn't scare him." Perhaps the only one who anticipated Bukharin's fall was a fortune-teller in 1918 in Berlin who told him, "You will one day be executed in your own country."

It was increasingly clear by the end of 1936 that Stalin was about to wage a mass purge against his enemies, a campaign that would wipe out millions of political rivals (real and imagined), military leaders, and ordinary people. Bukharin's illusions about his own survival dissolved. After a Party meeting at which it became evident that his arrest was imminent, Bukharin sat at his desk and wrote a letter, eight paragraphs long, and brought it to his wife.

"He read it to me very quietly. We knew the rooms were bugged," Larina said. "I had to repeat the words back to him and to learn it by heart, because he was afraid that if the letter was found during a search, I would be hurt. He couldn't imagine that they would persecute me all the same."

With tears in his eyes, Bukharin dropped to his knees and begged Larina not to forget his appeal. Read today, it gives an eerie sense that it was addressed directly to Mikhail Gorbachev:

"I am leaving life. I bow my head, but not before the proletarian scythe, which is properly merciless but also chaste. I am helpless, instead, before an infernal machine that seems to use medieval methods, yet possesses gigantic power. In these days, perhaps the last of my life, I am confident that sooner or later the filter of history will inevitably sweep the filth from my head. . . . I ask a new young and honest generation of Party leaders to read my letter at a Party plenum, to exonerate me. . . . Know, comrades, that on this banner, which you will be carrying in the victorious march to Communism, is also a drop of my blood."

Larina was terrified as she listened, but she memorized the letter and never forgot it.

Bukharin's trial was an exercise in the surreal. The Central Committee had already condemned him thirteen months before with a simple instruction: "Arrest, try, shoot." Stalin's lead prosecutor in the purge trials, Andrei Vyshinsky, compared Bukharin to Judas Iscariot and Al Capone, a "cross between a fox and a pig," and accused him of leading a bloc against Stalin, of working as a foreign agent, of organizing a plot to murder Lenin. "The weed and the thistle will grow on the graves of these execrable traitors," Vyshinsky said in the courtroom. "But on us and our happy country, our glorious sun will continue to shed its serene light. Guided by our Beloved Leader and Master, Great Stalin, we will go forward to Communism along a path that has been cleansed of the sordid remnants of the past."

Larina could not attend the trial. She had been arrested as a "wife of an enemy of the people" and sent off to Astrakhan, the start of a twenty-year odyssey of prisons and exile all over Russia. The Bukharin's thirteen-month-old son, Yuri, was put in the care of relatives. It was the last time Anna saw Yuri as a child. And as for Bukharin, Anna knew he was dead from the day he was arrested.

In court, Bukharin played an astonishing linguistic and moral game with Vyshinsky, admitting to generalities but denying every specific trespass. Bukharin at once confessed and conducted his own countertrial of the Stalinist regime, all in the accustomed Party language of indirection and euphemism. Fitzroy MacLean, then in the British embassy, attended the trial, and believed then that Bukharin meant his general confession as a "last service" to the party. The same assumption is the basis for Arthur Koestler's novel

Darkness at Noon. Cohen, however, makes the case that Bukharin confessed to the general charges to save his wife and child but made it clear to everyone in his testimony that he was not guilty at all.

While Larina sat in a cell in Astrakhan, MacLean observed the drama from the Hall of Columns: "On the evening of March 12, Bukharin rose to speak for the last time. Once more, by sheer force of personality and intellect, he compelled attention. Staring up at him, row upon row, smug, self-satisfied and hostile, sat the new generation of Communists, revolutionaries no longer in the old sense, but worshipers of the established order, deeply suspicious of dangerous thoughts. . . . Standing there, frail and defiant, was the last survivor of a vanished race, of the men who had made the revolution, who had fought and toiled all their lives for an ideal, and who now, rather than betray it, were letting themselves be crushed by their own creation."

Bukharin was sentenced to die after a six-hour "deliberation" at 4:30 A.M., March 13, 1938. According to the death certificate, the date of execution was March 15, 1938. No place or cause of death was given on the document.

In her apartment, fifty years later, Larina's eyes filled with tears as she talked about those hellish days. She had no idea how her husband died or where he was buried, but it was probably safe to say that, like so many victims of the purge in Moscow, he was shot in the Lubyanka prison and cremated at the Donskoi Monastery.

From prison, Anna wrote a letter to Stalin: "Iosif Vissarionovich, Through the thick walls of this prison, I look you straight in the eyes. I don't believe in this fantastical trial. Why did you kill Nikolai Ivanovich? I cannot understand it." The letter may never have reached Stalin. Larina's wardens told her she would be set free if she would denounce Bukharin. She refused. She spent eight years in prison and was in internal exile until the late 1950s, well after the rise of Khrushchev. For years she lived adjacent to a Siberian pig farm.

When the authorities finally agreed to let her son visit her in exile, Yuri was already twenty years old and had never been told who his father was. Anna and Yuri arranged to meet on a railway platform near the Siberian village of Tisul. On the platform that morning, Larina looked all around for a face she could recognize, a sign of her own face, of Bukharin's. But Yuri recognized her first. Only seconds after they embraced, he wanted to know who his father had been.

"I put the answer off one day after another," Anna told me, smiling now. "Then he said, 'I'll try to guess, and you just say yes or no.' "

Yuri's grandparents had already told him he was the son of a revolutionary leader. But who? Trotsky? Radek? Kamenev? Zinoviev? When he finally guessed Bukharin, Larina said, simply, "That's it."

"I told Yuri he couldn't spread this news around," Anna said. "When necessary, he told his friends that his father had been a professor."

While she was in jail, Anna had never dared write down her husband's last testament. Instead, she lay awake at night in her cell reciting it "like a prayer." But by the time she returned home—weak and sick from tuberculosis—Khrushchev had delivered his speech denouncing the Stalinist "cult of personality." At last, she wrote down the testament. "Finally," she said, "I had to get rid of this burden."

Larina lived in Moscow with her mother, who herself had been in prison and was now very sick, and Yuri, who was suffering from a life-threatening tumor. They all lived on Anna's tiny pension. "Despite my sufferings and the camps, I always thought we would live through this, that this terrible business was just something on the surface and the real thing, socialism, would prevail in the end. I always felt that Bolshevism had been liquidated by one person, Stalin."

Larina tried to win rehabilitation for her husband under Khrushchev. Years later, dictating his memoirs in retirement, Khrushchev said that he regretted rejecting the application. In the late 1960s and 1970s, Bukharin became a kind of banner for relatively liberal Communist parties in Europe, especially in Italy. But in Moscow, Brezhnev and his neo-Stalinist ideologists held out no hope. Once more, Anna Larina would have to wait.

———

On February 5, 1988, the foreign ministry announced that the evidence for the 1938 purge trials had been "gathered illegally" and the "facts had been falsified." Bukharin and nineteen other Bolshevik leaders were rehabilitated. The Party was immensely proud of itself. "I do think we are witnessing a grand and noble deed," said Gennadi Gerasimov, the spokesman who made the announcement at the foreign ministry press center.

This was front-page news around the world, and for good reason. Bukharin's rehabilitation was not so much an act of kindness or justice as it was a theoretical justification for the reformist principles of Gorbachev's perestroika. Trotsky, with his call for "world revolution," provided nothing of the kind, and to the day of the regime's collapse, Trotsky was never officially rehabilitated.

Bukharin's name, which once carried with it the awful ring of "Nicholas II" or "Hitler" in official Soviet history books, was now glorified. Bukharin's essays and Cohen's biography were published officially. Anna Larina emerged from obscurity with a series of interviews to the press and appearances at "Bukharin evenings." One afternoon at the Museum of the Revolution on Gorky Street, I saw Larina and Cohen walking together through the latest exhibit: the world of Nikolai Bukharin. The rooms were filled with Bukharin's papers, his mementos, even his watercolors.

"I believed," Larina said. "I believed. I wrote letter after letter. I kept going. But I was never sure that this would happen in my lifetime. Nikolai Ivanovich suffered so much because he thought that he had destroyed my life. It was awful for him. He loved me so."

CHAPTER 6

NINOTCHKA

The season of Anna Larina's euphoria turned quickly into the season of a coup. Not a coup with soldiers and tanks. That would wait. This was a quiet counterrevolution that the public hardly noticed, a struggle at the highest level of the Communist Party over the most vital questions of ideology and history. The only visible evidence of the coup was scraps of paper: a very dull play about Lenin, a pair of conflicting newspaper articles. But if this "silent coup" had succeeded, the drive for reform could have been stifled once more, perhaps for years. The process was still, as it had been thirty years before during the Khrushchev thaw, reversible.

The conservatives in the Communist Party did not pounce on the high art of the season. Their targets were not Joseph Brodsky's lyrics or Andrei Platonov's prose. They worried more about the transmission of heresy through cartoons, tabloid journalism, television, and dramatization. They worried, in short, about what they still called so lovingly "the masses."

In their January 1988 issue, the editors of the monthly journal *Znamya* published Mikhail Shatrov's play about Lenin and Stalin, *Onward, Onward, Onward*. To a Western ear, *Onward, Onward, Onward* seems yet another example of the classic "Lenin play," a form of staged ideology and glorification that had been described and endorsed by a meeting of the Party Central

Committee as early as 1936. It was a Bolshevik version of the miracle and passion play, a ritualized epic of a savior's arrival, his life and afterlife. In Shatrov's work, as in all such plays, the characters take center stage and give long speeches; they are cardboard.

But now it was clear to the ideologues of the Party, led by Yegor Ligachev, that millions of Russians would see the subtle heresies within Shatrov's version. They would read the play as a total denunciation of Stalin as a destroyer of all that was fine and good in Lenin. They would understand contemporary Soviet life as a tragic failure and the men who ruled them as inheritors of a tyrant's system. They would see the play as an endorsement of the "liberal Lenin," the gentler revolutionary figure who died "too soon." The critical moment in *Onward, Onward, Onward* comes when Rosa Luxemburg steps center stage and reads a letter she wrote from a German prison cell in 1918. She celebrates the Bolshevik Revolution but then predicts disaster ahead:

"Without general elections, without unrestricted freedom of the press and assembly, without a free struggle of opinion, life in every public institution dies out, becomes a mere appearance, and bureaucracy alone remains active. Public life gradually falls asleep; a few dozen extremely energetic and highly idealistic Party leaders direct and govern; among them, in reality, a dozen outstanding leaders rule, and an elite of the working class is summoned to a meeting from time to time to applaud the speeches of the leaders and to adopt unanimously resolutions put to them. In essence this is the rule of the clique, and of course their dictatorship is not the dictatorship of the proletariat but the dictatorship of a handful of politicians. . . . Socialism without political freedom is not socialism. . . . Freedom only for active supporters of the government is not freedom."

When Luxemburg finishes, Shatrov has his Lenin cry out, "Bravo, Rosa!"

An incredible moment. Shatrov had given theatrical shape to the new, approved, Gorbachev-version of things. If only Lenin had lived! A life of tolerance, the shining future! Historically, it was preposterous. While Luxemburg's prophecy could not have been more accurate, Lenin's approval of a Bolshevik Bill of Rights is, and was, pure fantasy. Lenin was a theoretician of state terror. In January 1918, he sent sailors from the Baltic fleet to put down the elected Constitutional Assembly—the Bolsheviks had lost in multiparty elections. And in 1921, Lenin eliminated official opposition, even within the Communist Party. But those were facts, details. They hardly mattered. Interpretation of history had always been politics in the Soviet Union, and Shatrov and Gorbachev bent the facts as long as the narrative had a pleasing conclusion. There was a noble end: to discredit Stalin and Stalinism. Other questions would have to wait.

Shatrov, a man of Gorbachev's generation, not only sympathized politically with the idea of a socialist "alternative," he was related to it by blood. He was five years old in 1937 when his uncle Aleksei Rykov, the former premier, was arrested and later sentenced to death alongside Bukharin. Shatrov's father was also arrested and shot, and twelve years later his mother was jailed as a wife of an "enemy of the people." Because of his own status as son and nephew of discredited Bolsheviks, Shatrov studied at a mining institute rather than at a more prestigious university. When he began writing, it was with a definite political purpose. Using the powerful vehicle of the ritual Lenin play, he would ever so slightly expand the form, drop hints, make rehabilitations and accusations of his own. Like the poet Yevgeny Yevtushenko, Shatrov was vain, at times rather loud about his moments of genuine daring; and like Yevtushenko, he had his privileges and patrons within the Party. Shatrov lived in a vast apartment with antique furniture in the famous House on the Embankment, once a stronghold of the Party elite. His dacha was next door to Pasternak's house in Peredelkino, a village just outside Moscow where the cultural elite spent weekends and summers. But for all his privileges, Shatrov was a figure the gray apparatchiks despised. He was a wooden writer and an unexceptional thinker—next to him, Neil Simon is Euripides—but he had the political skills to make himself a presence, the dramaturge of a threatening new script.

On January 8, at a meeting of Party leaders and newspaper editors, the editor of *Pravda,* Viktor Afanasyev, attacked Shatrov's play, telling Gorbachev that the text was filled with "inaccuracies" that "blackened" Soviet history. Afanasyev, like the majority of the members of the Central Committee, was a relic of the Brezhnev era, a self-proclaimed Marxist philosopher with an aristocratic passion for water skiing. He was not an editor in the Western sense. As editor of the Party daily, Afanasyev was an immensely powerful figure in the Communist hierarchy, a member of the Central Committee who often attended meetings of the Politburo. "Of course, I don't vote," he told me. But on his desk there was a cream-colored phone which provided the ultimate access. There were no buttons or dial on the phone, only the printed word "Gorbachev." "All I do," he said, "is pick it up and I'm connected."

But Gorbachev was clearly not in synch with Viktor Afanasyev. Two days after the meeting, *Pravda* published an attack on Shatrov, excoriating the playwright for "mistakes" and unthinkable "liberties."

On February 1, the letters department of *Sovetskaya Rossiya,* a particularly conservative Party paper, received a letter from a reader named Nina Andreyeva, a chemistry teacher in Leningrad and a Party member of two decades' standing. The letter approved the paper's own negative review of

Shatrov's play and said that an "internal process in this country and abroad" was out to "falsify" the "history of socialism." Andreyeva wrote that the play proved that the author had "turned away from Marxist-Leninist theory" and ignored the "objective laws of history" and the "historic mission of the working class and its role in a party of the revolutionary type."

Sometime in the first week of March, the editor of the paper, Valentin Chikin, came to Vladimir Denisov's office with a small stack of papers. Denisov was the science editor, but lately he had been handling ideology. He had good connections, too. Denisov had spent years working in the Siberian city of Tomsk when Yegor Ligachev was the party secretary there.

"Read this," Chikin said, giving Denisov a photocopy of the original Andreyeva letter. "Let me know your opinion."

Denisov knew Chikin had undoubtedly made up his mind. Chikin was not the sort to care about an underling's opinion.

The letter began with a scathing critique of Shatrov. Nothing unusual on the face of it. *Sovetskaya Rossiya,* which clearly spoke for the most conservative wing of the Communist Party, had been getting many such letters since the publication of *Onward, Onward, Onward* in *Znamya.* But Chikin came clean, according to Denisov's account. He told Denisov that he had been forwarding the letters to Ligachev at the Central Committee's ideology office. One morning, Chikin said, Ligachev called him on the Kremlin's secure phone-line system—the *vertushka*—and said, "Valentin, what are you planning to do with this letter? It must be used in the paper!"

Ligachev, for his part, would deny this. Years later, he made a great show of being honest about his role in what came to be known as the "Andreyeva Affair." Speaking imperiously in the third person, Ligachev lied like a thief. "Okay, I'm ready to answer everything," he told me. "The first thing is, as for the publication of this material, Ligachev had nothing to do with it. . . . Ligachev learned about Nina Andreyeva's article like all readers—from reading *Sovetskaya Rossiya.*"

But not only did Ligachev "advise" Chikin to print the letter, Denisov recounted, he also sent him an annotated copy with certain passages underlined.

Still, the piece needed improvement, sharpening, expansion. Chikin ordered Denisov to go to Leningrad and meet Andreyeva to work further on the letter. On March 8, Denisov called Andreyeva and arranged to meet her the next day. She told him to meet her on a square outside the institute where she taught.

"How will I know you?" he said.

"I'll find you," she said.

On the 9th, Denisov's train pulled into Leningrad station ahead of schedule early in the morning. He was exhausted. Not to worry. Someone had reserved a room for him at the plush Smolenskaya Hotel, the hotel of the Party bosses. It would not have been in the power of an obscure chemistry teacher to make such a reservation. The Central Committee apparatus was on the case and leaving nothing to chance.

Rested now, Denisov came to the square at the appointed hour. Then he heard a voice behind him.

"Are you Denisov?"

"I'm Denisov."

"Then let's go," said Nina Andreyeva.

For the rest of the day, they worked on expanding the ideas in the original letter. Denisov was no great liberal, but he was shocked to discover the depths of Andreyeva's conservatism.

"I'm a Stalinist," she told him in the matter-of-fact way an American might say she was a Democrat.

"Well, what about the Stalinist economic system?" he said. "Hasn't it shown its lack of viability?"

"Just the opposite. The system hasn't had a chance to show its real capabilities."

Denisov decided not to argue. It was going to be Andreyeva's name on the piece, not his, he figured.

The next day, on the 10th, Andreyeva gave Denisov additional material in typescript. He was surprised at how quickly she had come through. He should not have been. Nina Andreyeva was, after a fashion, a woman of letters. Years before she had been thrown out of her institute's Party cell for writing a stream of anonymous letters condemning her colleagues for various ideological shortcomings. More recently, she'd written letters to *Pravda, Sovetskaya Kultura,* and other papers condemning the drift of the Gorbachev line. Just before he left for Moscow, Andreyeva told Denisov, "I trust you and the editors to make whatever changes you think are necessary. *Sovetskaya Rossiya* is not the sort of paper that would meddle with my thoughts." Then she asked whether the piece really would be published.

"I am sure of it," Denisov said. He did not reveal the source of his confidence.

The next morning at the newspaper's offices in Moscow, Chikin said, "Have you brought it?" Chikin seemed as excited as a schoolboy on his birthday.

"I've got it," Denisov said.

"Good. We'll put it in Sunday's paper." That was just two days away, March 13, just as Gorbachev would be preparing to leave for an important trip to Yugoslavia. Aleksandr Yakovlev, Ligachev's ideological opponent, would be leaving for Mongolia. In Gorbachev's absence, Ligachev was the first among equals in the Politburo. His influence in the Central Committee was, perhaps, even greater. Gorbachev had put Ligachev in charge of personnel, and there were dozens of men in the Central Committee who owed their jobs to Yegor Kuzmich Ligachev.

Chikin himself came up with the headline for the piece: "I Cannot Forsake Principles." With unguarded irony, Andreyeva had used the phrase in her piece. It came from Gorbachev's speech to a Central Committee plenum in 1987: "We must act, led by our Marxist-Leninist principles. Comrades, we can never forsake our principles under any pretext."

At the Saturday-afternoon editorial meeting, Chikin told the staff he'd be putting the Andreyeva piece on page three of the Sunday edition. No one gave it much thought. It was a relatively lazy day at the office, a day to chat, drink tea, and keep the paper moving along. Some of the editors did not bother even to read the proofs. They should have. The text, a full page in the paper, was a complete contradiction of everything Mikhail Gorbachev, Aleksandr Yakovlev, and the liberal intelligentsia had been saying for more than a year. The Andreyeva article, Yakovlev would say later, was "nothing less than a call to arms, a counterrevolution."

"The subject of repressions," Andreyeva wrote, "has been blown out of all proportion in some young people's imagination and overshadows any objective interpretation of the past." Stalin may have made some "mistakes," but who else could have built the country so quickly, prepared it for the great victory against the Nazis? The country, she said, was suffering from "ideological confusion, loss of political bearings, even ideological omnivorousness." Shatrov, of course, came in for scathing criticism for daring to deviate "substantially from the accepted principles of socialist realism."

"They try to make us believe that the country's past was nothing but mistakes and crimes," Andreyeva wrote, "keeping silent about the greatest achievements of the past and the present."

There were also some less-than-subtle anti-Semitic remarks, especially to carve up Trotsky, émigrés, and the intelligentsia. "There is no question that the [Stalin era] was extremely harsh. But we prepared people for labor and defense without destroying their spiritual worlds with masterpieces imported from abroad or with home-grown imitations of mass culture. Imaginary relatives were in no hurry to invite their fellow tribesmen to the 'promised land' turning them into 'refuseniks' of socialism."

The piece ran on Sunday, March 13, and within hours, telegrams of support started pouring into the *Sovetskaya Rossiya* offices from war veterans and local Party offices. Chikin boasted to Denisov that even Gorbachev's own military adviser, Marshal Sergei Akhromeyev, had phoned to say that he "fully supported" the piece.

On the same day, in Ligachev's home city of Tomsk, Shatrov's play had its national stage premier. A great battle for history had begun.

———

On the morning of the 14th, with Gorbachev in the air to Belgrade, Ligachev used his position as ideologist to call a meeting of the leading editors and broadcast agencies. He did not invite the two best-known liberal editors, Yegor Yakovlev of *Moscow News* and Vitaly Korotich of *Ogonyok* magazine. Chikin came back from the meeting at the Kremlin beaming. He told Denisov and other editors that Ligachev had told everyone to read the article by Nina Andreyeva, which "in all respects," Ligachev had said, "is a wonderful document." Ligachev also told the head of the Tass news agency to put out the word to all provincial papers across the country that the leadership "recommended" they reprint the Andreyeva letter. By the by, Ligachev said, he was hoping that the Central Committee would soon pass a resolution "not allowing destabilization in the country."

"I was in Mongolia and Mikhail Sergeyevich was in Yugoslavia," Yakovlev recalled years later on Russian TV. "They phoned me from Moscow that the article had appeared. It was quickly sent to me; my aide telephoned Irkutsk, and they sent it and I read it. Well, my reaction was understandable. . . . I know the ways of the apparatus—and I knew it had been clearly sanctioned. Such an article could not appear without being sanctioned by the leadership, because this was indeed an anti-perestroika manifesto. It was meant to overturn everything that had been conceived in 1985. What especially surprised me was the form in which it was done. . . . It had a firm, sort of Stalinist accusatory form as in the style on the front pages of our old newspapers. In other words, there was a shout of command. You know, if this had been an average article based on this theme, I would not have paid any attention. But this was a harsh bellow of a command: 'Stop! Everything is over!' I returned to Moscow the same day. . . ."

For the next three weeks, as the infighting within the Politburo developed, the liberal intelligentsia fell into a state of despair. *Ogonyok*'s editor, Korotich, half in jest, but only half, told friends he was keeping a packed bag handy in case there was a knock at the door. A few editors went to Aleksandr Yakovlev saying they wanted to respond. Cryptically, Yakovlev told them to wait.

There was really only one instance of outright protest. On March 23, a friend of Shatrov's, the playwright Aleksandr Gelman, stood up at a Party cell meeting at the Filmmakers' Union and said the neo-Stalinist attack in *Sovetskaya Rossiya* was designed to prolong the current system and its millions of Party bureaucrats. The Party apparatchiks, Gelman said, wanted only a slight tinkering with the system, a moderate, technocratic liberalization instead of a genuine democratization which would redistribute power. Such a liberalization, he said, was merely an "open fist," a kinder, gentler version of business as usual. The Filmmakers' Union, by far the most liberal in Moscow, endorsed Gelman's statement and sent it on to the Central Committee.

Provincial editors, though, understood the Andreyeva letter to be an official change of course, and very few dared ignore it. As Ligachev had hoped, the article ran in papers across the Soviet Union. One signal that the old Communist guard was on Ligachev's side came from as far away as East Berlin. East Germany's version of *Pravda, Neues Deutschland,* published "I Cannot Forsake Principles" in its April 2 edition. The Party apparatus in Moscow also gave signs of waging an underground agitprop campaign. *Moscow News* reported that conservatives were passing out unsigned leaflets, including one called "Information for Reflection" that said that perestroika would lead to "economic disaster and social upheaval and then to the country's enslavement by imperialist states."

"It was a terrifying time," said Yegor Yakovlev, the editor of *Moscow News.* "Absolutely everything we had ever hoped for and dreamed of was on the line."

———

Lost in all of this was the woman herself.

Nina Aleksandrovna Andreyeva lived on Komintern Street in the Leningrad suburb of Peterhof. All day tour buses roared to and from the czar's summer palace about a mile away. On Komintern Street, though, it was quiet. The shops were empty. The air was still and redolent of gasoline.

I knocked at her door.

Andreyeva opened the door and invited me in. Somehow she did not fit the role of a polemicist, not physically anyway. With her hair swept up in a loaf, her eyes narrow and darting deep within the plump meat of her face, she looked rather more like a head nurse, a starched and angry woman of fifty trying, when the occasion demanded, to be nice. I'd called ahead, but she seemed to have forgotten my last name. I reminded her. Smiling stiffly, she repeated the two syllables, sifting through them for ethnic clues, shifting the accent fore and aft, searching for a nugget of recognition. She was too polite, though, to ask any questions. Finding nothing, she smiled and invited her guest to sit down to tea and a box of candy.

I had decided on the way that it was best not to break with the custom of foreigners visiting Russians. Nina Andreyeva was nothing if not a traditionalist. And so I presented her with a box of German chocolates and a $7 bottle of Bordeaux.

"How lovely," Nina Aleksandrovna said.

She lived in the smallest apartment I had ever seen. There was a minuscule kitchen and, next to it, a room the size of a king-size bed that served as living room, dining room, and bedroom. There were books all over, Party histories and the like, and a huge box of letters. Seven thousand of them, she said, and nearly all in support.

For a while, the discussion buzzed this way and that, confused, frenetic, like a wasp caught between double-paned windows. The train trip from Moscow. The weather. The remarkably low price of books. The train trip again. Finally the talk alighted, somehow, on rock-and-roll.

"Do you like it much?" I asked.

Nina Aleksandrovna's eyes widened just a bit, scandalized. Rock was "mindless rhythms," she said, songs that were "half-animal, indecent imitations of sex." She'd read in the Leningrad magazines about a singer named Yuri Shevchuk. "He sings a song called 'Premonition of a Civil War.' What in God's name is that? I saw this picture of him, showing him dancing, and he's wearing a pair of cutoff jeans and a waistcoat with his belly button showing. Okay, let him do it, but excuse me, everything was unbuttoned so his chest was showing and, down below, his male dignity was protruding! He is dancing with his male thing jutting out in front of all those young girls. How can you talk about purity anymore after that?"

The question seemed to ring in the air, unanswered. Then Nina Aleksandrovna enlarged on her point. "The thing is, we may not need an iron hand, but in any state there must be order," she said, her voice rising to meet the higher theme. "This is not a state we have now, it is like some anarchistic gathering. When there is such a gathering, there is no state, no order, no nothing. A state, above all, means order, order, order."

The labels of public life had long ago become meaningless in the Soviet Union. If Mikhail Gorbachev had been a politician in the late 1920s and had gone around Moscow peddling privatization of farms, democratization of the government and the Communist Party, free markets, and the rest of the pretty-colored bottles in the sales case called perestroika, he would have been branded, with Bukharin, a right-wing deviationist. And then they would have put him up against a wall.

"Now 'right' is left and 'left' is right and no one knows what anything means anymore. Who is who?" Nina Aleksandrovna said. She rolled her eyes like an exasperated teenager.

Her husband, Vladimir Ivanovich Klushin, a whey-faced scholar of "Marxist-Leninist concepts," sat across the small card table, interrupting every so often until his wife resumed her train of thought and cut him off. He tried to put in his two cents on the left-right problem, but she would not hear of it.

"Volodya, quiet. I'll tell it, thank you," she said.

"You see, if Bukharin had been our leader," she went on, "there would have been no Soviet Union today. The Soviet Union would have been destroyed completely during World War II. Bukharin as a personality was fine, a good man. He went skiing with his students in the hills, and anyone could talk with him. But he lacked character and principles. He was for collective farms, but only step by step. He would have dragged it out until the fifties. But if there'd been no collective farms in the beginning of the thirties, then in 1941 we would have been destroyed. Demolished."

And with that, Nina Aleksandrovna smiled queerly and poured out tea and a few tiny glasses of cognac.

Since 1985, she said, the country had been awaiting the results of Gorbachev's reforms. Where were they? "During four years of Lenin, the country succeeded in revolution and won the Civil War and we were saved from foreign invaders. In four years under Stalin, the people rebuffed the Nazi attack and became a part of the vanguard of nations. Approximately the same amount of time was needed to heal the wounds after the war and achieve the prewar levels of production."

And what of perestroika, the "brainchild of the liberal intelligentsia"? Humbug. "The political structure of an antisocialist movement is taking place in the form of democratic unions and popular fronts. The number of ecological disasters is growing. There is a decline in the level of morality. There is a cult of money. The prestige of honest, productive labor has been undermined. We have also aggravated the situation of our socialist brethren. Poland and Hungary are running ahead of us, straight toward the abyss."

It was these feelings of horror, the fearful sense that the country had lost its way and was sprinting hellbent for oblivion, that caused Nina Aleksandrovna Andreyeva to write her famous letter. In her way, she was a defender of "traditional values"—the homey Stalinist verities of collectivization, central authority, the dictatorship of the proletariat. She said she had begun thinking about writing after reading two articles on politics and Afghanistan by Aleksandr Prokhanov in the conservative tabloid *Literaturnaya Rossiya* and the labor paper *Leningradsky Rabochy*. Prokhanov romanticized the Afghan adventure, made it seem like a great imperial quest. She approved, but found them "wanting."

———

Nina Aleksandrovna left me with her husband, tied an apron around her thick waist, and retreated to the kitchen. She prepared an enormous lunch of salads, roast potatoes, vegetables, and meat and only occasionally ducked her head into the sitting room to punctuate her husband's sentences.

While Nina Aleksandrovna cooked, the windows steamed and Vladimir Ivanovich came to life once more. He had been mostly silent in her presence, having learned the price of his wife's celebrity and severity. In her absence he was unbound. As he unleashed a great tirade on the "tremendous value of Stalin," I had the feeling that he was speaking for them both. Where she would temper her comments about Stalin, Vladimir Ivanovich was unapologetic. His lack of fame loosened his tongue.

"What is the younger generation learning from the liberal magazines like *Yunost* and *Ogonyok*? That Stalin was a paranoiac, a sadist, a skirt-chaser, a drinker, a criminal. They try to equate him with Mao Zedong, as if there were no achievements under Stalin.

"As for the repressions, I cannot talk about their scale. Because now people just feel free to present any old figure. Khrushchev, when he was working on the commission about those times, found that eight hundred and seventy thousand were repressed in this country. This is a lot, but it is not a million, not twenty million or fifty million as some people are trying to say it was. Everything now is based on inventions and concoctions.

"Look," Klushin said sternly, "in a struggle there are always victims. But I was at the front in 1943. I knew common soldiers, officers. And they treated Stalin differently. . . . The majority of our farmers and intellectuals respected Stalin. At any holiday, people drank their first drink to the commander in chief, to Stalin. No one was forced to do that.

"My own father was repressed according to Article 58 of the criminal code. So what of it?"

Vladimir Ivanovich told the story of how his father, an engineer, had lost "some kind of state secret or another" during the war. He was sent to a labor camp for ten years. It was harsh punishment for "a slip-up," he conceded, "but, after all, he was to blame for something."

"You," he said, pointing at me with a wagging finger, "you represent a younger generation. Ask your parents who might have fought in the war. During that time, man's life was not as valuable as it is now. In this country, we had war from 1914 to 1917, then again in 1918 to 1921. In wartime, when perhaps a simple punishment is enough, people are executed. This is very cruel . . . but had there not been such cruelty, everyone would have just run around in different directions. Sometimes brutality can be justified."

———

The lunch was hot, long, and filling. Russian reactionaries, I had been discovering, were fine cooks. Nina Aleksandrovna was exceptional. Considering Leningrad was almost empty of food and the provinces were worse, the lunch was a miracle of shopping and preparation.

As she savored her own meal, Nina Aleksandrovna sat back in a hard chair and talked of her life.

"I was born October 12, 1938, in Leningrad to a simple family," she began. "I was baptized and still remember the church bells at Easter. They elevated you to great heights. But I believe in reality. Religion is just a wonderful fairy tale that while we suffer here, tomorrow will be better. Communism is based on your real actions, on what you have done today.

"My parents were peasants from the Kalinin region of central Russia. In 1929, when the famines started, they escaped to the city. My father, my mother, and my elder brother all joined the ranks of the proletariat. My father had only four years of education and my mother less. My mother's family had been considered middle-class. They had ten children, they had a horse and a rowboat with a little motor. There was a cow, too, but the children were always half-starved.

"At the start of the war, my mother dug trenches in Leningrad. She and one of my sisters worked in a hospital where the wounded soldiers came. I was three years old when I was evacuated from the city with two of my brothers and their school class. Mama left Leningrad on the very last train out of the city. After that, all links with Leningrad were broken.

"My eldest sister went to the front and was killed in 1943 at Donbass. Her husband, a commissar with an antitank battalion, was killed a week after she was. My father was at the Leningrad front, and my eldest brother was also at war.

"My sisters and mother and I lived in a place called Uglich until 1944. It was a communal apartment, twenty-two or twenty-four square meters, that we shared with two other families. There was a table—I always wondered why it wasn't used for firewood—and an empty bed and nothing else. No bowl, no spoon, no glasses. Absolutely zero. We were loyal and kept a 'red corner,' a place for a portrait of Lenin; the same place where Christians used to keep their icons. One day they came and told us that my brother and my father, who had been in the artillery battalion, had been killed at the front.

"In 1953, back in Leningrad, we heard the news that Stalin had died. I was in the sixth or seventh form. It was a time of total mourning. All the children stood in a line as the director spoke to us about Stalin. All the teachers were crying. The deputy master of the school was sobbing so hard she could not speak. We all stood there, holding back our own tears. It was a gloomy day, a spring day without sun. We put on our coats and went out onto Nevsky Prospekt to the monument of Catherine the Great. Funeral music was playing on all the radios. Everyone was sad, and everyone was thinking about the same question: What will we do now?"

There was a catch in her throat. For a moment, Nina Aleksandrovna could not go on telling the story of her life. Then she raised her head and waved it all off, half angry, half sad. Why continue the story, after all? It seemed that nothing would fulfill Nina Aleksandrovna's hopes. Khrushchev was a failure, a debunker of Stalin. Brezhnev was corrupt and a fool. Now she was living through an age when dissidents were suddenly dominant, legal voices, and Stalin was compared to Hitler on national television. When Nina Aleksandrovna considered it, her eyes narrowed; a stony anger overtook her.

"Stalin is the leader under whose leadership the country built socialism for thirty years," she said. "We were poor, illiterate people shod in slippers. The majority of the peasants were so poor they could hardly exist from harvest to harvest.

"Our media are lying about Stalin now. They are blackening our history and erasing the world of millions of people who were building socialism in terrible conditions. We are saying, 'Look at how awful our lives were.' Well, our lives were hard, but everyone had the belief that we would live better and our children and grandchildren would live better still. People with nothing could achieve something. And now what? Now do we have such trust and faith in the future? I think in the four years of perestroika, they have undermined the trust of working people—I emphasize working people, decent, normal people—because they have spit on our past.

"An unpredictable future cannot be a basis for a normal working existence of the current generation. In the past, a person going to bed at night knew that in the morning he'd go to work and have free medical care—not very skilled care, but free nonetheless. And now we don't even have these guarantees."

———

We cleared the dishes and took a walk along Komintern Street. The meal had been fine, the talk clear and frank, but by now something had gone very wrong. For a while Nina Aleksandrovna's opinions seemed mainly those of a woman of her particular age and circumstances. She had been poor, she'd lost a brother, her father. She had survived, and all in the name of Stalin. Guarded from real accounts of history, Nina Aleksandrovna made sense to herself, just as so many people had made sense to themselves for so long. But now she was faced with an avalanche of contradictions, an army of "pseudo-intellectuals" telling her that the history of Bolshevism was a litany of horror, and this she could not, and would not, accept. Although she was merely a tool, a curiosity, in a greater political struggle, Nina Aleksandrovna seemed to think that she herself was the lead crusader of the party, its Saint Joan.

Late afternoon was coming on, the long-shadowed moment in the day. But just before the conversation turned into the timeworn suburban ritual of helping the guest figure out the quickest way back to the city—the electric train? the ferry across the gulf?—Nina Aleksandrovna somehow slid into the subject of Jews. She had not been asked. She knew there were subjects to avoid with a stranger, especially an American journalist. It was as if she had been driving and had suddenly fallen asleep and lost control:

"Switch on Leningrad TV," she said. "If you watch it you see that they are mainly praising Jews, whether you like it or not. They may call the person 'Russian,' but that is only for naive people. If they show a Russian on TV, they'll always find a fool with horrible bug eyes and protruding teeth. A caricature. Then they'll show an artist, a painter, who is supposedly a representative of Russian art. But excuse me, he is not Russian. He is a Jew.

"In our society there are less than one percent Jews. That's just a very few. So then why is the Academy of Sciences in all its branches, all the prestigious professions and posts in culture, music, law—why are they almost all Jews? Look at the essayists and the journalists. Jews, mostly. At our institute, people of all different nationalities defend their theses. But Jews do it illegally. We can see that the work they hand over is a simple dissertation, but they insist that they have made a world-class discovery. And there's nothing in it at all. This is how the department is formed.

"Certain Zionist organizations are carrying out their work here. You have to take that into account. They are clever conspirators. I know that our Leningrad professors—I got this information from someone who is no longer at the institute—they go once a month to the synagogue and give them money on the day they get their salary. This goes on. This is constant mutual aid. In such a way, the Jewish people keep getting into the institute.

"You are not even allowed to say someone is a Jew. You aren't even supposed to pronounce the word! You can say Russian, Ukrainian, so why not Jew? Does it diminish the person? Why hide him behind some other nationality? 'Jew' and 'Zionist' mean different things, but all Zionists are Jews. Life has proved this, and not just to me.

"Among our friends, there are some wonderful Jews. In our society, there are some interesting Jews, clever professors, economists, and they don't accept the political positions now being advertised. Do you understand?"

Of course, I said. I understood.

Nina Aleksandrovna looked around a bit. At first she seemed a bit surprised by her own outburst, and then she gave a quick nod, as if to say, "Well, so I said it. So what?"

We kept walking. In the czar's summer gardens, no one knew Nina Aleksandrovna. They knew her name, perhaps, but not her face. In high heels and a white outfit that made her seem even more the head nurse, she had a proud strut, and her husband kept pace, describing this fountain, that historic bench. At one point the talk was of beauty and then beauty contests in the Soviet Union, a new phenomenon. Nina Aleksandrovna made a face that one would have thought she saved specially for rock-and-roll.

"The most beautiful thing in a woman is her charms and femininity, the richness of her soul, her purity. She must clean and purify a man, to lead and raise him to something higher, to take away from him all that is wild and animal. In the sex act, she must enrich him, raise him above animal desire. These girls, they strip themselves down to their God-knows-what, and wiggle their backsides."

After that, we walked along in silence. What more could be said? This was the woman, I thought, who was the ideologist's ideologist. She was both pawn and theoretician, no more ignorant than her sponsors, just less of a politician. At last, we reached the ferry dock. As I climbed into the boat, Nina Aleksandrovna waved and then turned toward home, her face to the palace of the czars and her back to the West.

———

By the beginning of April, Gorbachev and Yakovlev were beginning to win their battle. Perhaps for the last time, they were able to rely on the key authoritarian principle of the Party—Party discipline—to bring the conservatives to heel. Even though the reformers were in a minority in both the Politburo and the Central Committee, Gorbachev was able to manipulate the situation so that defiance of the general secretary would be impermissible. They still had control over the main party newspaper, *Pravda,* and they began to prepare an article that would make it clear that the "Andreyeva coup" and its sponsors had lost.

"The Politburo spent two days going over this article," Yakovlev said. "All the members of the Politburo had their say and expressed their views. Mikhail Sergeyevich's opening remarks were very harsh—he gave a severe assessment of the article—and as a result, as it always happens with us, with our very high sense of principle and probity, everyone agreed with his view!"

Ligachev recalled that two-day-long session of the Politburo as a "witch-hunt in the spirit of [Stalin]." He said that before the meetings began, several members of the Politburo expressed support for the Andreyeva article, but folded under pressure from Yakovlev and Gorbachev.

Gorbachev's article, as drafted by Yakovlev, denounced those who would "put the brakes" on perestroika or indulge in "nostalgia" for the old order. It ran on page three of *Pravda* on April 5. As they read the text that morning, the liberals in Moscow, from Dima Yurasov to Yuri Afanasyev to Yegor Yakovlev, all breathed a little easier for the first time in three weeks.

"It has proved harder than we had presumed to rid ourselves of old thoughts and actions, but there is no turning back," Yakovlev wrote in the *Pravda* piece. "The [*Sovetskaya Rossiya*] article is dominated by an essentially fatalistic perception of history which is totally removed from a genuinely scientific perception of it, by a tendency to justify everything that has happened in terms of historical necessity. But the cult [of Stalin] was not inevitable. It is alien to the nature of socialism and only became possible because of deviations from fundamental socialist principles."

Just after the affair was over, Gorbachev and Yakovlev pretended it had never happened. When asked about Ligachev, they said that all was well and unanimous in the Politburo. To state otherwise would be to mouth the lies of the Western press and its intelligence organs. But long after, Yakovlev would be more candid. "Did you notice that the article against Nina Andreyeva in *Pravda* didn't even mention her name? That's not by chance," he told me. "It was all part of a process that snowballed. Besides, we knew how the whole thing had been organized, who was behind it, who revised the article, who went to see her in Leningrad. Had it been just some lady named Nina Andreyeva writing an article that somebody published, it would have been different. The article in response did not mention her because it was not addressed to her."

In private, Yakovlev urged Gorbachev once more to reconsider his attitude toward the Communist Party. In December 1985, Yakovlev had written a confidential memo to Gorbachev asking him to consider splitting the Communist Party and then siding with the more liberal faction. After all, the Andreyeva affair had already proved just how deep the splits actually were. There could be no acceleration of change while the dead weight of the Party apparatchiks hung on the shoulders of the reformers. Eventually, Yakovlev insisted, they would have to consider the idea not only of two or three Communist parties but of a true multiparty system.

Sooner or later, Yakovlev knew, the Party would have to break with its own history, or it would collapse entirely. The Party was filled with ministers and apparatchiks who swore their fealty to the general secretary, but they were always prepared to betray him in the name of the System. Years later, in retirement, Gorbachev would admit that even he did not understand fully the "monster" he was trying to transform. "At least Ligachev was out in the open," he would say. There were others who would pretend loyalty and then send tanks into the streets of Moscow.

CHAPTER 7

THE DOCTORS' PLOT
AND BEYOND

Sometime between the Andreyeva affair and the start of the Nineteenth Party Conference in June 1988, the anti-Semitic incidents began. In a suburb of Moscow where Jewish intellectuals often rented dachas for the summer, vandals burned one house to the ground and broke into a few others, smashing windows, knocking over furniture, and spray-painting swastikas on the walls. Members of Pamyat and other hate groups toppled Jewish headstones and tacked up handbills signed "Russia for Russians: The Organization of Death to Yids."

Judith Lurye, a longtime refusenik, called me one night and said that she and her friends were terrified. That night they had gone to a hall they'd rented at the Yauza Club for a meeting of their new Jewish cultural organization. When they arrived, the door was padlocked and a pair of KGB officers were on guard. A leaflet was nailed to the door.

"How long can we tolerate the dirty Jews?" it said. "Scoundrel Jews are penetrating our society, especially in places where there are profits to be gotten. Think about it. How can we allow these dirty ones to make a rubbish heap out of our beautiful country? Why do we—the great, intelligent, beautiful Slavs—consider it a normal phenomenon to live with Yids among us? How can these dirty stinking Jews call themselves by such a proud and heroic name as 'Russians'?"

Many of the same Jews who were calling to warn me were also publishing their literary or scientific work for the first time and getting visas to travel abroad. Some were getting permission to emigrate. They had high hopes for perestroika, but they could not let down their psychological guard. A historic dislocation had begun. The economy was in serious decline. If things got much worse, the Jews understood, they would be among the first ones blamed. Far-right intellectuals writing for *Nash Sovremenik* ("Our Contemporary") and *Molodaya Gvardiya* ("Young Guard") were already shaping a fanatic Russian nationalist ideology that made all Jews devils, and all enemies Jews. If they came to despise a Russian, they then wrote that the person in question had obviously changed his name from Goldshtein or Rabinovich.

Igor Shafarevich, a world-renowned mathematician who joined both Sakharov and Solzhenitsyn in the seventies in a number of dissident causes, turned out to be one of the most dangerous of the intellectual anti-Semites. His long essay "Russophobia" proposed that "the Little People"—mainly Jewish writers and émigrés—had ruined the self-respect of "the Big People"—native Russians—by describing them as a nation of slaves who worship power and intolerance. Jews, he wrote, had managed to create an image of themselves as reasonable, cultivated, and European and of Russians as barbaric.

I visited Shafarevich one evening at his apartment on Leninsky Prospekt. He eyed me suspiciously and denied he was an anti-Semite. His enormous hound circled the floor of the study, never stopping. Such accusations, he said, were the result of Jewish "persecution mania."

"There is only one nation whose needs we hear about almost every day," Shafarevich had written in *Nash Sovremenik*. "Jewish national emotions are the fever of the whole country and the whole world. They are a negative influence on disarmament, trade agreements, and international relations of scientists. They provoke demonstrations and strikes and emerge in almost every conversation. The Jewish issue has acquired an incomprehensible power over people's minds and has overshadowed problems of Ukrainians, Estonians, and Crimean Tatars. And as for the Russian issue, that is evidently not to be acknowledged at all."

When I read this passage back to Shafarevich, he nodded in agreement, enthusiastically, as if hearing it for the first time. Then he said, "The term 'anti-Semitism' is like an atom bomb in our heads. Against the background of violence against Armenians or Russians, it is impossible even to speak of anti-Semitism. I haven't heard about a single quarrel or of people being beaten in the face because of anti-Semitism. It is absolutely incompatible with the real problems present now. I am just amazed to hear such things."

Shafarevich was not alone. While many leading Russian writers spoke out against anti-Semitism, the Russian Writers' Union leadership promoted a nationalist ideology steeped in hatred of Jews. In an open letter signed by seventy-two of its leading members and published in the house organ, *Literaturnaya Rossiya,* the union declared: "It is precisely Zionism that is responsible for many things, including Jewish pogroms, for cutting off dry branches of their own people in Auschwitz and Dachau."

———

For months, Jewish friends called saying they were convinced that there would soon be pogroms. Not more abuse, not the occasional attack, but pogroms, a word that evoked the memory of massacres of Jews a century ago in Kishinev, Odessa, and Kiev, a word that implied the tacit participation of the state. The Kremlin did nothing to help the situation. The official Tass news agency ran an item saying that Natan Shcharansky, who had spent eight years in the camps on trumped-up charges before he was allowed to leave the Soviet Union for Israel, was now "scrambling back into the news" as an army conscript. "As he was issued his brand-new Israeli uniform, Shcharansky declared pompously that he had finally found his place in life," Tass reported. "Walking on Palestinian corpses is indeed a logical and natural campaign in the life of that sham advocate of human rights."

It was hard to judge what all this amounted to. One of the older leaders of the Jewish community in Moscow told me he had not seen such threatening signs of anti-Semitism in Moscow since Stalin's time.

I had been complacent about all this until the first night of Passover the previous spring. After all, hadn't vandals desecrated Jewish cemeteries at home? Why was this more of a threat? Esther and I went to evening services at the Choral Synagogue, itself a depressing sight. Outside on the steps, KGB goons kept a careful watch on who went in the building. In a way both cloying and threatening, the agent of the evening (dressed in the easily recognizable black plastic topcoat and red-and-brown plaid scarf) asked questions as if he were taking a poll: "Do you believe in almighty God? Have you ever been to Israel?" Usually, a couple of his buddies waited in a car across the street. Inside, on the main floor of pews, where the men prayed, there were only a few dozen ancients gossiping in Yiddish and some curious tourists from New York and Buenos Aires. The young had long since written off the synagogue as an impossible place to meet or pray. The few observant Jews who had not already gone to Israel or the West prayed in their homes. Even those who didn't care much about the KGB presence outside felt the rabbi had been too compromised over the years.

Upstairs, sitting with the women, Esther got into a discussion about Passover rituals and discovered that they knew next to nothing.

"My grandfather used to do all this," one old woman said, casting back her memories to the last century, "but I forget: how many cups of wine must we drink?"

Esther, who was raised in an Orthodox home and knew the language and rituals as second nature, was astonished. She explained as well she could, but it broke her heart to see how desperate they were to know. "Can you really not eat bread on Passover?" another woman said.

We left the services early to get back and prepare the seder at home for a half-dozen Soviet friends. But when we got to the car I noticed that someone had written on the grimy door a huge Y with a circle around it. Y for Yid. If the leaflets and vandalism had not focused my attention, the writing in the dust certainly did.

As it turned out, there would be no pogroms. But the anxiety was real. As the state structures began to disintegrate, so too did the old facade of a "friendship of peoples." The glasnost that had begun to encourage genuine historical debate also, inevitably, revealed the depths of historical resentments and hatred in Stalin's empire. In Tallinn, I heard Estonians describe Russians as cretins and brutes, and Russians describe Estonians as Nazi collaborators. In Yerevan, Armenians were sure that Azerbaijanis had deliberately "set off" the earthquake that killed at least 25,000 people with an underground nuclear test and were about to carry out an Islamic crusade against them more bloody than the Turkish massacre of Armenians in 1915. In Baku, Azerbaijanis knew with absolute certainty that the Yerevan government was preparing to grab all its territory and assert an Armenian kingdom with the help of émigré millionaires in Los Angeles.

For Jews in cities like Leningrad, Moscow, and Novosibirsk, the new street-level face of hatred was the group known as Pamyat, "Memory." Pamyat began in the early 1980s as a group attached to the Aviation Ministry and was organized by a few cultural activists to help preserve Russian monuments and buildings. But after years of expansion, infighting, and splits, the most vocal group still calling itself Pamyat turned out to be a band of anti-Semitic fanatics, a motley bunch of Russian factory workers, Party members, teachers, career military officers, and street thugs. Their feeling for imagery was impeccable and historically resonant. They wore black T-shirts, a symbol that linked them to the Black Hundreds, the anti-Semitic mob that carried off dozens of pogroms under the last czars.

While he was still in the Politburo, Boris Yeltsin met with representatives from Pamyat on the grounds that as Moscow Party secretary he should get to know a broad range of public groups. He went away from the session disgusted. "Pamyat began as something interesting and then turned out evil," he said. He never had anything to do with it again.

I met leaders of Pamyat at various apartments and rallies in Moscow, Leningrad, and Siberia, and they were uniformly, and not surprisingly, supreme dolts. Dmitri Vasiliyev, a former photographer and bit player in the movies, boasted of having only an eighth-grade education, a claim that did not stretch credulity. At one small rally, this doughy little man barked into a megaphone for a couple of hours, berating Zionists and "those who would humiliate the Russian people." He said that Russian children were being turned into alcoholics because "sinister forces" were slipping alcohol into the yogurt supply. Jewish editors were guilty of subliminal conspiracy because they used six-pointed stars in their papers. Jewish architects "by no coincidence" designed Pushkin Square so that Pushkin's back was to the movie theater, the Rossiya. It was unclear whether Vasiliyev was the most dangerous of the Pamyat leaders. His rival Valery Yemelyanov, after all, spent a few years in a mental institution after murdering his wife. He left the institution just in time to enjoy the fruits of the new glasnost.

The clearest and most comprehensive representation of Pamyat's "ideas" I saw was contained in a twenty-four-page manifesto that had been passed along to me. The document was written in a less hysterical tone than Vasiliyev's rants, but, all the same, it attacked the "satanic" cultural influence of the West and a "genocide of the Russian people." Jews and Zionists were responsible for the ills of Russia. Jews, homosexuals, and Masons were responsible for rock music, drug addiction, AIDS, and the dissolution of Russian families. Brodsky's poems, Chagall's paintings, and Pasternak's "antipatriotic" novel *Doctor Zhivago* were all worthless, a blot on "true Russian culture." The Russians, the manifesto said, "saved" the Jews in World War II, but the Jewish media only mocked and degraded Russians and their suffering: "It's as if the mass media told us that only Jews were killed on the front during the war."

Pamyat members circulated copies of the "Protocols of the Elders of Zion" and won support from *Literaturnaya Rossiya, Molodaya Gvardiya,* and other right-wing magazines. In Leningrad, one of the most active centers for Pamyat, the group denounced Isaak Zaltsman, a Jew who headed the production of Soviet tanks during World War II, for organizing "a chorus of sixteen-year-old Russian virgins" and then seducing them. Elsewhere, Pamyat blamed Jews for food shortages, sex on television, and the nuclear accident at Chernobyl.

———

Compared to what was going on elsewhere in the empire, the real threat to Jewish life was relatively slight. Yet the rise of glasnost, the loosening restrictions on emigration, and the atmosphere of tension and fear of an uncertain future all helped to produce the moment that Jews around the world had awaited for many years. An exodus had begun. Soviet Jews who wanted to leave now for Israel, for the most part, could. In 1989, 100,000 Soviet Jews left for Israel and the West. Hundreds of thousands more were waiting for visas, invitations, and tickets. A people that had once seemed destined for oblivion were getting visas for a new life.

There would be no second "Doctors' Plot." In fact, the only living survivor of that ugly affair, Yakov Rapoport, declared he would not join the new wave out. "My time is past," he told me. "I'm ninety-one years old. It's too late for me. I'll be buried here." And yet his story, and his family, seemed an emblem of the history and the future of the Jews of Russia.

Yakov Rapoport, like many Jews of his generation, well understood that the purges of the 1930s were not an aberration of the moment. Cruelty had preceded 1937 and cruelty was sure to follow. Stalin was indulging his hatred of the Jews. In 1948, Stalin ordered the execution of Solomon Mikhoels, the legendary director of the Jewish State Theater and the leader of the Jewish Anti-Fascist Committee as a presumed enemy of the state. After the murder of Mikhoels—called a car accident by the authorities—the KGB arrested the leading members of the Anti-Fascist Committee, citing a "postwar return to normalcy." Almost as a warm-up to the Doctors' Plot and the coming purge, the KGB killed twenty-three Jewish intellectuals in 1952 on trumped-up charges of spying and treason. Then, in the first weeks of 1953, Stalin ordered the arrest of a group of nine prominent doctors, six of them Jewish; the Party papers claimed the doctors were poisoning the Kremlin leaders and covering up the conspiracy. Stalin's murderous paranoia appeared ready to soar once more. Most historians now agree that Stalin's order to arrest the doctors was similar to the Kremlin-ordered assassination of the Leningrad Party chief Sergei Kirov in 1934—a prelude to a wave of mass terror. Khrushchev said as much in his speech at the Twentieth Party Congress in 1956:

"Stalin personally issued advice on the conduct of the investigation and the method of interrogation of the arrested persons. He said that Academician Vinogradov should be put in chains, another one should be beaten. Present at this Congress is the former minister of state security, Comrade Ignatiev. Stalin told him curtly, 'If you do not obtain confessions from the doctors, we will shorten you by a head.'

"Stalin personally called the investigating judge, gave him instructions, advised him on which investigative methods should be used. These methods were simple—beat, beat, and, once again, beat. Shortly after the doctors were arrested, we members of the Politburo received protocols containing the doctors' confessions of guilt. After distributing these protocols, Stalin told us, 'You are blind like young kittens; what will happen without me? The country will perish because you do not know how to recognize enemies.' "

Of the nine doctors arrested, only Yakov Rapoport lived to see the advent of glasnost. I got to know him, his daughter Natasha, and his granddaughter Vika and visited them several times at Natasha's apartment. The old man was long retired, but his memory was good, his voice as clear as that of a man half his age. "I thought I was finished, a dead man," he said, remembering his despair in prison. "Then one day they let me out of jail—for no reason at all, it seemed. I didn't understand what had happened until I came home and my wife told me that Stalin was dead. It was just dumb luck, for me—and probably for hundreds of thousands of other Jews."

The furious anti-Semitism of the Stalin era and the Doctors' Plot itself were merely two of countless "blank spots" in official versions of Soviet history. The first official publications on the period were Yakov Rapoport's memoir in the magazine *Druzhba Narodov* ("Friendship of Peoples") and Natasha Rapoport's memoir in *Yunost* ("Youth")—both in April 1988. Both father and daughter began writing years before the rise of Gorbachev. But it was only in 1987 that either one thought it might soon be possible to tell the story of the Doctors' Plot. Natasha visited her friends Irina and Yuli Daniel in the country and read them her manuscript. She could not have chosen a better audience. Yuli Daniel, along with Andrei Sinyavsky, had been jailed for seven years in the sixties in one of the very first dissident cases. Daniel's father was Mark Meyerovich, a celebrated Yiddish writer. When Natasha finished reading, Daniel told her it was time to publish.

At Daniel's suggestion, Natasha took her manuscript to *Yunost,* a monthly famous for publishing young talents during Khrushchev's thaw. The new, relatively liberal editors were impressed, but she was told there were "too many Jewish names" in the story, too much explicit discussion of anti-Semitism. Natasha laughed and said, "I told them it reminded me of the joke about the boy who asks his grandfather, 'Is it true Christ was a Jew?' And the grandfather says, 'Yes, it's true. At the time, everyone was a Jew. Such were the times.' Well, during the Doctors' Plot, such were the times." The editors said they would try to publish, but they didn't want to "irritate" the audience. They asked Natasha if she could remember any "good Russian people who had helped" her. The meetings ended vaguely, with no promises, no rejection. The editors had not yet gotten the necessary signal from above, and so they waited.

"Then came November and Gorbachev gave the history speech," Natasha said. "He even mentioned the Doctors' Plot. Two days later there was a telephone call from *Yunost* congratulating me. They had decided to publish.

And then they said, 'Only don't think that it is in any way connected to Gorbachev's speech.' Well, no, of course not! They got Yevtushenko to write the preface. He wrote rather a lot about anti-Semitism, but they cut that, insisting, after all, that Russians, too, had been arrested. There was also a sentence saying that there were rumors of pogroms in 1953, that concentration or labor camps were being prepared to accept Jews after the doctors were executed on Red Square. We fought over that, but what could I do? They cut that, too."

Despite the cuts, the appearance of both Rapoports' memoirs marked the first attack in the press on anti-Semitism. "We took a walk in the forbidden zone," Natasha said.

———

The generations of Rapoports were tied to one another in an easy, undramatic way. Their stories, even their sentences, elided into a single line of thought and memory. Their family narrative was nothing less than the Jewish experience in the Soviet Union in this century. "There is a whole age behind these eyes," Yakov said, "from Nicholas II to Gorbachev." Natasha smiled and put her hand over her father's knobby wrist.

There was great love between them, but tension as well. "I've wanted to emigrate since the sixties, but my parents refused to go," Natasha said. "They were afraid, and I couldn't persuade them. They decided it was too late for them and that they should die here. My mother is gone now. I cherish her memory and I love my father very much. But still, I cannot forgive them this."

As he listened to this, no doubt for the thousandth time, Yakov Rapoport's left hand trembled slightly. He said nothing, just stared at the teapot and let it pass. He feigned a kind of nonchalance that his hands betrayed. When Natasha began talking about her fears that a worsening economy would provide "openings" for groups like Pamyat, he said bravely, "I've seen this before. I'm not afraid," but his hands shook once more.

It must have seemed to him that little had changed. Weekend mornings sometimes, Yakov Rapoport looked out his apartment window and saw the Pamyat boys in their black T-shirts carrying placards around All Saints Church. "Yids Out!" "Down with the Judeo-Masonic Conspiracy!"

"I have seen this before, too," Yakov said.

Rapoport grew up in the Crimea. His first memory was of a pogrom in 1905. "I was six years old. My father was teaching Russian and mathematics where I went to school. We were having a science lesson when the Cossacks rushed in. The school was destroyed. I remember the globes were smashed, there was broken glass everywhere, and my father was badly injured. The police brought the bodies to the morgue, and my father along with them because they thought he was dead. One of our friends saw my father there, only by chance, and they could hear him moaning. He was unconscious, covered with blood. His fingers and hands had been broken by the truncheons. He had tried to guard his face, so they just broke the arms. It took months for him to heal.

"This friend of ours tried to drag my father through a gate to a cab. The school principal was there, and he was shouting, 'Go away, you Jew!' When my father finally returned to the school weeks later, the other teachers shunned him. They would not speak to him, and he finally had to leave the school. This is what was first imprinted on my memory as a child."

As a boy, Rapoport was also caught up in reports of the Beilis case in Kiev. For the Jews under the czars, the case had an impact equal to that of the Dreyfus affair in France. In 1911, police in Kiev found the corpse of a thirteen-year-old Russian boy. His mother, a poor prostitute, accused "the Jews"—that scheming mass—of murdering her son to use his blood to make Passover matzoh. The "Blood Accusation" was rooted in anti-Semitic folklore in Ukraine—and was, of course, preposterous. Nevertheless, the czarist police arrested a Jewish factory worker, Mendel Beilis, and thought they were sure to win a conviction. With the world press watching, the prosecution brought in witnesses to testify that such ritual murders were widespread. "It was an accusation against all Jews, not just Beilis," Rapoport said. "In our school, about half the class believed the accusations, and half did not." But the jury, made up mostly of illiterate Ukrainian peasants, rejected the Blood Libel and set Beilis free.

"It was a great miracle," Rapoport said. "One of the jurors was asked why he had voted for acquittal, and he answered, simply, 'My conscience.' I found out later that those peasants in the jury were seen praying before they brought in the verdict. So religion, at least in this case, was a carrier of conscience."

From one year to the next in Rapoport's life, there were attacks on the Jews in schools and in the courts. There were always pogroms and the threat of pogroms. Discrimination, life-threatening and petty, touched every facet of ordinary life. Jewish students like Rapoport even paid extra fees to study in the state schools. "My family was never religious, but my whole life in the czarist times let me know who I was," Rapoport said.

A keen student of natural sciences, Rapoport set off to study medicine in Petrograd, the city of the czars that would soon be the city of revolution and renamed Leningrad. Petrograd was outside the Pale of Settlement, the only region where Jews were allowed to live, but for some reason the university officials let Rapoport study there. "All in all," he said, "I think the czars were somehow more liberal than the Bolsheviks were." Rapoport arrived in 1915 and rented the corner of someone's room.

Those years were for him a mix of laboratory study and street revolt. After mornings in class and autopsy rooms, he sat in the gallery of the Duma, the Russian legislature, listening to the charges of repression and incompetence gather against the czar. Later he stood on the street and watched Lenin preach workers' revolution from the apartment balcony of the city's richest ballerina. Soon there were food riots and student protests. "When the first— the February—Revolution took place and the czar fell, I was there," Rapoport said. "I was armed with a rifle and a pistol. Together with the workers I helped arrest the czarist ministers. It was a real bourgeois revolution. . . . We thought we would have a constitutional state, as in France and other parts of Western Europe. I don't think that was a naive hope.

"At first, I was taken by the ideas of the revolution, but then I became much more realistic. I had no admiration for the Bolshevik Revolution. I saw it as a terrific threat because of the mass of illiterates inside it who hated intellectuals. That spelled the elimination of the intellectuals. I thought there would be chaos, and I turned out to be right.

"Lenin was surrounded by both Russians and Jews. There was not such a differentiation then. They were just members of the Party, and this ethnic question was not raised there. But there is an interesting detail which quite often evades many people. I remember reading in the complete works of Stalin, where Stalin describes the Third Party Congress, where there was a split between the Bolsheviks and Mensheviks. At the Third Congress, Stalin wrote, the majority of the Mensheviks were Jews and the majority of Bolsheviks were Russians. Malinovsky, a friend of Lenin's, said there should have been a Party pogrom. For Stalin that was no joke. Stalin understood that suggestion as guidance for action.

"In the Crimea after the Revolution, I saw terrible things happening to the White officers. Zemlyachka and Bela Kun came to the Crimea and started to gather lists of people who had taken part in the White movement. They promised not to kill them, just to register them. And then they killed everybody, many young men among them. Those who did register were shot. Those who did not survived. I realized what was going on by then, and who was who."

Rapoport quickly became a prominent pathologist in Moscow. He tried to avoid politics as much as possible. But the better known he became in his field, the harder it became to stand apart. With Stalin in power, Rapoport was constantly being asked to join the Communist Party. Over and over again he refused. He got into trouble in the late 1930s when, as the head of the admissions committee at a medical institute in Moscow, he would not discriminate against children of the "enemies of the state"—those who had been arrested or shot for no reason by Stalin's secret police. Rapoport guessed that the only reason he himself had avoided arrest and execution in the camps was that the country could ill afford to wipe out all its best doctors. "But the truth is I really don't know why I got through the purges," he said. "Good luck, maybe?"

During the Battle of Stalingrad in 1943, the pivotal point in the war for the Soviet Union, Rapoport finally gave in and joined the Party—"for patriotic, not political reasons. At that time the Party was the only force that held the country together. What I will always remember is the interview I had at Party headquarters. The first thing they asked me was 'What is Zionism? What do you think of it?' I was angry with this, but I answered: 'Zionism is the national liberation movement of Jews aimed at the organization of their own territorial state.' They were stunned."

———

Natasha Rapoport was fourteen when the doorbell rang. It was the night of February 2, 1953. One of the family's closest friends, Dr. Myron Vovsi, had already been arrested, and the newspapers and radio had begun a crude propaganda campaign against the "murderers in white smocks," the Jewish doctors.

"There were rumors that, for the sake of 'protecting' the others—the 'innocent' Jews—from the mass hatred, camps were being set up for them in Siberia. All of them would be sent there soon," Natasha said. "The question of how to execute the criminals was widely discussed. Informed circles in my class contended that they would be hanged in Red Square. Many were worried whether the execution would be open to the public or only to those with special permission. Someone consoled the disappointed: 'Don't worry. Surely they will film it.' I had nightmares about Vovsi on the gallows."

Now, with the doorbell ringing incessantly, the secret police had come for her father. The agents rifled through every drawer and book, noting a few volumes of Freud as further evidence for the court protocols against Yakov Rapoport. During the search, one of the agents happened to cut his finger. Terrified that Natasha's mother would poison him with contaminated iodine, he refused treatment. "They phoned somewhere for a car," Natasha said, "and the suffering one was taken away—most likely to a special clinic where his scratch would be treated by a trusted, dependable Russian surgeon."

The arrest was, for Natasha, what the 1905 pogrom in the Crimea had been for her father—the pivotal memory of what it means to be a Jew in a hostile place. "Stalin is a bastard and a criminal," Natasha's mother told her, "but never say this to anyone. Do you understand?" Natasha's friends scorned her, stared at her in class. The children in the courtyard mocked her, telling her that her father had taken pus from cancerous corpses and rubbed it into the skin of healthy people. They hurled rotten tomatoes, stones, and dead mice at her. The police confiscated all the family's money, bonds, and bank passbooks. Natasha's mother sold the family's copies of Tolstoy, Pushkin, and Hugo to buy bread and milk. Natasha lay awake nights wondering when the police would come for her mother, too.

An anti-Semitic hysteria engulfed Moscow. Party committees met in every school, institute, and factory to denounce the doctors and instruct "the workers" to be "on the lookout" for other Jewish plotters. At Moscow State University, Mikhail Gorbachev sat through a painful session of his Komsomol organization and heard a colonel, a decorated veteran of the war, denounce Gorbachev's close friend Vladimir Lieberman. Many years later, at a class reunion, Lieberman told a reporter, "Some comrades sniffed the wind, tried to criticize me. I was the only Jew at the law faculty's Communist Party meeting. Gorbachev had entered the Party right before this event, but it was he who tried to prevent the attack on me and did so very sharply, using some unparliamentary words. He called one of our old and respected veterans a 'spineless animal.' That just stopped them."

But very few rebelled, and few did not believe the Doctors' Plot was a prelude to something more ominous. Within a few weeks of the arrest, the Rapoports were convinced that Yakov was dead. The prison officials said it was no longer "necessary" to deliver food parcels to the jail. Hundreds of thousands of families during the purges recognized this as a sign that their loved ones were already dead.

———

On March 5, the director of Natasha's school gathered all the students in a huge recreation hall. Comrade Stalin was no more, she told them. For forty-five minutes, Natasha looked around her and saw everyone crying, her teachers, the students. She could not cry but tried not to seem too obvious. "Finally they let us go home," Natasha recalled. "My friend and I were walking home and we started to discuss some absolutely other problems and we started to laugh. We had forgotten completely that Stalin had died and we should be mourning with all the others. As we laughed, the people around us on the street were furious, they were shocked. We had to run home because we were afraid we'd be beaten right there on the street."

Three days after Stalin's death in March, there was a phone call, a stark male voice: "I am calling at the request of the professor. The professor asked me to tell you that he is healthy, feels fine, and is concerned about his family. What should I tell him?"

He was alive! Yakov Rapoport came home on April 4. Before coming up to the apartment he called from a phone downstairs: "I didn't want them to have a heart attack at the sight of me," he said. Every year thereafter, the survivors of the Doctors' Plot gathered for a party on that day as an anniversary of freedom. Around thirty people—the doctors who had been arrested and a short list of other "suspects"—celebrated their own survival and the survival of the Jews in Russia.

"Now there is only me," Yakov Rapoport said. "My family and I, we celebrate alone."

———

Yakov Rapoport came home a grateful man. Even now it was hard for him to find much fault with Nikita Khrushchev—"not after he freed hundreds of thousands of people and gave them back their good name." But for Natasha, the Doctors' Plot was a great divide between childhood and adulthood, innocence and alienation. The end of the plot meant freedom for her father, but a different quality of mind and trust for the daughter: "I began to see all the lies around me. I began to have a double life, one outside of my circle when I had to be careful what I did and said, and one inside my circle of family and friends, when I could have my own thoughts, my real life, the times when I could be myself.

"My attitude toward people had changed. There were so many who had betrayed us, people I never would have suspected. I stopped trusting people. And I began to understand—really understand—that I was Jewish. I understood that to be Jewish was to be persecuted. Years passed until I understood that, and maybe I don't have a full understanding even now. After all, I am deprived of Jewish history, Jewish culture, Jewish language.

"For all of us, this is the saddest thing. We know nothing of ourselves. We have had in here in our building a Jewish boy, with a Jewish face and appearance. A funny little boy. Another boy came from Central Asia. And there was a fight between the two boys. One mother asked the Jewish boy why he was fighting the Central Asian. The little Jewish boy said, "Because he is not Russian!" The poor child didn't even understand that he was not Russian either. The first time he'll understand it is when a Russian comes after him, with a leaflet, or a club."

State anti-Semitism followed Natasha Rapoport throughout her life and career as a chemist. After graduation she and the rest of her Jewish classmates were sent off to work in factories while others got far better work at academic institutes. Eventually she won a spot at a prestigious institute, but she was told she could not advance very far. "I don't have anything against you or your abilities, Natalya Yakovlevna, but there are just too many Jews in your department," said one of the institute chiefs. "The regional Communist Party committee is already angry with your lab boss for hiring too many Jews. Do you want him to have more problems?"

In 1978, she watched with astonishment as a less deadly version of the Doctors' Plot was played out at her father's institute. Local authorities received an anonymous "tip" that Russian patients were dying while Jewish patients were being cured. The letters charged the Jewish doctors at the institute with carrying out Nazi-style experiments on the Russians and that the crimes were being covered up. "Instead of throwing the accusations in the garbage, the authorities made a thorough investigation," Natasha said as her father smiled weakly at the absurdity of it all. "Can you imagine? Ancient history all over again. And guess what? It turns out that there had been no experiments after all.

"There is something special in *Homo sovieticus,* in this special nation of people, and the scale of anti-Semitism here is unique," Natasha said. "Here, anti-Semitism is political, it is a weight on the political balance. Our government will sell Jews or not sell Jews, will let them go or not, depending on what it gets in return. Jews are a card in the political game. And this makes anti-Semitism more dangerous, because you never know how politics will change and what they will do with us the next time around."

Natasha was thwarted in her attempts to leave the country for Israel or the United States. Israelis promised her an immediate post at the Chaim Weizmann Institute in Jerusalem, but she could not persuade her parents to move. And her husband, Vladimir, was also hesitant. "He is a very indecisive man," she said. "This issue almost broke up our marriage. I think my life would have been different in Israel. As a scientist I could have worked as far as my talents could bring me. Here I am trapped, kept in a cage."

Natasha was determined that at least her daughter, Vika, would learn to live and think like a free woman. At first, when the little girl came home humming and singing the Bolshevik hymns she had been taught in school, Natasha was furious. "I told her to shut up," Natasha said, "but she loved those songs. When I tried to counter the lies she was being told in school and I told her to look around at the real life around her, she started crying and shouting, defending what she was told in the second and third grade. She was struggling for the sake of these beautiful lies."

But as Vika grew older, she began to understand the deep contradictions between the textbooks in school and everything she knew about the real history of her own grandfather and the world around her. Like so many, she grew cynical, alienated from anything that smacked of official Soviet life. She decided she would emigrate if she could. "By the time I was thirteen I already knew that I could no longer live here," Vika told me. "I was still in the Soviet Union, but I knew it was temporary. Just thinking that way set me free.

"I'm not scared of the latest wave of anti-Semitism. They are pathetic people, and they will always be around. I'm leaving because I cannot stand it here any longer: the rules, the psychology, the gray sameness of everything. If I stay here, I will suffocate. Unless a brick were to fall on my head, I could predict every moment of my life here until I die. I want to have children one day, but I will not have them here. I will miss everyone, but I am gone."

A few nights before she was to leave for Israel, Vika and her mother staged an extraordinary puppet show for all their friends and relatives. Around seventy-five people were packed into a single tiny room. The puppets, with voices supplied by Vika's friends, played out her own personal history and coming exodus. When it was over, and the puppets lay in a heap, some people were still laughing, the rest were in tears.

Until the last minute, Vika was reminded of just why she was leaving. On the night of her departure, she and Natasha were driving through their neighborhood in north Moscow in Natasha's tiny orange Lada. Natasha glanced in the rearview mirror and noticed they were being followed. She pulled into the local police station and said, "What the hell is going on? Why are you having me followed?"

"It's for your own protection," the police captain said.

Natasha was furious, but her daughter smiled, as if in justification of her decision to go. That night, Vika flew to Budapest, then switched planes for the flight to Tel Aviv. When Vika left, Natasha said, "it was the first time in weeks that I had a good night's sleep."

A little while later, I visited Natasha Rapoport once more. With her daughter in Jerusalem and her father still in Moscow, Natasha said she felt like a "woman in the middle." Whenever we talked, she did everything she could to avoid the inevitable question of her father's death and her long wait to emigrate. Finally, she brought it up herself.

"I know what you are thinking," she said. "And the answer is yes. When he is gone, I will be gone, too."

CHAPTER 8

MEMORIAL

Esther has no idea where her grandfather died or where he is buried. Most likely, he was shot in the back of the head. Probably he is buried in a mass grave somewhere near the city of Gorky. She can guess, but she does not know.

In the Soviet Union, an empire of holocaust survivors and the children of survivors, this gnawing uncertainty was the usual condition of life. As Hannah Arendt writes, "The concentration camp, by making death itself anonymous (making it impossible to find out whether a prisoner is dead or alive), robbed death of its meaning as the end of a fulfilled life." I am not sure we met anyone who did not have a grandparent, a parent, a sibling, a friend, someone who still wandered through his dreams, still ghostly because there was no way to fix the dead one's end in time and place. The survivor can usually imagine the death in a generic way—the executioner's rubber apron, the ditch dug in frozen mud. But the suffering continues because there is no closure. It's as if the regime were guilty of two crimes on a massive scale: murder and the unending assault against memory. In making a secret of history, the Kremlin made its subjects just a little more insane, a little more desperate.

Awake, the people lived in the ruins of their nightmares. In their daily lives they lived in apartment buildings that had been built by prisoners, sailed through canals dug by slaves of the state. One afternoon in Karaganda—an industrial city in central Kazakhstan that, seen from the air, looked like an ashtray stuffed with cigarette butts—I wandered into the woods and discovered an abandoned school. The coal miners showing me around pointed to the bars in the windows. "It was a pretty good school, but it was a wonderful prison camp," one miner said bitterly. His father spent a year for "anti-Soviet activity" in a room that later became the second grade. The rooms were dank, and a bitter wind blew through them. In the basement playrooms, the miner said, the guards carried out their nighttime executions. There were drainpipes in the floors to catch the blood, zebras and wildebeests on the walls to amuse the children.

Much later on, I took another trip, this time to Kolyma in the Russian far east, the old prison camp region just across the water from Alaska. At least two million prisoners died in Kolyma. The survivors went home years ago, but the place was still haunted. The Russian north was once the region of "little peoples," hunters and nomads, Eskimos, Yakuts, Chukchis, Yukagiris. A friend told me that one hundred or so Eveni people lived in the village of Godlya an hour north of Magadan. Would I like to see them?

We arrived in Godlya at about eight-thirty in the morning. The village was a sea of mud, a few heaps of garbage, an empty store, a couple of wooden houses tilting into the mud, and the sort of poured-concrete barracks you'd see on the outskirts of almost any Soviet city. We saw a young woman—a beautiful woman, with a round Eskimo face—stumble drunkenly through a puddle. She sort of squinted at us and dropped to one knee. Farther on, we saw a few more people, some leaning against a wall, a couple more passing a bottle back and forth and saying nothing. Half the town was smashed before breakfast. It was always this way in the morning, and by sundown hardly anyone was awake, my friend told me. They drank vodka, bathtub gin, hair tonic, eau de cologne, even bug spray. It had been that way for years. The Eveni had been herded into these villages after centuries of hunting reindeer in the forest; once they ceased to wander, they were lost. The regime, in order to create a more perfect Soviet Eveni, or Chukchi or Eskimo, took children away from their parents and villages and "educated" them in state boarding schools, sickening little places in the middle of nowhere. By the time the schools got done with them, there was no Eveni left in them at all. Now they spoke Russian miserably and Eveni not at all.

One of the few sober men around, a squat young man with a withered arm, introduced himself. He said his name was Viktor, and I asked him my earnest questions. "The Eveni are dying out," he said. "They have nothing to do and they drink until they can't drink anymore. I spoke Eveni until I was four years old. That's what they tell me. Then they sent me off to the schools. It wasn't school really. They just let us sit there and made sure we spoke only Russian. So most of us didn't say anything at all."

I asked him what chances he thought he had in life and whether the changes in Moscow might help. By now a small crowd of drunks had circled round us. Their eyes were glassy and their heads swayed slightly, like dandelions in a breeze.

"We are done for," Viktor said, looking at his neighbors. "It's too late. They killed us."

Viktor led us over to two other Eveni men. They were wearing cheap Soviet coveralls and University of Alaska baseball caps that must have floated across to Siberia on the Bering Strait. They were the only two men in town working. They had a curious job. With huge blowtorches they scorched the skin on a huge dead hog until it was pink and dry. Then, they cut the skin in strips and fried and salted them. "Very tasty with vodka," one said. Bar food, Eveni potato chips.

Another man, Pavel Trifonov, came over and watched this strange ritual with us for a while. "This is the sort of thing we do now," he said. "The state won't let us fish. And there are no reindeer left. They call this village a state farm, but there hasn't been any farming here in a long time. It's way below zero most of the time. What are we supposed to raise? Lemons? Most of the time, this place is a sheet of ice."

I asked him what his family had done before they settled here in Godlya.

"My grandfather was a trapper and a hunter and he traded with the Japanese," Pavel said. "And what am I? I stand around and watch this. I don't feel like an Eveni and I am not a Russian. I don't feel like anyone. They are killing us. No, they already have. This is slow genocide, and it's almost at its end."

———

How to put a limit on these stories, this sense of hauntedness? On a winter afternoon in Leningrad, I paid a call on Dmitri Likhachev, a distinguished scholar of medieval Russian literature at the Leningrad institute known as Pushkin House. Likhachev was eighty-four at the time, and his office seemed designed to ignore all things Soviet. The feeling of entering that room was the reverse of what happens to the pitiful exile in Nabokov's story "The Visit to the Museum," who wanders through a museum in France and magically finds himself "not in the Russia I remembered but in the factual Russia of today." One entered Likhachev's study as if into another time. There was Dal's great dictionary of the Russian language, a prerevolutionary clock, a stunning portrait of Pushkin where the dull face of a general secretary might have been. But it somehow avoided fakery. This was not fantasy, but rather an act of attention and defiance. In a city where thousands of volumes in the main library had been burned and ruined from neglect, where Rembrandts faded needlessly on the walls of the Hermitage, Likhachev created an idealized room in which to read and think.

"Most of all, I like the quiet," he told me that winter afternoon. "Russia is a noisy state." When he was a boy, Likhachev watched the February and October revolutions from his window. A decade later he had an even closer view of the rise of Soviet civilization, courtesy of a five-year term in a labor camp. Likhachev was arrested in 1928 for taking part in a students' literary group called the Cosmic Academy of Sciences. The club posed about as great a threat to the Kremlin as the *Harvard Lampoon* does to the White House. For election as an "academician," Likhachev presented a humorous paper on the need to restore to the language the letter "yat." The Bolsheviks banned the letter as part of a campaign to "modernize" Russian after the revolution. Later, one of Likhachev's interrogators railed at him for daring to waste his time on such things.

"What do you mean by language reform?" the interrogator shouted. "Perhaps we won't even have any language at all under socialism!"

Likhachev spent most of his term in Solovki, a labor camp established by Lenin in 1920 on a White Sea island. The monastery on the island had been used as a prison before, but a single statistic gives some idea of the difference between the czarist repressions and the Bolshevik Terror. From the sixteenth century to the end of the Romanov dynasty in 1917, there were a total of 316 inmates at Solovki. On a single night—the night of October 28, 1929—Likhachev listened to gunfire as three hundred men were executed.

"It was autumn and my parents had come to visit me. We had rented a room from one of the guards," he once said. "A man came running to see me on that night saying the wardens had just been to the barracks to get me. Well, I told my parents that I had to go because I was being summoned for night work and that they shouldn't wait up for me. I could not tell my parents that they were coming to take me away and shoot me. I hid myself behind stacks of firewood so they would not see it happening.

"Meanwhile the shooting was in full swing. I was not found. It meant that I was also included in that number, I was also meant to be one of those three hundred. So they took somebody else instead of me. And when I emerged from my hideout the next morning, I was a different man. So many years have passed since then, more than half a century, sixty years in fact, and I still cannot forget it. Exactly three hundred people were mowed down just like that, as a warning. . . . Three hundred shots, one per man. The executioner was drunk, so he did not manage to kill them all immediately. But all the same, they threw all the bodies in a big pit. The executioner is older than me, and he is still alive."

———

A little while after the Nina Andreyeva affair in the spring of 1988, I was walking along the Arbat, the pedestrian mall in downtown Moscow, and saw a young woman in her twenties collecting signatures. This was still dangerous business in 1988. I'd seen people arrested on the Arbat and near Pushkin Square for handing out petitions or organizing an "unauthorized" demonstration. Sasha Podrabinek regularly got himself arrested when he passed out his underground paper, *Express-Khronika,* on the street.

There were about a half-dozen people huddled around the woman. A couple signed; the others kept a step back and listened, passing the time. She said her name was Elena and her petition, a sheaf of onionskin sheets riffling in the wind, was for a new "historical, anti-Stalinist" group called Memorial.

Memorial, Elena said, wanted to "give a name" to the victims of the Stalin era; they wanted to build monuments, research centers. The more she explained the group, the more it seemed to me their goal was to build a kind of Soviet Yad Vashem, the memorial center in Jerusalem dedicated to the memory of the six million Jews killed in the Holocaust. She kept talking about "the names," giving people back their names, and as I stood there, I remembered going to Yad Vashem nearly twenty years before and walking into a vast, dark library, a room filled with immense volumes containing the names of the lost. I had never even begun to understand the immensity of the Holocaust until that moment. I'd had teachers who had asked us to imagine four of the five boroughs of New York gassed to death. But it was only in that simple room, surrounded by the names of all of them, that I felt it. And what had Solzhenitsyn written? What was his count of the victims of the Soviet regime? Sixty million?

The woman told me how I could find out more about Memorial. She said I should find Lev Ponomarev or Yuri Samodurov, a human rights activist and a friend of Sakharov's. Lev Ponomarev lived on the very outskirts of Moscow, a neighborhood that had apartments on one side and miles of birch forest on the other. He was in his forties but looked many years younger. Unlike the shaggy Russian intellectual of legend, Ponomarev looked like an astronaut, fit, clean-cut. With his daughter running in occasionally with a shriek and announcements about the weather ("huge snow!") or dinner ("coming soon!"), Ponomarev brought me up to date on the start of Memorial. He said that he and most other intellectuals in their twenties, thirties, and forties viewed the advent of Gorbachev skeptically. But when Sakharov was released from internal exile, he said, "We began to come around."

"Like a lot of people," Ponomarev said, "I thought that what had to be done at the start in order to dismantle the system was to tell people how many victims there have been, to plant the idea that monuments should be erected to those who had perished, archives should be published. This is the real start of perestroika. The truth. And with that, the process can become irreversible. Without that, without everyone acknowledging that the system is discredited and guilty, a crackdown can always succeed.

"In the winter of 1987, I got together with Yuri Samodurov. We formed an action group of about fifteen people. This was at a time when many informal groups were being launched. A general meeting was held in someone's apartment. We started drafting a one-page-long appeal in order to begin a petition campaign. To get the language of it just right was very tricky. For example, we knew that millions of people had been killed, no one doubted it, and yet we didn't know whether we ought to include the word 'millions' in our document. We still had no legal proof to substantiate it. We were afraid of turning people off."

The Memorial founders, a group of mainly young unknown scholars and writers, first tried to collect signatures at their various offices. That seemed to be the safest route. But Ponomarev and the others found that even close friends they had known for many years were refusing to sign.

"A lot of them agreed with what we were after," he said, "but they were suspicious. You could see they were wondering if their friends had suddenly become agents and the petition was some kind of trap. So then we decided to take the more anonymous route and go to the streets and ask passersby to sign. And since we wanted our appeal to have legal force, we asked people for both their names and their addresses. We all had our doubts about this. This is something that is terribly dangerous in our country. The levels of suspicion run so deep. But people responded! After all these years, people were just ready for this. It was such an amazing sociological experience. We discovered that there were people willing to give a name and an address and yet they had no idea that we were not KGB agents. They trusted us."

The Memorial people usually went to the streets in groups of threes. One held a poster saying "Sign this appeal," another collected signatures, and the third held up a quotation from Gorbachev's speech saying there should be no "blank spots" in history. Gorbachev still had tremendous authority and popularity; what's more, Lev said, Memorial hoped that a quotation from the general secretary would ward off the police. It did not always work. The petition groups were often arrested, until, finally, mysteriously, they found themselves getting hauled into the police stations less and less often. Divine— or Party—intervention, they supposed.

If the Memorial group was to become the preeminent historical preservation society, it needed historians to help. This was an almost impossible order. The field of Soviet history had become so degraded over the years that the Memorial people felt they could not trust anyone; the ones they could trust, people like Dima Yurasov, were not professionals.

There was one exception at first, a young scholar named Arseny Roginsky. Roginsky's father was arrested twice in the Stalin era and died in 1951 at a camp near Leningrad when his son was five years old. But, typically, the KGB did not bother to tell the Roginsky family about the death. Month after month, until 1955, Arseny's mother sent parcels to her husband in the camps, all the while planning for his eventual return. The family learned about the death only when they received a telegram informing them that the "packages are no longer being received." Later on, the Roginskys were given a packet of documents that claimed the cause of death had been a heart attack. "When I saw that document I was eight or nine years old," Arseny told me one afternoon at the Memorial headquarters. "I saw the stamp and the seal of the Soviet Union, and yet I knew it was false. They were telling us lies and they didn't care how absurd they were. That's when I decided to become a historian."

Roginsky took his university degree in Tartu, a university town in Estonia that had about it the air of the Berkeley academic underground in the sixties. The most influential teacher there—and Roginsky's mentor—was the cultural historian Yuri Lotman. While it was impossible to conduct courses and draw up reading lists on subjects considered "anti-Soviet," Lotman and his students looked at the structure of literary texts and cultures in a way that they all understood as a thinly veiled critique of the society they were living in. Their refusal to use Newspeak and channel everything into Marxist-Leninist categories was a form of dissidence. At Tartu, Roginsky's classmates included Natalya Gorbanevskaya, who joined Pavel Litvinov on Red Square for the 1968 demonstration, and Nikita Okhotin, another future leader of Memorial.

After graduating and moving to Leningrad, Roginsky took a tremendous risk. He founded an underground group called Pamyat, or Memory (not to be confused with the racist Russian nationalist group of the same name). Roginsky's Pamyat was a forerunner to Memorial. Working secretly and with friends in the dissident movement, he began building an archive of Western and Soviet documents on the Stalin period. Roginsky followed Solzhenitsyn's lead in *The Gulag Archipelago* and interviewed dozens of camp survivors about their experiences. "More than anything, I wanted to prove that the study of history actually could exist in this country," he told me. It was not long before the police and the KGB were on to him. They searched his apartment seven times, bugged his telephone, and called him in for questioning. But while the KGB obviously knew what Roginsky was up to, he made it difficult for them, carefully burying his tapes and papers. The KGB never found that evidence. Then in 1981 the KGB ended all pretense toward the legal niceties. They arrested Roginsky and he was sentenced to four years in the camps. They moved him from camp to camp in order to prevent him from "infecting" the other inmates with anti-Soviet ideas and to make sure he never got too comfortable. When Roginsky finally returned to Moscow in August 1985, Mikhail Gorbachev was in power. He was ready to try the same crime again. "I had to assume that history would outlast stupidity and cruelty," he said.

———

Through the spring of 1988, Memorial was adding thousands of names to its petition lists. Gorbachev planned on holding a special conference at the end of June to plant the seeds of a more democratic political system, and Memorial wanted to find some way to use the historic meeting to establish itself. For that it needed support at a higher level; it needed backing from people who would command the attention of at least the reformist flank in the Party leadership. The activists needed a core of names that would lend some political heft to Memorial. Most of the names were obvious: Sakharov, of course, writers such as Ales Adamovich, Dmitri Likhachev, Daniil Granin, Lev Razgon, Anatoly Rybakov, and Yuri Karyakin; the editor of *Ogonyok,* Vitaly Korotich; and Boris Yeltsin, who had become a mythic figure of defiance after his ouster from the Politboro in 1987.

And there were two historians on the list. The first was Roy Aleksandrovich Medvedev. Throughout the Khrushchev and Brezhnev eras, there had been other scholars who tried to work honestly, to conduct research outside the system of Party rules and guarded archives. Mikhail Gefter, another of Arseny Roginsky's mentors, was well known to historians in the West for his essays on what he saw as the Stalinist "aberration." Viktor Danilov's groundbreaking first attempts to describe the scope and brutality of the collectivization campaign had also won respect abroad.

But while Western historians trying to piece together the scale of the Soviet catastrophe relied almost solely on published Soviet documents, literature, and émigré sources, only one historian still living in Moscow played a major role in deepening the world's understanding of Stalin and his successors. The publication in the West of Medvedev's *Let History Judge* in 1971 astonished foreign scholars with its unstinting denunciation of Stalin and the sheer accumulation of evidence.

I came to Moscow thinking that Roy Medvedev was the man to know. Dozens of my predecessors—especially the American and Italian correspondents—depended mightily on him for analysis and high-grade gossip: who was fighting whom, who had a fatal cold in the Politburo. The same sources in the world of Communist Party politics, bureaucracy, and journalism who had informed *Let History Judge* also provided Medvedev with nuggets of information that, for foreigners, could be mined almost nowhere else.

Roy and his wife, Galina, lived on Dybenko Street in a distant part of town not far from Sheremetyevo Airport. Medvedev's tiny study was a meticulous arrangement of books and files, a masterly use of space imposed by necessity. File cards peeked out of the shelves announcing "early Leninists," "Beria," or "Brezhnev." Roy's twin brother, Zhores, who had lived in a middle-class section of London called Mill Hill since his exile in 1973, had arranged his own office in the same fashion. London street life murmured outside, but inside, Zhores had recreated Russia. All through their separation, Roy and Zhores exchanged necessities with the help of obliging Western diplomats and journalists. For Zhores's books on Soviet agriculture and the Chernobyl nuclear disaster, Roy sent clippings and source materials; Zhores handled Roy's foreign-language publication rights and sent him packages of books, rubber bands, envelopes, folders, and underwear, socks, and shoes.

Before Gorbachev came to power, Roy Medvedev was considered a dissident. After years of study and teaching school in the provinces, Medvedev took Khrushchev's "secret speech" in 1956 at the Twentieth Party Congress and the further anti-Stalinist mood of the Twenty-second Party Congress in 1961 as a signal of permission. Year after year he accumulated source materials and interviews with Party officials, camp survivors, and other witnesses to the era. As a scholar he pushed the limits of the possible. But Medvedev's timing was dangerous. By the time he finished *Let History Judge* and sent it to the West for publication, Khrushchev was out of office and Brezhnev had already begun a movement to rehabilitate the reputation of Stalin.

Medvedev, who had maintained his membership in the Communist Party, was soon banned from its ranks. But while he was rejected by officialdom, he was also never really accepted by the dissidents. In his memoirs, Sakharov rarely levels any personal attacks, but in several spots he makes it clear that by the early seventies he not only disagreed with Medvedev's Marxism but also did not entirely trust him. Without saying so directly, he wonders if Medvedev did not have at least the tacit support of, or some kind of unsavory relationship with, the KGB. Other dissidents were far less guarded in their conjectures.

I find it hard to believe the worst. In the early eighties, a KGB guard sat outside Medvedev's door, and I doubt he was there to give out flowers to foreign guests. The specter scared off some visitors, but not all, and by the time I arrived, Roy still gave help to anyone who asked for it. I think his

fallen reputation among the dissidents and then, later, among the liberal
intelligentsia as a whole had more to do with his refusal to shed Marxism
than with any shady dealings with the Party and its organs. It seemed strange
to me that people who had never made a peep for thirty years could forgive
themselves rather quickly for their cowardice, but were brutally critical of
Medvedev's constancy. This was a man who first made sense of his life as a
scholar during an interrogation at Lefortovo Prison in the mid-seventies.

"Comrade Medvedev, tell me, please," the KGB officer had said, "would
you have written your books about Stalin if your father hadn't been sent
away to the camps?"

For nearly two decades before the start of glasnost, the KGB had regularly
shown its interest in Roy and Zhores Medvedev. Zhores was Roy's equivalent in the scientific world, a biologist and gerontologist who wrote about the
abuse of genetics under Stalin and the use of psychiatric wards as prisons for
dissidents under Brezhnev. In 1970, the authorities declared that Zhores
suffered from "paranoid delusions of reforming society" and threw him into
an insane asylum. Only Roy's intervention, his rallying of Soviet and Western scholars, forced the Kremlin to release Zhores within three weeks.

The KGB officer at Lefortovo had surely asked Roy the right question.
"Why?" No one had ever posed it to him quite so directly or with such
perverse intent. "I realized then just how closely my destiny was intertwined
with my father's," Roy told me one day in his tiny study. "I was sitting there
in that prison room, and it all came back."

On an August night in 1938 there was a knock on the door. The familiar
scene had begun. Working with their uncanny efficiency and speed, KGB
men introduced themselves and went to work. The twins, fair and thin, sat
up in bed and tried to make out the muffled commotion outside the bedroom
door.

"Why do you come so late, comrades?" they heard their father say.

They could not make out the answer.

For weeks the boys had noticed that their father was depressed, eating
almost nothing. It was a mystery to them why their father, Aleksandr Medvedev, a respected officer in the Red Army and a professor of philosophy and
history at the Tolmachev Military-Political Academy, had been fired from his
job. And why had they been sent home early that summer from Pioneer
camp? Some of the family's friends had been arrested, but the boys could not
understand what their father understood only too well, that the defining
principle of the terror was its randomness. There was no reason for any of
this except the ruthlessness, perhaps the pathology, of Josef Stalin and the
system he had built.

When the boys woke the next morning, the visitors were still there, opening and slamming cabinets, pushing aside furniture, rummaging through every-thing. The bedroom door opened and the boys' father walked in. He was dressed in a military tunic, but wore no belt. He looked as if he'd gone days with no sleep. Without a word, he sat down on the bed and embraced his sons. There was something final and desperate about his grip. Zhores told me he still remembered the feel of his father's prickly, unshaven face scratching against his cheek, how his father's wordless terror was so obvious, so physi-cal, that all three began to cry at once.

A few minutes later, the visitors left with Aleksandr Medvedev.

In the first months after the arrest of their father, Roy and Zhores and their mother received a series of letters from Aleksandr Medvedev. He was writing from Kolyma, the camps of the far east. Some of the letters from their father were addressed for forwarding to the Communist Party Central Committee, the Supreme Court, the secret police. They all protested his innocence.

"There was always the sense that this was odd, a mistake that could not have happened to us," Zhores said. "Of course, everyone in the country, when it touched them, felt that way."

Roy and Zhores had idolized their father. He had been a strict teacher and a scholarly example to them, urging them to read everything from Jack London to the Russian classics. His letters to them from Kolyma betrayed none of his own suffering. They concentrated instead on the boys' future.

My dear Roy and 'Res:
    At last, spring has come, a rare guest in this part of the country. I am very far from you, but in my thoughts and in my heart, I am very close, closer than ever. You fill my everyday thoughts, and you are the aim and essence of my life. You are on the threshold of becoming young men. I so want to be beside you and give you all my experience and deliver you from youth's mistakes. But destiny has decided otherwise. I do not want my absence from your lives to sadden your youth.
    The main thing is that you must study persistently and not limit your-selves just to the school program. Use your time when your perceptiveness and memory are especially keen. Try to be disciplined in your work, for even a mediocre man can accomplish a great deal if he is disciplined. You are talented capable boys. You must learn to think and be well organized. What you need above all is patience. You must learn to overcome difficulties no matter how large. I am sorry for the preaching tone . . .

Love,
Your Father

In the winter of 1941, the Medvedev family received a letter from Alek-sandr saying he was in the hospital and needed vitamins. A few months later, a letter they had sent to him in Kolyma came back unopened and stamped: "The money is returned on account of the death of the addressee." For a while, the family could not accept this all too obvious reality and continued sending parcels. But each time they were returned with the same dark stamp.

When he was just a teenager, Roy's mother told him, "Don't be a philosopher or a historian. It's too dangerous." And too painful. When Roy was studying at Leningrad State University in the forties, he began to do some independent research. He slowly uncovered who had betrayed his father. At the height of the terror, Boris Chagin was both a military officer and an intelligence agent of the NKVD, the precursor to the KGB. He was the author of numerous letters slandering his fellow officers. Those letters helped send many men, including Aleksandr Medvedev, to the camps. In Leningrad, Roy discovered that Chagin held a prestigious position in the same history department in which Roy was studying. Chagin was a professor of dialectical materialism.

The Medvedev brothers stood off to the side, observing the man who had betrayed their father. Zhores especially made a thorough study of Chagin's books: *The Struggle of Marxism-Leninism Against the Philosophy of Revisionism* and *The Struggle of Marxism-Leninism Against Reactionary Philosophy.* They took no action. They did not confront him. They learned. "I felt disdain for him, but not hatred or the desire for revenge," Zhrores said.

Decades later, when Roy was interviewing camp survivors for *Let History Judge,* a woman called him at home. "Are you the son of Aleksandr Medvedev?" she asked. Roy said he was, and the woman invited him to visit her at her apartment, which she shared with several other survivors from the Kolyma camps. There, for the first time, Medvedev heard the story of his father's death, how he had injured his arm in an accident while working in a copper mine and was sent to work in a greenhouse. He developed cancer and was admitted to the camp infirmary. The inmates knew their friend was gone only when they saw the camp foreman walking like a peacock around the muddy yard. He was wearing the dark wool jacket Aleksandr Medvedev had had on his back when he arrived in Kolyma.

———

For all his credentials as a scholar, Roy Medvedev was not for Memorial, and Memorial was not for him. Although he was nominally a member of the group's "public committee"—its council of well-known senior figures—Medvedev did not attend meetings and even doubted the value of the group. Roy believed in Gorbachev and in the Party as the only legitimate body of power. Memorial, to him, seemed ragtag, beside the point.

The man who quickly took the lead as Memorial's chief scholar-politician and was an admitted hypocrite, a calculating man who had been on the editorial board of *Kommunist* and was an instructor in the Higher School of the Young Communist League. Yuri Afanasyev had no illusions about his past. "For more years than I care to remember," he said one night on television, "I was up to my neck in shit."

His ascendance was astonishing. In my first year in Moscow, Afanasyev was already the democratic movement's master of ceremonies. At nearly every meeting you'd go to—at the Saturday-morning sessions of Moscow Tribune, at the lectures on Stalin—Afanasyev was invariably the man at the microphone, mediating, introducing, lecturing. He was a specialist in French historiography, and yet he looked, with his bullfrog neck and barrel chest, like a high school football coach. He had the gruff confidence of a man who had led many a committee meeting, first in the Young Communist League (the Komsomol), later in the radical opposition.

His metamorphosis was not so much laughable as pitiable. Here was a man who never would have dared defend Roy Medvedev in the seventies and then scorned him as "hopelessly reactionary" in the late eighties. But I found that for all his presumption, his gall, Afanasyev's analyses of what was happening in the country and where the situation was leading were uncanny. There were times when Afanasyev, with his supreme confidence, reminded me of Norman Mailer. He knew he had lived a life full of mistakes but he insisted on being heard. His campaign for the "return of history," his early attacks on the "Stalinist-Brezhnevite" Supreme Soviet and on Gorbachev himself, always preceded fashion. He was not much loved—he had none of Sakharov's subtlety or carriage—but he was often right. In contrast, Medvedev's predictions now were not nearly as reliable as his gossip had once been. Typically, the day that Eduard Shevardnadze resigned as foreign minister in December 1990 predicting the rise of a dictatorship, Medvedev declared to all who would listen that Shevardnadze was stepping down because of trouble in the Georgian Republic.

Afanasyev grew up in Ulyanovsk, the town where Lenin was born. His father, a household repair man, was sent to jail for several years in eastern Siberia on the usual false pretense: he had pilfered a few kilos of flour from the collective farm to give to a poor family. "But the strange thing," Afanasyev told me one afternoon at his office at the Historical Archives Institute, "is that we did not experience it as a grief or tragedy, because literally every other person we knew then was in prison for collecting leftovers on the farm or for missing a day of work. We never had any conversations about Stalin and I had no doubts about him."

Like Gorbachev, Afanasyev was a provincial boy whose grades were good enough to gain him admission to the best university in the country, Moscow

State University. As a student, Afanasyev said, "I was like everyone else. I memorized *The Short Course* like any good Komsomol boy, like any other Communist." On the night before Stalin's funeral in March 1953, Afanasyev wandered the streets near the Kremlin. Tens of thousands of people jammed the streets headed for the Hall of Columns, where Stalin lay in his coffin. People were hysterical, wracked with fear after the death of their living god. Dozens, perhaps hundreds, of people suffocated to death in the mad crush to get to the hall. Afanasyev broke free of the crowd. As he walked, he could hear some drunks singing in an alleyway. He had never heard such joyous singing. The drunks were celebrating the death of Stalin.

"I suppose once or twice in a lifetime you have those moments when you see something or hear something that tilts your life just slightly in another direction. When I heard those men, well, suddenly the purity of my political consciousness was stained," Afanasyev said. "I felt the first moment of doubt. It wasn't until Khrushchev's speech three years later that I really started to rethink things more thoroughly, but it was this drunken celebration in the dark corners of Moscow that made me start to doubt. I was never quite the same."

After graduation, Afanasyev worked as a Komsomol leader in Krasnoyarsk, not far from where his father had been in jail. He certainly was no radical. He believed in the "infinite possibilities" of the Party. He and his friends talked about the great vistas of Leninist ideology, the great hydroelectric power station they—or at least the workers—were building.

"That enthusiasm," he said, "lasted until the late sixties, when Brezhnev tried to reanimate Stalinism."

Back in Moscow, Afanasyev worked in the national leadership of the Komsomol organization and then took his graduate degree in history, specializing in French historiography. Afanasyev knew enough to stay away from Soviet history as a field—"That's where all the real idiots and timeservers were"—but even in his own work he made sure to glorify the obvious and denigrate "foreign influence." For years his published works set out to prove that the "bourgeois" historians had grossly misinterpreted the October Revolution. Basically, he said, "I scoured the texts for their 'glaring insufficiencies.'"

But like so many others of his generation, Afanasyev developed a kind of two-track mind. Because he was such a loyal servant of the official line, he was sent abroad several times to study in France. In Paris, Afanasyev read books by the dissidents and émigrés. He lived in an academic atmosphere where he could speak a little more freely. So by the time he returned to Moscow, Afanasyev had changed just a little more. Once more he had heard the shouting from the dark corners, and he responded—or at least part of him did. Little by little, it became harder for him to resist the evidence. His faith—what little there was of it—eroded. Polish students at the university told him about Stalin's massacres of Polish officers in the Katyn Forest. Afanasyev saw how senior professors of history at the university were arrested, or at least fired and silenced, when they strayed too far from doctrine.

In the late seventies and early eighties, Afanasyev was a resident scholar of "the critique of bourgeois historiography" at a Moscow institute and was an editor at *Kommunist,* the Party's chief theoretical journal. When Gorbachev came to office, Afanasyev wrote him a series of daring letters about the situation in Soviet historical science, calling on him to use his position as general secretary to end restrictions on academic study and open the archives of the Party and the KGB. Afanasyev got no direct answers. But he did win the key appointment in 1986 to take over as rector of the Historical Archives Institute and quickly used that position to give the first public lectures criticizing Stalin and introducing to the public several new faces—Dima Yurasov included.

Afanasyev was determined to use his new post to help open up the study of the Soviet past. Exploiting his new access to at least some Party archives, he reviewed the letters of Olga Shatunovskaya, a woman who had been a member of the Communist Party Control Committee under Khrushchev. In those letters Shatunovskaya wrote that she had collected sixty-four folders of documents saying that according to KGB and Party data, between January 1935 and 1941 19,800,000 people had been arrested; and of these, seven million were executed in prisons. Her statement was supported by specific data describing how many were shot and where and when. But the files Shatunovskaya described were declared "missing." By reading such letters, Afanasyev began to realize that the Party and the KGB had probably destroyed many of the most incriminating documents in the archives.

Afanasyev got into some of his first battles with the Party hierarchy when he began to insist that professional scholars and not the Central Committee—not even the general secretary—should be the country's principal historians. Although Gorbachev's 1987 history speech helped open the process, Afanasyev said that there could no longer be such speeches. "As long as such things still exist," he said, "there will still be the idea that history should be made not in the archives and universities and by writers, but rather at Party conferences and committees. That way history remains a handmaiden of propaganda and an extension of policy rather than a sphere of knowledge on the level of science or literature. If power wants to gain authority, then it has to say honestly, 'We are not linked in any way with the previous regime.'

"When we talk about perestroika, we see it in the following way: the former model of socialism was no good, so let's work out a new model and put it into life. Again, we have it backward. We must give up this idea of a conscious construction of a more perfect society, the whole culture of belief in the limitless capabilities and opportunities of the human mind, and the ability to construct a model of socially engineered society and then realize it all.

"Educators and utopian thinkers used to think that the opportunities were endless. That the idea of a just society could be formed by the human mind, that it could be discovered on a theoretical basis; and it seemed to them that those theories could be realized in practice. In other words, a society of universal justice and prosperity could be built by thinking things out. We are now living through the final stages of that culture. Marx and Lenin are vanishing. They are being swept away in the same way that the 'truth' of Newtonian mechanics was swept away by Einstein and relativity."

———

By June 1988, Gorbachev's victory in the Nina Andreyeva affair had given the Memorial leadership a sense of hope and expectation. Afanasyev and the liberal head of the Filmmakers' Union, Elem Klimov, decided to seize on the Nineteenth Party Conference as Memorial's moment. Both men had been elected delegates to the conference and here was a chance to propose the Memorial platform to the top officials of the Communist Party.

Afanasyev had already helped to lay the political and intellectual groundwork for Memorial's plan. A few weeks before the conference, he produced the most important political book of the Gorbachev era: *Inogo ne dano* ("There Is No Other Way"), a collection of thirty-five essays by the leading intellectuals of the "thaw" generation, men and women who had become the torchbearers of the glasnost era. While Gorbachev's own book, *Perestroika,* was sodden with Party cliché, "There Is No Other Way" provided dazzling clarity and a sense of possibility. Published by the huge state-run firm Progress and edited by Afanasyev, "There Is No Other Way" read like an underground manifesto but it was printed officially and on good paper. Afanasyev, Mikhail Gefter, the renaissance scholar Leonid Batkin, and the journalist Len Karpinsky all wrote essays on the persistence of Stalinism and the need to evaluate the past in order to create a humane future. In one way or another, the need for truth, for a clear-eyed view of history, was behind every piece in the collection, among them Vasily Selyunin's analysis of the Soviet bureaucracy, Aleksei Yablokov's survey of ecological disasters, Yuri Chernichenko's essay on the "agro-gulag" of the collective farm system, Gavriil Popov's piece on the absurdity of the centralized economic system. Nearly all the authors were scholars and journalists who had, for years, pulled their punches, spoken in euphemism, or spoken not at all. The presence of one author, however, honored the entire project. The simple addition of Andrei Sakharov, and his essay "The Necessity of Perestroika," showed that an alliance existed between the dissidents and a much wider category, the liberal intelligentsia. Sakharov's article was not much different from his underground manifestos; what was different now was the audience. The first printing alone was 100,000. Until Sakharov's release from exile there were probably not ten thousand people in the country who knew the name Sakharov as anything other than an odious figure in the pages of *Pravda* and *Izvestia.* In his essay, Sakharov wrote that perestroika "was like a war. Victory is a necessity." To even begin to win that war, he wrote, the leadership had to end the folly in Afghanistan, sponsor a thorough rewriting of the criminal code, endorse freedom of speech, and agree to a radical reduction in strategic and conventional weapons. In the next two years, Gorbachev would follow Sakharov's prescriptions almost to the letter.

A few days after buying my blue-and-silver copy of "There Is No Other Way," I went to a demonstration organized by Memorial outside a sports arena in Moscow. It was a brilliant sunny day, and the people on the streets outside the arena took obvious delight in their freedom to chant slogans and carry signs reading "No to Political Repression," "Death to Stalinism," "Stalin's Boot Still Endangers Us." A half-dozen of the contributors to "There Is No Other Way" gave speeches on the steps. But one moment struck me above all. Not far from Sakharov, a young man carried a sign saying, in Russian, "I would like to call you all by name," the famous line from Anna Akhmatova's long poem *Requiem.*

During Stalin's Terror, Akhmatova spent seventeen months, day after day, waiting in long lines to find out what had become of her son, who had been arrested at the height of the purges. "One day someone 'identified' me," she wrote in a preface to the poem. "Beside me, in the queue, there was a woman with blue lips. She had, of course, never heard of me; but she suddenly came out of that trance so common to us all and whispered in my ear (everyone spoke in whispers there): 'Can you describe this?' And I said, 'Yes, I can.' And then something like the shadow of a smile crossed what had once been her face."

I quote a few lines here (in a translation by D. M. Thomas) because, in them, Memorial found its voice and credo:

> Again the hands of the clock are nearing
> The unforgettable hour. I see, hear, touch
>
> All of you: the cripple they had to support
> Painfully to the end of the line; the moribund;

And the girl who would shake her beautiful head and
Say: "I come here as if it were home."

I should like to call you all by name,
But they have lost the lists. . . .

I have woven for them a great shroud
Out of the poor words I overheard them speak.

I remember them always and everywhere,
And if they shut my tormented mouth,

Through which a hundred million of my people cry,
Let them remember me also. . . .

And if ever in this country they should want
To build me a monument

I consent to that honor,
But only on the condition that they

Erect it not on the seashore where I was born:
My last links there were broken long ago,

Nor by the stump in the Royal Gardens,
Where an inconsolable young shade is seeking me,

But here, where I stood for three hundred hours
And where they never, never opened the doors for me.

Lest in blessed death I should forget
The grinding scream of the Black Marias,

The hideous clanging gate, the old
Woman wailing like a wounded beast.

And may the melting snow drop like tears
From my motionless bronze eyelids,

And the prison pigeons coo above me
And the ships sail slowly down the Neva.

A few days after the demonstration, Afanasyev and Klimov hauled their huge sacks of petitions through the gates of the Kremlin. It was the opening day of the Nineteenth Party Conference, and the Party apparatchiks eyed them suspiciously. Afanasyev and Klimov presented the petitions to Gorbachev and his aides and waited for a response.

On the last day of the Nineteenth Party Conference—after Boris Yeltsin's dramatic appeal for rehabilitation, after a war over the direction of reform—Gorbachev took the podium and delivered a long speech. Just before he finished, he said that an idea had been "introduced," one that echoed a similar suggestion in 1961 by Khrushchev—to build a memorial to the victims of the Stalin era. Now the Party, he said, must finally approve the idea. Gorbachev's words had a tacked-on feel to them; they sounded like an afterthought. In fact, it was one of the most critical moments in the political and emotional life of the perestroika era. Although the Party would later try to block Memorial, although it would try to deny it funds and meeting places, the group had sown the first seeds of a struggle far deeper and more unpredictable than anyone had imagined.

CHAPTER 9

WRITTEN
ON THE WATER

Just as Memorial's demonstration outside the sports area was ending, Arnold Yeryomenko's plane was landing. Yeryomenko lived in Magadan, the city that had once been the "capital" of the Kolyma region of the gulag archipelago in the Soviet far east. The rest of the passengers were worn out from the ten-hour flight to Moscow aboard Aeroflot's cramped and creaky liner. The one meal served had been a Dixie cup of green mineral water and a greasy chicken wing. Somehow, Arnold bounded off the plane "refreshed," he said. He'd come to Moscow on a mission.

Yeryomenko was the leader of Democratic Initiative, the first non-Communist political group ever in Magadan. The group's membership decided to send him as a "delegate" to the Nineteenth Party Conference. "We figured that if democracy is starting in this country, then we ought to be heard, too," he said. The membership passed a hat and collected his 800-ruble round-trip airfare.

Before he left, Arnold called me in Moscow. He said he had heard my articles read in Russian on Radio Liberty. Could we meet? Of course. Not only had Yeryomenko managed to sound engaging at a distance of six thousand miles, I was also eager to talk to someone from Magadan. Magadan had always defined distant to me, an almost mythical outpost, closer to

Los Angeles than Moscow, where the winters are ten months long and a mild day in January is forty degrees below zero. Magadan is the setting for two of the best books ever written about Stalinism: Yevgenia Ginzburg's memoirs *Journey into the Whirlwind* and her son Vasily Aksyonov's novel *The Burn*. Magadan "was, in a sense, the freest town in Russia," Aksyonov wrote. "In it there lived the special deportees and the special contingent, which included those categorized SHE (Socially Harmful Elements) and SDE (Socially Dangerous Elements), nationalists, social democrats, Catholics, Muslims, Buddhists . . . people who recognized themselves as the lowest slaves and who, therefore, had challenged fate." In June 1988, Magadan was still closed to foreigners. The only way to get there was on an official Potemkin-village tour with the Foreign Ministry. It was on such a trip in the summer of 1944 that Vice President Henry Wallace decided that Kolyma was wonderful and the regional secret police chief, the infamous General Goglidze, was "a very fine man, very efficient, gentle and understanding with people."

I met Arnold at the Lenin statue on October Square near my building. He was in his early fifties with the silver hair and fine features of Cesar Romero, quick and jaunty as a bantamweight.

"You are Remnick?" he said. "Well, come, I've got great things to show you."

Arnold spoke such good English that when we switched to Russian I had the odd sensation that he had an American accent. Probably he was just dumbing down his Russian for my sorry self. He told me he had learned his English in school "but mostly from listening to 'the foreign voices,' " Radio Liberty, the Voice of America, and, especially, the BBC. Evidently the jamming system had been less efficient in Magadan than in Moscow. On the short walk to my apartment, Arnold told me he was born in 1937, the year the purges really began. His father was an engineer who had been assigned to Magadan for his technical expertise. In those days, Magadan was still short on barracks and ports for the slave ships that came in every few days from Vladivostok.

"It was kind of a gulag boomtown," Arnold said with a terrific smile; it was the "gateway to hell." Even in late spring, the ice was thick near the shore. It was on days like those that the tramp steamers could not make it through to the docks. The prisoners, many of them barefoot and dressed in rags, had to walk on the ice for the last mile to shore. A camp orchestra would assemble on the ice and play for the new prisoners, usually a march or a waltz.

In a way, arrival was a relief, the journey had been such hell. The train trip to the far east from Moscow and European Russia was in cattle cars, and it took a month at least. The prisoners were packed together so tightly that it was said there were those who starved to death and were found still upright at the end of the journey. At the embarkation points on the Pacific, inspectors went up and down the line looking for slaves. Like horsemen before an auction, inspectors checked the prisoners' teeth and eyes. They pinched their biceps and buttocks to see how much muscle tone there was left after more than a month in the cattle cars. At Vanino in the late 1940s the NKVD had a contract to supply some state firms for 120,000 slave workers a year.

The rest of the prisoners were then packed into the holds of tramp steamers headed for Magadan. As the purges became a permanent condition of state in the thirties and forties, rumors of the sea journey reached Moscow and the other big cities on the "mainland." But no rumor could capture the horror of the voyage itself. Michael Solomon, a Romanian prisoner, wrote of his shock as he was herded into the hold of the ship *Sovlatvia* headed north to Magadan. It was a scene, he said, "which neither Goya nor Gustave Doré could ever have imagined": thousands of men and women, dressed in rags, half-dead and covered with boils and blisters. "At the bottom of the stairway we had just climbed down stood a giant cask, on the edges of which, in full view of the soldiers standing on guard above, women were perched like birds, and in the most incredible positions. There was no shame, no prudery, as they crouched there to urinate or empty their bowels. One had the impression that they were some half-human, half-bird creatures which belonged to a different world and a different age. Yet seeing a man come down the stairs, although a mere prisoner like themselves, many of them began to smile and some even tried to comb their hair."

Later, the officers would load on board even more prisoners—not more "politicals," but murderers, thieves, rapists, whores: "When I saw this half-naked, tattooed apelike horde invade the hold," Yevgenia Ginzburg wrote, "I thought that it had been decided that we were to be killed off by mad women. The fetid air reverberated to their shrieks, their ferocious obscenities, their wild laughter and their caterwaulings. They capered about incessantly stamping their feet even though there appeared to be no room to put a foot down. Without wasting any time, they set about terrorizing and bullying the 'ladies'—the politicals—delighted to find that the 'enemies of the people' were creatures even more despised and outcast than themselves. Within five minutes we had a thorough introduction to the law of the jungle." Feeding time came and the warders dumped a cartload of bread down the hold and into the gaping mouths of the beasts.

The killing went on and on, day after day, and in every form. The ships would often get caught in the ice far from any shore, and the crew had no choice but to wait out the weather and keep the rations for themselves. The wait could go on for weeks, even months. Thousands of prisoners would die of hunger and disease. Sometimes the guards left the corpses in the hold with the living. Sometimes they pitched the dead over the rails onto the ice, where they stayed, day after day, rotting, until the thaw came and the sea swallowed them and the ship sailed on, to Magadan.

That was the world Arnold Yeryomenko grew up in, the landscape of his childhood and youth. "The ships would come in to shore all the time," he said as we sat down to some coffee in my kitchen. "I remember seeing the prisoners in huge lines, five, six thousand men and women in rags, exhausted, being marched from the ships and onto the shore and up to the barracks. The guards were always beating them in the street, and sometimes you heard the pistols going off. Sometimes you'd see a dead man in the street. Maybe no one had time to cart him off."

Arnold's professional life never really got going. He studied engineering and foreign languages in the early 1960s. But he was broke, and, to make some extra money, he tried to trade on the black market. He was arrested and put in jail for ten years. When he was freed, he was not allowed to live in Moscow, and he moved back home to Magadan. The humiliation of his arrest and imprisonment and his growing sense that the cruelty he had seen as a child was still an essential part of the social order of the Soviet Union helped make Yeryomenko an angry man, a political man. In 1981, he wrote a book condemning the Communist Party and circulated it in samizdat editions. For that he got two more years in prison.

When perestroika finally started in Moscow, Arnold was impudent enough to think that reform ought to come to Magadan as well. He started Democratic Initiative. He stood outside KGB headquarters—he and a few kids and housewives—shouting slogans into a bullhorn. He was summarily fired from his construction job. The local Party committee and the KGB began to treat this out-of-work engineer and his younger friends in Democratic Initiative like an invading army. They bugged, harassed, and occasionally jailed the members on false charges.

Arnold said I should come see for myself. I told him I'd always wanted to go to Magadan, but it was still a closed city.

"Well, you don't have to go," he said. "I can show it to you on television." He took a videocassette out of his briefcase and said, "Do you have Beta or VHS?" He explained that one of the members of Democratic Initiative had bought a videocamera on a trip to Alaska. "It's better than having a newspaper, which of course, we can't," he said.

The tape flickered and jerked and then finally found its focus on a crowd of about 2,500 people on the city's main square. Lenin Square, of course. There were signs protesting that the city's leading Communist Party officials had grabbed up all the delegate seats to the Party conference in Moscow.

There was Arnold shouting into a bullhorn, demanding that the Party, the "sole possessor of power in this country," let representatives from outside the Party apparatus represent Magadan in Moscow. Another speaker pointed to the "White House," the relatively elegant-looking building that was the Party headquarters, and asked why the "Communists always hogged all the wealth."

"That's where the mafia lives!" the speaker shouted. "That's why they have to be guarded day and night by the militia! They're criminals!"

Another speaker demanded that a special hotel for visiting Party officials be converted into a kindergarten. It wasn't easy to make out all they said. The police had hooked up a set of speakers near the demonstration and played deafening Soviet pop music to drown out democracy.

The most dramatic moment came when Ludmila Romanova, a local Party official, accepted Arnold's invitation to address the crowd. The young woman spoke with a kind of hyped-up spirit, but she could only talk in the old Party way. She told the anti-Party demonstrators that they had assembled "without proper permission from the Party." But she did say that workers would be "invited to participate" in discussions about new schools and other civic improvements.

"We're sick of your promises!" "We don't want your words!" came some of the more polite replies.

Then Romanova ended with a prim reminder of "Soviet legality."

"You must know," she said, "that according to the Constitution, the political rights given to the people should not damage the rights of others." The crowd was less than impressed with her insinuation and booed her off the platform.

Now Arnold was laughing. He got up from his chair and pointed to a building and a set of windows in the top right-hand corner of the screen.

"There," he said. "Look at that building. You can see the KGB guys in the windows taking our picture."

———

The next day, Arnold tried to deliver Democratic Initiative's manifesto and petitions to the Party conference. We stood about half a mile from the Kremlin and watched one black limousine after another ferry the visiting Party hacks to the conference.

"They won't let me near the place," Arnold said.

After he dumped off his documents at a Party "reception hall," he booked a seat back to Magadan. Back at my place, we watched some of the conference on television. We were like football fanatics on New Year's Day. We could not take our eyes off the set. Arnold hissed the hacks and cheered on the liberals.

"You know what will bring these people down?" he said. "Embarrassment. One day they will just slink off the stage."

Like most of the liberals in Moscow, Arnold was all for Gorbachev's scheme to create a new legislature, but suspicious that it would be rigged and loaded with Party leaders. He loved watching Yeltsin's confrontation with Yegor Ligachev, his plea to the Party for rehabilitation and his call for a faster, more radical, program of democratization. Looking dazed by the task ahead, Yeltsin jutted his jaw and barged on, evoking in speech if not in manner nothing less than the return of Nikolai Bukharin and other Old Bolsheviks who had been shot in the purges and restored to the Party ranks under Gorbachev:

"Comrade delegates! Rehabilitation fifty years after a person's death has now become the rule, and this has a healthy effect on society. But I am asking for political rehabilitation while I am still alive."

Yeltsin also lambasted Ligachev for trying to railroad him and obstruct reform, in general. Ligachev had his chance at the podium and replied, "Boris, you are wrong!" To Yeltsin's barrel-chested, hangdog heavyweight, Ligachev came across on television as a street-tough middleweight. He was furious, accusing Yeltsin of sitting mute at Politburo meetings. The nomenklatura in the hall roared their approval while most of the country made a hero of Yeltsin.

Yeryomenko reveled in this liberating theater. Like millions of others, he was delighted to see the Party begin, at last, to feed on itself, to expose its corruptions and splits, live on television. But most of all, Arnold was thrilled that Memorial had won its great victory at the conference. By allowing the construction of a memorial to the victims of the regime, the Party, largely in spite of itself, had begun a period of national repentance.

"At least the conference wasn't a complete loss," he said from the airport. I told him I still wanted to come to Magadan. "I'll see you soon," I said. We both laughed. The possibility still seemed very far away.

———

Memorial's victory at the Party conference was sweet, but even its leaders knew that there was something too easy and superficial about it. "Stalin Died Yesterday" was the title of Mikhail Gefter's contribution to the "There Is No Other Way" collection and by that he meant that Stalinism infected everything and everyone in the Soviet Union. Every factory and collective farm, every school and orphanage was built on Stalinist principles of gargantuan scale and iron authority. In every relationship—in trade, on buses, in almost any simple transaction—people treated each other with contempt and suspicion. That was Stalinism, too. Only now were people beginning to wonder out loud about the efficacy of such a life. Only now were they permitted to express those doubts in the papers, in books, on television. "Stalinism is deep inside of every one of us," Afanasyev told me after the Party conference. "Getting rid of that spirit is the most difficult thing of all. Next to that, getting the Party to permit a monument is nothing."

I met a filmmaker named Tofik Shakhverdiyev, an Azerbaijani who had made a documentary called *Stalin Is with Us.* He interviewed Stalinists all over the country: a Cossack on the Don River, a cab driver in Tbilisi, the man who was Bukharin's guard during the purge trial. At one point in the film, a group of veterans is sitting around a table singing songs in praise of Stalin. The old soldiers seem transported.

I told Tofik about my Kaganovich obsession, and instead of giving me a patronizing look, he laughed and said, "Me, too. But he just won't answer the door." Lately, *Moscow News* and a few other papers had been trying to figure out, through interviews and polls, how people felt about Stalin. Just the idea of political opinion was new. But the polls were primitive, and I thought Tofik would have as good a sense as anyone what it meant now to be a Stalinist. Who were they? What did they want?

"The number of people who openly defend Stalin, really admire him, is limited," Tofik said. "But if you talk about people whose first instinct is a passion for order, then I think you are talking about not less than half the people in the Soviet Union. You see, we use fashionable words like 'democracy' and 'pluralism' now, but so few people can really live without the security of complete order and control.

"In a perverse sense, the dissidents and the nonconformists of today are Stalinists. We democrats have become like-minded in a way. We ignore or ridicule what's really out there. But off to the side, the Stalinists are going against the current, and this halo of being dissidents, strange as it seems, gives them a sort of dignity. They believed in their great cause and the creation of a great society, of Communism. They see democracy and capitalism as a matter of the rich exploiting the poor, while in our system, we are all poor. For them, the lack of an iron hand means prostitution, AIDS, emigration to the West. Stalinists derive their sense of themselves from their connection to the memory of the great man himself. When a slave kisses the hand of the master who whips him, he is getting some of the power of the master. A belief in his greatness appears."

That spirit remained on view, at least physically, in the Republic of Georgia, among other places. Like all reporters in Moscow, I eventually made a trip to

Gori, Stalin's hometown. As if that would tell me much. Gori was about an hour's drive through the mountains from the Georgian capital, Tbilisi.

The centerpiece of the town was one of the most spectacular bits of kitsch on earth. The Gori Party authorities, with some funding from Moscow, had moved Stalin's ancestral house—a tiny two-room structure—to the center of town in 1936. In an attempt to make a hut into Olympus, the Party had built neoclassical columns to frame the great man's childhood home. The rooms themselves were intended to speak for Stalin's Leninist modesty. One room had a simple wooden table, the other a portrait of Stalin with his beady-eyed, black-shrouded mother. Next door, the vast Stalin Museum, as grandiose as the columns, was closed—"pending reconsideration," the guard told me.

People who had finished looking around the Stalin house sat outside in the park under the trees eating sausages and apples. Not a single visitor I spoke to said he had any problem with Stalin. They said the country needed someone just like him to put an end to all the "confusion." A factory worker I talked with showed me the tattoo on his chest. It was an impressive double portrait of Lenin and Stalin. I asked the worker about Gorbachev. Was there room for him?

"Gorbachev?" he said. "I wouldn't tattoo his name on my ass."

———

Stalin was born Iosif Vissarionovich Djugashvili on December 21, 1879. His father was a drunk and beat his wife. He died young. When he was a boy, Stalin's favorite story was Aleksandr Kazbeg's *The Patricide,* the tale of an avenging hero of Georgia named Koba. After he read the book, Stalin demanded that all his friends call him Koba. "That became his ideal," wrote a childhood friend. Stalin's closest comrades in the party called him Koba— sometimes until the day he had them shot.

Stalin studied at a Russian orhthodox seminary. The monks said he was "rude and disrespectful." His mother always wanted him to enter the clergy. When he visited her in 1936—by then he was already the Soviet leader and planning the Great Purge—she said, "What a pity you did not become a priest."

In 1895, Stalin wrote:

> Know this: He who fell like ashes to the ground
> He who was never oppressed,
> Will rise higher than the great mountains,
> On the wings of a bright hope.

In 1926, Stalin's wife, Nadezhda, left him. He begged her to return, and at the same time had her followed by the secret police. Six years later they fought over Stalin's brutal treatment of the peasantry in Ukraine. When the row was over, Nadezhda left the room and shot herself. Her daughter, Svetlana, later said, "I believe that my mother's death, which he took as a personal betrayal, deprived his soul of the last vestiges of human warmth."

Stalin lived for years by himself in the Kremlin. One of his guards said that Stalin bugged the phones of all his advisers and spent long periods of the day listening in on their conversations. Aleksei Ribin, a secret police officer and Stalin's guard, wrote in *Sociological Research* magazine that Stalin loved to tell his limousine driver to pull over to the side of the road to give old women rides home. "He was just that kind of man," said Ribin.

In the Homeric tradition, *Pravda* used countless titles to refer to Stalin: Leader and Teacher of the Workers of the World, Father of the Peoples, Wise and Intelligent Chief of the Soviet People, the Greatest Genius of All Times and Peoples, the Greatest Military Leader of All Times and Peoples, Coryphaeus of the Sciences, Faithful Comrade-in-Arms of Lenin, Devoted Continuer of Lenin's Cause, the Mountain Eagle, and Best Friend of All Children.

There were many Western intellectuals who were all too willing to indulge Stalin in his cruelties. In the midst of a state-imposed famine, George Bernard Shaw looked up from his plate at the Metropole Hotel and said, gaily, "Do you see any food shortages here?" Later he added that he "took his hat off" to Stalin "for having delivered the goods." In a meeting with Stalin, Shaw's traveling companion Lady Astor asked, "How long will you go on killing people?"

"As long as necessary," Stalin replied.

Lady Astor quickly changed the subject, asking Stalin if he could help her find a good Russian nanny for her children.

After his own audience with Stalin, H. G. Wells reported he had never "met a man more candid, fair and honest." The American ambassador in Moscow, Joseph Davies, wrote of Stalin that "a child would like to sit on his lap and a dog would sidle up to him."

Stalin, who was five feet four, wanted a court portrait done showing him as a tall man with powerful hands. The painter Nalbandian complied by portraying Stalin from a flattering angle with his hands folded, powerfully, across his belly. Stalin had his other portrait painters shot and their paintings burned. Stalin rewrote the official *Short Biography of Stalin,* personally adding the passage "Stalin never allowed his work to be marred by the slightest hint of vanity, conceit, or self-adulation."

Stalin died of a stroke on March 5, 1953. He once said that those revolutionaries who refused to use terror as a political tool were "vegetarians."

According to Roy Medvedev, Stalin's victims numbered forty million. Solzhenitsyn says the number is far greater—perhaps sixty million. The debate continues even now.

———

It was the trial of the season. Since the rise of Gorbachev, a retired lawyer from Kharkov named Ivan Shekhovtsov had filed repeated lawsuits against various intellectuals and newspapers for "slandering Stalin." He made a career of these suits. Sixteen so far. This time his opposition was *Vechernaya Moskva*, the city's evening newspaper.

STALIN IS THE FATHER OF OUR PEOPLE.

SLANDER IS THE DIRTY WEAPON OF THE ANTI-STALINISTS.

"Get those signs out of here," said the judge.

At the witness table, Shekhovtsov sat taking notes. He wore a suit and a row of military medallions. He had been a tank gunner on the Baltic and Ukrainian fronts in the war and had lost part of a lung in a firefight. There were a half-dozen benches, all crammed with Shekhovtsov's supporters. Most of them were older men and women, and nearly all wore ribbons and medals from the war. They were angry that they had to get rid of their banners, but they made up for it with loud gossiping. There were some nasty remarks about the Jews and Armenians, about Raisa Gorbachev, about Memorial. They carried copies of right-wing journals, *Nash Sovremenik* ("Our Contemporary"), which was hard-line Russian nationalist, and *Molodaya Gvardiya* ("Young Guard"), which was hard-line Stalinist. There was a lot of whispered speculation about whether the representative from *Vechernaya Moskva* was a Jew. Of course, they concluded. She must be.

"We spent our lives building socialism, and now these people—Afanasyev, Adamovich, Korotich—they are getting rid of socialism and they are succeeding," a woman named Valentina Nikitina told me as we waited through the lull in the proceedings.

She, too, was a decorated veteran of the war. She said she had lost many friends and relatives in the war—"half the people I knew," she said—and the idea of reforming, much less dismantling, the system was unconscionable. "These people are like the Hungarians in 1956. They are staging a counter-revolution. The majority of our people support Stalin as a builder of socialism. The kulaks, most of them, were Jews. The secret police at the Belomor Canal were Jews. The leader was a Jew! The chief engineer was a Jew! If the Jews would only move to an autonomous region, they would have a wonderful life!"

I thanked her for sharing her thoughts with me and turned to Shekhovtsov himself. He looked imperious and bored. He drummed his fingers on the witness table, making sure the three judges could observe his superiority even as they conferred. Shekhovtsov had no lawyer. He was his own advocate.

A few yards away, the woman from *Vechernaya Moskva* finally stood and told the judges that her lawyer could not make the session. Could she have a continuance?

"He's on vacation," she said uncertainly.

Shekhovtsov rolled his eyes. The crowd chuckled and hissed. The judge set another court date.

"A lot of rubbish that is!" my seatmate muttered. We all stood to leave. As the woman from *Vechernaya Moskva* left the crowded little room, she kept her head down and took quick, purposeful steps toward the door.

"Slanderer!" the crowd hissed at her. "Shame on you!"

Out in the parking lot, Shekhovtsov's supporters unfurled their banners and celebrated. I introduced myself to Shekhovtsov.

"Then I suppose you want to interview me," he said. "Well, I could use a lift to the train station. And maybe something to eat, if you don't mind too much."

I asked Shekhovtsov why he bothered. Why was he spending all his money and energy filing suits and always losing? He looked at me, not angrily, but with a sort of kindly eye. I was a foreigner and didn't know any better.

"It is I who is restoring the historical truth," he said. "I didn't know anyone who was repressed. In the press now they are saying that in every house everyone at least knew someone who was repressed. In Kharkov, I investigated one hundred and fifty households and not one said it was waiting for a knock on the door. These numbers you are hearing are all sensations, pure libel. During collectivization in 1929, my grandfather was kicked off his land and exiled. But people gave us clothing and food, and after six months we returned to the land. During the exile, my brother died of an inflammation of the lung, but my mother never blamed Stalin. It was the local officials! My mother is eighty-six and she understands this with her woman's mind!

"From the point of practical deeds, Stalin did more than even Lenin. But that, of course, is probably a matter of longevity. I get letters all the time from people nostalgic for the life under Stalin—their joy in labor and love of the Motherland, how they lived with heads raised high and sang patriotic songs. Right now we don't hear anyone singing. And it's not that there is an absence of songs to sing. There is an absence of faith. You see, people forget. They need to be reminded. In the thirties, when I was in the Young Pioneers and in Komsomol, there was unprecedented patriotism in this country. There was a willingness to sacrifice personal needs for the good of the nation. People had in mind great aims and a wonderful future, and so they endured. Stalin is with us and Stalin will come. That is the mind-set of a generation. We went into battle with his name on our lips. He took Russia, which had a wooden plow in its hands, and he left it with an atomic bomb. Such a man cannot be slandered. The young should learn their history."

In his most celebrated suit, Shekhovtsov charged that Ales Adamovich, the Byelorussian writer and one of the leaders of Memorial, had slandered Stalin in a film called *Purification.* To Shekhovtsov, Adamovich represented the "worst kind of liar," a "man old enough to know better" who was trying to lead the youth of the Soviet Union astray.

"People have lost the ability to learn the truth for themselves," Shekhovtsov said. "They listen to Korotich and Yevtushenko. They don't read the truthful histories that have been published by the Institute of Marxism-Leninism."

And what about Sakharov? After all, Sakharov was now the nominal chairman of Memorial. Could he not be trusted either?

"Under Brezhnev, Sakharov was exiled to Gorky so that he would not have the chance to talk about nuclear secrets or slander the system," Shekhovtsov said. "Now, under Gorbachev's instructions, he has been returned. But in revenge, Sakharov is trying to slander us, and he is guiding the greatest power in the country—Memorial. Memorial can one day turn into an alternative party."

Shekhovtsov said he knew Nina Andreyeva and thought her a "good worker." Their acquaintance seemed confirmed when he said he was quite convinced that "the majority of people who slander Stalin and the homeland are Jews."

A few weeks later, Shekhovtsov called to tell me he had some news. He'd won his suit against *Vechernaya Moskva.* Not that it had slandered Stalin. But the court did rule that the paper had libeled Shekhovtsov when it said that he had used "Stalinist methods" when he was working as a prosecutor. The paper printed a long apology, and Shekhovtsov said he had won a great victory for himself and, most of all, for "Stalin's good name."

"The day I stop my fight," he said, "is the day I die."

———

In the courtroom, I'd gotten a dinner invitation from a woman who described herself as a "great lover of Stalin," Kira Korniyenkova. She was a matronly woman in her late fifties. Plump and stern, she wore wire-rimmed glasses, and her hair was done up in a bun. She looked like a teacher who specialized in handwriting and never gave an A. Her apartment was dim, dowdy, crammed with books. She lived with her two parakeets, Tashka and Mashinka. "My children," she called them as she poked the cage. She had never married. Never wanted to. "I wanted to be free," she said. "When you have close

relatives living with you, they get in the way. They are a hindrance. I've got
my plan and I am fulfilling that plan."

If she ever had a passion, it was Stalin. "I have always loved him. I have
dedicated my life to him and his memory." Kira Alekseyevna was a woman
unstuck in time. She spent countless days at the Lenin Library researching
the "scandalous" charges of Western and Soviet scholars writing on Stalin.
Medvedev, Solzhenitsyn, Afanasyev, Roginsky—they were all "enemies" to
her. She wanted to disprove "everything they say about how Stalin killed
millions. He didn't. He only attacked enemies of the people." Sometimes she
wrote letters to the Central Committee to complain about one point or
another in the avalanche of articles in the liberal press.

"Feel right at home," she said, and left me in the dining room with the
parakeets. She went off to cook. The room was decorated with dozens of
pictures of Stalin. Stalin as a boy. Stalin with Lenin in Gorky. Stalin on the
front page of *Pravda*. Stalin in white military dress. She had hundreds more
photographs in albums and shoeboxes. She had stacks of photos wrapped
with purple silk ribbons.

"I've never seen anything like this," I said, shouting politely down the hall
as if I were admiring my hostess's Matisse.

"Oh, I've got lots of them!" she said, shouting back from the kitchen.
"Look, look . . ."

She came running down the hall, flushed. She started shuffling through a
stack of pictures.

"Look!" she said, thrusting them a few inches from my eyes. "Each one
shows a different emotion, every stage of that great man's life." Kira glowed.

Like a lover of Wagner who goes every year to Bayreuth, Korniyenkova
took an annual pilgrimage to Gori. Sometimes, she said, she went twice a
year: once on the anniversary of Stalin's death, once to celebrate Victory
Day. "There are a lot of people who think as I do. In 1979, we gathered there
for the centenary of his birth. I think more than thirty thousand people
visited the Stalin Museum that day. People who want to build a monument
to the so-called victims of Stalin should think about that a little. It's not
necessary to build a monument to people who were imprisoned. They had
something to answer for. It's not necessary to build monuments for rich
peasants who were purged. They should build monuments to the Communists. Traitors don't deserve monuments."

Kira served pot roast and potatoes. By the by, it seemed, she said that two
of her relatives had been sent to the camps during the purges. Their crime had
been being late to work.

"They were properly judged," Kira said. I didn't say anything at all.
Tashka and Mashinka twittered in their cage. Kira's voice rose in anger.

"Was it Stalin's fault that my uncles were out late drinking and came in late for work? They had to be punished for that. I am a person who loves order. I am for real order, an iron hand or some other kind of hand. I am for a situation in which people are answerable for their deeds."

The food was delicious, but Kira Alekseyevna did not eat. She lectured. She swooned. She ascended to rapture. "I only wish we could be living in such merry days as we had then," she said. "When you see the documentary films, you can see how animated people were, how happy they were. Their faces glowed. They had poor tools, but they worked and they loved working. And now we are supposed to think that labor is 'monkey's work.' It was always so wonderful for the people to tell Stalin about their successes. I was only eighteen when Stalin was alive, but I could see how my mother worked in those years. She didn't work because she was afraid of anything, but for the sheer pleasure of it. Those parades on Red Square were some of the happiest days of our lives."

I asked her if she had ever actually seen Stalin. Kira's eyes watered as if she had suddenly been swept by a wave of memory, love recalled. "The last time I saw Stalin was in 1952. I remember the mood of the workers when, at first, Stalin could not be seen standing on the Lenin Mausoleum. They mourned. But then he appeared, and you cannot quite imagine the happiness we felt. He was quite old by then, and we greeted him with such joy. We were all fulfilling the tasks he had set out for us. We were ready to go to the moon for him. We loved Stalin, we believed in him with all our hearts."

When I asked Kira how she had reacted to Stalin's death, she told me, and cried all the while. After she heard the news, she said, she felt ill and would not leave the apartment for several days.

"On the day of the funeral I went out into the street, and you could hear all the factory sirens wailing," she said. "They used to do that when a worker left a plant forever, and now they were wailing for Stalin. Nowadays we have no such passion for our leader. Everyone gets his salary, but there is no food. How can I believe in these rulers? I believe in real things."

After dinner, Kira told me that she had once been friends—"oh, well, not friends, but comrades"—with a few of Stalin's relatives. She had even visited Molotov at his dacha. Molotov, she said, had "the eyes of wisdom." Until he died in his nineties, Molotov would tell all his visitors that Stalin had acted rightly. There had been enemies, and enemies, he said, had to be eliminated.

But hadn't there been mistakes? I asked Kira Alekseyevna. Did Stalin never commit a mistake?

"Mistakes?" she said. "Yes, he made one. He died too soon."

———

There was one other visitor to the Stalin trial I wanted to see: Stalin's grandson, Yevgeny Djugashvili. There were four Stalin grandchildren still living in Moscow: a housewife, a surgeon, a theater director, and Djugashvili. The first two begged off from a meeting. I spoke with the director, a slender and quiet man named Aleksandr Burdansky, at his office at the Soviet Army Theater, a vast building shaped like a star. All his life, he had done what he could to distance himself from Stalin. He changed his name. ("I think Burdansky sounds better than Stalin. Don't you agree?") He quit military school and always tried to look at Stalin "the way an artist would."

"I have to carry a burden, but I am not to blame for having such a grandfather. I think and act like a normal man. I have no extreme views about Stalin. I try to understand him as a phenomenon. Shakespeare's *Richard III* helped me understand Stalin. Not the play so much as Richard's biography. Richard was born a hunchback, but he had talent and a quick mind. So the man wanted to prove his right to be on an equal footing with everyone else."

If Burdansky had not pushed Stalin off to the boundaries of his mind, then he certainly liked to think he had. I had never known anyone to talk about Stalin with such an air of boredom and abstraction. "Looking at it from a civilized point of view," he said professionally, "it would be naive to regard Stalin as pure evil after he was portrayed by everyone as the friend of all peoples, children, and animals, the most outstanding personality of the age, and so on. I think he correctly translated Marx's ideas into life. It was the only way to carry them through, alas. . . ."

Burdansky did have one public moment of pique—an appearance on television in which he made it plain that he despised his grandfather. He outraged the Stalinist wing of the Stalin family. When I called Yevgeny Djugashvili on the phone, he said, "Just one thing. Don't talk to me about that faggot half brother of mine. He betrayed Stalin. His grandfather."

Djugashvili was the son of Yakov, who was captured by the Nazis and, when Stalin refused or failed to win his release, was executed. The day I met him, Djugashvili was preparing to retire from his job in the Defense Ministry in Moscow and retire, at the age of fifty-five, to Tbilisi. The man who opened the door looked exactly like Stalin: a little thinner, perhaps, his mustache more a pencil line than a hairbrush, but, still, the resemblance was chilling. He was in full military dress and, at first, conducted himself with the formality of a Politburo member. We entered a room that had several portraits of Stalin on the wall and a bookcase crammed with Party and military histories published in the Stalin era. There was a simple table and on it a stack of fresh paper and several sharpened pencils.

"So, what is question number one?" he said as he stared hard at me across the table. This was not a naive man. He was not so foolish as to think that an American reporter was visiting in order to do anything other than harm— and, in this, I suppose, he was right. But there was no point in confronting him. I simply asked him what he thought about his grandfather, what he thought of the attacks in the press and within the Party. It was the question he had expected.

"I always adored Stalin," he said. "No congress, no book or magazine article is ever going to change that and make me doubt him. He is my grandfather, first of all, and I adore him."

Solzhenitsyn was "an immoral scum," and, as for Gorbachev, "The Party's authority has fallen, this is obvious. They say the fish rots from the head. And when the fish is rotten, people throw it away. Everything is moving in that direction. In the end, I think the party will be disbanded."

Djugashvili had a nasty word to say for all the obvious people—Shatrov, Afanasyev, Sakharov, Yeltsin, the leaders of Memorial. He went on for a while, too, about the latest plays and television programs that had slandered his grandfather. He clearly kept up with it all. The only thing that seemed to lift his mood was his own recent appearance, as Stalin, in a Georgian film production.

"They say I'm a real chip off the old block!" And then he stopped and stared at me once more. For a moment it really felt as if Stalin were there. But Djugashvili broke the spell.

"Enough!" he said, slamming his hand down on the table. His face broke into a weird grin. "I like you! I have decided that! Now I will make you my real guest!"

In Georgia, a good host usually shows his guest around the farm and the farmhouse. Stalin's grandson showed me his kitchen, then his bathroom shelves.

"I built these myself!" he said, waving his hand across them lovingly as if they were a prize in a game show.

"And here is the bedroom . . . and over here . . . the living room! . . . By the way, you know, I never got anything out of being Stalin's grandson. But, of course, when I needed an apartment I wrote a letter to Brezhnev. They gave me this place. And they jumped me ahead on the waiting list for a car, too. So it hasn't all been bad.

"And this," he said, entering the kitchen, "is the kitchen again."

Djugashvili yanked a jerry can out from under a table. "Here is cha-cha," he said, lifting the moonshine. Then he put a watermelon in my arms, and we marched back to the living room.

"Pour out two glasses of cha-cha," he said. Djugashvili cut thick slices of the watermelon with a curved dagger and salted them. He stood and lifted his glass and waited. I stood.

"We shall drink to friendship between nations!" he said. Fair enough, I thought, and we both downed the cha-cha, a home brew from Tbilisi. On first gulp, the drink did not seem as obvious or as strong as Russian vodka.

Djugashvili stood again. "In a Georgian house," he said, "the host makes all the toasts, and in my house, the second toast is always to Stalin!"

I felt a wave of nausea sweep through me and weaken my knees. But I kept my glass high and my eyes fixed on my host's. "The Soviet Union took on the brunt of the war, and Stalin was at the head of all that," he went on. "He took a backward country, with peasants in felt boots, and made it great. And yet we still curse him. These people should be punished and their lies exposed! I think there will come a day when the Soviet people will give their evaluation. And so . . . to Stalin!"

"To Stalin," I said. And may God forgive me.

———

By the end of 1988, there were chapters of Memorial in over two hundred Soviet cities. A debate was beginning between members who wanted to limit Memorial's attention to the repression during the Stalin period and those who thought it should widen to include all acts from the first arrests and executions under Lenin to the death of the dissident writer Anatoly Marchenko in a prison camp in December 1986. In other words, some Memorial members were beginning to speak not merely of the "aberration of Stalin" but of a criminal regime.

Novy Mir, Neva, and other journals began to publish articles critical not only of Stalin, but of Lenin and even the Revolution. In January 1989, Yuri Afanasyev presided over a two-day constituent congress of Memorial. Vadim Medvedev, a leading member of the Politburo, tried to shut down the session before it ever began, citing obscure reasons of "permission" and "sanction." Sakharov called Medvedev and informed him that the Politburo had no business getting involved. "If you shut us out of our meeting hall, we will hold the congress in apartments all over Moscow," he said. Medvedev gave up, and the congress went on. The Communist Party was beginning to lose control of history, and a Party that could not be sure of its hold on the past had to be nervous about its future.

But even as Memorial expanded its definition of the past, its essential purpose remained the same: to honor the dead, to give them back their names. Some of the younger historians and volunteers worked on their own to accumulate more information on arrests, executions, exiles. Others made careful studies of existing history textbooks and won a series of critical victories when the Party decided to rewrite the schoolbooks, eliminate high school ideology exams, and make mandatory university courses in Marxism-Leninism and scientific socialism as optional as basket weaving.

No one took the mission of Memorial more literally than Aleksandr Milchakov. A journalist whose father had been the general secretary of the Young Communist League and head of one of the industrial ministries, Milchakov grew up in the House on the Embankment. When he was a child, he saw guards in the courtyard carrying what seemed to be violin cases. "In reality, they were cases for their machine guns," he told me. "They were ready for action at all times."

Milchakov was in his fifties and still lived in the apartment of his childhood when I got to know him. As one of the leading figures of Memorial, he decided to narrow his journalism to a single investigation. According to Roy Medvedev's *Let History Judge,* around one thousand people per day were killed during the height of the purges in the late thirties. Milchakov wanted to know where the dead of Moscow were buried.

Milchakov's own father was arrested and spent fifteen years in internal exile. "During those arrests I was only around eight or nine, but I was a curious boy and liked to hang around the courtyard. I saw the reaction of the other boys when their parents were taken away. It was a time when you could hear the clomp of high boots on the staircase. The police were in the habit of never using the elevator. I remember clearly how they took my father down the stairs, not the elevator. And so we all listened every night for footsteps.

"Most of the parents truly believed that there were enemies in the Party and that there was a genuine political struggle going on. They were always surprised when someone was arrested. But their surprise was that someone who they thought was honest turned out to be a traitor. When my father was arrested and our belongings were confiscated, I remember how we children were ousted from our own apartment and we sat in the courtyard on wooden sleighs and no one, none of our old friends, would come near us or talk to us. To talk to a relative of an enemy of the people was the gravest sort of sin."

Using Western and Soviet published sources, Milchakov began researching the location of the biggest mass graves in the Moscow area: the Donskoi Monastery, the grounds of a KGB colony in the village of Butovo, the Kalitnikovsky Cemetery near the city pet market, the fourteenth-century Novospassky Monastery, the banks of the Moscow-Volga Canal.

Early one morning, my friend Jeff Trimble of *U.S. News & World Report* and I met Milchakov outside the House on the Embankment and headed for the Donskoi Monastery. The flower ladies in their blue canvas jackets sat near the entrances selling carnations, 5 rubles a bunch. Milchakov led us toward the main building on the cemetery grounds, the crematorium. We walked to the back of the building where an old man, an attendant, was watching over a small bonfire of garbage. A few broken tombstones lay on the ground.

"See this gate?" Milchakov said. "Well, every night trucks stacked with bodies came back here and dumped the dead in a heap. They'd already been shot in the back of the head—you bleed less that way—at the Lubyanka prison or at the Military Collegium. They stacked the bodies in old wooden ammunition crates. The workers stoked up the underground ovens—right in through that door—to about twelve hundred degrees centigrade. To make things nice and official they even had professional witnesses who countersigned the various documents. When the bodies were burned they were reduced to ash and some chips of bone, maybe some teeth. Then they buried the ashes in a big pit."

We walked for a few minutes up and down rows of tombs, elaborate monuments that would not have seemed out of place at Père Lachaise Cemetery in Paris. We stopped at a tomb marked "The Grave of Unidentified Corpses, 1930–1942." There were four white plastic tulips stuck in the ground and a stack of rotting carnations that smelled like spilled wine. Someone had also put a tiny icon of Saint George near the base of the monument. Milchakov said that the pit had been five yards deep and twenty feet square and when it was filled completely with ashes—"hundreds and hundreds of pounds of ash"—the secret police paved it over with asphalt. He said there were rumors that Bukharin was buried at Donskoi, but he was not sure.

"When the purges were at their peak," he said, "the furnaces worked all night and the domes of the churches and the roofs of the houses here were covered with ash. There was a fine dust of ash on the snow."

We drove to Kalitnikovsky Cemetery, a dumping ground for thousands of corpses. There was a sausage factory nearby, a fetid place, and Milchakov said, "In the purges, every dog in town came to this place. That smell you smell now was three times as bad; blood in the air. People would lean out their windows and puke all night and the dogs howled until dawn. Sometimes they'd find a dog with an arm or a leg walking through the graveyard."

At the Novospassky Monastery, Milchakov showed us the steep bank near the pond where the NKVD buried the bullet-riddled corpses of foreign Communists: John Penner of the American Communist Party; Herman Remmele, Fritz Schultke, Herman Schubert, and Leo Fleig, leaders of the 842 German antifascists arrested in April 1938; Bela Kun and Laiosh Madyr of the Hungarian Communists; Vladimir Chopich of the Yugoslavian Party; Marcel Pauker and Alexander Dobrodzhanu of Romania.

"There used to be apple trees along the bank," he said. "They burned them off. They took the prisoners to the monastery church to a room they called 'the baths.' They stripped the prisoners, weighed them, and shot them in the back of the head. In the records, this was called the 'medical process.' They had them shot in a sitting position. A little window would open behind the prisoner's head and the executioner reached in and fired. They used that method so they could avoid strokes, heart attacks, and hysteria. They stacked the bodies like pencils in a box and carried them off in a horse-drawn cart to a crematorium."

Milchakov struggled constantly with the KGB to get permission to carry out excavations on all these sites. The "glasnost" KGB, under Vladimir Kryuchkov, was engaged in an extraordinary public relations maneuver. Kryuchkov tried to humanize the secret police, declaring to the press that he was a great lover of theater and dogs and children. At the same time, the KGB did what it could to deflate the likes of Aleksandr Milchakov. They rebuffed his requests for documents, denied him access to Butovo, and made sure he was followed and harassed when he went on one of his field trips. But the better-known Milchakov became, the more he publicized his findings in a series of articles in *Vechernaya Moskva,* the more he accomplished. The KGB didn't help him much, but they did not stop him either.

A couple of weeks later, we went together to the very edge of town near a water-treatment camp on the banks of the Moscow-Volga Canal. Stalin ordered the construction of the nearly useless canal in 1932, and it was finished in 1937. The workers were slaves, prisoners, most of them peasant farmers who, because they owned a horse or a cow, were declared kulaks and arrested. Genrikh Yagoda, the secret police chief at the time, worked the prisoners to death.

Milchakov said that around 500,000 prisoners died working on the canal, most of them from cold and exhaustion. Even in winter they were given nothing more to wear than a thin jacket. The prisoners lived in shabby barracks next to the construction site. They built the 127-mile canal using shovels, picks, and wheelbarrows. Their diet was dismal. Scientists have done analyses of the teeth of the prisoners. From the way the enamel has worn off, it appears that many of the prisoners ate bark, roots, and grass to supplement the bread and thin gruel they were given.

Milchakov was not prone to superstition, but in order to find the graves along the canal he resorted to divining rods when witnesses and guesswork proved unavailing. He had arranged for us to meet with an expert diviner near a certain row of birches. Milchakov assured us that in the past he'd been able to dig up several long mass graves with this man's help. And so for a couple of hours we watched in silence as the diviner paced and weaved through the woods and a flock of jays rioted in the trees.

"Someone else is meeting us here, too," Milchakov said. He led me to a monument in the woods: a towering cross wrapped in barbed wire. Memorial had constructed it to honor the prisoners who died building the canal. Next to the cross stood an old, stooped man who introduced himself as "Sergei Burov, pensioner."

He said that when he was a child of ten or eleven, he had lived near the barracks. Every morning, on his way home from the store, the workers would call out to him to throw them pieces of bread.

"I'd wrap the bread in newspaper and throw it," he said. "Sometimes I saw the guards catch them and beat them. I saw the burial teams, too. They were prisoners, and for their work they were given bottles of vodka to keep them drunk. I remember running around, quite innocently, playing, and seeing these men in their prison clothes throwing bodies into the ground. Our parents told us about it and they would say, 'There is some sort of wildness going on.' They just had no idea. They did not want to know."

One morning, years after the canal had been completed, Burov said, he was walking beside it and saw some families on the bank. They were all crying. They folded pieces of paper, letters, and put them in bottles. They corked the bottles and threw them into the water.

"I asked them what they were doing and they told me they were sending messages to people they had lost on the canal," Burov said. "They said they hoped that sometime in the future people would find the bottles and read the letters and remember. They said they were sending the names of their loved ones into the future. They cast their names on the water."

PART II

DEMOCRATIC
VISTAS

CHAPTER 10

MASQUERADE

After the Bolsheviks sacked the Winter Palace and seized power in 1917, they still had an empire to win. To help conquer the hearts and minds of the people, Lenin declared cinema the most important of the arts and sent propaganda films and projectionists by train across Russia to advertise the Revolution. Stalin, too, saw the value of the new art. Though his preferred instrument of enculturation was the pistol, he told the Communist Party that cinema was "the greatest means of mass agitation." And so for years after the Great October, workers and peasants in makeshift tent-theaters and railroad cars watched *The Extraordinary Adventures of Mr. West in the Land of the Bolsheviks, Strike, October,* and *Kino-Eye,* imbibing all the while the spirit of revolution.

But with new revolutions come new media. When Gorbachev rose to power in 1985, his chief ideologist and propagandist, Aleksandr Yakovlev, declared, "The television image is everything." Yakovlev had been for ten years an ambassador in Canada, and he often sat at home in Ottawa, watching the Canadian and American networks. Yakovlev also studied television in Moscow. For years he worked in the Central Committee's ideology department. Better than anyone around him, he understood the potential of television as an instrument of persuasion, coercion, and homogenization in an empire as vast as the Soviet Union.

Though the Soviet Union was poor and primitive, nearly everyone had a television. Everyone watched. Yakovlev understood that if there was one ritual that could unite Baltic intellectuals and Siberian peasants, it was television. Above all, he understood the essential value of *Vremya* ("Time"), the official evening news program, a prime-time ritual for nearly 200 million people every night of the week.

———

Stalin had been an untelevised tyrant. He was like some magical Eastern god, unseen, rarely heard. The media technology of the day allowed him easy control of his own cult. To a great extent, Stalin's cult was a phenomenon of print: histories, newspapers, textbooks, posters. It was so easy to manipulate. His photographs in *Pravda* were retouched. Pockmarks disappeared. He grew a head taller. It was impossible to tell he had a withered arm.

But as the system loosened somewhat and technology advanced, the people of the Soviet Union came to know the leaders of the post-Stalin era— Khrushchev and Brezhnev—more intimately, mainly through television and the evening news. *Vremya* was an invention of the Central Committee in the sixties. It was a product designed to be the high mass of a closed, atheist state. The Party ideologists shaped the look and sound of the program with pains-taking care. After a long search, they discovered their Big Brother in Igor Kirillov, an unassuming actor of deceptive skill. For twenty years, Kirillov would anchor *Vremya*. He was slender and wore serious glasses, giving him the unthreatening look of a kindly teacher of mathematics. Such was the public face of the Kremlin.

Kirillov was the master of his own voice and presence. Using the slightest gesture or shift in intonation, he made the declarations of the Central Committee seem the revealed wisdom of heaven; he could also report the most ordinary events in the capitalist West as if they were scandals against human-ity, a mockery of all that was good and decent. Above all, he commanded attention. "Today, in the Politburo . . ." Kirillov would begin gravely, and every subject would listen, waiting for instruction.

Kirillov, like so many servants of ideology, went through a conversion experience born of necessity under Gorbachev. When I saw him at the state television studios in 1991, Big Brother wore a sweater and the hound-dog look of repentance. He was grateful for a second chance, and now introduced various youth programs. He apologized for himself constantly and wore his cardigan as if it were sackcloth. "The sweater shows I've changed," he said. "The system survived as long as it did thanks to the ideological service of the Communist Party and television. It was a kind of mass hypnosis." For that Kirillov seemed genuinely sorry.

Kirillov had been chosen for his great role thanks to his training in the Stanislavsky Method. "I had the ability to make people believe," he said. Kirillov remembered being overcome with emotion in 1961 when Khrushchev declared on television that the Soviet Union would achieve Communism in his lifetime. "And as Khrushchev spoke those words, the sun came out— and the entire Hall of Congresses seemed to light up. See, we told each other, even nature believes in our cause. That's when my wife and I decided to have our first daughter. We hoped that she would live under Communism. Now I am ashamed that I was used as a marionette and that, through me and through television, a fog was created in the minds of the people."

The producers of *Vremya* knew precisely how to create an imagery of empire and to win over, or at least befuddle, the people. They surrounded Kirillov with the aural and visual symbols of Bolshevik grandeur. When the question arose about what music to use for the opening of the show, the TV ideologists immediately ruled out Mozart and Beethoven. To use German music would have violated the Russian imperial spirit.

"The opening showed the Kremlin as the symbol of empire. The idea was for information to flow from this mighty pinnacle downward," said Eduard Sagalayev, who ran *Vremya* for a while under Gorbachev. *"Vremya* was a medium not only to convey information but also to give instructions, especially to provincial Party leaders and to the most ordinary person. It was the singular connection between supreme authority and the people. I personally saw letters from old ladies addressed to Igor Kirillov saying, 'Please, dear Igor Leonidovich, tell Gorbachev to do such-and-such.' Kirillov was for many people right between general secretary and the Lord God. In fact, he was higher than general secretary, because, after all, it was *Vremya* that prescribed precisely how to live. Kirillov would read the decrees of the Central Committee without any editing or compression, for such decrees were on the order of the Ten Commandments. It was a biblical phenomenon. How could Moses compress the commandments God had handed down to the Israelites?"

The rituals on *Vremya* were always repeated precisely. Even during the Gorbachev era, there was little room for improvisation. If the general secretary was leaving for a trip abroad, the producers of *Vremya* knew precisely how to portray the scene. First, the establishing shot at the airport with a red banner reading "Long Live the Party"; then the Politburo members in their hats and overcoats coming out of the building to wait by the plane; then the general secretary himself saying good-bye, kissing each of his comrades on the cheek; then the general secretary at the top of the airplane stairs, waving farewell.

"Faith was the issue," Sagalayev said. "People swallowed the stereotypes they were fed, they believed everything was all right, everything was fine, as long as the rituals were in place. Even the kisses at the airport were a cause for pride and joy. Provincial Party secretaries watched and dreamed of the day when they'd be shown on television, leaving for Zimbabwe."

In Brezhnev's dotage—an interminable stretch on the critical list—*Vremya* began to work against him. For a man who could barely function in office, television was a cruel medium. Leonid Parfyonov, a popular television host in the glasnost era, told me with just a touch of irony that after Andrei Sakharov, the most effective dissident of the 1970s was *Vremya.* "It was only then that people could see how decrepit our leaders were," he said. "They'd watch Brezhnev talking, losing his place in his speeches, mumbling like an old man falling apart, and they began to think: 'This is the leader of our great state?' It had never been like that." Not a few viewers understood Brezhnev's deterioration as a new symbol: the symbol of the deterioration of the Soviet Union itself.

————

Gorbachev knew that he could use *Vremya,* and television in general, to create a public image of himself as new kind of czar. His image, and no other, would embody his policy. Television was still his tool, his to use as he liked. In his first major public appearance as general secretary, a speech in Leningrad, Gorbachev was so vigorous compared to his predecessors, so critical of the status quo, so informal and unembarrassed by his southern accent and grammatical slips, that he was quickly dubbed "the chairman of the collective farm." On television, Gorbachev dove into crowds. No one had to know that the KGB had carefully screened those crowds or that the producers had carefully edited the footage to the general secretary's own specifications. The entire state media apparatus was dedicated not to reporting the news but rather to the evolution of a personality and the promotion of a policy, a new way of doing things.

The Kremlin inner circle was obsessed with Gorbachev's television image. Just before airtime, Sagalayev said, Gorbachev himself frequently called the *Vremya* producers at the studio to go over the details of his appearance. No editing, no visual image or remark, was left to the judgment of anyone but Gorbachev and his aides. "Gorbachev's image," Sagalayev said, "was carefully planned and organized with the help of the KGB, Gorbachev's staff, and the ideology department of the Central Committee. And most of all, Yakovlev and Raisa Maksimovna helped develop the new image of the general secretary—open, democratic. They wanted him to resemble Lenin, for Lenin's image was that of a simple man who received ordinary people and peasants and drove in a car with no bodyguards. They wanted perestroika to be a return to Leninism, a purification of the Party from Stalinism and totalitarianism."

Every night, people would turn on *Vremya,* and, inevitably, Gorbachev would be up to something: speaking off the cuff at a provincial Party meeting, wading through crowds in New Delhi or Bonn, greeting a foreign delegation in a room with a green baize table and a red runner carpet. Gorbachev was never interviewed in the conventional Western sense. A nervous state broadcaster, carefully briefed, would ask a fuzzy, open-ended question ("Mikhail Sergeyevich, what hopes do you have for your trip to London?"), and then Gorbachev would go on for fifteen or twenty minutes. By mid-1987 at the latest, urban intellectuals especially sat in front of the television watching this new figure, captivated, a little bit in love. The intellectuals were like film critics who, after sitting through years of depressing schlock, were suddenly shown a print of *Citizen Kane.*

Probably the height of Gorbachev's television career, in Soviet eyes, was his performance at the Nineteenth Party Conference. Not only did he read his own part well, he also directed "spontaneity" to his advantage, sending up obscure speakers to excoriate and embarrass hidebound Politburo members, setting Ligachev up against Yeltsin to enhance his own stature as the wise, liberal center flanked by ideological and emotional extremes.

Never again would Gorbachev's mastery be so complete; never would he be as in control of the spectacle of politics. But for several years, Gorbachev not only was the lead actor, producer, and director in his nightly drama, he also had no competition. *Vremya* played on all the main channels. The educational channel's Italian lessons were not exactly an ideological challenge. For nearly four years, there were no competing political actors to speak of. None, that is, who had access to prime time. Yeltsin did not really appear until June 1988, and even then the focus of his attack was Ligachev, not Gorbachev. Sakharov also did not get much airtime until mid-1989. And the right wing was still too bound by the traditions of Communist Party discipline to go on television in the spirit of contradiction.

Gorbachev was a lecturer, a cajoler. At conferences and in his meetings on the street, he was a relentless pedant. But for all his power and self-possession, Gorbachev did allow a bit of humor about himself. This, too, was revolutionary. Political humor had always been a staple of private life in the Soviet Union, starring Brezhnev as the doddering fool or the corpse of Lenin as *kopchushka,* the "smoked fish." But such jokes were never permitted in official publications. In the March 1988 issue of *Teatr,* the satirist Mikhail Zadornov adopted the voice of a resident of a town Gorbachev had just visited. He writes a letter to the general secretary telling him how the once dingy town had been transformed. "It is true that you informed our local authorities about your visit just three days in advance," the mock letter to Gorbachev says, "but even in those three days they managed to do more for our city than they had in all the years of Soviet power. All the buildings that you were supposed to pass were painted, but then someone said that you like to swerve off your planned course and so our authorities were obliged to paint all the other houses in the city. They worked so hard that they painted the windows, too."

The joke was less on Gorbachev than on the vanity of the Communist Party and the Russian tradition of Potemkin villages. But a year later, as glasnost expanded farther beyond the strict control of the Politburo, the humor cut deeper and Kremlin patience wore a bit thin. The Gorbachev family was no longer amused. On the stage of the Satire Theater, one of the actors starring in Vladimir Voinovich's political satire *The Tribunal,* Vyacheslav Bezrukov, spun out a long and hilarious imitation of Gorbachev, complete with his signature hand motions (karate chops, raised index finger), odd grammar, and accent. Gorbachev's daughter, Irina, was sitting in the third row, and she had been laughing throughout the show. But when Bezrukov started his Gorbachev imitation, Irina scowled. The moment the curtain fell, she headed for the exit, unsmiling, not applauding.

Gorbachev did not shut down any theaters, but he did guard his image, and his life, jealously. Despite his policy of democratization, he never suffered the scrutiny of a real political campaign, much less the assault of a hungry press corps in search of his "character." Gorbachev's climb to power took place inside the Soviet Communist Party, an institution that valued aggressive obedience and secrecy. The initiator of glasnost revealed little of himself except through political performance. When it came to unsanctioned exploration of his personality and his past, Gorbachev was not, at first, much more forthcoming than his predecessors. Even the most liberal papers and magazines did not dare publish what a Westerner would call a profile. Gorbachev insisted on communicating directly with the Soviet people, and the only filter permitted would be the one that he and his staff designed and approved.

For all his support of glasnost, for all his talk of the need to fill in the "blank spots" of history, Gorbachev kept to himself a central fact of his early life for more than five years after coming to power. It was only in December 1990, when he was alienating the entire liberal intelligentsia, including Shevardnadze and Yakovlev, by cooperating with the hard-liners in the Party, that Gorbachev revealed that both of his grandfathers had been repressed under Stalin. You had to be listening carefully to catch it. Late one night, Central Television broadcast a tape of one of Gorbachev's meetings with a large group of leading writers and journalists. Somehow, Gorbachev was trying to justify his swing to the right but at the same time to win back the respect of the intelligentsia.

"Look at my two grandfathers," Gorbachev said. "One was denounced for not fulfilling the sowing plan in 1933, a year when half the family died of hunger. . . ."

Why now? Why hadn't he said anything in 1988 when the battle for history had been raging?

". . . They took him away to Irkutsk to a timber-producing camp, and the rest of the family was broken, half-destroyed in that year. And the other grandfather—he was an organizer of collective farms, later a local administrator. This was quite a figure for those times. He was from a peasant family, a peasant of average means. He was in prison for fourteen months. They interrogated him, demanded that he admit what he'd never done. Thank God, he survived. But when he returned home, people considered his house a plague house, a house of an 'enemy of the people.' Relatives and dear ones were not able to visit him, otherwise 'they' would have come after them, too."

It was as if Gorbachev's family was a paradigm of the Stalinist era: one grandfather was punished for failing to fulfill the absurd and brutal demands of collectivization; the other, a leader of collectivization, suffered for no reason other than to be a victim of Stalin's scheme of organized, random terror. "When I was up for membership in the Communist Party, I had to answer for all this," Gorbachev told me later, in an interview. "It was a very painful moment." Throughout the speech, Gorbachev made plain that he himself was the leader of a particular generation with a particular vision: a man of late middle age, born into a system that betrayed his family, but one who is convinced nevertheless that "genuine" socialism was possible and still "my banner." The tragedy of the Stalin era and the farce of the Brezhnev period represented for Gorbachev not the failure of ideology, but rather its perversion.

But Gorbachev had not finished. There was a reason for his revelation. It turned out that he had saved his confession for traditional ends. "I've been told more than once that it is time to stop swearing allegiance to socialism," he was saying now. "Why should I? Socialism is my deep conviction, and I will promote it as long as I can talk and work." By late 1990, political opinion polls showed that only a minority of Soviet people—not more than 20 percent—still shared Gorbachev's faith in the efficacy of socialism. But attempts to turn away from the "socialist choice" were inconceivable to Gorbachev—a betrayal, a "counterrevolution on the sly." The Baltic independent movements were a threat to his notion of the Soviet Union as "one people"; he saw the calls for private property as a threat to the psychology of a people who spent years being taught to despise it. The opposition to such foreign ideas, he said, were "last stands," comparable to the battles of Moscow and Stalingrad.

"Am I supposed to turn my back on my grandfather, who was committed to the [socialist] idea? . . . And I cannot go against my father, who defended Kursk, forded the Dnieper River knee-deep in blood, and was wounded in Czechoslovakia. When cleansing myself of Stalinism and all other filth, should I renounce my grandfather and my father and all they did?"

———

In 1989, I traveled to the scene of Gorbachev's youth, the southern Russian city of Stavropol and the farming villages nearby. When I showed up at the Hotel Kavkaz, a forbidding old woman with bandaged legs sat squat on a stool, her gaze set on me, barring the door. I tried to get an explanation from her but I could not.

"You'll have to excuse us, but we're having a mass killing in there," said a voice over my shoulder. The local tourist guide, Valentin Nizin, as it turned out. "We're wiping out the cockroach population. But don't worry. When you get to your room, I'm sure you won't be disappointed."

Nizin was right. Roach platoons raced down the linoleum in columns.

Nizin, who seemed like something more than a tour guide, was extremely interested in why I had come to Stavropol "when there are hundreds of other places for you to go in the Soviet Union." Except to protect friends and sources, I did not conceal much when reporting in the Soviet Union, even in conversations with people I took to be informers. I printed nearly everything I knew anyway. So I told Nizin that I was there to learn what I could about Gorbachev's past. I was not the first, and Nizin kindly helped me find a few of Gorbachev's old friends in town. But when I said I wanted to go to Privolnoye, the village nearby where Gorbachev was born and raised, Nizin stiffened. He would get back to me on that, he said, and disappeared into his office.

Within an hour, he told me I could not go.

"There is a quarantine in Privolnoye," he said. "It is forbidden to you."

"What sort of quarantine?"

"The cows are diseased, apparently. They do not want any foreigners to come and get sick."

"The cows are against it?"

"No," Nizin said. "Not the cows."

I knew very well what this meant and could guess with even more accuracy with whom Comrade Nizin had just been talking. But I was tired and angry, and so I pushed things a bit too far.

"Mr. Nizin, I do not plan to interview any cows, nor do I plan to exchange fluids with one. I told the Foreign Ministry I was going to Privolnoye and they had no objections, and I don't believe there is any quarantine."

"Oh, but there is," he said. "Hoof and mouth disease."

Or whatever. Nizin smiled and shrugged in a way to let me know that he knew that I knew, but that was too bad, you'll have to limit yourself to the city, where we can keep a good eye on you. It was no use, and we both knew it. I gave up, bought Nizin a drink, set my alarm for 5:00 A.M., and went to bed.

———

When I woke it was snowing, fat flakes that whitened the grim city. I dressed quickly and walked past the concierge, who was slumped in her chair and snoring. The halls still stank of pesticide, and there were still roaches, thousands of them skittering along the linoleum.

On the street, I got lucky. I was looking to hire a car, and I found one after only fifteen minutes or so. A tiny orange Zhiguli with bald tires and a smashed windshield pulled over. Perfect. It would not have been so smart to go to Gorbachev-land in a bright yellow taxi. I got in the car and quickly explained to the driver, a young farmer out to make some extra money before breakfast, where I wanted to go. When he squinted quizzically, I added that I was willing to pay $25 in hard currency, a sum that would surely put him in feed until harvest time. Off we went.

The driver and I figured that it would be best if we just drove through Privolnoye to get a quick look and then went to Krasnogvardeiskoye, a much larger town where Gorbachev went to high school, entered Communist Party politics, and fell in love. If I was still undetected after talking to people there, we'd stop in Privolnoye on the way back to Stavropol. With so many KGB men around, my luck would surely run out; it was just a question of when.

The road was among the most beautiful I'd ever seen in the Soviet Union, including the Georgian Military Highway through the Caucasus and the flat road through the Kara Kum desert in Turkmenia. Snow dusted the rich fields like confectioner's sugar over a Black Forest cake. In two hours of driving, we passed more horse carts than automobiles. Peasant women with silver teeth, humped backs, and mud-covered boots led cows down the side of the road. The lushness of the farmland seemed to me the very soil of Gorbachev's optimism. "You could shove a stick in the ground around here and you'd get a harvest," people told me in Stavropol, and now I could believe it.

Privolnoye was not much different from the village before it and the one after. Peasant huts, livestock, fields. The air was cold and sweet with the smell of fertilizer, hay, and loam. There was one paved road and some dirt ones, all near the muddy stream known as the Yegorlik River. A black bull was tethered to the green fence surrounding Gorbachev's first schoolhouse. Ducks and geese waddled down the road.

Privolnoye, which is roughly translated as "free and easy," could no longer be called an entirely typical village. Not when the KGB was in town keeping a close watch on the white brick house with blue-green shutters where Gorbachev's mother, Maria Panteleyevna Gorbacheva, lived. Gorbachev's mother was in her late seventies, a stout and friendly-looking woman in support hose. Her accent was southern, a peasant's accent. The KGB took great pains to shield her from journalists, but she did appear on television on one of Gorbachev's birthdays, informing the nation that young Misha had worked hard on the farm, read all the books in the collective farm library, and played a mean balalaika. "And my how he could sing!" According to people I met who have lived in the village and in villages nearby, Maria Panteleyevna rarely went out anymore. A few years later, when her son was on the brink of resignation, she said perhaps that might not be so bad, since he'd had no time to visit her in years. Accustomed to the pace and the faces of the village, Maria Panteleyevna had always refused Gorbachev's requests to move to Moscow. She did have a few modern conveniences that had not been around when her son lived there: television, indoor plumbing. She was too old to care for the animals anymore. "She said, 'At least let me keep the rooster so I'll get up in the morning,' " Georgi Gorlov, an old family friend, told me.

———

At the very moment when Gorbachev was born in March 1931, southern Russia and Ukraine were living through the collectivization campaign and the starvation that went along with it. According to Western studies, more than thirty thousand people in the Stavropol region died during the terror-famine of 1931–32. Despite the horror of those years, Gorbachev, like so many "reform Communists," believed in the idea of collective farms, but abhorred what Bukharin called the "Genghis Khan" methods of Stalin.

Without plunging into the puddle of psychohistory, one might fairly say that Gorbachev's early sense of himself as a success was tied to the collective farm. Working with his father and the family of fellow farmworker Aleksandr Yakovenko, Gorbachev spent his teenage summers on a rickety S-80 combine harvesting grain. It was hard and filthy work, usually under a broiling southern sun. To cool off, the two boys, Gorbachev and Yakovenko, stripped and sat in barrels of river water. The Gorbachev-Yakovenko team was a local success, so much so that they earned a banner headline in the June 20, 1948, edition of the *Road of Ilyich,* the local newspaper: "Comrade Gorbachev Is Ready to Harvest."

The next year, while Gorbachev was in high school, the team won a coveted honor, the Medal of the Red Banner. Such an honor was the first step toward a life in the Party. Many years later, when he was the regional Party leader in Stavropol, Gorbachev would visit the farms in the region and stun his traveling party when old farming friends like the shepherd Vasily Rudenko would greet him with a bear hug and "Hey, Misha! Have you eaten?" With that, they would march into Rudenko's hut for a plate of jellied innards and a bowl of borshch.

———

After the brief and unnerving driving tour of Privolnoye, we headed for the town of Krasnogvardeiskoye, or "Red Guard." Gorbachev knew this stretch of road well. Four decades before, he woke early in his parents' house, a two-room hut made of mud, manure, and straw with pigs and chickens and an outhouse in the yard. The harvest was over. The village schools were opening. Gorbachev tucked a package of home-grown food under his arm, met up with his friend Dmitri Markov, and began the walk to Krasnogvardeiskoye's High School No. 1. Gorbachev rented a bed in the house of an old retired couple there. Weekends he returned home to Privolnoye to work in the fields.

The two-story brick high school fast became the center of Gorbachev's universe. He was the classic small-town overachiever, a class-president type who scored high marks, starred in the school plays, and won the heart of the best-looking girl in the school. For half a day, I buzzed around the town, talking to teachers, old friends, people on the street. There was, of course, something preposterous about the entire mission, something straight out of the old television series *This Is Your Life*. Yekaterina Chaika, Gorbachev's old chemistry teacher, was one of several people to deliver twinkling remembrances and boilerplate as if on cue. "He is a man of his time," she said, "and there are countless factors of history that come into play. But if you want to understand him better as a man, it doesn't hurt to know where he came from. Like anyone, he has roots. And those roots are right here." Others who probably did not know him at all conjured visions of the ideal. "You know," one man told me, "I don't think Mikhail Sergeyevich even had that birthmark on his head when he was here."

But there were others in town who had something to show me. The high school principal was Oleg Sredni, a man at least fifteen years younger than Gorbachev. He seemed unfazed by the prospect of helping an uninvited foreigner find out more about the general secretary of the Communist Party.

"You want to see Mikhail Sergeyevich's grades?" he said. "I think we have them here in the safe."

Plump and graceful, Sredni darted across his office to the safe and brought out a musty, Dickensian ledger. He opened to 1950, the year of Gorbachev's graduation, and there, in a formal hand and cloudy ink, was "Gorbachev, Mikhail Sergeyevich" and a line of numbers. On a grade scale with 5 being the highest to 1 the lowest, Gorbachev had a nearly uninterrupted row of 5s: algebra, Russian literature, trigonometry, history of the Soviet Union, the Soviet Constitution, astronomy, and so on. The one blemish was a 4 in German. "Apparently his class in Privolnoye refused to take German after the war, so he was a bit behind when he got here," Sredni said in a tone of churchly reverence. "That is why he got the silver medal here, not the gold."

Except for the portrait of Gorbachev on Sredni's office wall, the school had not paid much attention to honoring their native son. In the school's hall of fame, Gorbachev was listed as just one medal winner among many, a future general secretary next to Gennadi Fateyev, the class poet. I had been to high schools in the United States where third-rate quarterbacks have been honored more grandly. Sredni had made sure there would be no personality cult in the halls of his school.

"In our day there were lots of pictures of Stalin, of course. I remember one especially, a portrait of Stalin and Mao called *The Great Friendship*," said Yuri Serikov, one of Gorbachev's classmates and now a history teacher at the school. "It was absurd, but what did we know?"

Gorbachev was a Soviet Best Boy, with conventional ambitions and ideas. He was the leader of the school's Komsomol organization and became a candidate for membership in the Communist Party when he was only eighteen. He was no high school rebel. "We were told that Stalin was doing everything perfectly, and we believed it all," Yuri Serikov said. "That was our level of understanding, and Mikhail Sergeyevich was no exception. None of us ever thought twice about it."

———

After interviewing fifteen or twenty people in town, the inevitable happened: the KGB caught up with me. Sredni, the school principal, took a phone call while I was in his office. "*Da,*" he said grimly. And *da* three or four times more, all with the same dead tone of obedience. He hung up the receiver and, lifting his eyes to me, said, "I'm afraid I can't talk with you anymore. Please wait here."

Someone had obviously called the authorities, and I was soon summoned to the office of the deputy Communist Party chief, the head chief being out of town on business. The deputy chief had a caveman brow and never smiled. When I told him that I had heard no objections from the Foreign Ministry in Moscow to my coming to the countryside, the deputy chief did not betray the slightest emotion.

"You will get in your car, and proceed directly to Stavropol," he said.

"What about Privolnoye?" I said. "I told the foreign ministry I'd go there, too."

"As you know, there is a quarantine."

"What quarantine?"

"You know very well. You were told."

"And how do you know that?"

The deputy chief blinked once, slowly, to indicate annoyance. I was not to be childish, he seemed to say. He had no time. He had an entire town to run into the ground before the year was out.

———

Before leaving Krasnogvardeiskoye, I had asked a dozen people if Gorbachev had a girlfriend when he was in school. Everyone remembered the same name: Yuliya Karagodina. "Very pretty, if I remember." "Played the Snowgirl in the play with Mikhail Sergeyevich." When I asked one local Communist Party official if she had Karagodina's number, she smiled girlishly, conspiratorily, and gave it to me.

Yuliya Karagodina, it turned out, had long ago moved to Moscow, where she was divorced, living with her mother, and teaching at a chemistry institute. When I called and asked to see her, Yuliya, as she asked me to call her, was nervous, but quickly agreed. "Make sure you use 'Karagodina,' my maiden name, and don't tell any other reporters my number. I knew this would happen sooner or later. I'll tell you everything and that'll be it."

A few days later, we met in a basement laboratory at her institute. Yuliya was no longer beautiful, not even a match for the woman she faintly regarded as the victor, Raisa Maksimovna. She was middle-aged, matronly, and sweet.

"Was it love?" I said.

"It was love, yes it was, for both of us," she said. "I was attracted to him, he was magnetic. But I'd be upset if you thought that our relationship was like those that young people have now. It just wasn't that way. We were close friends, and we cared for each other and helped each other. It was—what would you say?—a specific kind of friendship, not just a Komsomol thing. Young love, you might call it. We met for the first time in the September he arrived at school, and after a few months we grew closer. He once told me that he had liked a blond girl named Talia in Privolnoye, but that was more a child's affection.

"You know, it's funny, but whenever I watch him now on television leading the Supreme Soviet, I think of Misha in school, playing the Grand Prince in Lermontov's *Masquerade* or heading the morning gym class, shouting into a big megaphone: 'Ready, class! Hup, two, three, four! Hup, two, three, four!' He was fearless for someone that age. I remember him correcting teachers in history class, and once he was so angry at one teacher he said, 'Do you want to keep your teaching certificate?' He was the sort who felt he was right and could prove it to anyone, be it in the principal's office or at a Komsomol meeting."

Yuliya said she had grown up in a village much like Privolnoye a few miles down the road. Her mother was a widowed schoolteacher, and so their circumstances were more modest than Gorbachev's. Yuliya put her briefcase on the table and took out a huge sheaf of old photographs. In pictures of the young drama costars, Gorbachev was dark and regal in his homemade costume and fake mustache. Karagodina was wide-eyed, delicate, a bit faraway. She looked like Lillian Gish in *Broken Blossoms*.

As Yuliya leafed through the pictures, slowly, like a child dealing cards, she said, "Once we were rehearsing Ostrovsky's play *The Snowgirl*. And there is a point when the Snowgirl—that was me—says, 'Dear Czar, ask me a hundred times if I love him, and I will answer a hundred times that I do.' I said those lines in open rehearsal, with the principal sitting right there in the audience. Suddenly, Gorbachev leaned over and whispered in my ear, 'Is it true?' My God! I was shaken. I could hardly go on with my monologue. Everyone was asking what had happened, and there was Gorbachev off to the side, smiling. Sometimes we spoke rather roughly to each other, but I was so dumbfounded, I couldn't answer.

"The truth is, he was a very good actor. There was a time when he even talked with me, and his friends Boris Gladskoi and Gennadi Donskoi, about trying for a theatrical institute. But I think he really always wanted to be a lawyer.

"We never really spoke about the future, except that we would go to Moscow and study there together. I'll tell you the truth. If we had been well dressed, well fed, and had everything like this generation, then maybe we would have talked about such things. But they were hard times, and we concentrated on our studies. . . .

"I was very proud and poor. Gorbachev was better off. He was better dressed. During the war, my family had been evacuated from Krasnodar to the Stavropol region. Gorbachev's family were living in their own house on their own soil. They always had enough to eat. He once invited me to come meet his parents in Privolnoye. I said that I had been brought up in such a way that I could not do such a thing. I was too proud. I think I must have felt that his parents would feel that I was offering myself to them. . . . I just imagined how they would look at me, a simple little girl.

"But Misha did visit my own home. At first we lived in a dugout hut, and then in a small house that we built ourselves. He had the bravery to tell my mother he liked me, but I kind of lied to my mother and said the two of us were just solving the problems of the Komsomol together. He spent the night on a little bed in the house, and I stayed with neighbors.

"He could be so cool and businesslike sometimes. Once at a Komsomol meeting, in front of everyone at the local cinema house, he was angry with me for not finishing on time a little newspaper we put out. And despite our friendship, he reprimanded me in front of everyone, saying that I'd failed, that I was late. He was shouting a bit, disciplining me. Then afterward it was as if nothing had happened. He said, 'Let's go to the movies.' I was at a loss. I couldn't understand why he did what he did, and I said so. He said, 'My dear, one thing has nothing to do with another.'

"That reminds me: Years later I was living way outside of the city with my mother, and the commute was very long and we had hardly any room. By then Gorbachev was in the Central Committee. And so I wrote him a letter, asking him to help me. I wanted to get permission to move into the city center and get an apartment. I reminded him who I was, in case he had forgotten. I got the letter back soon after, and on it he had written simply that it wasn't his area, it wasn't his job, and that I should apply to the city authorities, not him. Just like that, so businesslike. Not one warm word. Deep in my heart I had hoped he would help me, but I suppose he wanted to avoid even the appearance of favoritism.

"In school, it was all very innocent. We never said things like 'I love you' to each other. He would never say such things. And on the rare times he put his arm around my shoulder, as if to say, come, let's go to the movies or somewhere, I would kind of glance over at his hand. No, it wasn't like our young people today. I finished school first, and went off first to Moscow. But I had no money and could not find any place to live. Remember, this was still a hard time, and so I returned to my village to work as a teacher. I've always thought that Gorbachev somehow thought I was weak for having come home.

"When he went off to the law faculty of Moscow State University, he wrote letters to me telling me how much he liked Moscow and the abundance of things and the fascinating people. There was never a sense in his letters that he felt any lack of confidence because he was a village boy. There were many letters, and later, when I was married, my husband was so jealous he burned them all. I suppose he didn't know Misha would be general secretary. I'm so sorry those letters are all gone.

"I'll tell you how it was. I think in the end I felt I was not really good enough for him, or we didn't really fit. He was too energetic, too serious, so organized. And he was smarter than I was. He was the center of attention. We drifted apart. Things were getting lost. But he did send me a letter at the end with his picture, and on it he wrote 'Dum spiro spero,' Latin for 'While I am breathing, I am hoping.' I suppose I didn't want to acknowledge that he was getting farther than me in life, so I said to myself, 'Okay, Misha, live and write as you like, but as for me . . .' I accepted a job in the Soviet far east, but even before I got there, on the road so to say, I was married.

"The few people now who know that Misha and I were good friends sometimes ask me about Raisa Maksimovna. I like Raisa. She plays her role very well. She's intelligent, and there's obviously a lot of love there between the two of them. She helps him greatly, that's clear enough. I'm not envious of her. I cannot say I am glad, just that my destiny is my destiny. I see things as a realist. When I do think back to those days, I see it as a pleasant island of time. Sometimes when I watch him on television I think to myself, 'Poor Mikhail Sergeyevich. He is so tired, and he has the weight of the world on his shoulders. If he could only take out ten minutes and just be Misha for a while.' I think of how nice everything was back then. I see that moon in the country sky, and the little river and everything was so lovely."

———

Gorbachev came to Moscow in September 1950. At Moscow State University, where he would study law until 1955, he took a room with six others at the Stromynka student dormitory. The crumbling, overcrowded dorm had once been a barracks for the soldiers of Peter the Great. Gorbachev had one jacket and one pair of decent pants to put in his closet. "Gorbachev was a villager, and you might have expected him to seem worse off than the city boys, but we were all poor then, and our new surroundings were no better," said Rudolf Kolchanov, an editor at the labor newspaper *Trud,* who roomed with Gorbachev for three years.

Zdenek Mlynar, a Czech Communist and another of Gorbachev's college friends, arrived at the same time in Moscow as an exchange student from Prague and recalled a Moscow of "poverty and backwardness . . . a huge village of wooden cottages" where people had barely enough to eat, where "most families lived in one room and instead of flush toilets there was only an opening leading directly to a drainpipe." In his memoir of the Prague Spring, Mlynar wrote that in Moscow at the time "what you didn't hold on to tightly would be stolen from you in a crowd, drunks lay unconscious in the streets and could be dead for all the passersby knew or cared."

Dressed in his baggy, hayseed clothes, Gorbachev tried doggedly to catch up with students who had gone to superior schools in the city. He often returned from the library at one or two in the morning and then stayed up another couple of hours talking with his roommates. Mlynar, Gorbachev, Kolchanov, and six war veterans would lock the door, turn a portrait of Stalin to the wall—revealing on the back an amateur portrait of a czarist-era courtesan—and drink and talk the night away. "Yes, it could be grim and wild even," Kolchanov said. "But Gorbachev seemed to avoid drinking too much. He was fastidious that way. That dorm room may have been the greatest classroom for all of us. We talked about everything from girls to more serious things: the latest exhibition or the latest artistic awards or historical event. Of course, one subject that was never mentioned was Stalin himself. That was too risky, even with the door closed."

The law class was dominated by some older vets and younger men, like Gorbachev, who had won academic medals in high schools. Unlike the politics or history departments, the law departments provided their students, by the standards of the time, with a relatively wide reading list. Along with the standard diet of Marx, Lenin, and Stalin, students read many of the essential works of Western thought: Roman law, Locke's treatises on government, Rousseau's *Social Contract,* and even the U.S. Constitution. But those texts served mainly as relics of bourgeois liberalism, and the core readings, the holy writ, were Stalinist textbooks.

Gorbachev, who as general secretary would campaign for a "law-base state," was steeped in the theory of its opposite: Stalinism. "The theme of political crimes was touched upon only in very brief and general terms," according to Mlynar. "There was nothing complex about it, as long as you accepted the fundamental principle that political activity upsetting to the government was comparable to any other form of criminal activity." Dissidence among the students was a crime; dozens of students were arrested for ideological missteps and sent to labor camps.

Mlynar, who returned to Czechoslovakia and eventually helped lead Alexander Dubcek's ill-fated Prague Spring reforms, now lives in Vienna. Some biographers have found a pleasant irony in what they see as Mlynar's influence on the man who would become the most powerful reformer in the Soviet Union and Eastern Europe. But Kolchanov said that "the influence is overrated. Gorbachev was intellectually curious, he was tolerant, but there were no signs of radicalism. You can't make those leaps. Remember, Stalinism was something deep inside us. We were only lucky that we were young enough and flexible enough to change later on."

But there was in Gorbachev and some of his friends a tendency toward independence, toward questioning authority, that was surprising, considering the times. Once, in 1952, as a professor teaching "Marxism and Issues of Language" droned on—he was reading straight from the works of Stalin— Gorbachev rose from his chair and said, "Respected professor, we can read for ourselves. What is your interpretation of the reading, and why don't we discuss it?" Gorbachev was summoned to the dean's office. But he was not punished. Probably his position in the Komsomol helped him avoid a suspension.

But at the same time, Gorbachev was a leader of the law department's Komsomol group, and in this position, he took no risks. Two émigrés now living in the West who were in Gorbachev's class remembered him as a hard-liner in the Komsomol who made speeches scolding the short-comings and improprieties of fellow Party members. Writing in the émigré journal *Possev,* Friedrikh Neznansky recalled hearing "the steely voice of the Komsomol secretary of the law department, Gorbachev, demand-ing expulsion from the Komsomol for the slightest offense, from telling inappropriate political jokes to trying to avoid being sent to a collective farm."

Midway through his five-year course, Gorbachev met Raisa Titorenko, a philosophy student from Siberia. A few of Gorbachev's friends were taking a ballroom dancing class, and one day Gorbachev and Kolchanov dropped by with the expressed purpose of mocking their buddies. "We were ready to say, 'You call yourselves real men and look at all this,' " Kolchanov said. "But then one of our friends in the class, Volodya Kuzmin, introduced Mikhail Sergeyevich to his dance partner. It was Raisa Maksimovna. I think for Gorbachev it was love at first sight. Just like in the movies. She was just so striking. And, as I think he discovered later on, she was extremely smart." Raisa, for her part, liked Gorbachev, according to Mlynar, for his "lack of vulgarity."

The marriage may have been the crucial personal event of Gorbachev's youth, but the signal political event for nearly everyone of his generation came in March 1953: the death of Joseph Stalin. In the years to come, Khrushchev would set free hundreds of thousands of prisoners and begin to tell the truth about Stalin. Although Gorbachev would choose the path of the Party apparatchik, scaling his way up through the hierarchy, flattering Brezhnev and his superiors, he would be one of thousands who would be changed by the Twentieth Party Congress in 1956 when Khrushchev gave his "secret speech" denouncing Stalin. Through a long process of personal and historical change, Gorbachev would recognize the need to transform the country and its relationship to the world. "Really, we have no alternative," he would say, decades later.

But at the moment Stalin died, there was for Gorbachev and his friends only stunning confusion. "There are a lot of things you could say about Mikhail in the old days that you could say now," Rudolf Kolchanov said. "He was hardworking, a good listener, tolerant, decent, but he was also much like the rest of us. In fact, he was not the most impressive student in our class by any means. And he believed what he was taught about Stalin. It's not as if he were always a great reformer and world leader just waiting to happen. Most of us were out all night in the freezing cold trying to see Stalin's body at the Hall of Columns. When we all got back to the room, in the early hours of the morning, we were sitting on our beds. We tried to talk, but mostly we were just silent, thinking. Some were crying, though I remember that I wasn't, and neither was Mikhail Sergeyevich. We were so accustomed to life under Stalin. We might find it strange and terrible now, but that was how it was. And then someone spoke the question that everyone had on his mind: 'What are we going to do now?' "

CHAPTER 11

THE DOUBLE THINKERS

A very popular error: Having the courage of one's convictions; rather, it is a matter of having the courage for an "attack" on one's own convictions!

—FRIEDERICH NIETZSCHE, *notebooks*

On a winter's night in 1986, two electricians and their KGB escort installed a "special telephone" in the apartment of Andrei Sakharov. For six years, Sakharov and his wife, Yelena Bonner, had been living in the industrial city of Gorky under government edict, and the phone seemed at first just another Orwellian moment in the day of exiles. Maybe the Soviet press would call for an interview, Sakharov thought. Two magazines had already put in requests. Turning the moral equations in his mind, Sakharov arrived at a finely calibrated stand of principle: he would refuse all interview requests until there was no longer a "noose around my neck." The KGB agent merely turned to Sakharov and said, "You will get a call around ten tomorrow morning."

The next day, the phone rang. A woman's voice said, "Mikhail Sergeyevich will speak to you." Now Gorbachev was on the line, telling Sakharov that he and Bonner could return home to Moscow.

"You have an apartment there," Gorbachev said without a word of apology or regret. "Go back to your patriotic work!"

Sakharov said a brief word of thanks, then wasted no time in going back to his "patriotic work." He told Gorbachev that for the sake of "trust, for peace, and for you and your program," the Kremlin was obliged to release the political prisoners included on a long list he had mailed to the leadership from Gorky. The Soviet leader said he did not quite agree that all the prisoners Sakharov was speaking for had been tried illegally. Then the two men said their awkward good-byes.

One week later, Sakharov arrived by overnight train at Moscow's Yaroslavl Station, an event of such moral and political importance that it evoked another homecoming decades earlier—that of Lenin at the Finland Station. But no one could have predicted what was ahead for Sakharov in the three years left to him. Exile had worn him down. KGB threats, a painful hunger strike, forced feedings, random attacks, thefts of his diaries and manuscripts—all of it had taken a toll on his health. Now, as he answered questions into the swarm of tape recorders and television lights, his voice was mumbly, hesitant at times. He walked with a stoop and had to catch his breath every few steps on flights of stairs. Bonner said at the time that Sakharov would limit his activities. He would read up on developments in cosmology and work on specific human rights cases. That seemed like more than enough.

A few days after his return to Moscow, Sakharov was sitting at the kitchen table of his close friend the human rights activist Larisa Bogoraz. Another of the guests, the historian Mikhail Gefter, turned to Sakharov and said, "How are you feeling, Andrei Dmitriyevich?"

Sakharov said sadly, "It is difficult to live now. People write me, they visit, and they are all hoping that I will be able to help somehow. But I am powerless."

For months Sakharov mulled over his role, tried to find his political voice. Some younger dissidents were impatient with Sakharov's hesitation and what they saw as his naive, uncritical support of Gorbachev.

Those young dissidents probably should have known better, but the rest of the country knew Sakharov hardly at all. They could not have known what sort of man he was. Until Sakharov returned from exile, most people knew nothing more about him than the slanders they had read for years in the press. Even intellectuals with some connection to the human rights movement knew little about him. "We knew he was out there, but for years Sakharov was almost like a myth," said Lev Timofeyev, one of the political prisoners freed shortly after Sakharov's return from Gorky. But when Sakharov did return home, his gift for judgment became an open secret and a public trust. Many ordinary people who had been instructed to despise Sakharov came to love and trust him. Through him they saw the hollowness of the old propaganda and the system itself. There was a sense of the uncanny about Sakharov. In 1988, at a discussion sponsored by and published in *Ogonyok* magazine, a group of Soviet and American intellectuals went around the table trading opinions on the myriad issues of perestroika. For nearly an hour, Sakharov seemed half asleep, but when it came his turn, he found all the inherent faults in the latest wave of political reforms. He zeroed in especially on the "unhealthy" way Gorbachev continued to control both the government and the Communist Party. No one had ever said that before, and yet, as we all left the room, Sakharov's brief exposition seemed like sense itself.

For anyone living in Moscow in those years, Saturday mornings were a time to listen to this voice. Sakharov was everywhere. He inevitably became either the chairman or the spiritual leader of all the key groups to the left of Gorbachev: first Moscow Tribune, then Memorial, and, later the Interregional Group of radical deputies in the parliament. Nearly every Saturday morning, Sakharov would sit in some dim auditorium, usually the House of Scholars on Kropotkinskaya Street, or the Filmmakers' Union near the Peking Hotel, and for half an eternity he would doze, his great dome of a head nodding off as the speeches went on. When it was his turn at last, Sakharov would take the lectern, and in a few minutes of very formal, incisive Russian, he would make the point that most needed making, invariably pushing public thinking ever closer to the creation of a civil society.

With the authority of his life and the clarity of his thinking, Sakharov became a one-man loyal opposition, a moral genius who was now, at last, able to speak directly to the people. "Sakharov was the only one among us who made no compromises," said Tatyana Zaslavskaya, a leading sociologist whose views helped shape the early reforms. "For us, he was a figure of the inner spirit. Just the bare facts of his life, the way he suffered for all of us, gave him authority that no one else had. Without him, we could not begin to rebuild our society or our selves. Gorbachev may not have understood it quite that way when he let Sakharov come home, but he would understand it eventually."

What made Sakharov unique was not his suffering alone. Others had suffered much more. And what made him unique was not his ideas. He shared his ideas with men and women who were dissidents even before he was—Larisa Bogoraz, Pyotr Yakir, Pavel Litvinov, Solzhenitsyn, and, for that matter, the first opponents of Russian totalitarianism, Aleksandr Herzen, Nikolai Berdyaev, Vladimir Solovyov. "My father's ideas were not original," Sakharov's son Efrem told me. "His ideas of morality and liberty had all been said before. It was his fate to bring received wisdom to a place where it did not yet exist." The story of the perestroika years—the years between the rise of Gorbachev and the collapse of the Soviet state—was, to a great extent, the story of change inside the hearts and minds of individuals. Sakharov's life and thought prefigured that change in such a dramatic way that I would not hesitate to call him a saint. He was the dominant moral example of his time and place.

Sakharov was a scientist whose metaphors and sense of truth were rooted in an understanding of cosmology, the "magic spectacle" of a thermonuclear explosion, the calculus of the Big Bang. His unerring sense of rightness, like that of scientist-moralists from Galileo to Oppenheimer, was steeped in his understanding of the scientific problems of light and time, his firsthand appreciation of both the laws of the universe and man's tragic tendency to turn progress into catastrophe. He held in mind, it seemed, a picture, even a music, of eternity. Sakharov once turned to his wife and said, "Do you know what I love most of all in life?" Later, Bonner would confide to a friend, "I expected he would say something about a poem or a sonata or even about me." Instead, Sakharov said, "The thing I love most in life is radio background emanation"—the barely discernible reflection of unknown cosmic processes that ended billions of years ago.

Sakharov was a man inclined toward the purities of theoretical physics but who became the conscience of the Soviet Union, a political actor in spite of himself. His physics and his politics grew out of the same mind, the same sense of wholeness and responsibility. "Other civilizations, perhaps more successful ones, may exist an infinite number of times on the preceding and following pages of the Book of the Universe," Sakharov wrote in his Nobel Prize lecture. "Yet we should not minimize our sacred endeavors in the world, where, like faint glimmers in the dark, we have emerged for a moment from the nothingness of unconsciousness into material existence. We must make good the demands of reason and create a life worthy of ourselves and of the goals we only dimly perceive."

———

For almost every young man and woman who would one day join the circle of Communist Party liberals around Gorbachev, the death of Stalin was the pivotal event of moral and intellectual life. The same was true for Sakharov. Like Gorbachev, Sakharov knew well the horrors of the age. When he was a boy, his aunt Zhenya received news of her husband's death in the camps when one of her letters was returned "Addressee relocated to the cemetery"; later one of Sakharov's friends died in the gulag, the authorities announced, owing to a "chilling of the epidermal integument."

And yet, Sakharov's response to the death of Stalin was utterly typical. He heard the news while he was working on the Soviet bomb project and wrote home to his first wife, Klavdia: "I am under the influence of a great man's death. I am thinking of his humanity." Even in his memoirs, written three decades later, Sakharov could not pretend to understand his own reaction:

"I can't fully explain it—after all, I knew quite enough about the horrible crimes that had been committed—the arrests of innocent people, the torture, the deliberate starvations, and all the violence—to pass judgment on those responsible. But I hadn't put the whole picture together, and in any case, there was still a lot I didn't know. Somewhere in the back of my mind the idea existed, instilled by propaganda, that suffering is inevitable during great historic upheavals: 'When you chop wood, the chips fly.' . . . But above all, I felt myself committed to the goal which I assumed was Stalin's as well: after a devastating war, to make the country strong enough to ensure peace. Precisely because I had invested so much of myself in that cause and accomplished so much, I needed, as anyone might in my circumstances, to create an illusory world, to justify myself."

Sakharov's sense of patriotic urgency after the American attack on Hiroshima and also the sheer seduction of the scientific world involved left him "no choice," he once said, but to move to a desolate weapons research center in Kazakhstan known only as the Installation, the Soviet Los Alamos. Even though he was immersed in what he called the "superb physics" of nuclear weaponry—"the sustenance of life on Earth but also the potential instrument of its destruction were taking shape at my very desk"—Sakharov still saw the gulag through the fence. The Installation, where Sakharov lived for eighteen years, was near a slave labor camp, and every morning he watched long lines of prisoners trudge to and fro, guard dogs at their heels.

Nevertheless, there was a determined innocence about Sakharov in those first years at the Installation. The prisoners and the guard dogs were a background that could be overlooked. But five months after Stalin's death, Sakharov began a personal and political conversion ignited by nothing less than the explosion of the first Soviet thermonuclear bomb. On August 12, 1953, twenty miles from ground zero, he watched the explosion, his eyes protected by dark goggles. The test was a success, and in his memoirs Sakharov describes the vision only in its incandescence, without a trace of regret: "We saw a flash, and then a swiftly expanding white ball lit up the whole horizon. I tore off my goggles and though I was partially blinded by the glare, I could see a stupendous cloud trailing streamers of purple dust." The government awarded Sakharov and his partner, Igor Tamm, 500,000 rubles each, dachas in the countryside outside Moscow, and the title of Hero of Socialist Labor. Marshal Kliment Voroshilov spoke for the state at the awards ceremony in the Kremlin: "I have been told that Sakharov's work was especially outstanding," he said. "Let me kiss you."

In the months to come, Sakharov grew more and more concerned about the effects of nuclear fallout. Secretly, he was beginning to make calculations, trying to figure out how many innocent people would likely be hurt by every nuclear test. Roald Sagdeyev, the former head of the Soviet space program, visited Sakharov at the Installation after the test and noticed how "this young, distant god of physics" drew little offhand doodles of airplanes dropping bombs as he talked. "Those were the first real doubts," Sagdeyev told me. The accidental deaths of a young girl and a soldier at the test site also startled Sakharov. Then, after another successful test in 1955, Sakharov's sense of complicity in these few accidents began to torture him.

At a banquet after the test, Sakharov gave the first toast, and said, "May all our devices explode as successfully as today's, but always over test sites and never over cities."

The table fell silent, Sakharov recalled, "as if I had said something indecent." Marshal Mitrofan Nedelin, the ranking military man at the banquet, rose to give a countertoast, the rebuke.

"Let me tell a parable," he said. "An old man wearing only a shirt was praying before an icon. 'Guide me, harden me. Guide me, harden me.' His wife, who was lying [in bed], said, 'Just pray to be hard, old man, I can guide it in myself.' Let's drink to getting hard."

Sakharov turned pale. He understood well that Nedelin's joke was a parable. "He wanted to squelch my pacifist sentiment, and to put me and anyone who might share these ideas in my place," Sakharov wrote. "The ideas and emotions kindled at that moment have not diminished to this day, and they completely altered my thinking."

Finally, Sakharov understood. His moral protests were nothing to the men of the Communist Party. The Party was way beyond the control even of a Hero of Socialist Labor. So gradually, Sakharov became a dissident, and the ideas of his dissidence, which crystallized in his 1968 manifesto *Reflections on Progress, Peaceful Coexistence, and Intellectual Freedom*, anticipated the ideas of perestroika.

———

But while Sakharov was the moral leader of the era, he was not a man of raw political power. There may have been no Gorbachev without Sakharov, no perestroika without the efforts of the dissidents to keep the idea of truth alive in a dead time, but there were other figures, less easy to love, more ambiguous, who had the political power to make something out of ideas.

Gorbachev and the most influential people around him were contradictory men, politicians, academics, and journalists whose lives were filled with doubt, small victories, and sorry compromises. They had done things of which they were ashamed or should have been. For the sake of ambition, they told themselves lies and half-truths. They served brutal masters and tried not to care too much. There was Vitaly Korotich, the crusading editor of *Ogonyok,* who had once been only too glad to write a scurrilous book about America called *The Face of Hatred.* There was the poet Yevgeny Yevtushenko, preternaturally vain, slippery, periodically brave. And there were the Gorbachev advisers who had worked in the Central Committee staff under Yuri Andropov and still remembered it as an oasis of free thinking: the Americanist Georgi Arbatov, the policy advisers Anatoly Chernayev, Georgi Shakhnazarov, and Oleg Bogomolov, the journalists Aleksander Bovin and Fyodor Burlatsky.

These were the *shestidesyatniki*—those who came of age during the thaw under Khrushchev, and grew disillusioned when Soviet tanks crushed the Prague Spring in 1968. They were the generation that woke to the horror of the Stalin era after Khrushchev's "secret speech" of 1956 denouncing the "personality cult." They harbored the dream of a humane socialism in Russia. They did not dare take the risks of full-blown dissidence, as Sakharov had, but they found a measure of independence and sanity in their work. There were scholars, like Abel Aganbegyan and Tatyana Zaslavskaya, who fled the oppressive scrutiny of Moscow for the relative academic freedom of Novosibirsk. There were journalists like Yegor Yakovlev and Yuri Karyakin who fled *Pravda* for Prague and wrote for the slightly liberal magazine *Problems of Peace and Socialism.* The *shestidesyatniki,* especially those from Moscow and Leningrad, were like an enormous floating club in which everyone had a nodding acquaintance with everyone else. They scrutinized each other's compromises and drew fine distinctions that would appear to be nonsense to anyone outside. The gossip in this crowd was as thick as it is in official Washington or the studios of Hollywood. Whether they worked in academia, for the press, or inside the Central Committee, it was all the same: every day they were faced with questions of what to say, whom to protect, when to withdraw. They thought one thing and said another, and sometimes, after speaking lies long enough, they believed them and were beyond redeeming.

"Gorbachev, me, all of us, we were double-thinkers, we had to balance truth and propaganda in our minds all the time," said Shakhnazarov, an elfin intellectual who was at Gorbachev's side from start to finish. "It is not something I'm particularly proud of, but that is the way we lived. It was the choice between dissidence and surrender."

Westerners were often fast to judge these people. They came from countries where liberty was almost a given, and still they mocked men and women in the Soviet Union who looked foolish in the act of trying to save both their families and their souls. The system made beasts of them, and it was a sorry sight. When the atmosphere of fear began to fade under Gorbachev, there were those who grabbed the public stage shamelessly, as if all that they had done in the past was of no matter. Some had trimmed their ideological sails for so many years that it was hard to take them seriously. They were indecent. But there were also quite a few who not only relished their new power, they understood their contradictions. They were complicated men and women who had done the best they could and knew their best was far from exemplary. Len Vyacheslavovich Karpinsky, a columnist and later editor in chief of *Moscow News,* was among the most likable because his case was one of the most complicated and tragic.

Len Karpinsky's parents were Old Bolsheviks. He was named in honor of his father's mentor and friend Lenin. "The name Len was pretty common then and so was Ninel, Lenin backward, or Vladilen for Vladimir Ilyich Lenin," Karpinsky said. "I'm just glad I didn't get a name like Elektrifikatsiya or some others my friends got stuck with."

Karpinsky's father, Vyacheslav Karpinsky, belonged to a generation of revolutionary romantics, the *fin de siècle* Communists. He joined the Communist Party in 1898, and in 1903, after his activities as a political organizer got him into trouble with the police in the Ukrainian city of Kharkov, he went into exile. In Switzerland he was Lenin's aide and copy editor. In Moscow, after the Revolution, he helped Lenin assemble his personal archives from exile and held various posts at *Pravda* and the Central Committee's Department of Propaganda. He received three Orders of Lenin and in 1962 became the first journalist ever named a Hero of Socialist Labor.

For the Karpinsky family, a life in revolution provided an elevated sort of existence. From 1932 to 1952, they lived in the House on the Embankment with the Kremlin elite: generals, Central Committee members, agents of the secret police. There were billiard halls, swimming pools, and, for the children, Special School No. 19. When Len Karpinsky was a boy, he was even friendly with a couple of Stalin's nephews. At a birthday party once, the playing stopped as the runty, pockmarked man with the withered left arm—the Mountain Eagle, the Friend of All Children—stood in the doorway. "Children!" one of the adults announced. "Iosif Vissarionovich is here!" Stalin waved and smiled. The children all waited in silence until he left, and then resumed their games.

That was in 1935. In the coming years, Len watched dumbstruck as one acquaintance after another in the building lost parents, aunts, uncles, grandparents, and friends to the great furnace of Stalin's purges. Nearly every night, secret police vans would arrive and there would be arrests—an admiral, a lecturer on Marxism-Leninism, the sisters of a spy in a foreign embassy. "There was a knock and then they disappeared," Len said. It had been the world of Yuri Trifonov's novella *The House on the Embankment*—a world where "a life went on that was utterly different" from the life of ordinary people. Now it was a world where the most devoted revolutionaries, the most obsequious ministers, suddenly found themselves declared "plotters" and "infiltrators" and "enemies of the people." Karpinsky's family was, by the standards of the building, not hard hit. One of his aunts and her two brothers were sent off to the camps. To this day, Karpinsky does not quite understand why his father, the very sort of Lenin loyalist who so threatened Stalin, was never arrested and executed. The only reason he can think of now, he said, is that by 1937 or 1938, his father was semiretired and out of politics.

————

From the moment that the leadership installed Karpinsky's old friend Yegor Yakovlev as editor in chief, *Moscow News* became the paper of the thaw generation, subtly breaking taboos formed over seventy years. From time to time I visited Karpinsky at the *Moscow News* office, on Pushkin Square, and he always seemed to me an honest man, if a limited writer—a representative figure whose life had been, as he put it to me, "the inner conflict between the ambition to be a boss in the Communist Party and the almost involuntary development of a conscience." His appearance, waxen and drawn, spoke of that struggle. He looked exhausted at every minute of the day. His face was long, lined, and worn. The fingers of his right hand were yellowed up to the first knuckle from tobacco. More often than not when I called and asked how he was, he would say dryly, "My health is awful. I'm spending the week in a sanatorium. I may die."

Karpinsky was so unassuming, so ironic about his own failures and hesitations, that it was hard to believe he was once, in the culture of Soviet politics, as ambitious as any flaxen-haired kid who takes a job as a Senate intern and starts talking about "the day I run for office . . ." He believed deeply in Communism and in himself, in his entitlement to success. After entering Moscow State University in 1947, he began working as a "propaganda man" at factories and construction sites during the days before the Party's single-candidate elections. "My assignment was to make the workers get up at six in the morning and go to the polls," he told me. "There was a competition among the propaganda men over whose group would be the first to finish voting. The limit was midday, by which time the whole Soviet people was supposed to have voted. That was a decision of the Party. We eighteen-year-olds were supposed to conduct propaganda among the workers, and the only tool was the promise to improve their housing conditions. They lived in horrible slums, railway cars with no toilets, no heat. I loved the work, thought it was a great service and, yes, a stepping-stone. At the university, Yuri Levada, who is now a well-known sociologist, wrote an article about me called 'The Careerist.' And it was true. I did it all with the idea of getting to the top. That was what it was all about: to be one of the bosses.

"But having said that, I have to say a few words in self-defense. Society during the Stalin era left open no real opportunities for self-realization or self-expression except within this perverted system of the Communist Party. The system destroyed all the other channels: the artist's canvas, the farmer's land. All that was left was the gigantic hierarchic system of the Party, wide at the base and growing narrower as one climbed to the top. You had to have a Party membership just for admission. That was the only opportunity. When you are engaged in that work, you forget about the social and political implications, and just do it. Gradually, this sort of life bifurcates your mentality, your intellect. You can begin to understand that life is life and it's better to do something good for thy neighbor than to climb upward stepping on their bones. But it all depends on moral principles. I suppose my first doubts came when I went to Moscow State University in 1948. A Jewish friend of mine named Karl Kantor was attacked at the university's Party committee at the start of Stalin's anti-Jewish campaign. That was just the start of a long transformation.

"After graduation, I was sent to the city of Gorky for Komsomol work. It was in 1952 and Stalin had one more year to live. I got to know the working class and the peasants there. I saw the utter degradation, the ruin. I saw Soviet society as it had really emerged. This 'intellectual conscience' that I talk about began to emerge. Some people still think, erroneously, that the life of the apparatchik breeds only conformists and subjects loyal to the regime. Actually, the regime splits people into two opposing factions: those who believe they can make it only through conformism and time-serving, and those who, thanks to a different structure of mind, dare to question the surrounding reality.

"So when Stalin died, I realized perfectly well what he had been all about. Still, I went to the funeral in Moscow out of curiosity. I felt like one of those prisoners in the camps who threw his hat in the air and cried, 'The man-eater has finally kicked the bucket!' My father's reaction to Stalin's death was interesting. By then he was retired, working for the Central Committee only as a consultant. He sat there in his office typing on an old Underwood which he had brought from the offices he had in Switzerland with Lenin. He called me into his study and said, 'Son, Comrade Stalin has passed away. And having been an epigone of Lenin, he created all the necessary conditions for our cause to triumph.' It was so strange. My father had never talked so formally before to me in his life. I think he talked that way because his generation had always carried a burden to promote at all times the Party line and he felt it was his duty to pass that down to his children. But in a way, this was a man, eighty years old, who had conceived of his idea of the Party before the Revolution and while living in exile. He had to convince not me, but himself. He was talking to himself."

———

When Karpinsky returned from Gorky to Moscow for good, in 1959, the thaw was in full swing. *Novy Mir,* Aleksandr Tvardovsky's monthly journal of literature and opinion, was publishing texts critical of the old regime. Khrushchev himself read a manuscript copy of Solzhenitsyn's *One Day in the Life of Ivan Denisovich* and sanctioned its publication in *Novy Mir.* Karpinsky's friends Yevgeny Yevtushenko and Andrei Voznesensky were winning a following with their lyrics and public performances. In various pockets of the Central Committee apparatus, young apparatchiks wrote proposals and outlines of economic and political reform—though all within certain boundaries of ideology and language. For his part, Karpinsky worked as head of the Komsomol's Department of Propaganda and Agitation and as the editor of *Molodoi Kommunist* ("Young Communist"). Then in 1962 he joined the empyrean of the adult Communist world. He was promoted to *Pravda*'s editorial board heading the department of Marxism-Leninism. He had made it.

"Once I was back in Moscow from Gorky, my critical approach weakened somewhat," Karpinsky said. "I was part of the elite again, and not merely as my father's son but as a real member. I was part of the top nomenklatura, and the nomenklatura is another planet. It's Mars. It's not simply a matter of good cars or apartments. It's the continuous satisfaction of your own whims, the way an army of boot-lickers allows you to work painlessly for hours. All the little apparatchiks are ready to do everything for you. Your every wish is fulfilled. You can go to the theater on a whim, you can fly to Japan from your hunting lodge. It's a life in which everything flows easily. No, you don't own a yacht or spend your vacations on the Côte d'Azur, but you are at the Black Sea, and that really is something. The issue is your relative well-being. You are like a king: just point your finger and it is done."

Karpinsky's potential as a man of the Communist Party elite was unlimited. It is conceivable that he could have won election to the Politburo one day. He was a Soviet Ivy Leaguer: bright, ambitious, a legacy. One afternoon, at a Kremlin ceremony, two of Khrushchev's most powerful partners in the leadership, Mikhail Suslov and Boris Ponomarev, complimented Karpinsky as their golden boy, their comer. One of them said Karpinsky was like a "son of the regiment" to them and they saw for him a great future in the ideological department of the Communist Party. "We are pinning our hopes on you," Suslov said.

Working in that rarefied atmosphere, Karpinsky got to know nearly every figure who would make a difference (one way or another) during perestroika. He was friendly with Yegor Yakovlev, the Lenin biographer who became the editor of *Moscow News;* Yuri Karyakin, a Dostoevsky scholar who was among the leading radical deputies in the Congress of Peoples Deputies; Aleksandr Bovin, the gargantuan journalist at *Izvestia* who promoted the "new thinking" in foreign policy; the reform-minded economists, Gavriil Popov and Nikolai Shmelyov and the sociologist Yevgeny Ambartsumov; Otto Latsis, the son of an Old Bolshevik and an editor at *Kommunist;* Gennadi Yanayev and Boris Pugo, who helped lead the August coup; and even the leading triumvirate of reform, Eduard Shevardnadze, Aleksandr Yakovlev, and Gorbachev himself.

"I first met Gorbachev in the sixties when I was working at *Pravda* and he was in Stavropol working in the Komsomol organization there," Karpinsky said. "He was not very well known at the time, but I must tell you that Gorbachev was saying the same things then that he did at the beginning of perestroika. He was in Moscow on some business trip or another—I forget what it was all about—but we met for a couple of hours, and I was impressed. He talked about the outrage of paying combine operators by the mileage and not their output. In a nutshell, he spoke about the absurd system of incentives, or lack of them, in the economy. He was excitable, but somehow very rational. And for the first two or three years of perestroika, Gorbachev was the same sort of innovator he was when he was young. The innovative projects were always limited, within certain boundaries, and that, of course, was telling later on. Well, I understand him. Like all of us, Gorbachev had to have a dual nature. It was in his mind and soul. He knew well that the idea of reward for work well done was considered out of the ordinary but not quite heretical. You could experiment with something limited like that. But we were not allowed to make any political or philosophical conclusions that the system itself was a failure. In your mind you avoided such conclusions.

You were simply incapable of thinking that way. To think that way was not only career suicide, it was a form of despair. And so, like the rest of us, Gorbachev hedged—outwardly, and within himself."

———

Karpinsky and his friends were, at first, not greatly upset with Brezhnev and Suslov's overthrow of Khrushchev in 1964. When Karpinsky heard the news, he and Yegor Yakovlev celebrated over a bottle of cognac. Khrushchev had long since tightened restrictions on the press and the arts, and he had become prone to unpredictable decisions—a manic "voluntarism," as the Party language had it. It was only years later, when Khrushchev was a sad old man living in the exile of his dacha, that Karpinsky called him to wish him well on his birthday. Karpinsky said he was calling on behalf of the "children of the Twentieth Party Congress" and that Khrushchev should know that one day history would make clear to everyone the importance of that session, in 1956, at which he leveled his first attacks against Stalin's "cult of personality."

"I have always believed this and I am very pleased that you and your relatively young generation understand the essence of the Twentieth Congress and the policies I initiated," Khrushchev replied. "I am so happy to hear from you in my twilight years."

It did not take Karpinsky or anyone else long to realize that Brezhnev had no intention of instituting reforms. Just the opposite—a neo-Stalinist movement was in the works. One night at dinner with Yevtushenko and Otto Latsis, Karpinsky began to pronounce aloud what was happening to his generation, to its way of thinking. "Our idea was this: when one has an education in philosophy and a certain intellectual background, one begins to understand the inner properties of reality, something I termed 'intellectual conscience.' It's not a natural, inborn conscience, yet a conscience that stems from a kind of thinking that links you with a moral attitude to reality. If you understand that everything in this society is soaked in blood, that society itself is heading toward collapse, that it is all an antihuman system—if you understand this instinctively and intellectually—then your conscience cannot remain neutral. Look, I never really took any risks, and didn't want to. I was sort of compelled to take the steps I did by my conscience. And once compelled to take those steps, I could never foresee the bad consequences. Every time I thought I'd get away with it. And every time I didn't."

Karpinsky made his first real foray into the netherworld of what he called "half-dissent" in 1967, and it was a personal disaster. He and a friend at *Pravda,* Fyodor Burlatsky, wrote an article in *Komsomolskaya Pravda* calling, in a euphemistic way, for an easing of censorship in the theater. Kar-

pinsky now says the piece was "half rotten," especially its solipsistic arguments that the best way to eliminate anti-Soviet sentiments from the theater
would be to let the people, and not the official censors, decide. That way, the
authors said, the playwrights would have no right to complain about the
government, and so would be deprived of a source of anger and subject
matter. But the article, "On the Road to the Premiere," contained one idea,
plainly stated, that caused an uproar when it appeared: the personality cult,
Karpinsky and Burlatsky said, had been criticized only lightly, and the
censors were preventing anything deeper.

Brezhnev, who had already begun the ideological rehabilitation of Stalin,
was furious when his aides brought the article to his attention. He took it as
a personal attack. By chance, the article appeared on the same day that a
member of the Central Committee criticized the country's enormous arms
industry, which had been Brezhnev's province before he became general
secretary. Karpinsky, Burlatsky, and the editor of *Komsomolskaya Pravda*
were all fired. Karpinsky was quickly appointed to a job at *Izvestia,* but after
he made a few critical remarks at a meeting of that paper's Communist Party
committee, he was eased out of that post, too.

Despite his inherited romantic view of Bolshevism and his own pleasure in
the perquisites of power, Karpinsky could no longer hide his disaffection.
The invasion of Czechoslovakia, in August 1968, was, for Karpinsky and
many of his friends, a breaking point. He did not join the seven young
protesters who went to Red Square. Nor did he form any close links with
Sakharov or other leading intellectuals who had decided, once and for all, to
give up their lives in the hierarchy for the dangers of political dissidence. But
he did act. Under the pen name L. Okunev, Karpinsky wrote a long article
titled "Words Are Also Deeds," for circulation only among a select group of
friends and would-be reformers within the world of the Party and its official
academies. (The pseudonym was an inside joke—"Karpinsky" derives from
"carp," and "Okunev" from "perch.") In the article, Karpinsky argued that
free thought—and not "rows of armed soldiers, insurgent crowds, columns
of revolutionary sailors, or a volley from the cruiser *Aurora*"—would one
day challenge the Soviet system. Furthermore, the state structures and ideological machinery would not be able to resist, for the system "lacks any
serious social basis. It cannot convince anyone of its viability and only hangs
on by the instinct of self-preservation. The face of neo-Stalinism we are
passing through is just the outward expression of the 'uneasy forebodings'
the petty tyrants feel. They long for the old regime, the 'Stalin fortress,' but
they find only decrepit foundations too weak to support such a structure."

The article, like nearly all of Karpinsky's writings, is clogged with indirection and filler, great clots of undigested verbiage typical of a Party ap-

paratchik. But this piece was remarkable not only for its points of clarity and daring but also for its prescience. Here was an apparatchik ("We are pinning our hopes on you," Suslov had said) who now believed no more in the viability of the Bolshevik state than did Sakharov himself.

"Our tanks in Prague were, if you will, an anachronism, an 'inadequate' weapon,' Karpinsky wrote. "They 'fired' at—ideas. With no hope of hitting the target. They 'dealt with' the Czechoslovak situation the same way that at one time certain reptiles 'dealt with' the coming age of mammals. The reptiles bit at the air, gnashing their teeth in the same ether that was literally seething with the plankton of renewal. At the same time, fettered by their natural instincts, they searched for 'hidden stocks of weapons' and diligently occupied the postal and telegraph offices. With a fist to the jaw of thinking society, they thought they had knocked out and 'captured' its thinking processes."

Karpinsky also provided an insider's view, identifying within the monolith of the Party structure "a layer of party intellectuals." He went on to say, "To be sure, this layer is thin and disconnected; it is constantly eroded by cooption and promotion and is thickly interlarded with careerists, flatterers, loudmouths, cowards, and other products of the bureaucratic selection process. But this layer could move toward an alliance with the entire social body of the intelligentsia if favorable conditions arose. This layer is already an arm of the intelligentsia, its 'parliamentary fraction' within the administrative structure. This fraction will inevitably grow, constituting a hidden opposition, without specific shape and now aware of itself, but an actually existing and widely ramified opposition at all levels within the administrative chain."

It was this "layer" that made itself known when Gorbachev came to power. The dissidents were the bravest and most clear-minded of all, but in the early Gorbachev years they did not constitute, in numbers or in force, an adequate army. As if from nowhere, intellectuals within the Party, the institutes, the press, and the literary, artistic, and scientific worlds slowly took a Soviet leader at his word when he said that this would be a different age. For once, the purposes of a Kremlin leader and the liberal intelligentsia intersected.

The tragedy was that by the time Gorbachev came to power there were so many broken lives: great minds lost to emigration, drink, suicide, despair, or sheer cynicism. It was a miracle, after seven decades of murder and repression, that there was any intelligentsia left at all. "So many people had been destroyed," Karpinsky said. "One can behave in that split way of thinking for a while, but then you begin to degenerate and start to speak only what is permitted and the rest of the conscience and soul decays. Many people did not survive to perestroika. We had to create an internal moral system, and not everyone could sustain it indefinitely. Solzhenitsyn spoke about this in his essay 'Live Not by Lies.' I understood his viewpoint, and we tried not to live by lies, but we couldn't always manage it. If you ignore the regulations of the state completely, and go into complete dissidence, then you can't have a family, you don't know where you will get rent money, and your children would have to go into the streets to scrape up money. To fulfill this principle of living not under a lie in every aspect is just impossible, because you live in a certain time.

"Compared to the people who were not afraid of prison, my friends were not heroes. We abstained from direct acts. This position was itself a compromise. But it was like the sort of compromises you make when you are in the same cage with a lion. It is understandable, though nothing to be proud of. When I myself was in the position of having to say what I felt, I said it. I just didn't deliberately try to put my head in a noose. I used Aesopian language. I had to use hints about progress, but nothing more. What we did publish only hinted at our real thoughts."

But Karpinsky's "Words Are Also Deeds" went far beyond Aesopian language. In 1970, Karpinsky gave a copy of his text to Roy Medvedev, the Marxist historian. One night, Medvedev called Karpinsky and told him that the KGB had ransacked his apartment and taken every manuscript in sight, including "Words Are Also Deeds." For a few years, Karpinsky was oblivious to the trouble he was in. He bounced around from job to job, from a sociology institute to editing Marxist-Leninist works at Progress Publishers. But in 1975, when he was caught working on the manuscript of his friend Otto Latsis's book *On the Eve of a Great Breakthrough,* an analysis of collectivization and Stalinism, the KGB called him in. Naturally, the interrogator was an old friend: a Komsomol buddy named Filipp Bobkov, who had become one of the most infamous figures in the Soviet secret police. Karpinsky tried to soften up Bobkov. "When you came to me there was tea and cookies," he told him. "You don't even offer me tea. It's not very polite." Bobkov was not amused. He had passed along the damning documents to the Communist Party Control Committee, and Len Karpinsky, son of Lenin's friend and the Party's great hope, was expelled. Suslov, for one, viewed Karpinsky's transgressions as a personal betrayal.

Now Karpinsky did whatever he could to make a living—among other things, commissioning paintings and monuments for a state agency, for which he received a minuscule salary. He kept up his friendships, talked politics, lived awhile at the dacha he had inherited from his father. The moment of reckoning he had written about in "Words Are Also Deeds," the advent of dissent as a cultural and political fact of life, seemed years and years off.

———

Even after Gorbachev took power, Karpinsky never dreamed change could come so quickly. And at first it did not. Although the liberals in the Politburo secured the editorship of *Moscow News* for Karpinsky's friend Yegor Yakovlev and told him to transform this tourist giveaway sheet, published in Russian and several foreign languages, into a "tribune of reform," glasnost was initially a process of hints, insinuations. To read now through a stack of *Moscow News* issues from 1987 and 1988 is to get lost in a blur of nonlanguage. The barriers were immense at first, the victories almost unbearably difficult. When the editors of *Moscow News* wanted to print a simple obituary of the émigré poet Viktor Nekrasov, the Politburo itself had to give permission, and did so only after long debate.

"But, still, the change was tremendous," Karpinsky said. "The difference between 'the thaw' and 'glasnost' was a difference in temperature. If the temperature under Khrushchev was two degrees above zero centigrade, then glasnost pushed it to twenty above. Huge chunks of ice just melted away, and now we were talking not only about Stalin's personality cult, but of Leninism, Marxism, the essence of the system. There was nothing like that under Khrushchev. It was just a narrow opening, through which only Stalin's cult could be seen. There were no real changes. And as we saw, it could all be reversed. The bureaucracy, the Party, the KGB, all the repressive apparatus in charge of the intelligentsia and the press, remained in place."

For Karpinsky, *Moscow News* provided the opening to a public hearing and a rehabilitation. In March 1987, he published a long article, "It's Absurd to Hesitate Before an Open Door." Like his other liberal pieces of the past, it was a mixed performance. Karpinsky made sure to blast the West for what he thought was its phony concern for the Soviet dissidents, but he also made a crucial point that was getting close consideration within the government but was rarely voiced in public: the critique of Stalin begun in 1956 would have to go deeper. Reform without a thorough consideration of the country's "core" problems, the rottenness of its history and foundations, would be meaningless.

Karpinsky wanted to rejoin the Party not only as personal vindication but also to play a role in what was still the central institution of political power. At a meeting with the chairman of the Party's Control Commission, however, the hard-liner Mikhail Solomontsev mocked Karpinsky. From a thick stack of papers that had obviously been compiled by the Party and the KGB, Solomentsev pulled out a copy of "Words Are Also Deeds" and, holding it up, he shouted, "You still have not disarmed ideologically! Nothing has changed in our party!"

But things had changed. The sharp ideological divisions within the Party had now become an open secret, an open struggle, and the trick was to get the support of powerful liberals within the structure. Three old friends—Yuri Afanasyev, Nikolai Shmelyov, and Yuri Karyakin—brought to the Nineteenth Special Party Conference, in June 1988, a petition demanding Karpinsky's rehabilitation. With the help of his old acquaintances Aleksandr Yakovlev and Boris Pugo, the tactic worked. By the next year, Len Karpinsky was in the regular rotation as a columnist at *Moscow News*—a golden boy, he says, "of a certain age."

CHAPTER 12

PARTY MEN

Geidar Aliyev was humiliated. After two decades as the Communist Party boss of Azerbaijan, he had been dumped in 1989 from Gorbachev's Politburo, vilified for corruption in the news columns of *Pravda,* and reduced to sharing the backseat of a dismal Volga sedan with an American journalist. The upstarts in the Party—the Karpinskys, the Yakovlevs, even Gorbachev himself—had all betrayed him. "When we made Gorbachev general secretary we had no idea what it would lead to!" he said. The pressures of Aliyev's decline wore on him. He had suffered mild heart attacks; his complexion had turned the shade of a votive candle. He complained of poverty to all who would listen. But Aliyev was still possessed of a certain unctuous charm, a parody of William Powell's parody of a regal smoothie. "You should feel quite honored," he told me as we drove to Moscow from his posh dacha in the village of Uspenskoye. "It's not often that I give an audience."

When he was a young man, Aliyev's ambitions were almost derailed when he was accused of sexual assault. He avoided expulsion from the Party by a single vote at his disciplinary hearing. There were, of course, no further "legal" proceedings. The Party's judgment was all. In 1969, as the republic's KGB chief, Aliyev launched a "crusade against corruption." He intended only to purge his enemies and elevate himself and his clan, and he succeeded spectacularly. Once installed as republican Party chief, Aliyev ruled Azerbaijan as surely as the Gambino family ran the port of New York. The Caspian Sea caviar mafia, the Sumgait oil mafia, the fruits and vegetables mafia, the cotton mafia, the customs and transport mafias—they all reported to him, enriched him, worshiped him. Aliyev even practiced hegemony over the intellectual life of Azerbaijan. He appointed his relatives chairmen of various institutes and academic departments, enabling them, in turn, to charge tens of thousands of rubles to scholars in search of meaningful employment.

The structure of state in Azerbaijan—and everywhere else in the Soviet Union—was itself a mafia. The Communist Party's dispensation of power and property was unchallenged by election or by law. Administrators of "socialist justice" were duplicitous props intended by the Party to give the appearance of civil society. These judges, police captains, and prosecutors were generally well fed and not meant to stand up for anything more than their share of the booty.

There had been, of course, some honest men in the Party structure. In one famous incident in Azerbaijan, a prosecutor named Gamboi Mamedov tried to investigate corruption in the Communist Party leadership. Aliyev had him fired and denounced. Later, at a session of the republican legislature, the inflamed Mamedov managed to grab the microphone, shouting, "The state plan is a swindle, likewise the budget—also, of course, those reports of economic success are a pack of lies, and . . ." Police hustled Mamedov off the speaker's platform and into a back alley of obscurity. Seventeen loyal legislators quickly lined up to defend Aliyev. "Who are you fighting against, Gamboi?" Suleiman Ragimov, a hack writer and deputy, cried out. "God sent us his son in the form of Geidar Aliyev. Are you then opposing God?" The legislature rose as one in a standing ovation.

When Gorbachev came to power in 1985, he became the boss of bosses, the leader of a Communist Party Politburo in which most of the leaders were unabashed mafia sultans, men like Aliyev of Azerbaijan, Viktor Grishin of Moscow, Grigori Romanov of Leningrad, Dinmukhamed Kunayev of Kazakhstan, Vladimir Shcherbitsky of Ukraine. In Russia, the principle of blood ties did not mean as much as it did in Azerbaijan or Central Asia, but the Party hierarchy, and the way it controlled all economic activity, was just as powerful. The Central Committee, too, was filled with "dead souls," Party hacks whose sole mission was the protection of the Party as a privileged class. They had all long ago turned the poverty of Leninist ideology to their own advantage. In a state in which property belonged to all—in other words, to no one—the Communist Party owned everything, from the docks of Odessa to the orange trees of Georgia.

Aliyev, like the others, knew that the only real imperative of stability under Brezhnev had been to grease the don. Leonid Ilyich did not require the genuine prosperity or happiness of his people to please him. He needed only reports of same. As long as the official-looking documents that crossed his desk informed him of record successes and overfulfilled plans, he was well pleased.

Of course, the traditions of tribute pleased him even more. When Brezhnev came to the Azerbaijani capital, Baku, in 1978, Aliyev gave him a gold ring with a huge solitaire diamond, a hand-woven carpet so large it took up the train's dining salon, and a portrait of the general secretary onto which rare gems had been pasted as "decoration." For an official visit in 1982, Aliyev built a palace for Brezhnev's use, an edifice with all the kitsch grandeur of the Kennedy Center in Washington. The great man slept there for a couple of nights and then the palace closed. To commemorate the same visit, Aliyev gave Brezhnev yet another ring that symbolized the worldview of the Kremlin better than any map. One huge jewel, representing Brezhnev the Sun King, was surrounded by fifteen smaller stones representing the fifteen union republics. "Like planets orbiting their sun," as Aliyev explained. This masterpiece of the jeweler's art was given the title "The Unbreakable Union of Republics of the Free." When he received the ring and listened to Aliyev's careful explication, Brezhnev, in full view of the television cameras, burst into tears of gratitude.

This system of shadows and gilt served the Party well while it lasted. But now Aliyev, who had grown accustomed to long Zil limousines while he was in power, found himself with his knees jammed into the seat ahead of him.

"Ach, I live badly," he said as we sped along the highway linking Moscow to the villages where the Party elite kept their dachas. "My pension is tiny. Believe me, you would never work for such a sum. The driver? The car? Not mine. I just have the right to order them up once in a while."

In office, Aliyev had grown used to ordering suits from the Kremlin tailor, to regular deliveries of Japanese electronics, American cigarettes, and delicacies from the special farms and shops run by the KGB. Now his world was confused and threatening. "Gorbachev says he is for the renovation of socialism and against capitalism," Aliyev said. "Fine. But what sort of renovation? What does it mean? Is it social democracy? That's not socialism. What exactly is his socialism? No one knows. They don't know what socialism is anymore, and they are all living in a fog. You Americans want everyone to follow your way, and the more things here are to the liking of George Bush, the better. But is Bush Jesus Christ or something?"

We rode on a while in an agreeable silence toward Pushkin Square. Then, suddenly, through the evening fog, the gleaming apparition of the future: a pair of yellow arches, a winding line of hungry Russians. Aliyev sneered.

"McDonald's!" he said. "There's the perestroika you all love so much."

———

The Communist Party apparatus was the most gigantic mafia the world has ever known. It guarded its monopoly on power with a sham consensus and constitution and backed it up with the force of the KGB and the Interior Ministry police. There were also handsome profits. The Party had so obviously socked away money abroad and sold off national resources—including the country's vast gold reserves—that just after the collapse of the August coup, the Party's leading financial officer took a look into the future and threw himself off a high balcony to his death.

The Party's corruption under Brezhnev was not a matter of exceptions, of rotten apples fouling the utopian barrel. No thorough prosecution could stop with a single indictment. "If it were a question of just one of the former leaders, the new government could easily give him up to be destroyed, presenting him as the black sheep—a sad exception to the general rule," according to Arkady Vaksberg, the top legal writer for the weekly paper *Literaturnaya Gazeta.* "But since it is a question precisely of all (or nearly all) of the members of the previous administration of autocratic old men, their exposure would lead to only one possible and inescapable conclusion from a historical perspective, that is, of the criminal character of the Party and the whole political system which enables criminals to make their way into positions of power and fanatically protects them from exposure."

In many ways, Stalin's Terror mirrored the tactics of the mafia. He used violence as an instrument of coercion and discipline; he fostered an atmosphere of secrecy and universal suspicion; there were "made" men (Party apparatchiks) and the outward appearance of legitimate business (embassies, diplomats, trade, etc.). As terror faded under Khrushchev and then Brezhnev, the Communist Party's business became business. "Sometimes you gotta get rid of the bad blood," Richard Castellano tells Al Pacino in *The Godfather.* But after an all-out war, the mafia always dreams of an Arcadian period of cooperation, of relations that are profitable, stable, and, always, "just business." Ideology in the post-Stalin era was not so much a system of beliefs or behavior as a kind of language, a password among the "made" men; if you could speak the language without deviation, you might be trusted to share in the loot. "More than anything else," the Yugoslav dissident Milovan Djilas wrote a few years after Stalin's death, "the essential aspect of contemporary Communism is the new class of owners and exploiters."

It was only in the post-Stalin era, after the violent period of collectivization and industrialization was over, that the Party-mafia structures took shape. Vladimir Oleinik, a famously honest investigator in the Russian prosecutor's office, published excerpts from his diary in *Literaturnaya Gazeta* that described the rapid growth in the 1960s of the trade mafia, a pyramid of corruption that began in the Communist Party Central Committee and the top ministers and went all the way down to butchers, bakers, and gravediggers, with everyone getting a piece. Oleinik wrote of how one Central Committee member filled his bank account by selling midlevel positions in the ministries for 50,000 rubles a spot.

The trade mafia worked thousands of scams. Even the small-time jobs had a certain beauty to them. In Central Asia, I was told about the fruit juice scam. Workers paid enormous bribes to get jobs servicing carbonated juice machines throughout the warm, southern republics. When the workers serviced the machines, they skimped on the syrup and then sold it elsewhere. They also skimmed some of the money out of the cash boxes. The workers used part of their gains to pay the foremen; the foreman, in turn, paid off the assistant minister; the assistant minister paid the minister . . . and all the way up the line and to the top of the Party structure.

In the same region, even high Party positions and awards were for sale. The magazine *Smena* ("Change") reported that the position of regional Party secretary in Central Asia cost a bribe of $150,000, and an Order of Lenin, the Soviet Union equivalent of the Congressional Medal of Honor, cost anywhere from $165,000 to $750,000.

It wasn't as if this swamp of corruption were a secret to the Soviet people any more than the existence of the mafia is a secret to the New York storekeeper forced to pay protection money. The mafia made itself known at every turn. You literally could not leave this earth without feeling its heavy hand on your shoulder. One afternoon, the nanny who took care of our son came to work exhausted and depressed. Her mother had died, but what had run her down most was the enormous effort and expense of getting the woman buried—a process that drained her as much as it enriched the "cemetery mafia" and its Party patrons.

"I knew immediately this was going to run into big money for us," Irina said. "We were supposed to get a free funeral and burial. But that is a joke. The first stop was the bank. First, Mother's body had to be taken to the morgue. We were told that the morgues were all filled up, and they wouldn't take her. But when we paid two hundred rubles to the attendants, they took her. Then there was the fifty rubles for her shroud.

"Then the funeral agent said he had no coffins my mother's size and that we could only buy something eight feet long. My mother was five feet tall. For eighty rubles he came up with the right size. Then the gravediggers said they could not dig the grave until two P.M., even though the funeral was set for ten A.M. So that took two bottles of vodka each and twenty-five rubles each. The driver of the funeral bus said he had another funeral that day and couldn't take care of us. But for thirty rubles and a bottle of vodka we could solve the problem. We did. And so on with the gravesite and the flowers and all the rest. In the end, it took two thousand rubles to bury my mother. Three months' income for the family. Is that what ordinary life is supposed to be? To me, it's like living by the law of the jungle."

In the West, the mob historically moves in where there is no legal economy—in drugs, gambling, prostitution—and creates a shadow economy. Sometimes, when it can buy the affections of a politician or two, the mafia meddles in government contracts and runs protection schemes. But in the Soviet Union, no economic transaction was untainted. It was as if the entire Soviet Union were ruled by a gigantic mob family; virtually all economic relations were, in some form, mafia relations. Between a government minister's order for, say, the production of ten tons of meat and Ivan Ivanov's purchase of a kilo of veal for a family dinner, there were countless opportunities for mischief. No one could afford to avoid at least a certain degree of complicity. That was one of the most degrading facts of Soviet life: it was impossible to be honest. And all the baksheesh, eventually, ended up enriching the Communist Party.

"Look, it's all very simple," Andrei Fyodorov, who opened Moscow's first cooperative restaurant in 1987, told me. "The mafia is the state itself."

Before opening his restaurant, 36 Kropotkinskaya, Fyodorov worked for twenty-five years in the state restaurant business. Over a cup of tea one morning in his empty dining room, Fydorov described how it all worked at his old place of business, the Solnechny Restaurant, a huge state banquet hall. "The game started at nine o'clock on Friday mornings when the inspectors came by. I soon realized they were not really interested in the state of things in the restaurant. Very soon we established good contacts in terms of giving them various foodstuffs, providing tables in the restaurant, arranging saunas. The director of the restaurant would just tell me which services I had to arrange for them. You see, every person working in services is always on a hook. The restaurant director's salary is one hundred ninety rubles a month, say. You can't live on that, and so he is forced to take bribes. But there is a system of bribing in the USSR. You can't get too greedy. A restaurant director cannot take more than two thousand or three thousand rubles per month. If he starts taking more, the system grows worried, and in the next five or six months new people will come around to inspect your place, which means that you can be arrested for violating the unwritten code of bribery.

"It goes from the bottom on up. From waiters, the bribes go to the maître d', and then on to the deputy director, to the director of the restaurant, and upward to various Party officials and auditing bodies. The same system applies to cafés, tailor shops, taxi depots, barbershops. A man who does not give bribes for more than six months is doomed."

———

Until his untimely arrest a few years ago, the most flamboyant mafia figure in the country was Akhmadzhan Adylov, a "Hero of Socialist Labor" who ran for twenty years the Party organization in the rich Fergana Valley region of Uzbekistan. Adylov was known as the Godfather and lived on a vast estate with peacocks, lions, thoroughbred horses, concubines, and a slave labor force of thousands of men. Anywhere Adylov went, he was accompanied by his personal cooks and a mobile kitchen. For lunch, he always ate a roasted baby lamb. He locked his foes in a secret underground prison and tortured them when necessary. His favorite technique was borrowed from the Nazis. In subzero temperatures, he would tie a man to a stake and spray him with cold water until he froze to death.

Adylov insisted he was a descendant of Tamerlane the Great. Considering his taste for ritual and cruelty, his blend of ancient and Bolshevik cruelty, it seems fitting. Adylov often sat in judgment, as if on a throne, under a portrait of the state deity, Lenin. When a Party hack named Inamzhon Usmankhodzhaev was nominated for high office in Uzbekistan, he had to appear before Adylov for approval. As a test of loyalty, Adylov ordered Usmankhodzhaev to execute an informer, but he could not bring himself to pull the trigger. Adylov could not excuse such a pathetic show of weakness and relented only when Usmankhodzhaev begged for forgiveness and, on his knees, licked clean the shoes of the Godfather.

From the Uzbeks, Brezhnev wanted only cotton and, more important, wonderful cotton *statistics.* The cotton scam was gigantic, yet elegant. Brezhnev would call on the "heroic peoples" of Uzbekistan to pick, say, 20 percent more cotton than the previous year. The workers, heroic as they were, could not possibly fulfill the order. (How could they when the previous year's statistics were already wildly inflated?) But the local Party leaders understood the overriding issue. They assured Moscow that all had gone as planned. If not better! The central ministries in Moscow would, in turn, pay vast sums of rubles for the record crop. The republican leaders would pocket the extra cash. Brezhnev, for his part, smacked his lips anticipating the gifts that would come, air freight, from Bukhara, Samarkand, and the other centers of Uzbekistan.

Of all the most famous Party mafias in the Soviet Union—the Kazakhs, the Azeris, the Georgians, the Crimeans, the Muscovites—the Uzbeks showed a certain flair. Sharaf Rashidov, the republican Party chief, was a soft-spoken sybarite with literary pretensions. He fancied himself a novelist. To fulfill his ambition, he hired two Moscow hacks, Yuri Karasev and Boris Privalov, to do the writing. The resulting potboilers were published in editions that would cause Judith Krantz profound envy. Rashidov also knew how to satisfy his appetites. After hours of waving to the masses from the podium on May Day, he would descend into the basement beneath the podium, where, as Vaksberg reports, there were tables "piled with festive fare and delightful young ladies ready to put the spring back in his step." Rashidov was awarded ten Orders of Lenin, and when he died in 1984 he was buried with pharaonic ceremony in the center of Tashkent near the Lenin Museum. For years, people brought mounds of roses and carnations to the tomb. Finally, the Uzbek leaders recognized the shift in political winds from Moscow and moved the grave to a remote village. But Rashidov's legacy lived on. In 1988, regional Party officials summarily pardoned 675 people who had been sentenced for their roles in the corruption scandals of the Brezhnev era.

These were the go-go years under Brezhnev, and Uzbekistan did not, by any means, hold a monopoly on the grotesque. In the Krasnodar region of southern Russia, a mafia stronghold, ordinary membership in the Party cost anywhere from 3,000 to 6,000 rubles. Vyacheslav Voronkov, mayor of the resort city of Sochi, hired an Armenian architect to construct a musical fountain in the foyer of his state mansion. Tourists were permitted to pay a few kopecks to hear their Party leader's fountain in full aria. When Communist Party chiefs in Russia went fishing, scuba divers plunged underwater and put fish on the hooks. When they went hunting, specially bred elk, stag, and deer were made to saunter across the field in point-blank range. Everyone had a wonderful time. When the king of Afghanistan visited the Tajik resort of Tiger Gorge, he blew away the last Turan tiger in the country.

The mutual congratulations, the feasts and wedding parties, the piety and self-righteousness all smacked of mafia culture. At a conference of the Soviet Writers' Union in 1981, Yegor Ligachev, who would later serve as Gorbachev's nominal number-two man and conservative nemesis, said, "You can't imagine, comrades, what a joy it is for all of us to be able to get on with our work quietly and how well everything is going under the leadership of dear

Leonid Ilyich. What a marvelous moral-political climate has been established in the Party and country with his coming to power! It is as if wings have sprouted on our backs, if you want to put it stylishly, as you writers do."

—

In Kazakhstan, a republic bigger than all of Western Europe, Dinmukhamed Kunayev showed a certain kindliness to his relatives and (a rare feature in mafia men) to his wife. Arkady Vaksberg confirmed a story about Kunayev's connubial bliss that I had first heard when I was in Alma-Ata.

It seems that Kunayev's wife became jealous after learning that the wife of the Magadan Party secretary had been given as a gift an extremely expensive Japanese tea service. Magadan, the former labor camp center in the far east, had unique access to Japanese goods, but Mrs. Kunayev would not be soothed. She had to have these cups and saucers. Party etiquette did not allow Kunayev simply to order the tea set from Japan or even Siberia. That was somehow too obvious. Even dispatching an aide to Tokyo was deemed unseemly.

"A way had to be found, of course," Vaksberg writes. "And such was its originality and refinement that it deserves its own little page in the history of the Soviet mafia." Kunayev could not merely send his private plane, a Tupolev 134, on the mission. Party rules dictated that a Politburo member's plane always had to be on the ready for emergency sessions in Moscow. So Kunayev told his aides to draw up an official report saying the plane's engine required repair. This would allow him to order another plane while the first was being "fixed."

Rules also dictated that after the repair, a Politburo member could not fly on the plane until it had been flown twenty thousand kilometers. "The point of this brilliant move is clear," Vaksberg writes. "Some of Kunayev's closest associates were happy to take on the 'kamikaze' role. They worked out a route which, there and back, would clock up the required distance of twenty thousand kilometers. There would be stopovers in Krasnoyarsk, Irkutsk, and Khabarovsk. They would return via Petropavlovsk-Kamchatsky, for it would have been unthinkable to visit the Soviet far east and not gawk at geysers and an active volcano. Everywhere they were received at the highest level—after all, they were emissaries from Kunayev himself. Those that have clawed their way to power have an astonishing passion for recording their pleasure on film. Thanks to this hobby we can today see with our own eyes how their trip went. Lavish picnics everywhere with the traditional shashlik and variety of vodkas, saunas, and royal hunting of boar, elk, and deer especially put up in front of them for easy shots.

"The first lady herself did not take the trip, needless to say. Like her husband, she was not allowed to take chances with her life. However, the jolly kamikazes came back with the passenger cabin and baggage hold crammed with gifts from the Soviet far east and Siberia. They brought not only dozens of Japanese tea sets but also Japanese sound and video equipment, furs, carvings on rare deer horn—the finest art of indigenous craftsmen—thousands of jars of Pacific crab and other fruits of the ocean. All these things were brought back to Alma-Ata like trophies."

———

After three decades as the Kazakh Party chief, Kunayev had been forced to retire for "reasons of health" in 1986. In retirement, he lived across the street from a park named in his honor. The focal point of the park was an enormous monument, a huge plinth with the great man's granite head perched on top. The building at 119 Tulebayeva Street looked like a second-rate Miami Beach motel. In addition to Kunayev, the two top-ranking Party leaders also lived there.

The first time I went to meet Kunayev, I tried to "doorstep" him, to show up and hope for the best. This was not a wise maneuver. A KGB guard in the courtyard stopped me and made it clear, as his hand flashed lightly to his holster, that one further step toward the Kunayev residence would be inadvisable. So I tried a more conventional tactic. Through a Kazakh journalist, a particularly obedient one whom I knew from Moscow, I asked to see Kunayev and sent along a list of questions of the "What are the key achievements of Kazakhstan under Soviet power?" variety. While we waited for word back from Kunayev, we ate a multicourse dinner at the apartment of the journalist's in-laws. It was a long evening. His father-in-law got badly hammered on the cognac I brought as a gift and spoke lovingly for some hours of Stalin's "iron hand." We all ate heartily of a dish that I was later informed was "delicious noodles" mixed with shredded horse heart. Tastes like chicken, my hosts assured me. They were wrong.

Finally, the call came from Kunayev. He was ready to see us the next morning at eleven.

We arrived, four of us, at the house five minutes early.

"Where are you going?" the guard asked us.

"We have an appointment with Kunayev."

"Impossible," the guard said.

"We do. An interview at eleven. He is expecting us."

"Documents!"

We all showed our various papers, and the guard went to his special phone. He talked for a while and came back smiling in triumph.

"The American is forbidden," he said. This seemed nonnegotiable.

Clearly, the ministers of Moscow had no interest in giving Kunayev a public platform, especially not in an American newspaper. They were prepared to let Kunayev live in relative splendor amid his beloved collections of cigarette lighters and foreign shotguns, but they did not want to be the agents of a resurrection. Gorbachev had already suffered once from Kunayev. When he fired Kunayev in 1986, Gorbachev made the mistake of appointing in his place an outsider and a Russian, Gennadi Kolbin. This was just what Kunayev needed. By all accounts, Kunayev's clan encouraged anti-Russian, anti-colonial riots, using a latent nationalism to do his own work. Gorbachev soon corrected the mistake, replacing Kolbin with a Kazakh, Nursultan Nazarbayev. But it was that incident in Alma-Ata that should have demonstrated to the Kremlin that, contrary to myth, the Soviet Union had not solved its national problems; instead, the abuses of a half-century had created an empire of resentments. Alma-Ata was prelude to a series of national movements Moscow never expected.

I waited on the street. An hour later, the Kazakhs came out of Kunayev's place, beaming. "Kunayev seemed sad that you couldn't come," one of them said. "He said, 'It seems I'm powerless in my own house.' "

It seemed I would never meet the fallen don. But later the same day, while I was with another Kazakh political official, one of the journalists walked into the room, tapped me on the shoulder, and told me to "wrap things up." He had called Kunayev and we were all set to meet on the street, outside the gates of the Communist Party's House of Rest.

A half hour later, a Volga, not unlike Aliyev's modest car, pulled up. Kunayev unfolded himself from the backseat. He was enormous, silver-haired, and dressed in a chalk-striped suit. He wore dark glasses and carried the sort of carved walking stick that gave Mobuto his authority. He had a fantastic smile, all bravado and condescension, the smile of a king. Without my asking a thing, he launched into a monologue about the such-and-such anniversary of Kazakhstan and wheat production and the need to preserve the monuments of the Bolshevik state. "I've never swayed," he solemnly reminded us. "I am a man of the Leninist Party line. Never forget that." We swore we would not.

When I finally asked my earnest questions—about Gorbachev, about politics—Kunayev laughed them off, fiddled with the mahogany knob of his stick, and set back on the course of his monologue.

There were, I said, interrupting, still many Kazakhs who wanted Kunayev to return to politics. "Are you ready to make a comeback?" I asked.

"I wouldn't be against it," he said. "Let the people decide. But tomorrow, I should tell you, I'm busy. I'm going hunting for ducks. I love hunting for ducks."

The decline of the Party mafia began with the death of Brezhnev and the brief reign of Yuri Andropov. Although Andropov was guilty of many things—most notably his brutally efficient campaign against the dissidents while he ran the KGB—he was a throwback to a tradition of Leninist asceticism. Andropov was profoundly corrupt, a beast. No man who ran the Budapest embassy during the Soviet invasion of Hungary in 1956 can be declared an innocent. "In a way I always thought Andropov was the most dangerous of all of them, simply because he was smarter than the rest," Aleksandr Yakovlev told me.

But Andropov's main virtue was that he was appalled by the kind of corruption and rot that had become endemic under Brezhnev. While he was KGB chief, Andropov conducted a wide-scale, independent investigation into Party business and the general state of the country's economic system. After Brezhnev's death, in his few months as general secretary, Andropov ordered arrests of some of the most obvious Party and police mafiosi. He frightened the worst elements in the apparatus so badly that a series of high-ranking officials in Brezhnev's old circle shot, gassed, or otherwise did away with themselves.

The remaining Brezhnevites at the top were not much grieved when Andropov became seriously ill. The Party mafia could not bear the thought of reforms that would endanger its comfort. As Solzhenitsyn wrote in 1991, "The corrupt ruling class—the many millions of men in the party-state nomenklatura—is not capable of voluntarily renouncing any of the privileges they have seized. They have lived shamelessly for decades at the people's expense—and would like to continue doing so."

Had it not been for that primal urge to power and privilege, Gorbachev might well have taken over as general secretary more than a year earlier than he did. Arkady Volsky, a former aide to Andropov and a leading figure in the Central Committee, told me how the Brezhnevites in the Politburo steered power away from Gorbachev, an Andropov protégé, to "their man," the moribund apparatchik Konstantin Chernenko. By December 1983, Andropov was in the hospital with kidney problems and blood poisoning. His aides would take turns visiting him in the hospital with important matters and paperwork. On a Saturday preceding a Tuesday plenum of the Central Committee, Volsky came to Andropov's room at the Kremlin hospital on the outskirts of Moscow to help him draft a speech. Andropov was in no shape to attend the plenum, and he would have one of his men in the Politburo deliver the speech in his name.

"The last lines in the speech said that Central Committee staff members should be exemplary in their behavior, uncorrupted, responsible for the life of the country," Volsky said. "We both liked that last phrase. . . . Then Andropov gave me a folder with the final draft and said, 'The material looks good. Make sure you pay attention to the addenda I've written.' I didn't have time to look right away at what he had written. Later, I got a chance to read it and saw that at the bottom of the last page Andropov had added in ink, in a somewhat unsteady handwriting, a new paragraph. It went like this: 'Members of the Central Committee know that due to certain reasons, I am unable to come to the plenum. I can neither attend the meetings of the Politburo nor the secretariat [of the Central Committee]. Therefore, I believe Mikhail Sergeyevich Gorbachev should be assigned to preside over the meetings of the Politburo and the secretariat.' "

Volsky knew well what this meant. The general secretary was recommending that Gorbachev be his inheritor. Volsky made a photocopy of the document and put the copy in his safe. He delivered the original to the Party leadership and assumed, naively, that it would be read out at the plenum. But at the meeting neither Chernenko, Grishin, Romanov, nor any of the other usual suspects in the Brezhnev circle made mention of Andropov's stated wishes. Volsky thought there must have been some mistake. "I went up to Chernenko and said, 'Sir, there was an addendum in the text.' He said, 'Think nothing of any addendum.' Then I saw his aide Bogolyubov and said, 'Klavdy Mikhailovich, there was a paragraph from Andropov's speech . . .' He led me off to the side and said, 'Who do you think you are, a wise guy? Do you think your life ends with this?' I said, 'In that case, I'll have to phone Andropov.' And he replied, 'Then that will be your last phone call.' "

Andropov was furious when he heard what had happened at the plenum, but there was little he could do. Even Lenin did not have the power to name his successor, and the Brezhnevites in the Politburo were just too powerful. When Andropov died in February 1984, Chernenko became general secretary, the ventriloquist's dummy of the Party mafia.

As a concession to the Andropov faction and over the objections of some of his own confidants, Chernenko made Gorbachev the nominal number-two man in the Politburo. This turned out to be a serious tactical mistake. Chernenko held office for only thirteen months, and much of the time he was sick and powerless. As Chernenko wasted away, Gorbachev was carefully consolidating power. He ran Politburo sessions and won the support of two critical figures—the foreign minister, Andrei Gromyko, and the KGB chief, Viktor Chebrikov. He also took his famous trip to Britain, where he made a lasting impression on Margaret Thatcher and the world press. When Chernenko finally died in March 1985, Gorbachev had the backing of the younger

Party secretaries and a few key members of the old guard, including Gromyko. He was in a position to head off any potential opposition from the mafia dinosaurs.

Gorbachev, for his part, took office without taint of blood or corruption, a first for a leader of the Soviet Union. But even this was relative. As the Party leader of a resort region in the Caucasus, a neighbor of the notorious Krasnodar region, he must have known about the Party way of doing business, both with Moscow and within the local structure. At best, it is unlikely that he could have avoided toadying to Brezhnev either as the Party chief of the Stavropol region in southern Russia or in Moscow as a member of the Central Committee. Roy Medvedev, a Gorbachev loyalist to the last, told a reporter for *La Stampa,* "I believe that presents for Brezhnev even arrived from Stavropol."

"Did Gorbachev give Brezhnev diamond rings the way Aliyev did? Of course not," Arkady Vaksberg told me. "But on the other hand, no provincial Party secretary could survive, much less advance, by ignoring the birthdays and so on of those superior to him. Even an 'honest' Party secretary coming to Moscow would have to bring gifts for his superiors: a few cases of good wine. You couldn't get away from that. Gorbachev included. That was life in the Communist Party."

On New Year's Eve 1989, the censors canceled an installment of the popular television program *Vzglyad* ("View") for "aesthetic reasons." Vaksberg claims that the aesthetic reason in question was that Brezhnev's daughter, Galina, had told an interviewer that Raisa Gorbachev had tried to curry favor with the Brezhnev family when Leonid Ilyich was in power and had given them a number of presents, including an expensive necklace. But Vaksberg is also quick to recount how after publishing a piece called "Spring Floods" in *Literaturnaya Gazeta* about the negligence of ministers while the harvest rotted in the fields, the paper got a dressing-down from the Ideology Department of the Central Committee. Just as the editor was instructing Vaksberg to print a retraction, Gorbachev called the paper to express his compliments for its crusade against corruption.

But Gorbachev knew that he could not conduct a genuine investigation into the Party's corruption. First, the Party, of which he was the head, would sooner kill him than allow it. Second, even if he could carry out such an investigation, Gorbachev would be faced with the obvious embarrassment: the depths of the Party's rot. Instead, taking a page from Andropov's style manual, he made a grand symbolic gesture. Yuri Churbanov, Brezhnev's son-in-law and a deputy chief of the Interior Ministry, was indicted and tried for accepting more than $1 million in bribes while working in Uzbekistan. At his trial, Churbanov admitted accepting a briefcase stuffed with around

$200,000. "I wanted to return the money, but to whom?" he said. "It would have been awkward for me to raise the question with Rashidov," the Party chief of the republic. Churbanov was sentenced to twelve years in prison at a camp near the city of Nizhny Tagil. Brezhnev's personal secretary, Gennadi Brovin, was sentenced to nine years in prison, also for corruption.

Like Andropov before him, Gorbachev believed in his ability to master the Party and reform it. Over a five-year period, he fired and replaced the most obvious mafiosi in the Politburo: Kunayev, Aliyev, Shcherbitsky. But just as he could never distance himself enough from a discredited ideology, Gorbachev's inability to jettison the Party nomenklatura and his political debts to the KGB spoiled his reputation over time in the eyes of a people who had grown more and more aware of the corruption and deceit in their midst.

———

In the meantime, a new wave of politicians saw Gorbachev's equivocations as an opportunity. Telman Gdlyan and Nikolai Ivanov, investigators who helped convict Churbanov, became two of the most popular legislators in the parliament purely on the strength of their public attacks on the Party. In their investigations of corruption under Brezhnev, Gdlyan and Ivanov were known for mistreating witnesses, manufacturing evidence, and committing other illegalities. They dismissed such charges with a smirk. Gdlyan, especially, was a wild man. He told me one day that Yegor Ligachev, the number-two man in the Politburo, had "definitely" accepted at least 60,000 rubles in bribes from an Uzbek official. When I asked for proof, Gdlyan laughed, as if such things hardly mattered.

Boris Yeltsin was the master of the populist attack, using the issue of Party perks and corruption as a way to discredit everyone at the top, Gorbachev included. In his memoir, *Against the Grain,* which was terrifically popular in Russia, Yeltsin writes about the "marble-lined" houses of the Politburo members, their "porcelain, crystal, carpets, and chandeliers." For an audience living in cramped communal apartments, he described his own house when he was in the Party leadership, with its private movie theater, its "kitchen big enough to feed an army," and its many bathrooms, so many that "I lost count." And, he wrote, "why has Gorbachev been unable to change this? I believe the fault lies in his basic cast of character. He likes to live well, in comfort and luxury. In this he is helped by his wife."

At times, Yeltsin seemed the Huey and Earl Long of Soviet politics, a theatrical populist. Relying on the politics of resentment, he won an angry public's affection. After he'd been fired from the Politburo for daring to confront the leadership in October 1987, Yeltsin was still a member of the Central Committee, with all the privileges that entailed. But in an interview with me at his modest office at the Ministry of Construction, Yeltsin swore that he had voluntarily given up his dacha, his grocery shipments, and his car. "All finished!" he said with the pride of the converted. For a very short while Yeltsin made sure that Muscovites saw him tooling around the city in a dinky sedan. Later, when he returned to power, however, Yeltsin lived no worse than Gorbachev did. He commandeered a splendid dacha, organized a regal caravan of limousines, and made a public show of his love for that proletarian game—tennis. Yeltsin's new double-breasted suits and silk ties were also, one supposed, not available for rubles.

Like Gorbachev, Yeltsin was an ambitious provincial who made good in the Communist Party. Like Gorbachev, he made absurd speeches at various meetings praising the wisdom of Leonid Brezhnev and the eternal goodness of the Party. But while Gorbachev spent all his working life in the Party, Yeltsin began late. He became a member of the Party to get ahead at the state construction agency in Sverdlovsk. In his autobiography, Yeltsin recounts with a brand of irony foreign to Gorbachev the preposterous oral exam at the local Party committee required for membership:

"[The examiner] asked me on what page of which volume of *Das Kapital* Marx refers to commodity-money relationships. Assuming that he had never read Marx closely and had, of course, no idea of either the volume or page number in question, and that he didn't even know what commodity-money relationships were, I immediately answered, half-jokingly, 'Volume Two, page 387.' What's more I said it quickly, without pausing for thought. To which he replied, with a sage expression, 'Well done, you know your Marx well.' After it all, I was accepted as a Party member."

After his fall from the Politburo, no statement, no amount of bombast, was out of bounds. In interviews, Yeltsin would suggest with a burlesque arch of the brow that the KGB could yet kill him with a high-frequency ray gun that would stun his heart. "A few seconds," he told me, "and it's all over." His paranoia was comic, but understandable. The Kremlin leaders despised him. They formed a commission within the Central Committee to investigate him and ordered wild stories in the state-run press to disgrace him.

As the man who would not go away, Yeltsin was, for the Communist Party, an intolerable dissident. Such was his vital importance, his first important contribution to the collapse of the regime. Despite the Kremlin's best efforts, the history of Soviet politics will show it was Yeltsin—vain, comic, clever, crude—who accelerated the essential step in political reform: the shattering of the Communist Party monolith. From the moment Yeltsin attacked Yegor Ligachev at the Party plenum on October 21, 1987, and rumors of this assault became the talk of Moscow, the facade of unanimity and invincibility, the hermetic code of Party discipline and loyalty, began to crumble. Although the proceedings of the plenum remained secret for months, Yeltsin quickly became an underground martyr. An actress performing in a hit play about the cleaning of the Augean stables, *The Seventh Feat of Hercules,* stepped center stage, abandoned her script, and accused the audience of sitting idly by as a new Hercules, come to purify the city, had been disgraced and persecuted. There were demonstrations at Moscow State University. Small independent political groups such as the Club for Social Initiatives petitioned the government for more facts on the Yeltsin case. Club members reported they were followed around town by men in small cars.

After failing to win back his position or good name within the Party at the Nineteenth Party Conference, Yeltsin took his campaign for revenge and rehabilitation to the public. His barrel-chested fury, his awkward candor, had an almost narcotic appeal for a people who saw the Party that ruled them for seven decades—the Party of Aliyev and Kunayev—as an ominous secret. To any reporter or crowd who would listen, Yeltsin insulted Gorbachev's "timidity and half-measures" and Ligachev's "dark motives."

The Communist Party, for its part, well understood not only the meaning of Yeltsin's attacks but also the much wider issue of what his political success would mean to its future. Yeltsin's ascendance embodied the threat to the Party's control of the economy and the Party mafia's system of tribute.

From the first appearance of cooperative businesses in 1987, the Party did everything it could to destroy the new movement it had ostensibly endorsed. One leading conservative in the Central Committee, Ivan Polozkov, made his name fighting the rise of semiprivate cooperative businesses in the Krasnodar region. He closed down more than three hundred co-ops in the region, calling them "a social evil, a malignant tumor." The KGB, under Vladimir Kryuchkov, waged a campaign against private business, all under the pretense of rooting out corruption. But Kryuchkov never got around to investigating the barons of the state military plants, men who would soon become his closest allies in the struggle against radical reform. The conservatives also knew they could play games with the psychology of a people grown accustomed to "equality in poverty." They knew they could arouse bitter jealousy in millions of collective farmers and workers by advertising cases of abuse under the new "mixed" economy. They portrayed the new wave of businessmen as hustlers (invariably Jewish, Armenian or Georgian hustlers) who made millions by buying products at low state-subsidized prices and then reselling the same products for three or four times more.

Undeniably, the first wave of private businessmen in Russia were no angels—no more than the first Rockefellers or Carnegies were. Racketeering, theft and bribery soared. But to the Party and the KGB, what these entrepreneurs and hustlers represented was not so much evil or capitalism as competition. This was intolerable. Lev Timofeyev, the journalist and political activist who spent 1985 to 1987 in a labor camp for writing a book describing rural corruption, wryly demanded that the Party men "transform themselves into men of property, landowners or shareholders.

"Let them make profits and reinvest them, let them outrun competition and become rich. Let them be useful at last. They have a right to do that. The only requirement is that they do not prevent others from doing the same," he wrote. "Unfortunately the party officials will hardly become successful owners of land or industries. They lack the qualities needed for becoming honest entrepreneurs and this is why they are so terrified of those who have them. They will stop at nothing trying to prolong the days of their rotten power and they are still strong enough to do it."

CHAPTER 13

POOR FOLK

There in some smoky corner which, through poverty, passes for a dwelling place, a workman wakes from his sleep. All night he has been dreaming of a pair of boots. . . .

—FYODOR DOSTOEVSKY, Poor Folk, 1845

W hen I first came to Russia in 1985, I rode through Moscow on a tour bus packed with a gaggle of British socialists. They were spindly fellow travelers who wore orthopedic shoes and plastic raincoats that folded away into envelopes "no bigger than the palm of your hand." They felt like complaining about the rotten breakfast—cold kasha, bad coffee, surly waiters—but they knew they should not.

We settled into our seats, and with a noxious wheeze, the bus headed north for the monastery at Zagorsk. The tour guide, who spoke English with the clutzy formality of a movie spy working undercover, chirped on about the "utterly ideal" marriage of atheism and freedom of religion in the Soviet Union. "It is epitome of social and spiritual," she said obscurely, but with a smile. The passengers had neither the strength nor the inclination to press her. They all wiped little circles in their misted windows and watched Moscow go to work on a dun-colored morning. Somewhere along the Avenue of Peace, we stopped at a red light. Through the gloom, I noticed a woman in a brown tattered coat begging in a doorway. She was hunched over and kept her gaze on the sidewalk so no one would see her face. She thrust her hand into the foot traffic. There were, I could see, a few 5-kopeck coins in her palm, though judging by the way everyone streamed by her, she probably had put them there herself, as a hint. A woman in the row behind me on the bus raised her hand and asked the guide what was going on. "Unlike in London," the woman said, "doesn't the state care for the poor?"

"This is quite unusual," said the guide without looking out the window longer than she had to. "It is quite likely, in fact, that precisely the woman you see is a foreigner. Or gypsy." Enough said. The guide was rattled and we were all a bit embarrassed for her. We rode the rest of the way to the center of Russian holiness in silence.

———

Those were the last days of illusion in the Soviet Union. Under Brezhnev, Andropov, and Chernenko, the regime floated on an immense sea of oil profits. At the height of the world energy crisis and its aftermath, the state plundered its vast oil reserves in Siberia, Azerbaijan, and Kazakhstan, giving Moscow the cash it needed to fund the vast military-industrial complex. The rest of the economy was a wreck and ran on principles of magic and graft, but so long as world crude prices remained high, it hardly mattered to the Kremlin. There was still enough wealth to fill the stores with four kinds of cheese, cheap boots in wintertime, and 3-ruble vodka.

But by the time Gorbachev took power in March 1985, the oil boom had vanished. The economy of illusion was dead. The Soviet Union entered the era of high tech with none of its own and could not hope to compete. It could barely hope to survive. The state of affairs was best summarized in the chestnut "The Soviet Union makes the finest microcomputers! They are the biggest in the whole world!" Although the West was slow to notice, its great enemy of the cold war was dangerous and broke. "Upper Volta with missiles," as the *Daily Telegraph*'s Xan Smiley put it.

At first it was hard to make any sense of the poverty, to quantify it. In 1988, there were still far more articles in the press about Stalin's mental health than about homelessness, infant mortality, or malnutrition. It was as though the press were in vague agreement with Edmund Wilson's observations of Moscow a half-century ago: "One gradually comes to realize that, though the people's clothes are dreary, there is little, if any, destitution; though there are no swell parts of the city, there are no degraded parts either.

There are no shocking sights on the streets; no down-and-outers, no horrible diseases, no old people picking in garbage pails. I was never able to find anything like a slum or any quarter that even seemed dirty." But decrepitude was everywhere now. Every sign of poverty that Wilson could not, or would not, see was now general and could not be overlooked. You wandered into poverty at every corner, in every city and village.

On a winter afternoon, I drifted away from a small street demonstration outside the offices of *Moscow News* and into a run-down cafeteria on Gorky Street. I was cold and hungry, and so I bought a bowl of watery borshch and sat down at one of the communal tables.

"You want a spoon with that?"

The woman next to me was smiling, her mouth filled with steel teeth. She gave me her spoon, a flimsy thing, and filthy, too, but a spoon. She said her name was Yelena and that for the past eight years she'd been living in train stations and airports. In summer she slept in some of the more obscure parks on the perimeter of Moscow. "Sometimes I get five rubles a day scrubbing the floors on the train after they pull in to Moscow," she said. "Right now I'm broke, and everything I have is what you see—the coat and the clothes I'm wearing." Yelena said that some of her friends had been thrown out of their apartments by husbands and boyfriends and they had nowhere to go. She wrote letters appealing for help to the Communist Party at every level and never got a response.

A friend of Yelena's, a homeless man named Leonid, joined us. "I've written Mikhail Gorbachev, Andrei Gromyko, everyone," he said. "I want my right to work and live guaranteed by the Constitution of the Soviet Union."

Yelena nodded. "You know," she said, "there are thousands like us in this country. Thousands."

"To tell you the truth, I probably make more money out here collecting empty bottles for twenty kopecks apiece than I would on a construction job in town," said Vitya Karsokos, who made his living searching garbage dumps. "My biggest problem is I have to sleep in the train station or out in a dump in a box somewhere. I'd get a job in town if I could, but good luck."

For years, while state television was still broadcasting documentaries about the street people of New York as an advertisement against capitalism, the Moscow police tried in vain to keep their own homeless out of sight. But as the number of homeless grew, their efforts collapsed. Moscow *bomzhi*—the acronym for "without definite place of residence"—slept in cemeteries, railway stations, construction sites, and basements. A favorite spot was the empty top floor of Moscow high rises with their ventilation pipes and heating ducts. There were drunks, abandoned children, the mentally ill—people who had fallen into the bureaucratic abyss and no longer had any right to a place on the apartment waiting list. *Bomzhi* sometimes worked, sometimes for money, sometimes for a bottle of vodka. You'd see them afternoons helping the local liquor store unload the vodka delivery truck. They'd collect empty bottles in the park and on garbage heaps and cash them in for change. At airports and train stations, *bomzhi* helped the drivers hustle fares and then took a small cut. In Moscow they might hold a place for you in line at a store; in Central Asia they'd take on migrant work at harvest time in the cotton fields.

At the Kazan Station in Moscow a wanderer named Alik said he'd talk my ear off if I'd only buy him a bottle. I suggested we go to a store and join the vodka line. When he stopped laughing, he said, "Just give me thirty rubles." He snatched the bills from my hand and set off down the sidewalk. We walked ten feet before Alik found what he was looking for. A ghostly woman in a ratty coat reached into her pocket and the silent exchange was done. Alik quickened his pace and we headed toward a place marked CAFÉ. Three feet inside the door, he screwed off the bottle cap and downed the entire liter bottle in a few magnificent swigs. "Usually, in the morning, I like some potatoes," he said and then stormed out the door, singing.

Alik was a sawed-off man with a two-week beard. He kept a change of clothes stuffed in a ventilation duct at the station. He said he refused to work collecting empties. "Too humiliating. What am I, a dog?" he said. "I'll tell you what I do. When I need money, I take it. Like, one minute you've got your rubles, then you don't!" For his adventures in pickpocketing, Alik had spent the better part of twenty years in prison camps and exile. Whenever he was released, he returned to "the station life." He had no residence permit— "In Moscow, I'm no one"—and hospitals and drunk tanks couldn't bear him for long. He didn't make it easy. He was a nasty drunk. Sometimes he went three or four days without eating—"just 'cause I can't stomach it." He was irritable, manic. In a moment, he would turn sentimental, an autodidact who recited the poems of Pushkin and sang the songs of the great bard Vladimir Vysotsky, screaming them all in your face as if they were a curse.

"My father and mother worked morning till night just to support us kids," Alik said, sitting in a deserted courtyard. "My brother was killed in Hungary in '56. He was nineteen. Sometimes I think if he had survived I might not have started the way I did. I ran away when I was sixteen or seventeen, went off to Kazakhstan. I was going hungry, and so I lifted my first purse. That's how my prison career started. I got five years in the Tashkent camp for teenagers. I've been all over the prison zone ever since. You sit in a rank cell and get twenty minutes' exercise a day and you're hungry, lying there on the cold concrete. I started getting sick that way. We *bomzhi* stay in these places twenty-four hours a day and we're always worried we're gonna get clubbed by the cops, day and night. We have nowhere to go. I'm telling you this on behalf of the Soviet homeless, who are punished for their destinies. No rights, no residence permit, no nothing. It's tough when you get out of jail. It's like you're a third-class citizen and nobody needs your life."

At times, Alik stopped talking and began humming and singing a Vysotsky song about a man going off to jail and never seeing his beloved again. Then he'd break it off and stare out into space and take another swig on a new bottle.

"So how do I break this cycle? I just don't know. One of my buddies comes up to me the other day, yesterday maybe, and says he'll smash my face if I don't stop drinking, and I said, 'You son of a bitch, I can't stop. I can't.' I worked some in Uzbekistan, but it didn't last. Never got along with the bosses. Worked on an oil rig once, too. I've never worked a single day in Moscow. For me, three hundred rubles a month and a flat, and I'd make it all right. But I don't have it. So where should I go? You tell me."

———

To describe the Soviet Union in terms of overwhelming national poverty was, by 1989, no longer the work of fire-breathing ideologues from abroad. Even the news organs of the Communist Party took up the survey of the wreckage of everyday life. *Komsomolskaya Pravda,* the Party's youth newspaper, blamed the Soviet system, pointing out that before the 1917 revolution, Russia ranked seventh in the world in per capita consumption and was now seventy-seventh—"just after South Africa but ahead of Romania."

"If we compare the quality of life in the developed countries with our own," the paper said, "we have to admit that from the viewpoint of civilized, developed society the overwhelming majority of the population of our country lives below the poverty line."

The people themselves began to make the connection between the grimness of their circumstances and the failure of the Communist Party leadership. In the streets, "the mafia" became the muttered explanation for every shortage and inequity, and only foreigners made the mistake of thinking the term referred exclusively to the hustlers at the bottom of the criminal structure.

For a while the Kremlin ministries set the poverty line at 78 rubles a month—a level fit for dogs. But no one, not even the government itself, took the official poverty line seriously. Most officials and scholars in Moscow and in the West argued that the figure should be doubled. Even then, about 131 million out of 285 million Soviet citizens would have been registered as poor. "For decades we were striving to translate into life the idea of universal equality," economist Anatoly Deryabin wrote in the official journal *Molodoi*

Kommunist. "So what have we achieved after all these years? Only 2.3 percent of all Soviet families can be called wealthy, and about 0.7 of these have earned that income lawfully. . . . About 11.2 percent can be called middle-class or well-to-do. The rest, 86.5 percent, are simply poor. What we have is equality in poverty."

Poverty in the Soviet Union did not look like poverty in Somalia or Sudan; it did not necessarily mean bloated bellies and famine, but rather a common condition of need. The self-deception and isolation of the Soviet Union had been so complete for so long that poverty felt normal. Even so, almost no one, save the government elite, could ignore the widespread misery. "Even the 'millionaire' farm chairmen don't have hot water out here," a cotton farmer told me in the Turkmenian countryside. Or as Joseph Brodsky writes, "Money has nothing to do with it, since in a totalitarian state income brackets are of no great variety—in other words, every person is as poor as the next."

Miners in the northern region of Vorkuta did not have enough soap to wash the coal dust from their faces; mothers on the far eastern island of Sakhalin gave birth in rented rooms for lack of a maternity hospital there; Byelorussian villagers scavenged scrap metal and pig fat to pay for shoes. A few early published figures began to give some sense of the scope of the problem: the average Soviet had to work ten times longer than the average American to buy a pound of meat; the riggers in Tyumen, a Siberian oil region with greater resources than Kuwait, lived in shacks and shabby trailers despite winter temperatures of forty degrees below zero; even Party officials estimated that there were between 1.5 and 3 million homeless, more than a million unemployed in Uzbekistan alone, and a national infant mortality rate 250 percent higher than in most Western countries, about the same level as Panama.

There was also the sheer crumminess of the things that you could find: the plastic shoes, the sulfurous mineral water, the collapsible apartment buildings. The decrepitude of ordinary life irritated the soul and skin. Towels scratched after one washing, milk soured in a day, cars collapsed upon purchase. The leading cause of house fires in the Soviet Union was television sets that exploded spontaneously. All of it kept people in a constant state of frustration and misery.

Glasnost meant admitting to all this, too. Sometimes the admission came in the shape of an earnest article in the paper, sometimes with a certain flair, a Russian irony that deflated Soviet pomposity. The Exhibition of Economic Achievements, a kind of vast Stalinist Epcot Center near the Moscow television tower, had for years put on displays of Soviet triumphs in the sciences, engineering, and space in huge neo-Hellenic halls. Vera Mukhina's gigantic statue *Worker and the Collective Farm Girl* (jutting breasts and biceps, bulging eyes) presided at the entrance, providing citizens with the sense that they were now part of a socially and genetically engineered breed of muscular proletarians. But with glasnost, the directors grew humble and put up an astonishingly frank display: "The Exhibit of Poor-Quality Goods."

At the exhibit, a long line of Soviets solemnly shuffled past a dazzling display of stunning underachievement: putrid lettuce, ruptured shoes, rusted samovars, chipped stew pots, unraveled shuttlecocks, crushed cans of fish, and, the show-stopper, a bottle of mineral water with a tiny dead mouse floating inside. All the items had been purchased in neighborhood stores. "It was time to inject a little reality into the scene here," one of the guides told me. The exhibit was unsparing, a vicious redefinition of socialist realism. In the clothing section, red arrows pointed to uneven sleeves, faded colors, cracked soles. One piece of jewelry was labeled, simply, "hideous," and no one argued.

"Let me tell you a little secret," a transport worker, Aleksandr Klebko, said as we filed past the display of rotten fruit. "This isn't so bad. I've seen worse. Most stores have less than this. Or nothing at all."

ASHKHABAD

Stalinism was still lethal a quarter century after Stalin was dead. In the mud-brick hovels on the outskirts of Ashkhabad, the capital of Turkmenistan, children were the first casualties of poverty. Every year, thousands of infants throughout the republic and the rest of Soviet Central Asia died within twelve months of birth. Countless others suffered more slowly, weakened by the heat and infected water, the pesticides from the cotton fields, a diet built on bread and tea and soup. "I consider myself fairly lucky. I've given birth five times, and only one child died," said Elshe Abayeva, a woman of thirty-one who looked twenty years older. Some of her children played on a hillock of mud and garbage as she cut grass with a blunt scythe. Farther up the road, Abayeva's neighbors, the Karadiyevs, were not so lucky. "Five children are alive and three died—two at birth and one after a month," the father said. "In Turkmenia, it's like this all the time. Worse in the villages."

Inside the Abayevs' two-room hut, the bare bulbs were furred with dust, flies buzzed around the children's faces. The children were filthy, their clothes in tatters. Only heavy stones kept the tin roof from blowing off the outhouse and the rusted chicken coop. Aba Abayev, Elshe's husband, earned 170 rubles a month as a video technician for state television—less than 6 rubles a day to support a family of six. The Abayevs had been waiting since 1975 to be assigned an apartment in the city. "When that child was born, it was a cold winter morning," Aba Abayev said. "No one has phones here, and there are no hospitals or doctors around. I ran two or three kilometers to the pay phone and called. It looked like the baby was dying—or was dead already, maybe—and it took the doctors more than an hour to get here. By then the child was dead. This is the way our lives go out here. I have no hope, to be honest. And for my children, I don't think things will change, unless they get worse somehow."

In Turkmenistan, the official infant mortality rate in 1989 was 54.2 infants per 1,000 births, ten times higher than in most West European countries and more than two and a half times that of Washington, D.C., the city with the highest rate in the United States. Turkmenistan was about on a level with Cameroon. In especially poor regions, such as Tashauz in the north, the rate soared to 111 deaths in every 1,000 births. Many experts in Moscow and the West said that even these statistics understated the problem. The Central Asian republics, they said, regularly underreported their infant mortality rates by as much as 60 percent.

Children fell sick for many reasons, but mainly they suffered from the effect of the cotton "monoculture," the obsession with a cotton crop at all costs. Working in the cotton fields, the children often drank from irrigation sources poisoned with pesticides and toxic minerals. In the regions near the Aral Sea, which had been ruined and drained through a mad scheme to irrigate the cotton fields by diverting the rivers that flow into the sea, the poisons in the drinking water were so intense that children were taking them in through their mothers' breast milk. Even seeing a doctor proved dangerous at times. In the first year of their lives, Turkmenian children were given an average of two hundred to four hundred injections, compared to three to five for American children. It was nothing systematic. The doctors threw everything they had at the children. Within a few years the effect of the vaccines was close to zero.

Everything that went wrong with the Soviet system over the decades—the centralization of authority, the vacuum of responsibility and incentive, the triumph of ideology over sense, the dominance of the Party and its police— was magnified in Central Asia. The system was known as "feudal socialism," a Soviet-Asiatic hierarchy led by Communist Party bosses and collective-farm chairmen.

At the Institute of Health Care for Mothers and Children in Ashkhabad, the head pediatrician, Yuri Kirichenko, treated dozens of patients every day. Outside Kirichenko's door, Turkmenian women, many of them pregnant, paced the hall and waited hours for treatment for themselves and their children. Some of the pregnant women were in their late forties and had already had a dozen or more children. Because of the tribal legacy, there was a high rate of marriages among close cousins and other relatives. Many Turkmenian men refused birth control, and women frequently gave birth twice in one year, believing that more children would bring greater wealth— "more hands, more rubles." The state, of course, encouraged the high birth rate, figuring that could only mean a boon for the cotton crop.

Kirichenko said he was a Communist Party member of twenty-five years' standing, but he was thinking about quitting after reading about what the Party hierarchy had done to the region. "We had always been brought up to believe that our system was the best, that our lives were the best, and now we find just the opposite," he said. "This is not Africa—children are not starving to death in the same blatant way—but there is no way to hide it anymore: we are poor and we are suffering. Of course, we need to educate people on birth control and all the rest. But as a Party member—and it hurts me to say this—the truth is that poverty here is tied to politics. Ninety percent of the blame lies with the system, the bureaucracy, the command system, the centralization of control. There is no escaping that."

In Ashkhabad, government and health officials did all they could to convince me that their horrifying infant mortality rate was "temporary" and had nothing to do with politics. They were furious that I had come to write about the problem at all. I asked local officials for permission to visit several of the collective farms west of Ashkhabad. They refused most of my requests on the grounds that they were too close to the Iranian border. Finally, I was granted permission to visit Bakharden, which was also close to the border, but, evidently, not so close that I would be tempted to make a run for Teheran.

The Mir Collective Farm was a pathetic sight. A mother and her dirt-caked, vacant-eyed daughter stood by the gate. A ragged dog slept curled in the road, flies buzzing around its sores. The "office of administration" was a shed with a few ancient desks, a half-empty bookshelf, and a portrait of Lenin framed in gold. At a small hut nearby, I struck up a conversation with a young woman named Aino Balliyeva. She was twenty years old and unmarried. She picked cotton in the fields and said she knew there were dangers in the work, that she was undoubtedly taking in pesticides and defoliants that would one day hurt her children. "But what can I do about it?" she asked. "I want to have children, because that is life. And as for the rest, I just don't know what to do."

As if on cue, a police car, lights flashing, pulled up. Two uniformed police told me and my friend—a Russian photographer, Edik Gladkov—that we were in a "restricted area" and that we should "come along." At the police station, we were interrogated by a couple of officers and then by a blond

Russian official who was clearly KGB. Like a fool, I told the KGB officer that if he called the officials in Ashkhabad he would find out that I had their permission to go to Bakharden. He called, and, of course, the very same official said no such permission had been granted and, in fact, he could not recall our ever having met. Edik pointed to one of the wall posters: under a portrait of Lenin, it read, "Socialism—is control." After a few hours, we rode back to Ashkhabad, this time with a police escort.

———

I did meet a brave man in Turkmenia. His name was Mukhamed Velsapar, a young writer who had grown up in a family of eight children near the town of Mary, east of Ashkhabad. He said he never knew, until long after he was a young man and had seen the relative wealth of Moscow, that he had been raised in poverty. "And that is the mind-set of nearly all Turkmenians: 'We have bread, we have tea, we have a roof, we are alive—therefore, we are not poor,' " he said one afternoon. "These people have no basis for comparison. There are seventy-three newspapers in the republic, and not one of them has any degree of freedom."

In 1989, Velsapar, along with a few hundred other writers, journalists, and workers in Ashkhabad, organized Ogzibirlik, a democratic advocacy group with two key aims: to bring glasnost to Turkmenistan and to encourage radical economic change to end what one member called "the cycle of poverty and the colonization of our resources." Members of Ogzibirlik met with nationalist leaders in the Soviet Baltic republics for crash courses on developing a mass movement. The Ogzibirlik activists believed that the ruin of Central Asia had been the decades-old demand from economic planners in Moscow that the republics turn most of their farmland into cotton fields. The cotton monoculture, directed by Moscow planners and Central Asian overlords, brought the region everything from the tragic infant death rate to the drying up of the Aral Sea. The rulers of the Russian empire had never been as cruel. Ogzibirlik was seemingly powerless to challenge the Communist Party boss, Saparmurad Niyazov, and his well-organized apparatus. Velsapar said he was often interrogated by party officials. "They'll just blatantly say they have been listening to my phone conversations and then make some wild accusation," he said.

Velsapar did succeed, however, in stirring up the Party. His weapon was a short article in *Moscow News*. "It is hard to believe," the piece began, "but the majority of Turkmenian children in our time are permanently undernourished." The article was merely a summary of the infant mortality crisis, but for local authorities it was a humiliation. Not so much because it exposed the horrific details of infant mortality in the region—there had been other such articles in local papers—but because it appeared outside Turkmenistan in a paper read by the liberal intelligentsia and Gorbachev himself.

"It was a libel on all of us!" Geral Kurbanova, vice president of the republic's Children's Fund, shouted at me. "No one goes hungry here. The Turkmenian people love to eat! And poor? Oh, they have lots of money, cars—two cars sometimes. They could buy proper food if they wanted, but instead they buy carpets and expensive dresses." Comrade Kurbanova was a Turkmenian version of those American demagogues who go on about welfare queens who buy Cadillacs with food stamps.

What intensified the furor over Velsapar's article was the accompanying photograph of an emaciated two-year-old child named Guichgeldi Sait-muradov. The image was hellish, like something out of the worst African famines—hollow, desperate eyes, a skeleton barely alive. Several sources corroborated the boy's fate: After repeated trips to a hospital near his parents' collective farm in the Tashauz region, the child died in 1988. Before Guichgeldi's death, however, Khummet Annayev, a physician and senior researcher at the Institute for the Health of Mothers and Children, made a research trip to the region. He reported dire shortages of meat, butter, chicken, and other foodstuffs over a ten-year period, abuse of pesticides and defoliants, miserable medical facilities. And when he saw Guichgeldi in a clinic, he asked someone to take the photograph that would eventually be published in *Moscow News.*

"An aberration," said the republic's deputy health minister, Dmitri Tessler, who pronounced Velsapar an "adventurer" and Annayev "out of his depth." The republic's newspapers never reprinted Velsapar's article, but they did run countless denunciations triple its length.

———

After the Bakharden incident, the republic's foreign ministry said I ought to see what a "typical" collective farm looked like. They sent me to a farm called Soviet Turkmenistan just outside Ashkhabad. The head of the farm looked like Burl Ives playing Big Daddy in *Cat on a Hot Tin Roof.* Broad-bellied and wearing a crisp suit and a panama hat, Muratberd Sopiyev was one of the most powerful men in the republic. He had been "elected" chairman of Soviet Turkmenistan thirty years running. "We have democracy here on the farm," he told me. "Every so often I'll tell the people they can nominate an alternative candidate, but they say, 'Oh, no! Never! No need!' and that's that."

Sopiyev said the rate of infant mortality on his farm was "not so bad" as in the rest of the republic—"forty-five out of a thousand"—but that is still more than double that of Washington, D.C.. Like the rest of the Turkmenian leadership, Sopiyev saw the "triumph of Communism" as the road out of poverty.

"We have to keep fulfilling, even overfulfilling, the five-year plans," he said. "We don't need private property. Not in this country. That will only bring exploitation. No one wants it. We know that in capitalist countries they have very, very poor people. We don't have that. We provide free apartments, gas, education, medical care. We don't need a multiparty system, either. We don't need the chaos that would bring. We need the Communist Party, and we have to follow the Party line. That is the way to wealth."

With that, Sopiyev got into his car, and his driver took him to a ministry in Ashkhabad where the republic gets its instructions from Moscow.

SPASSKAYA

At the height of spring planting, Edik Gladkov and I visited the farm villages outside Vologda in northern Russia. At midday, with the sun high and the weather ideal, we drove past one field after another—all empty, all unplowed and unplanted. There were tractors and trucks leaning at crazy angles, stuck in the mud. We stopped at the gates of one of the biggest state farms in the Vologda region, the Prigorodni Sovkhoz, which allegedly grew vegetables and raised livestock.

The usual cheap irony greeted us at the entrance: a faded portrait of Lenin and a tattered banner—"We Shall Witness the Victory of Communist Labor." We drove down the long road to the farm center, its headquarters, its store, and its three-story concrete barracks. Everything looked abandoned, the fields, the road. Where had everyone gone? Certainly not into the fields. In the store, the shelves were bare of everything except some canned eggplant and pickled tomatoes.

"Most people go on the buses and buy food in Vologda," the counterman said. "Probably they're off in the city now."

And where does the food in Vologda come from? Why weren't there any vegetables in the store here?

The counterman rolled his eyes. He explained patiently, as if to idiots, the problems on the farm. The ministry still hadn't delivered seed. Wages were low, so no one wanted to work. They couldn't get spare parts for the machinery. And so on for a half hour. "So you see," he said, "there is no point."

The farmers and their families who were not in Vologda standing in grocery lines were in their concrete apartments. They all had televisions and they were all watching the same game show.

One member of the farm who showed both anger and initiative was a young man named Yuri Kamarov. He said that of the hundreds of people on the farm, he was the only one who thought the idea of giving some land back to the peasants would come to anything good. Everyone on the farm had parents and grandparents who had been jailed, starved, or deported for their dreams of ownership and prosperity. "I guess I'm the only true believer here, the only one," Kamarov said. He was twenty-seven and dreamed of raising livestock and vegetables on a plot that was now little more than a swatch of mud and rubble. Every day after work, Kamarov worked alone, building a house for his wife and daughter. The neighbors came by sometimes and laughed. Others made threatening remarks about destroying his project. Kamarov was suffering from that terrible envy born of years of serfdom under czars and general secretaries, an envy embodied in a classic Soviet joke: A farmer's cow dies, but a great spirit grants him one wish. And what is the wish? "Let my neighbor's cow drop dead, too," he says. Kamarov persisted, nonetheless. He took out a 24,000-ruble loan, which meant, he said, "I'm up to my eyeballs in debt for the rest of my life. That's the gamble. Let them laugh. Maybe they're right, and nothing will ever change," the true believer said, "but it's time I started living a real life, a life like my grandfather had long before the disasters began."

The legacy of collectivization was everywhere in the Soviet Union. In the Vologda region alone, there were more than seven thousand "ruined" villages, ghost towns of collapsing houses and untended land that had once been working farms. For decades, the young had been abandoning the wasted villages in droves, searching for a decent wage in the textile and machine-tool plants of Vologda. Like others before them, their search for the industrial utopia turned out to be fruitless. They found only miserable work in textile plants and lived in vast dormitories.

Edik and I spent a few days at one of the villages near Vologda, a row of two dozen houses called Spasskaya. Behind an abandoned church, the cemetery was filling up. Every six months or so, a workman arrived from the city, borrowed a shovel, and dug a grave. No one had been born in Spasskaya in twenty-five years. A prosperous village before the Revolution, it was now little more than a few collapsed cabins, a graveyard, and wheel ruts in the mud.

Mariya Kuznetsova, a stooped old woman with fierce, squinting eyes, spent her days tending her chicken coop and gossiping with her neighbors along the rails of a rotten pine fence. There were seventeen people left in Spasskaya. Once there had been hundreds. At seventy-five, Mariya was among the youngest. "On winter days," she said, "we check the other houses.

If there's no smoke coming out of one of the chimneys it usually means another one of us is dead."

Mariya Kuznetsova said she lived on a pension of less than 3 rubles a day. Not long ago, before new pension levels were adopted, retired farmers got a ruble a day. Kuznetsova's meals were mainly bread, milk, macaroni, cabbage soup, potatoes, and salted fat. If she needed to see a doctor or go to the store, she had to walk two miles down a road of mud and stones to catch a bus that "comes when it comes." During the winter, when temperatures hit thirty and forty degrees below zero and the snow piled up, she said, "we are prisoners."

"We listen to the radio and hear all that talk about 'Land for the Peasants' and private farming, but who's going to do the work?" she said. "Who is going to save the countryside? One generation should hand down what it knows and what it has collected to the next. But all that is broken. Everyone has long since left for the cities. The collective farms are a disaster. There's nothing left. It's all lost."

One of Kuznetsova's neighbors, Anatoly Zamokhov, leaned out the window of his cabin and cackled viciously. He spit at the sound of the word Moscow. "I'll tell you about Moscow," he said, taking an angry drag on a foul cigarette. "Before the Bolsheviks, my parents and their parents lived decently. They weren't rich—not by any means, God knows—but they had food and a cow and a table to call their own. We were all supposed to be one big family after collectivization. But everyone was pitted against everyone else, everyone suspicious of everyone else. Now look at us, a big stinking ruin. Now everyone lives for himself. No one visits anyone on Easter. What a laugh, what a big goddamn laugh."

During collectivization, people in Spasskaya told me, police crammed countless peasants into a complex of labor camps that was just north of the village. The police ripped the crosses and icons out of the churches and used the transepts and basements as holding cells. In the Vologda region, 25,000 children died in the churches over a three-month period. In a matter of a few years, an entire fabric of social relations, of village life, was in shreds. The "masters of the land" were suddenly servants of the state, stripped of their religion, their traditions, and their will.

The Bolshevik contempt for the peasant was rooted in the works of Lenin, who called them *myelki khozyaichiki*—roughly, "little landlords." Before the Revolution, Solzhenitsyn has estimated, the peasantry constituted more than 80 percent of the Slavic population. Today, many of those "little capitalists" not already in mass graves, urban bunkers, or dying villages live in the "inter-nats," state-run homes for the aged.

Not far from Spasskaya, about a hundred villagers lived at the inter-nat in the town of Priluki, near an abandoned monastery. The place was run by a well-intentioned, kind woman named Zoya Matreyeva. She and her small staff did what they could to keep the place clean, care for the sick and dying, and arrange decent burials when the time came. She had lived in the area for many years and said that the old people yearn only for the village life before the ruin began. Soviet and Western historians have described the harsh conditions, drunkenness, and bigotry of the prerevolutionary villages in such stark terms that it seems impossible for anyone to be nostalgic for them. Impossible, that is, until the surviving villagers describe what came afterward, in the early 1930s.

"We even have a few old Communist Party members here, people who worked half their lives and more on the collective farms, but you won't find one who believes in collectivization," Matreyeva said. "They talk about the cows and chickens they had, how it was theirs and they cared about it. Then it was all stripped away."

The inter-nat dining room was a dim place of buckled linoleum, fluorescent light, and Lenin's portrait. The old women, plump and toothless, peasant scarves tied around their heads, shuffled to their seats. The men ate in a separate room, and there were only a few of them—nearly all the men in the area were killed in World War II. Each place was set with a bowl of soup, a tin spoon, and two small pieces of brown bread. Zoya Matreyeva, for forty years a loyal employee of the state, had a point she wanted to prove.

"Grandmothers!" she said. "Maybe you can tell our visitor about what you remember about the old days. The old days before you were on the collective farms."

The old women stopped stirring the sour cream into their soup and looked up. "These gigantic state farms killed the villages and put nothing in their place," said one, and then they all began to chime in.

"Six of the families from our village were dragged away and we never saw them again."

"In my village, there were one hundred and twenty houses. Now there are ten, and the only people who live there now are people who use the houses on weekends to get out of the city. They garden, they don't farm."

"I had to spend my life feeding something called the state. Now at least the state feeds me."

"My grandchildren wouldn't know what to do with a piece of land. Even my own children have a hard time telling the difference between a horse and a cow. Are these the new 'masters of the land'?"

"One generation is supposed to show the next how to live. One generation is supposed to build something so the next can carry on. That was all cut off. Destroyed. Do they think you can rebuild that in a day? In five years?"

After a while, the old women quieted down. In a way they seemed happy for a moment to have a visitor ask a question or two, but as the memories rushed forth, the women grew sullen and tired, and they ate.

MAGNITOGORSK

At the height of the Depression, John Scott, a young socialist from Philadelphia, decided to quit his academic work and join in the creation of what *The Nation* was then calling "the world's most gigantic social experiment." Scott arrived in Moscow in 1932, desperate to find a future that worked. Stalin's bureaucrats promptly sent Scott, and hundreds of other young American socialists, to one of the "hero projects" of the first five-year plan, to "Magnetic Mountain," the steel town of Magnitogorsk in the Urals.

In Magnitogorsk, Scott discovered a city that was one massive construction site: workers pulling eighteen-hour shifts, families living in tents and ramshackle barracks. The vast majority of the Soviet workers at Magnitogorsk had come not out of any ideological commitment to the "shining future" of socialism, but because they were forced to. Many of them had been peasant farmers, forced off their private plots during the collectivization campaign. Scott saw priests in their cassocks digging coal with picks and wheelbarrows, workers killed by falling girders. But in his memoir of working at Magnitogorsk between 1932 and 1938, *Behind the Urals,* Scott noenetheless remembered a "city full of vitality and life. . . . Tens of thousands of people were enduring the most intense hardships in order to build blast furnaces, and many of them did it willingly, with boundless enthusiasm, which infected me from the day of my arrival."

Magnitogorsk became a legend of the war. Because it produced the steel for half of the tanks and one third of the artillery used to defeat the Nazis, people began referring to the mills as "Hitler's grave." But Magnitogorsk never stopped running on a wartime mentality. The ultimate bosses, the ministers in Moscow, measured success in sheer quantity. Never mind that other countries were beginning to produce modern steel alloys that brought the weight of a refrigerator down to a hundred pounds, not four hundred; never mind that pollution got so bad that the clouds of poison above the city decreased sunlight 40 percent. But the Lenin Steel Works, the biggest mill in the world, kept churning on in ignorant isolation. And always the command was "More steel!"

"Magnitogorsk is a classic Stalinist city," Aleksei Tuplin, a correspondent for the local paper, the *Magnitogorsk Worker,* told me. "We built an autonomous company town here that pushed away every cultural, economic, and political development in the civilized world. We existed, and still do exist, for the sake of a machine that doesn't even work." When Premier Aleksei Kosygin proposed a massive retooling project in the 1960s that would have put an end to Magnitogorsk's antiquated open-hearth mills in favor of more efficient conversion techniques used elsewhere in the world since the 1950s, Brezhnev and the rest of the leadership pronounced the project too expensive. "All they ever wanted was more steel," Dmitri Galkin, the plant director during the Brezhnev era, told me. "That's all they ever cared about."

I stayed a week in Magnitogorsk as a guest of the city coroner, Oleg Yefremov. Oleg was in his early forties, and he had a smoker's cough that plagued him without end. He did not smoke. He suffered, as did most of the citizens of Magnitogorsk, from the habit of breathing.

"I should quit inhaling," he said.

We woke early and drove to the top of a hill to get a sense of the biggest company town I'd ever seen. The Lenin Steel Works stretched seven miles along the left bank of Factory Lake. The plant was in full operation day and night, grinding out sixteen million tons of steel every year. The smokestacks never stopped pumping poison, a sickly mix of yellow, gray, green, and bluish smoke that shifted in color, depending on the light. According to a report by the local environmental protection committee, the city's industries dumped one million tons of pollution annually. "There's four hundred and thirty thousand of us, so that means more than two tons for everybody," said Yuri Zaplatkin, the committee's chairman. Satellite pictures show that the mills have produced a zone of ruined air and soil 120 miles long and 40 miles wide. In winter, the snow was crusted black; in summer, the grass grew in sad, brownish tufts.

Oleg said that at one time or another in their lives, 90 percent of the children of Magnitogorsk suffered from pollution-related illnesses: chronic bronchitis, asthma, allergies, even cancers. The local environmental protection committee reported that birth defects in Magnitogorsk doubled between 1980 and 1990. At the city morgue, Oleg surveyed the morning's corpses. A worker with collapsed lungs. A little girl dead from asthma, a weakened heart, or both.

Oleg lived on the "good side" of Magnitogorsk; the bad side being downwind from the plant, the "left bank." One of the worst neighborhoods in the city was one of the oldest, Hardware Square. The air there was especially foul and gassy; you could taste the dust on your tongue. In room after room in one of the barracks, old women stared blankly out windows, children were as filthy as any street kid in the barrios of Lima. At eight o'clock in the morning at the health clinic on Hardware Square, groups of a dozen children got ultraviolet treatments and drank their daily "oxygen cocktails," a viscous soup of fruit juice, herbs, and sugar infused with pure oxygen. Older patients came in just to take a few pulls from an oxygen tank.

Down the road at the steelworks' own pulmonary ward, one of the doctors, Natalya Popkova, said that she had seen thousands of workers and their children who came in for a few days suffering from "what the plant provides us." "The patients, all of them, become permanently angry at the mills," she said. "They know why they are sick, but what choice do they have? Where can they go?"

The apparatchiks who ran the mill and the city were masterful in the way they headed off any potential political conflicts with the work force. The mill owned everything in town, from the sewer system to the streetcars; the mill directors had an iron grip on food supplies and distribution of the goods they earned in barter deals with the West. When companies from West Germany or Japan offered televisions, washing machines, and vacuum cleaners in exchange for scrap metal, the bosses used the goods to bribe the workers. "We are a poor people," said Viktor Seroshtanov, a judge in the municipal court. "If you throw us a little piece of meat, a VCR, something, we'll be happy. In a way, the foreign companies that do business with the mill are contributing to a kind of colonial system." When the Communist Party organization in the mill sensed there might be a strike coming in 1989, they tipped off the factory bosses, who quickly sold barrels of cheap beer to the workers. When the threat of strikes disappeared, so did the beer. "What am I supposed to do about it?" a mill worker named Viktor Oyupov told me. "Should I rebel and not eat? Then what?"

The trap seemed inescapable, as inescapable as the system itself. For all the excitement in the big cities over glasnost and the new parliament, the great majority of the people in the Soviet Union felt trapped, cogs in a system that not only oppressed them, but also failed to provide a decent, minimal standard of living. "Our workers are soldiers, shock troops who serve a machine," said Oleg Valinsky, a liberal member of the Magnitogorsk city council. "They wear the shoes the factory gives them. They kill themselves working and they go home. All the spirit is drained out of them. We created a city of robots."

CHAPTER 14

THE REVOLUTION
UNDERGROUND

The life of the underworld was now rumbling around them, with deputies
continually running to and fro, trains going up and down, drawn by trotting
horses. The darkness was starred by countless lamps.

—EMILE ZOLA, *Germinal*

For the first few years of the glasnost era, *Moscow News, Ogonyok,* and the rest of the liberal press had only hinted at the connection between the seventy-year rule of the Communist Party and the disastrous state of the country. The year of miracles in Europe, 1989, began with the first opportunity for the people of the Soviet Union to make that connection for themselves. On March 26, the people would vote in multiparty elections for the new Congress of People's Deputies. Despite Aleksandr Yakovlev's advice to split the Party, to separate the progressives from the conservative majority, Gorbachev believed that by strengthening the government, by creating this new Congress, he could gradually diminish the role of the Party regulars.

In the months before the balloting, I spent many nights at election meetings and debates—in Moscow, Leningrad, the Baltic states, in provincial

Russia. The issues varied somewhat. In the Baltics, of course, the emphasis was on sovereignty, on gaining greater distance from Moscow; in the Russian provinces, the emphasis was on empty stores, ground-level economics. But everywhere the talk was of freedom, of learning democracy. Confronted for the first time by the prospect of political choice, people were both confused and exhilarated. They had no prior experience of genuine debate or choice, and yet they seized the opportunity immediately. Nowhere was that more the case than in my own precinct—Gorbachev's district—the October Region of Moscow.

On a January afternoon, after the first shift had let out, the bureaucrats and workers of the Red Proletariat machine-tools factory filed into their auditorium and saw their boss and director, Yuri Ivanovich Kirillov, waiting onstage to greet them. For once, Kirillov was all smiles, saccharine and ingratiating. He looked like a game-show host in a bad suit. With his seigneurial handshakes and shoulders-back posture, he showed every sign of expecting the 325 "electors" for the six thousand workers to fall into place, to rise as one and nominate him as their candidate for the March 1989 elections.

The workers stashed their heavy wool coats under their chairs, settled down, and quickly chose a secretary and a chairman. Then the chairman called a factory foreman named Nikolai Blinkov to the rostrum. Blinkov read a long, formal speech, talking of the "grave responsibilities" of political reform. "There were so many mistakes in nominating candidates in the past," he said. "This is why we are so nervous now." Then, "without further ado," Blinkov proposed the nomination of Yuri Ivanovich Kirillov. Surrounded by his deputies in the first row, Kirillov crossed his legs suavely and smiled, the master of all he surveyed. The election meeting was going splendidly, just as he had planned it. The birth of democracy was going to be wonderful.

"This man," Blinkov said, pointing to Kirillov, "this man is a simple Soviet worker. He is not spoiled by applause." Blinkov praised Kirillov's "magnificent" two years as factory director, his "extraordinary facility with problem-solving," his "superlative" relations with the workers, his "uncanny" ability to remember everyone's name. The applause was furious in the front rows near Kirillov, and softened out in the rear.

Then someone on the aisle rose and asked Blinkov the first impertinent question of the afternoon.

"Are there any other candidates proposed?"

There followed a moment of tense silence. Clearly, this question was not part of the script. Blinkov blinked, then scanned the first row, a rabbity panic in his eyes. But the denizens of the first row could not help him, Kirillov least of all. They had not anticipated the messiness of democracy any more than Blinkov had.

Blinkov conceded the obvious. "On my way over here," he said, "I was told that in all the work collectives there were no other names suggested."

The chairman edged Blinkov away from the podium and called on a succession of Red Proletariat employees to sing the praises of Yuri Ivanovich. "From the day he walked in the door, our director was already a well-formed organizer," said a worker named Sergei Khudyakov. "And thanks to him, our factory has a resort home for the workers in the Crimea." A Komsomol leader pledged the "fealty of our youth to Yuri Ivanovich." A foreman described the director's "generosity of spirit" and "high intelligence."

And so it went. For nearly an hour, the meeting seemed like a grass-roots version of Brezhnev's Central Committee circa 1978, a mix of oleaginous praise and muggy boredom. Through it all, Kirillov relaxed in his seat and smiled his kingly smile.

But in the transitional moment between the last speech and what would have been the call for a voice vote of acclamation, all hell broke loose. A balding engineer named Viktor Oskin asked for the floor.

"You are not on the schedule," the chairman scolded him.

But after some catcalls and shouted comments about "learning democracy," Oskin got the microphone.

"I've just got one question," he said. "Yuri Ivanovich already has so many duties. When will he find the time to work as a deputy in the legislature?"

No one could quite believe this display of impudence.

"Get off the stage!" one person shouted.

"Who asked you to speak? Get off!"

"Away with him!"

But Oskin was unafraid. He dipped his face closer to the mike and shouted over the noise.

"You all say Yuri Ivanovich is such a good man," he said. "You act as if there are no problems at all in our factory. This man has too many duties. He should refuse some. They've been telling us all along that we should have two or three candidates, and once again we've only got one. We are supposed to be talking about democracy, but we only have one candidate."

There was some hissing and booing, but just as many workers in the audience were quiet or nodding slightly, as if in agreement. Something had happened; there had been a breakthrough. Oskin plopped down in his chair, and his friends around him eyed him nervously.

Now a younger man asked for the chance to speak. He said his name was Konstantin Yasovsky and he represented a work collective. "Our collective doesn't want to approve this man Yuri Ivanovich!" he said.

Yuri Ivanovich, for his part, was now squirming in his seat in the front row like a man with the bends.

Yasovsky went on: "We don't know his program or what he'll do. What is he for? What is he against? Our opinion is that we need him as a factory director, but only that."

The boos rolled over Yasovsky like a wave, and the undertow of hostility brought him sliding back to his seat. But then there were some cheers, here and there. Then catcalls, and arguments in patches of the crowd. The meeting had gotten distinctly out of hand. With a nod from one of the assistant directors in the front row, the chairman snatched the microphone off its stand and said, "Well, I guess it's time for a vote."

But by now there were enough voters in the hall who knew something was wrong. The present seemed too much like the past. This time they would not be deceived. They would not be fooled or ignored. There were insults from every direction. Of course, no one had any illusions. There would be no alternative candidates, no rebellions, certainly. But there was at least a feeling, an insistence, that the appearance of democracy had to be served.

"A vote?" one man shouted from the back of the hall. "All our lives we've been raising our hands. Let the man tell us who he is and what he stands for before he gets our vote."

And so, finally, Yuri Ivanovich Kirillov spoke. This was his magnificent concession to the democratic process. He said he didn't mind the criticism, "though it wasn't very pleasant to sit through it." He made no mention of a platform in his long, rambling speech. His only idea for reform at the national level was his "firm intention to build a recreation center for the workers of the Red Proletariat machine-tools factory."

The applause was polite. The chairman got his way, and there was, at last, a vote: 308 for Kirillov, 10 against, and 7 abstentions. The hands went up slowly, more in concession than affirmation. After all, what choice did they have? No one was prepared to rebel. The idea did not yet exist. At least not here, and not yet. The catcalls, the insistence on hearing the candidate, had been rebellion enough. The electors filed out of the auditorium in silence, guilty and downcast, as if they knew they had not gotten things right and did not yet know what it was they had to do.

———

The Communist Party, of course, wrote the election laws for the 1989 elections to ensure that it would have the vast majority of seats, and that is the way it turned out. More than 80 percent of the 2,250 deputies were Party members, the vast majority of them local secretaries, military officers, and other loyalists. The reason was simple. Every imaginable Party front group, from the Komsomol to the Union of Stamp Collectors, was guaranteed a raft of seats. Only one third of the deputies would come from open races. In conservative regions, especially Central Asia, single-candidate races were the rule, not the exception. "This was not a democratic election," Sakharov told me. "It was rigged quasi-democracy. The only oases of democracy were where the system was somehow imperfect." In those few spots where the elections were imperfect—meaning open—the establishment Party candidates invariably lost. Central Committee members, admirals, generals, apparatchiks of every sort suffered the humiliation of public rejection.

Such was the case in the October Region when Comrade Kirillov was one of a half-dozen apparatchiks who didn't even come close. The runoff came down to a popular, and not very intelligent, television commentator and Ilya Zaslavsky, a textiles engineer, not quite thirty years old, who walked on canes and spoke in a barely audible mumble. Zaslavsky, running on a platform of general reform with an emphasis on the rights of the disabled, won easily.

When the Congress opened in May, Zaslavsky was one of dozens of young liberals who had gotten into politics only because they had finally seen a leader they thought they could trust. Zaslavsky, Arkady Murashev, and Sergei Stankevich of Moscow, nationalists from the Baltic states, Armenia, and Georgia, environmentalists from Ukraine, Byelorussia, and Siberia—they all had seen the elections as an opening. That period just before and after the first Congress was a time of euphoria. These were days when radical democrats thought that reform of the Party was not only possible, but the only route to change. Somehow the chance of a reactionary counterrevolution seemed academic, remote.

That first session of the Congress was an endless series of astonishments. In the opening minutes of the Congress, Sakharov ambled to the podium to make the first speech. Later on, Sakharov would make specific proposals about the creation of a multiparty system and a "decree on power" that would lead to constitutional democracy, but now he kept his remarks general, trying, it seemed, to serve simply as a model of patience and openness. But the Congress quickly became something hotter, as if the crises of seventy years could wait no more; what followed was an explosion of public debate and revelation. A former Olympic weightlifter, Yuri Vlasov, blasted the KGB, saying that the secret police ran an "underground empire" in the Soviet Union and had not reformed at all. A law professor from Leningrad, Anatoly Sobchak, attacked the generals and Party officials who had sanctioned and led the assault in Tbilisi against a peaceful demonstration in April 1989 which left at least nineteen people dead. Yuri Karyakin, the Dostoevsky scholar, called for the removal of Lenin's remains from the mausoleum on

Red Square and for their "decent burial." The liberals in the Congress also were beginning to make clear they would criticize Gorbachev, even oppose him, when they thought it necessary. When Gorbachev was put up for election by the Congress as chairman of the legislature, an obscure and slightly woolly delegate from northern Russia, Aleksandr Obolensky, nominated himself. "It's not a question of winning," he said. "It's a matter of creating a tradition of political opposition and competition."

The action in the hallways during the frequent recesses was almost as dramatic as the speeches inside. At first, the young Soviet reporters watched with amazement as the Westerners walked up to the most powerful men in the country and pestered them with cameras, tape recorders, and notebooks. Within a few days, the Soviets were getting the hang of it. For the first time in their careers, members of the Politburo and leaders of the military and the KGB were subjected to embarrassing questions. For decades, no one had dared ask them about the weather, much less the erosion of the Communist Party. Now they were being chased to the bathrooms and the buffet tables for their opinions, for accountings of themselves.

Gorbachev quickly mastered the art of spin control. Accidentally on purpose, he would wander into a huge crowd of journalists just after the lunch breaks, make his case, and disappear. *Vremya,* of course, would run his comments in full, giving him the role as both chairman and media commentator over his political creation.

Sakharov, for his part, endured interviews with a wistful patience. The camera lights, he must have understood, were part of modern democracy. Everyone talked, and talked. Or almost everyone. Day after day I stalked Viktor Chebrikov, the head of the KGB until 1988, a man with a gnarled face and the posture of a Roman emperor. As he paced the halls, very few deputies dared approach him. Those who did say hello were grasped by the elbow and taken off to a private corner. Chebrikov would not talk where other deputies or foreigners could overhear him. I kept after Chebrikov, and at first he shooed me away as if I were a small cloud of gnats. When I would not go away, he said, "We'll talk tomorrow." Or "after the next break." Finally, toward the end of the session, he said, "Mr. Remnick, there will be no interview." Strange, but I had never told him my name.

No one in the country could tear himself away from these televised sessions of the Congress of People's Deputies. No newspaper, no film, book, or play had ever had such an immediate political effect on the people of the Soviet Union. The sessions were broadcast live for two weeks, and factories and collective farms reported that no work was getting done. Everyone was gathered around television sets and transistor radios. People simply could not believe what they were hearing. Though the reform-minded deputies were in a distinct minority—no more than three or four hundred out of 2,250—they were much more savvy about getting to the microphone, and Gorbachev was usually eager to hear from them. It was only when someone went beyond the barriers of the official conception of perestroika—most famously, Sakharov's demand for a repeal of the Party's hold on power—did Gorbachev grow impatient and call for the next speaker. Gorbachev ruled his Congress with the swiftness and guile of Sam Rayburn in his House of Representatives. When Sakharov's criticism exceeded Gorbachev's tolerance, he dropped all pretense of democracy; he switched off the microphone and sent Andrei Dmitriyevich to his seat.

The reformers were overcome with a sense of triumph and possibility. While the session was on they had seen the Chinese leadership order the slaughter of hundreds of peaceful demonstrators in Beijing, and they had the sense that for once, the leader of the Soviet Union was not the same sort of butcher. Vitaly Korotich, the sly editor of *Ogonyok,* walked with me toward the Kremlin gates talking of how the conservatives were in for a "crash," how the country had changed in just two weeks. "The people in this country have always been afraid of power," Korotich said. "Now, maybe, the powerful are becoming a little afraid of the people." By the end of the session, the conservatives in the Politburo were impossible to find. They were finally embarrassed and tired of all the criticism and challenges. They made liberal use of their private, guarded entrances and exits and were rarely seen on the way from the Hall of Congresses to their waiting limousines.

But for all the exhilaration of the elections and the catharsis of the Congress, no one had any idea what it would lead to. From start to finish, the Gorbachev era was an improvisation, with alternating dull spots and high-wire periods. Until now, the politics of the country had gone unseen. Politics had been a matter of the Kremlin, the closed, untelevised sessions of the Politburo and Central Committee. The gulf between the state and the individual was unbridgeable. Even the huge street demonstrations in Yerevan and the Baltics went nearly unreported in the main Party newspapers.

But now almost everyone had seen the accumulated anguish of seventy years broadcast live. They had become familiar with the ideas and personalities not only of the country's leaders, but of Sakharov, Zaslavsky, and Afanasyev of Moscow. They had seen a bookish Estonian woman, Marju Lauristan, challenge Gorbachev's authority as if it were almost . . . normal. They had even seen a half-articulate cabdriver named Leonid Sukhov take the podium and warn Gorbachev that, "like Napoleon," he was being led by the nose by his own "Josephine," his wife, Raisa. Another deputy demanded that Gorbachev answer for his new expensive dacha on the Crimean coast. Until now, Kremlin power had run on mystery as well as might. The Congress had ended all that in one two-week-long television extravaganza. The Congress hinted at something new, a revolution from below. But what form would it take? Who would lead it, and when?

———

Little more than a month after the Congress closed and Moscow shifted into its mode of summer torpor, perestroika spun out of control, first in the coal mines of Siberia, then in mines all across the country, from Ukraine to Vorkuta to Sakhalin Island. After July 1989, the Kremlin could never again have any confidence at all that it was the master of events. After July 1989, the illusion of a gradual, Gorbachev-directed "revolution from above" was over.

The "revolution from below" began when a group of coal miners in the Siberian town of Mezhdurechensk walked off the job at the Shovikovo mine, led by their shift leader, Valery Kokorin. The main issue was soap. The miners were angry, too, that their equipment was pitiful, that the work was wretched and underpaid, that food supplies were meager and benefits nonexistent. But what galled them most was the grit in every crevice of their bodies, the inability to come home from work and wash themselves clean. There was no soap.

All around the Kuznetsk Basin (the Kuzbass) of Siberia—in Mezhdurechensk, Prokopievsk, Novo-Kuznetsk, and Kemerovo—miners had been grumbling for years among themselves. They had never dared take their protests outside a small circle of friends and family. Their poverty—like the poverty of the farmhands in Turkmenia or the steelworkers of Magnitogorsk—was, simply, the way things were. But within twelve hours of the walkout in Mezhdurechensk, nearly every mine in the Kuzbass was on strike. "You cannot imagine how off-the-cuff this was. It became so enormous so quickly, but it started from almost nothing," one of the miners at the Severovo mines, Ilya Ostanin, told me. Soon the strike spread to Vorkuta in the far north, to the Don Basin (the Donbass) in Ukraine, to Karaganda in northern Kazakhstan, to Sakhalin in the far east.

Gorbachev went on television looking stricken and exhausted, but still pretending to complete mastery. He had no choice but to try to make the strikes his own, to describe them as a healthy manifestation of a very young democracy and then pray they would end before the railway workers, collective farmers, or oil riggers got any ideas in their heads. He could not control an entire nation in rebellion. Even the conservatives in the leadership could not ignore the miners. The miners had the ability to shut down heavy industry and force the Kremlin to contemplate what a long, cold winter could mean.

After a five-hour flight and a half-hour ride through the Siberian taiga to the city of Kemerovo, I got my first glimpse of the working-class rebellion. In Armenia I had seen hundreds of thousands of demonstrators on the streets and almost as many in Lithuania, Estonia, and Latvia. But there had never been anything quite so dramatic as this, nothing that had so vividly illustrated the disintegration of the workers' state and the changing mind of a broad sector of the people.

In a hard afternoon sun, miners dressed in their work gear, tens of thousands of them, sat in the main square of Kemerovo outside the headquarters of the local government and Communist Party. "Get Up and Show Your Anger!" one sign read. "The Kuzbass Is Not a Colony!" said another. When some of the local Party officials took the microphone to tell the miners that the strikes were hurting old people and schoolchildren, they were shouted down and booed off the podium. The local Party press denounced the strikes, but one local television host, Viktor Kolpakov of *Kuzbass, Day by Day,* read straight, informative reports on the strikes around the country every night at eight.

The Siberian miners had an instinctive sense of media and imagery. They made for great television, and they knew it. Though they were not working, they came to the meetings dressed as "miners," smeared with coal dust, wearing their helmets and gritty work clothes and boots. At dusk, they created an even more spectacular image when they turned on their Davy lamps. It seemed as if tens of thousands of huge fireflies had invaded the square and gone into a frenzy. The speakers, of course, took their turns under the feet of the city's biggest statue of Lenin. The irony was lost on no one.

At first, only a few strike committees called for a Solidarity-style union. The initial demands were economic: more soap, detergent, toothpaste, sausage, shoes, and underwear, more sugar, tea, and bread. Vacations and a regular work week were at stake, not Gorbachev. He still represented, for the miners, a shining possibility, a figure of integrity. Almost everyone was careful to praise him, or at least show a measure of respect. One of the speakers, Pyotr Kongurov, a member of the strike committee in Prokopievsk, said that while ecological conditions and the standard of living remain "a focus of despair" in the mining town, "people are not blaming Gorbachev. They know they are able to strike because of Gorbachev. But on the other hand, they are waiting—and we can't wait forever."

There had been strikes before in the Soviet Union: bus drivers in the city of Chekhov, airline pilots who refused to fly until safety standards were improved. But the symbolism of the miners' strike was extraordinary. The miners embodied the vanguard of the proletariat, a bastion of Bolshevism in the old days. To look out at the great crowd of them in Lenin Square was to see a kind of poster for what had once been called "the masses." And now the masses were walking off the job and declaring that socialism had not delivered anything—not even a bar of soap.

———

Soon the word came to Siberia from Moscow that the Coal Ministry was ready to promise more supplies, higher salaries, and other benefits. At a huge public meeting in the Kemerovo city square, the miners gathered to hear the details and vote. They heard promises from Moscow's emissaries that planes would soon land loaded to the ribs with soap, meat, lard, cooking oil, and detergent. Salaries would be increased, vacations lengthened. Most of the miners were relieved. At least for now they had reached the limit of their daring and were ready to go back to work. They were ready to believe Moscow. Some miners warned that the deal would fall apart, that Moscow was "up to its old tricks," but when it came time for the vote, nearly everyone agreed to end the strike. Tens of thousands of hands shot into the air to vote yes, to accept the deal.

That night, workers arrived at the Yagunovsko mines for their first shift. They seemed happy to be back, but wary, as if they were already losing conviction in their decision to return. "I'm down in these mines for thirty-nine years, and I'll walk out again without any hesitation if Moscow tries to go behind our backs," said a tunneler named Leonid Kalnikov. "I believed in Communism, once our great dream, and now I believe in the power of our strike. We're not very experienced with this, but we are ready to learn." Kostya Doyagin, who had worked in the mines near Kemerovo for seven years, said that with the thirty-five-point settlement worked out between the Kremlin and the local strike committees, "we've won a small victory. But it's still small. We have to wait and see if they deliver." The miners did not get much done that night. Mostly they stood around in the offices and down in the shafts talking through what had happened in the days before.

Even in the beautiful summer weather, the villages near the Yagunovsko mines were dismal places, more miserable than anything I had seen in West Virginia or the north of England. The miners and their families lived either in tiny wooden houses, shacks with a tin chimney, or, more often, two- and three-story apartment flats known as barracks. Families were packed into these dwellings, and somehow they could not keep them clean. No one took the garbage away. There was no hot water. Indoor plumbing was rare; in winter, that meant a trip to the outhouse in temperatures forty degrees below zero. Men confided that they and their wives were humiliated that they had to make love in rooms while their children were sleeping, or pretending to sleep. They had not been able to buy contraceptives of any kind for months.

"The abortionist is the busiest man outside the mine," one woman told me. The children in the villages seemed to have no toys and wandered through the streets, playing army, hurling sticks and stones. They were filthy and their teeth were already yellowing. Their parents' teeth were rotten, and the lucky ones had caps made of brilliant silver or gold. They all looked older than they were. Men in their fifties who had just gone on pension were hunched over and sinewy from crawling through the mines and swinging a shovel since they were fifteen. They wore greasy jackets and caps. When you shook their hands, they felt like a fighter's hands, rough and pillowy, swollen from too much work. Their eyes were vacant and filmed with rheum. The women, at least the ones who worked above ground, seemed to have more spirit in them, but not much. They were women who, after a certain age, had seen their husbands fall sick or break down and die.

It was a miserable life. Near the mines, I saw a ten-year-old runaway begging for coins. There were ration coupons for cooking oil, butter, vodka, meat, macaroni, and fat. There were coupons, but not always the products themselves. The main grocery store near the Yagunovsko mines had nothing but canned tomatoes, oatmeal, and rotting cabbages. People didn't go hungry, but they did not have enough. Many people told me they got by mostly on bread and macaroni. Sausage was a twice-monthly treat. One morning my cabdriver swerved crazily, nearly plowing into a tree. He pulled over to the side of the road. He was disoriented and knew it. He apologized, saying, "I haven't eaten much in a while."

The drugstores were empty unless you counted the bottles of leeches and the jars of aspirin. An old woman named Irina Shatokhina, who worked twenty years underground as a ventilator specialist, told me that one of her friends had had a mild stroke and could not get the medicine he needed. "Because of that," she said, "he is now a vegetable."

If there were pleasures in the life of the miners beyond those of good talk and family, I did not see them. The most obvious pleasure killed them: in the morning, retired miners lined up at a vodka truck, and seconds after they'd made their score, they drained the bottles. When they could not get the real thing, they made moonshine out of everything from hair tonic to canned peas. I saw one drunk lying in the street drinking water out of a puddle.

Everywhere, the air was thick with gas. Around the mines, the leaves on the trees were filmed with a gray dust. One pond in Kemerovo was so thoroughly contaminated with toxic waste that municipal workers got rid of dead stray dogs by throwing them in the water. After a few days, even the bones disintegrated.

The mines themselves pretended to be offices. Blocking the view of the elevators and the open pits, there was invariably a brick office building where the engineers and administrators had their cubicles and the workers had their lockers and showers. There was the illusion of "going to work" instead of plunging straight down to hell.

I met a few men outside the headquarters of the Yagunovsko mines one afternoon and asked where I could find the director. I wanted permission to go down the coal shaft.

"Why do you want to bother with the director?" one of them said. "He'll just tell you a lot of shit and send you on your way. Come with us."

The miners took me inside to the locker room. I stripped to my underwear and T-shirt and they gave me a full set of gear. Without a moment's condescension or mockery, they showed me how to wrap my feet in long white bandages and pull on black rubber boots. The miners' suits were made of heavy, fireproof cloth, a thick canvas, and felt strangely light; there were thick rubber gloves that made your hands sweat, a plastic helmet, an emergency oxygen supply, and an extra flashlight. The miners flipped on their suits easily; they had spent most of their waking hours dressed like this and underground since their mid-teens.

We walked clunkily down a set of stairs and outside to the elevators for mine No. 6. The iron door slammed shut, and, packed shoulder to shoulder, we began our descent a quarter mile into the Siberian earth. Thirty miners dressed in greasy coveralls stared at their boots, then at the dents in the ceiling. Irritable, still half asleep, they shuffled and fidgeted. It took a while to get to where the coal was. Their helmet lamps darted nervously in the dark. There was no talk, only coughing and a few long yawns. The elevator went down and down, and my ears ached, then popped. The iron walls rattled against the shaft. Finally, we hit bottom and the door opened onto a labyrinth of dark halls of stone. A blast of cool air from the ventilators hit us in the face. It was the freshest air I had smelled since arriving in Siberia.

"Sometimes this town stinks so bad that the air down here is better than the air up there," said Leonid Kalnikov. Even before the day's mining had begun, his face was black, and I supposed mine was, too. As we walked through a long tunnel, Kalnikov said he was sixty years old and kept working because his family could not survive on his pension. There was no other way for him. He had no illusions; "I'll probably drop dead down here one of these days," he said, without self-pity. Forty years before, he had been a young, muscular man and had helped build this shaft, digging through the stone and putting up steel struts. "Now almost all the coal is gone," he said. "It's got some years left, but it's just about dead. I'm not so eager to stick around for the last lump. But I may have no choice."

During the strike, the mine had been neglected. The labyrinth of alleys and tunnels and chutes had filled with water, which made the walking all the harder. As we made our way down the main shaft we began to stumble along through water a foot deep. The bottom was like the muck at the bottom of a pond, and after a few minutes my boots were filled with bits of coal, sharp-edged chunks that began to slice my ankles and blister the soles of my feet. Not one of the miners said a word about it. Along the way, we passed men, many of them in their fifties and sixties, tucked into crevices and cracks only a couple of feet high. They lay on their backs, or in some other contorted position, chipping at the coal face or repairing some part of the support structure. When they opened their mouths, coal dust would fall in. The men who had been working for an hour or more were completely black, and all you could see in the half-dark was their flashlights, their eyes, and their teeth. I glanced into one corner and saw three miners, black figures in shadow-light, and they did not move or speak. They were on their ten-minute break.

After a long walk—how far I could not tell—we reached a tiny railcar, a steel contraption that rides on tracks through the mine shafts. The "metro" took us another four miles farther along the mine, rumbling and rattling along like the Seventh Avenue local in New York. "It's about the last chance you get to relax all day," one of the workers said as he slumped in his seat and caught a nap. He slept soundly and then woke with a start when the brakeman put an end to the reverie.

Once the work began there could be no relaxing. To relax, to let attention drift, could mean a horrendous accident, an explosion or a collapse. The miners lived with this fear all the time. Each year a few men died at every mine in "minor" accidents, the sort that are never reported in the news, the undramatic kind. It was November when the mine last blew up. Vladimir Gaponyuk, who put in twenty-four years "underground," told me he remembered the strange muffled sound of it. "It was close to silence, but you knew exactly what had happened." Someone broke a safety rule, then a stream of methane caught a spark, and, in the end, four miners were crushed to death. "We've got accidents like that all the time," Gaponyuk said. "We lose a couple every year." Outside the mine shaft there were two posters: "Hail to the Work of the Twenty-seventh Party Congress" and "We Need Your Hard Work, But What We Need Most Is You Alive."

Valentina Alisovna, a member of the mine's Party committee, was one of my guides. She watched me listen and take down the long, numbing litany of complaints: the horrible work conditions, the danger, the disgust with a life that goes nowhere. Party leader or not, she seemed ashamed, and at one point her eyes filled with tears. "We live like pigs, I'm sorry to say it, but it's true," she said. "The mine is a century behind the times. When we go home we can't count on electricity. The water goes out on us. I'm no capitalist, but it's obvious this system has done nothing for us." All the miners were listening and nodding. Alisovna's comment hung in the dank air. I had thought this had not been a political strike. That is what I had been told. No one said anything, and we got down on our knees and crawled through another tunnel. The ventilator wind whistled across the stone.

———

In the afternoon, while more teams of miners tried to clear the shafts of water and sludge and to get production moving once more, the Yagunovsko strike committee met in a wooden shack where the Communist Party committee had its offices. Across the country, the strike committees had become the center of political power at the mines. The Party and the official unions were doomed. Six men and Valentina Alisovna sat down to a table, the inevitable portrait of Lenin staring down over them. A poster on the wall read: "The Party is the mind, honor, and conscience of our epoch." Everyone was anxious. They had some sense that all of the Soviet Union, and all of the world, had seen the images from the mines of Siberia, Ukraine, and beyond, but the strike committee had no idea of what would come next. There was no pleasure in their voices, only the suspicion that they were about to be betrayed, the conviction that there were more strikes, more trouble ahead.

"Look, it's a long time before we have any real money in our pockets from this strike," one of them said. "We have to watch out."

The talk bounced around the room, picking up speed and fury all the time.

"No one's paying any attention to the fact that this mine is the worst around the Kemerovo region. It's exhausted. There are two villages to feed, and we're going to be out of coal in a few years. Some of the mines have no coal left in them at all."

"We've got to talk about redundant work. Sixty percent of us are working, and forty percent are standing around 'supervising' or smoking cigarettes upstairs."

"Not true. People are breaking their backs down there."

"We need a united front. Obviously, our union is nothing. And we can't stand alone, we're just one little committee. We miners have to unite, form a real union or something."

"The Politburo can't do everything for us. Perestroika has to move faster. Maybe we need new tires."

"It's time to get rid of the bosses. We don't need them."

"We have to answer two simple questions: 'How are we going to live?' and 'What do we do now?' "

The meeting lasted an hour.

———

Afterward, I walked with the shift leader of mine No. 6, Anatoly Shcheglov, a huge man with a broad smile and mouth filled with gold teeth. The day had begun for him at five forty-five in the morning. He woke in his izba, a small log cabin two miles from the mine, and took a look at the *Kuzbass,* the morning paper, for more news about the mines still out on strike. His address was 2 Second Plan Avenue. In the summer, Shcheglov said, it was easier to get out of bed. The sun was already high. "At least you can walk outside without snow up to the waist in the dark," he said.

Now the kitchen garden outside his door was rich, green with basil and cucumbers. Shcheglov said he ate a lot of cucumbers, "raw or pickled, there's not much else." He opened his refrigerator, a squat primitive thing that buzzed, and searched it for something for dinner. It was filled with food that he was lucky to have: a grayish roll of sausage, a few eggs, a cabbage, a cut of pork that was no less than three-quarters fat, a half-bottle of vodka. Lucky, because the stores were nearly empty. Nearby, at Fruit and Vegetable Store No. 6, known as the best in town, Anatoly went looking for something more to eat. The groceries available were these: half-brown cabbages, rotten tomatoes, cans of tomato juice and sardines, salt, and jars of pickled cabbage. And at the state "products" store off Johann Sebastian Bach Street there were more half-brown cabbages, more rotten tomatoes, smelts, five wan chickens, bins of white bread, and sacks of dried corn. To do better, they say here, you need *blat,* or connections. The only way to do better was to make a deal, to trade a bottle of home brew for a bag of decent carrots, an auto part for a cut of meat.

"The only other way is to buy from the private market," Anatoly said, "and the prices there are impossible for anyone but a Party big shot, the guys who have the dachas down the road."

About a half mile from Shcheglov's place was a prison camp: Prison 1648-043. Every day the convicts—thieves, rapists, murderers—were shuttled in railway cars between their cells and the "zone," the work camp. People in town despised the prison, mainly because when the convicts were released, they said, they took jobs at the mines and the factories nearby, and many of them went back into crime. "But I'm not so sure it's a bad thing," Shcheglov said. "We have three guys down in our mine who were prisoners there. One of them stabbed his wife in the stomach. Another beat someone over the head. I think he killed him. And another guy's wife was involved in some sort of scandal, and so he beat her to death. But they served their time. They work all right."

During the Stalin years, Shcheglov's father was thrown in a labor camp for ten years for no crime at all. Anatoly remembered the day Stalin died, and how everyone around, even those with parents and friends in the camps, wept as if the world were lost. "It was March 1953," he said. "I was a Young Pioneer, and we always wore those orange scarves. They gave us black ones to wear. And when the teachers started crying, we cried, too. Children always imitate the emotions of their parents."

Shcheglov was no radical. He heard the news that the miners in Vorkuta in northern Russia were still on strike and demanding an end to the Party's constitutional hold on power. "I'm not sure that's right," he said. He was a trusting man who spoke with only the slightest bit of irony when I asked him about the effect the dust had on him after working in the pits for so long. "My lungs?" he said, taking a long drag on a cigarette butt. "The doctors always tell us our lungs are fine. They give us a checkup every year. And why shouldn't I trust the doctors? If you can't trust them, who can you trust?"

For years, his dream had been simple: finish working at fifty or so, take his pension, and move outside of town to the taiga, the vast Siberian forest. What he wanted from the strike, he said, was just the chance to live "decently," to have a cake of soap or toothpaste when he needed, to eat a cut of meat worthy of the word, to wear a pair of shoes that could last six months, and to have the chance to earn a profit if, by some miracle, his work brigade could squeeze some extra coal out of mine No. 6. And then, when it was time, he'd move out to the forest, where the fishing was good, the air was clear, and life was lived above ground. "I'm used to the dark," he said. "But enough is enough."

———

The Siberian miners had no single leader, no Lech Walesa. The unions were a farce. They did not protect the workingman so much as they ensured his passivity and obedience to the Party. That had been Lenin's design. Lenin declared Western-style labor unions "narrow-minded, selfish, case-hardened, covetous, petty bourgeois." The unions under socialism, he said, would be "conveyor belts" of the Party. One of the first thing the miners did during the strike was to box out the union leaders and set up strike committees. Taking their cue from the miners, all kinds of laborers set up "workers' clubs" in the Baltics, Byelorussia, and Ukraine, and in Russian rust-belt cities like Magnitogorsk, Sverdlovsk, and Chelyabinsk.

But there was no Walesa. Probably, Walesa had been a particularly Polish phenomenon, a figure able somehow to unite workers, Catholic clergy, and urban intellectuals. Anatoly Malikhin was as close as it came to a Walesa in the Soviet miners movement, but because of the vastness of the country, his influence was mainly in western Siberia.

Malikhin was an eloquent tunneler from Novo-Kuznetsk. He had the muscular, squashed-down, weary look of a man who had played fullback for one year too many. He was in his early thirties and looked ten years older. All that was left of his hair was a kind of monk's tonsure. Malikhin said he was a "congenital enemy of the people," a bitter joke. His grandfather, a Cossack, was arrested in the purges of 1937, and his father, as a child of an "enemy of the people," was deported to Siberia. Malikhin's mother, a Ukrainian, was also a political deportee.

For years, he said, he had led the same "unconscious existence" his father had, that everyone around him did. There was never any thought of protest, much less mutiny. Miners were serfs in a patrimonial system in which the lord was the Communist Party and its instruments were the schools, the trade unions, the mine directors. "Our system and our propaganda didn't allow people to grow as individuals, to ask questions. We were raised to be uninterested," Malikhin told me. "We had no idea how the state was run. We went to elections having no idea what they were about. They told us, 'You are a small man, a punk, and why should you care? You just do what your boss tells you.' The principle was this: 'I am the boss and you are an idiot.' If you tried to argue, even slightly, you were immediately thrown to work in the worst spots. You were crushed, humiliated. We are still dogs with three different kinds of collars: green, yellow, and red. They are the colors of the passes to the mine, and they can be changed or taken away for the slightest violation. Everyone violates the rules sometimes—that is the only way you can work with the equipment we have—so if they don't like you, they seize on that and you'll never work again. People who tried to preserve their dignity were crushed and thrown away.

"This is not a life for human beings. We have no time for leisure. We have no decent clothes. We spend our entire lives making just enough to feed ourselves and our children. The shift starts at six A.M., so you have to be up at four-thirty. You go to the mine, work eight hours underground, and all your life is work. When you come home you are too exhausted to do anything but collapse. On the weekend there are chores to do at home. About the only leisure we have is a mug or two of beer in the morning after the night shift. That's it. And then you quit—if you haven't already been killed in an accident. A few years later, your lungs give out, or your heart goes. Bye-bye. You're dead."

———

In the coming months, I went to mines in Ukraine, Sakhalin, and Kazakhstan. As it became clear that Moscow would not—and, probably, could not—come through on the economic deal, I heard more and more miners and other workers talking about a political strike. They were giving up on the system. But I had also heard those very things on the afternoon before I went back to Moscow from Kemerovo. Another of the workers at mine No. 6, Ivan Narashev, invited me home. His hut, at 6 Krupskaya Street, was smaller and even plainer than Shcheglov's. He could barely control his anger. He had voted against going back to work. "We should have stayed out until there was money on the table," he said. "We should have been like bulls and waited until we got exactly what we wanted." Hunched forward in his pine chair, Narashev talked about how the "party big shots" were trying to break the strike with "sweet words and no deeds." He remembered being on the town square in Kemerovo one afternoon at the height of the general strike meetings and seeing the local KGB chief hovering near the speaker's platform.

"I'll tell you, I'm only thirty-seven but I'm ready to go for early pension," he said. "I've had it. Ten years underground is enough for me. I'd like to get a car and put my wife and kids in it and drive away from here, somewhere where the air doesn't burn your eyes. We should have had these strikes years ago. We've been destroyed by Stalinism and Brezhnev's cronies. I'm ready now for a leader other than Gorbachev. Someone more like Boris Yeltsin. Yeltsin's a man of concrete deeds. How is it possible that until now our leaders eat all the pork and we chew on the bones? If Yeltsin were sitting where Gorbachev is, maybe it would be different."

What seemed to burn in him most was the feeling that the strike would turn out to be not the glorious victory that everyone at mine No. 6 was saying it was, but another humiliation, like gray sausages and no electricity. It was not yet clear that the miners' strike of July 1989 was the first and most dramatic step in the creation of a link between the revolt of the intelligentsia in the cities and the nationalists in the republics with the political uprising of workers across the country. "Think about this country for a minute," Ivan Narashev said as the room began to darken. "Our leaders have always divided us, kept us down. I think they're doing that now, and they will rule again."

CHAPTER 15

POSTCARDS FROM THE EMPIRE

V alentin Falin, a rumpled, weary man high up in the Central Committee apparatus, was always prepared to serve the Party. But now he had an impossible task. With Eastern Europe beginning its democratic revolution, with evidence of the same in Lithuania, Latvia, and Estonia, he was instructed to go before the press and deny the existence of a Soviet empire.

The Kremlin had long since given up trying to rein in Eastern Europe. "We made that decision in 1985, 1986," Yegor Ligachev, of all people, told me. "We already had the example of Afghanistan before us." That is not to say the Kremlin was overjoyed with the triumph of Solidarity or other non-Communist parties in Eastern Europe. Officials in the Kremlin simply could not believe that the Eastern Europeans were rebelling on their own. Ligachev told me that had it not been for Western "provocateurs," the Eastern Europeans would have chosen "reformed socialism" and not "bourgeois" democracy. The leadership had hoped for Eastern Europe what it hoped for itself: the victory of the Communist Party's liberal wing. "I am confident," Gorbachev said in an interview with *The Washington Post* in the spring of 1988, "that the vast majority of people in Poland favor continuing along the path on which the country started after World War II." But no matter how disappointed the Soviet Communist Party was in the nature of the Eastern European revolution, it could not afford intervention—not if it was going to get Western support for rebuilding the Soviet economy.

Moscow, however, was absolutely determined to hold together the union, the "internal empire." The preservation of the union, Gorbachev said repeatedly, was "a last stand," and yet his strategy was all muscle-flexing and expulsion of wind, the threat of force and a fraudulent argument that all the republics, including the Baltics, had joined the Soviet Union willingly and happily. For all his democratic pretensions, Gorbachev never saw the Soviet Union as an empire, a product of czarist and Bolshevik conquest, but rather as a "multinational union." He saw the union as inexorably linked not only by economic ties, shared history, and intermarriage, but by an ineffable sense of commonality. Gorbachev portrayed himself as a kind of Soviet one-worlder and the proponents of republican independence as retrograde nationalists doomed to the tribal battles of centuries past. "We are looking ahead," he told the Lithuanians, "and you are looking to the past."

To preserve the union, the Party was still willing to use its airbrush on history. The leaders of the Baltic independence movement, backed up by nearly every reputable Western historian, argued that Latvia, Estonia, and Lithuania came under the Soviet sphere of influence as the result of a secret deal between the Kremlin and the Nazis. The Molotov-Ribbentrop Pact of August 1939 surreptitiously divided Europe into Soviet and German spheres of influence. One of the secret protocols gave Moscow control over Latvia, Estonia, and parts of Poland and Romania. A second protocol, signed a month later, gave the Kremlin control over Lithuania. In 1940, Stalin annexed the Baltic states and forced their puppet legislatures to "request admission" into the union. And now Valentin Falin, chief of the Party's international department, was on the stage of the Foreign Ministry press center telling us that even if there had been such protocols, so what? They had nothing to do with "present realities." Falin's excuses would have shamed a schoolboy. The dog, he seemed to say, had eaten the secret protocols of the Molotov-Ribbentrop Pact.

When perestroika began, Gorbachev had at least some sense of the deterioration of the national economy and the difficulty of creating semidemocratic politics in a totalitarian state. But he and his colleagues started out nearly oblivious to the nationalities question. In December 1986, Gorbachev fired the Kazakh Party chief, Dinmukhamed Kunayev, and replaced him with an ethnic Russian, Gennadi Kolbin, never anticipating that the people of the republic would object. The ensuing riots in the republic's capital, Alma-Ata, eventually forced Gorbachev to replace Kolbin with a Kazakh, but the incident did not seem to impress the Kremlin very strongly. Even the massive demonstrations in Armenia and Azerbaijan in early 1988 seemed to Gorbachev a matter of local interest, a petty squabble over Nagorny Karabakh that could be resolved by replacing the local Party leadership. He saw no threat there. After all, hadn't the protesters in Yerevan carried portraits of Gorbachev?

But the Balts spoke more clearly; their demands were easier to discern. They began with demonstrations about the environment, then about the need to preserve Baltic languages and cultures. Step by step, the Baltics grew more political, more self-confident. By early 1989, the most popular politicians in the region were non-Communists, and by May the parliaments of Estonia, Latvia, and Lithuania had all declared their sovereignty. It was unclear what sovereignty meant, or could mean. Even the leaders of the main opposition groups—Sajudis in Lithuania, the popular fronts in Estonia and Latvia— were careful not to talk of outright independence as anything other than a remote goal; when they spoke of independence it was in the wistful tones of scientists planning on the colonization of Mars. "We cannot afford illusions," said Marju Lauristan, a leader of the Estonian Popular Front. Lauristan least of all. Her father had been a leader of the Estonian Communists who welcomed Stalin's annexation in 1940 with open arms.

At first, the Kremlin had not seemed so threatened by the Baltic republics. They were, after all, a "special case," minuscule states absorbed into the Soviet Union more than twenty years after the Bolshevik Revolution. And just as important, there was the matter of temperament. The Balts were calm and measured, reasonable. Their demonstrations—next to the huge and noisy marches in Yerevan, Baku, or Tbilisi—were as gentle as a Save the Whales march on a summer's day in Sausilito. The Balts were "more European" somehow than the rest of the Union, and their traditions of small-scale farming and business, Gorbachev supposed, might even set a healthy example in Russia.

But the Baltic example became the model not for the revitalization of the Union, but rather for its collapse. In the three years it took to win independence, the Balts were never violent, only stubborn. It was that very temperament—Sakharov's calm confidence on a mass scale—that characterized their revolution. None of the other republics organized quite so well or thought with such precision and cool.

At first glance, the idea of Lithuania standing up to Moscow sounded like an episode from *The Mouse That Roared.* It was too comic to consider. Sajudis headquarters, a small building near the main Catholic cathedral in the capital city, Vilnius, was filled with well-scrubbed volunteers. They had a couple of PCs, a fax machine, satellite phones, and sweet wall posters showing Balts holding hands and singing songs. One afternoon I watched as a young woman, wearing Birkenstock sandals and humming a Tracy Chapman song, pumped press releases through the telex machine and sent them to news bureaus all over the world. She was announcing a demonstration for August commemorating the fiftieth anniversary of the Molotov-Ribbentrop Pact. I thought of how blithe she seemed next to the traditional Bolshevik image of "real" revolutionaries: sweaty, bearded men in the Smolny denouncing "factionalism," Lenin speaking from an armored car, the stink of bad cigarettes. And yet she was their master; here she was, playing a vital role in the creation of a mass movement that would eventually liberate Lithuania and give the rest of the Soviet Union . . . ideas.

In their public statements, the leaders of the Baltic popular fronts had a knack for echoing Gorbachev's own rhetoric and then applying the principle to their own situation. When the Central Committee issued a threatening statement directed at the Balts, the popular front groups in the region issued a counterstatement that sounded much like Gorbachev's address to the United Nations: "The time when military force can solve everything has long since passed. Tanks are not only an immoral argument, they are no longer omnipotent. The main thing is that such a turn of events could once and for all put the Soviet Union back into the ranks of the most backward of totalitarian states." The Latvians, Estonians, and Lithuanians were keenly aware that for Moscow, the price of violence would be much higher than it had been in 1956 or 1968; this time Moscow made no secret that it needed the help of the West to survive. A bankrupt empire would be forced to shrink. That equation gave the Balts their confidence, a confidence that was shaken only when the governments of the West were weak, or tardy, in their support. "How can there be a 'threat' of tanks when there have already been Soviet tanks in the Baltic states for fifty years?" said Trivimi Velliste, president of the Estonian Heritage Society. "Tanks will not help them, even if they do move them into our city streets. The only thing they will do is cause a lot of trouble for our road repairmen. India used a passive resistance and India became independent in the end. In terms of that kind of strategy, we can learn a lot from India."

In Lithuania, especially, you could see with the greatest clarity the Baltic strategy. The Estonians, the saying went, were the brains of the movement, the Latvians the organizational spine, and the Lithuanians the heart, the moral force. The key leader of Sajudis, and eventually the president of the republic, was Vytautas Landsbergis, a man of almost infuriating confidence and righteousness, a moody academic who drove Gorbachev and even George Bush to distraction with his disdain for "playing politics" and moral compromise. A musicologist at the Vilnius conservatory, Landsbergis was no less a pedant than Gorbachev himself. When the Lithuanian parliament—in what seemed like a moment of fantasy—took up the question of a national anthem, Landsbergis went into a long discourse about how the song could not be sung, as it had been traditionally, in the key of F sharp. "No one can sing that high," he said, and thus launched into a long disquisition.

Like many other intellectuals in the Baltic states, Landsbergis had not lived the dangerous life of an outright political dissident. But unlike the older Moscow intellectuals who worked within the Party and saw its reform as the only avenue of change, Landsbergis kept his distance from officialdom. In the years before Gorbachev, he saw the preservation of the Lithuanian culture as the only possible political act. "If we could keep alive the language, our religion, the culture, everything Moscow was trying to kill, then we had a chance," he said. Landsbergis's cultural dissidence was a family trait. His maternal grandfather, Jonas Jablonskis, was a linguist who fought for the primacy of the Lithuanian language after it was banned by the czars; his paternal grandfather, Gagrielus Landsbergis, was arrested and deported by the czarist government for the crime of writing for an underground newspaper; his father, Vytautas Landsbergis, Sr., was an architect during Lithuanian independence who fought in the resistance against the Nazi occupation. In the "years of stagnation" under Brezhnev, Landsbergis himself tried to preserve Lithuanian culture by studying the music of the composer Mikalojus Ciurlionis.

When the political opportunity came in 1989, Sajudis and Landsbergis led a cultural revolution, a revival of historical memory. I was in Vilnius to see a political act that would, in the next few years, become the ultimate symbol of the return of history. I saw members of Sajudis, after a vote of parliament, ripping down the signs reading "Lenin Street" along the main drag in Vilnius and replacing them with signs reading "Gediminais Street," named for one of the great dukes of Lithuanian history. The highway between Vilnius and Kaunas was changed from Red Army Avenue to Volunteer Avenue, celebrating the volunteers who fought for Lithuanian independence in 1918. On Sunday mornings, Lithuanian television broadcast Catholic mass on a new program, *Glory to Christ*. The young quit the Komsomol and the Young Pioneers. The Lithuanian Communist Party even conducted its sessions in Lithuanian, a great departure from the days when sessions were held in often clumsy Russian, the "Soviet language."

Western visitors, still flush with Gorbymania, would, with increasing frequency, come to Vilnius and hope that they could bridge the differences between the Kremlin and Sajudis. No matter how distinguished the visitor, Landsbergis would greet such attempts only with weary condescension. "We are an occupied country," he told me once. "To pretend we are grateful for a little democracy, to go through some sort of referendum to prove our commitment to independence, to talk with Mr. Gorbachev as anything other than a foreign leader, is to live a lie. . . . It is very simple. We are an occupied land. Only now we can say it, of course, but we have never considered ourselves a genuine part of the Soviet Union. That is something that Gorbachev does not quite understand. We wish his perestroika well, but the time has come for us to go our own way."

In the end, the Baltic strategy was excruciatingly simple. They would speak the truth and then press the Kremlin to make good on its own moralistic rhetoric. As Gorbachev himself had done, the Balts defined their direction by first clarifying the facts of history. The secret protocols of the Molotov-Ribbentrop Pact made clear that the Baltic states were occupied as part of a geopolitical deal with the Nazis. The second step was a matter of logic: if the occupation was illegal in 1939, then it had always been such; therefore the Baltic states need only reaffirm their independence. Once they had established this logic of revolution, the other Baltic leaders followed Landsbergis's strategy and spoke of Moscow as a foreign state. Nearly all the Baltic representatives in the Soviet parliament suddenly declared themselves "interested observers" rather than deputies. They also played a kind of moral game with Gorbachev, insisting on his goodness, his distinctiveness. "We in the Baltics look on Gorbachev as the 'good czar' and try to pretend that the 'czar doesn't know,' it's his ministers who are up to mischief,'" said Andres Raid, a television journalist in Tallinn. "In a way, we are playing a political game, using Gorbachev's name. He is an anchor for us, a shield, a shelter. Of course, we disagree with him on some things, but we try not to be too harsh about it. We have no one else looking out for us in the political hierarchy. We have nowhere else to go for help."

The Balts were determined to prove that they were tougher than the Kremlin, that their moral certainty would result in either victory or annihilation. Perhaps what gave them their confidence, and what distinguished them from most of the rest of the Soviet Union, was that the Lithuanians, the Estonians, and the Latvians enjoyed and remembered a legacy of at least intermittent independence. The Lithuanians, for example, had been dominated by the Danes, the Teutonic Knights, the Swedes, the Russians, and the Nazis, but there were periods of freedom, most lately between 1918 and 1940. In the most recent period of domination, under the Soviet Union, Stalin deported hundreds of thousands of Lithuanians to Siberia and "replaced" them with Russian workers. But now the Baltic leaders would not accept a middle ground, for the middle ground meant continued occupation. And they were right. The Kremlin capitulated, slowly, step by step. On July 23, Aleksandr Yakovlev, as chairman of a legislative investigating committee, conceded the obvious: the secret protocols existed. Landsbergis could not help but be amused. "This announcement," he said, "comes to us as a great shock." History had once more been returned.

———

A few months after Yakovlev's announcement, I had a chance to see glimpses of the worst nightmare of those who had once dreamed of an eternal Soviet empire.

In early October 1989, Gorbachev visited Berlin, ostensibly to help cele-brate the anniversary of East German statehood. The cracks in the wall were already visible. Thousands of East Germans were fleeing across border points for West Germany, Hungary, Czechoslovakia, and Austria. But the East German leader, Erich Honecker, was as obstinate as any of the Eastern European dictators; he was the sort of tyrant who could begin a proclama-tion, "If I die . . ." He had every intention of outlasting Gorbachev and the pressure to change. To make himself understood, Honecker orchestrated a grand ceremony of state in Gorbachev's presence: a day of speechmaking in the main government palace, a goose-stepping military parade, fireworks. One night, tens of thousands of the Party youth league members marched through the streets of Berlin carrying flaming torches and singing songs of socialist brotherhood. (In a few weeks, they'd be marching through the Berlin Wall to buy steaks and singing praises of the gods Nike and Reebok.)

The Berlin visit was one of Gorbachev's finest moments, the sort of subtle exchange that he was made for. A year later, when blunt decisiveness was needed at home, when democratic politics demanded an end to backroom maneuvering, Gorbachev would hesitate and fail. Boris Yeltsin would fill the vacuum. But Gorbachev was the man for this moment. In public, he played along nicely with the East German leadership. In his own speeches and comments, he never drifted far from his host. He kissed Herr Honecker firm on the lips. But in the end that kiss was the kiss of farewell. In private, Gorbachev hinted broadly that the leadership could either begin its own massive reforms or end up defeated and defunct. Gorbachev trotted out one of his favorite aphorisms for the occasion: "Life itself punishes those who delay." He repeated it here and there, and his spokesman made sure to emphasize it at a press conference.

Such hints can spark a revolution. As the East German folksinger and dissident Wolf Bierman said of Gorbachev's phrase, "the tritest common places, launched into the world at the right moment, become magic spells." Many factors led to the collapse of the East German regime—the action along the border, dissension in the ruling Politburo, the rise of opposition groups—but Gorbachev's hint surely let the people know where the Kremlin, the center of the empire, stood. Within hours after he left for Moscow, an uprising had begun, angry confrontations between demonstrators shouting "*Freiheit! Freiheit!*" and the Stasi police on the Alexanderplatz. According to reports on the radio, the demonstrations were far bigger in Leipzig. Erich Honecker may not have been listening to Gorbachev, but the people of East Germany were. On November 9, just one month after Gorbachev's visit, the Berlin Wall collapsed.

———

To live anywhere between Bonn and Moscow in 1989 was to be witness to a year-long political fantasy. You had the feeling you could wander into history on the way to the bank or the seashore. Esther and I had bought cheap tickets to Prague for Thanksgiving week, thinking we'd have time to see the city and some friends and relax. There was little chance of that. The day we arrived, we checked in at the hotel and walked to Wenceslas Square, where there were no fewer than 200,000 people marching for an end to the Communist regime. A couple of days later at an even bigger demonstration, I was leaning out a window watching Alexander Dubček, fifty feet away, declare his return to Prague after two decades of shame.

Dubček's return was remarkable enough—he was the living personification of the 1968 Prague Spring—but it was even more extraordinary that he now seemed antique. The crowds roared for him when he walked out on the balcony, but the enthusiasm faded steadily as they listened to him. His was still the old dream of "socialism with a human face." The tens of thousands of students who led the 1989 revolution, who were pouring into factories and bringing the workers out to join them on the city squares, looked on Dubček as a well-intentioned but slightly out-of-it grandfather. Dubček sounded as if he had been frozen in time from the moment he was arrested by the Soviet authorities in 1968. His language was still stiff, his cadences metronomic. Like Len Karpinsky's articles, Dubček's speech could not quite dispense with the Communist Party habit of euphemism, pomposity, and cliché. By the time he finished that day on Wenceslas Square, the applause was only polite.

With each demonstration Václav Havel's voice grew more and more hoarse, but his expressions of liberty and passion transcended the dead language of the official newspapers and Party pronouncements. It was as if by writing and speaking clearly, honestly, Havel helped keep alive principles and a language that would inevitably triumph over the regime. His opposition was to act outside the system, to act decently. How lucky the Czechs were to have such a voice among them! Havel was no less a hero than Sakharov or Walesa, and his greatness, like theirs, was in his absolute belief in himself and the rightness of his cause.

In Prague I read a collection of letters Havel sent to his wife, Olga, from prison. They were filled with philosophical discussion, abstract exploration of the reasons for existence and faith, but I found myself just as moved by "overhearing" Havel describe the routine of prison life, his reading of Max Brod's biography of Kafka and Bellow's *Herzog;* his progress in English and German; his hemorrhoids; the pleasure of smoking two cigarettes a day and intensifying that pleasure by smoking slowly in front of a mirror; his reasons for living, his reasons for hope. Most of all, I found myself nodding with admiration at Havel's description of the insidious way the Prague regime (or the Moscow or Beijing regimes) had made language "weightless" by twisting it, pacifying and corrupting it.

"Words that are not backed up by life lose their weight," Havel wrote, "which means that words can be silenced in two ways: either you ascribe such weight to them that no one dares utter them aloud, or you take away any weight they might have, and they turn into air. The final effect in each case is silence: the silence of the half-mad man who is constantly writing appeals to world authorities while everyone ignores him; and the silence of the Orwellian citizen."

A man of the theater, Havel held his press conferences onstage during those weeks of revolution. On November 24, after Dubček's speech on the square, he and Dubček answered the nightly questions from the press at the Magic Lantern Theater and even got into a mild debate on socialism. Dubček was all for a "purified" socialism, once rinsed of Stalinist "deformations." A familiar, Gorbachevian theme. Havel said he could no longer discuss "socialism," that it was a word and idea that had been rendered meaningless. After about an hour of this meeting of the generations, Havel's brother walked on the stage, which was still set for a production of Dürrenmatt's play *Minotaurus.* He whispered in Havel's ear. Havel smiled, a radiant smile. Dubček was talking, and Havel interrupted with a polite gesture.

"The entire Politburo has resigned," Havel announced.

Suddenly there was a bottle of champagne and glasses all around.

Havel and Dubček rose and toasted a free Czechoslovakia.

Curtain.

In the epilogue a few weeks later, Havel appeared not onstage, but on state television. He was now president of Czechoslovakia. Citizens, he declared, "your government has been returned to you!" This was not theater. This was really happening.

———

Inside the Soviet Union itself, republican independence leaders celebrated the end of the external empire. Except for Romania, where the revolution ended in bloodshed and political ambiguity, the liberation of Eastern Europe seemed almost effortless. But they were careful not to let themselves believe that their own freedom would come soon. The Kremlin gave them every reason to think otherwise. Writing in *Sovetskaya Kultura,* the Kremlin's arch spokesman, Gennadi Gerasimov, said that the West was showing "malignant pleasure" in the Baltic independence movements. Such movements, he wrote ominously, "threaten our reforms and are provoking use of the 'iron fist.' "

In early 1990, after the string of revolutions in Eastern Europe had come to an end, an American historian, Eric Foner, conducted a seminar with his history students at Moscow State University. Foner was a specialist in the American Civil War, and the afternoon I sat in on his class, he and his students discussed the parallels between Gorbachev and Lincoln and their quests to keep together a union. For a while, Foner and his students compared the two leaders, but soon the students began to talk about what they thought their country would look like in a few years. Every one of them predicted collapse, and every one was frightened that the old regime would resist to the end.

The Soviet Union is a great empire, and we are now watching its disintegration, Igor, a student from Byelorussia, said. "Assuming that by my early thirties I have not been killed in a civil war, I think what will be left will be Russia—the original core territory. And that is what happened to the Roman Empire, isn't it? It shrank. I just hope that it all happens without haste, and peacefully."

"I'm frightened," said another student, a Russian, Aleksandr Petrov. "Power is still in the hands of the Communist Party and the KGB. They can stir it all up if they want. And if there is violence, they'll say they had to do it all to preserve peace."

Their fears and visions of the future differed, but all of Foner's students fully expected the Union to collapse. "The old regime," Petrov said, "is not just old. It's dead."

———

As I traveled around the Union, opinions varied on when and where the old regime died. Uzbeks in Tashkent and Samarkand told me that the exposure in around 1988 and 1989 of the callous way Moscow had turned all of Central Asia into a vast cotton plantation—in the process destroying the Aral Sea and nearly every other area of the economy—was the turning point. In the Baltic states, the official "discovery" of the secret protocols to the Nazi-Soviet pact was the key moment. But it was in Ukraine that I found the most unifying event, the absolute metaphor for the explosion of the last empire on earth.

On a trip to the western Ukrainian city of Lvov in 1989, I met with small groups of nationalists who promised that "one day" their republic of over fifty million people, the biggest after Russia, would strike out for independence and do far more damage to the union than the tiny Baltic states ever could. They knew their history. "For us," Lenin once wrote, "to lose the Ukraine would be to lose our head." Bogdan and Mikhail Horyn, brothers who had spent long terms in jail for their pro-independence activities before Gorbachev took power, said that while an independent, post-Soviet Ukraine may be years off, the old regime collapsed, practically and metaphorically, at 1:23 A.M., April 26, 1986, the moment of the nuclear accident at Chernobyl. That devastating instant had from the start been wrapped in a mystical aura. Within weeks of the accident, people realized that "Chernobyl" meant "Wormwood" and then pointed to Revelations 8:10–11; "A great star shot from the sky, flaming like a torch; and it fell on a third of the rivers and springs. The name of the star was Wormwood; and a third of the water turned to wormwood, and men in great numbers died of the water because it was poisoned."

The accident at Chernobyl embodied every curse of the Soviet system, the decay and arrogance, the willful ignorance and self-deception. Before leaving for Chernobyl, I arranged to see Anatoly Aleksandrov, the physicist who designed the reactor model at Chernobyl. Aleksandrov was in his nineties, the dean of Soviet science. He was the former head of the Academy of Sciences and the head man at the Kurchatov Institute of Nuclear Energy. During the Brezhnev era, Aleksandrov had written that nuclear power plants were 100 percent safe and ought to be built as close to population centers as possible, the better to solve the country's heating problems during the winter.

Aleksandrov's office was grander than any I had seen before, grander even than most of the palatial offices at the Kremlin. He and a group of his top aides and engineers sat in a semicircle and he talked of the accident. No, he felt no remorse. Yes, the reactor was sound and reports of future accidents were absurd. "If there was a defect or two, we've fixed it, you see." And as for reports that hundreds, if not thousands, of people would die over the years from the effects of radioactivity unleashed at Chernobyl, Aleksandrov lifted his enormous, aged hand and flapped it in derision.

"Oh, really now," he said. "That's wild exaggeration. Stop worrying so much!"

There remains every reason to worry. The Chernobyl explosion released a radioactive cloud ten times more deadly than the radiation following the blast at Hiroshima. There were children in the region who absorbed radiation equivalent to a thousand chest X rays. More than 600,000 workers took part in the cleanup, a deadly job; more than 200,000 people were evacuated from the region, but only after a thirty-six-hour delay and after absorbing dangerous amounts of radioactivity. There are thousands of people in Ukraine, Byelorussia, and other republics who eat food grown in radioactive earth and drink contaminated water. At the Petrovsky Collective Farm in Narodichi, the farm directors reported that sixty-four farm animals were born with serious deformities in 1987: calves without heads, limbs, ribs, eyes; pigs with abnormal skulls. In 1988, the rate continued to rise. They recalled only three or four such instances before the accident. *Moscow News* said that the radiation readings in the area were thirty times greater than normal, but that local farm animals were still fed fodder from the contaminated fields. People in the region received 35 rubles a month from the state as a subsidy—money the people called the "coffin bonus." The various bureaucracies seemed not to care about, or believe in, the perils of radiation. As late as 1990, more than 180 tons of contaminated meat was shipped to stores in Siberia and northern Russia from a processing plant in Bryansk where the sausage was being made from beef and pork with radiation levels ten times normal.

"Chernobyl was not *like* the Communist system. They were one and the same," said Yuri Shcherbak, a physician and journalist who led the fight in Ukraine to publicize the medical and ecological hazards of the accident. "The system ate into our bones the same way radiation did, and the powers that be—or the powers that were—did everything they could to cover it all up, to wish it all away."

From the moment that the engineers in the control room of reactor No. 4 at Chernobyl reported a disaster beyond imagining, their superiors refused to act. The top bureaucrats at Chernobyl kept repeating the same fiction: that there had been a "mishap," but nothing terrible, the reactor had not been destroyed. They quickly passed on this fiction to the leadership in Moscow. The next day, the people of Chernobyl, Pripyat, and the neighboring villages acted out their lives under a radioactive cloud. Children played soccer in radioactive dust. There were sixteen outdoor weddings sponsored by the Young Communist League. Old men fished in a contaminated river and ate the contaminated fish. When he was told by his engineers that the radiation at the plant was millions of times higher than normal, the plant director, Viktor Bryuchanov, said the meter was obviously defective and must be thrown away. For more than a day, Boris Shcherbina, a deputy prime minister, refused suggestions to carry out a mass evacuation. "Panic is worse than radiation," he said. The world got word of the seriousness of the accident only when Scandinavian scientists reported dramatic increases in radiation levels. Even as they were evacuating their own families, Ukrainian Communist Party officials insisted on holding the annual May Day parade; the children of Kiev kicked up radioactive dust to celebrate the victories of socialism. After a long filibuster in the Politburo and strict controls on public information about the disaster, Gorbachev went on television to discuss Chernobyl a full sixteen days after the accident, and much of his talk was taken up with denunciations of the Western press.

"Meanwhile the reactor was burning away," wrote Grigori Medvedev, an engineer who once worked at Chernobyl. "The graphite was burning, belching into the sky millions of curies of radioactivity. However, the reactor was not all that was finished. An abscess, long hidden within our society, had just burst: the abscess of complacency and self-flattery, of corruption and protectionism, of narrow-mindedness and self-serving privilege. Now, as it rotted, the corpse of a bygone era—the age of lies and spiritual decay—filled the air with the stench of radiation."

In the aftermath of the accident, Shcherbina, the deputy prime minister, issued a secret decree in force from 1988 to 1991 telling Soviet doctors they could not cite radiation as a cause of death. Shcherbina, who had himself been exposed to high doses of radiation, died in 1990. The cause of death was marked "unspecified."

One morning in Kiev, an official from Spetsatom, one of the cleanup bureaucracies, picked me up in a van and we drove north for Chernobyl. I had visited cities that were often described as "frozen in time": Havana, with its faded hotels from the era of gambling and Battista; Rangoon, with its stopped clocks, reworked English cars, and the battered English silver at the Strand Hotel downtown. Usually it was a matter of faded colonialism matched against the poverty of the native regime. Chernobyl was something else again, a kind of ruin of the Soviet system, a horrible metaphor for the era that began with the Revolution in 1917 and was now ending. We passed a series of checkpoints, changed into a "dirty" radioactive van, and headed into the haunted "zone." In the town of Pripyat there were abandoned apartment buildings, dilapidated as any other buildings in the Soviet Union. The workers and administrators of the power plant lived there. It was a moonscape of abandoned playgrounds, half-buried cars, buses, railroad wagons, abandoned fields. After the accident, people desperate for cash would dig up the buried cars and sell the radioactive parts or just drive the whole car off to Kiev. I met older people who had been evacuated but now had come back to the "zone" to live and die. They had never believed anything the state had told them, and why should they begin now? They drank poisoned tea and ate poisoned potatoes. A few hundred yards away was reactor No. 4, now encased in layers of concrete. Engineers were still trying to work out how they would finally eliminate the near-eternal danger posed by the core. The concrete would not hold forever.

Most of the people still living in "the zone" were cleanup workers, and most of them stayed "inside," working for fifteen days, and then went home to Kiev and other towns for fifteen days of recuperation. That was the rule. But there were also some who were so dedicated to the cleanup project that they rarely left "the zone" except to visit family for a day or two every month. The Spetsatom director, Yuri Solomenko, and the chief engineer, Viktor Golubyev, spent nearly all their time in the zone and vowed to stay on until the Sarcophagus—the nickname for reactor No. 4—was "cleaned out." Once, while I was interviewing the two men, Golubyev excused himself. He had another meeting. As soon as he left the room, Solomenko told me his friend "was all but finished." After getting news of the Chernobyl accident while working at a reactor site in Cuba, Golubyev had volunteered to help put out the fire. In those rescue operations, he absorbed so much radiation that his skin turned deep brown and had to be peeled away. Solomenko explained that his friend's body had been "utterly degraded." And yet he would not leave Chernobyl until the damage was cleared away.

"Chernobyl was like everywhere else in this empire," Yuri Shcherbak said. "The only thing that stood between us and total oblivion was a few good people, a few heroes who told the truth and risked their lives. If it weren't for the danger, they should leave the Chernobyl plant standing. It could be the great monument to the Soviet empire."

CHAPTER 16

THE ISLAND

I met a free man on the island of Sakhalin. His name was Nikolai Batyukov, a would-be intellectual turned itinerant fisherman, and he knew only vaguely of the political fervor thousands of miles to the east in Moscow. He did not have much to say about Gorbachev or Yeltsin or any other figure in the political life of the capital. "As you can see, I keep my distance," he said.

Batyukov was one of the few men or women I had encountered in Russia who seemed at ease with what he had made of his life. He was in his fifties, and many years before he had been, in the loose, Russian sense, an intellectual, a serious student, but he saw "no future at all" in a life of the mind. "Not in this country, not in the Soviet Union." He gave it all up to live as a "half-legal, independent" fisherman. "In this country, the only way to be free was to run away from it," he said. "I couldn't run to Tokyo so I ran for the hills."

In the warmer months, Batyukov set up camp in the pine woods overlooking the Sea of Okhotsk, a landscape as jagged and beautiful as the coast of northern California. He fished mainly for salmon and spiny crab and sold his catch at markets in the capital city, Yuzhno-Sakhalinsk. Batyukov had a hermit's wild gray beard, and today he said he felt more worn out than usual.

All day he had been hauling nets heavy with salmon; it was the summer run. There were more fish around than he could possibly catch. What made him furious was to see the "government nets"—the nets set out along the shore by the state fishing boats—filled with rotting fish, big, glorious salmon going gray and belly up while the captains idled at sea, waiting for Moscow to give them the order to bring the fish on board. Those fishing nets held at least 150,000 pounds of salmon, Batyukov reckoned, but because the local bureaucrats had to wait for orders from the central bureaucrats of the "central command system," a million-dollar catch would soon be little more than rotting guts, bones, and scales. "Can you imagine anything so stupid?" he said.

As if to make his guests taste the loss, Batyukov set out one of the most splendid seafood feasts I have ever eaten. He cooked it all outside over a fire, in dented tin pots and an ancient fry pan. He worked with speed and skill; he was the fifteen-minute gourmet. There was a fish soup as fine as any in Marseilles, a mound of steamed spiny crabs, glossy red salmon caviar smeared on fresh bread, glasses of home-brewed vodka, and mugs of hot *chaga,* a chocolaty tea made from the sap of birch trees. Most people in the Soviet Union got fat on bad sausage, potatoes, and butter. Batyukov had clearly built his magnificent pot on finer things.

"I live the way I want to live," he said, "but the only way I do it is to keep low and out of sight. In your country, I'd be a worker, maybe a businessman. Here, I'm like an outlaw. An outlaw fisherman. So, sure, I like what I'm hearing on the radio about Sakharov and glasnost. Fine. But I'll believe it when I can see it. Tell me. You've been in Yuzhno-Sakhalinsk. Do you figure everything's different? You figure there's a place for a free man like me?"

———

In 1890, Chekhov left behind his literary triumphs in Moscow and traveled by rail and riverboat to the prison colonies and fishing villages on Sakhalin. "This seems to be the end of the world," he wrote in his journal as he approached the coastline, "and there is nowhere else left to go." In Chekhov's day, Sakhalin was Russia's Australia, a penal colony so distant that it seemed the very definition of exile. The camps were places of arbitrary cruelty and violence; one prisoner finally murdered a sadistic guard by suffocating him in fermenting bread dough. Working conditions were miserable. Migrant coal workers ate candles and rotten wood while the czar's ministers sold the island's salmon and caviar abroad. Chekhov visited Sakhalin to work as a census taker, to talk with prisoners and vagrants, and to write a long, and strangely dispassionate, account of life there, *The Island.* Sakhalin seemed to him as remote as Patagonia; Sakhalin, for Chekhov, was as much an idea as a place, a representation of Russia's vastness and the czar's reach across it. In his census, he discovered a people who took on names that somehow reflected their remoteness and conditions. "The most common surname is Nepomnyashchy [Unremembered]. Here are some of the vagrants' names: Mustafa Nepomnyashchy, Vasily Bezotechestva [Without Parents], Franz Nepomnyashchy, Ivan Nepomnyashchy 20 Years, Yakov Bezpozvaniya [Nameless], Vagrant Ivan 35 Years . . ."

The czar's prison camps closed long ago. Stalin favored the slightly closer, but less accessible, Kolyma region as his favorite murder site. The Soviet regime did what it could to Sovietize Sakhalin, building squat, shabby apartment houses in Yuzhno-Sakhalinsk and crabbed collective farms in the ports and provinces. The government populated the island by offering extra pay for miners, fishermen, and farmers.

Sakhalin was considered a border frontier, and so, until just a few months before my visit in the summer of 1989, the island was closed to foreigners and even to nonresident Soviet citizens. Even when I was there, Sakhalin was covered with concrete guard shacks. The KGB border troops were the age of college sophomores and wore daggers in their belts. They were stunned by the presence of foreigners: a reporter from *The Washington Post* one day, a Korean computer salesman the next. It seemed to them an invasion, but they were under orders now to let us through.

I went to Sakhalin to see if the political reforms going on in Moscow had taken root at the edge of Russia. By the time I got to the island, there had already been an awakening. The first sign of trouble for the local Party apparatus came in May 1988 when a few hundred men and women staged a demonstration outside the Chekhov Drama Theater in the capital to accuse the Party chief, Pyotr Tretyakov, of doling out apartments to his relatives and generally padding his own patronage rolls. The police and KGB circled the small demonstration but were too stunned, too confused, to act. The Party tried to wish it all away. To acknowledge the demonstration would have been "a situation." That was impermissible, unthinkable. The next morning, the official papers made the requisite noise about "a handful of extremists," then ignored the issue entirely.

But soon, as if sensing the Moscow breeze at their backs, the local democrats staged even bigger demonstrations on the squares and streets of Yuzhno-Sakhalinsk. The island's Party leadership was suddenly, and unalterably, on the defensive. A triumphant banner appeared over Lenin Avenue: "Get Rid of the Bureaucrats and Give Them a Shovel." Tretyakov, the Party chief, would have fought back if he could have, but he got no support from Moscow. He was fired by the Central Committee and fled Sakhalin for Moscow on a military transport jet. He never returned to the island. In the meantime, the new Party leaders knew well enough to halt construction of an expensive new headquarters and said they would let the people of Sakhalin decide whether to make a hospital or a school out of the building. In fact, everywhere I went in the Soviet Union in 1989 and 1990, the Communist Party was always in a state of "halted construction." Dozens of expensive headquarters never opened, were turned into schools and hospitals, or, more often, sat empty, dark, haunted.

This tiny revolution became an instant legend on the island. It was known as the "May events," a distinct echo of the legendary "July events" that led to the Bolshevik uprising of October 1917. Gorbachev was so pleased with the sign of an awakening in the hinterlands that he told reporters, "Finally, perestroika has come to Sakhalin."

But for all of Gorbachev's triumphalism, the Party still could not grasp the depths of people's anger with the old structures of power and the hegemony of Moscow. The Central Committee replaced the old apparatchik, Tretyakov, with a new one, Viktor Bondarchuk. Sakhalin Island had to wait only a few months before it showed its opinion of Comrade Bondarchuk. In the race for the Yuzhno-Sakhalinsk seat in the Congress of People's Deputies, an obscure and dyspeptic journalist named Vitaly Guly trounced Bondarchuk. Guly had been an ardent Komsomol boy, dutifully traveling the island preaching ideology. But he had changed radically by the mid-eighties. Now in his late thirties, he wrote many of the opinion pieces and embarrassing investigative pieces that led to the "May events."

One afternoon, we rode around in Guly's tiny Moskvich "looking for constituents." He wanted to talk with workers about the Congress and the miners' strikes. "I can't exactly say all I need to say in my paper—*Sovetsky Sakhalin*—so they have to hear it from the horse's mouth." The roads were generally miserable, but suddenly we found ourselves on a strip as fine as a German autobahn. Guly laughed and said, "You want to know why the road is so smooth? This is the road from Party headquarters downtown to where all the Party big shots had their dachas. They wanted a good road for themselves, and that's all there was to it. Presto! It was built! As for the rest of us . . ."

We headed toward a fishery and caviar-processing plant on Freedom Peninsula. To get there, we had to get through yet another KGB checkpoint, which consisted of a crumbling concrete shack, two teenage guards, and a boom box booming "I Saw Her Standing There." The guard poked his head inside. He asked for our documents. While he checked them over he was still tapping his foot to the music.

"Okay," he said. "We were expecting foreigners. Go ahead through."

After I got over my awe at the sight of the caviar—women in white fingering their way through bucketfuls of wondrous, slick goo—I could concentrate on how easily Guly mixed with the workers. He had the knack of listening to their complaints, remembering their names, and laughing at their jokes. Many of the workers referred to the first session of the Congress simply as "the show," the "great show in Moscow," and they wanted to know much more about immediate things: their salaries, housing. One woman told Guly with no embarrassment that "the main method of birth control on this island is abortion and the only way you can get one is to hire a doctor and rent a hotel room."

Guly said he would look into the possibility of building a clinic and making birth control available on the island. But there was also a grim understanding between the woman and Vitaly Guly: only the Communist Party had the power to do anything. And it would do nothing. Guly and his constituent smiled thin smiles at each other and parted.

Guly headed for the car, boiling. "Sakharov is right," he said. "I'm a member of the Party, but the Party has to go. The rest is details."

————

But the Party remained and the Party was still all-powerful, especially in a distant province like Sakhalin. The Party had rigged the elections so that it could stock the Congress with obedient servants. These were, in the main, dim-witted hacks who had very little idea at all what words like "perestroika," "glasnost," or "democratization" meant. Since the days of Stalin they had been hearing the Kremlin boast of its democracy, its constitutionalism; the Constitution written under Stalin, after all, sounds no less glorious than the American version of 1789. But it hardly mattered. Words, much less slogans, had long ago lost their meaning. What really meant something was belonging. Membership in the Party apparatus was all.

During my stay in Sakhalin, I shuttled back and forth between one host and the other, between Guly and a happy lug named Anatoly Kapustin. Both were deputies in the Congress, but they could not have been more different. Kapustin was elected not by people in his territory, but rather to a seat specially reserved for fellow Party and labor union officials. According to the more polite critics in town, he was a time-server, a low-rent apparatchik who had worked his way up from the coal mines to a soft office job in the union bureaucracy. He was in no way nasty, and friendlier even than Guly. Kapustin was eager to please. He had voice like a bassoon and a crushing handshake. He smiled constantly, like a maniac. But now he was in deep trouble. After the triumph of his election, he was having a very bad summer.

"Things are out of control," he said, "and that's not good."

There had been strikes at the Sakhalin coal mines, and in their aftermath

Kapustin wanted badly to show us that he was "working closely with the working class." One morning we watched him try to negotiate his way through a meeting with about 150 miners at union headquarters in Yuzhno-Sakhalinsk. Kapustin did the best he could. He pledged "openness" like Gorbachev. He chopped the air and wrapped the lectern like Gorbachev. But his moves were unconvincing. The poor man was too weighed down by his own meager talents, his dubious résumé and election, his habits of thought and speech. He was a cliché, an earnest windbag of the apparat. His new role as a "man of perestroika" was beyond him. He was no more convincing to the miners than he was to himself. Kapustin was like a dinner-theater extra asked to play Hamlet at the Old Vic with an hour's preparation. He knew some of the lines—"We will work together, hand in hand!"—but he fooled no one. The miners rolled their eyes and hooted like a flock of owls.

Afterward, Kapustin was embarrassed and sad. He thought he was getting it. He thought he'd been brave. "I used to toe the line all the way," he said. "The big guys would say what to do, and I would do it. It was just 'Kapustin do this' and that was that. Now I think if something is wrong, I try to speak up." But it wasn't enough.

Nearby, in the hallway, one of the strike leaders, Vitaly Topolov, said he was trying hard to work with Kapustin, but the prospects were not good at all: "I suppose he was an apparatchik, but Gorbachev was an apparatchik under Brezhnev, too. I keep hoping."

Kapustin bumbled on. We drove through the hills to Sinegorsk, a tiny mining town built by the Japanese when they were in control of the island in 1905. There, in the mine director's office, Kapustin was suddenly at ease. These were his friends, the midlevel bureaucrats who were marginally competent in their jobs, marginally honest. They all regretted the passing of time and apologized for the meager spread of ham sandwiches and fizzy water.

"Too bad this isn't the Brezhnev era," one of the mine directors said. "Back then we really would have laid out a banquet for you."

It wasn't their arrogance that hampered them so much as their complete lack of comprehension. When it came to simple economics, they could not connect the dots. The mine director complained that production had fallen at the mine by half, but at the same time he launched into a glorious paean to the central planning system and the web of state orders and subsidies. The fact was that his mine was badly equipped, primitive, and probably defunct. It was a dangerous place to work and an ecological disaster, and would never be profitable in a normal economy.

After lunch, Kapustin led us on an expedition of the mine, and it was worse than anything I'd seen in Siberia, Ukraine, or Kazakhstan. The mine was a horror. There were no elevators, and the shafts were brutal and tight. It took some of the miners two hours of sliding and creeping along stone just to get to their work stations. Later, my back and legs were covered with bruises and I was more sore than I would have been if I'd run ten miles. Until the strike, the miners had not been paid for this "commuting" time: they tore themselves up, four hours every day, for free. "And we've taken you down the best mine we've got here," the director said. "This one's dry. In the others, you've got water running down your back all day."

Outside, in the daylight at last, Kapustin wiped the soot from his eyes and put on his Gorbachev face again. Two dozen miners, exhausted and instantly bored, circled around. They wanted to go home but had been told to wait. "I'm here to listen to your problems," Kapustin said clumsily. "Please, tell me your problems." The men wore the bemused expressions of high school students watching their teacher trying too hard to be hip. They could not wait to go home and soak in a bath. They were in no mood to perform for a union hack like Anatoly Kapustin.

———

And yet, for a few days, I liked him. Kapustin was trying so hard to be admired, and the rewards for toadying were next to nothing: a slightly better salary, a better summer vacation. As a member of the Congress, he was the Soviet equivalent of a congressmen, and yet no American—much less a member of the House of Representatives—could have lived the life of Anatoly Kapustin. He lived just about as badly as anyone else in the Soviet Union.

A couple of days after our trip to the mine, Kapustin took us out to a huge fishing trawler. I thought we'd get a chance to see how a state boat operated, why it was that so many tons of salmon were rotting in the nets a few hundred feet away. But Kapustin had no interest in that. He was a close friend of the ship captain, and, as Kapustin said, "It's time we kicked back and relaxed. You relax sometimes in America, don't you?"

He led us to the captain's stateroom, a wood-paneled affair of surprising elegance. The table was already set with china, decent silverware, dishes heaped with food, and a half-dozen bottles: Georgian champagne, Ukrainian beer, pepper vodka. There was no way out. We were in for a time of it, and I prayed only that the seas would stay calm.

Amazingly, Kapustin was a worse drinker than I am. After three vodkas he was expressing his eternal fealty to Yegor Ligachev and the "wisdom" of the Party hard line. The strikes were an outrage, private property impermissible, the independence movements in the Baltic states treason. After just one more drink, he was making horrible sport of Sakharov, calling him "self-righteous," "anti-Soviet," and "useless."

"Just who does he think he is?" Kapustin said, his face darkening. "The man talks too much for his own good. He's a slander-monger."

It was a nasty performance, and I was—to my surprise—surprised. So many Party apparatchiks in so many situations had performed prettily for me, the foreign journalist. But now Kapustin was unbound. The vodka and the days of proximity had worked on him like a key. He was a man who instinctively felt the moral and political threat that Sakharov posed to him and the Party. Sakharov and his followers were challenging the very existence of the Party, the power of the Kremlin, the way of doing business. "Sakharov and his bunch think we don't understand them," Kapustin said, lifting his glass one last time, "but we do. We understand them. All too well."

CHAPTER 17

BREAD AND
CIRCUSES

W hen Gibbon wrote the saga of Rome's decline and fall, he relied on the written word, on memoir, epic, and history, for his source material. But the scholars of the collapse of the Soviet empire will go not to the library so much as the videotape. And in this video revolution, Anatoly Kashpirovsky played the role of Rasputin, the crazy wisdom man.

In a thousand years of Russian history, there have always been healers, mystics, and "holy fools." Usually they came to prominence in periods of rapid change, disaster, and disorientation. The sixth-century historian Agathias recalled "charlatans and self-appointed prophets roaming the streets" after an earthquake in Byzantium. "Society," he wrote, "never fails to throw up a bewildering variety of such persons in times of misfortune." In the last years of the czarist regime, Rasputin, an illiterate Siberian, convinced the Romanovs of his magical powers. The royal family was sure Rasputin was curing the heir to the throne of his hemophilia.

But while Rasputin's mesmerizing influence was limited to the czar's family and high society, Kashpirovsky was a man of the global village and the world tour. His healing "séances" captured television audiences of 300 million in the Soviet Union and Eastern Europe and filled huge concert halls and football stadiums. Kashpirovsky's medicine show had been kicking around for years, but it was at the end of 1989, when the economy was plummeting and people began talking about a new "Time of Troubles," that the Communist Party officials who ran state television decided it was time for a grand diversion, a video healer.

I saw the first of Kashpirovsky's broadcasts, and, like everybody else, I was hooked from the opening credits:

A logo announced the "tele-séance." Kashpirovsky came on the screen dressed all in black. He had the hyped-up glare, the scissors-and-a-bowl haircut of Brando in *Julius Caesar*. He started talking about his method of reaching the "bio-computer" inside his "patients," how he had healed "hundreds of thousands, perhaps millions" of people of their tumors, hernias, and heart pains. His voice was 16 rpm, low and even, like a threat. He claimed medical successes never known in "human history," successful cures of impotence, frigidity, blindness, baldness, emphysema, ovarian cysts, kidney stones, psoriasis, eczema, varicose veins, scars, tuberculosis, asthma, diabetes, allergies, stuttering, astigmatism, and, in four "documented" cases, the AIDS virus. He was at once God and Ponce de León: amputated limbs and extracted teeth regenerated at his mere suggestion; gray hair turned glossy and dark. Thanks to him, a woman of seventy began menstruating again and Mikhail Gorbachev's mother got over her arthritis. And then there was the Kashpirovsky Diet: one of his patients dropped 350 pounds, "and without the skin hanging off or anything." Or so the doctor said . . . so he said.

The soundtrack picked up now, a great wash of synthesizer music, switched-on baroque.

"Rid your mind of everything," Kashpirovsky purred. "Get rid of all those goals and ambitions. Everyone, close your eyes. No matter what emotional reactions you have, don't suppress them. And you will have different kinds of emotional reactions. Our silence is like a pause, a pause without words. Words don't matter. There's no work involved in this. It's hard to understand, because all their lives people have been taught to try and understand. . . . Forget everything. . . . Listen to the music. . . . Don't be afraid of the process that's starting within you. . . . If something is moving, pay no attention."

The man seemed never to blink. He glistened, and for long periods he said nothing, just stared and smirked a little, the way a tyrant dinner guest does when he is half soused and certain you should be fascinated by everything he says.

". . . Some of you are seeing forests, mountains. One . . . two . . . three. . . . Others are having very sad memories. Five . . . six. . . . Others are making plans for tomorrow, weighing, weighing everything. Seven. . . ."

By "ten" Kashpirovsky was gone.

"The séance," he said, "is over."
We were healed.

———

Since his first televised séances, Kashpirovsky's popularity—his cult of personality—went unmatched. Everyone knew his name and thought him either a genius or a confidence man. He told me once that he had an archive of more than a million telegrams and letters mainly from grateful viewer-patients. Schoolgirls and pensioners wrote in hinting they would do anything to be near him, learn from him, sleep with him. Older women wrote saying they had redecorated their *krasny ugol*—"red corner"—by taking down the traditional portrait of Lenin and replacing it with his. In the provinces, street vendors sold picture postcards of Czar Nicholas II, John Lennon, Jesus Christ, and Anatoly Kashpirovsky. He may have been the only man in the city of Kiev with three cars in his garage and a bank account to match. Newspapers that debunked his legend did so at their peril. After the weekly *Literaturnaya Gazeta* printed an article calling Kashpirovsky a dangerous charlatan, the protest mail grew into such an avalanche that the editor canceled a second article.

There were those who thought of Kashpirovsky as a healer not only of stretch marks and wens, but of nations as well, and he was loath to dismiss the claim. "If I were president, people would kiss my footprints after I died because I would go out among the people and work for their interests," he told me. His constituency was uncertain, but, he insisted, it was vast. "Ukraine is too small for me."

Kashpirovsky first appeared on the scene with a series of six nationally televised séances in the last few months of 1989. With the rise of independence movements and a workers' revolt, perestroika was spinning out of Gorbachev's control. The health care system was a shambles, with officials saying that only 30 percent of all basic medicines were available; even aspirin and penicillin were impossible to find. There were constant reports of hospitals without running water, doctors operating by candlelight. Kashpirovsky's rise came precisely at the start of this extreme uncertainty, confusion, spiritual search. And, as happened so often in Russian history, disruption gave rise to an increased interest in black magic, prophecy, and wizardry. *Bogoiskatelstvo,* the search for God, in Russia led not only to the church, mosque, and synagogue, but to such frauds as Rasputin and Kashpirovsky.

Always, even during the purges, there were village healers and mystics in Russia. In his dotage, Leonid Brezhnev secretly invited the healer Dzhuna Davitashvili to the Kremlin to work her magic. But now there were no taboos, no hiding. During the Gorbachev era, old women sold copper bracelets in city parks swearing they would work as a vaccine against AIDS; horoscopes ran in Communist Party newspapers; the official news agency Tass announced that "humanlike" giants and a midget robot flying in a "banana-shaped object" had landed in the city of Voronezh. Witnesses described the craft in question as a "large shining ball" and the "one, two, or three" creatures as being "three or four meters high but with very small heads." In Moscow, a healer named Alan Chumak opened shop on the program *120 Minutes,* the Soviet version of the *Today* show. Waving his hands as if he were petting an invisible cat, Chumak "charged" glasses of water and tubes of cold cream that people put in front of their television sets with "healing energy."

"I am in touch with another world," Chumak told me. He dug his hand into a garbage bag and pulled out one of his "countless" telegrams: SINCERELY GRATEFUL STOP HAD CHRONIC TACHYCARDIA AND GASTRITIS STOP DOCTORS COULDN'T CURE ME STOP NOW THANKS TO YOU I LIVE WITHOUT MEDICINE STOP THANKS SERGEI OF NOVOCHERKASSK

I followed Chumak as he rode the elevator downstairs and stepped out into his building's parking lot to heal a crowd of a few hundred people. This was a biweekly event, weather depending. A big crowd had gathered. Some of the people held up pictures of their sick children or parents, in hopes that the healer could radiate his energy through the photographic medium. Chumak stood on the steps and invited all to gather around and feel his aura. He had only one warning: he could not cure any former functionaries of the Communist Party.

"Their souls are already too hardened," he said.

———

Kashpirovsky, of course, regarded Chumak as "a quack" and himself as above all this common magic. He was the *über* doctor, a secular priest of mind and body. "I've outgrown the title of 'doctor,'" he said one night backstage before a séance. "That's child's play. It's not healing. I have a Great Idea. But I'm not pushing religion. What good does it do if Jesus walked on water two thousand years ago? What does it do for these people?" He rubbed his chin and wondered where his marvelous gift came from. "The spiritual power that drove Jesus Christ very possibly exists within me," he said, "and, in fifty years, I think I will be remembered as a saint."

Kashpirovsky trained as a psychologist in Vinnitsa, a provincial city in Ukraine, and worked in a hospital there for twenty-eight years. He earned a tiny salary, and to earn 100 rubles a month extra, he worked at night loading trucks with cement and lumber. For a while he was a fanatical weight lifter and boxer, and even now, in his early fifties, he was physically vain, claiming,

"I can beat any champion of the world." But in 1975, Kashpirovsky said, he had severe pancreatic disorders and nearly died. He spent a year in a hospital in Ukraine and then decided to go to Sakhalin, where he wandered the island, like Saint John the Baptist, eating one cookie a day. "Thanks to my hunger," he said, "I was cured."

It was only in 1988 that Kashpirovsky began his public experiments in hypnosis and mass healing. He held five tele-séances in Kiev and, he claimed, cured thousands of children of bedwetting. His technique was as obscure then as now, a talking cure in which the healer somehow sets right the organic balance of the body. "Happiness and sadness have some sort of material basis, biochemical substances behind them. When I am afraid, I have a lot of adrenaline. When I'm depressed, I have more," he said, beginning a lecture of sorts. "The gates open up inside of you and you accept information. You don't know how those gates open—that's my method—the information comes in, but because you don't know how it comes in, it can't get out. I reach beyond the mind, into the innermost being, to heal the body. The mark is left."

In 1988, the head of Soviet television was Mikhail Nenashev, a doltish apparatchik who told his aides that the primary aim of television was to soothe and reassure the troubled masses. In Kashpirovsky, who had strong support from people high up in the Ukrainian Communist Party organization, Nenashev found his soothing and reassuring voice. He signed him up for séances that were broadcast in 1989 not only in the Soviet Union, but in Bulgaria, Poland, Israel, Czechoslovakia, and Scandinavia. "In a country where you can't even find aspirin, you begin hoping for a miracle," said Yelena Chekalova, a television critic for *Moscow News.* "Then along comes this man and he offers you an easy way out, a miracle. It's a phenomenon inherent in a poor and miserable country." Leonid Parfyonov, a well-known broadcaster, said, "Kashpirovsky's role has been similar to Gorbachev's role in '85 and '86. They even have common gestures. They both come up with tremendous patches of meaninglessness in their speeches, and yet they were mesmerizing and inspired confidence."

Kashpirovsky's most theatrical bit of psychic trickery came in a "tele-bridge" between Kiev and the Georgian capital, Tbilisi. A woman named Lesya Yershova needed a major abdominal operation at a Tbilisi hospital. Rejecting ordinary anesthesia, she allowed Kashpirovsky to hypnotize her, via television from Kiev. The resulting tape, a split-screen extravangnza, was grotesque.

"Just close your eyes and sing 'The Poplar Tree,' " Kashpirovsky tells the poor woman. The poor woman actually squeezes out a few wobbly notes.

"Close your eyes! You're floating!" Kashpirovsky says. "You have no pain from your stomach to your spine! Close those eyes! . . . Yes, yes, you do feel the surgical instruments in your body, but you feel normal. Soon everything will be all right! People will ask me later if you are asleep. Are you?"

"No," she says meekly. "I feel someone doing something to my body." Indeed they are. The operation requires a forty-centimeter incision.

When it is over, Kashpirovsky tells the audience, "Now all of you who have watched me can go to the dentist and get a tooth pulled. There will be no pain at all. I assure you."

Kashpirovsky claimed he had made medical—"no, spiritual!"—history with that performance. But then the patient rebelled. Lesya Yershova told reporters that, in fact, she had been in "monstrous pain" during the operation and had cooperated only because she "didn't want to let Kashpirovsky down."

Yuri Savenko, the president of the Independent Psychiatric Association, said the Ministry of Health's cooperation in Kashpirovsky's broadcasts was an outrage and part of a broader bread-and-circuses conspiracy engineered by the Communist Party. He was far from alone in believing that the Party was using the broadcasts to divert the attentions and sorrows of the people. "With the Russian people," he said, "Christianity is superficial. They are largely pagan. They observe rituals without understanding the essence. Under the political situation today, mysticism increases, and with such a low cultural level it acquires outrageous forms." Savenko said that one of his colleagues had "firm data" proving that Kashpirovsky's séances had not only done nothing to heal people of their ills, they also caused some Russians to have psychotic episodes. But there was no investigation. Journalists and doctors alike had a difficult time attacking a figure so popular that he won Man of the Year honors in various newspapers in 1990 and had a following no politician or movie star could match. Savenko said that some of his psychologist and psychiatrist "friends" were reduced to pranks: "I know some people made fun of Kashpirovsky by sending him cables saying things like 'Thanks to you, my amputated stump has grown five centimeters longer.' Then they waited for him to read them out in public as a testimonial."

———

On tour, Kashpirovsky packed concert halls, factory courtyards, and even soccer stadiums. His videocassettes were passed hand to hand the way Solzhenitsyn's manuscripts once were. In the provinces, where very few people had VCRs, video salons and movie theaters organized Kashpirovsky Nights and showed the great man's tapes. As a businessman, he was not altogether happy with this underground trafficking. At the beginning of one tape put together in the United States, the usual FBI warning that it is a crime to copy the tape dissolved into Kashpirovsky's own message: "Warning! Duplicating this tape will result in losing its medical properties!"

I saw Kashpirovsky in Moscow and on his world tour in the West. It was always the same scene, a mix of spooky New Age and Beatlemania. One night in New York, at a school in the Pelham Parkway section of the Bronx, Kashpirovsky hid in a corner, trying to avoid the stares of the bulky, perfumed émigré babushkas as they filed into the auditorium. The healer was in an awful mood. A few nights before in Queens he had had a good time of it. The adulation level was just right. "I believe in you like a god," one woman told him. "Someone should blow up your enemies. Thank God that you were delivered to us. You are a god on earth." Another man threw away his cane and started limping joyously around the apron of the stage, yelping his thanks in Russian. Kashpirovsky accepted all this as his due. He feigned boredom. Sure there was a "cult of Kashpirovsky," Kashpirovsky allowed, but it wasn't "as if I'm going to tell them to blow up a nuclear power station. . . . You shouldn't be afraid of a repeat of Stalin or something."

But now, Kashpirovsky wore the collapsed look of the doomed. He was sure everything would go wrong. His manager, Mikhail Zimmerman, darted around like a wasp, frantic to know why the microphone crackled with static, why his star was so riddled with gloom. "Anatoly Mikhailovich is like a great instrument," Zimmerman said. "Sometimes he is just not in tune."

Kashpirovsky was feeling the despair of all self-declared prophets. The world, the very universe, was not prepared for his wonderfulness. "Humankind is not ready yet to be saved," he said. "There is not yet the technique. Imagine that everyone is healthy, no one is dying, and people keep reproducing. Where will they go? The other planets aren't inhabitable yet. It's some kind of law."

Once he was on stage, Kashpirovsky gave it a valiant try but never caught the groove. Never mind the inadequate universe; hell, as Robert Frost said, is a half-filled auditorium. He was angry at the middling ticket sales. He was used to 300 million on TV and 25,000 live, and now he had three hundred, if he was lucky. He recited his accomplishments and theories with all the tricked-up enthusiasm of a guy selling toupees on late-night television. Then the testimonials began. A woman's neck no longer had its crick. Hallelujah. Another woman's rheumatism was gone, her gray hair had darkened. "I feel like thirty, not sixty," she said. She looked seventy. Kashpirovsky hardly acknowledged the miracles he had wrought. He had his eye on the clock on the back wall, and, after a decent interval, he declared it time for the real séance, the synthesizer music and the purring into the microphone, the healing. But even this, his centerpiece, wilted.

As he strolled up and down the aisle, Kashpirovsky spotted people who had not closed their eyes, others who fidgeted in their seats.

"Don't look at me!" he shouted at one woman. "You're irritating me! Turn away from me!"

As he turned away, the music swelled, and Kashpirovsky reddened: "Where did you get that music?!" he barked at his assistant at the mixing board. "This is not human music! This is the sort of music they play at the May Day parade! Quieter! Turn it down!"

When it was over, Kashpirovsky waited at the lip of the stage as grandmothers and mothers and children all rushed at him in a frantic grab for the star's handshake and his healing glance. A few tried to corner him and describe their cancers, their migraines and tumors. "Look, I'm not an ordinary doctor," he answered in a huff. "Don't address me with your concrete illnesses." Sometimes when the ailing and the weak approached him with their ills, their pains, Kashpirovsky was even more specific.

"Take a couple of pills," he said.

CHAPTER 18

THE LAST GULAG

The country in which my books are printed will not be the same country that exiled me. And to that country I will certainly return.

—ALEKSANDR SOLZHENITSYN

On a summer afternoon in 1988, Yelena Chukovskaya was leading a tour through the small museum in the village of Peredelkino dedicated to the life and work of her grandfather, the children's-book writer and eminent literary scholar Kornei Chukovsky. One of the tourists fixed on a small photograph of Solzhenitsyn, a friend of the family. "Why doesn't Solzhenitsyn just come home?" the tourist asked. "What is he waiting for?"

Yelena was stunned. "I could not believe how naive, how unknowing, the question was," she told me. "And the younger people, they just had no idea who Solzhenitsyn was. A generation had already gone by since his exile, and he'd become little more than a legend to them, almost forgotten in his own country."

By that summer, Gorbachev's glasnost had already opened the door to many of the "anti-Soviet" classics: Anna Akhmatova's *Requiem,* Mikhail Bulgakov's *Heart of a Dog,* Boris Pasternak's *Doctor Zhivago,* Vasily Grossman's *Life and Fate.* After a comic court case, the government even let Nabokov's *Lolita* go through. But nothing of Solzhenitsyn. The Politburo would not sanction it. I asked Yegor Ligachev, Gorbachev's conservative rival, about Solzhenitsyn, and he made it plain that the Politburo felt, for a long time, that it could not tolerate a writer—especially a living, exiled writer—who considered the entire reign of the Communist Party an unmitigated crime and catastrophe. Ligachev wanted me to know that he was no critic but he knew obscenity when he read it. Ligachev was in charge of presenting a report to the Politburo on Solzhenitsyn, and he portrayed himself as the put-upon Party apparatchik, staying up night after night at home reading through the entire oeuvre, from *One Day in the Life of Ivan Denisovich* to the historical volumes known as *The Red Wheel.*

"You know that adds up to a lot of pages," he said proudly.

It was Solzhenitsyn's merciless portrait of Lenin as a fanatical revolutionary, as the originator of a system based on state terror, that most disturbed Ligachev and, for a time, Gorbachev himself. "After all, Lenin is ours!" Ligachev said. "We adhere to his viewpoint, to Leninism, and we must defend him."

But why should the Politburo decide instead of the reader? I asked.

Ligachev grimaced and waved the question away in disgust. After all, it had always been so. It was Khrushchev himself, after a long day's reading in 1962, who gave the word that *One Day in the Life of Ivan Denisovich* could be published in *Novy Mir.* And it was also Khrushchev who led the campaign against Pasternak. It was the Party's absolute right to decide.

"We have sacred things, just as you do," Ligachev said dryly.

But why use censorship to enforce it?

"Okay, pardon me, but we have a different psychology, a different worldview," he said, his voice rising. "I respect you and you should respect me. For me, Lenin is sacred."

———

A few days after the incident at the museum in Peredelkino, Yelena Chukovskaya sat down at her desk determined to "do something—and fast." She wrote a brief article outlining the facts of Solzhenitsyn's life and appealing to the government to return his citizenship. Then she sent it to *Book Review,* a weekly with a good reputation among the intelligentsia. The act seemed natural to Yelena, an extension of family tradition. Her mother, Lydia Chukovskaya, set an example in the 1970s when she went before the Writers' Union and, at great risk, swore to it that despite its evil denunciations,

Solzhenitsyn would return to Russia. For her troubles, Lydia Chukovskaya was denounced and *Sofia Petrovna,* her extraordinarily personal novel about the purges, banned. Now Yelena was picking up the battle. Just hours after receiving the piece, the editor of *Book Review,* Yevgeny Overin, took an enormous risk. He accepted the article for the August 5 issue on "editor's responsibility," an extraordinary step meaning that he did not wait for clearance from the censors.

Yelena Chukovskaya's piece was an immediate sensation. Thousands of letters and telegrams of support arrived at her door and at *Book Review's* ramshackle offices. Officials in the Central Committee reported that they, too, started getting more and more mail demanding the rehabilitation of Solzhenitsyn and his works. Chukovskaya's article and the response to it were signals, hints of what was politically possible and morally necessary. Other publications quickly took the cue. The editors of *Rabochoye Slovo* ("Worker's Word"), an obscure newsletter for Ukrainian railway workers, acted first, becoming the first aboveground publication to print Solzhenitsyn for nearly three decades. On October 18, the paper's 45,500 subscribers heard the old vatic voice, Solzhenitsyn's appeal to the young from 1974, the year he was exiled, to "Live Not by Lies":

"Let us admit it: we have not matured enough to march into the squares and shout the truth out loud, or to express openly what we think. It is not necessary. It is dangerous. But let us refuse to say what we do not think. This is our path, the easiest and most accessible one, which allows for our inherent, deep-rooted cowardice."

From his home in Cavendish, Vermont, Solzhenitsyn tried to manage the terms of his return. The editors of *Novy Mir* talked with him by phone and telegram and asked for permission to publish the two early novels, *Cancer Ward* and *First Circle.* Solzhenitsyn refused, insisting instead they they publish *The Gulag Archipelago* before any other of his books. Not only was *Gulag* his monument to the millions of victims of the Soviet regime, it was also the book, when it was published abroad, that hastened his arrest and his forced exile to the West. Solzhenitsyn's demand was also a way of attacking in the quickest way possible the latest official version of the Soviet past. Unlike the Gorbachevian scheme of socialism-gone-errant, of blaming all sins on Stalin, Solzhenitsyn's three-volume "literary investigation" argued that the forced labor camp system was no aberration, but began instead with Lenin.

The editors agreed to Solzhenitsyn's demand. Now they had to deal with something only slightly less intimidating: the Communist Party. At first, *Novy Mir*'s editors thought they could somehow ignore the Party and slip Solzhenitsyn into the pages of the magazine, as if through a hidden door.

On the back cover of *Novy Mir*'s October 1988 issue, the editors printed a cryptic announcement, saying merely that Solzhenitsyn had given them permission to publish "some of his works" beginning in 1989. But the Central Committee's ideological department, which certainly had its informers at the *Izvestia* plant where *Novy Mir* was printed, quickly suppressed the plan. In the middle of the night, the printers got a firm "stop work" order from an anonymous official in the ideological department of the Central Committee. "The printers were indignant," said Vadim Borisov, the editor at *Novy Mir* who was working most closely with Solzhenitsyn. "They felt great respect for glasnost, democracy, and the name of Solzhenitsyn. They were furious and invited reporters from the newspapers and television to come to the print shop to see what had happened. But no one came." The printers were forced to pulp more than a million covers and print new ones—without the Solzhenitsyn announcement. Only a few subscribers, mainly in Ukraine, got the journal as it was originally printed.

Not long after, Vadim Medvedev, who had replaced Ligachev as the chief Party ideologist in a shift in the leadership, attacked Solzhenitsyn for his "disdain" of Lenin and the Soviet system. *The Gulag Archipelago* and *Lenin in Zurich,* he told reporters at a news conference, "undermine the foundations on which our present life rests."

That foundation, however, was crumbling fast. The momentum of glasnost, fueled now by the publications of Solzhenitsyn in *Book Review, Worker's Word,* and other journals, as well as by rumors of the *Novy Mir* incident, could not be contained or ignored. *Novy Mir* was well positioned to press the issue. The editor in chief, Sergei Zalygin, was a contradictory figure, an elfin man in his seventies who had "played the game" in the Brezhnev years, constantly compromising principles to stay afloat. Like Len Karpinsky at *Moscow News* or Vitaly Korotich at *Ogonyok,* Zalygin had much to regret. But he saw glasnost "as my last chance," he told me. He would try now to right a great wrong. Zalygin adopted a strategy of defiant persistence. For six months running, he kept including Solzhenitsyn's Nobel Prize lecture in the galleys for the next issue—and for six months, the censors kept removing it. Aleksandr Tvardovsky, a legendary figure during the thaw, had used the same strategy when he ran *Novy Mir* in the sixties. Zalygin also made his rounds, campaigning quietly for publication with various members of the Politburo, including Gorbachev himself. Zalygin knew there were sharp ideological divisions in the leadership—especially on questions of history and glasnost—and he was prepared to wait for his opportunity. He knew, most of all, that Gorbachev was in an extremely difficult position. Many members of his earliest constituency, the middle class and the intelligentsia, were growing impatient, disillusioned with reform. Any further resistance to publishing Solzhenitsyn could only damage his popularity further.

But as an avowed Leninist, a "committed Communist" dependent on the support of the Party apparatus, Gorbachev also had to find a graceful way to change the policy and, at the same time, keep his distance from a writer who despised the system.

On a June afternoon in 1989, Medvedev summoned Zalygin to his office at the Central Committee. The meeting, *Novy Mir's* Vadim Borisov told me, was "extremely unpleasant," and gave Zalygin the distinct impression that the delay in publishing Solzhenitsyn could be indefinite. The next day, the Politburo gathered for its usual Thursday meeting. To the surprise of some Politburo members, Gorbachev broached the "Solzhenitsyn problem." He suggested that the Soviet Writers' Union meet and decide the issue for themselves.

The *Novy Mir* contingent did not know what to expect of the union, an organization famous for its cowardice. Many of the leaders who still ran the union headed the smear campaigns against Solzhenitsyn in the early 1970s which led to his exile. Zalygin and Borisov settled uneasily into their seats at the Central House of Writers.

The first speaker was the union first secretary, Vladimir Karpov, a veteran toady of the regime. Karpov was one of those hack novelists who, in return for unstinting obedience, won huge printings for his books, a large apartment, and a dacha in the shade. Just a year before, Karpov had told reporters at a news conference that Solzhenitsyn would never be welcomed back in the Soviet Union if he did not renounce his views: "If someone wants to come back to take part in our reform process, then he is welcome. But if a person has lied through his teeth and slandered our country from abroad and wants to come back and do the same from here, then there is no place for him." Surely, Karpov would do the Kremlin's bidding, Zalygin thought. But what would that bidding be?

"Comrades," Karpov began, "we used to think one way about Aleksandr Isayevich, but now things have changed. . . ."

Borisov felt his entire body lighten with happiness. The long wait was over. Solzhenitsyn's Nobel lecture appeared in the July 1989 issue of *Novy Mir* along with an announcement that the first of several installments of *The Gulag Archipelago* would appear in August. The state-run publishing house, Sovetsky Pisatel, announced that it would issue a multivolume *Collected Works.* After long exile, Solzhenitsyn had returned.

———

A few days after I got the first "Solzhenitsyn issue" of *Novy Mir* in the mail, I went with my friend Lev Timofeyev to see a theatrical version of *One Day in the Life of Ivan Denisovich* at the Independent Studio. There were no ads, no posters around town. The Independent Studio group was a poor, obscure troupe working out of a dank basement just around the corner from one of the most ominous buildings in Moscow: 38 Petrovka, the headquarters of the Interior Ministry police.

Backstage, I met with the lead actor, Yuri Kosikh. His head was shaved clean and he was dressed in his costume, the filthy padded jackets that prisoners wore in the camps throughout the Stalin era. Could it be that labor camp prisoners, like eccentric English colonels or French roués, were now "characters" on the Moscow stage?

Kosikh was quick to say, however, that the play was not distant to him. In rehearsals, he heard the voice of his father ringing in his head. His father had spent ten years in the labor camps of Kolyma. "I've played Chekhov, Shakespeare, every kind of role," Kosikh said. "But never has it come so smoothly. It's as if I'd internalized the being of Ivan Denisovich through my father."

Like the novella, the play began with five-o'clock reveille and ended with Ivan Denisovich falling asleep "fully content." And as in the novella, Kosikh's Ivan spends a day—one of hundreds—filled with petty humiliations, brutalities, and small triumphs of the spirit. The set was dreary, barbed wire draped over heating ducts, dirt scattered in clumps on the concrete floor. The light flickered weakly, even at "midday," like winter afternoons in Siberia.

The production was sometimes overwrought, but, all the same, Lev was deeply moved. He idolized Solzhenitsyn. Lev spent more than two years in the labor camp at Perm in the Urals—more than six months of that time in an isolation cell. He was a Gorbachev-era prisoner who was released only during the "amnesty wave" following Sakharov's return to Moscow from Gorky and the superpower summit in Reykjavik. No writer meant more to him than Solzhenitsyn. He had read *Gulag* in an underground edition, and just the memory of certain passages about the spiritual life of the prisoner helped sustain him throughout his own term. "Aleksandr Isayevich leveled the telling blow against the system," he said. "*The Gulag Archipelago* is the criminal and spiritual indictment of a sick society."

Onstage, Ivan Denisovich was falling asleep. There was darkness for a while, then the dawn of the house lights at half power and a stunned, desultory applause. The people in the audience finally rose to their feet, everyone weary and stretching, stunned to be in a theater and thinking, suddenly, of ordinary things: the walk home and how to buy some milk and bread for breakfast. But the feeling stayed with Lev for hours. As we walked down the street, he said, "That smell. Even that smell of wet leather and wet wool and sweat is the smell of the camps. It takes me back."

By 1990, political prisoners became a new breed of politician. In Ukraine, nationalists looked to former "politicals" to lead them: Bogdan and Mikhail Horyn, Stepan Khamara, Vyacheslav Chernovil. I met the philologist Levon Ter-Petrossian in Yerevan a week after he was released from prison; two years later he was elected president of Armenia. Georgia adored the former political prisoner Merab Kostava, and then mourned him endlessly after he was killed in a car crash. A far lesser man, Zviad Gamsakhurdia, filled the gap. Gamsakhurdia was a paranoiac, an untrustworthy fool, but he was, after all, a comrade to Kostava. That was his selling point. He would be elected Georgian president and then chased out of Tbilisi in a coup d'etat. Sakharov's protégé the biologist Sergei Kovalev, a prisoner in the Urals for many years, became a key leader in the Russian parliament. As a deputy, he suddenly found himself in a suit touring prison sites and instructing the commandants in the rudiments of decency and human rights.

According to the main human rights organizations in the Soviet Union and in the West, the last island of the gulag, the last outpost for political prisoners, was a camp in the Ural Mountains called Perm-35. Anatoly Shcharansky, Vladimir Bukovsky, Sergei Grigoryants, Timofeyev, and Kovalev had all spent time in Perm. Now the number of political prisoners had become so small that some of the Perm camps closed and were consolidated into just one, Perm-35.

Perm was a classic Soviet city—that is, an urban mass indistinguishable from hundreds of others, with a Lenin Avenue and broad and pitted streets and apartment blocks so ugly and uniform that you could weep looking at them. For a long time, Perm was closed to foreign journalists. Like many cities in the Urals, it was a center for military production. But now Perm was open, and getting to the camp turned out to be no problem at all. Accompanied by a local journalist I had gotten to know in Moscow, I paid a call on the chief of police. The Interior Ministry in the region was thoroughly bored by then with occasional visits by journalists or members of Congress. Colonel Andrei Votinov, the man in charge, was just a harmless wise guy. He wanted me to tell him why "in God's name" I wanted to drive for hours to see "a rathole." And after I explained my worthy reasons, I asked what conditions were like at Perm-35.

"You'll see," he said. "It's just like Switzerland."

I was told to return to my hotel and wait.

At eight the next morning, Major Nikolai Dronin, an unsmiling officer of the law, rapped on my door.

"So now we go to prison," he said.

It was a four-hour drive to Perm-35 from the city, but I was happy for the boredom. In Moscow, and even on trips to other republican capitals, it was easy to lose the sense of the vastness of the country. Out here it was easier to understand how so many hundreds of islands in the gulag archipelago could go unseen, tucked away in forests and mining villages and on mountaintops. All the banalities of the size of the Soviet Union—the eleven time zones, the number of times you could fit France into Kazakhstan, etc.—took on real meaning just by driving hour after hour. In the Urals, as in so many other places, Russia seemed like an unending frontier, wild and huge with only occasional settlements, hastily built towns, unlivable places where tens of millions of people lived, not villages so much as population clusters, work forces built around workplaces: lumber works, chemical plants, coal mines. All along the road, we saw peasant men riding wooden carts heaped with coal, humpbacked women carting their heavy sacks down the road. We could have driven for a week or more to the east and seen little else.

Finally there was a turnoff, primitive and unmarked. "The road to Perm-35," the major said.

My host would be Lieutenant Colonel Nikolai Osin, who had been running the camp since it went up in 1972. Shcharansky, Bukovsky, Marchenko, Stus, Orlov, Timofeyev: they all knew Osin. Shcharansky, especially, remembered his eyes, the dull gleam in the ruddy meat of his face. "Osin was an enormous, flabby man," Shcharansky wrote, "with small eyes and puffy eyelids, who seemed to have long ago lost interest in everything but food. . . . But he was a master of intrigue who had successfully overtaken many of his colleagues on the road to advancement. . . . I could see that he enjoyed his power over the prisoners and liked to see them suffer. But he never forgot that the zeks—the prisoners—were, above all, a means for advancing his career, and he knew how to back off in a crisis."

Once, when Shcharansky was refused permission to celebrate Hanukkah, he went on a hunger strike. Osin didn't want a scandal and cut a quick deal: if Shcharansky would end the hunger strike, he could light his Hanukkah candles. Shcharansky agreed, but demanded that while he said the appropriate prayers, Osin would stand by with his head covered and, at the end, say "Amen."

"Blessed are You, oh Lord, for allowing me to light these candles," Shcharansky began in Hebrew. "May you allow me to light the Hanukkah candles many times in your city, Jerusalem, with my wife, Avital, and my family and friends."

Inspired by the sight of Osin, Shcharansky added, "And may the day come when all our enemies, who today are planning our destruction, will stand before us and hear our prayers and say, 'Amen.'"

"Amen," Osin repeated.

Shcharansky quickly spread the word in Perm-35 of Osin's "conversion." This meant a freezing stint in the isolation cell, but Shcharansky could not resist. Today, Shcharansky lives in freedom in Israel. After his release, his mother sorted through photographs of her son in Jerusalem. She wanted to send a little memento to Lieutenant Colonel Nikolai Makarovich Osin.

———

Perm-35 was a tiny place, five hundred yards square, a few barracks, guard towers and razor wire everywhere. Osin was there to greet us, and he was much as Shcharansky had described him, enormously fat with dull, pitiless eyes. We went up a flight of stairs, past a few Party propaganda posters— "Socialism Is Order!"—to his office. Osin had a broad desk and a well-padded armchair, and he affected the pose of a contented chief executive officer. He was humbled only by the size of his work force. Just sixteen men remained in his charge. The Interior Ministry was planning to get rid of the "politicals" and bring in a "full population" of common criminals: rapists, murderers, thieves.

"So it's time to retire," the commandant said, leaning back as if waiting for the gold watch. "I'll be on a pension by the end of the year."

Osin tried, but failed, to conceal his disdain for the latest turn of Soviet history, the fitful lurch toward a civil society that was making him a relic of the totalitarian past. For years, he had inflicted punishment on dissident poets, priests, and mathematicians. He was, to use the Stalinist accolade, an exemplary "cog in the wheel." He did what he was told, "and all the prisoners were the same to me." Equal under lawlessness.

"You know, they talk about political prisoners, but there were never any political prisoners here," Osin said. "There were laws, and they were convicted on those laws, and that was it. They betrayed their Motherland. Later, the laws changed, but that's something else." There was no hint of repentance, or even self-doubt. "What do I have to regret?" he said. "People were sent here under the law, and I did what I was told to do. This was the work I chose, and I did it. This is what was required of me. I think the prisoners here have better living conditions than some people who are free. They have meat, after all." At this, Osin grabbed his belly and shook with laughter. He was a card.

Osin was not completely out of work, of course. The courts were still capable of indulging the political intrigues of local and regional Communist Party bosses, and, of all the branches of government, the judicial system has probably been touched least by reform. But most of the remaining cases were not, in the jargon of monitoring groups, "pure" political cases. In fact,

Gorbachev and the administration at Perm-35 claimed that there were no political prisoners in the country at all. "Most of the remaining cases are mixed—people who tried to flee the country illegally, people with ambiguous contacts with foreign groups," said Sergei Kovalev, a former political prisoner who eventually became the chairman of the human rights committee in the Russian parliament. "What I'm mainly working on is the length of their terms. People with ten, fifteen years in a camp for trying to row a raft to Turkey is absurd."

Like a good host at a housewarming party, Osin rose from behind his desk and said, "So! Let's give you the tour!"

Osin's tour, with an emphasis on the quality of the paint job and the cleanliness of the floors and toilet, was significant insofar as we saw no prisoners.

"They're off at work," Osin said.

When will they be back? I asked.

"Let's have lunch," Osin said.

And so we did, a meal beyond the imagination of the prisoners—cabbage soup, brown bread, salad, chicken, mashed potatoes, fruit juice. Then, like hurried tourists, we were off for more touring. We saw the infirmary. We saw the barracks where the men slept. But suddenly, as Osin was demonstrating the firmness of the camp beds, a pasty, middle-aged man with a shaved head and wearing prisoner coveralls burst through a door and down the hall, screaming.

"I must talk with you! They are beating me!"

"Yasin," Osin said glumly, his eyes still on the mattress. The commandant pursed his lips. His neck turned crimson.

"I must talk to you!" Yasin said. The guards tried to wrestle him back down the hall and into a room where they had been keeping the prisoners. I asked Osin if it would be all right to talk to the man, fully identified later as Valery Yasin. The commandant rolled his eyes and made a signal with his hand to suggest that Yasin was mentally unbalanced and not worth listening to. Still, Osin said, "Bring him back in."

The guards led Yasin back into the room. He was out of breath and his skin was pale and damp. He had been in and out of prisons, mental hospitals, and camps like Perm-35 for more than fifteen years. He had been accused of fleeing the country illegally, consorting with foreign intelligence. His term was set to run until the year 2003. Yasin's case, according to an official at Helsinki Watch, was murky—"the political and the criminal aspects are all tangled, confusing." There was, however, no doubting Yasin's fury. His words tumbled out between gasps for breath.

"For seven years I refused to go out for walks or to go out to the street.

This was my protest. I also demanded to stay alone in a one-man cell. I was in despair, sure I would be killed. They beat me. They demanded evidence that the KGB needed. They wanted me to cooperate with them and said that otherwise I'd be left to die here.

"I was desperate and slashed my arm. I was beaten and put in an isolation cell. This was in February. I lost one and a half liters of blood. I was half dead, and in this state I was dragged into the isolation cell, which was extremely cold, and they threw me in there naked. This was the order of Lieutenant Colonel Osin."

Osin, sitting nearby, rolled his eyes. He said nothing. A guard near the door spoke: "Let him say why he cut his veins!"

"I have a written document stating why I cut my veins," Yasin said. "They did barbaric things. On December 10, Human Rights Day, they forcibly shaved off my hair. I was beaten, my hands were twisted, my arms were twisted. This is how they celebrate Human Rights Day here."

The guard said, "You can only grow hair three months prior to release. How long until your release?"

"My hair was already short," Yasin said.

"If someone passes a new law, then maybe we won't shave your hair," the guard said. "Until then, if you don't get it cut voluntarily, then we'll do it by force."

Osin was silent.

Yasin was sweating. "So, this is how they abide by the law," he said. "They put handcuffs on people and beat people, under the pretext that the guy will resist. People are forced to submit to this humiliating procedure. All over the world, when your head is shaved bald, it is considered a humiliation."

With an imperial wave of the hand, Osin signaled the guard to lead Yasin out of the room. I asked to talk to a few more of the prisoners. Osin rolled his eyes, but agreed. The first man I asked to see was Yuri Pavlov, who had been sentenced to seven years on charges of espionage for the United States. The man I met did not seem capable of dialing the United States on the telephone. He was lethargic and distant and admitted to some sort of "brain injury." I asked him about the treatment of prisoners in Perm, and he said mechanically, "There are changes for the better. I remember how it was before, and I can compare with the present. When I was in Perm-36 with Timofeyev it was much worse. Now my complaints are mostly medical." Pavlov asked to be remembered to Timofeyev and walked slowly out the door.

Then the guard brought in the last prisoner on my list, Vitaly Goldovitch, a physicist who had worked in defense research and had been charged with treason and other crimes when he tried to row a rubber raft across the Black

Sea to Turkey. Goldovitch was nervous, his hands fluttering at his sides. Months passed with no visitors, no company except the guards and his fellow prisoners. No one had told him a reporter was coming, and now the words, half-pronounced, flew out of him. To try to calm him, I repeated what Pavlov had told me, that the treatment had gotten better lately. But Goldovitch said that was nonsense, that he was still manhandled and berated.

All the same, he said, "I'm trying to see the human being under the guards' uniforms. I can see that some of them may be good people, but they are crushed psychologically. There are almost no free people in the Soviet Union." Osin listened to all this with bored amusement. Once more he twirled his index finger around his ear, signaling that the charge was mere fantasy, craziness. Who would believe such a thing could happen in Perm-35?

As we left Goldovitch, I asked Osin to see the "isolators," the punishment cells. Nearly everyone in Perm-35, nearly every political prisoner in the history of the Soviet Union for that matter, had spent time in such places.

"Is this really necessary?" Osin asked.

Still, Osin walked outside in a huff, opened a huge gate, and pointed to a small field covered with snow and mud. There were rusted soccer goals at either end of the field. "Recreational facilities," he said angrily. "Here we let them play soccer, volleyball, whatever. I don't suppose they have that in prisons where you live, do they?"

Osin opened the door to a shed with a narrow hall and a series of tiny cells—the punishment cells. For now—perhaps for the benefit of the day's visitor—they were empty. Each one had a wooden plank for a bed. "See?" Osin said. "Not so terrible." In our talk, Goldovitch had said he spent more than a year in a punishment cell after a rebellion in Perm-35 in 1989. Some prisoners had refused to work, attend roll calls, or wear their names on their shirts. "We refused to do everything that was required as if we were soldiers of the army," he said. "We wanted to make this revolt in compliance with the law, in the framework of the law. Nine people ended up in the isolation cells after that.

"It is very hard but you get used to it. The cell is three meters long, one meter wide, two meters high. The cell is like your clothes. You are very cold, but in three days your body heat keeps you warmer. You walk around all day, don't sleep, look for some trifles, like filling the cracks with paper, to avoid going crazy. Or you wash your handkerchief over and over again. You think a lot and it helps."

Osin slammed shut the door to the cell and led me to our car. He said good-bye and did not smile.

During the ride back to the city, Major Dronin got to talking about politics, about the "lawlessness" in the country these days.

"There will be a dictatorship soon," he said with a certain relish in his voice. "It won't be the Communist Party organs, it will be the real organs— the KGB. They will try to develop the economy, but there will be a strict discipline."

As in Stalin's day? I asked.

"No, that was too harsh," he said. "But maybe as it was under Brezhnev or Andropov."

Dronin stared out the car window as the camp disappeared into the milky fog behind us. His eyes were open, but he seemed to be dreaming.

The decay of the old regime was evident in the old prison camp city of Magadan, where a statue of Lenin stood before a Communist Party headquarters building abandoned for lack of construction funds.

(*Edik Gladkov*)

Mikhail Gorbachev, the catalyst for the collapse of an empire and an ideology, began life as an actor in high school plays like *Masquerade* and *The
Snow Girl* and, as a provincial, came to Moscow for an education. He
played alongside his first girlfriend, Yulia Karagodina.

(*Courtesy of Yulia Karagodina*)

The most important element of glasnost was the ability to unearth the horrors of the regime. For the first time, people saw abandoned prison camps and, like this woman in Lithuania, the remains of relatives slaughtered by the secret police and buried in mass graves.

(Aleksandr Kuznetsov) *(Reuters/Bettmann)*

Pavel Litvinov, seen here with his wife and child in Siberian exile, was the grandson of Stalin's foreign commissar. In 1968 he helped organize a stunning protest against the Brezhnev regime. *(Courtesy Flora Litvinov)*

In Lithuania, Estonia, and Latvia, the popular fronts began their independence movements with protests against the 1939 Hitler-Stalin pact that led to the Soviet annexation.

(*David Remnick*)

Anna Larina, the widow of the Bolshevik revolutionary Nikolai Bukharin, who was killed in Stalin's purge. For Gorbachev, Bukharin represented an anti-Stalinist alternative in Soviet history and he sanctioned his rehabilitation after fifty years.

(*David Remnick*)

The poverty of everyday life in
the Soviet Union wore on the faces
of everyone, including these two
Siberians.

(*Aleksandr Kuznetsov*)

Three who made a revolution: Within the Communist Party hierarchy, adviser Aleksandr Yakovlev, Gorbachev, and foreign minister Eduard Shevardnadze were the chief architects of reform and fought an unending battle with more reactionary elements in the Party, the KGB, and the military.

(Reuters/Bettmann)

After he returned from forced exile in the city of Gorki, Andrei Sakharov was the spiritual leader of the democratic forces in Russia. Tens of thousands of people lined up to wish him farewell after his death in December 1989.

The author with archrivals Yegor Ligachev (top) and Boris Yeltsin. Ligachev bemoaned the "radicalization" of perestroika while Yeltsin left the Communist Party to lead the radicals and, eventually, Russia itself.

Journalist Len Karpinsky was an exemplar of the Gorbachev generation of officials and intellectuals who had lived lives of compromise and small gestures of protest until their moment arrived. Karpinsky, the "golden boy" of the Party as a young man, was a loyal Gorbachev supporter until the army massacre in Vilnius in January 1991.

In Siberia, faces of
rebellion and defeat.
(*Aleksandr Kuznetsov*)

In a time of revolution, despair took different forms. Nina Andreyeva, pictured here with her husband, wrote a neo-Stalinist manifesto that became a tool of the Communist Party's right wing in March 1988. (*David Remnick*)

In Moscow and in many other cities, people fell for the bread-and-circuses of faith healing, in person and via television. Here a woman holds the passport of her sick son and a bottle of water. The healer promises to "charge" the water and the photograph with "healing energy."

(*David Remnick*)

The coal miners' strikes in 1989 were the first signs of a "revolution from below." *(Reuters/Bettmann)*

Anatoly Shcheglov, a miner in Kemerovo, Siberia, said
he was through with a lifetime of unquestioning "slavery"
and led his brigade out of the pits.

(*David Remnick*)

Father Aleksandr Men, a defiantly independent Russian Orthodox priest in
a village outside Moscow, was murdered by someone wielding an ax. Many
Muscovites suspected the KGB or the right-wing Pamyat organization.
Though there was never an arrest, this shadowy, Dostoyevskian incident
was seen as a sign of conspiracy and a reactionary crackdown.

In the battle for Baltic independence, Estonia was the brains, Latvia the organizer, and Lithuania the moral leader. The Balts also sent emissaries to Georgia, Armenia, Central Asia, and other regions to help organize anti-Kremlin revolts. Here a woman in Vilnius, the Lithuanian capital, joins in an anti-Moscow demonstration. *(Reuters/Bettmann)*

Even on the first day of the August coup, there were signs that it would not succeed. Here a woman gives a young soldier some hard-boiled eggs for lunch as he stands guard outside the Russian parliament building where Boris Yeltsin was leading the resistance. *(Reuters/Bettmann)*

After the collapse of the coup, the streets of Moscow were a scene of celebration and the old Russian tricolor replaced the red Soviet flag forever.

Lenin's remains are still in the mausoleum on Red Square, but, despite all of Russia's lingering crises, there is little chance of his resurrection. *(Reuters/Bettmann)*

After the coup, a couple of workers play dominoes at a foundry that used to make busts of Lenin. The factory now operates for the tourist industry. *(Reuters/Bettmann)*

PART III

REVOLUTIONARY DAYS

"TOMORROW THERE WILL BE A BATTLE"

The facts of history evolve into the mythologies of history, but I had never realized just how quickly. Everything I was watching in Moscow, Vilnius, Siberia, and beyond instantly transcended "the facts"— the meetings, the demonstrations, the newspaper accounts, the transcripts and videotape. No part of the narrative, no conflict or uprising, was without its mythic dimension: the revenge drama of Gorbachev-and-Yeltsin, the David-and-Goliath drama of Lithuania-and-the Kremlin, the ironic drama of the coal miner proletariat. Most mythic of all was the presence of a saint among the foolish and the vain, among the insulted and injured. Sakharov was the founder of fire (the hydrogen bomb) who renounced his gift; who dedicated himself to the rescue of the Land of Nod when rescue seemed quixotic; who returned from exile to reveal his wisdom and prod the czar.

But there was the man, too, and, by the end of 1989, Sakharov looked as though he had wrung the last ounce of blood and energy from his body. He was sixty-eight and his face was delicate as parchment. He spoke in a slurred mumble. He had trouble walking up more than seven or eight stairs before gasping for breath; he was stooped, listing a little to the right. And yet the demands on his time and energy only increased. There were more visitors now to the apartment on Chkalova Street than there had been in the seventies when Sakharov's kitchen table was the crossroads of the human rights movement. Now no one had reason to be afraid to come, and so they all did, reporters, filmmakers, friends, foreigners on the make, acolytes, deputies, scholars from abroad.

In bringing home Sakharov from Gorky, an act that met with much grumbling in the Party nomenklatura, Gorbachev felt himself to be the kind and benevolent czar. He was proud. But Sakharov refused to indulge Gorbachev's vanity. Even in that first telephone conversation from Gorky, he quickly reminded Gorbachev of the death of one political prisoner, his dear friend Anatoly Marchenko, and then pressed for the release of a long list of others. Sakharov did what saints do; he lightly complimented the czar when he did right, but never let him relax. Sakharov's support was conditional; his decisions were based not on intra-Party realities—though he understood them well—but on a set of moral standards that could be etched on two small tablets of stone.

Sakharov respected Gorbachev as a brave politician, but he was not in awe of him. During the first session of the Congress, Gorbachev had given Sakharov the floor immediately and often, but when Sakharov tried to press Gorbachev into endorsing a "decree on power" that would end the Communist Party's guaranteed ascendancy, Gorbachev's response was haughty disdain. Saints annoy, and Sakharov annoyed Gorbachev profoundly. Even the transcript, devoid of the glares, the peremptory, bullying tone of Gorbachev's voice, showed that much:

GORBACHEV: Anyway, finish up, Andrei Dmitriyevich. You've used up two
    time allotments already.
SAKHAROV: I'm finishing. I am leaving out arguments. I have left out a great
    deal.
GORBACHEV: That's it. Your time, two time allotments, has run out. I beg
    your pardon. That is all.
SAKHAROV: [Inaudible]
GORBACHEV: That's all, Comrade Sakharov. Do you respect the Congress?
SAKHAROV: Yes, but I respect the country and the people even more. My
    mandate extends beyond the bounds of this Congress.
GORBACHEV: Good. That's all!
SAKHAROV: [Inaudible]
GORBACHEV: I ask you to finish. I ask you to conclude. That's all! Take
    away your speech, please! [Applause in the hall] I ask you to sit down.
    Turn on the other microphone.

There was part of Gorbachev that could not help but respect Sakharov, even envy him; but it rankled him, too, that the man he had deigned to release was, somehow, untouchable, uncontrollable. Sakharov seemed, somehow, to float above politics even as he was engaged in the most critical debates. When an Afghan vet attacked him and Sakharov was booed and whistled at by the hard-line majority, some viewers called in worried that Andrei Dmitriyevich would suffer a heart attack. But he was serene, absolutely serene. Perhaps it was that quality that helped drive Gorbachev to distraction. When the weekly tabloid *Argumenti i Fakti* published a poll showing that Sakharov was, by far, the most popular politician in the country, Gorbachev was incensed. He even threatened to fire the editor.

It was very simple: Sakharov represented the hard and inescapable truth. One evening during that first Congress session, Sakharov requested a private audience with Gorbachev. In his memoirs, Sakharov remembers waiting for the meeting:

"I could see the enormous hall of the Palace of Congresses, semidark and empty. There were guards at the distant doors. Finally, around a half hour later, Gorbachev came out with [his deputy, Anatoly] Lukyanov. Lukyanov had not been part of my plans, but there was nothing that could be done about it. Gorbachev looked tired, as did I. We moved three chairs to the corner of the stage at the table of the Presidium. Gorbachev was very serious throughout the conversation. His usual smile for me—half kindly, half condescending—never appeared on his face.

"I said, 'Mikhail Sergeyevich! It is not for me to tell you how serious things are in the country, how dissatisfied people are and how everyone expects things to get worse. There is a crisis of trust in the country toward the leadership and the Party. Your personal authority and popularity are down to zero. People cannot wait any longer with nothing but promises. A middle course in situations like these is almost impossible. The country and you are at a crossroads—either increase the process of change maximally or try to retain the administrative-command system with all its qualities. In the first case you must use the support of the 'left,' you can be sure there will be many brave and energetic people you can count on. In the second case, you know for yourself whose support you will have, but you will never be forgiven the attempt at perestroika.' "

In other words, side with the radicals, who you know are right; the Party apparatchiks, the military-industrial complex, are enemies no matter what you do. They will betray you no matter how long you coddle them. Do not delude yourself. But Sakharov could not break through to Gorbachev.

Just after the strikes broke out in Siberia, Sakharov, Yeltsin, Yuri Afanasyev, and the economist Gavriil Popov put together a radical opposition faction in the legislature, the Inter-Regional Group. That development only increased the tensions between Gorbachev and Sakharov at the next session of the Congress in December 1989. To his credit, once more Gorbachev made a point of calling on Sakharov to speak, but when the speech was too radical, he dismissed him summarily. "That's all!" Gorbachev barked as Sakharov tried to present him with tens of thousands of telegrams sent him in support of eliminating the Party's monopoly on power. At home, Sakharov despaired so of Gorbachev's "half-measures" that he wrote out in a thick spiral note-book his own proposed constitution envisioning a Eurasian commonwealth in which participation was voluntary and the Communist Party was one among many. Just as his essays in 1968 anticipated the ideas of perestroika, his constitution envisioned what would one day seem like sense itself. ("If we had only listened more carefully to Andrei Dmitriyevich, we might have learned something," Gorbachev would say three years later.)

Late in the afternoon of December 14, the Inter-Regional Group held an open caucus at the Kremlin. Sakharov looked worn out, and he dozed off during some of the other speeches. Yeltsin would say later that Sakharov was "obviously suffering," but no one said a word at the time and the session dragged on. Sakharov delivered a typically understated speech. He said he despaired of the current policy of half-measures and an opposition force was the only way to accelerate the reform process. Gorbachev's government, he said, was "leading the country into catastrophe and dragging out the process of perestroika over many years. During this period it will leave the country in a state of collapse, intensive collapse. . . . The only way, the only possibility of an evolutionary path, is to radicalize perestroika." Once more he pressed Gorbachev to repeal Article 6 of the Constitution, which gave the Commu-nist Party a guaranteed monopoly on power. Instead of heading home when the session was over, Sakharov agreed to meet with some Kazakh journalists at a hotel near the Kremlin for a long interview.

Back at his apartment, Sakharov told his wife, Yelena Bonner, that he was going downstairs to his study. He wanted to take a nap and then get up to write another speech. He asked Bonner to come wake him at nine. He had a lot of work to do before morning. "Tomorrow," he said, "there will be a battle."

When Bonner went downstairs to wake her husband, she found him in the hallway on the floor, dead. "The totalitarian system probably killed him," Vitaly Korotich said later. "I'm only glad that before he died Sakharov dealt the system a mortal blow. If God sent Jesus to pay for the sins of humankind, then a Marxist God somewhere sent Andrei Sakharov to pay for the sins of our system."

By nine in the morning of the 15th, as the deputies milled around in the vast foyer of the Palace of Congresses, everyone knew, was finding out, or was about to know. The men and women closest to Sakharov looked stricken. They stood alone or with friends, saying nothing, smoking and staring through the windows that looked out on the churches and spires of the Kremlin. Yuri Karyakin, the Dostoevsky scholar who had helped found the Moscow Tribune study group with Sakharov, told me the country had lost its "perfect moral compass." Yeltsin wandered the hall, loose-limbed and aimless, until a few of us asked him about Sakharov. Yeltsin seemed relieved to have a task, to deal with the cameras and the notebooks. "We must come to the end of the path that Sakharov began. Our duty is to Sakharov's name, to the persecution he suffered," he said, sounding very much like a man talking to himself.

Gorbachev, in his constant need to appeal to the majority of deputies in the room, played politics. It would take him years to admit fully to Sakharov's influence, and now he chose not even to announce the news himself or comment from the rostrum. He expressed his regrets to the liberal weekly *Moscow News,* but would not do the same in front of this audience. He lost the moment. Instead, one of the thickest men in the Politburo, Vitaly Vorotnikov, was in the chairman's seat and his gavel came down at ten o'clock. Vorotnikov stood and droned that "one of the country's greatest scientists and a prominent public figure," Andrei Dmitriyevich Sakharov, was dead. "His contribution to the defense capability of the state was great and unique," he allowed. But when it came to politics, Vorotnikov was all euphemism: "The objective analysis of various aspects of his activities is the province of history." No mention of the dissident movement or the new opposition, nothing of his moral leadership or example.

Then we all rose for a minute of silence.

From there, Gorbachev just let Vorotnikov go on with business. Members of Sakharov's circle found it astonishing that the session was not called off for the day or that the day of the funeral was not declared a day of national mourning. Ilya Zaslavsky, the thirty-year-old engineer crippled by a childhood blood disease, hobbled on his crutches to the podium. He represented the October Region of Moscow. Before the session, Zaslavsky had approached Gorbachev and asked that he declare a day of mourning in honor of Sakharov. Gorbachev refused, telling him it was "not the tradition." And so now Gorbachev knew very well what Zaslavsky wanted to say, and before the young deputy could open his mouth, Gorbachev said firmly, "Sit down!" But Zaslavsky would not move. Again, Gorbachev told him to sit. And again Zaslavsky stood his ground and waited only for the deputies to stop their murmuring and hear him out. From the side of the stage came a flunky who tried deftly to "help" Zaslavsky down the steps. Zaslavsky cast him a withering look, the look of a boxer staring across the ring at a presumptuous opponent. The flunky slunk away. And so now Gorbachev had the choice of either forcing a young cripple to his chair for the crime of wanting to speak out for a fallen saint, or to give in. It was an amazing standoff, and even from my gallery seat, I could see (with a pair of binoculars) the fury in Gorbachev's eyes. But he gave in. Zaslavsky demanded a day of mourning, and the chairman said the suggestion would be taken under advisement. It never was.

Later, Zaslavsky told me about the encounter. "I considered it my duty not to sit down," he said. "Sometimes a person has to say his piece. Sakharov was the conscience of our country. I have admired him since childhood and I felt this was my duty to him. At the beginning of the session I approached Gorbachev and asked him to call for national mourning, but he said he could probably not do that because it would defy tradition. We have a procedure, it seems, for this: a general secretary gets three days of mourning, a Politburo member one, and none for an academician. Gorbachev said that according to precedent, there should be no such mourning. But all the other countries will be in mourning. What about us?"

Meanwhile, the hard-liners in the Congress could not restrain their scorn for Sakharov. They, too, played their part in the mythic narrative, the unbelievers, the heathen raging against the saint. They had jeered him when he was at the rostrum and now they disdained him in death. Tatyana Zaslavskaya, a sociologist who had given Gorbachev invaluable advice on public opinion before he came to power, told me she was filled with shame and disgust hearing the "mocking, filthy remarks made by the apparat" about Sakharov. When it was finally announced that the session would be suspended for a few hours on the day of the funeral, the conservatives hissed. There was hypocrisy everywhere. Tass, which had slandered Sakharov in his lifetime as a "foreign agent" and "moneygrubber," was now spitting out shameless tributes over the wires. And by the way, came one announcement, exclusive videotape of Sakharov's last days is available to foreign television stations—for $1,500, hard currency only. There were other squalid moments, too. Yevgeny Yevtushenko scurried around the Congress buffet, handing out to correspondents (in Russian and English) a copy of the poem that he had written, instantly, in honor of Sakharov. "Maybe you will print it on your editorial page?" he said.

The people of Moscow were fast turning 48 Chkalova Street into a shrine. They came alone and in groups and heaped carnations at the doorstep. Someone tacked a photograph of Sakharov to the wall, and, as if this were not icon enough, others put lighted candles and flowers around it. One of the first mourners at the building put out a thick notebook for the people to write out messages of farewell. "We are orphans," one entry said. "Without you, there is no one to defend us and our children." "Shame on the murderers," said another. "Forgive us for all the misfortune that we caused you. Forgive us for the fact that now only good things will be said of you by those who did not do so while you were alive. Words will not help, and we did not safeguard your life. But I believe we will safeguard your memory. Forgive us."

Upstairs, Bonner was frantic with grief. With her husband's body still in the apartment, she had to go through the ordeal of planning the funeral with Gorbachev's man, Yevgeny Primakov. Finally, an ancient and humpbacked ambulance pulled up in the slush near Primakov's limousine. Three medics in dirty smocks went up to Sakharov's place. They strapped the body to a stretcher and carried him down seven flights of stairs to the car. Then Bonner had to deal with the reporters out on the stairs. She stuck her head out the door and lost it: "You all worked hard to see that Andrei died sooner by calling us from morning till night, and never leaving us to our life and work. Be human beings! Leave us alone!"

Bonner did have a terrifying temper, but she, too, had to be admired deeply. She was indispensable to Sakharov, his lion at the gate. She protected him, inspired him, and he loved her ferocity. In their human rights work, Sakharov and Bonner were a team. They suffered, physically and psychologically, as equals. The KGB harassed the Sakharovs every way they could, even mailing them "Christmas cards" with grotesque images of mutilated bodies and monkeys with electrodes stuck in their skulls. There were threats against their children and grandchildren. Tass, *Izvestia,* and *Pravda* spewed reams of slander. In Gorky, thugs broke into the apartment waving pistols. After threatening to turn the apartment "into an Afghanistan," one of the men turned to Sakharov and said, "You won't be here long. They'll take you to a sanatorium where they have medicine that turns people into idiots." A "historian" named Nikolai Yakovlev wrote a book insulting Bonner as a "sexual brigand . . . who foisted herself on the widower Sakharov." In the most memorable moment in the history of Russian chivalry, Sakharov— good, gentle Andrei Dmitriyevich—confronted Yakovlev and slapped him square in the face.

"A year ago, Yelena Georgiovna and I went to Paris together for a conference on human rights," Lev Timofeyev told Esther at the wake. "Andrei Dmitriyevich was coming from the States and had met us at the airport. They hadn't seen each other for a month and a half, and when they saw each other, their faces lit up like young newlyweds. Such clear young faces. They saw nothing except one another. All the journalists who were waiting there seemed out of place, and I felt like an interloper at a meeting of two lovers."

Primakov offered Bonner a general secretary's funeral for Sakharov. He could lie in state at the Hall of Columns across from the Kremlin—the same place where the corpses of the various Bolshevik leaders had been put on display in their time. Bonner said no. She wanted something less official, and unique to Sakharov. She chose the Palace of Youth, an enormous hall on Komsomolsky Prospekt.

The next morning it was so desolate and cold that it hurt to breathe. Esther and I picked up Flora and Misha Litvinov and some of their friends and walked along the ice to the Palace of Youth. We were an hour early for the wake and were stunned to see that a line of thousands of people had already formed. We found people in line who had flown from Leningrad, Armenia, and Siberia. There were Azeris and Crimean Tatars, teenagers and children, old men and women who suffered terribly in the cold. Some of them waited three or four hours, their faces red and chapped—but they waited.

Inside, Sakharov was laid out on a coffin festooned in red and black crepe. Within moments after the doors had opened, mountains of flowers accumulated at his feet. Yelena Georgiovna sat off to the side with her children and other family from Russia and the United States. Yeltsin, Timofeyev, Sergei Kovalev, and many others stood near the coffin as honor guards. And for the next five hours the long flow of people streamed by at a slow, unceasing step.

"Forgive us!" one woman cried out as she passed. "Forgive us, Andrei Dmitriyevich!"

Yelena Georgiovna walked over to the coffin and bent over her husband, kissed his forehead, smoothed his cheek with the back of her knuckles. She stood a long time there, her elbow draped over the coffin and her face buried in her hands.

———

If the day of mourning at the Palace of Youth had shown the general grief set off by Sakharov's death, the next day made clear the political dimension of his loss.

At nine-thirty on December 18, a string of black limousines pulled up to the front entrance of the Academy of Sciences building on Leninsky Prospekt. Gorbachev and a half-dozen other Politburo members got out of their cars and walked up the stairs past a banner of Lenin that read: "Under the Banner of Marxism-Leninism, the Leadership of the Communist Party, Forward Toward the Victory of Communism! Proletarians of the World, Unite!" It had gotten slightly warmer, and there was a mix of drizzle and fat snowflakes that melted when they hit the ground. A few minutes later, the funeral train arrived, a police Mercedes leading a few decrepit yellow buses. As

Sakharov's coffin was unloaded from the back of one of the buses, Bonner spoke briefly with Gorbachev and the other members of the Politburo. She told Gorbachev that with the death of Sakharov he had lost his most loyal opponent. He asked if there was anything he could do for her. Yes, she said. Memorial had still not been registered as an official national organization. It will be done, Gorbachev said.

A member of the honor guard lifted the lid of the coffin. Gorbachev took off his gray fur hat and stepped to the foot of the casket. The other members of the Politburo took off their hats and flanked their general secretary. They stood in silence for two or three minutes, all of them staring at Sakharov's pale and regal face. Someone held a black umbrella over the coffin. Then, with two quick nods of the head, as if to say, "Okay, enough," Gorbachev signaled that the moment was over. The group went inside the Academy of Sciences and signed a memorial book. The general secretary wrote "M. S. Gorbachev" in a bold script and the rest of the Politburo signed below in more modest hands.

Before Gorbachev left, a reporter asked him a question about Sakharov's Nobel Prize for Peace in 1975, an event that the Brezhnev regime had taken as a humiliating international endorsement of state treason.

"It is clear now," Gorbachev said, "that he deserved it."

Early in the afternoon, the funeral cortege slowly wended its way from the physics institute where Sakharov had once worked to the parking lot of the Luzhniki sports complex near the Moscow River. I was just a few yards behind the lead bus. The back door was open and Bonner sat on a bench next to the coffin. Yeltsin was walking just ahead of me. Even then it was clear that if anyone was going to take the lead of the political opposition, it was Yeltsin; and yet he knew that Sakharov and the people closest to Sakharov regarded him with apprehension. Yeltsin was not one of them. He was, after all, a former member of the Politburo. But while Yeltsin already had tremendous support as a populist, he wanted badly to widen his appeal, to learn from the radical democrats and to get their support. By walking just behind Sakharov's casket he was not so much grandstanding as he was keeping himself as close as possible to everything he was not, but wanted to be.

The march went on for hours. It was not until we reached Luzhniki that I could see how many people had come to say farewell to Sakharov. No fewer than fifty thousand people had packed into a vast parking lot. And there was something far more striking about the crowd than its mere size. It was the first time that I got any sense that there could ever be a unified democratic movement in the Soviet Union. Until now, the miners, the Baltic independence groups, the Moscow and Leningrad intelligentsia had all seemed spread out, loosely knit at best. But now I saw Baltic flags, a Russian tricolor, banners supporting the Rukh independence movement in Ukraine, miners from Vorkuta, students. There were placards with a huge "6" crossed out—meaning that Article 6 of the Constitution, which guaranteed the Party's "leading role" in society, should be eliminated.

Oginsky's "Farewell to the Motherland" played through the loudspeakers. The speakers included former political prisoners—Kovalev and dissident priest Father Gleb Yakunin among them—and the politicians who would now have to begin filling in the enormous vacuum: Yeltsin, the Lithuanian independence leader Vytautas Landsbergis, the Leningrad law professor Anatoly Sobchak, Ilya Zaslavsky, Yuri Afanasyev, Gavriil Popov. Sakharov's casket was hoisted up in front of the flatbed truck where the speakers stood, and Bonner, wearing Sakharov's gray fur hat, stood near the microphone smoking cigarettes. She stepped up to speak only once, asking everyone to make room so that the ceremony would be peaceful and safe. Only a non-Soviet would have missed the reference: in the days after Stalin's death, the crowd outside the Hall of Columns was so dense and emotional that hundreds of people were crushed to death—a fitting tribute.

Dmitri Likhachev, the scholar of Russian literature and the oldest of all the deputies in the Congress, was the first to speak: "Most respected Yelena Georgiovna, relatives, friends, colleagues, and students of Andrei Dmitriyevich! Respected comrades! We are gathered here to honor the memory of a very great man, a citizen not only of our country, but of the whole world. A man of the twenty-first century, a man of the future. This is why many did not understand him in this century.

"He was a prophet, a prophet in the ancient sense of the word. That is, he was a man who summoned his contemporaries to moral renewal for the sake of the future. And like every prophet, he was not understood. He was driven from his own city."

Afanasyev said that in the future the union of democratic forces should be named for Sakharov. Father Gleb Yakunin compared Sakharov to a holy man; others mentioned Martin Luther King, Gandhi, Tolstoy. Landsbergis said that on Cathedral Square in Vilnius, church bells were ringing out in tribute to Sakharov. As they listened to the speeches, many people held candles and wept. As darkness gathered, the service broke up. The huge crowd shuffled to the metro stations and the bus stops. I have never heard so many people be so quiet.

The burial was an hour later on the outskirts of Moscow at Vostryakovskoye, a cemetery cut out of a pine forest. The snow was falling once more, and everywhere was the smell of pine and snow. A military band played Chopin's "Funeral March" and Schumann's dirge "Traumerai." Sakharov's grave, fresh and deep, was dug out next to two straight pines and the grave of Bonner's mother, Ruf. Bonner let a cigarette drop from her hands into the wet earth. She pulled back the thin white cloth that covered Sakharov's face, kissed him one last time, covered him, and stepped away. But she could not bear it. She came back, kissed him once more, and lingered there. I was near Timofeyev, who stood at attention, tears flowing into his beard. Finally the music stopped. Two workmen closed the coffin and lowered it into the grave. Bonner threw a bit of dirt down onto the coffin. Others did the same, with dirt and pine branches still dusted with snow, and everywhere there was quiet except for the thud of the dirt and the branches on the coffin. The gravediggers filled in the hole and Bonner watched, smoking. Soon the mourners, carrying candles, covered the grave over with flowers, red carnations and yellow roses. Then they stepped back and lingered. There was nothing left to do. Once more the rain began to fall.

———

I felt hollow that day and for days after. I have never felt that way about anyone's death except the death of those whom I have loved. Many people I knew in Moscow felt the same, and even more strongly for having lived their lives under the regime. In March 1953, the bewitched people of the Soviet Union learned of Stalin's death and asked themselves, "What now?" Now, the spell was finally gone, but the question was the same. "What now?" Sakharov was just better than the rest of us. His mind worked on an elevated plane of reason, morality, and patience. Valentin Turchin, one of Sakharov's closest associates both in physics and the human rights movement, remembered one typical episode:

"It was September 1973, soon after the infamous letter of forty academicians condemning Sakharov. I was sitting with the Sakharovs—in their kitchen, as usual—and discussing the letter. The Sakharovs had just returned from a Black Sea resort, and Yelena told me about a funny occurrence which took place a couple of days before they left. They were taking the sun at the beach when a short man ran up to Andrei Dmitriyevich, said how glad he was to meet him, shook his hand, and several times repeated how fortunate it was that such a person was among them.

" 'Who was that?' Yelena asked when the short man departed. Andrei Dmitriyevich answered that it was Academician so-and-so. Three days later, when the letter of forty was published, that academician was among the signers. Yelena, who is generally emotional, spoke with contempt and indignation, which were certainly well justified. I looked at Andrei Dmitriyevich: what was his reaction? It was very typical of him. He was not indignant about the episode. He was *thinking* about it."

The Soviet Union could ill afford to lose such a man.

CHAPTER 20

LOST ILLUSIONS

Aleksandr Yakovlev thought he was a dead man. He lay on a swampy battlefield outside Leningrad, his body and legs riddled by Nazi machine-gun fire. It was dark and cold and he was terrified. He was a village boy, so sickly as a child that his mother waited two years before she registered his birth. Now he was eighteen and a lieutenant in the Baltic marines' 6th Brigade and he was going to die. His only chance for survival was the tradition of the Soviet marines: no one was to be left on the battlefield, not the wounded, not even the dead. Tradition saved him. Five of Yakovlev's buddies sprinted onto the field to get him. The first four were shot down and killed. The fifth scooped Yakovlev up in his arms and ran. They made it. Yakovlev came home to his village outside Yaroslavl on crutches. His mother was so horrified at her son's condition that he felt as if he had failed her. There were three younger sisters to feed and the country was a ruin. What was he going to do with his life?

A half century later, after he had become known as Gorbachev's closest adviser and the intellectual architect of perestroika, Yakovlev told a group of students at Moscow State University how he, a wounded teenaged veteran of war, became a man of the Communist Party. He went to a pedagogical institute and dreamed of a career in teaching. But he had also become a Party member in 1944. With millions of Party activists dead or still in battle, the local bosses scrambled to train young Communists, to fill up the ranks. They urged Yakovlev into political work and out of academia. "Then, after a number of years, enrollment began for the Higher Party School," Yakovlev told his audience. "I was invited for an interview to the regional Party committee. I didn't know what they wanted of me. In those times, everything was done in an atmosphere of utmost secrecy. I was asked to sit for exams, which I passed to become a trainee of the Higher Party School. That was how I started."

For liberal students in Moscow in February 1990, Yakovlev was about the only figure in the Politburo who could be trusted—Gorbachev included. The Communist Party was, for them, a dead issue. No one took the old exams in Party history anymore; those who specialized in Party history did so with the dispassionate interest of anthropologists studying the lives of cannibals and fire-eaters. Downstairs, in the main lobby of the university, students pinned up the most notorious quotations of Lenin and Stalin; they started clubs in honor of the Beatles, Iron Maiden, banned Russian authors, and American baseball. But they were young and still wanted to know what it was like to have lived through a nightmare.

Yakovlev told the students he was a typical member of his generation. He and his buddies had run into battle shouting, "For Stalin! For the Motherland!" They believed in the "shining future" promised by the Party. In Korolyovo, the tiny village where Yakovlev grew up, no one could even begin to understand the great tragedy the country was living through. When one of Yakovlev's great-uncles was thrown off his land and deported in the twenties, no one understood that this was part of a far greater collectivization campaign in which millions would die. There were few newspapers around, and the ones that could be found were filled with lies. Many of the people in the region, including Yakovlev's mother, were illiterate; his father had four years in a Russian Orthodox school, his mother no schooling at all. It was only through an accident of kindness and loyalty that Yakovlev's father did not disappear into the meat grinder of the purges.

"Our district military commissariat was headed by a man named Novikov. As it turned out, he was the commander of my father's platoon during the Civil War. He was an extraordinary person. I remember how he would ride through our village high on his horse, talking with all the kids and conscripts. He was the only one we knew from the district leadership. One day he came and knocked on the window with his whip handle. My father was not home, and Novikov told my mother, 'Tell him that he should go to the conference, which—only be sure to get this right—will last three days at least. I'll come later.'

"Mama didn't understand. When she went to tell my father, he questioned her several times—especially about that last phrase, 'I'll come later.' My father packed some things in a bag and went to a neighboring district, to mother's sister Raya—'to the conference.' He told mama where he could be found, just in case. Mama was a quiet woman, a peasant.

"That night, there was a knock at the door and they asked where my father was. Mama said, 'He went to the conference.'

" 'What conference?'

" 'I don't know,' she said. 'He didn't say.'

"They left. They came again the next night. . . . And after three days, Novikov showed up. That's what the friendship of the front meant. Not everything was inhuman. Then Novikov told Mama it was time to tell her husband to come home. The 'conference' was over! Mama sent me off to get him."

As Yakovlev well understood years later, the local Party committee probably had a "plan" to fulfill: kill X number of people in Y number of days. When Nikolai Yakovlev could not be found, they just found someone else.

By 1956, Yakovlev was living in Moscow and working at the Central Committee headquarters. As a young instructor—in fact, the youngest in the building—he received an "observer" invitation to attend the Twentieth Party Congress in the Kremlin. He sat in the balcony and listened to Khrushchev deliver his breakthrough report on Stalin's personality cult. As Khrushchev described the purges of the Party and military ranks, the delegates sank into a state of shock. The complicit were humiliated, the ignorant stunned. "There was a deathly silence," Yakovlev recalled. "People did not look at one another. I remember sitting in the balcony and from up there you could hear just one word spoken, the same word, one after the other: 'Yes.' You could hear only that: 'Yes.' There were no conversations. People went around shaking their heads. What we had heard did not quite penetrate right away. It was very hard, very hard. It was especially hard for those of us who had not become hardened by cynicism, who still had ideals and yet did not know the truth."

Khrushchev committed a heroic deed at that Twentieth Congress, Yakovlev told me. But the tragedy was that "he never could take the next step toward democratization. . . . Instinctively, he understood it was necessary to move forward, but he was thigh-deep in the muck of the past and he couldn't break free. When he grew older in his memoirs he regretted that he had not gone forward. But memoirs do not make up for a man's life."

By his early thirties, Yakovlev was the deputy head of the Central Committee's Department of Science and Culture, and there he began to learn about "that cruel force" the Party apparat. He arrived an ideological romantic, a believer in Leninism and the new thaw. But he found himself inside the most Orwellian world of all, one of whispered threats, hermetic codes of behavior and privilege, black comedy. He was at one meeting at which a department chief accused someone of "Trotskyism" as it related to his supervision of animal husbandry. Yakovlev, too, was subject to the "petty brutalizations" of a life in the apparat. "For example, I once received a prize for a review of a film I never saw," he said, recalling an incident in the Yaroslavl Party organization. "There came an order from 'the center' to publish in all the papers a review of the movie *The Battle of Stalingrad.* They called the editor and said the review had to be in the next day's paper. The film hadn't come to our region and no one had seen it. We called the local film purveyor and it turned out that he had a list of the actors and the plot of the film. I wrote off of that. I knew some of the actors from other films, and I could say how they had 'profoundly revealed their characters' or some such. It goes without saying that the review was positive."

———

Yakovlev's career before 1985 was a mix of the academic and the apparatchik. After he won an advanced degree in history and philosophy, the Party thought him reliable enough to send to New York for a year of study at Columbia University. Yakovlev's classmates in New York remember him as doctrinaire and defensive, but intellectually curious. He traveled around the northeast and midwest and wrote a thesis on the politics of the New Deal, a program that he would later take as a kind of inspiration for perestroika. Yakovlev enjoyed the experience, but he was also haunted for years by the ignorance of Americans about the Soviet Union. For many years to come he would tell people a story about a New Yorker who asked him if all Russians had horns.

As Brezhnev took power, Yakovlev's work back in Moscow took a curious turn. He was highly valued in the propaganda department of the Party—the department that ran television and the press—but he was increasingly thought of as not quite reliable. In 1966, when the writers Andrei Sinyavsky and Yuli Daniel were arrested, Brezhnev's "gray cardinal," Mikhail Suslov, asked Yakovlev to handle the "propaganda side" of the trial. The Sinyavsky and Daniel affair was one of the first major dissident trials, and Yakovlev, repulsed by the incident, found a way to keep his distance. He did not have rebellion in mind. He valued his career and comforts too much for that. But Yakovlev did tell Suslov that the trial should be handled by the some other department. "I said that I was not sufficiently 'in the know' to take part," Yakovlev told me. "I wouldn't exactly call that bravery of the highest order." After that and similarly subtle "defenses" of dissidents such as Sakharov and

Lev Kopelev, Yakovlev said, "the Brezhnev leadership treated me with the utmost distrust" and refused to make him head of the department instead of acting head.

In the 1970s, Yakovlev even helped protect a young Party leader in southern Russia, Mikhail Gorbachev, who was carrying out experiments by hiring student brigades during harvest time. "He was organizing these brigades and paying them, and this was thought to be ideologically unsound," Yakovlev said. "He was obviously an impressive man and I did what I could for him."

As a polemicist for the Central Committee. Yakovlev wrote his share of agitprop monographs and books, wooden diatribes mainly about the American "empire" and "imperial ideology." He even edited a volume of the Pentagon Papers. These labors were all greatly appreciated by the Central Committee. But Yakovlev ended his career as a Party propagandist by writing a long, and unusually pointed, article directed against Russian nationalism. In November 1972, the weekly *Literaturnaya Gazeta* splashed the article, "Against Anti-Historicism," across two full pages. Yakovlev lashed out at the hard-line nationalists for making a "cult of the patriarchal peasantry," for romanticizing the prerevolutionary past. The article was directed especially at writers for the journal *Molodaya Gvardiya* ("Young Guard"), who saw the rise of Western intelligentsia both inside and outside the Party as a grave threat to Russia's "national spirit." Yakovlev couched his argument in the ritualistic language of Leninism, attacking the writers for their "extra-class and extra-social approach," but he also made a veiled defense of "intellectualism," a term understood as thinking outside the boundaries of official dogma.

Brezhnev and his ideological guard dogs did not like the article at all. Yakovlev knew now for sure that he no longer had a place in the Central Committee apparatus. As if to head off the punishment from above, he invented his own. He asked about diplomatic work, perhaps in an English-speaking country. Within hours, it was done. Yakovlev was sent to Canada, and there he stayed for ten years, an ambassador and an exile.

At the embassy in Ottawa, Yakovlev improved his English and marinated in the books, articles, and pop culture around him. He met regularly with Canadian officials, diplomats, and intellectuals. And he continued to write. "Canada was wonderful for me. It was a way out," Yakovlev told me. It was in Canada that Yakovlev also forged his relationship with Gorbachev. In May 1983, Gorbachev was a leading member of the Politburo. He came to Canada and traveled with Yakovlev across the country, from Niagara Falls to Calgary, in an old Convair prop plane. They visited farmers and businessmen, but the most important talks they held were with each other. According to both men, they spent hours talking about the disasters awaiting the Soviet

Union, the rot at the core of the economic system, the self-crippling lack of openness in the press, the cultural and scientific worlds. "The most important common understanding," Yakovlev told me, "was the idea that we could not live this way anymore. . . . We talked about absolutely everything, openly, and it was clear to me that this was a new kind of leader. It was a thrilling experience politically and intellectually."

Yakovlev wanted to return to Moscow, and Gorbachev had the power to give him his wish. Within a month, Yakovlev became the director of one of the most prestigious and liberal-minded think tanks in Moscow, the Institute of World Economy and International Relations (IMEMO).

For Western Sovietologists trying to figure out the thinking of the team forming around Gorbachev both before and after he took power in March 1985, Yakovlev was a beguiling figure. Cold warriors took one look at Yakovlev's book of the early Reagan era, *On the Edge of an Abyss,* and decided he was a hard-liner, a figure who would do nothing at all to ease Soviet-American relations in the near future. Scholars searching for flexibility in the nascent Gorbachev team found none in Yakovlev's opus. *On the Edge of an Abyss* reads like the sort of tract the Young Spartacus League might have been passing out on college campuses twenty years ago. In a voice of rage inherited from *What Is to Be Done?* Yakovlev lit into the United States as a smug, soft, and warped country sporting a "messianic ideology" and the urge to police and "dominate the world." John Wayne, TV evangelists, the "bourgeois press," and Norman Podhoretz all made him sick. For Yakovlev, the United States was "a miserable sight. A miserable democracy. Unfortunately, many Americans still harbor illusions. They are used to believing that they elect law-givers, benefactors and defenders and are shocked to discover that some of them sold themselves out long ago. This is an indisputable fact. However, the bourgeois propaganda media go out of their way to prove the contrary. . . . The romanticizing of brutality, approval of violence, the relishing of sex exploits and the portrayal of murder as an ordinary and normal phenomenon are characteristic features of the mass media and culture. . . . The main hero Americans see everywhere—in the movies, on television, in books, magazines and newspapers—is a gangster, sleuth, or sadist."

And yet, read in retrospect, *On the Edge of an Abyss* showed Yakovlev was a consumer of rigorous books and articles about the United States. He read everything from *Foreign Affairs* and *International Security* to the memoirs of Henry Kissinger. He also had a better sense of humor than most ideological warriors: "Some say, for example, that of all the superficial roles Reagan played while a film actor, the most successful one was as the sidekick to a chimpanzee named Bonzo. This film has not been forgotten by the public.

Demonstrators in Toronto, Canada, who came out to protest Reagan's militarist policies, carried placards admonishing Americans for having chosen the wrong chimpanzee."

Years later, when I asked him about his pre-perestroika books, Yakovlev said that they, like their author, were "prisoners of the time." "Had I not been in the U.S.A. and Canada, I would never have written such books about America," he said. "But being an impulsive man, when I read newspapers and books criticizing my country, well, this hurt me deeply. For example, I know that I am crippled. But when every day people tell me, 'You are crippled, you are crippled,' I get furious! And then I answer back: 'You are the cripple! You yourself are the fool!' "

———

From the moment Gorbachev took power, Yakovlev was an essential, if not lead, player in every progressive idea, policy, or gesture coming from the Kremlin. Yakovlev was a peculiar animal in the Communist Party leadership. Unlike most of the men in the Politburo, he never ran a republic or a region or even an industrial plant; he was never at the head of one of the major institutions like the army or the KGB. "The truth was he didn't know anything about ordinary life or practical politics," Yegor Ligachev, Yakovlev's nemesis in the Politburo, told me.

Yakovlev was simply the man at the leader's side, the homely intellectual with twitchy brows and goggly glasses whispering into the ear of the general secretary. "Seneca to Gorbachev's Nero," a Russian friend said. "Or maybe Aristotle to Alexander the Great?" In any case, it turned out that the obligatory language and fury of *On the Edge of an Abyss* masked a unique intelligence and a powerful urge to remake the Soviet Union. Yakovlev explored the New Deal, Kant's *Critique of Pure Reason,* the early socialists, and far less exalted texts for answers. One afternoon, Vitaly Korotich came to the Kremlin to see Yakovlev about an issue of *Ogonyok* and was amused to discover that the Communist Party's chief ideologist had his team of aides spend the afternoon "studying" a video of *Raiders of the Lost Ark*—presumably to understand the peculiarities of American media and self-image. It is not known whether Yakovlev's antipathy toward John Wayne extended to the more politically correct adventures of Harrison Ford.

Between 1985 and 1990, Yakovlev's accomplishments were legion. He helped draft the foreign-policy principles of "the new thinking." Because it dispensed with the classic Leninist approach of a class-based approach to foreign affairs, "the new thinking" gave an ideological rationale for everything from the withdrawal from Afghanistan to the rapprochement with the United States to the policy of noninterference in Eastern Europe.

Yakovlev engineered the cultural revolution known as glasnost by using his power to appoint liberal editors to publications like *Ogonyok* and *Moscow News*. Republican leaders from Armenia to the Baltic states found in Yakovlev a sympathetic ear. At one Politburo meeting in 1988, the KGB chief, Viktor Chebrikov, said that the Baltic national fronts were conspiring to create a counterrevolution, while Yakovlev, just returned from the region, said that there was no threat, "only the manifestations of perestroika and democratization." As the Politburo's house historian, he headed the commissions which rehabilitated political exiles and prisoners, investigated the Kirov murder of 1934, and "discovered" the secret protocols of the Molotov-Ribbentrop Pact.

As an ideologist, Yakovlev's predecessors had been men like Mikhail Suslov, dogmatists, enforcers of the faith. Yakovlev was charged with changing that faith. He and Gorbachev began with the idea of "cleansing" socialism and the Party, but they had precious little idea of how they would do it and where it would all lead. The truth is that Yakovlev, Gorbachev, and Shevardnadze—the lead reformers in the Politburo after Yeltsin resigned in 1987—were flying almost blind, and against a terrific conservative headwind, from the start.

"Speaking generally," Yakovlev said, "our baseline principle was that some things could be improved: more democracy, elections, more in the newspapers—limited, but slightly more open—the management system should be improved, centralization should be less strict, power should be redistributed somewhat, maybe the functions of the Party and the government should be divided. But you can find all of these democratic axioms since 1917, even under Stalin. 'Socialist democracy' was talked about as an ideal even then. But speeches are speeches. In 1985, for the first time, we started implementing things so that our words were matched by deeds. But as soon as these words became reality, a logic of development began to develop, and that dictated the next steps. Perestroika acquired its own logic of development, which dictated what to do. This logic of development led us to the 'conclusion' that the concept of improvement will not do us any good. One can fix up a car, add some oil, tighten some bolts, and you can drive on. But with a social organism you cannot always do this. It is not enough. It turned out that everything had to be made over.

"The ideological disputes began right away, in 1985. We clashed openly on questions of glasnost. The reformist wing had their own understanding of perestroika from the start. The conservative wing thought only that something needed to be changed. They thought we had to change a little bit, but always relying on the Party apparat. It was then that the tributes to the conservative spirit appeared: state factory inspections, the anti-alcohol campaign. They were all administrative methods and had nothing to do with a real economy. For example, we tried that—what did we call it?—*khozra-shchet* . . . regional, or local, cost-accounting . . . whatever! It was rubbish!

"After losing two and a half years we began searching for new types of society, radical restructuring on entirely new principles, and we realized that it was a more formidable task than we had anticipated. . . . It was not the Party, it had nothing to do with the concept of perestroika. It was a limited group of people who started that."

By 1989, Ligachev and the orthodox wing of the Communist Party came to blame Yakovlev, Gorbachev, and Shevardnadze for radicalizing pere-stroika to the point of creating a "bourgeois" state, for abandoning the "class approach" to politics, for failing to provide a blueprint for the future. "Some of our conservatives now say that a group of adventurists began to restruc-ture things without a concept," Yakovlev replied. "But imagine what would have happened if we'd just gone into an office and created an entire scheme. Marx did that and look what it led to! One should take things from life, and adjust them every day. Our whole trouble is that we are inert, we think in dogmas. Even if reality tells us to change things, we always check first in a book.

"Let's imagine if Ligachev had come to power. Would he have started perestroika? Yes. But it would have been of the Andropov sort: restore law and order in the economy, but only with administrative methods. But he would have done it. The result might even have been better. There might have been better conditions, more bread, more grain. But the old system of fear would have remained, the same lack of democracy and antihuman relations."

———

In the first years of perestroika, Yakovlev was careful about his terminology. As a political loyalist, he did not want to go too far beyond Gorbachev's own public expressions. But still, there were times when Yakovlev played the role of stalking horse and outraged the Party apparat. "I was under constant attack beginning with those first careful speeches," he said. "It was enough for me just to mention the word 'market' [in 1988] and there was an attack. Now everyone talks about the market. But back then you had to put your words in a special sort of wrapping paper."

Yakovlev's most radical proposal in the early days of power was to dis-mantle the one-party system. In his secret memo to Gorbachev dated Decem-ber 1985, Yakovlev suggested as a first step toward the creation of a democratic, multiparty system that the Communist Party be divided into progressives and conservatives. Such a split would acknowledge the obvious: the Party was unified by nothing but its pretenses and camouflage. Yakovlev hoped that such a move would either eliminate or silence the most hidebound elements in the Party. In the time-honored Russian tradition, it would show who was who. But Gorbachev knew the Party at least as well as Yakovlev, and he rejected the idea as out of the question, too dangerous. We could lose everything, he told Yakovlev. You'll see, he said. The Party can be reformed. But slowly.

By July 1989, the Party was proving unchangeable. The leading reformers still in the Party talked about quitting; hundreds of thousands of members did just that. Komsomol chapters were closing or dying out. Yakovlev, for his part, was under constant attack in *Pravda, Sovetskaya Rossiya,* and the rest of the Party press. So he finally decided that it was time to dispense with the wrapping paper. It was time to deal with the Party's dismal history and its dubious future. Yakovlev chose an extraordinary occasion for his "coming out": a July 1989 speech given in honor of the bicentennial of the French Revolution.

Before an audience of Party members, intellectuals, and foreign guests, Yakovlev deepened his scrutiny of the past. Gorbachev had already denounced the "crimes" of Stalin, but now his intellectual alter ego was launching a public attack on the founding myths of the Soviet Union. The Bolshevik Revolution, he told his audience, quickly dissolved into a reign of terror, one that far outstripped the Jacobin use of the guillotine.

"The idealization of terror was starkly evident during the October Revolution," Yakovlev said. The Bolsheviks looked back on the terror of 1793 as a model and "faithfully believed in violence as a cleansing force . . . a salvation for the country and the people. . . . The edifying thirst for freedom degenerates into the delirious fever of violence which ultimately extinguishes the flames of the revolution."

Then Yakovlev made a connection between Lenin and Stalin that was still considered radical even for non-Party intellectuals. To hear it from the main ideologist of glasnost, perestroika, and the "new thinking" in foreign policy was absolutely stunning: "Today, when we are asking ourselves the excruciating question of how it was possible for this country and Lenin's Party to accept the dictatorship of mediocrity and put up with Stalin's abuses and the shedding of rivers of innocent blood, it is obvious that one of the factors that nurtured the soil for authoritarian rule and despotism was the morbid faith in the possibility of forcing through social and historical development, and the idealization of revolutionary violence that traces back to the very sources of the European revolutionary tradition."

In other words, the appearance of Stalin was no aberration, but rather the direct result of Lenin's "revolutionary romanticism" that idealized violence as an instrument of class struggle and a force of purification. Until perestroika, even the most radical underground historians in the Soviet Union denied this. Roy Medvedev saw Stalin only as a pathological rupture with Leninism. Some Western historians tended to play down, or deny, Lenin's ruthlessness. But the evidence was undeniable, and no one knew it better than Yakovlev, the chairman of the Politburo's commission on history. As the émigré scholars Mikhail Heller and Aleksandr Nekrich point out, it was Lenin and Trotsky who were the first Europeans to use the term "concentration camp" and then use the device to such effect. Three months after Trotsky used the term, Lenin sent a telegram to the Penza Executive Committee on August 9, 1918, demanding the local Red leaders carry out "ruthless mass terror against the kulaks, priests, and White Guards; confine all suspicious elements in a concentration camp outside the city."

Yakovlev demanded that the Party recognize its past and renounce the old methods. "History cannot be different but we must be different," he said. "The idea of violence as the midwife of history has exhausted itself, as has the idea of dictatorial power based on violence."

It was a terribly difficult speech for Yakovlev to make. He had been working in one capacity or another in the Communist Party since just after the war. He said his first doubts about the Soviet leadership came when he saw how Stalin greeted returning prisoners of war by sending them directly to labor camps for fear of their "foreign influence." His thinking had developed radically since those days, and so had the thinking of many men and women of his generation; but he knew all too well that the majority of Party officials had changed only slightly. Despite their outward obedience to the vocabulary of the Gorbachev era—"perestroika," "acceleration," "democratization," and all the rest—they were deeply resistant to a fundamental change in the political system. In the French Revolution speech, Yakovlev acknowledged as much. "The need for radical renewal is born of the times, but, on the other hand, is always ahead of them," he said. "A rise to a new spiral of civilization does not occur without pain. Acute dramas are generated by the inertia of the outgoing social structures, the refusal to accept the new things, and revolutionary impatience."

Yakovlev even tried, in an oblique way, to address "the problem" of how revolutions consume their children, to reassure the right-wingers that there would be no hunt for enemies. He did not lash out at his antagonists; rather, he warned them. "A party that revels in myths and vain illusions," he said, "is doomed."

————

By the beginning of 1990, the collapse of the Communist Party monolith was at hand. Sakharov was gone, but his demand to eliminate the Party's guaranteed hold on power had become a banner of the growing democratic opposition. Nevertheless, Gorbachev needed convincing. The proposals of Sakharov or Yakovlev—and the rise of dozens of new parties across the country—were not enough for him. He had to be beaten over the head before he dared make a move on the Party. Lithuanians, as usual, were only too pleased to provide the drubbing.

In January 1990, Gorbachev went to Vilnius, confident that he could find a way to finesse the alarming developments there. He was sure he could slow down the sprint to independence and convince the republic's Party organization to come back into the fold. Yakovlev had already been to Vilnius and said it would be "immoral" to deny the Lithuanian argument that Moscow was still running a coercive empire. Gorbachev plainly disagreed. He berated the Lithuanian Party leader, Algirdas Brazauskas, for splitting with the all-union organization and for letting the "romantic professors" of the Sajudis popular front assume such power there. In Vilnius, Gorbachev's fury and confusion were obvious at every meeting and encounter. As long as the progressive elements of the country followed him, Gorbachev had been happy; but now his erstwhile followers were in the lead, and this was intolerable. Gorbachev had lost control of the political world.

At one point on the trip, Gorbachev confronted an elderly factory worker who was carrying a sign reading "Total Independence for Lithuania."

"Who told you to write that banner?" Gorbachev asked angrily.

"Nobody. I wrote it myself," the worker said.

"Who are you? Where do you work?" Gorbachev said. "And what do you mean by 'total independence'?"

"I mean what we had in the 1920s, when Lenin recognized Lithuania's sovereignty, because no nation is entitled to dictate to another nation," the worker replied.

"Within our large family, Lithuania has become a developed country," Gorbachev said. "What kind of exploiters are we if Russia sells you cotton, oil, and raw materials—and not for hard currency either?"

The worker cut off Gorbachev. "Lithuania had a hard currency before the war," he said. "You took it away in 1940. And do you know how many Lithuanians were sent to Siberia in the 1940s, and how many died?"

Gorbachev finally could not bear this impudence. "I don't want to talk to this man anymore," he said. "If people in Lithuania have attitudes and slogans like this, they can expect hard times. I don't want to talk to you anymore."

Raisa tried to calm down her husband.

"Be quiet," he snapped.

———

On the last day of his trip to Lithuania, Gorbachev finally conceded the obvious. A year before he had called the idea of a multiparty system *chepukha*—rubbish. Now, he said, "We should not be afraid of a multiparty system the way the devil is afraid of incense. I don't see a tragedy in a multiparty system if it serves the people."

By now, Gorbachev knew that tragedy might come if he did not make his run at the Communist Party. From a distance, he watched what had become of Jaruzelski in Poland, Honecker in East Germany, and, most vividly, the Ceauşescus in Romania. Gorbachev did not need to strain very hard to see the same rage gathering at home. Everywhere there was an urge to clean house. In the northern Ukrainian city of Chernigov, crowds gathered around a car crash and discovered that the drunken driver of one car was a leading Party official. It turned out the official was carrying around a trunkload of various delicacies that had not been seen in the city in years. The official resigned. In Volgograd, the entire Party leadership was forced to quit when tens of thousands of people protested the construction of special housing for the local officials. In the Siberian city of Tyumen, the entire Party leadership resigned after it was accused, en masse, of corruption. And in Leningrad, the former Politburo member and local Party chief Yuri Solovyov was expelled from the Party after hundreds of people demonstrated outside his home demanding to know just how he was able to buy a Mercedes-Benz sedan for 9,000 rubles when the usual price was more like 120,000.

On February 4, 1990, a bitter cold day in Moscow, around a quarter-million people marched halfway around the Garden Ring Road, down Gorky Street, and toward the Kremlin for a rally on Manezh Square that could only have scared the wits out of the denizens behind the great brick walls. It was the biggest demonstration in Moscow since the rise of Soviet power, and there was nothing polite about it. The banner "Party Bureaucrats: Remember Romania!" was just one of the helpful reminders they provided. While the crowd clapped their gloved hands and stamped their feet to keep warm, Yuri Afanasyev climbed onto the bed of a flatbed truck and shouted into the microphone, "All hail the peaceful February revolution of 1990!" The reference was lost on no one: it was the February Revolution that toppled the established order, the czar, in 1917. The Central Committee was scheduled to gather for a plenum a few days later and a vote on the fate of Article 6, the clause guaranteeing the Party primacy in public life. For the first time, the opposition seemed sure of a great victory. "When the [members of the Central Committee] show up at the Kremlin Monday morning they had better have in mind the image of hundreds of thousands of people you see here today," Vladimir Tikhonov, the head of the Union of Cooperative Businesses, said. In his speech, Yeltsin barked that this would be Gorbachev's "last chance." And the crowd—the vast brew of democratic socialists, social democrats, greens, monarchists, Hare Krishnas, veterans, housewives, and students—roared its approval.

At the plenum, Ligachev and various other members of the Central Committee complained about the "loss" of Eastern Europe, the "chaos" on the streets. But then they fell into line. On February 7, 1990, the Central Committee passed a platform that effectively opened the way for a multiparty system. They really had no choice. They had seen the crowds. They had read the placards and the future they promised.

———

Yakovlev never gave up his loyalty to Gorbachev, but now they were clearly split over matters of ideology and tactics, especially where the Party was concerned. "I am a convinced Communist," Gorbachev kept saying. But for Yakovlev, socialism meant little more than the idea of a welfare state, a government that could "protect people against calamity and misfortune." His attitude toward Lenin also grew more and more critical. "Oh, yes, it did change," he told me. "As the Bible says: there is much grief in wisdom. . . . [Lenin] was an extremely talented politician. There is no question about it. But he was geared only toward power and power alone. Everything else was subordinate to that. He thought morality was of no value in the proletarian revolution."

The Party scheduled a congress for July—a congress that Yuri Afanasyev predicted would be its "funeral." In the weeks before the event, the Party press steadily increased its attacks on the reformers in the Party, describing them as "traitors" to socialism and the state. Invariably, the named targets were Yeltsin and Yakovlev. At the congress itself, deputies were handed leaflets allegedly reporting Yakovlev's comments at a meeting with the radical and conservative factions. The "answers" made Yakovlev seem disloyal to Gorbachev, insulting to the army, and even more radical than he was. Later, an investigating committee discovered that the organizer of the leaflet was General Igor Rodionov, the military commander who won national fame for leading the assault in Tbilisi against a crowd of peaceful Georgian demonstrators.

Yakovlev had rarely stepped out in public over the years, preferring to stay at Gorbachev's side and influence events with his advice. But at the congress he took the rostrum in his own defense, and his performance was devastating. After debunking the leaflet attacking him, he held up yet another leaflet that had been circulating among the Party delegates, a photocopy from the newspaper *Russky Golos* ("Russian Voice"). It said, "We need a new Hitler, not Gorbachev. We are badly in need of a military coup. There is still a lot of undeveloped space in Siberia waiting for the 'enthusiasts' who have buried perestroika."

"My name is there," Yakovlev said. "So, Siberians, await the arrival of new gulag inmates. That's what's happening, comrades. A massive attack has been launched and all means, including criminal ones, are being used in this campaign. True, all this leaves scars on the heart, but I want to say this to the organizers of this well-orchestrated campaign and those who are behind it: you may shorten my life, but you can't silence me."

———

Yakovlev's despair over the Party led to even more probing about the viability of Marxism itself. Soon he would be telling all who would listen that Lenin's intolerance was matched by Marx's irrelevance. "A great deal has been rejected by life," he told the newspaper *Rabochaya Tribuna* ("Worker's Tribune"). "Marx said, for instance, that revolutions would take place in several industrialized European capitalist countries at the same time. That did not happen. A revolution took place in Russia, but even there it resulted from a queer concurrence of circumstances. Marx said that capitalism was a rotting society that impeded scientific, technological, and social progress. He was wrong about that, too. . . . But this is not even the main point. Life corrects many a theory. The problem is that a rash experiment was performed on Russia. An attempt was made to create a new model of society and put it into practice under conditions that were unfit for socialism. No wonder the new way of life was imposed by terror."

On August 20, 1990, Gorbachev had signed a decree rehabilitating all those who had been repressed in the twenties, thirties, forties, and fifties and repealed any orders that had stripped dissidents of their citizenship. The Party, of course, thought it was being awfully generous in this. But then Yakovlev came on the evenings news program *Vremya* and made a short statement worthy of Sakharov or Havel.

The president's two decrees, he said, "are, in my view, acts of repentance. . . . When we say that we are rehabilitating someone, as if we are mercifully forgiving him for the sins of the past, this smells of cunning and hypocrisy. We are not forgiving him. We are forgiving ourselves. It is we who are to blame that others lived for years both slandered and oppressed. It is we who are rehabilitating ourselves, not those who held other thoughts and convictions. They only wanted good and freedom for us, and the leadership of the country answered with evil, prisons and camps.

"As we breathe the air of freedom, it is already becoming difficult today for us to remember what happened in the distant and not so distant past. There were hundreds of thousands of brutal trials, people who were shot and killed, people who killed themselves, people who did not even know what they were charged with, but who were destroyed. . . .

"For us, they are not a reproach but a harsh reminder to all those who still have a yearning nostalgia for the past, for those who would turn everything back to the fear. . . . I want to pay special attention to the tragic fate of our peasantry, which paid the price in blood for the criminality of the Stalinist regime. This is not only an unprecedented reprisal against the peasantry, which disrupted the flow of the society, but it also brought the development of the state into crisis. History has never known such a concentrated hatred toward man."

CHAPTER 21

THE OCTOBER REVOLUTION

As the Party was collapsing, I got to know one of its last high priests. Vyacheslav Shostokovsky, an ally of both Yakovlev and Yeltsin, ran the Moscow Higher Party School, the ultimate training ground for young Leninists. In a matter of months, he undid the work of a thousand ideologues, firing faculty, bringing in new, younger teachers, revising the curriculum to include every possible idea and thinker. Suddenly, the students were reading Mill and Locke along with Marx and Lenin. Much of what they read of Soviet history came from foreign and underground editions; there was no time to wait for the Party publishing houses to catch up with the world. It was a desperate mission. Either Shostokovsky would revive the Party with a new crop of young social democrats, he told me one afternoon, "or we die."

"We're moving toward a multiparty democracy, to a political marketplace, and the Communist Party is just not ready for that," he said. "I'm afraid even Gorbachev himself is not ready for this marketplace."

After my meeting with the dean, I headed for the exit. On my way out, I noticed a handwritten sign advertising a showing of "an American movie tonight in Lenin Hall." No title given, but I went anyway. Lenin Hall was packed. The lights dimmed and the familiar faces of Michael Douglas and Charlie Sheen flickered on the screen: the Communist Party Higher Party School presents *Wall Street*.

If I hadn't known then that Communist ideology was dead, I knew it by the final credits. The young acolytes, presumably the next generation of Leninist priests, reacted to this morality play of American finance in a way that would have made poor Oliver Stone weep. They did not see it as a warning about the perils of greed, not a propaganda cartoon meant to steer the best and the brightest toward a life of goodness and social work. Not at all. They audibly lusted after the goods on display: the stretch limo (with bar and TV), the sushi-making machine, the steak tartare at "21," the fabulous cuffs on Michael Douglas's Turnbull & Asser shirts. God, they loved those shirts. When Charlie Sheen, the young stud stockbroker, first checked out his new East Side apartment, with the wraparound windows and the view to die for, you could hear the sighing of the young Leninists.

"Models are out. Dogma is out," Shostokovsky had told me. "Now we can only speak about goals." Precisely. It was pretty clear what the goals were here. The climax of the film came when Douglas, doing his best Ivan Boesky imitation, delivered the killer line: *"Zhdanost—eto khorosho!"* ("Greed is good!") The Communists went wild. There were whoops of approval. Unironic whoops.

As we were all leaving Lenin Hall, the student next to me, Muen Tan Kong, an exchange scholar from Vietnam, said, "All I can tell you at this point is that Communism is the contradiction of capitalism—I think," he said. "And the Party is the vanguard. We're studying that now. It's all very confusing. But the movie was good, wasn't it?"

———

Local elections were scheduled for early March 1990, and they held out the promise of a new vanguard of mayors and ward heelers. Such a sudden test of a multiparty system still in swaddling clothes seemed unfair. The Communists had the resources, the money, and, when all else failed, the KGB to keep them afloat. Most of the new parties consisted of a few dozen people in a rented auditorium making terrifically dull speeches. Sometimes there were sandwiches.

But the democrats were confident of victory. In those first weeks after the collapse of the one-party system, one young politician, Moscow's Ilya Zaslavsky, made a startling campaign promise. He told the voters of the October Region that if he was elected to the local council and made its chairman, he would do nothing less than reverse seven decades of economic disaster. "We will build capitalism in one district," he declared. The reference was clear. Zaslavsky would counter Stalin's greatest ambition to build "socialism in one country."

It was quite a campaign promise. All anyone could do was wish him the best of luck. The same Communist Party apparatchiks I had visited not long after moving in two years before were still running the October Region with singular incompetence. Like everyone else in the neighborhood, I was appalled at the decay: the heaps of uncollected garbage, the empty shops and decrepit buildings, the abandoned construction sites. The district looked like a slum. In this way it looked like almost everywhere else in the country. Now Zaslavsky was proposing as a remedy the very sort of free enterprise that Lenin had long ago declared "parasitism . . . a thing of the past."

The leaders of the democratic opposition—Zaslavsky included—had all but given up on the national parliament as anything more than a televised debating forum. They knew well that the majority of deputies were at best obedient to Gorbachev and at worst potential followers of a harder line. After that initial burst of drama and glasnost during the first session, the radicals despaired that the Congress did not have the means to push the program of economic or political changes faster or further. And so now the leading reformers of Russia had shifted their focus from national to local politics. Democratic Russia—an alliance of everyone from Memorial to the latest social democratic party—hoped to fill the city halls and regional soviets, or councils, with their people. Popular-front groups in the Baltics, Central Asia, and the Transcaucasus hoped to do the same. Just as Yeltsin wanted to win a seat in the Russian parliament and turn that institution into a power base, Zaslavsky wanted to do the same "at the sidewalk level."

As a Democratic Russia organizer, Zaslavsky advised candidates not only for the October Region, but for the entire city. In a country that had little experience of elections and none at all of the gimmickry of the West, Zaslavsky hired pollsters, ran seminars on campaign techniques, and even found psychologists to help draw up effective campaign literature. He called on well-known writers, who used their own connections to get leaflets printed when the main Party printing plants refused.

Disabled, a little snide and condescending, Zaslavsky was not a natural politician. His teachers, his bosses at the textile plant where he worked, even his parents could not comprehend his becoming a politician—much less one of the most famous new names in Russia. He was just thirty years old. But the voters never forgot it when he insisted on calling for a day of national mourning when Sakharov died; and they never forgot that when Gorbachev told him to sit, he did not. Now all the reform candidates for the Moscow city council or the regional councils wanted his endorsement and his organizing talent.

Zaslavsky won his race in the October Region easily. The local council was filled with Democratic Russia candidates, who quickly made Zaslavsky the regional chairman. His personal victory was one among hundreds for Democratic Russia and other reformist groups throughout the union. Many people had, as they put it, "voted a straight democratic line." Yeltsin was elected to the Russian parliament, and it was obvious that he would try to become its chairman. Gavriil Popov, the economist, went to city hall and became the mayor of Moscow. Anatoly Sobchak, the law professor who became a star of the Congress, was now mayor of Leningrad. Once more, there was a brief wave of euphoria in the most politically active pockets of the Soviet Union, a sense of possibility and confidence. When I went to see Sobchak in Leningrad, he had commandeered an enormous office in the Mariinsky Palace. And yet I could not get past the fact that he still kept an enormous painting of Lenin hanging behind him.

As I was leaving the office, I whispered to an aide, "What's the painting doing there?"

He laughed. "Pay it no mind," he said. "We tried to take it down, but we found a huge stain on the wallpaper. We don't have the money for new wallpaper."

In his first months in office, Zaslavsky came to an even deeper understanding of the Communist Party's legacy. The Party, which had complete control over every store and factory, every police station and fire brigade, had let the October Region fall into a state of economic decay—a typical situation throughout the Soviet Union. Food supplies were erratic; there were days when even the bread shops were empty. The housing shortage was pitiful. Many people lived in studios the size of walk-in closets or in communal apartments with fifteen or twenty people to a bathroom. By reading district documents, Zaslavsky also discovered that the huge showpiece statue of Lenin on October Square had cost 23 million rubles—7 million of which had come from the local budget. In the meantime, garbage lay rotting for days on the streets, uncollected; doctors at the local state hospitals were paid half as much as bus drivers.

One night a week, Zaslavsky sat in a dismal office near October Square listening to residents' complaints. Widows, pensioners, drunks, and young parents would sit on narrow benches in the hall and wait their turn. To sit next to Zaslavsky from six until long past midnight was to hear a catalog of the failings of "socialism in one separate country":

"Ilya Iosifevich, my husband and I are divorced, but we still have to share the same one-room flat. We've been in line for a new apartment since 1978. . . ."

"Ilya Iosifevich, my mother died this week, but they say the only way they will bury her is if I pay bribes to the cemetery manager. I have no bribe money. . . ."

"Ilya Iosifevich, my son has leukemia, but the doctors say they can do nothing. They say the only place he can get treatment is in the West. We have no visa and no money. . . ."

Zaslavsky slumped in his chair, not so much from the specific complaints—everyone knew the problems—but from the sheer number of them, the weight of his responsibility. The self-confidence was slowly draining out of him. He was powerless and sad. After he began his comeback in the Congress of People's Deputies, Yeltsin had also allowed me once to sit in on his office hours, and while the complaints were similar, he was often able to do something. The apparatchiks may have despised Yeltsin, but they had to listen to him. He was still a former Politburo member and a member of the Central Committee. Yeltsin could make a quick phone call and get his constituent just about anything: an apartment, a wheelchair, a visa to see a daughter in Warsaw. But that was mainly because of his immense authority and connections as a former member of the Kremlin leadership. Zaslavsky could only leaf through the growing stacks of papers and complaints his constituents brought him. He would look into the problems, he told them all, he would do what he could. He wrote letters, he made phone calls. But the system he relied on considered him its enemy.

Zaslavsky knew real change would come only with political and economic reform far beyond the boundaries of the October Region. In the meantime, he could hardly look his constituents in the eye. "They think of me as their last hope," he said one night between visitors, "and there is so little I can do. How do I tell them it will take years?"

———

At first, Zaslavsky's only successes were symbolic. New parties were required by law to register, and every new party in the city and Russia itself, it seemed, registered in the October Region because it had the most accommodating regulations. Nearly every Saturday another party would hold its founding congress in the October Region. "It got a little absurd. We'd already registered three different Christian Democratic parties before we ever made a move on economics," said Grigori Vasiliyev, a thirty-two-year-old economist who was Zaslavsky's choice to head the region's *ispolkom,* or executive committee.

Zaslavsky also recognized that glasnost was still far from free speech, and so he registered and helped fund newspapers that were too small or too radical to get help from the Party bureaucracy and its printing presses. Sergei Grigoryants, an underground editor whom Gorbachev, in an interview with *The Washington Post,* described as a parasite, was able to take over a small building and run his magazine *Glasnost* without government or Party interference. Zaslavsky also opened a book and magazine store in the lobby of the regional headquarters on Shabolovka Street where you could buy émigré journals like *Kontinent* and *Posev.* Later he sponsored the openings of newsstands in the metro stations.

The October District also began to wage war on the Communist Party organization that had run things for so long. Zaslavsky stripped the Shabolovka Street headquarters of all its Communist trappings—the busts of Lenin, the hammers and sickles—and then pushed the Party bureaucracy out of the way. He gave them a few bad offices on a high, drafty floor and took away their internal phone lines.

"Let them fend for themselves," he said. "These people have no more right to this building than the Christian Democrats or the local bird-watchers' association."

Zaslavsky and his colleagues knew what they wanted to do, but they wanted at least the pretense of consensus before they did it. I went along and heard Zaslavsky tell the local police force that the city, and not the Interior Ministry bureaucracy, should be hiring and firing police officers. I saw him try to describe to a room filled with befuddled factory workers how it was time that they had shares in their own workplace, that inefficient or polluting plants should be shut down and replaced with factories that "worked cleanly and made things that people need." Zaslavsky also knew that the creation of a real market would lead to higher prices, unemployment, bankruptcies, and the end of relatively equal incomes, and he said so. He was cold and honest, and the reception he got was never easy or enthusiastic. At a machine factory one afternoon, Zaslavsky sat on the podium under a huge banner—"The Name and Work of Lenin Will Live Forever!"—and, once more, got an earful:

"What are you going to do about all those Azerbaijanis selling in our markets?"

"These kebab salesmen are making a fortune on our backs! They buy up all the meat and they sell it for three and four times the original price!"

"Don't make us your lab rats for capitalism!"

The workers were understandably more concerned with their daily disasters than with grand designs and new October revolutions. Zaslavsky tried to explain the difference between the black market and a real market, the need for competition, regulation, incentive. He was getting nowhere. "If I had known about all this, I never would have voted for you!" one worker shouted.

By the end of the session, Zaslavsky and Vasiliyev were depressed. The euphoria of the election campaign was fading fast. "We never understood just how deep the psychology of Bolshevism is in every one of us," one aide, Ilya Gezentsevei, told me. "The harder we try to push, the harder that psychology pushes back."

For months, they floundered. But slowly, Zaslavsky and Vasiliyev's economic planning began to pay off. Their first stroke of genius was to make the October Region the Delaware of Moscow. The regional council passed measures making it easy for private businesses to register in the region. With no Party bureaucracy to impress or bribe, the businesses came in droves. More than 4,500 small enterprises registered in the region within twelve months— nearly half of all the new private businesses in Moscow. Restaurants, brokerages, commodities exchanges, private research labs, construction firms, law firms, and an electronics store opened. Taking in a percentage of the business profits as tax, the October Region raised its annual income from 73 million rubles to 250 million rubles in one year.

In the October Region you could see the first signs of a market economy: the ambition, the fast profits, the crime, the bewildering greed. The "October Revolution," as the local papers called it, was a gold rush for a hustler like German Sterligov, a twenty-four-year-old college dropout and one of the self-proclaimed pioneers of Soviet capitalism. He set up a private commodities brokerage and named it after his dog, Alisa. Just like that. And within six months, he told me, he was worth "tens and tens of millions of rubles." Sterligov made his fortune in the vacuum left by the collapse of the old command system. As the system deteriorated, it was becoming impossible for builders to get bricks, for truckers to get oil and gas. Alisa filled in where the old ministries would not, or could not. When I visited him at the brokerage house on Leninski Prospekt, he acted like a child sultan. Everywhere there were pretty young blond women wearing spandex miniskirts: Sterligov's angels. "They are assisting me," Sterligov said with a leer. He had big dreams and, what was more, he was fulfilling them. Sterligov was the owner of the country's first professional hockey team and the founder of the Young Millionaires Club, a place where like-minded tycoons could get together and make big plans. "Oh, and another thing," he said as his secretary stooped to light his Marlboro. "We're going to take over the Moscow racetrack and bring in the Kentucky Derby people to set up some big-time international racing."

As he grew rich, Sterligov developed a stony heart. "Why should I pity the poor and the lazy?" he said. "Pity the sick and the weak, okay, but if the rest want to live in poverty, God help them. If they want to be slaves—well, then, every slave has his dignity before God. But history is made by the individual, not the crowd. It is only when the ignorant crowd takes part in the historical process that it turns into a mess.

"My generation despises the system. It killed everyone and everything it touched. This was the richest state in the world and they destroyed it all down to the bone! But older people don't understand us. Their psychology is all screwed up. They are so used to being equal in poverty that they assume if you have any money, you are a crook."

Sterligov was not a lonely robber baron. The newspaper *Tochka Zreniya* ("Point of View") reported that there were at least 150,000 "ruble million-aires" in the Soviet Union by the end of 1990. "But look, a million rubles on the open market is now twenty-five thousand dollars. Is that really so much?" Sterligov said. "And I don't have a single free ruble. Everything is tied up in the business."

After our talk, one of Sterligov's men showed me around the trading floor, which was buzzing with brokers and angels. "Welcome to the future," said Yevgeny Gorodentsov, an Alisa broker who had just put together a brick deal that brought him 750,000 rubles in commissions. He was twenty-one years old. The brokers all talked of Sterligov as if of a god—a slightly mad deity. His people reminded me of the inner circle around Citizen Kane. They knew he would crash, but they wanted to be next to something transcendent and new. Sterligov's ambitions were boundless and wild, a mix of Thatch-erian free-market zeal, Chicago in the twenties, and P. T. Barnum myth-making. When I last saw him, his newest scheme was to buy a huge tract of land 150 miles from Moscow and build a self-contained "mini Western country," with factories and accredited schools and universities, airports and heliports, satellite dishes and a "Japanese TV for everyone."

Perhaps the singular feature of Sterligov's wealth was the envy, and the harassment, it attracted. Once a week, police inspectors showed up at Alisa demanding to see his books. The KGB dropped in too. To avoid racketeers demanding protection money, Sterligov, his wife, and their infant daughter moved from apartment to apartment. The same dangers appeared to await anyone who succeeded in the new marketplace. Of the twelve new members of the Young Millionaires Club, only Sterligov would reveal his name. Doz-ens of others told him they wanted to join but feared kidnapping and attacks. The Communist Party weekly *Glasnost* printed an article accusing Sterligov of a "pathological hatred of Communism," a history of racketeering, and a "real lack of intelligence." The attacks came from all sides. So successful was

Alisa in its first six months of existence that rival entrepreneurs told me that they were sure Sterligov had a working relationship with the KGB. There were rumors that one of his uncles was a minister.

Sterligov, like most plutocrats, immunized himself from criticism and convinced himself that everyone was simply jealous. "It's still a sin to be rich in this country," he said. "But we're going to change all that. It won't take long."

———

Liberals in their late thirties and forties were not so much angered as amazed at this new, younger generation. My friend Alex Kahn, a music critic from Leningrad, grew up in semi-dissident circles reading samizdat and listening to pirated tapes of John Lennon. Now the young seemed entranced by money and the possibility of money. "Every month, every week, you see more of these guys around town," he said. "My generation, in our late thirties and forties, worshiped the ideas and ideals that were forbidden to us. We looked to the poets and the bards. These guys are sick of all that. What they want most is a society that works."

The young millionaires were an arrogant lot, young men (never women) acting without a developed code of behavior or common language. Primitive capitalists, as Marx called them. The hard-liners despised the new breed, and the liberals saw them only as a necessity, a first step toward a decent material life. "Some of them are a crude bunch, but to develop wealth, you need these people. We can't wait for angels to do the spadework," said Igor Svinarenko, a reporter for the leading newspaper of the Soviet business world, *Kommersant*. "These businessmen who make their money selling rotten meat or lousy computers or patched-together trade deals, they'll accumulate money and build things and set up factories and stores. Some of them may do ugly things or act like barbarians. But they'll also educate their kids, maybe send them overseas to Harvard. And then the kids will come back with their high-minded ideas and they'll say, 'Dad, you are a scoundrel.' And so they'll do things in a more refined way. They'll act on their guilty conscience. And so society will develop from there."

If there was a Soviet model for the young millionaires it was Artyom Tarasov, a high-tech and trading magnate in his forties who was a constant target of KGB and police investigation for the allegedly illegal export of capital. Tarasov was the first of the Soviet millionaires to flaunt his wealth publicly, even describing his real estate deals and foreign trips at a press conference at the Foreign Ministry. He once suggested publicly that Gorbachev might sell the disputed Kuril Islands back to the Japanese for billions of dollars. Infuriated, Gorbachev threatened to sue, and the KGB investigations increased. By 1990, Tarasov was spending most of his time on the French Riviera, fishing and waiting for the right moment to come back home. "I've been fascinated watching this generation—these young Tarasovs—and it's clear they love the game more than the money as an end in itself," said Vladimir Aleksanyan, an émigré who ran an import-export business with offices in Palo Alto, California, and Moscow. "They work sixteen, eighteen hours a day. Their mentality is completely different from anyone I ever knew before I left twelve years ago. They speak foreign languages. They come to the States and they rent cars, move around. They are absolutely fearless. They talk about renting military transport planes from the army to fly over some product, and they don't even realize how mind-boggling this sounds to anyone over the age of thirty."

An example of the breed was Anton Danielets, a twenty-four-year-old information services and real estate czar in Leningrad. He was a moon-faced naïf with the bovine grace of a young Jackie Gleason. He claimed by 1991 a fortune of 20 million to 30 million rubles and $1.5 million in foreign banks. Danielets used a dying Communist institution, the Komsomol, to build his nascent empire. In the first rush of cooperative businesses in 1987 and 1988, he opened a video theater with Komsomol help and made 500,000 rubles in personal profit within a year. He learned management from a pirated copy of a business text published abroad. One of the first things he did next was to hire lawyers to "guide me through the thicket of laws." The key to business amid the "war of laws" between Moscow and the republics, between cities and districts, he said, was to know just who owns what, who has the right to issue licenses.

Racing around Leningrad from morning till night in a dilapidated Soviet Fiat, he quickly used his savings to rent and buy valuable properties and put some of his long-held ideas to work. He rented a run-down indoor pool and gym that the city had left for dead and turned it into a profitable sports center, popular with his fellow Soviet millionaires and the foreign community. He saw business on the rise and started a financial information center, a kind of Dow Jones in Leningrad. He started a popular newspaper, *Nevskoye Vremya* ("Neva Times"), and bought a printing press that had once belonged to the local Communist Party. In Siberia, the Urals, and Karelia, he traded in raw materials "whenever the deal looks good." He had more than a thousand people working for him. After a while, Danielets finally decided that the backseat of his car was not quite adequate as a corporate headquarters, and so, for 300,000 rubles, he bought the glorious three-story mansion at 47 Herzen Street—Vladimir Nabokov's childhood home.

"My forebears too were business people, gentry, and we're going to make this place look like it once did," Danielets said, pointing to rooms immortalized in Nabokov's memoir *Speak, Memory.* "I think of this place as our connection to what we lost and what we want to regain. People forget that there was something known as a Russian business life before the Revolution. Now we are nothing more, nothing less, than a Third World country—at best. I want to restore what we had. So when people come to me with interesting projects, I invest, maybe with cash, maybe with equipment or space.

"Everyone knows that the smart guys in the Communist Party are trying to grab up as much as they can before they finally leave the stage. My attitude is this: Let them. Most of them are so stupid they don't even know what real business is. It's the young who are going to do the work over the years. We're building empires, but not evil ones."

———

In classical Marxist theory, the initial stages of the accumulation of wealth produce "morbid symptoms." Chief among them in the Soviet Union was the rapid rise of thuggery: protection rackets, Ponzi schemes, the occasional murder and night of arson. Zaslavsky and the police faced problems with crime all over the district, especially on blocks with new private businesses. For some reason, though, I had better luck meeting the mob in Leningrad.

Alex Kahn said he knew someone who knew someone who sold computers "and whatnot" out of a storefront in the Vasilievsky Region of the city. The businessman, who was named Aleksandr, told us just to bring a bottle or two of Scotch—"Johnnie Walker if you've got it"—at two in the afternoon and we "might meet some interesting people." Happily, the hard-currency store in the Astoria Hotel was well stocked with Johnnie Walker.

The office was a shambles, a room filled with spiderwebs, scrap lumber, dust, and a desk and a phone. Aleksandr quickly said the Scotch was not for him and, "under the circumstances," he would prefer I didn't print his last name. It was soon clear why.

Within five minutes, four brawny types arrived. "The Charity Society," they called themselves. It was time to collect the weekly 5,000-ruble "donation" from Aleksandr. I handed over the Scotch, Aleksandr handed over a paper bag, and the Charity Society boys seemed happy. They were only too pleased to talk, they said brightly.

"Some people call us gangsters," an ex-athlete named Sergei explained as he popped a knuckle. "We like to think of it this way: we protect people. We persuade them to let us protect them." Sometimes, Sergei said, they used pistols and Uzis bought on the black market as their instruments of persuasion. Pasha, a wiry hood who "went a little crazy" fighting in Afghanistan, explained how he and his partners did their business during what economists in the press were now calling "the transition period" from a centralized, socialist economy to a free market, and what the punks referred to as "the Wild West" and "Chicago in the thirties":

"First, everything is explained to the businessman in question. Very slowly and carefully. Then if he doesn't seem to understand the kind of payments he has to make, he's beaten up. But professionally. A couple of broken ribs, a few nights in the hospital. The next step is, he's hustled into a car, driven out to the woods, and given a shovel. We tell him to start digging his own grave. That's usually when they crack."

There was no way to know whether their stories were fact or cheap bravado. But such rackets did exist, such murders went on all the time, and Aleksandr, a Nordic-looking man in his late thirties, tried hard to keep from trembling as he listened. Occasionally he shot me an anxious glance. To make everyone just a little more nervous, Sergei broke into the sort of half-mad giggle that Robert De Niro used to great effect in the film *Mean Streets.* The mannerisms, it turned out, were as imported as the Reeboks on their feet. Sergei admitted that he had seen the films *Once Upon a Time in America* and *GoodFellas* on the Charity Society's video system. "We learn a lot of what we do that way," he said.

With private business growing by the day here, life was good for the Charity Society. They shook down everyone from the owners of newspaper kiosks to department stores selling foreign goods.

"Just the price is different," Sergei said.

"When I get about two or three million for myself, then maybe I'll go out and get some principles," Pasha said. "I've got plenty of time later on to buy a farm and live quietly."

After the Charity Society left, Aleksandr said paying protection money was "just part of doing business nowadays." His only other expense was his phone bill. "This country is in a state of transition, a wild time, and so there are no rules, no stability. It's open season," he said. "I know of one guy who couldn't make his payments and they tortured him with a soldering iron. Ninety-nine percent of the businessmen in town—me included—violate a lot of rules. Taxes, hard-currency restrictions, the laws on hiring people. We have to break the law if we want to get anything done. And so the racketeers know we can't resist. Calling in the police is hopeless. That is, unless you want to spend the rest of your life in a fortress. Or dead in the canal."

———

During the Brezhnev era, the personification of sleazy business dealings was the *tolkach,* the weary factory representative who would travel the country to make sure he got the supplies his firm needed. Bribes and gifts were his stock in trade. If he was from Moldavia, he would bring cases of wine to sway his clients; if he came from Astrakhan, it would be quart-size tubs of black caviar. But the *tolkach* was only the comic face of a degraded, dishonest system. Corruption permeated the centralized economy from the bottom to the top: from the state butcher shop manager who sold his best beef on the black market to the members of the Council of Ministers who lied about production levels to curry favor with the general secretary.

That legacy of cynicism and lawlessness, despite all the talk of reform, still lingered. "The standard of 'dual honesty' for seventy years here has led to a deterioration of ethical standards," said Vladimir Aleksanyan, the émigré import-export executive. "You rob your workplace. You cut in line. You skip out on contracts if it's convenient. Dishonesty is deep-rooted. When a person in business is honest, it is because he has made a conscious, and usually temporary, decision to be honest. There is not a deep-rooted sense of ethics."

Corruption was a matter of course. In Leningrad's Kirov District, officials and businessmen said, merchants quickly discovered that to do a simple remodeling job on a building or to get a decent location for a kiosk they had to pay off the district government's architect. Finally, the local police caught the architect, Timur Kuriyev, taking a 9,000-ruble bribe in a public bathroom. One of the great scams of the Gorbachev era was known as the "convenient collapse." In an effort to encourage semiprivate cooperative businesses, the government issued huge start-up loans at low interest rates. Some cooperators used the funding to open stores or services. But others, who did not believe the period of liberalization would last more than a few months and wanted to make a quick fortune, grabbed the money and, when the loan came due, said, "Sorry, the business failed." The bank could do little more than put a 12 percent lien on the debtor's meager state salary. Every time a new form of commerce began, it seemed, a new racket appeared alongside it. After Sotheby's held its first auction of modern Soviet paintings in Moscow in July 1988, black marketeers discovered a source of quick income. Soviet artists told me that a man identifying himself as Oleg Petrovich—alias "the Gypsy"—showed up with his henchmen at various artists' studios demanding works that he knew would bring in big money when sold abroad for hard currency. "Friends of mine were hit bad, and they told me that I was on the guy's list for four or five paintings—specific ones that they saw in the Sotheby's catalog," said Lev Tabenkin, a Moscow painter who had sold many of his canvases abroad. "They're very systematic. So far they haven't gotten to me, but I haven't been working very much in my studio these days either."

Lieutenant Nikolai Mirikov, chief of the Moscow police investigations department, said the "evolving economic situation," the conversion to a market economy, will keep the rate of crime soaring for years. He said that while he needs five thousand police to cope with rising crime rates, he has lost more than a thousand officers in the past two years. "They mainly go off to work in cooperatives, where their salaries are a lot higher," he said. KGB officers, some of them at the highest levels, often took an early retirement to use their connections in the official and underground economies and make a killing as businessmen. Sometimes the police went into business without turning in their uniforms. A Moscow detective was caught shaking down street vendors for bribes of 10,000 rubles a month, the business newspaper *Kommersant* reported. In 1990, the same officer had been voted the city's Detective of the Year.

———

Businessmen in the October Region and elsewhere told me it was easy to make millions of rubles. Step One: Get a short-term loan of, say, 10 million rubles. Step Two: Launder the rubles. That is, convert them into dollars. One of the most common back-channel methods is to buy from a third party a paper obligation for money owed in "semihard" currencies: Indian rupees, Chinese yuan. The paper obligation, for which you have paid dearly, makes the transfer to dollars much easier. Step Three: Buy goods—Japanese VCRs, Hong Kong computers, American blue jeans. Volume and a foreign label matter far more than quality. Step Four: The easiest part—sell the goods to a middleman or a commission store or a workplace. Make sure your prices are absurd; Soviet consumers are desperate, and the demand curve knows no bounds. Step Five: Collect your money and pay off the bank. In three or four months, if all goes smoothly, you will be several million rubles richer.

It seemed painless. But then I met Oleg Falkovich.

A plump man with a heavy measure of guile, Falkovich worked for twenty-five years in the state economy in Siberia and the far east before he began dealing privately in construction materials, clothes, and video equipment. Eventually, he became a buyer for a company called ARTO, which was looking to obtain millions of rubles' worth of video equipment for resale on the Soviet market. Falkovich contacted another firm, Terminal, which agreed to get the televisions and VCRs from Japanese suppliers. A few weeks later, however, Terminal said the deal in Tokyo had fallen through, and Falkovich had to give the bad news to ARTO. But ARTO said it was going to suffer losses in the millions as a result of the deal's collapse because it had taken out short-term loans with high interest rates. The ARTO bosses told Falkovich that the burden for getting back the money was on him.

One spring afternoon, Falkovich said, and other sources confirmed, three men forced him into a car and drove him to the Rossiya Hotel near the Kremlin. "Once we were in a room, they started threatening me, saying that unless I signed a contract handing over to them five million rubles, they would rape me, kill me, kill my wife and daughter. This went on for days. But when they got to my family, I signed. I would have signed anything."

Falkovich managed to reach one of his partners by phone, and the partner called some members of their acquaintance in the Uzbek mafia to come to Moscow and set their boss free. The team flew to Moscow and knocked on the door of the hotel room. But Rustam, the Uzbek leader, recognized one of the three men as an old friend and colleague. "It was a nightmare," Falkovich said. "Instead of freeing me, Rustam turned to one of the others and said, 'Once you beat the five million out of him, we'll beat out another million.' "

Eventually, the police arrived at the Rossiya and sent everyone home. Later, they arrested the three men whom Falkovich accused of kidnapping him. But the men were released after three days of questioning; the police said there was insufficient evidence to prosecute. "Falkovich claims the men were extortionists and the three said they were not. The whole situation was a blur," said Genri Reznik, the lawyer for ARTO.

In the meantime, Falkovich said he is sure he is "a hunted man." He has moved his family from their home in Magadan to a secret location, and he is hoping to emigrate to the United States. With no relatives there, his chances for an entrance visa are not good. "I can't live this way any longer," Falkovich said. "In a normal world, they settle these things with contracts or, if it comes to that, with lawsuits. This kind of thing will go on and on in this country until we have real laws, real business, and not the kind of insanity we have now."

———

Despite the "morbid symptoms" of the new capitalism, Zaslavsky and Co. had no intention of scaling back their ambitions. They were world-beaters. Dmitri Chegodayev, the twenty-seven-year-old chairman of the district's media committee, began holding meetings with foreign investors about setting up a thirty-two-station cable television system featuring an "October channel." "We want to hook into Europe via cable TV," he said. There were meetings about how best to attract foreign investors—the "capitalist leeches" of Stalinist legend. The most ambitious plan—one that smacked of megalomania to Communist Party loyalists—was to create a huge business center on Gagarin Square modeled on the La Defense complex in Paris. Important-looking documents were drawn up. The center would include luxury hotels, office buildings, underground parking lots, an exhibition center, a computer and communications center, a trade center, and a medical complex.

But by the summer and fall of 1990, something else was happening. The Communist Party newspapers were beginning to hint at a counterrevolution. Suddenly, the most prominent free-market advocates in the country were under attack—Zaslavsky included. Like the Soviet Union itself, Zaslavsky was flying into the heavy weather of a market economy without a flight plan or a radar screen. His vision of the future—a world of stock markets, computer centers, and shopping malls—met head-on with the endless barriers of habit and instability: the obstinate psychology of a people grown used to "equality in poverty." Perhaps a little sooner than the rest of the country, the radical free-market leaders of the October Region encountered the limits of people's tolerance. Some workers in the district were growing angry with the new businesses. There were small demonstrations. Some of Zaslavsky's supporters began to turn on him. "Many people in the district saw businesses like Alisa succeeding very quickly while they still had to stand in lines for food. It outraged them, and they started screaming, 'Give us! Give us!' " said Zaslavsky's aide, Gezentsevei. "Many people could not understand that the idea of government is not to provide, the way parents provide for a child. What we were trying to do was set up the structures, the possibilities for everyone to have the chance to work and succeed."

———

It came as no shock to Zaslavsky that a lot of the negative letters he got in the mail, to say nothing of the articles in the nationalist press, were anti-Semitic. As the business explosion intensified and the average wage bought less and less, resentment eventually made its way toward that fine end. Anyone with a little extra was a Jew. You heard the grumbling on the buses, on the streets, on park benches. Sometimes it became the stuff of public meetings and demonstrations. On June 6, 1990, at the Red October cultural hall in Moscow, seven hundred members of something called the People's Orthodox Movement met, and the level of hatred was startling. "We declare that the Jews bear collective responsibility for the genocide of the Russian people and other peoples of our country!" said one speaker, Aleksandr Kulakov. "And we demand that Jews be forbidden to leave the country until a tribunal of the Russian people decides their fate. We express solidarity with the Arab world, which struggles with this evil! We also express solidarity with the German people. The Jews were never victims of the German people. The Germans were the victims of Jewish deception!"

Groups like the United Workers' Front, Motherland, and Unity all emit-

ted similarly horrifying grunts, all in the name of "proletarian justice" and
the call for a class war. Zaslavsky showed me some of his mail, where the
word *Zhid*—Yid—appeared more frequently than commas. It was as if he
had ended up on the wrong side of a perverse class war, a focus of class
resentment. *Nash Sovremenik, Moscow Worker,* and *Molodaya Gvardiya*
were the main publications supporting this strange amalgam of nationalism,
neo-Stalinism, and pure resentment that was fast becoming known as National Bolshevism. "We face a paradox," wrote Richard Kosolapov in the
Moscow Worker. "An actual ban on the class approach and its false contrast
with universal human values is happening at a time when the gap between
rich and poor is widening. We are stubbornly being told that there is a need
for fraternization between striking coal miners and the growing ranks of
millionaires . . . despite the fact that our entire historical experience is literally
crying out about the inevitability of conflict."

——

Zaslavsky had begun his term in early 1990 with the support of more than
a hundred of the 150 October Region deputies. But by winter, he could rely
on only forty or so. The rest, with help from various Communist Party
organizations, began to plot against him. Articles began appearing in the
Russian Communist Party paper *Sovetskaya Rossiya* accusing Zaslavsky of
incompetence, of "aggressive anti-Communism," of taking power out of the
hands of the people and putting it in the hands of a few young millionaires.
"Zaslavsky was not the man we thought he was," said Alla Vlasova, a
conservative on the council. "He turned arrogant. He would only listen to the
inner circle around him. He has to go."

Inexperience and a measure of arrogance also gave Zaslavsky's enemies
ammunition for the approaching political battle. Some members of the city's
executive committee, it turned out, were also businessmen. Vasiliyev's deputy, Shota Kakabadze, for one, was president of the law firm Assistant,
which did legal work for the region. Although the lawyers said they did their
municipal work free, the impression of a conflict of interest became indelible.
"We started falling victim to our own stupidity and inexperience," Chegodayev said.

The biggest mistake was in the way Zaslavsky handled the privatization of
several thousands parcels of land and new enterprises. The Municipal Property Board was in charge of holding auctions and selling off land in order to
help create businesses, hotels, or plants that fit in with the October Region's
plans for the future. Zaslavsky saw the dilemma of mixing the state and the
private sectors, but he argued that this was often done in other developing
countries. "And that," he said, "is what we are, let's face it. A developing

country that happens to have nuclear weapons." Upper Volta with rockets. Zaslavsky's enemies pounced all over him, accusing him of funneling profits to his cronies. And while the charge was never proved, it hurt him badly. Suddenly, the young politician who had started with a pristine image was stained.

To make matters worse, Zaslavsky took a hit from a powerful corner. For months, Zaslavsky had been telling the press and even audiences abroad that Gorbachev was a "lost cause" who was getting far too much credit for even beginning perestroika. He said that it was Ronald Reagan's strategy of negotiation through strength that brought the Kremlin to its knees. "I will never forget what Gorbachev did at the start," Zaslavsky said, "but it would be a mistake to put all our hopes in one man anymore. Thank God, we're beyond that." Gorbachev, who was then turning sharply to the right, went before a meeting of the Moscow Communist Party organization and railed against the "so-called democrats." It was one of his most conservative speeches during a conservative winter in the Kremlin. Zaslavsky in particular, Gorbachev said, had "disappointed" him.

On the bitter cold afternoon of February 13, 1991, Zaslavsky's opponents called a council session and put a no-confidence vote on the agenda. To bring down Zaslavsky, however, they needed a quorum of ninety-nine deputies. Zaslavsky's only remaining strategy was to block the quorum, to keep his people outside the hall. As he sat in his second-floor office, his opponents hammered him in the auditorium.

"All summer Zaslavsky was in the United States. He is learning to destroy our political, economic, and ideological system!" said Alla Zhokina.

"Zaslavsky's emissaries took their training in the United States!" said Gennadi Markov. "All his people now have cushy jobs." Yuri Mazenich said Zaslavsky's team "tried to establish a totalitarian regime based on the arbitrary seizure of regional property."

The denunciations went on from five to nearly midnight. Although the deputies were five short of a quorum, they held a no-confidence vote anyway, with seventy-eight voting for Zaslavsky's resignation. It was beginning to look as though the October Revolution would not lead to the shining future of "capitalism in one district." Zaslavsky sat in his office exhausted. He was surrounded by the mementos of his rise to fame: the bric-a-brac from his trip to the United States, the aides who doted on him, the map of the future—the gleaming region he saw in his mind's eye. The revolution was at a stalemate. "It turns out this is going to be a very long game," he said.

MAY DAY!
MAY DAY!

I woke early on May Day, 1990, the annual festival of labor, sunshine, and kitsch. The weather was perfect, a sweet astonishment in the perpetually dreary city of Moscow. Rumor had it in the past that the Communist Party, in its constant attempt to tame the heavens and the earth, seeded the clouds so it would rain before and after—but never on—the parade.

May Day was a cartoon of what was happening in the country. You could just plant yourself on Red Square and watch it all go by. Under Stalin, May Day raised the cult of personality to the level of communal entertainment. Every float and billboard, every song and banner was devoted to the worship of his greatness. Under Khrushchev and Brezhnev the atmosphere was still grotesque, but more jolly. Unsurpassed achievements of the workingman at least equaled the unsurpassed wonderfulness of the Leader.

By 1988, there were still some portraits of the Politburo leaders and Central Committee–approved slogans ("Acceleration!") floating by, but Gorbachev had reduced the ceremony mostly to a bit of tacky fun, a production worthy of halftime at the Sugar Bowl: strongmen flinging golden dumbbells into the air, gymnast-nymphets jackknifing at the waist in honor of the working class. Harmless Sovietiana. The banners were more in the spirit of self-help than national vanity. The country was collapsing, after all, and everyone knew it. It was in the papers every day. That year I also managed to run into Yeltsin as he wandered toward his modest car. He had not been seen around Moscow since his fall from power nearly a year before, and this was probably his last moment of shyness. Oh yes, he said with a fantastically broad smile, he was quite healthy. We would hear from him soon.

By 1989, the slogans had turned to a sugary mush. "Peace for Everyone!" one said. Or the touching "We're Trying to Renew Ourselves!" It was all so innocent, a Fourth of July barbecue without the hot dogs. Ideology had disappeared. There were no "our rockets are bigger than your rockets" signs anymore, no boasting of magnesium production rates, no Uncle Sams stepping on the neck of the Third World. An empire with thousands of nuclear warheads was eager to show just how toothless it had become. The Soviet Union was in the midst of a self-actualization craze.

For 1990, Gorbachev decided to account for the new wave of young politicians in the various legislatures, city halls, and town councils. The Kremlin announced that the liberal mayor of Moscow, Gavriil Popov, would be on the reviewing stand of the Lenin Mausoleum along with the Politburo and a few selected government honchos. Yuri Prokofiyev, the astonishingly dense leader of the Moscow Party organization, also declared that factory workers would no longer be compelled to celebrate. This year May Day would be "completely voluntary," he said. Only banners bearing "anticonstitutional" slogans would be discouraged. "What a gesture!" everyone was supposed to think. "What a kind and liberal leadership!" But, as usual, the Party was acting more out of anxiety than generosity. They opened up the parade only in exchange for an agreement from Democratic Russia, Memorial, and other opposition groups that there would be no embarrassing "countermarches" across town. In Leningrad, the Party was taking no chances; it canceled the parade altogether.

The morning was reliably gorgeous—a hard bright sun and a cool breeze washed along faces that had turned the lightest shade of pale after the long winter. Along the walk north from October Square to Red Square, I saw a few people carrying a Lithuanian flag and some rolled-up banners. I didn't think much of it. I got to the reviewing stand early, bought an ice cream, and gossiped with some of the other reporters. The public address system pumped out some treacly Soviet pop tunes and Pete Seeger's "We'll See That Day Come Round."

Finally, it was time for the ceremonies to begin. As always, the reporters took careful note of the order in which the various leaders walked up the stairs of the Lenin Mausoleum to the reviewing stand. Yeltsin and Geidar Aliyev had told me how Gorbachev, like a baseball manager, would give everyone his place in the order just before showtime. "Usually, it was written on a little card or piece of paper," Yeltsin said. He also said that at lunch breaks during Politburo sessions, everyone sat in his usual May Day order.

For the reporters, it was still considered slightly important who chatted with whom, who wore a fedora, who a homburg, and, above all, who was missing. This was called "Soviet watching." At least for me, the ritual lost its aura with the discovery that underneath the mausoleum there was a laboratory charged with monitoring the temperature and rate of deterioration of "the living Lenin." Below that, there was a gymnasium where the guards could work out on off hours. The idea of some pimply kid from Chelyabinsk doing squat thrusts in the bowels of sacred territory somehow erased all mystery from the grand procession and the leaders who watched it.

For about an hour, May Day was as calm and uneventful as the Macy's Thanksgiving Day parade. One merely had to substitute images of heroic labor for Underdog and Bullwinkle. Gorbachev watched with a bored, kingly smile, as if he were pleased to live through this hour of his life without crisis. The first marchers were mostly factory workers and members of official unions, and the signs they carried reflected their fear that a market economy would leave them without money or a job. "Enough Experiments," one said. "A Market Economy Is Just Power to the Plutocracy," said another. "Down with Private Property." Even while they mouthed the slogans of the right wing, those workers demanded our sympathy. They had lived for decades in a world of guarantees (however meager) and absolute truths (however false), and now everything had been denounced, undercut, found out. They felt threatened to the core.

The crowd moved from left to right, from the brick Museum of the Revolution across the cobblestones of Red Square then down the slope past St. Basil's Cathedral and toward the steely Moscow River, glinting now like the oiled barrel of a .38. But suddenly, the march seemed to run out of marchers. We all looked left and saw that another wave had gathered, but they were waiting, and they looked . . . different. What was this? There were red, yellow, and green Lithuanian flags, black, blue, and white Estonian flags, Russian tricolors from the czarist era. There was shouting, more young people, an entirely different feel. Something was about to happen. You could feel it. Everyone could. These were the very people who would have gone off to "counterdemonstrations" had the Party not cut a deal with them. Soon the Party would wish it had never had this stroke of genius.

The democrats started marching onto the square, and now their placards became visible from the reviewing stands. I'd seen the same ones at other demonstrations, but on Red Square? With Gorbachev watching?

"Socialism? No Thanks!"

"Communists: Have No Illusions. You Are Bankrupt."

"Marxism-Leninism Is on the Rubbish Heap of History."

"Down with the Politburo! Resign!"

"Ceaușescus of the Politburo: Out of Your Armchairs and Onto the Prison Floors!"

"Down with the Empire and Red Fascism!"

There were no portraits of the Politburo members, but there were numerous posters featuring Yeltsin ("Tell 'em, Boris!") and Sakharov ("Conscience of the Nation"). Then came the most chilling symbol of all: red Soviet flags with the hammer and sickle ripped out—an echo of the opposition flags on the streets of Bucharest during the uprising of December 1989. The demonstrators all stopped and turned toward the Lenin Mausoleum. The square was filled with tens of thousands of people now, waving their fists, chanting "*Doloi KPSS!*" ("Down with the Party!") "*Doloi Gorbachev!*" "*Doloi Ligachev!*" I borrowed a pair of binoculars and glimpsed the faces of the men on the reviewing stand. (Later I got a closer look on television.) Ligachev glared and nodded, his face hard as a walnut. Yakovlev was impassive, Yoda-like; Popov looked utterly serene, even pleased, though hesitant to let it show in such company. Gorbachev, as always, was a master of his emotions. As tens of thousands of people denounced him, he never let the minutest flicker of anger crease his face. I remembered other men in similar situations, how confused and frightened Ceaușescu had looked when he listened to those first demonstrators from his balcony in Bucharest. Gorbachev's performance was as amazing as the demonstration itself. He watched and watched and occasionally chatted with those next to him, as if this were the most common May Day parade in memory. As if it were normal!

The confrontation seemed as if it might go on endlessly. The demonstrators were ready to stay in Red Square all day. We all stood there, watching, still as lizards in the sun. The men on the mausoleum did not move. They merely stood there, as if they were watching something else, some other parade, instead of their own last judgment. Finally, someone ordered the Kremlin loudspeakers turned up and they started churning out patriotic slogans and marching music. But it was no match for the chanting on the square, a surge that grew louder with every minute. This was their square and there was not a goddamn thing anyone could do about it. At the center of the crowd stood a Russian Orthodox priest, his beard from the pages of Dostoevsky; he carried a seven-foot-high crucifix and shouted, "Mikhail Sergeyevich, Christ Has Risen!"

Finally, after a full twenty-five minutes of this, Gorbachev nodded, turned on his heels, and walked off the tribune. What else could he do? Everyone, Popov included, followed. Later, I visited Popov at city hall and asked him how he and Gorbachev had felt standing there on the mausoleum.

"For me, it was interesting," he said. "For Gorbachev? I would say the word is . . . uncomfortable."

I also spoke to Yegor Ligachev, who told me that he had been deeply disturbed by the incident. "Not just me, but Mikhail Sergeyevich, everyone had this feeling," he said. "On the one hand, we gave the chance for any force to march on Red Square and express themselves. On the other hand, we witnessed such extremist outbursts, such blatant aggressiveness, that if they would come to power and we would organize such a demonstration, we would be sent directly to jail from Red Square. No doubt about that. I watched for a long time and Mikhail Sergeyevich came up to me and said, 'Yegor, probably it's time to finish it.' And I said, 'Yes, it's time.' And we left, with me walking beside him. It was uncivilized. I said to Mikhail Sergeyevich, 'Once again we are seeing what a deplorable state the country is in.' These were my exact words."

After Gorbachev and the rest left the reviewing stand on Lenin's tomb, I walked into the square and joined the march at its tail end. Everyone was jazzed with a sense of power. "The leadership may try to dismiss what happened here today as just some extremists blowing off a little steam, but it runs deeper. Gorbachev has done a lot of good, but when it comes to us, the radical, he turns away from his natural allies," one demonstrator, Aleksandr Afanasyev, told me. His face was streamed with sweat, flush with the thrill of the standoff. A young man named Vitaly Mindlin, who was carrying a pro-Lithuanian banner, told me, "I've been forced to go to these rallies for years, and this is the first time I've come voluntarily, acting from my own soul. Gorbachev may have been insulted by our openness, but we have to take that risk. We can't afford to act as if we were someone's subject. We are our own masters. The people dictate the moment now, not Gorbachev."

The Party, of course, tried to make sure the country did not hear about the demonstrations. Official television gave blanket coverage to the first hour of the parade, but once the radicals crested the hill and entered Red Square, the broadcast ended. Of course, glasnost subverted any attempt to control the information. The more liberal papers were filled with accounts of the May Day events, and the public read not only about Moscow, but about the anti-Communist demonstrations in Eastern Europe and the "anti-empire" demonstration in Ukraine. The Party had been humiliated nearly everywhere. In Lvov, the center of the Ukrainian independence movement, demonstrators carried icons of the Virgin Mary and signs saying, "USSR: The Prison House of Nations." The mayor of Lvov, Vyacheslav Chernovil, could not help but applaud. He'd spent the better part of his adulthood as a dissident and political prisoner. "Happy May Day," he told everyone. "Happy May Day."

A few days later, Aleksandr Yakovlev had the pitiable job of facing the press. Playing against type, the most liberal man in the leadership denounced the May Day demonstrations as "insulting" and "freakish." Yakovlev turned demagogue as he singled out the few kooks in the march, war veterans with pictures of Stalin, monarchists with icons of Nicholas II. He made out this lunatic fringe to be the main current of the demonstration itself and then pompously declared that what we had witnessed that day were "anti-reform" forces trying to frighten the goodly men of the Kremlin. What a strange and terrible thing it must have been for Yakovlev to carry out such a task. Yuri Prokofiyev, the Moscow Party chief, was more honest in his anger. The crowds, he said, "carried insulting slogans exceeding the limits of decency. They smeared the leaders of the country, the Communist Party, and the president and chanted rude, almost obscene words and whistled. The goal of these people was explicitly clear: to spoil the holiday with the poison of confrontation." What a phrase! "Almost obscene words!"

The Party press scolded the "tastelessness" of the demonstration, as if the demonstrators had used the fish fork for the steak. Gorbachev, for his part, just kept away from the subject. What could he say? What he felt standing there on the mausoleum? What had Lyndon Johnson felt as he sat in the Lincoln bedroom or the Oval Office and heard the great throbbing coming from Lafayette Park: "Hey! Hey! LBJ! How many kids did you kill today?" In his own perverse way, Johnson had started out thinking of himself as doing good, raising up the poor, giving black folks a chance. And now he was a baby-killer, a demon. Gorbachev's indignation on May Day must have gone even deeper. He had challenged institutions and a system many times more monstrous than anything a modern American could imagine. His maneuvering, his attempt to erode the power of the Party and slowly build up democratic institutions, was the political feat of an age. No czar or general secretary had ever put himself and his power in such jeopardy. And now it had all gone wrong. Day by day, the people of the Soviet Union were developing minds of their own. Gorbachev cheered that—at least in principle. But the reality of a new psychology, independent and defiant, confused him, sent him running to the reliable bases of traditional power. He ignored those who told him what he did not want to hear. The only men who would flatter him were precisely those who would one day betray him. His tragedy had begun.

———

The liberal press was forever wringing its hands over the lack of young people in politics. I found that strange. Red Square that May Day was filled with men and women in their thirties, twenties, and teens. Unlike Karpinsky,

Afanasyev, Yakovlev, and Gorbachev—men who had been raised as true believers and then begun the long process of awakening after Stalin's death— the young had never believed for a minute. They did not believe in Communism, the Party, or the system. They did not believe in the future. As a secret Politburo analysis dated May 19, 1990, described the phenomenon, there was now in Soviet society an utter "disrespect for the organs of state power."

The Gorbachev years were not a negation for the young, but rather a chance to fill a void, to move from a despairing cynicism toward something resembling normal modern life in all its multiplicity. For the young, the instructions and pretensions of the existing system constituted a separate world of the absurd, a realm of lies so funny you could die laughing.

The official indoctrination had started in the first grade. On the first day of school, the principal would gather all the children in an auditorium and tell them, "You are so lucky to be living in this country where all childhoods are happy ones!" The first words in their readers were "Lenin," "Motherland," and "Mama." The flyleaf bore a picture of the Lenin Mausoleum, and in the sixties the last page of all textbooks had a portrait of Khrushchev with the caption "Nikita Sergeyevich is a fighter for peace. He says to all peoples, 'Let's live in peace!' " On Revolution Day, the children were declared *Oktyabritsti,* "Children of October," and they wore star-shaped badges bearing little pictures of Lenin as a cherubic child. In the essay "Less Than One," Joseph Brodsky captures the experience of school under the regime in two sentences: "It is a big room with three rows of desks, a portrait of the Leader on the wall behind the teacher's chair, a map with two hemispheres, of which only one is legal. The little boy takes his seat, opens his briefcase, puts his pen and notebook on the desk, lifts his face, and prepares himself to hear drivel."

In summer, the luckier children went to Pioneer camps, where they played war games with balsa rifles and acted out "The Siege of Sevastopol" in evening song competitions. They were raised on a quaint prudery. During the Brezhnev era, the weekly *Ogonyok* magazine advised that "girls should learn self-respect, then there won't be any need to pass laws prohibiting kissing and hugging on the street. A woman's modesty increases the man's sexual energy, but a lack of modesty repels men and brings about total fiasco in their intimate relations." In 1980, an American researcher published *Sex in the Soviet Union* and cited one article in the official press declaring that premarital sex caused neurotic disorders, impotence, and frigidity; another article said that the "ideal duration of the sexual act" was two minutes, and a man who delayed ejaculation for the pleasure of his partner was doing something "terribly harmful" which could lead to "impotence, neuroses, and psychoses." All this while many Russian girls, in the absence of effective birth control, were having one abortion after another.

Those who grew up under Brezhnev were slowly crushed by a great, invisible weight. "Most conformed out of laziness, hopelessness," the music critic Alex Kahn told me one night. "When I was eighteen and in my first year of college, I was picking apples on a collective farm and I was talking to a friend of mine every day in the field. And I remember how we concluded that we were living in the most sophisticated dictatorship that has ever existed on this planet. The force of the propaganda was so strong that there could never be a revolution from below. I knew all about Sakharov and the other dissidents, but they were a tiny island off by themselves. The system had permeated society at every level. It was everywhere. No one was being tortured, as in the Middle Ages or under Stalin—or, at least, not many. But the system was unshakable because it penetrated society so thoroughly. You could talk openly only with your closest friends, and even that was not always safe."

But people of Alex's generation and younger grew up without the same sense of ever-present fear that their parents had known. The "era of stagnation" demanded obedience, but usually not your neck, not even your soul. For the first time, a generation began to distance itself from the system and look at it with disdain; it saw the strangeness and horror in all that had gone on before. Its relation to the state and its institutions was purely ironic.

What seemed to save people was the cocoon of friendships, the feeling of independence and intimacy that long nights of talk could provide. My tutors in this were, above all, a quartet of friends in their mid-thirties so close to one another for so many years that I feel presumptuous even now saying I was part of their circle. At least I was a kind of tangent to the circle of Masha Lipman and her husband, Seriozha Ivanov, and Masha Volkenshtein and her husband, Igor Primakov. They were the sort of people you'd see in the audience at meetings of Memorial or Moscow Tribune or, joking and paying half attention, at a rally somewhere on the outskirts of Moscow. Seriozha was a historian, Igor a seismologist, Masha Lipman a translator, Masha Volkenshtein a pollster. They were not famous, but they knew people who knew this well-known artist or that reform politician. Of the four, I knew Masha Lipman best, because she eventually came to work for the *Post*. When we finally had the nerve to stop hiring the KGB-approved informers that the Foreign Ministry had always sent us, Masha went to work as a researcher and translator, finally displacing a harpy of the higher organs.

Most nights when we got together, the talk was about politics. I supposed that was always the way in a city of revolution. But after a while Masha and Seriozha talked about their families, typical stories for educated people of their generation.

"My maternal grandfather, David Rabinovitch, was born in Kharkov, in the Pale of Settlement, and he became enthralled with proletarian ideas,"

Masha told me. "He was a typical Jewish intellectual, enthusiastic about a new era, a new art. He was a musician. When he came to Moscow and graduated from the conservatory, he taught Marxist political economy and was a member of the Russian Association of Proletarian Musicians. He wanted a new proletarian culture, loved Mayakovsky. For Jews, the Revolution meant the idea of an end to the Pale of Settlement. Grandmother was an actress who studied with Meyerhold, worked in his Theater of the Revolution. My grandfather knew Shostakovich, and my grandmother played a vendor who sold fur-lined brassieres in a Mayakovsky play.

"It was incredible. They and their friends developed a revolutionary style even in the way they lived at home. They had no dishes, no real furniture. They decided it was all too bourgeois and left it all in Kharkov. Birthday parties, weddings, and New Year's trees were also gotten rid of. Bourgeois. To make a table, my grandmother found a few boards, scrap wood, and asked the super to make a table. They thought that traditional Russian felt boots, *valenki,* were also bourgeois, so the children walked through the slush and the snow in their thin leather shoes, crying of the cold. They just mocked all traditions of the old order. So they had my mother call them by their first names and they ate their meals off of butcher paper."

Nevertheless, Masha's maternal grandfather was sent to the camps for espionage. He had met a few times with an American reporter. He survived, returning home after Stalin's death. Her paternal grandfather was not as fortunate. Aleksandr Levit was a revolutionary who worked in the Komintern and attended the Seventeenth Party Congress in 1935. He used the pseudonym Tivel. The year after the congress, he was arrested and disappeared. During the Moscow purge trials, Masha's grandmother turned on the radio and heard the voice of one of the accused, Karl Radek, testifying. "It was Tivel who came to me suggesting we kill Comrade Stalin," Radek said. Masha's grandmother fainted straightaway: "She knew it was the end."

Seriozha's family history was less dramatic and, perhaps, more typical. "My first clear memories can be easily dated. My parents had sent me to bed. Guests were coming over. My uncle brought a typewritten copy of *Paris Match,* which had run excerpts of Khrushchev telling the story of Stalin's death. I was in bed, trembling with curiosity. I had the door opened slightly and listened. I remember I was incredibly interested, even though my parents tried to fight this interest. They knew it was vaguely dangerous.

"When I was thirteen I had some very sharp political discussions with my parents, about history, about Bolshevism, about conformity. I was insisting that Bolshevism was a mistake that had caused incalculable suffering. I knew it from the beginning. I listened to the 'foreign voices' even though they were jammed. You had to sit out those long *wooo wooo* sounds. But you could hear the stations better out in the country where the jamming wasn't quite as good as it was in the center of Moscow."

At about the same age, Masha said, she was in a ninth-grade class that was reading *Crime and Punishment,* and the discussion turned into a political event, a moment when Masha realized that she was growing slowly and inexorably away from the mythical Soviet childhood. "I raised my hand and said I thought the killing of another human soul was prohibited, and what's more, there was nothing more precious than a human life. No one in the class agreed. There were those who said, 'What if the person is an enemy?' The teacher accused me of sharing an 'abstract concept of humanism.' At the next parent-teacher meeting, this teacher told my mother with great assurance, 'Don't worry. I will struggle with her.' "

As a teenager, Masha listened carefully to the talk at her kitchen table. Her parents were on the margins of dissident society. They knew people who knew Solzhenitsyn. They visited Nadezhda Mandelstam, the great memoirist; as always, Mandelstam greeted her guests in bed, in her nightgown and covered with the husks of sunflower seeds and cigarette ash. Masha listened to her parents' underground music tapes—the *magnitizdat*—of Aleksandr Galich and Bulat Okhudzhava. "The tapes were a big secret. Not all of my friends had a tape recorder, and my friends would come and listen to other things. Once a girl opened a drawer and saw the tape marked 'Galich' and I will never forget the terror of that moment. I was sure that we'd end up at the KGB."

Masha and Seriozha traveled in the same circles during the Brezhnev years. When they first met, they discovered that they both adored the same book: Venedikt Yerofeyev's comic epic *Moskva-Petushki.* "That was the book of what our lives were, the pain of it and the irony, too," Masha said. "It was a book about trying to escape when no escape was possible." Their friends were students, young men and women who lived on the edge of dissidence, who were absorbed in books and talk. "In school and university, to be an intellectual meant that you got together all the time, talking and drinking and talking about how drunk you got the night before," Masha said. "I think of it now as a life of meaninglessness. It was considered the height of good taste to disdain your studies, to skip classes. A job was valued insofar as how often you could call in sick without losing it."

"My choice of occupation was a form of escape," Seriozha said. "I really wanted to be a diplomat, but I realized what that led to. Then a journalist. I was sent by my school in 1971 to sort of hang around the paper *Moskovski Komsomolets,* and I realized very quickly that it was impossible to be a journalist and a decent person. The means of escape for intellectuals were ancient history, theoretical physics (if you could avoid military research), structuralism. Or you could be a *dvornik,* a caretaker or an elevator operator, and spend your vast amounts of spare time reading. It was a bit easier to be a scientist, but in the humanities you always had to be on the watch for the dead hand of ideology. So that's what I did. I raced into the past, far past the Bolsheviks, to Byzantium."

The circles of urban intellectuals whom Masha and Seriozha knew so well played at escape, at separateness, through style as well as substance. Unlike their Bolshevik grandparents, who affected the lives of ascetics, these Westernized intellectuals made a point of having good manners, of an almost stylized politeness, with men holding open doors and helping women on with their coats. They used a slightly ornate vocabulary, one as distant as could be imagined from the crude, politicized speech of *Pravda* and *Izvestia.* "There was a time when you would even kiss a woman's hand as a greeting," Seriozha said. "What could be more opposite from 'Greetings, comrade!' "

Real escape was possible only through emigration. And even though Masha and Seriozha both saw many of their friends off at the airport, they could not bear the idea of leaving, of living a life outside the Russian language and culture, of forcing their children to imagine their Russianness from a tremendous distance. "I went many times to get the forms and applications, but finally I just could not imagine myself stepping off a plane in another country and saying to myself, 'Where I am now is where I will be for the rest of my life.' I could not do it."

And so they staked their lives on a new Russia and tried to understand the pathology of the old. "Igor would quote Paul Tillich, who said there are two great fears: the fear of death and the fear of vastness, senselessness," Seriozha said. "Death and suffering are the same for all, but senselessness means different things in different cultures. Europe chose the undeniability of death as a principle, refusing to construct anything everlasting, so life ends with the end of life and is senseless. Previous old cultures and modern Oriental cultures chose another explanation. One possibility is to create something that lasts forever, a form of eternity. So we are together and there is no death. When some cells in an organism die in one organ, the organism still lives on, because it is social and not individual. The problem of death is solved. The idea that the ego has borders that are the same as the borders of the self is a new idea; it began with Descartes's idea 'I think, therefore I am.' If you ask a representative of old Roman culture or European medieval culture, 'Does human life coincide with the life of one man?' he'd say no.

"This was the case with Russian culture. And in Russia, this medieval mind-set has lasted until very recently. The serfs in Europe were liberated in the mid-fifteenth century, but it happened in Russia in the mid-nineteenth century. The idea of community was more important; that way the physical unit lasted eternally. The idea that the individual was of absolute value appeared in Russia only in the nineteenth century via Western influences, but it was stunted because there was no civic society. This is why human rights was never an issue. The principle was set out very clearly by Metropolitan Illarion in the eleventh century in his 'Sermon on Law and Grace,' in which he makes clear that grace is higher than law; you see the same thing today in our great nationalists like Prokhanov—their version of grace is higher than the law. The law is somehow inhuman, abstract. The attempts to revise this principle were defeated. The Russian Revolution was a reaction of absolute simplification. Russia found its simplistic and fanatic response and conquered its support. What we are living through now is a breakthrough. We are leaving the Middle Ages."

———

The young people in Red Square on May Day had changed not only in intellectual terms. Many of them were fairly ordinary, if being a worker or a student or running an elevator is ordinary. Simply because the intellectuals and the articles and books they wrote might have given the best expression of the times, the perestroika phenomenon was also a matter of the pleasure principle, the Id unleashed. The Id of sex, of self-expression, of rock and roll, of materialism, of even the junkiest impulse. The Id of tabloid accounts of the murderous past, the ruined landscape.

The war in Afghanistan, for example, was just one reason among many that the young had come to despise anything that smelled of official Soviet life. More and more, the worst insult you heard was *sovok,* a slang word for Soviet. If you called someone *sovok* you were saying he was narrow-minded, officious, weak, lazy, obsequious, a hypocrite. After years of reducing the West to a swampy hell of imperialism and homelessness, Soviet television and the press now romanticized "over there" as an attainable paradise. The movie *Little Vera,* with its brutally realistic view of Soviet family life, was a hit, but eventually people tired of putting the mirror to their own sorry selves. The state film industry quickly realized that the way to fill the theaters was to buy up Hollywood movies—surf movies, second-rate police thrillers, *Porky's II,* anything smacking of dumb pleasure.

In Leningrad, I met a man, no longer young, named Kolya Vasyn. He was a genuine dissident in the Brezhnev years, but his dissidence consisted of his worship not of Jefferson or Mill, but of Chuck Berry, Keith Richards, and, above all, John Lennon. "Lots of things can liberate people," he told me as we listened to a tape of *The White Album.* "For me it was the freedom in John Lennon's voice." Since the early sixties, he and his friends had been collecting pirated tapes of Western rock and roll and listening to them with the same furtive pleasure and sense of revelation as the intellectuals who read Sakharov in onionskin underground editions in one night-long sitting. He told me that when he first started listening to rock and roll, it was impossible to get records and it was before the era when audio cassettes were easy to find. "We had friends who worked in medical clinics and they would steal used X rays," Kolya said. "Someone would have a primitive record-making machine and you would copy the music by cutting the grooves in the material of the X rays. So you'd be listening to a Fats Domino tune that was coming right off of the X ray of someone's long-forgotten broken hip. They called that 'on the bones.' "

Kolya Vasyn's closet-sized apartment, decorated with Beatles memorabilia and a massive reel-to-reel tape recorder, became the equivalent of Sakharov's kitchen for the rock-and-roll set. Every major rock and jazz talent in Leningrad—the Soviet Union's Liverpool—came through, talked the night away, and, inevitably, collapsed in a corner. The native rock scene there was interesting enough: Kolya, Alex Kahn, and a bunch of others started a rock club on Rubenshtein Street, and Boris Grebenshikov's group, Aquarium, was as innovative as many of the top bands in the West. But what was most important was not the Soviet version of rock and roll, but the way that rock and roll brought kids into the greater world.

The Soviet regime had long worried about the lures of Western pop culture. Even the dullest ideologues, men who had never traveled much farther west than Minsk, knew that somehow James Brown and the Rolling Stones were nearly as dangerous as Helsinki Watch and the Voice of America. "The enemy is trying to exploit youthful psychology with dubious programs," Konstantin Chernenko declared at a 1983 plenum of the Central Committee. The Party's youth paper, *Komsomolskaya Pravda,* said of rock and roll, "Those who fall for this bait are playing into the hands of ideological opponents who sow in immature minds the seeds of a way of life alien to our society." But by 1989 and 1990, *Komsomolskaya Pravda* was earnestly reporting the latest news about Pink Floyd, the Talking Heads, and the *kheepkhope* (hip-hop) phenomenon. On my trip to Perm to visit the prison camp, I heard an odd throbbing sound coming from a vegetable stand. It was the first time I had ever heard a Russian rapper.

Rock and roll brought along with it sexier clothes, Reeboks, commercials, McDonald's. To the ideologues and nationalists nostalgic for an imagined Russian past, *Purple Rain* and Metallica were more of a threat than the idea of a stock exchange on Revolution Square. Now even the conservatives admitted that the country needed wealth, but in any issue of *Molodaya Gvardiya* or *Nash Sovremennik* you could read raving polemics about the evils of rock music, the encroachment on traditional Slavic music. "Live rock has become the scourge and poison of our lives," wrote Valentin Rasputin, Vasily Belov, and Yuri Bondarev, all prominent novelists and cultural conservatives. "Pop music, with its stupefying, monotonous, hollow pulsation, absurd texts, completely lacking in poetry, is kicking every new stream of youngsters into a spiritual void." I was even told that the Politburo would frown severely upon the rise of a rock culture in the Soviet Union. Alexsandr Yakovlev's view is what passed for liberalism. "It's not exactly my sort of thing, but I don't think banning it is the answer," he said. Ligachev, for his part, wanted to prevent Elton John from getting an entry visa. I am not sure what dire order Yegor Kuzmich would have given had it been Ice-T and Public Enemy on the passport line.

Most of the men who ran the Kremlin had never been to the West, or when they had been, it was in the "bubble" of an official visit. It was not by chance that the two men who had traveled in the West extensively before coming to power were also the two main figures of official reform: Yakovlev and Gorbachev. God only knows what the hard-liners thought the Soviet Union would look like if the West moved East. But you could guess. When a young activist named Roman Kalinin registered a gay newspaper with Moscow City Hall in 1990 and published personal ads and some fairly tame articles on gay life in Moscow, *Pravda* accused the paper, *Tema,* of telling necrophiliacs where they could find corpses and pedophiles where to buy children for sex. Kalinin seemed unfazed. He started passing out fliers for a gay rights demonstration: "Turn Red Square into the Pink Triangle."

———

For the older generation that had finally given up the Communist dream, the West was the land of their defeat, a smug and garish landscape of success. It was as if all the dreams of utopia had evaporated and they were stranded between McDonald's and the gulag. What could they do but order a Big Mac?

But for the young, the West was the dream itself. Compared to the hole they were in, the problems of the West seemed laughable. The West was romanticized, sure enough, but why not? How could you begin to talk about the decline of the American economy with a thirty-year-old woman who still had to live with the husband she had divorced five years before because there was nowhere to move? By 1990, one of the fastest-selling books in the street kiosks was *How to Find Work in America,* followed quickly by *How to Find Work in Europe.* This lust for all things Western could break your heart. For a couple of weeks, I watched the making of *Russia House.* The director, Fred Schepsi, set John le Carré's novel against all the most predictable postcard backgrounds. Off to the side, dozens of young Russians worked in odd jobs, as translators, stand-ins, technicians. I talked mostly with a young woman named Kira Sinyeshikova, who helped the Americans communicate with the Russians in the crew. I watched her watch Hollywood; I watched her bask in the glow of Michelle Pfeiffer. Kira could not get over the organization, the equipment, the treatment of the stars. And after a while she giggled at the way the Americans thought they were "capturing the true Russia" as they filmed Red Square, the Zagorsk cathedrals, the radiant parks of Leningrad. A few weeks after the production closed, Kira was back in her regular job as a tour guide at the Museum of the Revolution in Leningrad. We had agreed to meet for dinner, and I joined one of her tours. It was late morning and she was leading around a bored group of tourists from Voronezh and Siberia. She told them all about the "wondrous" documents stored there, the "unique" memorabilia of Lenin. The tourists did not care, and Kira cared less. I have rarely seen eyes so blank.

Things Western opened the world up. That spring and summer of 1990, I spent a couple of afternoons a week in Lenin Hills, where the Japanese had built a pretty decent baseball park for Moscow State University. I sat in the dugout with a kid from Sioux City named Bob Protexter who had come all the way from Iowa to coach baseball.

"I read this was happening in *Sports Illustrated,*" he said. "I wanted adventure, but what the hell would I do in Tahiti? So I figured I'd teach Russians how to turn a double play."

When the baseball craze began in 1986, traditionalists were gravely concerned. Somehow it never occurred to them that the country had also gone basketball-mad in the seventies without causing the sudden implosion of the Soviet nuclear force. Nevertheless, *Izvestia* published a frenetic editorial claiming that baseball was a foreign intruder and that, anyway, Russian *lapta* was a superior game that gave America the idea for baseball in the first place. Sergei Shachin wrote that *lapta,* which dates back to the days of Ivan the Terrible, came to California when Russian émigrés settled there in the nineteenth century. Hence, baseball. "It was a guess," Shachin admitted later.

The Soviets were getting an all-star team ready for an American tour, and they looked raw but not without talent. The field was filled with former javelin throwers, former water polo players, and former hockey players. Protexter's friend Richard Spooner was the Johnny Appleseed of the game in Moscow. He worked days at an American business consortium and spent weekends preaching the wisdom of the infield fly rule. Spooner managed to supply the Chemists, his team at the Mendeleyev All-Union Chemical Society, with gloves, balls, helmets, and even videocassettes of Los Angeles Dodgers highlights. The more they watched the tapes, the more the Russians developed the tics and affectations of their American brethren. Scratching, spitting, bubble-blowing. It took a while to get them all down pat. In one game, a guy took his gift of Red Man chewing tobacco and gobbled it down like chocolate. He threw up and spent the rest of the game in a hopeless daze. He struck out three times, looking.

"Now they chew and spit all right, but so far they haven't caught on to the tradition of grabbing your balls before the pitch," Protexter said.

Vadim Kulakov, Spooner's catcher at Mendeleyev, was a fanatic devotee of Gary Carter, later of the Mets and Expos. "If I ever have a son," Kulakov said, "I shall call him Gary, after the great Gary Carter." Kulakov used a curling iron to affect the cherubic look of Gary Carter. On the field, he had the same frenetic style, the same showy sense of hustle as "Mr. Hustle." And when he went on road trips with the team, Vadim Kulakov gave his girlfriend a Gary Carter 1988 Topps baseball card "so she will remember me."

So far, no Russian had ever hit a home run at the Moscow State University park. The Big Bear was still a nation of spray hitters. So far, no one had thrown a proper curve, and the slider was as distant a dream as shopping malls and microwaved tacos. But the fielding was surprisingly good. The country boys, the kids from the collective farms, had a good sense of outfield play. The only thing that seemed a little precarious was the decision-making. Billy Martin–Reggie Jackson-like squabbles were a common sight in the Moscow dugouts, and I was told that was likely to last a good while. "We decide everything together," said the leading Soviet manager, Vladimir Bogatyryov. "Despite all that's happened, we still have more of a collective mentality here in Russia."

It was nice to see that the Russian ballplayers had developed a sense of style despite the obvious impediments. Most of the players wore caps from major-league teams, though one wore a Minute Maid model and another, as if in the worst nightmare of the KGB, sported a model with the bold logo "Radio Liberty." In the other dugout, one of the coaches was writing a new lineup combination on the pale-blue cover of an old copy of *Novy Mir*. For a while I watched the action with Bill "the Spaceman" Lee, late of the Boston Red Sox. Lee was entranced with the players, the way they strived equally for mannerism and real skill, as if they knew, instinctively, that the quirks of the American game were not irrelevant, but the beauty part. He tried to show the pitchers that they had to "respect" the mound, to care for it "like your home, your office." And they loved the Spaceman.

"I'll tell you this, speaking as a red-blooded American who has no beef with the Russians: I hope they get this game down," Bill Lee said. "Because if they learn how to play, they'll discover it beats the shit out of working.

Take anything. Take music. When they can turn on the TV and they can see Joe Cocker singing 'Civilized Man' with fifty thousand people going apeshit and everybody's got their tops off and their tits jiggling, well, they'll say, 'You know, I want that! I gotta have that!' The same with baseball. They want what we have. And why the hell not?''

CHAPTER 23

THE MINISTRY
OF LOVE

Until I got to Moscow, I never caught the spy bug. In college, there were rumors that a professor might tap you for the work, the way the Communist dons of Cambridge had done for Philby, Burgess, and Blunt. I never heard of it happening, though I suppose that was the idea. As a reporter in Washington, I felt ridiculous the few times I was called upon to write about espionage and its entertainments. Inevitably, someone was feeding you a hunk of fakery: a "scoop" that won an obscure political point, an alluring narrative cooked up in some embassy basement. Once I wrote a story about a Soviet defector, the wife of an embassy official. She betrayed her country and fled into the arms of a used-car salesman. She was known, in the headlines and elsewhere, as "the Woman in the Blond Wig." On television, she wore her wig and big sunglasses. Later she signed a six-figure book contract. I knew I was somebody's fool. But whose?

In Moscow, it was understood that we, the foreigners, were under careful watch by the KGB. People talked about other reporters making graceless exits from Moscow after having been shown eight-by-ten glossies of themselves in sexual rapture with someone not their spouse. No matter how dramatic events became in Moscow, our friends and relatives at home wanted to know most of all what it felt like to be listened to, to be watched. After it became an instinct to avoid any mention of our Soviet friends, a life overheard felt like nothing at all, or almost nothing, like a slight numbness on your forearm that you forget until you touch it. Mostly, you stopped caring. Stupidly, arrogantly, you felt invulnerable. Go ahead. Let them listen. The cold war was over, wasn't it?

———

Vladimir Kryuchkov, who took over as KGB chief in 1988 from Viktor Chebrikov, tried hard to convince the world that he had created a kinder, gentler secret service. The Ministry of Love, as Orwell called it. Taking a page from Gorbachev's own stylebook, Kryuchkov tried to "personalize" himself and the institution he represented. He described for the press his great love for Bellini's *Norma*. If only Van Cliburn would move to Moscow, he said, the KGB would build him a wonderful apartment. Kryuchkov even begged for the workingman's sympathy. "The KGB chairman's life is no bed of roses," he told the editors of *New Times*. So much work, and so little time. He gave press conferences. He fielded (carefully screened) questions on a television talk show. He met with foreign visitors. There were even tours of Lubyanka on which guides would point to display cases filled with preposterous spy equipment—telephones in the heels of shoes, things like that. Kryuchkov never mentioned that he took part in planning the invasion of Budapest in 1956 and Prague in 1968. This did not quite fit with the new image.

Without cutting his forces by a single spy or border guard, Kryuchkov had embarked on one of the most curious public relations campaigns in history: trying to portray the spy apparatus of Dzerzhinsky, Yezhov, Beria, and Andropov as an earnest government servant of legality and democratic reform. One evening, the press was invited to the Foreign Ministry press center and treated to a documentary about the "new KGB," in which officers swooned over the food ("Can I have the recipe?") and generally acted like the corn-fed careerists in a U.S. Army recruiting film. Kryuchkov was eager not only to gild the present, but also to whitewash the past. "Violence, inhumanity, and the violation of human rights have always been alien to the work of our secret services," he told the Italian paper *L'Unità*. Although the Brezhnev era was "not the best in our lives," Kryuchkov said the KGB acted at the time in "compliance with existing legislation."

Kryuchkov's self-advertising was born of necessity. For the first time in its existence, the KGB was subject to public criticism. The former Olympic weight lifter Yuri Vlasov took the podium at the Congress of People's Deputies in May 1989 and denounced the KGB as a vast "underground empire" that had been using its troops and prisons to slaughter the best and brightest of every Soviet generation since the Revolution. Vlasov, a Hercules with horn-rimmed glasses, said the KGB was the "most powerful of all the existing tools of the apparatus" and must be put under strict control of the new, elected legislature. Needless to say, such a thing had never happened before, especially not on live national television. Kryuchkov admitted he had an "unpleasant" reaction to Vlasov's speech, "but then I asked myself: I must think about what is taking place. . . . He is just not aware of the many things we are now engaged in and what we are planning to do. If all Soviet people are as ignorant as he is, then many of them must think along the same lines." After all, he said, Western reports that the KGB somehow represented a reactionary, antireform force in the leadership were "unsubstantiated. . . . The KGB and the army both are closely connected with the people. They entirely accept the program of perestroika worked out by the Communist Party and are ready to support it and defend it."

Kryuchkov really must have thought he was fooling everyone. There was no shame to his public relations schemes. A man of the old order, he was sure he could master the new. He had the arrogance of a man who watched television once and was convinced he understood it. By 1990, the KGB even opened a press office and put a general in charge of "facilitating press relations." At one affair, Kryuchkov invited all the female correspondents in Moscow for an "interview," where he treated them with all the courtliness a scoundrel can muster. Waiters in formal dress brought the ladies their parting gifts: bottles of sweet Soviet champagne and a red, ersatz-leather-bound two-volume history of the Soviet secret services, autographed by Kryuchkov himself. What did he want out of this? Did Kryuchkov expect the reporters to rush to their keyboards and tap out feature stories comparing the KGB to the League of Women Voters?

One morning, on *Komsomolskaya Pravda*'s front page, under the headline "MISS KGB," there was a photograph of a pretty young woman named Katya Mayorova, the holder of the world's only "security services beauty title." It was a curious pose. She was making erotic work of strapping on a bulletproof vest. The article said that Comrade Mayorova would soon appear on the television program *Good Evening Moscow* to make "announcements" about KGB operations. It said that Katya wore her bulletproof vest with "an exquisite softness, like a Pierre Cardin model." Beyond "mere beauty," among her many charms was an ability to "deliver a karate kick to her enemy's head."

I called the press center and asked if I might interview Miss KGB. I thought everyone at the KGB's Lubyanka headquarters would get a good laugh out of that. But ten minutes later a call came back, confirming an interview appointment at the headquarters of the KGB.

"May I bring a camera?" I said.

"We would expect you to," came the answer.

At the appointed hour I parked in front of one of the auxiliary buildings just off Lubyanka Square. I gave my name to a receptionist and sat down to wait for my audience with the reigning queen. In the meantime, I noticed that every so often an ordinary person off the street would come in and shove an envelope or even a packet of documents into a large mailbox. This was where people came with their appeals and their complaints. It was a bitter reminder of what this place was—still was. I thought of Lydia Chukovskaya's novel *Sofia Petrovna,* her fictionalized account of her days spent trying to get the secret police to tell her what had happened to her husband; I thought of Akhmatova's days in line, waiting to know the fate of her son. And I imagined the scene downstairs at the end of the day, a few agents sitting around the furnace, laughing and emptying the mail into the fire.

"Mr. Remnick?"

It was Katya Mayorova, splendidly turned out in an angora sweater and a pair of tight Italian jeans.

In the presence of a KGB "press officer," Katya answered my questions— or didn't. She said the contest had taken place "in private" and even the number of contestants was a secret. That there obviously had never been any contest at all was, I supposed, a given and did not bear mentioning. But Katya, for someone trained in "kill methods" and marksmanship by the most feared organization in the world, was charming. She was making terrific work of this. With her combination of Miss America sweetness and a veiled sense of danger, she was satisfying some base fantasy that I could not quite identify. What? The Rosy Executioner? Mata Hari? No, she said she doesn't "necessarily only date KGB men." Yes, she had been getting quite a number of calls since the *Komsomolskaya Pravda* item appeared. "Men are the same everywhere," she said, rolling her eyes like a true Valley Girl. When I asked her to pose for a picture, she sidled up to a statue of "Iron Feliks" Dzerzhinsky, the founder of the secret police, and cooed.

———

It was getting late, and I wanted to stop by Lubyanka Square outside. The city's leading democrats were going to unveil the first major monument to the victims of the regime: a huge stone taken from Solovki, a labor camp established on a White Sea island by Lenin. I asked Katya if she would be going to the ceremony. She blushed, but then recovered with an answer that I imagined was highlighted in the daily briefing book of the KGB's public relations campaign. "Tens of thousands of innocent KGB men were also killed," she said. "And so I'll go to the monument tonight. I think of it as my monument, too. All of ours."

Outside it was snowing lightly and a small group of demonstrators had already begun to gather. They carried signs saying "The KGB Can Never Wash the Blood from Its Hands" and "Bring the KGB to Justice!" Slowly, several hundred people assembled around the stone as darkness fell. The ceremony began. Yuri Afanasyev, representing Memorial, took the microphone and in a voice that rang out across Lubyanka Square, he said, "Never before has a regime spent seventy years waging such a brutal war against its own people. Blessed are those who died in the camps and were hungry and cold." Oleg Volkov, a former prisoner of Solovki, pointed across the traffic to the statue of Dzerzhinsky and declared that the time had come for "false idols to be toppled." Priests in dark cassocks chanted prayers over the rock. People laid flowers on the stone and wept. Others carried candles and shielded the flames with their hands from the wind. The cars coming around the traffic circle slowed to catch a glimpse of this strange ceremony, and the snow fell harder, and then one of Sakharov's closest friends, the human rights champion Sergei Kovalev, warned everyone. He said what everyone really needed to hear, that "nothing has changed yet, that we the people are still down here, and they, the KGB, are still over there."

———

No lie was too big for Vladimir Aleksandrovich. When a *New Times* correspondent asked whether the KGB kept files on Soviet citizens, Kryuchkov was adamant: "Ask a KGB man that and he will laugh. You might find such things in other countries, but not here."

The "new KGB" under Gorbachev fed the correspondents spy stories as if they were bird seed, and they were impossible to resist. Even before Kryuchkov's arrival, they let a British journalist spend a few days debriefing the defector Kim Philby. Philby, a rat forever pretending to be a mouse, did his Honorable Englishman routine to perfection, waxing on about his service to ideals and complaining about the delay in getting copies of the *Times* and the *Independent*. Actually, Philby was a terrible drunk and the KGB treated him like a pathetic dependent whose bedpan needed constant changing. When Philby died in 1988, the KGB managed to leak very selectively the time and place of the funeral. Some of the British papers played the story as if it were the signal event of the century.

With Kryuchkov, the public relations campaign widened. An official in the Foreign Ministry press department—a KGB man himself, to be sure—let me know that if I wanted, I could have "a cup of tea and a chat" with Yevgeny Ivanov. In British tabloid language of the time, this was Yevgeny Ivanov, the "Slavic Mystery Man," who slept with "Good Time Girl" Christine Keeler, who "Coaxed Valuable Secrets" from John Profumo, the minister of war, who "Toppled Tory Government." In setting up the meeting with Ivanov, the KGB showed a New York publicity agent's sense of timing. *Scandal,* a breezy reenactment of the 1963 Profumo affair, was, at that very moment, playing in theaters in Britain and the United States. The film had a lot of yuppie appeal, what with its orgies and *Decline and Fall* accents.

I sat waiting for Ivanov in the dim Foreign Ministry café, wondering what this spy-novel figure would look like, how he'd behave. He'd been the Red Rogue in a story hardly anyone remembered anymore. The year was 1963. Under the tutelage of the osteopath Stephen Ward, Christine Keeler and her friend Mandy Rice-Davies slept their way to greater glory. The war minister, Profumo, who was married to a movie actress named Valerie Hobson, had his affair with Keeler and fell into disgrace after he lied to Parliament. He fell lower still when Keeler claimed that she had also slept with Ivanov, a KGB agent working undercover in the London embassy as Soviet military attaché. Keeler later made money telling her story. Ward, her mentor, killed himself. And so on.

A rumpled older man approached my table. He moved with a shy shuffle and seemed vaguely sad, as if he had gotten terribly lost and was too embarrassed to ask directions to the exit door.

"I am Yevgeny Ivanov," he said. "Sit down? Yes?"

In the legend of the Profumo affair, Ivanov had fluent English and public-school manners. Lord Astor liked to have him around. The man at my table could barely speak English and was very grateful when we switched to Russian.

"Slava Bogu," he sighed. Thank God.

I told him the critics in the West thought *Scandal* was a pretty good movie and had stirred interest once more in the Profumo affair and the name Yevgeny Ivanov. "Your name is in the papers. You're famous again," I said.

"Ach, ach, why is everyone so interested in this?" he said. "Why bring up this whole dirty story again? Our relations with the English are getting better. There was just a summit meeting with Thatcher and Gorbachev. We're waiting for Queen Elizabeth, to see and listen to her. And against this background, to stir up mud from twenty-five years ago? What forces can gain from that?"

Ivanov said he had worked for the Defense Ministry "analyzing documents" until 1982 and then for Novosti, the press agency that was also a well-known center for the KGB. He was vague about what he had done at Novosti, yet everyone knew that it was a holding pen for agents. Despite Ivanov's stagy lack of interest in the headiest days of his life, he said he was thinking of writing a memoir.

In that spirit, I asked him if he had ever slept with Keeler. And had he coaxed her to give up Profumo's whispered confidences?

"Never, never, never," Ivanov said. "My relationship? None at all. I never paid any attention to her. I say this honestly. Never. What kind of star was she? Okay, she had long legs, but that kind of girl exists even in Moscow.

"Some people say I gave her the task of pumping Profumo on where and what kind of nuclear weapons would be delivered to West Germany. That's nonsense. I could have done that better myself, just asking. It wasn't a secret that I, as a military man, as a Soviet man, am interested in those nuclear weapons and when they'll be delivered to Germany. And they called me a spy!"

Ivanov said he thought that he'd been trapped in a conspiracy that had nothing whatever to do with him or the Soviet Union. When the news broke, he said, he quickly realized that all his "old friends" in the British Parliament and the dinner party circuit would no longer talk with him or be seen with him. It was time to close up shop.

"I left London and a week later Keeler's 'life story' was in the press," Ivanov said. "I don't know if she ever went to college, but she could never have written that stuff herself. She could not even have imagined it by herself. It was all prepared beforehand. Some sort of group was interested in Profumo's downfall. What group, I don't know. He had enemies and they needed material to compromise him."

Ivanov shrugged. His whole physical bearing was a shrug. He reminded me of a retired ballplayer who had ended his career on a missed shot, a dropped pass in the ultimate game. He was famous when he would have been happier in obscurity. He was there eating with me because someone told him he had to, because it would serve an interest. "I guess I may be able to travel now to Britain, but I don't want to," he said. "And why? Because there is so much press in England. And if I go to England, and if Christine Keeler hears I'm there, she'll just call in the press and say, 'I slept with him,' once again. She needs more money and she'll make it if I go to London. It's just not worth it."

And so I wrote my story. Months later, Ivanov got a fat advance from some foreign publishers. He was ready to tell all. Had he slept with Keeler? Had he pirated secrets from the War Department? Of course, Ivanov wrote. Of course!

———

A few months later, at an interminable press conference at the Foreign Ministry, I was tapped on the shoulder and told there was a very important phone call for me. It was General Karbainov, the KGB's press officer, asking whether I would like to meet Edward Lee Howard.

Howard was the first CIA operative ever to defect to the Soviet Union and the KGB. He had been forced out of the CIA in 1983 as a bad security risk for failing a series of polygraph tests about his private conduct. The CIA was also convinced Howard had sold out a number of key "assets" in Moscow, including one aviation expert who was eventually executed for espionage. Howard defected in 1986, a "walk-in" at a Soviet embassy in Eastern Europe—probably Budapest.

Karbainov told me to go home and expect a phone call "confirming everything" at noon.

I was at the apartment in five minutes. The phone rang precisely at noon.

"You know the cuckoo clock at the 'Mezh'?" the voice said, using the foreigners' nickname for the Mezhdunarodnaya, the International Hotel. "I'll meet you under the cuckoo clock tomorrow at ten-thirty in the morning."

I said a quick okay and the line went dead. (As it always does in these stories.)

So once more, life would imitate trash fiction. Or the other way around. No doubt, by arranging a meeting with *The Washington Post,* Howard and probably the KGB itself were playing yet another clever game of "international intelligence." And yet it all seemed so . . . dumb.

On Saturday morning, at the appointed hour exactly, under the monstrous cuckoo clock with a squawking copper rooster on top, a man neither short nor tall, neither skinny nor fat, neither handsome nor ugly, tapped me on the shoulder.

"Hi. I'm Ed Howard," he said. "Good to meet you. Why don't we go?"

The International Hotel was the one place in the entire Soviet Union in the glasnost era that resembled Business-Class America. There were upholstered "conversation areas," an atrium with glass elevators, shops with goods in them, restaurants with food in them. Nothing like Russia.

"I like it 'cause it looks like one of those malls back home," Howard said. "Sometimes I eat upstairs at the German beer place, and I like the ice cream parlor a lot."

Howard headed toward the door, walking in that quick two-step that hit men use after they've finished a job. He seemed nervous, jumpy. But he never ran, never hid his face. The lobby was filled with Westerners, businessmen mainly, tired-looking men who roamed the lobby waiting for the next meeting, aimless as guppies in a bowl. Possibly one or more of them knew who Howard was, if only vaguely, as a distant scandal in a newspaper story, a man who humiliated the FBI and CIA when he slipped through their surveillance in New Mexico and left for Soviet sanctuary. Possibly—possibly not. No one seemed to be paying him special attention.

How was it that a defector—one suspected of selling secrets to the KGB—could roam around in public? I asked him. Wasn't he afraid that someone from the CIA station at the U.S. embassy here might try to grab him? Wouldn't he be recognized by some computer-chip salesman from Tacoma who all of a sudden would point and say, "Hey you, aren't you . . . ?"

"No way," Howard said. "If you asked a thousand people on the streets in Washington, D.C., or in a normal American city, say Cleveland, Ohio, 'Who is Ed Howard?' nine hundred and ninety-nine would never know who I am, much less what I look like."

And the CIA?

"They have better things to do with their time."

Outside in the driveway, Howard opened the rear door of a black Volga, the preferred car of countless midranking Communist Party, military, and KGB officials.

"We're going to the dacha," Howard said in terrible Russian, and the KGB driver, whose English was undoubtedly fluent, headed out Kutuzovsky Prospekt toward the southwest outskirts of Moscow. After leaving the main road, the driver took a deliberately circuitous route toward Howard's place. He took every curve at stomach-turning speed and kept glancing at us in the rearview mirror.

Howard rolled his eyes.

"On the way back, don't bother going this way," he told the driver. "After all, what's the point?" The driver was clearly not just a driver, but he indulged Howard with a nod just the same.

Dachaland, at least Howard's neck of it in the town of Barvikha, was a mix of ordinary peasant huts and the soaring brick-and-glass cottages of the Soviet power elite. Not far away from Howard's place, the notoriously anti-Semitic and unconscionably popular painter Ilya Glazunov lived in a multistory brick monstrosity; elsewhere there were KGB officials, Communist Party men, retired generals.

We pulled up to a smart, two-story brick house surrounded by a fence. There were two car sheds in the yard, one for the Volga, the other for Howard's own Volvo. A retired couple lived in a small cottage on the grounds; the woman cooked and cleaned for Howard and the man tended the garden, growing apples, strawberries, roses, and potatoes. The couple called Howard "Ivan Ivanovich," Mr. Nobody. In the backyard there was a guard booth where two young KGB men kept a round-the-clock watch on Howard. Inside the gate there were infrared devices to signal the presence of intruders. Howard, who also had a spacious apartment just off the Arbat in downtown

Moscow, was quick to mock his landlords as poor, shiftless Russians. He pointed to the second-floor window. "They never finished the construction up there. Typical. They probably ran out of money three quarters of the way through."

Inside, the house was set up with well-made, if wan, Soviet furniture and top-of-the-line Western video and audio equipment. There were two bedrooms, a large living room, a deck, and a study. The living-room ceiling was twenty-five feet high. Howard's library was slim: *Lenin: His Life and Work,* the Bible, *Russian for Everybody,* and a Len Deighton thriller. He said he picked up *USA Today* and *Newsweek* on his trips downtown, and the KGB bought him subscriptions to *National Geographic, Money,* and *Computer World.* To pass the time, Howard played chess with his guards or watched one of his three hundred videocassettes. In his study, an aerie that overlooked the living room, Howard kept two computers. He used them for his "economic consulting work" at a Soviet bank, he said. He also loved to play computer games for hours: "My favorite is this one, SDI," he said. "It's American-made software. The premise is that the KGB has taken over the country and is going to attack the West. So you fight the KGB. I always win. But my friends always lose."

In a country of general poverty, Howard lived like a pasha, mainly at KGB expense. "Oh, I'm comfortable," he said, sounding like a periodontist trying to downplay the expense of his new rec room. Howard said he earned 500 rubles a month at his institute job and some "paltry" hard-currency commissions at the bank. He had access to the well-stocked diplomatic stores where Westerners bought their groceries. But he denied the KGB ever paid him major sums of money for information or for his simple presence as a defector-trophy.

"When I got here I had one suitcase of clothes," he said. "Basically, when I got to work, they said make sure the boy has some good clothes. That's what Kryuchkov said. They gave me an allowance to buy clothes. Maybe a couple thousand rubles. Also, the first three months until I could work out my situation they gave me some money, some rubles. It wasn't a big amount. I don't want to specify how much."

All the guards and tails didn't seem to bother him. "The KGB is responsible for my security. They take it seriously. Sometimes I get lectures from them about why do you not take your security seriously and so on," he said. "But it's my decision. I made the decision on my own to take you out to the dacha today. Kryuchkov said, 'It's your decision.' They don't like it but they said I was responsible. We have a good relationship and I respect them in regard to the security they are providing. . . . As long as they give me the freedom to operate—well, 'operate' is a bad word—but the room to move around, to associate with who I want, to do what I want, it's okay. And they do."

Howard said he was even free to make his own travel decisions. In the past four years, he said, he had wandered Eastern Europe, Nicaragua, Cuba, Mexico, France, and Canada—"for fun." He said he had visited his wife and son in Minnesota and even gone to Cuba. I guessed he was lying, bragging for some complicated spy-versus-spy reason. And when I told him so, he got testy in a weird sort of way.

"Cuba's got some awfully nice beaches," he said. "Have you ever been to Cuba and seen those beaches?"

———

Howard was a small-town boy from New Mexico who grew up reading James Bond novels. Working for the Peace Corps in Colombia and the Agency for International Development in Peru, he got a taste for travel (and a bit for cut-rate cocaine). In 1980, when he was twenty-eight, he had a job interview with the CIA. "I must admit there was the aura of adventure," he said. At first Howard remembered his original image of the CIA. "But then, after meeting some agents in the Foreign Service, I thought, hey, they're human just like us. They like to party."

With his graduate degree in business administration from American University, Howard thought he'd spend his career abroad as an intelligence officer specializing in economics, "finding out what's in people's accounts and stuff." Instead, in 1982, the CIA put Howard in the "pipeline" for the Moscow station. "When I told my classmates that I was going to Moscow, everybody kind of opened their mouths. 'Ah, the Big M!' I thought, well, I'll put up with it and then I can name where I want to go next, like Zurich." For months, Howard trained in Virginia and Washington, learning "dead drops" and countersurveillance techniques, putting little pieces of film in tree stumps and not blinking. He learned terms like "wet assets" (Russian terminology for liquidated spies), "honey pots" (women used as sexual lures), and "ravens" (male homosexual lures). He learned of how the agency kept the names of its "live assets" in Moscow in separate black envelopes in a basement safe.

Howard loved the memory of it: "Ah, very holy and all that sort of thing."

But then Howard failed the polygraph tests and was forced to resign. According to CIA sources quoted in David Wise's book *The Spy Who Got Away,* Howard began acting strangely, phoning the U.S. embassy in Moscow and leaving messages for the CIA station chief. He also admitted later that he stood outside the Soviet consulate in Washington and contemplated "going over." There were unexplained trips to Vienna—practically an espionage playing field because of its position in Central Europe and its former status as a divided city in the days of *The Third Man.*

When the CIA forced Howard to resign from the agency, they had uncovered evidence of his personal problems, especially his history of heavy drinking. When he showed up at the hotel to meet me he was carrying a shopping bag with two bags of liquor, but, he said, "that's just for the guests."

"I think my drinking problems came from a lot of stress factors, especially when I was in the CIA," he said. "And there were some adjustment problems here. No doubt about it. And now I am mainly a beer man. I admitted to myself that I can't handle hard liquor. And that's the big step. I got depressed the last time I drank too much."

It was only after the Soviet spy Vitaly Yurchenko defected to the West and reportedly told the CIA about Howard that the CIA let the FBI in on the secret and the surveillance began. Howard was living at the time in Santa Fe, working in the New Mexico legislature. Trained by the CIA in countersurveillance, Howard soon realized he was being followed and watched. He said his shadows were "incompetent" and "fools." "I'd see the same guy all the time riding around the house. I mean, really. And then I took a trip to Seattle. I see people on the flight with me to Los Angeles, then on the flight to Seattle, and then all of a sudden back in Santa Fe."

Howard denied he ever had contact with the KGB until he finally defected in June 1986. Under pressure and drinking heavily at times, Howard felt he could no longer stay in the United States. In September 1985, he made his escape. Once more he used the techniques he had learned in CIA training. With his wife behind the wheel of their Jeep on the night of September 21, Howard rolled out of the passenger door. A dummy popped up in his place. Then he was gone. While her husband began a half-year odyssey through Latin America and Europe, ending with defection to the Soviet Union, Mary Howard went through a long interrogation by the FBI. According to David Wise, she admitted that her husband had collected $150,000 in a Swiss bank account and buried a small cache of Krugerrands and silver bars in an ammunition box. She also admitted that the Soviet Union had paid for her husband's trip to Vienna in September 1984. All of which reflected rather badly on Howard's claim that he had never had any relationship at all with the Soviet Union or the KGB until he defected. Every time the subject of that period came up, Howard looked away and said, "Let's please get off the subject of '85."

Where the United States was concerned, Howard enjoyed an exquisite sense of *Schadenfreude.* He was delighted with the KGB's bugging of the U.S. embassy in Moscow and the celebrated incidents of marines romping around with Soviet spies with names like Big Raya. Howard said, "I thought it was comical, funny. I think it turned out that only one guy went to jail after all that. The rest of the guys were just normal, young, red-blooded, horny Marines. And they were having some fun with some Soviet girls. Ha! Ha!"

———

At times, Howard acted as though the interview was a painful task done at someone else's beckoning. But at other times he rose to the subject, especially that of his own innocence. It was strange to hear him discourse on one of the other spy cases of his time, the Walker family of U.S. Navy spies who sold the Soviets codes and other key military secrets. His views were one part gall, one part moral relativism. "Oh, they should answer for their crimes, but in the intelligence business it's very difficult to say what is a crime and what isn't. Maybe I'm trying to back off here a bit, but God, it's a land of mirrors. I mean, it's very hard to moralize. . . ."

The long gray Saturday shoved on outside. At first, Howard played his character nicely, waxing cynical even about the KGB's current "kinder, gentler" public relations campaign: "Oh, Americans should believe that about as much as they believe the CIA press campaign." But as the day went by, the character seemed to drain out of Howard. He seemed to get bored with himself, bored with his story. Here was a man, after all, who was a bit player, a waterfly, in the great drama of the superpowers. And after all, wasn't the cold war over? Who needs Ed Howard? He was no Kim Philby or George Blake; there was no romance, no matter how perverse, about the Howard case. He didn't "come out" for ideals or fortune. He defected, and probably sold secrets, mainly out of panic and anger.

We drove back to Moscow and had lunch at the German beer hall on the second floor of the International Hotel. Howard hacked away solemnly at his roast chicken. All around him businessmen were laughing and hoisting their steins of beer and talking about their flights to Copenhagen and Paris and London. They were relieved to be going home.

Howard said he was thinking of living one day with his family in a "neutral country." "The Soviets haven't stopped me from seeking that alternative," he said. "I still consider it a viable option." In the meantime, from "a material point of view, I have pretty much everything I want." Including free court time at the Central Committee tennis courts.

At the dacha, his second bedroom was cluttered with huge stuffed animals and other toys. They were for his son, Lee, he said. So far, Lee Howard knew only that his father did "financial work" in Moscow. "I suppose one day I'll explain it all to him. I don't know at what age, but I will," Howard said. "He'll evaluate the situation against what he knows of me as a person, whether I've treated him well, whether I've raised him well, whether I love him. And eventually, after the shock, I think it will settle down into a relationship. I mean, you look at Kim Philby's sons. They used to visit him here regularly. They came to his funeral and everything."

Finally, Edward Lee Howard had nothing more to say. It was time to go back to the dacha. "I suppose they'll call tonight and ask how it went," he said. They probably already knew. But why did they care? I called a few days later and Howard was stone drunk. He had no idea who I was.

———

Sakharov had always said that compared to the hierarchy of the Communist Party, the men of the KGB were relatively honest and well educated, even a possible breeding ground for reformist tendencies. KGB analysts and agents, he reasoned, traveled and read widely, and they knew far better than anyone else the true picture of desperation within Soviet borders and the realities beyond them. Sakharov's thinking made sense, but it did not hit home with me until I spent a Saturday at the October movie theater on Kalinin Prospekt where the liberal wing of the Party, Democratic Platform, was holding its founding congress.

All morning the speeches had been predictable and by predictable people. By June 1990, with the Twenty-eighth Party Congress just weeks away, it was no longer a novelty that there were democrats in the Party. In fact, in Russia, most of the key reform leaders were still Party members, including Yeltsin. But an odd thing happened. One of the Democratic Platform leaders asked everyone to pay special attention because a special guest—Oleg Danilovich Kalugin, a former major general of the KGB—had decided to speak. Kalugin had the razor-sharp features and icy glare of a movie spy. In fact, he looked like a younger Zbigniew Brzezinski. His speech was untheatrical, but stunning all the same. He described his career as a KGB operative, including stints as the press attaché in the embassy in Moscow and as the chief of foreign counterintelligence in Moscow. He did not give many details then, but later he told me how he had helped run the famous Walker spy ring and was Kim Philby's designated "conversational partner" in Moscow: "I did not get all these medals for my good works as a Boy Scout, after all."

Kalugin's message was simple: the KGB, despite any public relations campaigns to the contrary, continued to infiltrate every workplace, church, artistic union, and political group in the Soviet Union. At the same time, many KGB officers, especially younger ones, could be called "dissidents," or at least in fundamental disagreement with the policies and ambitions of Vladimir Kryuchkov.

"The role of the KGB hasn't changed. It's got a new image, but it's the same old horse," he said after the speech. "The KGB is everywhere—omnipresent—and this is true today. As long as they are an instrument of the Communist Party, they are going to do this. We do not murder anyone on political grounds, but we can murder a person with character assassination. Thousands and thousands of human lives and careers are broken because of the manipulation of the KGB."

As a specialist in foreign intelligence, Kalugin learned to speak fluent English, Arabic, and German. As an exchange student at Columbia University in 1958, he became friends with another fellow Russian—Aleksandr Yakovlev. When he was in New York, Kalugin even scored a publicity coup in *The New York Times.* Max Frankel, who became executive editor many years later, wrote a "man in the news" profile of Kalugin in which he was described as a "real personality kid" who liked to sneak backstage at Lincoln Center and take photographs of the ballerinas "sometimes in ungraceful poses."

A few days after the speech, I went to see Kalugin at his apartment in Kuntsevo, a relatively tranquil district of Moscow. He and his wife, Ludmila, lived in a special KGB building, and outside there were several black Volgas ready to take their charges to work at Lubyanka and God knows where else. It was one of the more comfortable apartments I had seen in Moscow, filled with Western appliances, a brass dog, a ceramic Cinderella, and countless souvenirs from a lifetime with the KGB.

"Be careful of that ashtray," Kalugin said. "One of the best African dictators gave me that."

Kalugin counted himself a great bibliophile. "Look at this," he said, pointing to a copy of Solzhenitsyn's *The Cancer Ward* bound in red leather. "I've always loved him. I had it specially bound. Look at the gold lettering." There were also spy thrillers, *Europe on Five Dollars a Day,* Akhmatova, Gumilyev, and a good selection of old KGB disinformation books, including the notorious *White Book,* which was used in the eras of Brezhnev, Andropov, and Chernenko to spread lies about the personal and political lives of the refuseniks. Moving farther along the shelves, Kalugin said that in 1971 he became the KGB's "caretaker" for Kim Philby. "Kim had been drinking heavily. His life was going to the dogs. It was Yuri Andropov's idea for me to help Philby. I used to go by and see him maybe once a month. I was responsible for his safety and well-being until he died in 1988. I was the first to lay a wreath on his grave." He showed me his copy of Philby's memoir, *My Secret Life.* On the flyleaf it was inscribed, "To Ludmila and Oleg, With deep gratitude and happy memories . . . Best, old boy, Kim."

The neighbors, of course, were "rather upset" at Kalugin for speaking out at the Democratic Platform meeting. Kryuchkov, who lived in an even more exalted building, had been angry with Kalugin for years. In 1987, Kalugin sent a letter to Gorbachev warning him that the KGB was out of control. The personnel of the KGB, he wrote, ought to be cut in half at the very least and ought to be put under strict legislative watch "as they do in civilized countries." In 1989, he wrote an article for the journal *International Life* criticizing the KGB for its foreign operations. The article identified its author only as a major general "formerly occupied for a long period of time with questions of diplomatic activity." Three months before his "coming out" at the October Theater, Kalugin received notice that he was being retired at the age of fifty-five.

What Kalugin was saying now about the KGB was no more a secret to the world than what Yeltsin had said about the Communist Party. His description of the close relationship between Gorbachev and Kryuchkov as a "bad omen" was nothing original. But Kalugin's position gave him a certain authority, and it humiliated the men in power. Here was a major general of the secret police telling virtually anyone who asked that the KGB was still the backbone of a totalitarian state. Sure he could be playing a game. But why? What was in it for him?

Two weeks after the speech at the Democratic Platform convention, the Tass wire ticked out the announcement: Oleg Kalugin had been stripped of his military rank and decorations by order of President Mikhail Gorbachev. The military men who had ordered the slaughter of peaceful demonstrators had gone unpunished, but Kalugin was out. It was a chilling moment—in a year that was going to get a lot colder. Either Gorbachev was acting on his own or he was under pressure from the KGB. It was hard to say which was worse. Either way, the Ministry of Love was still in business.

CHAPTER 24

BLACK SEPTEMBER

What is written with a pen cannot be hacked away even by an ax.

—RUSSIAN PROVERB

In the morning twilight, the village priest opened his front gate and headed for the train platform a half mile away. It was Sunday, and Father Aleksandr Men always caught the 6:50 train from the village of Semkhoz near Zagorsk to his parish church in Novaya Derevnya, a small town thirty miles outside Moscow. He had a full day ahead of him: confessions to hear, baptisms, a lecture in the evening.

Father Aleksandr, a robust man of fifty-five with a thick beard of black and gray, was an emerging spiritual leader of the Russian Orthodox Church. Some of his followers compared him to Sakharov, "a spiritual Sakharov." Unlike countless other priests and church leaders, Men had kept his independence through the Brezhnev years. He refused to cooperate with the KGB. He taught underground Bible classes and published his theological works abroad under a pseudonym. He endured the harassment, sat through long searches of his home and interrogations, came home to open his mail and read death threats, threats against his wife and two children. All because he was an honest priest and served his flock honestly. But he had survived. Now, he told his brother, Pavel, he felt like "an arrow finally sprung from the bow."

In the old days, Father Aleksandr's meetings with intellectuals like Solzhenitsyn, Nadezhda Mandelstam, and Aleksandr Galich were more or less a secret. Now he had become, in spite of himself, a central figure in the rebirth of a degraded church. In the past couple of years, he'd been able to preach and lecture in churches and auditoriums, even on radio and television, all without fear. Just the night before, Men had given a lecture in Moscow and spoken of the spiritual quest as an endless ascent: "We climb breathlessly. Truth is not given easily. We look back down and know there is a great climb ahead. I remember the words of Tenzing, who climbed Mount Everest with the British. He said that you can only approach a mountain with respect. The same is true with God. Truth is closed to those who approach it without respect."

Father Aleksandr never seemed to tire, and he was intent now on getting an early start on Sunday. He kept walking along the asphalt path through the Semkhoz woods toward the train. The narrow macadam path had proved dangerous at times. There had been rapes, a few beatings. Drunks in town sometimes took their bottles into the woods and harassed the passersby. Not long ago, the local authorities had cleared away some of the trees to make the path to the train platform less forbidding. Still, a couple of weeks before, Men asked his young assistant, Andrei Yeryemin, to help find him a place to stay in the city on nights when he was teaching or lecturing late. He said it was getting dangerous to walk too late at night. "I was amazed to hear him say it after all the things he'd been through in 1981 and 1982 when he could have been hauled off at any time," Yeryemin said. But it wasn't just that. Lately, the priest had betrayed a tone of fatalism in his voice. He told one friend that he hadn't much time to live. He gave no explanation.

Suddenly, from behind a tree, someone leaped out and swung an ax at Aleksandr Men. An ax: the traditional Russian symbol of revolt, Raskolnikov's weapon in *Crime and Punishment,* one of the symbols of the neofascist group Pamyat. The ax hit Men on the back of the skull. The killer, police said later, grabbed the priest's briefcase and disappeared into the woods. Father Aleksandr, bleeding terribly, stumbled toward home, walking a full three hundred yards to his front gate at 3A Parkovaya Street. Along the way, two women asked if he needed help. He said no and continued on. From her window, Natasha Men saw a figure slumped near the gate, pressing the buzzer. She could not quite make out who it was in the half-light. Then she

did. *"Gospodi!"* Good Lord! She called an ambulance. Within minutes, her
husband was dead.

———

The murder of Aleksandr Men on September 9, 1990, was an ominous,
almost supernatural portent of a time of troubles, and it had come just when
political expectations seemed once more on the rise.

All summer it appeared as if Gorbachev was preparing to accelerate the
pace of reform, if only to keep up with the events around him. As one
republic after another, including Russia, took its cue from the Baltic states
and declared itself sovereign, Gorbachev made the dramatic step of joining
with Yeltsin to draw up a radical economic program that would encourage
the creation of a market and, even more important, redistribute power from
"the center" to the republics. In a government dacha outside the city, a witty
old economist named Stanislav Shatalin and a plump wizard of market
principles named Grigori Yavlinsky plotted, in civil tones and bureaucratic
language, the dismantling of the System. On the face of it, the "500 Days"
plan was an ambitious and amazingly facile prescription to begin the cure of
a ruined economy. Few had any illusions about the 500 Days part. It would
certainly be more than a year and a half before the empty lots of Moscow
were transformed into shopping malls of plenty. When I asked Shatalin how
long it would be until the Soviet Union had what passed for a modern
economy, he said, "My optimistic scenario?" Yes. Be optimistic, I said.
"Generations," he said. No, it would be a good while before there was a
Silicon Valley in the Urals and the people of eastern Siberia were cruising the
supermarket aisles choosing among Tide, Ajax, and Solo. It was the set of
principles behind the 500 Days that made it so revolutionary, so immediate.
Realization of the plan would mean the shutdown or conversion of hundreds
of defense plants, the rise of private property, radical cuts in the budgets of
the army, the police, and the KGB. What could that mean for the lords of
the System? It was very simple. It meant the end.

When Gorbachev returned from his annual summer holiday on the Black
Sea he told the legislature he was "inclined" to support the plan. That was
all the hard-liners had to hear. The fight for their political life, a war that
would rage for the next eleven months, had begun. The KGB chief, Vladimir
Kryuchkov, piled dozens of reports on Gorbachev's desk insisting that the
500 Days plan was nothing more than an attempt, supported by the West, to
crush socialism, destroy the Party, and weaken the country. At various
meetings, leaders of the Party and the military-industrial complex threatened
to revolt against Gorbachev if he gave his final support to the plan. A

creeping coup was under way, but Gorbachev was so vain, so sure of his ability to master both the machinations of the System and the passions of the people, that he thought he could control it all, finesse it as easily as he had the Nina Andreyeva affair in 1988.

One Politburo document, dated March 12, 1990, revealed the dark sense of foreboding in the Communist Party leadership and the attempt to exaggerate the situation in order to encourage emergency tactics. "The popular consciousness is being radicalized," the memo said. "Distrust in official structures and administrative structures grows. The criticism of the 'partocracy' and the local and central apparatus is more acute. . . . The opposition forces are attempting to exploit the situation. In fact, plans are being made to seize power by clearly antidemocratic means—through pressure, rallies, and the 'roundtable' tactic, which is completely antidemocratic." The "healthy forces in society," the memo added, want "decisive measures based on the law. . . . Use all means of propoganda to stop the discrediting of the army, the KGB, and the police. . . . Disarm the [opposition] ideologically and undermine them in the eyes of society."

For thousands of believers and nonbelievers in the city of Moscow, the first portent of the grim year ahead came with the swing of an ax in the village of Semkhoz. When I first heard about the murder of Aleksandr Men, I did not understand the importance of the event or of the man himself. He was a village priest whose church was an hour's drive from Moscow. And yet within days of the murder, I heard over and over how much he had meant.

In theory, at least, perestroika liberated the realm of the spirit as much as it did political and economic life. After seven decades of dogmatic atheism, the regime ended the persecution of religious believers and the institutions of worship. Suddenly, the word *bogoiskatelstvo*—"the search for God"—was the vogue. There were plenty of frauds around like Anatoly Kashpirovsky, but there were good signs as well. The churches were no longer the domain only of ancient women with childhood memories of a czarist world. Religious classes were no longer dissident activities. Gorbachev returned to the Russian Orthodox Church its ruined monasteries and cathedrals. Synagogues and mosques reopened. But just as the attempt at political reform slammed into one wall of resistance after another, the revival of spiritual life could not, in an instant, transcend a history of political repression. The nomenklatura of the Russian Orthodox Church, put in place by the ideologists and intelligence operatives of the Party, was at least as strong as the nomenklatura of the Party.

The history of the spirit's subservience to state authority goes back centuries before the first Bolshevik. As opposed to the Catholic Church, which developed its independent structures after the fall of the Roman Empire, the

Byzantine Church was always dependent on the state. The Byzantine emperors presided over all the synods of the church and were considered "God on earth." In a sign of things to come, the great dukes of the early Moscow period urged the clergy to reveal the mystery of confession, especially if state security was at issue. Ivan the Terrible tortured priests and jailed one metropolitan for life. The word "czar" is a Slavic form of the word "Caesar," but Iosif Volotsky, a great religious philosopher, wrote that the czar was simply the highest of all priests. When Napoleon met Aleksandr I in East Prussia, Napoleon said, "I see that you are an emperor and a pope at the same time. How useful."

The Bolsheviks despised the Russian Orthodox Church as an embodiment of old Russia. Lenin planned a soulless utopia. But when the Revolution needed to mobilize millions of illiterate people, it couldn't preach Marx to them. As the spiritual inheritor of Russian statehood, the Party needed to co-opt, not destroy, the church, bring it to its knees but not cut off its head. Stalin knew well how deeply the appeal of the church echoed in the Russian soul. To gain the allegiance of the population during the war, he appealed not so much to Communist ideology as to a mystical sense of Russianness, to Holy Russia and its warriors Nevsky, Suvorov, and Kutuzov. In his radio addresses to rally the country, Stalin would put aside the language of atheism. He returned some priests from prison camps and gave them decent positions and salaries. He was their emperor and pope. How useful. And when the war on Germany ended, the war on religion resumed. The dynamiting of churches, the imprisonment of priests, rabbis, and muftis, the prosecution of believers as "enemies of the state"—it all resumed.

———

Aleksandr Men was born a Jew. His father was a nonbeliever, and his mother converted to Russian Orthodoxy. In a country where Jewish religion and culture had been assaulted even more severely than the church, many families of the intelligentsia gravitated to Russian Orthodoxy, if only because they were able to feel their Russian identity more closely than their Jewishness. Men's mother, Yelena, saw the church as a place apart, a refuge. "In our family there was a personal religious search," said Men's brother, Pavel, a computer programmer. "Like so many people disgusted here by the life around them, our family tried to look within themselves for a religious way out." Yelena Men took her sons to pray under the guidance of an honest priest named Serafim who evaded the authorities by moving from apartment to apartment. The "catacomb church," they called it. Most of the parishioners were believers who had been in the prison camps, people who had lost relatives and friends for their faith.

"And so Aleksandr saw around him a kind of elevated moral life, God's people," Pavel Men said. "He made a decision when he was just twelve to study for the priesthood. He went to the local priest and asked what he would have to do to get into the seminary one day. The priest said Aleksandr was not 'one of ours.' Meaning he was Jewish. But Aleksandr set out to overcome that kind of thinking." As a boy and young man, Men found religious books in ramshackle country stores, "there among the nails and the guinea pigs." He began reading the great religious philosophers of the early part of the century, such writers as Vladimir Solovyov, Sergei Bulgakov, and Nikolai Berdyaev, who wrote in spiritual opposition to the Bolsheviks. Such reading, Men once said, "inoculated me against the cult of Stalin. I trembled as I read them."

As a young man, Men went off to study biology at an institute in Irkutsk, a Siberian city on the shore of Lake Baikal. His closest friend there was another Orthodox believer, a temperamental redheaded student named Gleb Yakunin. Men and Yakunin lived together in a tiny wooden house. Men brought with him huge trunkloads of books and kept Yakunin up nights at their rickety kitchen table talking about issues forbidden or, at least, discouraged by Soviet law. They talked about the sham that Soviet biology had become, about questions of Christian ethics and the way they contradicted the rules they lived under. "The Russian character, as you may have noticed, can be very lazy and unambitious," Yakunin told me, "but Aleksandr knew just what he wanted to do. He was interested in all subjects, and he had a purpose. Unlike me, he always knew he was meant to serve God, no matter the consequences."

One day the two city boys wandered into a village church looking, as Yakunin said, "like a couple of white elephants." Someone told the local KGB about these strange creatures. For making their religious faith so public, the two men risked their academic careers. The institute director barred Yakunin from finishing his studies and wanted to throw Men out, too. But the students, feeling the first flush of the post-Stalin "thaw," went out on strike in support of Men, refusing to go to lectures or classes. Men completed his degree.

Yakunin and Men returned to Moscow to follow their varying paths. Yakunin became Father Gleb, a priest and an unabashed political dissident who wrote letters to the Kremlin and the church hierarchy calling for religious reforms. For that he got nine years in prison camps and internal exile. Under Gorbachev, Yakunin returned home from exile and in 1990 was elected to the Supreme Soviet of the Russian Republic.

Men became a spiritual dissident, a less dangerous path than Yakunin's, but still perilous. "Each man has his own talent, his own way, and I moved toward the politics of religion," Yakunin said. "Aleksandr had another kind of gift. In a church that suffered from inaccessibility, he had the ability to explain, to make the teachings of the church available to people." Men's form of dissidence meant being an honest, uncompromising priest; it meant providing the means for internal, spiritual rebellion in individuals. While his friend Yakunin organized political groups to defend the rights of believers, Men tried to instill a kind of spiritual dissidence in his parishioners, an independence of soul. He was a man of faith, but his own man, and God's. Especially for urban intellectuals, Men became a link to turn-of-the-century religious thinkers and philosophers such as Bulgakov and Solovyov who stood apart from this tragic tradition of subservience and obscurantism. Even in the darkest moments under Brezhnev, Moscow intellectuals made Sunday pilgrimages to the village of Pushkino to hear Aleksandr Men. The crowds only increased with the gradual erosion of fear under Gorbachev.

"In general, I think politics is a transitory thing and I wanted to work in a less transitory way," Men told the newspaper *Moskovski Komsomolets* just before he was killed. "I consider myself a useful person in society, which like any society needs spiritual and moral foundations." Men once said, "Dissent is the individual's way of protecting his right to perceive reality in his own way, not to yield to the views of the mass. When an individual calls such views into question, he shows his natural independence, his freedom. It is only when such a personal appraisal is lacking that the law of the mob prevails and an individual turns into a particle of a mass which can easily be manipulated."

After such a long period when he was called in for interrogations by the KGB, Men suddenly found himself a very public theologian in the Gorbachev era. He gave lectures in meeting halls and spoke on the radio. He taught courses on religion at the Historical Archives Institute, Yuri Afanasyev's outpost for nonconformist academics in Moscow. Young people who attended his lectures taped them and then circulated the tapes throughout the country. Just days before the murder, officials at the Russian Republic's new television station were discussing ways to give Men airtime at least once a week to speak on religious topics.

"This was a man who could speak to all of us, from Sakharov to the simplest person," said the writer Yelena Chukovskaya. The literary critic Natalya Ivanova said, "In a country where the regime managed to eliminate, in a sort of grotesque genetic engineering, its best minds, its most honest souls, Men survived to teach, to be an example."

All that was cut off in the woods of Semkhoz. Andrei Bessmertni, a young filmmaker and "spiritual child" of Father Aleksandr, said Men "could have reached millions of young people." Men, he said, saw how at a time when faith in the "bright future of Communism" had faded away, young people had begun a spiritual quest. To overcome their profound cynicism, their sense that history had provided them nothing to rely on or believe in, younger people had turned inward, more in search of themselves than the next political sensation. "These times are not just about getting blue jeans and a McDonald's hamburger," Bessmertni said. "Some people actually want meaning in their lives, spiritual food."

———

On the day of the funeral, thousands of people, including religious leaders from the West, crowded the grounds of the village church in Novaya Derevnya. In Men's hand was placed a small Bible and a golden cross. People wept, and some sank to their knees in prayer. Several of the Orthodox priests who did their best to ignore or suppress Aleksandr Men in his lifetime made sure to speak his praises in eulogy. "My stomach turned as I listened to it all," Yeryemin said.

The eulogy that seemed to speak most eloquently for Men's followers and admirers was published a week later in *Ogonyok*. The article, written by a young journalist named Aleksandr Minkin, revealed that Men, as an honest, charismatic, and, not least, Jewish-born priest, had scores of enemies: the anti-Semites of Pamyat, the conservative zealots in the Russian Orthodox Church establishment, the police, the KGB. Minkin was convinced that the murder was not simply a random disaster, a mugging that went too far, the grotesque folly of an angry drunk. He was sure that this was an assassination intended to scare anyone else who would dare to challenge the System. A thief, Minkin wrote, "goes after a woman wearing jewels on the street or a well-dressed man with a fat wallet. But rich people don't go to work at 6:00 A.M. on a Sunday morning. The rich don't live in Semkhoz. . . . Humanization and democratization are one side of our system. The other is murder. We have been freeing ourselves from fear, but the ax is an instrument to remind us of our fear. They are reminding us that we are defenseless." Minkin compared Men's murder with the Polish secret police's assassination of the pro-Solidarity priest Jerzy Popieluszko in 1984—"an event that once and for all set the people against the forces of power in Poland." But in the Soviet Union, Minkin wrote, "people are standing in lines talking about other things. They have fallen lower into the muck than our brothers in the 'socialist camp' in Eastern Europe. So much the worse for us. We have not revolted, we have not become indignant. . . . This is a turning point in our history and we do not realize it yet. When we do become aware, what will we do?"

———

On the fortieth day after the murder, the day in the Orthodox faith on which the soul of the deceased either ascends to heaven or descends to hell, I drove out to the church in Novaya Derevnya. Even now, weeks after the funeral, people walked down the muddy road to the church to stop awhile at the grave, to lay down fresh flowers. The rotting flowers smelled like old wine, fruity and sour. I met a woman, eighty-six years old, named Maria Tepnina near the grave. She had known Aleksandr Men since he was a child; she knew the whole family. She stared a while at the grave and her face darkened with grief and confusion. After we stood there a while in silence, a light rain slowly soaking us, Tepnina invited me to her house. She lived just up the road from Father Aleksandr's church. Half the floor was covered with just-harvested potatoes, the walls were covered with family pictures and small icons.

For many years, Tepnina said, she helped Men with his secretarial work. "He'd get threatening letters all the time. He just threw them all away, never paid any attention. They accused him of everything from insulting the church, to being a 'rotten kike,' to serving the powers that be. Awful things, and they meant nothing to him."

From 1946 to 1954, Tepnina was in a prison camp near the Siberian city of Kemerovo and then in exile in Krasnoyarsk. In the camps, she met priests and believers, "real holy men." She saw people baptized secretly in their cells, priests shot muttering their thanks to God. But, she said, she had never met anyone with Men's gift for sympathy. And so she made sure, in her old age, to live near his church. Now, she was trying to make sense of the murder. "I think he was a genuine apostle, and all apostles end their lives as martyrs," she said. "So maybe there is a certain justice in this. All his life, Father Aleksandr prepared himself for this, daring to speak from his soul."

Another of Men's parishioners, Tatyana Sagaleyeva, came in and sat down with us. She had just moved from the nearby village of Abramtsevo to Tepnina's house. She also came to be closer to Men's church and to care for her aging friend. And now she was crying, and angry. "The murder of Father Aleksandr is a mystical event, not just a simple killing, an accident," she said. "God has taken this man from us, a spiritual leader who was at the prime of his life. His appearance was a miracle, a man who could, despite it all, despite an aggressive atheistic state, penetrate the sufferings of a great writer like Solzhenitsyn or of a simple woman like me. And suddenly he disappears. How to understand it? Why did God take him from us? Why now?"

———

The day after the murder of Aleksandr Men, a convoy of paratroopers from the Ryazan Airborne Division headed north for Moscow, 125 miles away. It was 3:00 A.M. Hours later, three dozen military transport planes carrying two regiments in full battle gear landed at airstrips in Ryazan. The KGB's elite Dzerzhinsky Division was also put on full battle alert.

For days after the newspaper *Komsomolskaya Pravda* broke the story, there were rumors that the military had staged a rehearsal for a coup d'état. Yeltsin appeared before the Russian parliament and said, "They are trying to prove to us that these are peaceful maneuvers connected with the November 7 Revolution Day parade. But there are strong doubts about this." A spokesman for the military, of course, declared the maneuvers were not maneuvers at all. The soldiers were merely helping out in the fields collecting the potato harvest. Which led *Komsomolskaya Pravda* to ask why soldiers gathering potatoes required the use of AK-47 machine guns and bulletproof vests.

By now, I had spent many nights in Moscow listening to the dark forecasts of one Russian friend or another. Every unpromising development, every hint of difficulty, was somehow part of a larger pattern, a murderous conspiracy. For a long while, I felt like Earl Warren at an unending convention of Kennedy-assassination theorists. What it took me a long time to realize was that in Moscow, being paranoid doesn't mean doom is not on the way. To live in a totalitarian world and not be paranoid—or at least pessimistic—was itself lunacy. When had events ever been benign in this twisted Oz?

As we would soon find out in the coming months, first in Vilnius and Riga, then in Moscow, there was indeed a conspiracy under way, and it was the most open, unguarded conspiracy imaginable. The hard-liners' struggle for power started with pressure, fleeting signs, random moments of psychological terror. Perhaps we would never know who had killed Aleksandr Men . . . but we could guess. We would never know what the troops were doing in Ryazan . . . but we could guess.

What was so strange about the times we were living in was that the press was free to guess, too. Political talk was no longer a dark parlor game among trusted friends. The week after the Ryazan "rehearsal," a well-known writer, Andrei Nuikin, published a piece in *Moscow News* called "Military Overthrow." Nuikin quoted a leader of the radical servicemen's group "Shield," who told him that "the leadership of the armed forces already had a clear plan to take control of the situation in the country." Nuikin said the plan was to start the coup, perhaps in the far east, with the seizure of television stations and newspapers and with the "neutralization" of foreign journalists and their ability to get information out of the country. The Shield supporter said the military would justify the coup not by campaigning directly against Gorbachev's reforms, but by claiming that ethnic tensions had gotten out of control, the economy was collapsing, and socialism was endangered and that the situation required emergency measures. Nuikin wrote that he had no evidence that the military actually had plans for such a coup but he added that the liberals had "grounds to consider means of responding."

———

The third omen of September arrived on the 18th with the morning mail. *Komsomolskaya Pravda* contained a special insert: a sixteen-thousand-word essay called "How Can We Revitalize Russia." The author was Aleksandr Solzhenitsyn, and the essay marked the first time in three decades that he had been able to publish a new work in a Soviet journal.

The article seemed like notes from the dead, as if Herzen or Dostoevsky had suddenly published from the Great Beyond a manifesto on the current state of things. Solzhenitsyn was being published everywhere now, but they were works from the sixties and seventies, historical works about twentieth-century tragedy written in an eighteenth-century language. Some readers were interested; some were bored with later works, especially the "Red Wheel" cycle of historical novels. But in either case, Solzhenitsyn himself was a gigantic absence, a legend living a ghostly life in a place that might as well have been a mountain palace in Brunei. And that mattered. In Russia, the presence of the writer was almost as important as the presence of the work. One writer after another—Vasily Aksyonov, Sasha Sokolov, Yuz Aleshkovsky, Vladimir Voinovich—came back, at least for long visits, to make contact with the audience and the language they had lost. Even in emigration they had always written for "home."

But Solzhenitsyn was secluded and mum. He was a legend. Russian intellectuals, especially, were alternately fascinated and repelled by the odd life the writer led in the woods of Cavendish, Vermont. Each new detail intrigued them. Solzhenitsyn lived in a good, but not indecently opulent, house, and he put up a chain-link fence to keep away unwanted visitors and snowmobiles. But in Moscow, I often heard people talk of Solzhenitsyn's "castle" and the "great wall" that surrounded it. When he first moved to Vermont, he spoke for twenty minutes at a town meeting and apologized to the people of Cavendish for the fence. He told them that when he lived without it, scores of uninvited visitors "arrived without invitations and without warning. . . . And so for hundreds of hours I talked to hundreds of people, and my work was ruined."

That Solzhenitsyn would insist on such a monkish life seemed incredible, especially in America, where publicity was the coin of the realm. Solemn, imperious, even righteous beyond measure, Solzhenitsyn had the nerve to make much of the contemporary literary scene look vaguely frivolous. He wrote gigantically (if not always well), as if from another age. He lacked the modernist leveler of irony. Instead, his rare public pronouncements were chillingly sarcastic. In political argument, disdain was his most common thread. He thundered against the "cowardice" of the West and the "liquid manure" of pop culture in the fierce voice of another era. Jeremiah was heroic, no doubt, but hard to love. He made no apologies. "The writer's ultimate task is to restore the memory of his murdered people. Is that not enough for a single writer?" Solzhenitsyn told his biographer, Michael Scammell. "They murdered my people and destroyed its memory. And I'm dragging it into the light of day all on my own. Of course, there are hundreds like me back there who could drag it out, too. Well, it didn't fall to them; it fell to me. And I'm doing the work of a hundred men, and that's all there is to it."

To me, Solzhenitsyn had a perfectly accurate sense of his mission and place in the world. No matter how dull some of the later work on the Revolution might be, *The Gulag Archipelago* would never fade from the history of Russian literature or the history of Russia. No single work, including Orwell's novels, did as much to shatter the illusions of the West; no book did more to educate the Soviet people and undermine the regime. So who cared if he had a fence? Who cared if some of his books were beside the point? But the price Solzhenitsyn paid for his sense of mission and its immodest expression was mockery. Both in America and in the Soviet Union, there were jokes about Solzhenitsyn's "gulag complex," speculations that he craved the isolation of prisons and prisons-of-his-own-making. He was a monarchist, an anti-Semite, a paranoiac. Voinovich wrote a satirical novel, *Moscow 2042,* that featured a Solzhenitsyn-like character who seemed a cross between a fundamentalist imam and a West Virginia hermit. Solzhenitsyn felt wounded. "They lie about me as they would about a dead man," he once said.

Aleksandr Isayevich, for his part, kept to his schedule. He worked twelve to fourteen hours a day at his desk filling notebooks with the tiny handwriting he learned while trying to conceal his drafts in prison. He also worked on assembling archives on the Revolution and the development of a fund to help the survivors of the gulag. In August 1990, he got back his citizenship. The Russian prime minister, Ivan Silayev, practically begged Solzhenitsyn to return home "in the interests of the state and its future destiny. . . . Your return to Russia is, in my view, one of those moves that our homeland needs as much as air." It seemed strange that Solzhenitsyn still had nothing to say about what was going on in the Soviet Union. When he caved in and granted an interview to *Time* magazine, he set down firm conditions: no questions about Gorbachev or politics, only literature.

"How to Revitalize Russia" came as a shock. After such long silence, Solzhenitsyn worked all summer on his essay and then published it in a paper with a circulation of between twenty-five and thirty million readers. (The next day it also ran in the weekly *Literaturnaya Gazeta,* which went out to another four million.)

———

The text began in prophetic voice:

> The clock of communism has tolled its final hour.
> But the concrete structure has not completely collapsed.
> Instead of being liberated, we may be crushed beneath the rubble.

That opening, and the essay as a whole, had much the same rhythm as his "Letter to the Soviet Leaders," which he sent to the Kremlin the year before his exile. "Your dearest wish," he had written to Brezhnev, "is for our state structure and our ideological system never to change, to remain as they are for centuries. But history is not like that. Every system either finds a way to develop or else collapses." He was now addressing a country that was doing both at once, though the collapse was ruthless and the development erratic. After a ringing restatement of the "blind and malignant" Bolshevik disaster—the murder of tens of millions of people, the destruction of the peasantry, the poisoning of the environment, the moral and spiritual degradation of the country—he provided what he called a "tentative proposal" but what sounded more like the vatic prescription of a convinced prophet:

"This is how I see it: We should immediately proclaim loudly and clearly: The three Baltic republics [Estonia, Latvia, and Lithuania], the three Transcaucasian republics [Georgia, Armenia, and Azerbaijan], the four Central Asian republics [Kirgizia, Uzbekistan, Turkmenia, and Tajikistan], and also Moldavia, if it is drawn more to Romania, these eleven—indeed!—definitely must be separated for good. . . .

"We do not have the energy to deal with the periphery, either economically or spiritually. We do not have the energy to run an Empire! And we do not need it, let us shrug it off: It is crushing us, it is draining us, and it is accelerating our demise. . . ."

The essay did not mention Gorbachev by name and gave him credit for nothing. Instead, the criticism, resounding and heavy with sarcasm, began in the third word of the title: *obustroit'* was a play on the word "perestroika." Gorbachev and the Communist Party used "perestroika" to mean the "rebuilding" or cleansing of socialism after Stalin's "deformation" of Leninism. Solzhenitsyn's verb, *obustroit',* could be translated as to reconstitute, fix, fix up, make comfortable, organize, or, more loosely, revitalize. The ironic echo of "perestroika" and the use of "Russia" instead of "Soviet Union" made it clear from the start that Solzhenitsyn's program had little to do with Gorbachev's idea of a "humane democratic socialism" or the maintenance of the "multiethnic state." Indeed, Solzhenitsyn showed little else but disdain for Gorbachev's efforts. The events of five years were reduced almost to nothing: "What have five or six years of the much-celebrated 'perestroika' brought us? Pathetic reshuffling in the Central Committee. Slapping together of an ugly, artificial electoral system, with a view solely to the Communist Party's clinging to power. Slipshod, confused, and indecisive laws. . . ."

Immediately after publication, there were varied complaints about the essay. The language, so full of archaic words, felt artificial, dusty. The Kazakhs were furious that Solzhenitsyn felt the northern part of the republic was, essentially, Russian. Ukrainians, especially, made it clear that independence, not a Slavic union, was their goal. Then there was the cranky side of Solzhenitsyn, the prig worrying that Russia would mindlessly pursue the road to Gomorrah because it couldn't find the off switch on the TV set: "Our young people, whom families and schools have overlooked, are growing in the direction of mindless, barbaric emulation of anything enticing coming from alien parts, if not in the direction of crime. The historic Iron Curtain protected the country superbly from everything good that exists in the West. . . . However, this Curtain did not reach all the way down, and this is where the liquid manure of debased, degraded 'mass pop-culture,' most vulgar fashions and excessive public displays seeped through. It was this waste that our impoverished, unfairly deprived young people swallowed greedily."

This old-mannish side of Solzhenitsyn seemed to me as marginal as Tolstoy's retrograde views on women and sex in *The Kreutzer Sonata.* But more important was that the right-wing fanatics, the monarchists and black-shirted nationalists, the anti-Semites of Pamyat, were deeply disappointed by the essay. They were looking for an endorsement of authoritarian rule, and what they got was a peculiar, but distinct, support of democracy and private property. What they got was a call for the breakup of the empire they worshiped.

There were serious mistakes and misjudgments in the essay. Solzhenitsyn did not recognize just how deeply Ukrainians, for example, had come to believe in their own distinctiveness, how much they wanted a capital in Kiev, not Moscow. And, as always, Solzhenitsyn created problems for himself with the pitch of his voice, its hyped-up grandeur. Somehow, the strength of his own hopes for a Slavic state drowned out the admission that he also makes: that, yes, of course, it must be the Ukrainians themselves who decide if they want to join Russia.

Solzhenitsyn's most curious critic turned out to be Gorbachev himself. A few days after the publication of "How to Revitalize Russia," a member of the Supreme Soviet asked the president to comment. (The idea of it! The general secretary responds in parliament to Solzhenitsyn!) To a hushed chamber, Gorbachev said he felt "contradictory" emotions after reading the essay twice through. Solzhenitsyn's views "on the future of the state," he said, "are far from reality and are being constructed out of the context of our country's development and bear a destructive character. But nonetheless there are interesting thoughts in the article of this undoubtedly great person." A splendid backhanded compliment. But then Gorbachev felt the need to distort Solzhenitsyn, to exploit the recurring stereotype of his views. Solzhenitsyn, Gorbachev said, "is all in the past, the Russia of old, the czarist monarchy. This is not acceptable to me." It was self-serving, a moment of demagoguery designed to present himself as the singular modern democrat.

———

On October 15, Gorbachev received the Nobel Prize for Peace.

On October 16, after the leaders of the KGB, the police, the army, and the defense industry made it quite clear that they would not tolerate a radical reordering of political and economic power, Gorbachev withdrew his support for the 500 Days plan. Gorbachev had caved in to the people who had everything to lose from the reform of the country. When he did that it was clear to everyone in the Soviet Union that Gorbachev had begun listing to the right. Soon he would reject all the reformers in his team, he would begin to speak, with a sneer, of the "so-called democrats." He would ignore one grab for power after another, ever confident that he was serving the cause of reform. The counterrevolution, which began with the swing of an assassin's ax, was now ascendant.

"When Mikhail Sergeyevich rejected the 500 Days program he was rejecting the last chance for a civilized transition to a new order," Aleksandr Yakovlev told me. "It was probably his worst, most dangerous mistake, because what followed was nothing less than a war."

CHAPTER 25

THE TOWER

On the December morning in 1990 that Eduard Shevardnadze resigned as foreign minister, I was in Riga to learn more about a strange series of dirty tricks aimed at the Baltic independence movements. There had been explosions near monuments and war memorials, the sort of incidents the army and the KGB could blame on the "radicals" and present as reasons to take "emergency measures" to "reassert an atmosphere of stability." They already had the language down pat. And why not? All they had to do was reach up to the shelf and bring down the handbook and look under "putsch, cf. Prague '68, Budapest '56, et al." The scenario was all there. All they needed now was the dossier, the pretext.

Shevardnadze, of all people, knew perfectly well what was going on. For months he saw how the military were trying to deceive him, how they tried to embarrass him before the West with their games in the Baltic states and ruin his arms negotiations by moving their tanks and missiles in just such a way that the Americans would catch it on their satellites and blame Moscow for bad faith. He and Yakovlev both saw how the Supreme Soviet chairman, Lukyanov, and the KGB chief, Kryuchkov—those gray Siamese twins— would sit in Politburo meetings and try to unscrew Gorbachev's head, try to convince him that the "so-called" democrats and Baltic independence people were going to take over with armed insurrections Vilnius, Riga, Tallinn, Tbilisi, and even the Kremlin. And Gorbachev would listen to every word, nodding sagely. These were the men he trusted, the Party men, the men he'd known since the early days. Sure, they were a little more conservative, but they spoke the same language, the language of the Party, and they knew what discipline was.

I spent the morning of Shevardnadze's resignation at the editorial offices of *Diena* ("The Day"), the main pro-independence paper in Riga. The rightward swing had already started, and so the reporters had no shortage of anecdotes about provocations and intimidation. It was an anxious newsroom. The place had the nasty edge of the family waiting room in intensive care. Something awful was going to happen, they said. It had to.

Then it did. One of the typists, who'd tuned in to the Congress broadcasts on the radio, slowly took off his headphones. He opened his mouth and nothing came out. He was ashen.

"Maybe I got it wrong," he said in a whisper. "Let me listen again."

Then he closed his eyes and listened.

"Shevardnadze," he said. "He's resigned. He said dictatorship is coming. He is sure of it."

Shevardnadze had warned that "dictatorship is coming" and that the democrats had scattered "to the bushes." Shevardnadze had not told anyone that he would make his speech except his family and a couple of his closest aides. As he spoke, his Georgian accent made thicker by the anger in him, the sense of moment, Gorbachev sat at the Presidium as shocked as anyone else in the hall. It was one thing for Moscow intellectuals at the kitchen table to talk about a nascent dictatorship, quite another for Shevardnadze, the second-most-recognized face in the leadership, to put an end to his career. What did this man, who was in a position to know so much, really know?

Everyone in the newsroom at *Diena* was shattered. Ever since the three Baltic states declared their independence a half year before, they had tried to sustain the conceit that they were already independent. They did not need to ask permission or hold a referendum or in any way pay much attention to the politics of Moscow, because Moscow was elsewhere, a foreign power. Now that conceit was finished, untenable. The Baltic leaders could always trust Shevardnadze (or at least as much as they trusted anyone in Moscow), and now he was telling them that their worst midnight fears were true. Dictatorship was coming, and a conceit of attitude and language, no matter how inventive or assured, would do nothing to stop the brutal charge.

———

I flew back to Moscow the next morning and went straight to the Kremlin. At the Palace of Congresses, military officers strutted in packs, back and forth across the main foyer. Before, the generals and admirals had always seemed to caucus down near the coatroom, away from the cameras and the reporters. They'd linger by the door in little crowds of olive green and navy blue. They seemed to laugh more than other deputies. After all, they were comrades. They had known each other for years. This democracy stuff, well, it was a lark, a sideshow. But now they were all over the main lobby, dumping one-liners off to the press, confident stuff about how they respected Eduard Amvrosievich, but, my dear American friend, not to fear, everything is under control, don't go worrying about coups and turns to the right. Everything is fine. Gorbachev's military adviser, Sergei Akhromeyev—a marshal much beloved by Admiral William Crowe at the Pentagon—chuckled through his teeth when I asked him about a military coup.

"How many times do we have to tell you people?" he said. "Relax! Stop inventing fantasies!"

Upstairs at the buffet tables, Communist Party hacks were stuffing themselves sick with state-subsidized caviar, smoked salmon, sturgeon, cream cakes, and tea. When they thought no one was looking, they bought ten sandwiches more and stuffed them in their briefcases, the better not to be hungry later on.

Meanwhile, the radicals did the death march, up and down the halls. Vitaly Korotich, with that ate-the-canary smile of his suddenly gone, said his friends and he had started making plans "for the trip to Siberia." He was only half kidding. Afanasyev was more bleary-eyed than usual. The Balts, those who hadn't left for home already, smoked furiously near the lavatories. Shevardnadze had said in his speech that "democracy would prevail," but he warned that the democrats, the radicals, were disorganized and dyspeptic, divided, egocentric, petty. They were risking everything. His language was cryptic, but he made it clear that they could no longer depend on the moral authority of Sakharov—he was gone—or the political strength of Gorbachev—that was in doubt.

Finally, toward the very end of the Congress, one of the democrats had a moment of eloquence that helped make sense of Shevardnadze's great gesture. Ales Adamovich, a war veteran, the best-known writer in Byelorussia, and a founder of Memorial, got up from his first-row seat, walked up the stairs to the stage, and took hold of the lectern, as if for balance. Gorbachev, Adamovich said, "is the only leader in Soviet history who has not stained his hands with blood, and we would all like to remember him as such." Then he turned for an instant behind him, as if to address Gorbachev directly: "But a moment will come when the military will instigate a bloodbath, and later they will wipe their bloodstained hands against your suit. And you will be to blame for everything. In the West, you are known as a political genius. I would like you to exercise your wisdom again. Otherwise, you will lose perestroika."

———

The truth was, it looked lost already. Day by day, the hard-liners made their moves, and there was nothing secret, nothing tricky, about them. Gennadi Yanayev, a witless apparatchik, philanderer, and drunk, was now vice president. Shevardnadze was replaced as foreign minister with Aleksandr Bessmertnykh, a liberal, but without any of the strength or authority of his predecessor. The KGB and the Interior Ministry gave themselves the right to patrol the streets of all major cities. Yazov went on the air complaining about provocations and warned that he would strike back whenever and however he deemed necessary. Kryuchkov announced that he might have to spill a little blood to keep the peace in the republics. And Anatoly Lukyanov, "Lucky Luke," the creepy chairman of the Supreme Soviet, was always eager to give the floor of the standing parliament to the colonels and crazies from Soyuz ("Union"), the right-wing faction that called, on a daily basis, for Gorbachev's neck and a state of emergency.

It was an ugly time, and everyone expected it to get uglier. Yakovlev said that the right wing was off on a "vengeful and merciless" counterrevolution, an echo from Pushkin's *The Captain's Daughter*. But Yakovlev, instead of resigning, quietly moved out of Gorbachev's orbit. Gorbachev would no longer listen to him anymore. What could he do? When I asked Yakovlev what he thought of Gorbachev's appointment of Yanayev, Yakovlev smiled wearily and said, "The president is a wise man, so I am sure it is a wise decision." But much later, when he could afford to be less cryptic, Yakovlev told me he saw an "eerie quiet" developing around Gorbachev that winter, as if all his ministers were merely pretending to obey the president, but then went off and did as they pleased. Slowly, they were making a hostage of Gorbachev, and they were counting on the man's powerful desire to stay in office to keep themselves in control.

Sobchak, the liberal mayor of Leningrad, was the coolest head among the democrats, and when I saw him at the Mariinsky Palace, the headquarters of the city government, he made perfect sense of what was going on. "We are living now through a transition from a totalitarian system to a democratic one, and the forces of dictatorship and democracy live side by side," he said. "Under these conditions, the danger of a new dictatorship, of military coups or the use of military force against the people, is absolutely real." It was all so ominous. And nothing had really happened yet.

————

By the winter of 1990–91, Moscow had become a newspaper fanatic's dream. Len Karpinsky's columns and *Moscow News* were only a part of the morning haul. Having started from nothing, from the wet wash of the Communist Party press, Moscow became the most exciting newspaper city since New York after the war. The Khrushchev "thaw" was a liberalization from which emerged a few works of real literature, but glasnost was a period of journalism, of investigation, sensation, commentary, and scoop.

At first, the most obvious mainstays of glasnost were *Moscow News* and the weekly magazine *Ogonyok*. But as glasnost evolved into more genuine freedom of the press, the democratic vista widened. There were breathless papers that rushed to the aid of the radical cause, especially *Komsomolskaya Pravda* with its circulation of twenty-five million. *Literaturnaya Gazeta* printed a blend of high-minded cultural criticism, political analysis, and Yuri Shchekochikhin's startling investigative work on the KGB. *Argumenti i Fakti,* with a circulation of thirty million, was a kind of bulletin board of two-hundred-word articles and factoids. *Izvestia* was solid, and for tabloid sensation there were *Top Secret*'s true crime stories ("Murder on Kutuzovsky Street!") and *Megapolis-Express*'s local muckraking. The puckish *Kommersant,* edited by Yegor Yakovlev's son Vladimir, covered the emerging business world, letting young entrepreneurs know which mafia clan ruled which district and how to find cheap computers on the black market. In the train stations and street corners, hawkers did a brisk business in Baltic sex papers, neo-Bolshevik mimeograph sheets, and copies of Dale Carnegie's *How to Win Friends and Influence People.*

For the hard-liners there was *Sovetskaya Rossiya,* which published the Nina Andreyeva letter in 1988 and the key manifestos leading up to the coup still to come, and *Dyen* ("The Newspaper of the Spiritual Opposition"), edited by Aleksandr Prokhanov, a theocratic-militarist wacko known affectionately as "the Nightingale of the General Staff." Among the wire services, the old Big Brother of the ticker, Tass, was as much a fossil as the evening news program *Vremya* or *Pravda,* while Interfax and a few others in some of the republics developed the manic intensity of the Associated Press on a good day. Interfax's leading reporter, Vyacheslav Terekhov, was a breeder reactor in a brown suit, badgering politicians and filing dispatches from breakfast till midnight.

Until 1988 or 1989 at the latest, *Moscow News* remained the iconoclast, always smashing idols just before the reformers in the leadership did. Ligachev called *Moscow News* an "ersatz" paper, and small wonder. *Moscow News* was clearly the voice of the liberals in the Politburo. But it was this lack of real independence at *Moscow News,* its obvious link to Gorbachev himself, that began to work against it in 1990 and 1991. As the country grew more diverse, as the liberal intelligentsia's ideas about the future of society and politics grew far more radical than Gorbachev's own, *Moscow News* under Yegor Yakovlev began to look a bit timid and almost comically protective of its original patron.

"Without realizing it, Yegor was turning *Moscow News* into *Pravda,*" said Vitaly Tretyakov, who was Yakovlev's deputy at the time. "Just as *Pravda* was the tribune of the old powers, he wanted *Moscow News* to be the tribune of the new power, the left-of-center position, the Gorbachev position in the Politburo. When I became Yegor's deputy, I began to see how many visitors and calls there were from the Central Committee and it was obvious the paper was not operating independently. Len Karpinsky was much more radical than Yegor, but *Moscow News* could only be as radical as Yegor would allow it to be. Yegor has the personality of a dictator, which may be necessary, but he always wanted to be in possession of ultimate truth, he claimed to know all the answers. None of us could take a step at *Moscow News* without Yegor's say-so. You couldn't mention Lenin, for instance, because Yegor thought he knew all there was to know. And then there was Gorbachev: we could not criticize him directly. And what could someone like Len Karpinsky do? After all, it was Yegor who pulled Len out of obscurity and got him a job."

By the summer of 1990, millions of people were quitting the Communist Party. The Party that called itself the "initiator of perestroika"—an appalling bit of self-congratulation considering the blood on its hands—had lost the power to convince many of its own members that it supported radical change. At *Moscow News,* Tretyakov proposed that the paper's Party committee all quit as one. But Yakovlev said no, they should "stay the course." As usual, Yakovlev had the votes—Karpinsky's included.

Vitaly Tretyakov was feeling more alienated from his colleagues at the paper by the day. At thirty-nine, he was not a man of the Gorbachev generation and he had none of the Old Bolshevik background and Party connections of so many of the *shestidesyatniki.* His parents were laborers. Tretyakov had worked for years on the sort of glossy propaganda magazines that the government printing organs ground out like sausage meat: *Soviet Life, Études Sovietique, Soviet Woman,* and the rest. His time at *Moscow News* was "a gift," but the time had come to quit, he decided. "My idea," he said, "was to start something new, a better *Moscow News.*"

Tretyakov had very little idea of what he wanted when he began his first planning sessions in the summer of 1990. He knew only that he did not want to tie the fate and tone of his paper to the fate of Mikhail Gorbachev or any other political personality. At first, he tried to lure some of the best-known writers in Moscow to join him, but they all turned him down. No one with a family and an established position was prepared to risk it all on an experiment, a notion. Tretyakov's one essential break came with the election of liberal democrats to the Moscow City Hall. The new mayor, Gavriil Popov, and his deputy, Sergei Stankevich, were intrigued by Tretyakov's idea and gave him a start-up grant of 300,000 rubles. No strings attached, Popov said. Remarkably, the city officials kept their word. They have never considered the paper their own and have not interfered in editorial or business policy. "It was just a small investment in the transition to a free press," Stankevich said.

I had heard about the paper a half year before its first issue appeared. One summer afternoon, I drove to the country town of Peredelkino to visit Andrei Karaulov, a young theater critic, and his wife, Natasha, the daughter of the playwright Mikhail Shatrov. Karaulov was a journalist-hustler the likes of whom I never had seen before or have since—at least not in Moscow. Even in the early days of perestroika he managed to get interviews with one Politburo member and spymaster after another. He somehow made patently evil and slimy men feel comfortable, then tortured them with his combination of unctuous charm and barbed questions. Andrei's knack was so uncanny that some of his rivals moaned that he must have "dark connections." At the Peredelkino dacha that afternoon, one of the other guests was a man in his early forties named Igor Zakharov. Zakharov, it turned out, was an extreme cynic who despised himself most of all. He worked for years at the Novosti press agency editing its propaganda sheets. "I am a born functionary," he said. "I never believed in anything official: not in Communism and not in the possibility of perestroika. I may have published all that shit, but I never believed it. You know that expression 'Life is elsewhere'?" Somehow this willingness to work with odious bureaucrats while believing "otherwise" seemed to wear less well on him than on an older idealist like Karpinsky. It was touching that Karpinsky actually did believe in something when he was young and then believed in something else later on. Zakharov believed in nothing but the hopelessness of just about everything, and the sudden advent of radical changes in the country made his cynicism seem worthless. There were times when Karaulov and Zakharov both made my skin crawl. So when they began telling me about their work with Vitaly Tretyakov on a new newspaper to be called *Nezavisimaya Gazeta*—"The Independent Newspaper"—not only did I think it would fail, I hoped it would.

I forgot about that discussion and *Nezavisimaya Gazeta* until six months later when I was flying back from Riga to Moscow on the morning after Shevardnadze's resignation. On the plane I borrowed two copies of an unfamiliar broadsheet—the first and second issues of *Nezavisimaya Gazeta*—and I was startled. The front page of the first issue featured little mug shots of the country's leading ministers—a loutish bunch who looked like the comic thugs in "Dick Tracy," Flattop, Mumbles, and the rest. Above the pictures was a triple-stack headline: "They Rule Us: But What Do We Know About Them, the Most Powerful People in the Country? Almost Nothing. . . ." On page five, Yuri Afanasyev published what was surely the most incisive and prescient piece of political commentary of the year: "We Are Moving to the Side of Dictatorship." In details that proved absolutely accurate, Afanasyev described Gorbachev's "tragedy," how his own internal and political limitations left him open to the pressures of the hard-line Communists in the regime. It was just the sort of pointed political critique of Gorbachev that *Moscow News* could not bring itself to publish. Then on page eight of the first issue—the back page—Tretyakov printed a manifesto declaring that there had never been "in the history of the Soviet Union" a paper independent of political interests. He promised *Nezavisimaya Gazeta* would be such a paper. The second issue led with the headline "Eduard Shevardnadze Leaves. The Military-Industrial Complex Stays. What Choice Will Gorbachev Make?" A few pages later, Karaulov weighed in with a fascinating interview with the number-two ranking man in the KGB, Filipp Bobkov—the same man who interrogated Len Karpinsky two decades before.

One day during those first weeks of *Nezavisimaya Gazeta*'s life, I went to the paper's offices with Karaulov. As we walked along the muddy streets near the KGB buildings on Lubyanka Square, he was trying to sell me—literally—some crackpot spy-story documents involving the Bolshoi Theater. Information was constantly for sale now in Moscow. When asked for interviews, some Kremlin officials had no shame. "How much?" they would say. When I refused Karaulov's "tip" on the Bolshoi and explained the rules about not paying for information, he seemed alternately bemused and hurt. "Besides, you'd never find the place without me," he said. "You owe me for that, at least." *Nezavisimaya Gazeta*'s offices were tucked away in an obscure courtyard building not far from Lubyanka Square. At the time, the paper shared the building with the Voskhod (Sunrise) printing company. Expansion eventually eased the printers out. The paper originally had twenty staffers and appeared three days a week, then built up to two hundred employees and five issues a week. When I first visited the office, the place was a sea of paper and ironic memorabilia—faded portraits of old Politburo members a specialty. No one looked as if he had slept, showered, or shaved in days.

Tretyakov wanted nothing more than to mimic the traditional model of a Western newspaper. His staff looked *Village Voice,* but he yearned for the style and substance of *The New York Times.* "It may seem boring to you,"

Tretyakov told me during one of our talks, "but I want to create the first Western-style, respectable, objective paper of the Soviet era."

Turned down by the older stars, Tretyakov got his journalists wherever he could find them. Most of them had worked at second- and third-tier publications, at movie and theatrical quarterlies, Baltic underground sheets, Komsomol dailies. Some had no experience at all. They were biologists, secretaries, workers, students, diplomats, anything. Whatever skills they did or did not have, they had a unanimous contempt for all things *sovok*—the slang term for "Soviet." (The staff's favorite early fan letter read, "Congratulations: You are neither pro-Soviet nor anti-Soviet. You are simply non-Soviet.") All were young, and they did not bother to struggle with the questions of their elders. The ideological ruminations of a man like Len Karpinsky were for these kids irrelevant and just a little bit sad.

Mikhail Leontyev, the paper's economics editor, was a typical hire. He had studied economics at the Plekhanov Institute in Moscow, but to avoid doing "idiot work for the regime," he quit the academic world and worked for years restoring old Russian furniture. He hardly ever wrote, he told me: "Why bother?" He did publish one prescient essay for the Latvian paper *Atmoda* in 1989 titled "The New Consensus," about the growing front of fascists, nationalists, and military leaders. "That was about all I could do," Leontyev said. "I just couldn't work for any of the old papers. Coming here, discovering *Nezavisimaya Gazeta,* was the revelation we were all waiting for. The coverage of economics in our paper starts from the principle that we don't need to tear our hair out about whether Marxism-Leninism or capitalism is the right way to go. That debate is dead as can be. Do we really have to go crazy over whether it is good to find a healthy balance between efficiency and social welfare? About whether the rules of the market are ultimately correct? I don't think so. I don't cover Communism or any other religions in these pages. That's not my business."

The darkening political mood that winter, the ominous sense that the army, the KGB, and the Communist Party now formed an open alliance against a radical reform of the country, had given *Nezavisimaya Gazeta* an immediate sense of purpose. Muscovites reading *Nezavisimaya Gazeta* in that first month or so had a sense of understanding and foreboding about the political earthquake to come. Not so with *Moscow News,* which still kept its reports within certain bounds. *Moscow News* was no longer responding to government censors—they had been either removed or rendered completely benign—but, rather, to an internal sense of propriety and caution, a lingering reverence for Gorbachev and the old hopes of the thaw generation.

Week after week, *Nezavisimaya Gazeta* was reinventing the newspaper in Moscow, and a twenty-seven-year-old reporter named Sergei Parkhomenko was consistently the paper's most incisive political commentator. The son and grandson of journalists, Parkhomenko first won a name for himself at the quarterly *Teatr* when he covered the first session of the Congress of People's Deputies in May 1989, a job he called the "ultimate in theater criticism." Gorbachev played the Great Reformer, Sakharov was the Conquering Saint, and the Communist Party hacks were the Evil Chorus. "Imagine if you in America had held the Constitutional Convention live on television," he said. "The old order died a little every day. No play ever changed an audience more thoroughly."

One night, I went with Sergei to the presses at *Izvestia* where *Nezavisimaya Gazeta* was printed. He was the duty editor, acting as a liaison between the printers and the editors back at the office, who were constantly trying to shove late items into the paper. He had already written a column in the morning and had called in a few items for his after-hours job as a stringer for other publications. Like many good young reporters in Moscow, Parkhomenko discovered he could make some hard currency on the side by working for a foreign news organization—in his case, Agence France Presse, the official French wire service. As it turned out, the experience expanded his sense of journalism. "With the French, I got a taste of real reporting," he said. "It was a new sort of game. Who can be the first to get the information? Who can get sources? Before it was all 'I think this,' 'I think that.' Now the game had changed and I loved it and the skills were just what I needed. You see, I somehow always knew I would work at a place like *Nezavisimaya Gazeta.* I knew it instinctively. I wanted a place that was born without any complexes. There are more radical publications, but I'm not interested in the contest for who can be the most radical or liberal. I can't stand unity and consensus."

Parkhomenko was best known in Moscow for his commentaries—mainly because he refused to shill for any one politician or party line—but he was also an instinctive investigative reporter. He caused a terrific scandal when he discovered that the Central Committee had been running for years a huge fourteen-room workshop for manufacturing fake Western passports. He reported that there were fake stamps, blank passport forms for dozens of foreign countries, and even false mustaches and beards and hats for the passport photos.

Investigative work was a signature of the front page at *Nezavisimaya Gazeta.* A married couple in their twenties at the paper, Anya Ostapchuk and Zhenya Krasnikov, enraged the Party when they scooped everyone by printing a copy of the Communist Party's proposed new platform endorsing a "democratic, humane socialism." Anya's methods were "quite simple and un-Soviet." She went to the apartment of a Central Committee member,

Vasily Lipitsky, and asked about the platform. He gave her the twenty-three-page document written by Gorbachev's aide, Giorgi Shakhnazarov, and said she could read it, "but no notes and no tape recorders."

"Then something odd happened," Anya said. "Lipitsky said he had to take a phone call in the next room. As soon as he left, I got out my tape recorder and read the thing as fast as I could. He didn't come back in time to stop me. I finished. But I'm sure he wanted me to do just that. It was terrific fun."

Presented with the scoop, Tretyakov was stunned. At *Moscow News,* his bosses would never have permitted such a thing. Too dangerous, a distinct lack of respect. But Tretyakov immediately published the piece. In a wry note to the readers, he wrote that ordinarily *Nezavisimaya Gazeta* did not print party manifestos and platforms "because that would be a form of advertising," and added, "but from such a party we would rather not take any money."

The next day, as every newspaper in Moscow scurried to catch up with the platform story, Parkhomenko got a swift lesson in the sensibilities of the powerful. At a small late-night press conference in the Moscow suburb of Novo-Ogarevo, Gorbachev looked at the reporters and said, "Okay, so who here is from *Nezavisimaya Gazeta?*"

The reporter from state television, a whinnying time-server, blanched and panicked.

"No, no, it's him," he said, pointing at Parkhomenko.

"Where did you steal it from?" Gorbachev said.

"I can't say," Parkhomenko said.

"And why not?"

"Because that's the way we work."

After the press conference, two of Gorbachev's aides tried to weasel the information out of Parkhomenko. "Oh, come on," one of them said. "You can tell me. I won't tell another soul!"

Shakhnazarov, for his part, told me he was shocked to see his work in the paper. "Woodward and Bernstein—that is not exactly something we're used to," he said.

Sometimes Tretyakov and Zakharov, the village elders at the paper, were scared by their own reporters, their relentlessness, their giddy fearlessness. They were well aware of just how inexperienced the reporters were, how little they knew about degrees of reliability and balance. Often, reporters turned in stories that were merely rumors that seemed a bit too good to check. But while the top editors often demanded more reporting and numerous rewrites, they seldom killed any stories. The only story that Tretyakov refused to run without further question was the rubbish about the KGB and the Bolshoi Theater that Karaulov had tried to peddle to me.

"The reason these kids do things like investigative work is that they not only don't fear the system, they don't even respect it," Zakharov said. "These kids are arrogant, silly, uneducated, undisciplined; they live only in the present. They don't care about yesterday and have no idea that there is nothing new under the sun. But they have no prejudices. They don't think ahead and wonder if someone at the Kremlin will think this or that. They just go ahead and do it."

The young reporters also changed the language of newspapers. They dispensed with the wooden bureaucratese and fanatic sloganeering of the Soviet period. "We don't talk *Pravda* language," Parkhomenko said. The change was incredible. Before I left for Russia, I took a course at George Washington University in something called "Newspaper Russian." For weeks, we memorized endless lists of political clichés: "The talks were held in a warm and friendly atmosphere"; "The peace-loving comrade-nations of the world will face the imperialists in a round of negotiations next week"; and so on. It was the language of Novoyaz, or Newspeak, and nowhere had it reached such a level of absurdity as in the Soviet Union. But *Nezavisimaya Gazeta*'s younger reporters had never had to write that way—or at least not for long. While someone like Len Karpinsky still had trouble clearing the Novoyaz from his prose—"I try, but I can't always get it clear"—the *Nezavisimaya Gazeta* crowd had no such handicap.

"Right away, we tried to imitate Western language," Parkhomenko said at the print shop. "In Russian, there had never been political language of a civilized country."

It took a while, but I was getting a better sense now of who was leading the right-wing counterrevolution. One night I went to the Red Army Theater for what the right-wing press promised would be an evening of "patriotic celebration." It was a full house, and nearly everyone was in uniform: army drab, priests' black, and, here and there, a writer in a pilled chocolate-brown suit. Onstage, one Father Fyodor, his robes festooned with military decorations, droned on about the greatness of Russia's warriors, "her Aleksandr Nevsky, her Dmitri Donskoi, her proud knights."

"God is our greatest general!" he cried out, and God's seconds, the teenage recruits who'd been bused in for the show, applauded dutifully.

"But what about Yazov?" one of these teenagers whispered to me. "Isn't he our general?"

Valentin Rasputin, a Siberian novelist well known for his moral indignation and attacks on the ecological ruin of Lake Baikal, sat off to the side of the stage, nodding solemnly at all the speeches. Rasputin was a writer of real talent. His stories about the degradation of the countryside and Communism's damage to the spirit were respected even by those critics who despised his right-wing politics. But he was not merely conservative. Rasputin was a hater, a brooding anti-Semite who blamed the Jews for the crimes of the Bolsheviks. And that was when he was giving an interview to *The New York Times*. He was less discreet at gatherings of the Russian Writers' Union.

For years the right-wingers lived in comfort. They controlled the unions, lived decently. But now, with the barbarians at the gate, they were ready to form even the strangest of coalitions. Rasputin's literary nationalists and the official priests of the Russian Orthodox Church aligned themselves with men like Akhromeyev and Yazov of the Red Army and Kryuchkov of the KGB, avowed Communists and party leaders. It was a confusing picture. But as I sat there that night in the Red Army Theater, I could see that they had forged a common language, one that had nothing to do with Communist ideology or theocracy. The unifying banner of this alliance of "patriots" was the imagery of empire, vast and powerful, unique and holy. Democracy, rock and roll, stock markets, foreign businesses, independence movements, uppity Jews, Balts, and Asians all undermined the empire.

After the priest blessed the military, and Rasputin blessed Mother Russia, Lieutenant General Gennadi Stepanovsky, one of the leaders of the army's Communist Party organization, gave the final benediction. The democrats, he said, were "auctioning off our tanks, destroying our monuments, destroying our ability to fight for freedom in the Baltics. But they will not win. They cannot wipe out our great history." Like Stalin during the war, Stepankovsky hoped a mystical stew of great-power nationalism would form the common bond. This time the enemy was not the Nazis, but the greater world itself, and its vanguard, the democratic infidels.

After the ceremonies that night I glanced through the latest issue of *Molodaya Gvardiya* ("Young Guard"), one of the exemplars of the new ideology. It was filled with the usual claims: "[Yeltsin's] Russia is a marionette of Western Zionism without a single shot being fired. One clearly sees a plan to draw the world into yet another world war in which Russians and other Slavs will be the cheap cannon fodder. A new spiral of historical genocide is being plotted against us." Another article warned against "strangers bearing gifts" and "cancer-causing shampoos" from Poland, "contaminated bread boxes and shopping bags" from Vietnam, and, of course, the American Big Mac ("too fast and very unhealthy").

———

The most powerful of the hard-liners—Kryuchkov, Pugo, Yazov, Lukyanov—knew better than to announce their leadership of the creeping, militarized coup d'état that Shevardnadze had warned of. They made threatening gestures and issued chilling proclamations, but, in general, they let others do the dirtiest work. In those winter months, the man who gave a face to the coup was an army colonel from Latvia, Viktor Alksnis. With his high black pompadour and black leather jacket, Alksnis was known in the liberal press as the "black colonel," the Darth Vader of the hard-line set. He loved his role and fairly chewed the scenery every time he appeared on the public stage.

"Before you stands a reactionary scum!" he once told the Congress. (Who would doubt him?) Then he pushed up his lower lip and affected the glare of Mussolini. Caricature, the picture of outsized badness, was just what the part required, and Alksnis played it beautifully. By comparison, men like Supreme Soviet Chairman Lukyanov and Kryuchkov thought they would look like the soul of sweet reason.

As a deputy, Alksnis represented the Soviet military bases in Latvia. He was not much liked. His own aunt went door to door campaigning against him. But Alksnis won, promising to restore the "honor of the military" after the "humiliations" of the withdrawal from Afghanistan and Eastern Europe, the arms reduction treaties with the West, and the cuts in the defense budget. As Party elders like Geidar Aliyev and Yegor Ligachev faded from view, Alksnis, and his counterpart from Kazakhstan, Colonel Nikolai Petrushenko, organized the Soyuz faction under Lukyanov's subtle patronage. Soyuz was a remarkably effective weapon for the right. It was Soyuz that pressured Gorbachev to fire his liberal interior minister, Vadim Bakatin, and replace him with a hard-liner, Boris Pugo. And it was Soyuz that constantly denounced Shevardnadze's foreign policy as treasonous. When he resigned, Shevarnadze angrily wondered why no one had defended him against the "boys in colonel's epaulets."

Alksnis's grandfather, Yakov, was head of the air force in the 1930s. In May 1937, at the height of the purges, Yakov Alksnis was a member of the three-man military tribunal that ordered the conviction and execution of Marshal Mikhail Tukhachevsky, the most brilliant military man of his time, on trumped-up charges of espionage. Alksnis then fell to the logic of the era. Eight months after Tukhachevsky's trial, he was arrested and shot.

"Those were complicated times," the grandson said blandly.

I met "the black colonel" at his suite at the Moskva Hotel, the vast home to out-of-town deputies in the Supreme Soviet. After looking me up and down, Alksnis said, "If you want to call me a reactionary, go ahead." A strange greeting, but then he was not an ordinary man. Even in his overheated room, Alksnis never took off his black leather jacket. He was like a teenager who could feel the length of his hair and the cut of his jeans at every moment like a second being. His look was his statement. He affected at all times an expression of bored disgust and quickly pronounced himself disgusted to meet me, a representative of the "lying bourgeois press." But, at the same time, he was eager to convey the greater disgust he felt with the way the Kremlin had gone all fuzzy and pusillanimous on him. "We are like Cupid: armed, naked, and we impose love on everyone," he said. "Sad as it may be, the reality of today's 'new thinking,' the priority on 'common human values,' well, the reality of it is that the Soviet Union has lost its status as a superpower. It is treated as if it should know its place. We are bullied now!"

And this weakness, I asked, was all the fault of Shevardnadze?

"The last myth of perestroika is collapsing: the myth of our wonderful foreign policy," he said, and then launched into an account of grievances, of being "sold out" by a government willing to debase itself before its rival, to grant every concession, to withdraw from every "interest"—all to get economic help that never came. It was humiliating! And now, he said, Washington was backing a Baltic independence movement that would tear apart the union and lead it to civil war. "Look at the technical equipment of the popular front of Latvia, the number of fax machines, computers, video machines. That kind of stuff can only be bought for foreign currency, and they had none of their own. It was all received from the West under the cover of various charities. I am acquainted with documents gathered by Soviet intelligence, and it is clear what measures the West has taken to support the separatists in the Baltic states. These are government organizations. They actively support them.

"The West," he went on, "has an official plan to break apart the Soviet state. Doesn't Bush's statement indicate that when he says he supports separatist movements in the Baltics? Doesn't the pressure indicate this? I think it does. This is called arm-twisting, and it's a policy. . . . The West wants to remove the Soviet Union from the political arena as a superpower. They have already managed to remove the Soviet Union as an ideological enemy. Now they want to remove them from the world arena. It is all being achieved without the use of force, just through exploiting the processes going on inside the Soviet Union. The West now thinks it can talk down to us. They used to think of the Soviet Union as Upper Volta with missiles. Now they just think of us as Upper Volta. No one fears us."

More than anything else, Alksnis wanted to be feared. This was his role, to give a face to intimidation. He wanted the democrats and the independence movements to fear the possibility of violence; he wanted the West to fear its own attempts at intervention. Fear, which had been so undercut by five years of reforms, was still the only weapon left to the hard-liners. Everything else—ideology, the promise of a shining future—was lost, forgotten.

Alksnis even had a prescription for the near future, and it went like this:

disband the democratically elected parliaments, arrest all resisters ("Landsbergis, Yeltsin, whatever it takes"), take control of the press, and install in power a "national salvation front." I said that sounded a lot like the scenarios for Prague in 1968 or, even more, the martial law in Poland.

"Yes," he said, "and you should not forget that martial law in Poland prevented a civil war there. It preserved the internal political stability in Poland and allowed a peaceful transition to reforms." Gorbachev, he said, could play the role of General Jaruzelski. "And then everything will be okay. There will be stabilization of the economic situation, the internal political situation. Gorbachev may not want it, but he is not in a position to dictate the situation. Events have gone too far, and Gorbachev is hostage to his own policy. It's gone beyond his control. It's a grass-roots policy. These processes will splash out into the streets in the next few months. It will be very hard to take any specific actions then. The situation is such that it will all happen in the next few months."

The tanks rolled in Lithuania on January 13, 1991.

For more than a year, the KGB and the army had been running operations in Lithuania designed to terrify the popularly elected government and the people. They arrested and beat draft dodgers; they seized various public buildings, institutes, and printing presses; they embarked on a propaganda campaign designed to convince the Russians, Poles, and Jews living there that the Lithuanians would turn them into third-class citizens; they ran military "exercises," including sending dozens of tanks rumbling past the parliament building in the middle of the night; they established a National Salvation Committee led by the few Communist Party officials in Lithuania still loyal to Moscow.

For more than a year, they hinted at an all-out offensive to unseat the Lithuanian government. On January 13, at around 2:00 A.M., the operation began. The National Salvation Committee declared itself in power and tried to take over all means of communication. With the KGB and ground forces commander General Valentin Varennikov in charge, soldiers fired on demonstrators at the Vilnius television tower. At least fourteen people were killed and hundreds injured: they were shot, beaten, or crushed under the tank treads.

But it was a botched job. Even as thugs, the organizers of the coup were miserable failures. The violence did nothing but intensify hatred toward Moscow. The attempts to control the media were halfhearted. The newspaper *Respublika* continued publishing daily eyewitness reports. The television station in Kaunas, a city two hours from Vilnius, jacked up its signal and broadcast the same footage that was going out on CNN, the BBC, and other foreign stations. The men who planned the operation had figured that the Western media would be too preoccupied with the war in the Persian Gulf to care much for Lithuania. They figured that the Bush administration would be too grateful for Moscow's support of the allied coalition against Saddam Hussein to show much public outrage. There was some truth in this. Americans were spending hours "watching the war" on CNN. The Lithuanians despaired that the West would overlook a series of events that could well mean the end of the revolutionary attempt to transform the Soviet Union.

"Of course, it depends on where you are sitting, but I am convinced that in the long run, what you are seeing now in the Soviet Union will prove more important historically than the war in the Persian Gulf," Algimantis Cekoulis, a leader of the Sajudis front in Lithuania, told me. "I don't think anyone doubts that the allied coalition will win in Iraq, but who will prevail in the Soviet Union? How much blood will be shed? This is not some isolated issue for the tiny Baltic states, or even for the Soviet Union. The course of events in this country will have a dramatic effect on the fate of Europe and even of the United States."

My colleague Michael Dobbs finished dictating his first eyewitness account to me from Vilnius at around four-thirty in the morning. I got a couple hours' sleep and went to Manezh Square. If there was going to be any demonstration at all, it would be outside the Manezh, an exhibition hall near the Kremlin gates. A few hundred people had gathered in the cold. Those with radios kept them tuned to the BBC or Radio Liberty. The main Moscow television and radio stations were broadcasting no news about what had happened in Lithuania except to say that there had been some sort of "incident," and it was all the fault of the sitting government, of course. But Radio Liberty and the BBC were reading back essentially what the Western reporters in Vilnius had put into the Sunday-morning papers.

The reaction was furious: "Gorbachev Is the Saddam Hussein of the Baltics!" one sign said. "Down with the Executioner!"

I ran into Sergei Stankevich, a charming baby-faced politician, and now the deputy mayor of Moscow. I'd first met him when he was campaigning for the Congress of People's Deputies wearing jeans and a T-shirt. He was furious. He had joined the Party because of the promise of Gorbachev and spent one night after another in political argument trying to defend the general secretary to his friends. "Now, that's over. No more," he said. "I'm finished with Gorbachev. There are just so many times you can let yourself be deceived."

Yuri Afanasyev climbed a platform and told the crowd that they would march toward the Central Committee buildings, the Party headquarters in Old Square. "The killings in Vilnius are the work of a dictatorship of reactionary circles—the generals, the KGB, the military-industrial complex, and the Communist Party chiefs," he told the small crowd. "And at the head of that Party dictatorship stands the initiator of perestroika, Mikhail Sergeyevich Gorbachev."

We marched up Marx Street toward the Central Committee, a series of dreary and imposing buildings around the corner from the KGB. A line of police had already cordoned off the area with sawhorses and a row of parked buses. But the crowd was in no mood to behave, and the people simply walked around the barriers and headed toward the entrances to the headquarters of the Communist Party. One man rushed by the cops and planted a six-foot crucifix at the front door. For a while, the people shouted up at the windows of the building and at the occasional apparatchik coming in to work. Then the police regrouped and cut off the marchers once more. Another charge could have led to blood. Stankevich and the other Democratic Russia leaders stepped in and said it was best to disperse, "to go home and figure things out."

The failed coup attempt in Lithuania changed everything for the middle-aged intellectuals who had remained loyal to the idea of a reformed Communist Party. They were the Gorbachev generation, the *Moscow News* generation, and they had lost a dream that many of them had held since the end of the war and the Twentieth Party Congress. While the young staff at *Nezavisimaya Gazeta* reported the story of the Lithuanian coup attempt as if it were the logical extension of the events of the months before, the writers and editors at *Moscow News* suddenly went through an ideological conversion. With the bloodshed in Vilnius, they lost all faith in Gorbachev. Len Karpinsky, Yegor Yakovlev, and a long list of *shestidesyatniki* including Vyacheslav Shostokovsky from the Higher Party School and Tengiz Abuladze, the director of the movie *Repentance,* signed a front-page editorial in *Moscow News* saying the regime, now in its "death throes," had executed a "criminal act" in Lithuania: "After the bloody Sunday in Vilnius, what is left of our president's favorite topics of 'humane socialism,' 'new thinking,' and a 'common European home'? Virtually nothing."

For so long, most of these men and women had hoped for a socialism made humane. They felt comfortable with the idea of the traditional power structure—the Party—leading the way. After all, weren't they all members? The idea of other parties was something foreign, bourgeois. The impudence of such people as Boris Yeltsin and Vytautas Landsbergis made them uncomfortable. Yegor Yakovlev, especially, had never liked Yeltsin, never liked the way he attacked Gorbachev or conducted himself. Now the men of *Moscow News* and their generation had nowhere to go but to the people Gorbachev had called, so venomously, the "so-called democrats."

"The Lithuanian tragedy must not fill our hearts with despair," the editorial continued. "While opposing the onslaught of dictatorship and totalitarianism, we are pinning our hopes on the leadership of other Union republics."

The crowd at *Nezavisimaya Gazeta* viewed the conversion of *Moscow News* with pity and condescension. "The truth is, I could never understand why those people only decided to make their split when the tanks rolled into Vilnius," Igor Zakharov said. "It's like trying to figure out why a woman who hates her husband for twenty years finally decides one day, after one little incident, to get up, walk out the door, and never come back."

Maybe the young could never understand. The editors at *Moscow News* sat a long and painful wake for their own dreams and delusions. Not long after the attack in Lithuania, Yegor Yakovlev invited Karpinsky and a few other friends to his apartment for a sixtieth birthday party. "It was a meeting of people who didn't know what to say to one another," said Yakovlev's son Vladimir, the editor of the business paper *Kommersant*. "The energy they used to have was gone, and the world around them was no longer their world. And, most important, they didn't know how to relate to this new world. It was the feeling you see at the gatherings in Russia forty days after someone dies. No one is crying anymore, but no one knows quite what to say. These birthday gatherings had always been such celebrations. Now it was just silence, a complete breakdown."

———

While the newspapers played out their generational drama, the most brutal struggle was the war for television. It was fitting that the scene of violence in Vilnius was the concrete television tower on the edge of the city, for this revolution was a battle for the minds of every person in the Soviet Union. "The television image is everything," Aleksandr Yakovlev had said, and now both sides knew it. For the reactionaries to recapture television would be far more than a symbolic defeat for democracy. It would be the beginning of the end.

When I got to Vilnius a week after the killings, young Red Army soldiers were still camped around the tower, guarding it as if it were the most precious property in all of Lithuania. And it may have been. The soldiers had AK-47s slung over their shoulders and wore tight, frightened expressions. These were kids, eighteen, nineteen, twenty years old, many of them unaware of what had happened. The crack troops who had carried out the assault had already been evacuated.

Outside the chain-link fence, on an incline leading away from the tower, a Lithuanian sculptor had carved out of wood a weeping, haggard Christ, a figure out of the paintings of Goya. People had made a shrine of the Christ, surrounding it with candles and flowers. Teenagers came and sat on the muddy hill and played tapes of Lithuanian folk songs and stared off into the pale winter sky.

Down the road a couple of miles, thousands of pro-independence Lithuanians had surrounded the parliament building with makeshift barricades, the better to guard against the next assault. They used huge blocks of poured concrete, steel scrap, sandbags, buses, trams. Outside the building, people sat in the cold, some of them around oil-drum campfires. One man made a fire for himself out of a dozen copies of *The History of the Communist Party of the Soviet Union.* Along the barbed wire that cut off access to the front entrances to the parliament building, people had thrown the symbols of their fury: plastic machine guns, water pistols, watercolors of the tanks painted by schoolchildren; there were portraits of Gorbachev as a killer, Gorbachev kissing Stalin on the lips, Gorbachev shoving Lithuanians into a meat grinder; some had spiked their red Party membership cards along the top of the razor wire, giving the fence a leafy, autumnal look. Inside the parliament building, everyone was waiting for the next move. Why would they stop at the TV tower? Landsbergis stayed in his office and slept a few hours a night on his couch. He refused to go home for fear of kidnapping, or worse. Kids who had run away from the Red Army acted as a makeshift guard. They carried ancient hunting rifles, rusty knives, and the sort of clunky revolvers you saw in Hollywood westerns. In the press room upstairs, young volunteers sent out faxes and telexes to news bureaus around the world: bulletins, appeals for help, official pronouncements of the president. Always, the televisions played. We watched the British Sky Channel and CNN to see what the world was seeing and *Vremya* in the evening to get a fix on the Moscow propaganda line. The Lithuanians despaired when the Gulf War news completely overwhelmed their own crisis on the Western stations. Rumors inside the building gave everyone a bad case of the jumps: "Tonight's the night." "They're going into Latvia tomorrow morning." "The roof's been rigged up so they can't land the helicopters." Lithuania was on the edge of a nervous breakdown, but there was no retreat.

"Why should we not win?" Landsbergis said.

———

At first, there were some heroic attempts in Moscow to bypass the censors and deliver the news. The cheeky late-night program *Television News Service* (*TSN*) broadcast footage of soldiers beating Lithuanians near the tower. The

Leningrad magazine show *The Fifth Wheel* also showed tape of the beatings and shootings.

But the Kremlin's new television czar, a fearsome hack named Leonid Kravchenko, quickly clamped down on all information broadcast about Lithuania. As the head of Gosteleradio, the huge bureaucracy that ran central television and radio, Kravchenko wiped out nearly all the major programs that had dared to report the news independently. In short order, Kravchenko banned *Vzglyad* ("View"), the most heroic of the glasnost magazine shows; he censored the reports on *TSN;* he darkened whatever glimmer of independence *Vremya* was beginning to show and returned it to the glory days of the Brezhnev era.

In the halls of the Supreme Soviet one afternoon, a reporter asked Kravchenko what he wanted in his broadcasts.

"Objectivity," Kravchenko said.

"And who decides what is objective?"

"I decide," he said.

Kravchenko said plainly that central television should reflect the view of the president and not attack him. "State television does not have the right to engage in criticism of the leadership of the country," he told *Nezavisimaya Gazeta.* What replaced much of the censored shows was even more insidious and cynical. Just as the Party had used the faith healer Anatoly Kashpirovsky to soothe a hurting country, they now filled the airwaves with other diverting junk. *Field of Miracles,* a rip-off of the low-rent American show *Wheel of Fortune,* was the new sensation. Contestants lined up to win such wonders as a rhinestone ring and a box of Tide. Kravchenko put on professional wrestling, Geraldo Rivera's interviews with dwarf transvestites, the *Death of Elvis* miniseries, schmaltzy World War II documentaries, and a Czech soap opera, *Hospital on the Edge of Town.* Kravchenko was willing to try whatever opiate on the masses that seemed to work. On the day after the bloodshed in Vilnius, while there were solemn marches in cities across the country honoring the dead, Kravchenko aired the *Aleksandr Show,* a variety hour so sleazy that Wayne Newton would have cringed.

In their front-page editorial, the *Moscow News* editors and their supporters echoed Solzhenitsyn's essay "Live Not by Lies" and put out the call to their colleagues: "We appeal to reporters and journalists: If you lack courage or opportunity to tell the truth, at least abstain from telling lies! Lies will fool no one anymore. They are evident today."

But because state controls were still relatively tight, television journalists had a much harder time following their consciences than print reporters. On *TSN,* Tatyana Mitkova ran a tape of Interior Minister Boris Pugo's fantastical testimony about Lithuania in the Supreme Soviet. Pugo's defense of the operation in Vilnius was a transparent lie. When Mitkova came back on the screen, she said, "Unfortunately this is all the information *TSN* has found it possible to provide." That was the best she could do.

In Kaunas, the Lithuanian television producers set up a relay system so that their broadcast could go to all the Baltics, southern Finland, and eastern Poland. When the Kaunas Party chief went on the air to defend the attack, the host stared him down and said, "After what's happened in Vilnius, how do you even look people in the eye?" The Kaunas station director, Raimondas Sestakauskas, told me, "Look, we don't have tanks, we don't have much at all to win our war for independence. But we're going to resist, and the resistance now is a matter of strength of character . . . and television."

————

No matter what the *Moscow News* appeal said, the Communist Party still thought it could lie to the people and get away with it. Their designated con man was Aleksandr Nevzorov, the right wing's video warrior. A former movie stuntman, he hosted *600 Seconds,* an immensely popular program on Leningrad television that featured gruesome true-crime stories and propaganda in the service of the Motherland. Like his friend Colonel Alksnis, Nevzorov was into leather. He always wore a black leather jacket and a matching sneer. As a journalist, he was equal parts Geraldo Rivera and propaganda minister, a master of the basest instincts of schlock and vengeance. For a couple of years, *600 Seconds* had been a semi-harmless distraction for hard times, the Soviet equivalent of a few minutes with the *New York Post* or one of the "real cops" shows on American television. Nevzorov won huge popularity by exposing his audience of around eighty million people to the world of corruption and vice. His was the scream in the agitprop cathedral, and the people loved it. Night after night, as the clock ticked away frantically in the corner of the screen (600 . . . 599 . . . 598 . . .), Nevzorov showed police dragging bullet-riddled corpses from the Neva River, cajoled rapists and murderers into "live on tape" confessions, and exposed the dalliances and secret luxuries of the Communist Party elite. Nevzorov was constantly sticking his camera in the snoot of some greedy apparatchik who'd just been caught getting a deal on a car or a house. "I'm probably responsible for the heart attacks of about forty apparatchiks," Nevzorov boasted when I went to see him at his studios in Leningrad.

Despite Nevzorov's attacks on the Party, few people ever had any illusions that he was a knight of liberal reform. He described himself as a monarchist and occasionally wore a czarist-era military uniform, thoughtfully sewn for him by his girlfriend. He bragged about his extraordinary rapport with the police and, especially, the KGB. "I have good relations with the KGB,"

Nevzorov said. "This is natural. They give us a lot of help and I highly value that organization. . . . They are incorruptable and not for sale." As the counterrevolution began to show its head, first in the Baltic states and then everywhere else, Nevzorov quickly became the televised face of Gorbachev's allies in the defense of the empire: the army and the KGB. As the semioticians might have said, he was the sign of the times.

One night when I was in Leningrad, *600 Seconds* showed a tape of a city council liberal frantically combing his bald spot. "So this is the last hope of the city?" Nevzorov growled in the voice-over. Then, armed with a minicam, Nevzorov and his crew stormed the headquarters of the Movement of Civil Resistance, one of the council's more radical factions, as if they had uncovered Hitler's bunker. "The place is a pigsty," Nevzorov said. Next, in a move that would have earned him an immediate libel suit in the West, he showed file footage of a pile of guns and said, "It's difficult to imagine how many arms these people have." There was never any proof that the guns belonged to the movement. But too late. It was time for the next item. On other nights, Nevzorov accused Leningrad city council deputies of welshing on their alimony payments, wandering drunk through the streets, and conducting shady business deals. And as for Sobchak, Nevzorov said, "His sole policy is survival at any cost. If the Germans attacked Leningrad again, he'd start learning German just to stay in power."

After years of grain harvest assessments, intermediate Polish lessons, and "Boy Meets Harvester Combine" movies, Soviet television may have needed Nevzorov badly. He was pugnacious, malicious, and wonderfully crude. He provided a thrill-hungry country with a nightly video *frisson* and his libels were somehow easy, or convenient, to overlook. Even Sobchak tried hard not to mind too much. "Nevzorov is a journalistic cowboy from the Wild West who does what he can to stay in the saddle" was about the worst thing the mayor would say.

———

But what was once a sordid amusement now became a centerpiece of the Kremlin's turn toward authoritarian politics. At times it seemed as if Nevzorov's role in the shift to the right ranked just below the ministerial level. *Vremya,* of course, tried to do what it could to stanch the propaganda wound of the Lithuanian assault with some bogus account of how the independence movement had itself caused the tragedy. Gorbachev waffled, and said the first he had heard of the assault was when he was wakened by his aides the next morning. Was he lying? It was hard to know which was worse: that he was telling the truth, and therefore not in control of the army and the KGB; or that he was lying, and at the head of a coup attempt against the Lithuanians. Later, when I asked Gorbachev's former economic adviser, Nikolai Petrakov, whether Gorbachev truly "slept through" the Vilnius events in ignorance, he said, simply, "Don't be naive."

The Kremlin and Kravchenko knew they needed a new form of public relations. Enter Nevzorov. If *Vremya* was Lawrence Welk, Nevzorov was Ice-T, the hip-hop artist of Soviet television. He didn't wear those mousegray suits like the announcers on *Vremya*. He was cool. When he lied, he did not sweat. His lip did not even twitch. And he had fantastic ratings. Boris Gidaspov, the conservative head of the Communist Party in Leningrad, told the city that "our Sasha Nevzorov" would soon deliver the "objective truth" on the situation in Lithuania.

The day after the shootings, Nevzorov and his crew piled into one of those tuna-can-sized Ladas and raced from Leningrad to Vilnius, where they quickly shot a ten-minute piece. Nevzorov called his film *Nashi*—"Ours," or "Our People," meaning . . . Russians. The idea was that the military was the defender of "Ours" and the Lithuanians an unruly—no, treasonous!—mob. Nevzorov called Landsbergis's pro-independence government "fascists" who had "declared war" on the state. In other words, the message was the same as Gorbachev's, the same as *Vremya*'s. But it was the imagery that did it. With a Kalashnikov slung over his shoulder and snippets of *Das Rheingold* booming on the soundtrack, Nevzorov inspected the fierce and sturdy faces of the troops inside the television center. They were defenders of the faith, defenders of the holy airwaves. They would save us all against the hordes of ungrateful Lithuanian college professors. Didn't they understand what an empire was? And as for the dead, Nevzorov had an answer for that, too. They had not died from the soldier's bullets; no one was crushed under the treads of the tanks or beaten to death with the butt-end of a rifle. No, they died in "car accidents" and of "heart attacks."

The funny thing about *Nashi* was that Nevzorov never interviewed a single Lithuanian. I asked him about that later in Leningrad. "I could have shown sweet Lithuanian flags waving in the air," he said, "but I didn't." Why should he? This was the army's show—with production credits to the KGB and the CPSU.

Nevzorov's broadcast and the endorsement it won from the Kremlin leadership were almost as chilling as the violence in Vilnius itself. The omen was nasty. The Supreme Soviet, with a push from Lukyanov, ordered Nevzorov's film shown three times on national television. The Communist Party daily, *Pravda*, which for years had suffered the scorn of *600 Seconds*, now praised Nevzorov as a "brilliant professional . . . an intrepid man." The paper said that Nevzorov's film was convincing proof that "the responsibility for the deaths of innocent people lies with the chief Lithuanian 'democrat'—Vytautas Landsbergis."

The broadcast cut into Nevzorov's ratings a little. Some of the democratically inclined said it made them just sick to watch him now. But that was all right with Nevzorov. His cubicle office at the Leningrad studios had turned into a political headquarters for local reactionaries. Every day, right-wing members of the city council, retired cops, and leaders of groups like Motherland and the United Workers' Front piled into the room to get a glimpse of him, to ask him to get their grievances (the Jews! the co-ops! Yeltsin!) on the air. To make everyone feel at home, Nevzorov decorated the place with some czarist memorabilia, a bulletproof vest, and a classic Bolshevik recruiting poster from the Civil War period that he'd doctored to read: "Have You Killed Any Democrats Today?"

In the weeks after the Vilnius affair, Nevzorov intensified his nationalist campaign in other films. In Riga, he hailed the decision of the shadowy Black Berets to storm the local police station, an incident that left at least five dead. He tirelessly promoted the career of Colonel Alksnis, who was now busy egging on Gorbachev to "finish the job he started" in Lithuania.

In all his reports, Nevzorov's methods were simple. He meant to scare the hell out of his viewers—all in the service of the Motherland. If the Baltics became independent, he warned, Leningrad would suddenly be overrun with hundreds of thousands of refugees: "There will be tent cities, hunger, fights, deaths, and with all those weapons we have!" Those who were with him were "ours." Those who were not were "radical scum."

Nevzorov insisted he was his own man, but at the same time he was quick to sing the praises of the KGB and the army—"the only institutions holding the country together." The local paper *Chas Pik* ("Rush Hour") reported that the "Public Committee for the Support and Protection of the TV Program *600 Seconds*" included eight directors of huge defense plants and leaders of the local military-industrial complex. Nevzorov made it a point to brag about a hunting rifle that the defense minister, Dmitri Yazov, had given him, and he went on and on about his grandfather who had been a KGB officer—in Lithuania. "They say I am the spitting image of my grandfather. He was a hero, wounded many times in the line of duty. This is a source of great pride for me," Nevzorov said. "The KGB is a great group of guys."

Nevzorov said his alliance with Gorbachev was probably only a temporary "coincidence of positions." He felt more at one with the men who carried the hardware, the soldiers who "bore the ideals of Peter the Great and Aleksandr Nevsky. These are our great Russian defenders. Look, there is chaos in the country. It's better to bring in the tanks now when we are not talking about hundreds and thousands of deaths. . . . A military coup, a military dictatorship, will be around for a while. It's only logical. If there are no healthy forces in society and everything is headed for chaos, then it is only natural that power should be seized by a structure that can maintain authority and order."

Nevzorov said he found my questions about television "whiny and pathetic." He was a pragmatist, he said. "Television and newspapers are nothing more than weapons," he said. "They brainwash the people. A journalist is always serving someone. I am serving my Fatherland, my Motherland. *The Fifth Wheel* is sophisticated propaganda against the state and order. I have no problems with censorship. If the head of Leningrad TV calls me up and tells me to do this or that, you just say, 'Fuck off.' "

And with that he stormed off to do battle for the Motherland. On the way out, I stopped off at the offices of *The Fifth Wheel,* where everyone was trying to figure out ways to beat the censors and undermine Nevzorov's broadcasts. Nothing was working and they were desperate. Viktor Pravdiuk, one of the lead reporters, told me, "They haven't strangled us yet, but their fingers are tightening around our throats."

CHAPTER 26

THE
GENERAL LINE

May the god of history help me.

—STALIN, 1920

As 1991 dragged on, the fury of the hard-liners deepened with every week; with every victory they won, the more brazen their demands became. There was no mystery about what was going on. In meetings public and private, Gorbachev was hearing the full-throated cry of the generals, the military-industrial complex, the Communist Party apparatus, and the KGB. They demanded he turn away from his most reform-minded advisers, and he did. They blamed him for the "loss" of Eastern Europe, the "triumphs" of Germany and the United States, the "ruin" of the union and the Communist Party, and the "degradation" of the armed forces. The KGB chief, Vladimir Kryuchkov, made speeches asserting that the policies of perestroika had evolved into a road map for the destruction of the Union, plans that were no less anti-Soviet than the darkest designs of the CIA. In a meeting in Moscow with Richard Nixon, Kryuchkov said, "We have had about as much democracy as we can stomach."

There was an acrid smell in the air, a sense of panic, fear of the past returning. The Moscow Spring of 1988 was long gone. Privately, Aleksandr Yakovlev told his friends that they would soon see each other in Siberia, "against a wall somewhere." There may have been something to his gallows humor. The press printed rumors that the KGB had even ordered the "reconstruction" of labor camps in eastern Siberia.

Gorbachev counseled calm, but you could see he was thoroughly spooked. At an afternoon session of the Congress that winter, I saw him mounting a short flight of stairs and, in the hasty, idiotic way of such encounters, I blurted, "Mikhail Sergeyevich, they say you are moving to the right."

Gorbachev stopped walking and fixed his eyes on me. His mouth clenched in a pained, ironic grin. The truth is, he said, "I feel as if I am going around in circles." It was the impish explanation of the confused schoolboy, the harried parent. But in Gorbachev's mouth, it was sad. What more was he willing to do to mollify these people? While Gorbachev may well have thought he was finessing the hard-liners and playing for time, he was ruining himself forever. The more he attacked Yeltsin and Landsbergis, the more he made cult figures of them. The man who had mastered his own personality and the tactics of the Communist Party now found himself unable to master the new form of politics he had set free. Gorbachev's compromises, his ugly language, betrayed him. A great man now looked weak, mean-spirited, and confused. There he was, in prime time, railing against the "so-called democrats" who got their marching orders from "foreign research centers." What fresh hell was this? Yeltsin accused Gorbachev of betraying the people, and who now was rushing to the defense of Mikhail Sergeyevich?

The generals, for their part, were so confident of their hold on power and the flow of events that they were ready at last to turn back history. They would reassert a "balanced" version of the past and rescue history from the historians. The hard-liners even had a new icon. Colonel Alksnis, Ligachev, and conservatives of all varieties wrote articles and gave interviews extolling the late KGB chief and general secretary Yuri Andropov for seeing the need for technocratic reform and for modernizing the economy. Andropov, they all said, had been a man of stability, one who never challenged the principles of socialism or the state.

To chart a new historical orthodoxy would not be easy for the hard-liners. The debate on Soviet history had long since gone beyond the boundaries set out by Gorbachev in 1987. Every leader, not merely Stalin, was now under question. The taboo against criticism of Lenin had weakened to such a degree that now even conservatives like Ligachev had to admit, with the gravity of sudden revelation, "Vladimir Ilyich was a man, not a god." Even Khrushchev and Bukharin were no longer held out as "alternatives."

At street demonstrations, however, there were signs calling for the criminal indictment of the Party and the KGB. The slogans of the old order gave way to a new irony and sense of repentance. "Workers of the World Forgive Us!" one banner read. The liberal intellectuals no longer debated whether the seventy-year history was a disaster; the argument was over the roots of that disaster. Igor Klyamkin, a leading economist, blamed Lenin for setting the tone of Soviet power with the Red Terror and the first labor camps. Aleksandr Tsipko, a former Central Committee official, argued that Marxism was the cause.

———

Of all the major events in Soviet history since 1917, the one that was preserved the longest as an unquestionable victory of the regime was the Great Patriotic War against Nazi Germany. Not even the Revolution held such an important place in the collective psyche of the Soviet people.

The May 9 victory parades were just one element in the cult of the war. Even in the mid-eighties, you could turn on the television any day of the week and there was a better than even chance that a group of veterans, old and festooned with medals and ribbons, would be talking about the Battle of Stalingrad to a group of theatrically interested schoolchildren. The war was the touchstone, the regime's lingering reason for being. When Gorbachev defended his allegiance to socialism in early 1991, he said, yes, his grandfathers had been persecuted, but how could he betray his father, who fought bravely at the Dniepr and was wounded in Czechoslovakia? Gorbachev recalled his train ride in 1950 from Stavropol to Moscow and looking out the window at mile after mile of devastation and misery. If he abandoned socialist principles now, he asked, would he not be betraying the memory of the twenty-seven million Soviet citizens killed during the war?

For the hard-liners, the meaning of the cult of the war went even deeper. Victory in the war served to legitimize the brutal collectivization and industrialization campaigns that went before it. Although these men no longer celebrated Stalin, at least not in public, their view of history was surely Stalinist. In textbooks and on television, the Party's propagandists portrayed the war as proof of the system's ultimate strength—the system that saved the world! Of course there had been excesses, the Stalinist pamphleteer Nina Andreyeva once told me, but without collectivization "we would have starved during the war," and without industrialization "where would the tanks have come from?"

Even as late as 1991, the military leadership held on to the habit of sponsoring official histories, and few projects were more important to the hierarchy than the writing of a new history of the war. This would be the third multivolume official history of the Great Patriotic War since Stalin's death. But the Ministry of Defense, which was in charge of the project, knew that this time, several years into the glasnost era, a completely bogus history was out of the question. The committee-written project would have to address the Molotov-Ribbentrop Pact and the purge of the officer corps in the late thirties. The new official history would have to answer the question why the Nazis were able to invade the Soviet Union in June 1941 with such ease.

The man in charge of the first volume, tentatively titled *On the Eve of the War,* was General Dmitri Antonovich Volkogonov. Marshal Dmitri Yazov, the defense minister, Marshal Sergei Akhromeyev, the leading military adviser to Gorbachev, General Valentin Varennikov, the commander of all ground forces, and the other hard-liners at the top of the army accepted Volkogonov as editor knowing they would not get a warmed-over version of the old histories of the war. His biography of Stalin, *Triumph and Tragedy,* published with the encouragement of the Gorbachev leadership in 1988, was the first objective study not written by a dissident. As the director of the military's main history institute, he had had access to all the major archives of the Party, the KGB, and the military while they were still closed to almost everyone else. He was the logical man for the job. They were prepared for a history that was more critical than those published under Khrushchev and Brezhnev. But they were not prepared for what they got.

In late 1990, Volkogonov's team turned in a draft that coolly assessed the relative evils of Stalin and Hitler and described in full detail the "repressive command system" which carried out, at Stalin's direct order, the wholesale slaughter of thousands of officers before the war. The draft explored the roots of Stalin's Terror and its origins in the Red Terror that followed the Revolution. They wrote critically of Stalin's negotiations with the Nazis that allowed Moscow to annex the Baltic states and other key territories. Most appalling of all to the hard-liners, Volkogonov's draft concluded that the Soviet Union had won the war almost "by chance"—despite Stalin, not because of him. They implied that perhaps the death of twenty-seven million Soviet people was in vain, that the victory of the Soviet Union represented the victory of one brutal regime over another.

The Ministry of Defense sent copies of the draft history around to various "reviewers": generals, admirals, officials in the Communist Party, and the heads of the major institutes. Their reaction was angry and quick. Akhromeyev gave an interview to the reactionary *Military Historical Journal* that accused Volkogonov of acting as a "traitor."

"Had Volkogonov succeeded in publishing the work, with its obviously false positions as set out in the first volume, it would have done great harm, and not only to history," Akhromeyev said. "The lies about the war would have been used for undermining the integrity of our country and the socialist choice, and for the constant defamation of the Communist Party. This could not be allowed." Volkogonov, he said, was an anti-Communist "turncoat" serving just one master: the equally anti-Communist Russian president, Boris Yeltsin.

———

The denunciations had only just begun. On March 7, at an elegant meeting hall in the Ministry of Defense, fifty-seven generals, Central Committee officials, and official academics gathered to review Volkogonov's work. The chairman of the editorial committee, General A. F. Kochetov, opened the session by reminding everyone that "when the original conception of the ten-volume work was discussed, everyone agreed with the idea that the driving force [of the victory] was the Soviet people, the people's army, the toilers, all led by the Party. But today, proceeding from the interests of the moment, everyone insults and blames the Party. Suddenly the people are to blame. . . . Many of the reviews asked the question: 'If things were so awful before the war, why did we win?' "

Kochetov pointed out incredulously that in the book there was an implicit (and intolerable) comparison of socialism with fascism. He said that some of the reviewers had also complained that Volkogonov betrayed the intentions of the volume by discussing the origins of the system leading up to the war, and others simply objected to the titles of chapters such as "The Political Regime Grows Stricter" and "The Militarization of Spiritual Life."

Kochetov then opened the session for "general discussion": an invitation to a beheading. General Mikhail Moiseyev, chief of the general staff, attacked Volkogonov, saying that he was merely out to inspire "today's destructive forces"—meaning Yeltsin and the pro-independence activists in the republics.

"Defend the army!" came the calls from the hall.

Later, Valentin Falin, the head of the Central Committee's International Department, took the floor. "We must point out the insufficiencies of this volume, its thousands of mistakes," he said. "I have not seen such fantastical stuff in thirty or forty years. . . . To waste government money on this is out of the question!"

Volkogonov turned pale. He had grown away from these men, but he was only now aware by how much. After more than an hour of denunciations, he finally demanded the floor.

"Respected comrades!" Volkogonov began. "My voice in this hall will no doubt be a lonely one. There is not likely to be a real scholarly discussion here. This is a tribunal on scholarship, on history, on a large group of writers.

Instead of an analysis of the issue, there is just unbridled criticism. . . . In the atmosphere that has been created here I cannot write a new history. To write only about the victory of 1945 means to talk nonsense about 1941, about the four million prisoners, about the retreat to the Volga. It is impossible to reduce history to politics."

Volkogonov had only begun, but now Varennikov, one of the most reactionary generals in the Ministry of Defense hierarchy, broke in, shouting, "There is a suggestion to deny him the floor!"

Volkogonov refused to back down.

"I am no less a patriot than Falin and love the Motherland no less than he," he said. "But you cannot change the consequences of history. I agree with those who say there are many faults in this volume. . . . But let's discuss and debate them. We'll give our points of view. But, no, Comrade Falin and some others do not engage in scholarly debate, but rather make accusations about a lack of patriotism."

"Enough!" one general shouted. "Listen to this!"

Somewhere in the hall came the shout "Stop his speech!"

Volkogonov kept going, arguing that unless the book and the Soviet people dealt with all the cruelty and misery that had preceded the war, there could be no understanding of what happened after the opening volleys of the Nazi invasion.

"How else can we look at the fact that forty-three thousand officers and other army officials were purged?" he said. "And what of the other victims? We don't need blind patriotism. We need the truth! . . . Mine is a lonely voice in this hall, but I want to see what you say about it all in ten years."

The chairman was appalled. He took personal offense.

Finally, the swarm overtook Volkogonov. The generals shouted him down, and he did not speak again. But the ritual was far from over. Two and a half hours after the session had begun, Marshal Yazov, the minister of defense, arrived. Yazov, with his lumpy face and bulbous nose, was none too bright. When it came time to appoint a new defense minister after a German teenager, Mathias Rust, managed to land his little plane on Red Square in 1987, Gorbachev went way down the ladder and found Yazov, the chief of military operations in the far east. The man had a reputation for mediocrity. But that was the point. Gorbachev wanted a man utterly without cunning. He wanted a pleasant mutt, a loyal friend.

But that was years ago, and now, with the conservatives in the midst of a full-fledged counterrevolution against radical reform, Yazov was showing his strength. He despised the direction perestroika had taken. Hundreds of thousands of young men in the Baltic states, the Caucasus, and other regions were ignoring their draft notices. Gorbachev was cutting troop levels and other liberals wanted even more reductions. Meanwhile, officers returning from Eastern Europe and Germany were living in crowded dormitories and even tents.

Yazov quickly addressed the group, and there was no doubt that his anger went far beyond any rough draft or a three-star general named Volkogonov. The battle over the book represented to him nothing less than the overall struggle for power in the Soviet Union.

"The 'democrats' now have made it their goal to prepare and carry out a Nuremberg II on the Communist Party," Yazov said. "The volume has in it the outlines for an indictment for such a trial."

"This book has at its foundation a libel of the Party," Varennikov pitched in.

"In this hall," Yazov continued, "I think, everyone is a Communist. And Communists cannot spit on their Party."

It was over. Volkogonov was dismissed from the editorial committee and his draft was "returned to the board for fundamental reworking." Another victory for the hard-line coalition. Five months later, in August, Yazov, Varennikov, Moiseyev, and other men in the room would go even farther and attempt a coup d'état.

———

I first met Volkogonov in 1988 when he was still in the official fold and about to publish his biography, *Stalin: Triumph and Tragedy*. (The English translation did not appear until 1991.) The publicity flaks around the foreign ministry were pitching him as their "breakthrough historian"—which caused immediate suspicion. For the liberal intelligentsia in Moscow and Leningrad, Volkogonov was not an inspiring choice. He had published dozens of books and monographs on military ideology, and none of them even hinted at independence, rigor, or critical thought. Here was a military man who had played the game; if he harbored dissident thoughts, he had not yet committed a whisper of them to paper.

But at a meeting with journalists at the Foreign Ministry, Volkogonov was impressive. He spoke without bluff or euphemism. He was familiar with all the major Western scholarship on Stalin, making detailed and admiring references to a number of books, especially Robert C. Tucker's multivolume biography-in-progress. As a way to defend himself against official Party historians who would attack his use of foreign scholars, Volkogonov wrote in the introduction, "Without realizing it, Stalin did far more to blacken the name of 'socialism' than anything written by Leonard Schapiro, Isaac Deutscher, Robert Tucker or Robert Conquest." Volkogonov clearly had full access to the *spetskhran*—the "special shelves" of Soviet libraries where banned books were secreted away. In his bibliography, he cites books that were, until glasnost, unavailable for ordinary Soviets: Adam Ulam's biography of Stalin, Deutscher's biography of Trotsky, Richard Pipes's *Russia Under the Old Regime,* Milovan Djilis's *Conversations with Stalin,* and the memoirs of Stalin's daughter, Svetlana Alliluyeva. In addition, Volkogonov read and made reference to the works of Stalin's enemies, the men he defeated and executed: Bukharin, Trotsky, Rykov, Kamenev, Zinoviev, Tomsky.

If Volkogonov had merely cribbed the Western biographies of Stalin and published the result under his name in the Soviet Union, his book would have had a certain notoriety. The mere notion of a Red Army general laying bare the awful facts of the Stalin era would have been an astonishing advance in the Soviet Union's attempt to recover its historical memory. But he did much more. Volkogonov will be remembered not so much as a great thinker or writer but rather for the uniqueness of his access, the way he made scholarly use of his political position. Volkogonov alone had the chance to exploit the paperwork of the totalitarian regime, and he went everywhere: the Central Party Archives, the USSR Supreme Court Archives, the Central State Archives of the Army, the Ministry of Defense Archives, the Armed Forces General Staff Archives, and the archives of several important museums and institutes, including the Institute of Marxism-Leninism.

On those shelves, Volkogonov found no definitive answers to the remaining riddles of history. For example, he did not come up with a "smoking gun" in the 1934 murder of the Leningrad Party chief Sergei Kirov. Nearly all Western scholars assume, with good circumstantial reason, that Stalin ordered Kirov killed in order to eliminate a potential political threat and to set the stage for the Great Terror. Volkogonov assumed the same and wrote:

"The archives that I have searched do not provide any further clues for making a more definitive statement on the Kirov affair. What is clear, however, is that the murder was not carried out on the orders of Trotsky, Zinoviev, or Kamenev, which was soon put out as the official version. Knowing what we now know about Stalin, it is certain that he had a hand in it. The removal of two or three layers of indirect witnesses bears his hallmark."

But while *Triumph and Tragedy* made no sensational advances, while it did not "solve" the enigma of Stalin's motives or produce a definitive death toll for the repressions of the era, the book was in no sense a failure. By providing excerpts from hundreds of memos, telegrams, and orders that had never been seen by scholars before, Volkogonov allowed the reader a terrible intimacy with the Soviet despot; *Triumph and Tragedy* gave new texture, at once horrifying and bland, to our knowledge of one of the worst passages in human history.

In his portrayal of Stalin, Volkogonov was more critical than many of his liberal critics might have expected. *Triumph and Tragedy* showed Stalin to have been a coward, a miserable commander in chief during the war, a "mediocrity but not insignificant," as Trotsky once put it. Volkogonov provided the conclusive documentary evidence that Stalin, using blue or red pencils, personally ordered the deaths of thousands in the same offhand tone as a man ordering a drink at a bar.

". . . According to I. D. Perfilyev, an Old Bolshevik who had spent many years in a concentration camp and who told me the story, once, in Molotov's company, while discussing a routine list with [secret police chief Nikolai] Yezhov, Stalin muttered to no one in particular: 'Who's going to remember all this riffraff in ten or twenty years time? No one. Who remembers the names now of the boyars Ivan the Terrible got rid of? No one. . . . The people had to know he was getting rid of all his enemies. In the end, they all got what they deserved.'

" 'The people understand, Iosif Vissarionovich, they understand and they support you,' Molotov replied automatically."

In Moscow, I got to know Volkogonov fairly well, first in his incarnation as a military historian, then as a political outcast, and, finally, when he became a radical deputy in the Russian parliament in 1990 and a top military adviser to Russian President Yeltsin. Even early on, when he had to take great care in how, and with whom, he talked about his work, Volkogonov never concealed just how deeply his days in the archives had moved him.

"I would come home from working in Stalin's archives, and I would be deeply shaken," Volkogonov told me. "I remember coming home after reading through the day of December 12, 1938. He signed thirty lists of death sentences that day, altogether about five thousand people, including many he knew personally, his friends. This was before their trials, of course. This was no surprise. This is not what shook me. But it turned out that, having signed these documents, he went to his personal theater very late that night and watched two movies, including *Happy Guys,* a popular comedy of the time. I simply could not understand how, after deciding the fate of several thousand lives, he could watch such a movie. But I was beginning to realize that morality plays no role for dictators. That's when I understood why my father was shot, why my mother died in exile, why millions of people died."

Volkogonov was born in the Siberian city of Chita in 1928 and later moved to the Pacific coast of Russia. His father was an agrarian specialist and his mother cared for the three children. In 1937, at the height of the purges, Anton Volkogonov was summoned to the local Party committee, where he was arrested for the crime of possessing printed matter of a "politically

questionable" origin—a pamphlet by the "right deviationist" Nikolai Bukharin. Volkogonov's father was never seen again. "He just disappeared into
the meat grinder of the purges," Volkogonov said. "When I was older, my
mother whispered to me, 'Your father was shot. Never, never speak of it
again.' "

This family of an "enemy of the people" was exiled to the village of Agul
in the Krasnoyarsk district of western Siberia, near an ever-growing complex
of forced-labor camps. When he was a child, Volkogonov saw long columns
of prisoners marching from the rail stations fifty miles away to the camps.
Guard dogs, barbed wire, and watchtowers were all part of his childhood
landscape. With each passing month, NKVD workers cordoned off more
land and built more camps. The guards dug huge trenches in the pine forest
and carried the corpses to the trenches at night on old-fashioned Russian
sleds. Schoolchildren would go looking for pine nuts in the forest and they
would hear gunfire, Volkogonov recalled, "like the sound of canvas being
ripped apart."

Volkogonov's mother died just after the end of the war. Like many other
orphans, Dmitri Antonovich entered the military as a draftee and never left.
His brother and sister were adopted by other families. As a young private and
officer during the late forties and the fifties, Volkogonov got a thorough
education in political orthodoxy. He learned quickly that no diversion was
too small to be noticed. Toward the end of *Triumph and Tragedy,* Volkogonov let himself enter the portrait of the system, here as a student of
military equipment and state ideology:

". . . Students were tested first and foremost for their ability to summarize
Stalin's works. I remember being kept back by the teacher when I was
attending the Orel Tank School. He was a lieutenant colonel, no longer a
young man, and was very much liked by the class for his good nature. When
we were alone he handed me my work, which was a summary of sources, and
said to me in a quiet and fatherly voice: 'It's a good summary. I could see
right away you hadn't just copied it down and had given it some thought. But
my advice is, summarize the Stalinist works more fully. Understand, more
fully! And another thing. In front of the name Iosif Vissarionovich, don't
write "Com." Write "Comrade" in full. Got it?' That night one of my
roommates told me they'd all had similar conversations with the teacher of
Party history. The exams were coming up and there were rumors that in a
neighboring school 'they had paid attention' to the sort of 'political im-
maturities' I had shown in my summaries."

As an officer, Volkogonov was prepared to do anything for the Motherland. At a nuclear test site, he was ordered to drive a new-model tank
straight through the area that had just been the epicenter of an atomic bomb test. And

he did. "There was nothing I would not do," Volkogonov told me. "I was a young lieutenant when Stalin died and I thought the heavens would fall without him. The fact that my father had been shot and my mother died miserably in exile, that didn't seem to matter: it was destiny, incomprehensible. My mind was contaminated. I was incapable of analyzing these things, of putting the pieces together."

In the Komsomol and the Communist Party organizations of the Lenin Military Academy in Moscow, Volkogonov became such a master of the standard texts of dogma that he gained a reputation among the senior officers as an especially reliable *polit rabotnik,* a political propagandist. Volkogonov got a doctorate in philosophy—which, in those days, meant Marxist-Leninist philosophy—and in 1970 was transferred to the army's Department of Propaganda. There he climbed the ladder steadily; he was promoted to general at forty, won a professorship at forty-four, and made it to deputy chief in charge of political instruction. Along the way, he also earned a doctorate in history.

With his high rank and credentials, Volkogonov was allowed access to all the most important—and closed—archives in the capital. "But make no mistake about who I was," Volkogonov said. "I was not a closet radical. I cannot distort history to suit my needs. The fact is, I was an orthodox Marxist, an officer who knew his duty. I was not part of some liberal current. All my changes came from within, off on my own. I had access to all kinds of literature. You know there were many people, especially young officers of the KGB, who thought liberally because they had more information than anyone else. That's why there have always been a lot of thinking people in the KGB, people who understand the West as it really is and what our own country really was.

"I was a Stalinist. I contributed to the strengthening of the system that I am now trying to dismantle. But latently, I had my ideas. I began asking myself questions about Lenin, how, if he was such a genius, none of his predictions came true. The proletarian dictatorship never came to be, the principle of class struggle was discredited, Communism was not built in fifteen years as he had promised. None of Lenin's major predictions ever came true! I confess it: I used my position. I began gathering information even though I didn't know yet what I would do with it."

While working in a KGB archive during the thaw, Volkogonov even read his father's file and learned that what his mother had whispered had been true. Anton Volkogonov had been shot in 1937 just after his arrest.

Almost as a dream, Volkogonov decided he would write a trilogy on Stalin, Lenin, and Trotsky. By the late seventies, Volkogonov was secretly working on the Stalin volume. His apartment was crammed with tens of thousands of photocopied documents and books, many of them banned. As time passed and times grew a bit more liberal, Volkogonov made little secret of what he was doing. The military hierarchy, however, decided that Volkogonov's historical research was not "consistent" with his position as a propagandist. He was shunted aside and installed at the Institute of Military History, a move that represented a demotion, Volkogonov said, of "three steps down the ladder." For a soldier, perhaps. But for a historian, the demotion was a gift. Now Volkogonov had more time and access to the archives. When the leadership finally came looking for a biography of Stalin, Volkogonov was there, ready to write.

————

Using his position as a general, Volkogonov was able to realize the dreams of such outsiders as Dima Yurasov. Volkogonov's work in the archives not only provided him international fame, it also shattered whatever last illusions he might have had about Soviet history. Now Volkogonov, like so many other intellectuals throughout the union, saw the roots of catastrophe in the ideology itself, in Leninism. "Abstract ideas give rise to fanatics, and such was Trotsky," he wrote. The utopianism, the ferocity, of Bolshevism gave rise to the totalitarian state.

In the spring of 1991, Volkogonov invited me to meet with him in his hospital room. He was exhausted by his battle with Yazov and the other generals. The hospital was tucked away on a side street off Kalinin Prospekt. Compared to other Soviet hospitals I'd seen, with their filthy floors, their crowded rooms, this special clinic for the military elite was a wonder. There were private rooms, wood-paneled hallways, a clean and efficient staff. Volkogonov told me he was ill and not sure how long he had to live. He had stomach cancer and would go for surgery to Western Europe. But he did not seem shocked or sad and wanted only to pick up on what we had talked about in his various offices.

"You see, I am now convinced that Stalinism created a new type of man: indifferent, without initiative or enterprise, a person waiting for a messiah, waiting for someone to come alive and solve all of life's problems. The most awful thing about it is that this cannot merely be shed, like taking off an old raincoat and donning a new one. There are many aspects of this mentality still inside me, and I lose them only slowly. This whole period we are living in now is about scrubbing this mentality from our minds. We are all becoming revolutionaries when it comes to our own individual way of thinking. For you it is so hard to understand. You are indifferent as to who will be in power in your own country. Democrats or Republicans, America is America. Only some nuances of the system change. For us, a mutiny is going on. The

Revolution was one sort of mutiny, and we are on the threshold of another. We are making our way through an intellectual and spiritual fog and all around us is collapse.

"The generals in the army reproach me for being a chameleon. They say I am a traitor or a renegade. But personally I think it is a more courageous stance to abandon honestly something which has been devalued by history instead of carrying it to the end in your soul. There are people among them who criticize me in public and in private say I am right but they can't say so.

"Now I am in complete isolation. I get support from the grass roots, from junior officers, and a couple of generals even support me secretly. The majority despise me. Even when I meet generals here in the hospital they pretend not to notice me. Others want to talk to me, but they fear the consequences.

"These people are frozen in the past. Even truth will not change them. Stalin died physically, but not historically. The image of Stalin lives because it has so many allies. No less than fifteen percent of the letters I get are from Stalinists, and the worse the situation gets, the more of those I get. The Party has sixteen million people in it. Thirty percent are like Akhromeyev or Nina Andreyeva. They won't change. Another thirty percent see the Party as a modus vivendi. They can't advance in their careers if they are not members. And the rest could leave at any moment.

"The army and the KGB were never for real perestroika. They were for minor repairs of the system, a little camouflage. They wanted to preserve the system intact by getting rid of the most obviously odious features: super-bureaucracy, corruption, and so on. Yet none of them wants to question the essence of the system. The Party ought to be in control, they say.

"Totalitarian systems usually absorb people absolutely. As I have come to realize, very few people have been able to transcend such a system, to tear themselves away from it. Most people of my generation will die imprisoned in this system, even if they live another ten or twenty years. Of course, people who are twenty or thirty are free people. They can liberate themselves from the system quite easily. The only thing I have to offer is my experience. Maybe my example will be valuable in tracing the crisis, the tragedy, and the drama of Communist ideas and utopia played out over the generations."

Volkogonov was getting tired. And at the same time, his mood was changing. The full weight of the news he had just gotten was beginning to hit him, and he began to talk about working "at full speed" to finish the volumes on Lenin and Trotsky and perhaps write a memoir. When we got to talking about the dark mood in Moscow, I finally asked him what he thought was ahead.

"Democratization is irreversible on the historic, strategic scale," Volkogonov said. "But on the tactical plane, in the short run, the right-wing forces still have a chance. They may even come to the head of the country and hustle us all back into the barn for another five or ten years. They could try. They are that crazy and that angry."

CHAPTER 27

CITIZENS

YAGUNOVSKO

In the summer of 1989, when the miners brought the revolution to Siberia, Anatoly Shcheglov walked me back from his village to the tram for Kemerevo and invited me back. "I'll take you fishing in the taiga," he said. Now, a year and a half later, the miners were on strike again and I was back in Siberian coal country. Most of the government's promises had been broken and conditions were as dismal as ever. Along the road to Shcheglov's hut on Second Plan Street, the snow was crusted black, the air was cold and gassy.

Anatoly Shcheglov had no phone. I just assumed he'd be at home. When he opened the door, he greeted me as if I'd been away a week and coming back to Yagunovsko were the most ordinary thing in the world for an American. He looked cleaner, more relaxed, but a good deal older. A lacework of wrinkles ate deep into his face. "I'm retired now," he said. "The expected happened." He said that the winter after we'd met, as he settled his huge frame into a chair one night after dinner, he had a heart attack. Like a horse kicking him in the chest, he said. He was fifty years old. "It's the usual thing for us underground men," Anatoly said. "You quit at fifty and you're lucky to make it to fifty-five. I doubt if I'll be around much longer."

Shcheglov now spent his days standing in lines at empty village stores, shuttling from one filthy hospital to the next looking for doctors, aspirin, glycerin pills. "An old man's life," he said. But what brightened him, he said, was the nerve and determination of his fellow miners across the country. The strikes now had nothing to do with the issues of July 1989. "It's not about soap or vacation pay anymore," he said. The miners wanted nothing less than the resignation of Gorbachev's government and the dismantling of the system of state socialism. "There are no more illusions left, no more socialist dreams," Shcheglov said. "The first strikes were for a crust of bread, a cut of meat. We got nothing that was promised us. Life just got worse. Now we know the secret. The system has to go."

Since the beginning of March 1991, over 300,000 miners had gone out on strike. The remaining 900,000 miners worked only to avert a complete collapse of the national economy. The strike leaders figured they would gain no supporters if it came to that. Their strategy was measured and effective. In the coming weeks there were warning strikes by machinists in Leningrad, electricians in Samara, Black Sea dockworkers in Odessa.

The strikes terrified the Kremlin hard-liners. They knew that the radicalization of the workers—the proletariat's evolving consciousness, to borrow from the Marxist phrasebook—could be the finishing blow to a tottering regime. Soviet power seemed able to withstand the demonstrations of urban democracy movements, but the workers had the power to turn the lights out in the Kremlin. And they were not kidding. "No more games," Shcheglov said. "No more games." At a session of the Russian Republic's legislature, most of the deputies did little more than echo softly Yeltsin's latest demands for Gorbachev's resignation. But late in the session, the Kuzbass strike leader, Anatoly Malikhin, took the floor and announced, "We are prepared to flood the mines." The miners, he said, had lost all tolerance for the system that had bled them white. Lead the attack, he told the Russian deputies, or the miners will.

A few days after the speech, I met Anatoly Malikhin at the Rossiya Hotel in Moscow. There were remnants everywhere of late-night strategy sessions: leaflets, stuffed ashtrays, and dirty glasses. Strike headquarters was wherever Anatoly Malikhin happened to be. His phone rang incessantly: strike committees from Siberia, Ukraine, the far east, and Vorkuta in northern Russia called with congratulations, questions, advice, more plans.

"Well, then fuck 'em," he said at one point on the line to the Kuzbass. "We'll go back when the demands are met. Not sooner."

Malikhin showed more certainty, more sense of purpose, than any of the liberal intellectuals in Moscow and Leningrad. He was absolutely serious; there was no theater to him, no veneer of irony. He and the other strike leaders had taken Gorbachev at his word when they negotiated a settlement to the strikes in 1989, and they would not repeat the mistake. Simple as that.

"No one is belittling what Gorbachev has already done, but every person has his moment, his moment of peak operation, like a machine," Malikhin said. "But Gorbachev thinks he is unique. At the beginning, he really did do a lot, and we take our hats off to him. But he should have changed the system radically a year or more ago. Then he could have found himself a place for himself in that new structure. But he didn't. He was stuck with his socialist principles. Now he is doing more harm than good. If Gorbachev is so smart, why is he still trying to protect the Party? There is a rumor that he is getting ready to send army troops to the mines. Well, believe me, if he does that the soldiers will die there by the thousands."

NOVOCHERKASSK

No one knew where the dead were buried. There were rumors: the KGB had pushed the corpses down a mine shaft or into a swamp, or the police had brought the bodies to a series of unmarked graves in cemeteries spread across the Black Earth zone of southern Russia. But no one knew.

For nearly thirty years, the story of the Novocherkassk rebellion was a secret of the state. The strike in June 1962 over price rises and wage cuts at the city's Electric Locomotive Works was the first workers' uprising in Russia since the fitful years immediately after the Revolution. At Moscow's orders, the military turned its machine guns on the unarmed demonstrators in Novocherkassk. At least twenty-four were killed, dozens more injured. Not long after, the Kremlin's judges ordered the execution of seven "ringleaders" who had survived. Within three days, all mention of Novocherkassk disappeared from the state-controlled press. Even Western specialists knew almost nothing of the bloody affair. Solzhenitsyn published a few pages of rough description in the third volume of *The Gulag Archipelago,* but that, of course, was considered "anti-Soviet propaganda" and banned until 1990.

Now, with the miners on strike once more, with the KGB, the army, and Gorbachev himself feeling threatened by nationalists and political opponents, in a time of increasing food shortages and ethnic division, there was constant talk of conflict, of civil disobedience, of the possibility of bloodshed. The massacre of demonstrators in Tbilisi, Baku, and Vilnius made it clear that the regime, despite all the reforms, could be expected to bring out the tanks and machine guns, even poisonous gas, if that was what it took to survive. What had changed, if anything, since that summer afternoon in southern Russia in 1962?

———

In addition to the twenty-four people killed in Novocherkassk, the massacre claimed at least one more victim: Soviet Army General Matvei Shaposhnikov, a true believer in the Bolshevik ideal who was awarded the title of Hero of the Soviet Union after leading a tank division to victory in some of the bloodiest fighting in World War II. Years before the emergence of Sakharov and the dissident movement, Shaposhnikov had done the unthinkable. Ordered to attack the demonstrators at Novocherkassk, he refused.

When I met him, the general was eighty-four years old. His political superiors forced him to retire three years after the Novocherkassk massacre, but he was active and strong. With his grip he could have crushed a walnut. His apartment in the city of Rostov-on-Don, which he shared with his daughter and son-in-law and their children, was military-neat, his books and memorabilia perfectly arranged and dusted.

"Let's talk, face to face," Shaposhnikov said, lifting a heavy chair and setting it down for his guest. He was older than the regime. "I remember clearly singing revolutionary songs as an eleven-year-old boy in 1917: 'Oh, march, march forward, working people . . . !' I believed all my life in Soviet power, and now I was being told to shoot at my own people, unarmed people. I had to pay for my decision with everything. They stripped me of my rank, my decorations, my membership in the Communist Party. They told me to retire for 'health reasons.' And my wife, my dear, dear wife, finally paid for it even more deeply. She died a few years ago, and I am convinced she died from the attacks on us. Finally, she just could not bear it."

There was not one hour, even now, the general said, when he did not think back to the days of the massacre. On the morning of June 1, 1962, the Communist Party press in Novocherkassk announced that the prices of meat and butter would go up at least 25 percent. When workers at the Electric Locomotive Works arrived at the plant, they discovered that their wages would be cut by as much as 30 percent. Both local newspapers, the *Hammer* and the *Banner of the Commune,* assured the people that these were merely "temporary measures," all in the name of "social progress." Somehow, the workers were not prepared this time to believe the usual doublespeak. Their anger was so intense that they forgot themselves. They forgot for a moment their "party discipline" and confronted the plant director, an odious bureaucrat named Kurochkin.

How would they live now? the workers demanded.

"You're used to wolfing down meat pies," Kurochkin replied. "Now you can stuff them with jam instead."

The workers were enraged. They blew the shop floor whistles and started gathering in the courtyards. There they talked of a strike and drew up placards: "Give Us Meat and Butter," "We Need Places to Live." They ripped down portraits of Khrushchev and burned them. Terrified, the plant managers locked themselves in their offices. The local Communist Party officials refused to meet with any of the strike representatives.

Meanwhile, the regional military command had been on alert for weeks in anticipation of the announcements of price hikes and wage cuts. According to Shaposhnikov, the regional military commander, General Issa Pliyev, received a stream of coded orders from the Ministry of Defense and Khrushchev himself. That first night, KGB officers and police arrested some of the most outspoken factory workers in an attempt to head off a potential strike.

Two members of Khrushchev's inner political circle, Anastas Mikoyan and Frol Kozlov, were already in the city. Shaposhnikov, who had been put in charge of the armed detachments stationed near the locomotive factory, told the two Politburo members that he was "gravely concerned" that the troops were carrying guns. A confrontation, he said, could lead to bloodshed.

"Commander Pliyev has been given all the instructions he needs," Kozlov replied angrily.

On the morning of June 2, at around eleven o'clock, seven thousand workers and other demonstrators began their protest march from the locomotive plant to the center of Novocherkassk. They ignored the troops and tanks that surrounded the plant. As they marched, some workers tried to block the railway line leading into town as a further show of protest. "But people were unarmed, peaceful. They even carried portraits of Lenin," said Vladimir Fomin, one of the region's deputies in the Russian parliament. The greatest offense of the marchers was their willingness to question Moscow. "Khrushchev for sausage meat!" the protesters chanted.

Anticipating violence, Shaposhnikov told all his soldiers to empty the ammunition from their guns and for the tank brigades to do the same. As the column of demonstrators passed, Shaposhnikov stopped one worker and asked where they were going.

"Comrade General," the worker said, "if the mountain will not come to Muhammad, then Muhammad will go to the mountain." They were headed for the police station and Communist Party headquarters. Shaposhnikov radioed ahead to Pliyev and told him that the column of protesters was now moving across the Tuzlov bridge and into town.

"Stop them! Don't let them pass!" Pliyev shouted into his radio.

"I haven't got enough men to stop seven thousand people," Shaposhnikov said.

"Send the tanks! Attack them!" Pliyev said.

Shaposhnikov said, "Comrade Commander, I see no enemy that our tanks ought to attack."

Pliyev slammed down the receiver in a rage. In that moment of dead air, Shaposhnikov sensed disaster, but he thought he might be able to head it off. He jumped in a jeep and tried to catch up with the protesters. But by the time he neared the city's central square, the marchers were at the gates of the police station, demanding that the strike leaders be let out of jail. Suddenly, soldiers started firing into the crowd. Some witnesses said the troops were issued dumdum bullets, which expand on impact. In a panic, the crowd turned and started to flee up Moskovskaya Street. The troops continued firing at their backs. One woman lay in a flower bed bleeding to death. Her arm had been shot off.

By the time the crowd was gone, Solzhenitsyn wrote, "the soldiers looked around for trucks and buses, commandeered them, loaded them with the dead and wounded, and took them to the high-walled military hospital. For a day or two afterward these buses went around town with bloodstained seats."

News of the killings spread to other factories. Workers left the plants and staged an even bigger rally in the center of town. "Trucks full of workers arrived from everywhere," one witness recalled. "It was a torrent of human bodies. No force on earth could have stopped them."

"Khrushchev! Khrushchev! Let him see!" the crowd chanted.

Soon Mikoyan was on the radio. He spoke of "hooligans" and "the tragic accident." The police issued a curfew order and sent the crowd home. The army left its troops and tanks in the city for weeks. Within two days, the official press ceased all mention of the Novocherkassk affair. And so it stayed for decades.

———

General Shaposhnikov was a loyal Party member with memories of the first days of the Revolution. He could not understand why the local Communists had not simply met with the workers as "comrades" and negotiated with them. He thought that he should write a letter to the Central Committee of the Communist Party. Maybe they would understand. After all, he thought, the Soviet army simply did not attack its own people. You could read it in Lenin, in all the Party rulebooks! He remembered how the Party always referred to "Bloody Sunday" when the czarist police in 1905 attacked a crowd of peaceful petitioners. The Party and its army would never act that way.

Shaposhnikov asked to speak with the Party officials. He was refused. Even after a few months went by, the general could not let the killings pass. He began sending anonymous letters to the Soviet Writers' Union in Moscow in the naive hope that their "great humanism" would be of help to him. And so Shaposhnikov, a Hero of the Soviet Union in his sixties, wrote: "The Party has turned into a car which is steered by a reckless, drunken driver who is always breaking the traffic rules. It's high time to take away the driver's license and prevent a catastrophe. . . . Today it is extremely important that the working people and the intellectuals should see clearly the essence of the political regime under which we live. They must realize that we are under the rule of the worst form of autocracy which rests on an enormous bureaucracy and an armed force. . . . It is necessary that people learn to think. Our blind faith is turning us into mere living machines. Our people have been deprived of all political and international rights."

Once more Shaposhnikov's idealism was betrayed. The Writers' Union was a hopelessly corrupt organization, a swamp of toadies, and its officers turned Shaposhnikov's letters over to the KGB. Shaposhnikov said his intentions were never "anti-Soviet" but rather "anti the bureaucrats and their arrogance." Somehow the KGB did not see it that way. The general began noticing that his mail was arriving already opened. He soon confirmed that he was under surveillance. In 1966, with no explanation, the army forced him out of active duty. In 1967, police searched his apartment and confiscated his archives. Without even pretending to secrecy, they also installed a listening device in the bedroom wall. "I was basically under house arrest, and I was followed by men in dark glasses all the time," Shaposhnikov said. "There was nothing I could do. Some friends remained loyal, but it was very hard for them, especially in a provincial place like this. They saw what was happening. People tried to avoid me. They would actually cross the street just to avoid saying hello to me in town."

Finally the KGB called Shaposhnikov to local headquarters for a prolonged interrogation. Over and over they demanded that he confess to "anti-Soviet" activities, and Shaposhnikov always described his work in the countryside teaching illiterate workers to read, his work in the mines for 20 kopecks a shift, his long and celebrated career in the army. "How could I have been anti-Soviet when I gave Soviet power everything?" he said. "If anyone had been dedicated to building Communism, it was me." He was stripped of his army rank and his membership in the Communist Party. Only by writing an impassioned letter to the KGB chief, Yuri Andropov, did Shaposhnikov save himself from jail.

Through the Brezhnev, Andropov, and Chernenko years, there was not much for the general to do except live in shabby retirement. While other Soviet generals had generous benefits—dachas, special food orders, generous pensions—Shaposhnikov lived no better than a retired factory worker. To pass the time and make a few extra rubles, he wrote memoirs of the war, about the tank assaults on the Nazis on the Ukrainian front. The books were published, but, of course, they had nothing to do with the massacre at Novocherkassk.

Throughout the sixties and seventies, the general never connected with the underground political ferment in Moscow and Leningrad. The truth was, the dissident movement confused him. It seemed directed not only at the leadership, but also at the foundations of Leninist ideology. "I could never understand that," he said.

When Gorbachev came to power in 1985, Shaposhnikov wrote five letters to the Kremlin. They all went unanswered. Finally, in 1988, he got an imperious letter from the Supreme Court: "Your case has now been dismissed in view of the absence of corpus delicti. . . . The acts perpetrated by you in the sixties provided ample grounds for bringing charges of anti-Soviet propaganda against you. It is only in the context of perestroika and the democratization of all spheres of life in the Soviet Union that it has become possible to find you not guilty."

It would be hard to find a more egregious example of indirection and self-righteousness in the service of simple justice. But Shaposhnikov was only relieved. He began going once more to his local Party meetings—"I am sixty years a Communist!" But his faith is of a certain kind. In 1990, when a group of young officers in the army scandalized the generals by forming the reformist group called Shield, they made Shaposhnikov their honorary chairman. They even asked him to speak at a huge antigovernment rally in Moscow just as troops were killing Azerbaijanis on the streets of Baku. "I thought a long time about what I wanted to say that day," Shaposhnikov said. "I thought about that afternoon in Novocherkassk and everything that is going on now, and so I said the army has to vow that they are always with the people and not against them. We can never shoot at our own people. Otherwise we are nothing. Otherwise, we have no future. We'd better remember that."

MOSCOW

Even after "Bloody Sunday" in Vilnius, the hard-liners wanted still more blood. They wanted to provoke a confrontation with the opposition forces that would *require* force; they wanted an incident so ugly that they would finally have the pretense they needed to step in, declare a state of emergency, and put an end to the strikes and the defiant leaderships in the Baltic states, Moldavia, Georgia, Armenia, and, most of all, Russia.

Gorbachev was showing no signs of relaxing his position. In early March 1991, he proclaimed victory in a referendum to preserve the union, but he knew well that he had been trumped by Yeltsin. Yeltsin added a second question to the ballot asking voters of the Russian Republic if they wanted direct elections for a Russian president. They voted overwhelmingly for a June election. Until now, Yeltsin had been the Russian leader, but only because he had been elected chairman of the republican parliament, and then only by a narrow margin. But Yeltsin knew two things: first, that he would run and win; second, that such a victory would force Gorbachev, who had never been elected to anything by the people, to deal more seriously with the opposition.

But for now, as president of the country and general secretary of the Party, Gorbachev still thought his power was with the Party, the KGB, and the military. He listened to them almost unquestioningly, even to their wildest deceptions. Shevardnadze, whose instincts and judgments had proved uncanny since the day of his resignation speech, saw in his friend Gorbachev a man who was a prisoner "of his own nature, his conceptions, and his way of thinking and acting." All through 1991, Shevardnadze wrote in his memoir, it was "none other than Gorbachev himself [who] had been spoon-feeding the junta with his indecisiveness, his inclination to back and fill, his fellow-traveling, his poor judgment of people, his indifference toward his true allies, his distrust of the democratic forces, and his disbelief in the bulwark whose name is the people—the very same people who had changed thanks to the perestroika he had begun. That is the enormous tragedy of Mikhail Gorbachev, and no matter how much I empathize with him, I cannot help but say that it almost led to a national tragedy."

Yakovlev told me that Gorbachev believed the chiefs of the KGB and the Interior Ministry police when they informed him that the reformers were actually planning to storm the Kremlin walls using "hooks and ladders." To tighten the screw, *Pravda*'s deputy editor, Anatoly Karpychev, repeated the same rumors in print, writing that the radicals were making "preparations for the final storming of the Kremlin." Yakovlev exploded, telling Gorbachev that these so-called intelligence reports were sheer nonsense and that he was making a fatal error in listening to all the sycophants and double-dealers around him. But Gorbachev was sure he knew better.

"You exaggerate," he told Yakovlev.

Against Yakovlev's advice, Gorbachev ordered a ban on demonstrations in Moscow from March 26 to April 15 and gave Boris Pugo's Interior

Ministry control of the Moscow police force, taking it out of the hands of the liberals who ran city hall. Gorbachev authorized all law enforcement bodies to "use all necessary measures to ensure appropriate public order in the capital."

The battle had reached a point of no return. Yeltsin called a demonstration for March 28. In his own legislature, he was facing a vote of no confidence from the orthodox Communist deputies. In February, Yeltsin had gone on television blaming Gorbachev for driving the country "to the edge of the abyss" and for flirting with military dictatorship. Gorbachev, he said, had to step down and power must be transferred to the collective rule of the republican leaders.

By March 27, the center of Moscow looked like an armed camp. Like the czars who once kept a cavalry unit stabled near Red Square in case of an uprising by university students, the Soviet police meant to deny the center of the capital to the pro-democracy demonstrators. More than fifty thousand Interior Ministry troops positioned water cannons and tear-gas launchers along the streets. Row after row of empty buses and troops cut off all access roads to Manezh Square outside the Kremlin.

The hard-line press and Tass ran ominous warnings, including the threat to use "all means at our disposal" from the KGB chief of Moscow, Vitaly Prilukov. Democratic Russia's leaders realized that they would never get to the Manezh, where they had held so many rallies before, but they did not call off the demonstration. Instead, they said, people should gather at two alternative spots: the Arbat metro station and Mayakovsky Square near the Tchaikovsky Concert Hall.

On the morning of the 28th, I walked with my friends Masha and Seriozha to the statue of Mayakovsky. We were more than an hour early, and while we waited to meet some other friends, we saw people selling pro-Yeltsin and anti-Gorbachev buttons; others listened to the new pro-opposition radio station, Echo of Moscow, which was describing the troop positions along Gorky Street and all around the Manezh. Like the Chinese demonstrators at Tiananmen Square in 1989, the demonstrators were going out of their way to seem casual, as if pretending that the worst could never happen. A bunch of teenagers were taking the afternoon as a *tusovka,* a hangout, and they were listening to a tape of *Exile on Main Street* on their boom box. For once, Mick Jagger's voice of threat seemed like more than puffed-up theater. As more and more people crowded onto the square, I was getting jumpy. What would prevent these generals from picking a fight? They had made a mess of their coup in Vilnius, it was true, but the KGB still had the means to provoke a conflict, to make it seem as if the demonstrators were out of control, and then "restore order." It hadn't been many weeks before that I was talking to

General Boris Gromov, the last Soviet commander in Afghanistan and now Pugo's deputy, and he was telling me that one "can stand back and be polite for only so long. But sooner or later, you have to take action." Not long before that I interviewed fifteen generals and admirals at the Congress of People's Deputies one afternoon, and all fifteen said they thought Viktor Alksnis, the "black colonel," had the right idea.

The demonstration began. The usual speakers—Afanasyev, Popov—spoke. There were the usual banners—"CPSU to the Ash Heap of History!"—and the usual chants. We marched a little this way, a little that way, but mostly we stood still. The simple fact that so many people had ignored the threat of violence was demonstration enough. We heard from other marchers, and even from an American senator who happened to be there, David Boren of Oklahoma, that plainclothes police, probably KGB, had punched and beaten a few demonstrators who had ventured too close to the armed cordon near the Manezh. But the incidents were few. The demonstration turned out to be boring, blissfully boring.

On the face of it, the day had been a political draw. The soldiers held their ground and the demonstrators marched in defiance of Gorbachev's order and avoided any serious provocations. But in this case, victory belonged to the opposition. The whole stew of opposition forces—urban intellectuals, teenagers, pro-independence people from the republics—proved that they were willing to face down a threat with their bodies as well as their slogans. As we walked home, my friends and I noticed that the crowd was full of itself. They were celebrating a great victory. If the attack on the Lithuanian television tower was the rehearsal for a coup, the protection of the Lithuanian parliament and now this demonstration were rehearsals for the resistance. The resistance looked far more impressive. How could the KGB ignore that? What's more, how could Gorbachev?

MAGADAN

For the first time in their thousand-year history, Russians were about to elect a president. In those last days of the old regime, in the last few days of the June 1991 campaign, I went to the farthest shore of the empire, to Magadan, where Stalin's slave ships docked and the labor camps of Kolyma began. I had never seen a city so desolate. In the days of the Great Purge and for years after, prisoners called the rest of the country the "mainland," as if Magadan and the wastes of Kolyma beyond were an island in the sea of nowhere. Even now it seemed to me a ghostly place, a landscape of the dead. Mornings, the water was the color of iron, the sky the color of milk. The black-green hills were shrouded in a dense mist and long wisps of smoke trailed into the sky from the tin-shack slums known as Shanghai. Even in the center of town, the loudest sound was from the desultory passing of beat-up cars, Ladas, Volgas, and Zhigulis, their tires smearing the slush.

I was also here to visit my friend Arnold Yeryomenko. We'd first met in Moscow during the Nineteenth Party Conference in 1988, and we saw each other whenever he returned to the capital. I sent a telegram to Arnold telling him I was on the way, but I knew he'd never get it. He was still a marked man in his hometown. The Party press in Magadan wrote denunciations of him as if he held it in his power to topple the regime and steal all its daughters. He was still the anti-Soviet devil.

After the nine-hour flight, I walked to Arnold's building and stuck a note under the door telling him where he could find me. The building was appalling. The concrete looked wet and ancient all at once and the yard outside was a sea of mud and abandoned construction junk. Kids had nothing at all to play with. They threw rocks against a wall, and when they tired they just sat down on a thick stick stretched across a sheet of abandoned concrete.

The next morning, Arnold found me at the Hotel Magadan. We took a long walk to the sea, and then headed back up the hill, the same path the prisoners took fifty years ago. "You see where that ship is now?" he said, pointing down a hill into the port. That was where the lines of prisoners began their march from the sea to the holding camps. Many of them would be marched hundreds of miles to camps throughout Kolyma. Arnold said, "Our house was fifty meters from a labor camp—now it's a movie theater. I could see them from my room, from the kitchen. None of it was ever out of my sight, and it went on from the time I was a baby until I was a young man. And I remember every day in school we ran to the windows and watched the prisoners go by in their chains: the Russians, later the Japanese POWs and the Vlasovites. I remember we'd come up to them and one might say, 'Boy, go get me some fish.' And he'd slip us a few rubles to buy it. But everyone knew they'd soon be dead. Getting them fish: it was like some horrible joke."

Magadan really was the history of the Soviet Union, its proper spiritual capital. Magadan and the vast territory of Kolyma had been all but wild, unsettled before the Revolution. Magadan was an invention of the Kremlin and the NKVD, an administrative center for mass murder throughout the Kolyma region in eastern Siberia. As a project of centralized planning, Magadan fulfilled and overfulfilled its five-year plans. In the one hundred camps of Kolyma, an area six times the size of France, around three million people were slaughtered between 1936 and 1953. They were shot, stabbed, beheaded, thrown into pits, or starved. Three million in just one corner of a country that was itself a vast network of concentration camps. There was no way to shove it out of the mind; in Magadan, the dead were everywhere, in the abandoned mine shafts, under the taiga, under the seabed. One of the roads to the northern camps was built on a bed of bones. The main street, Lenin Prospekt, was a road to oblivion. Starting from the center of downtown, the prisoners walked to their camps, sometimes to an outpost a thousand miles away. You could walk all the way to Yakutia, where the reindeer run. And now nearly all the living in Magadan slept in the houses of the dead. Eighty percent of the standing structures in Magadan were once barracks or headquarters for the secret police administration or "shooting halls."

Varlam Shalamov was the poet of Kolyma. He survived seventeen years in a camp there, all for the crime of declaring Ivan Bunin, who had won the Nobel Prize, a "classic author." Shalamov's own classic stories, quick narratives, sharp and glinting as mica, so pierced Solzhenitsyn that the younger man invited Shalamov to help him with the massive project of *The Gulag Archipelago*. Shalamov was too old and sick. He declined. But the work he did leave behind provided the clearest picture of the Kolyma nightmare that exists. In one story, he described the officer Postnikov, who made a blood sport of hunting down escapees:

"Drunk with murder, he fulfilled his task with zeal and passion. He had personally captured five men. As always in such cases he had been decorated and received a bonus. The reward was the same for the dead and the living. It was not necessary to deliver the prisoners complete. One August morning a man who was going to drink at a stream fell into an ambush set by Postnikov and his soldiers. Postnikov shot him down with a revolver. They decided not to drag the body to the camp but to leave it in the taiga. The signs of bears and wolves were numerous.

"For identification, Postnikov cut off the fugitive's hands with an ax. He put the hands in his knapsack and went to make his report on the hunt. . . . In the night the corpse got up. Pressing his bleeding wrists to his chest, he left the taiga following the trail and reached the prisoners' tent. With pale face and blue eyes, he looked inside, holding himself at the opening, leaning against the doorposts and muttering something. Fever devoured him. His padded coat, his trousers, his rubber boots were stained with black blood. They gave him warm soup, wrapped his chopped-off wrists in rags, and took him to the infirmary. But already Postnikov and his men came running out of their little hut. The soldiers took the prisoner. He was not heard of again."

As late as 1988, the Communist Party allowed no monument to the dead of Kolyma. In fact, the Party chief, Aleksandr Bogdanov, did unveil one monument in 1988: a bust of Reingold Berzin, the founding director of the Far Northern Construction Trust and the concentration camps of Kolyma.

Berzin himself was purged after Stalin's Central Committee decreed in 1937 that prisoners could no longer be "coddled."

But by June 1991, times had changed. For one thing, foreigners were allowed to visit, and I saw Russians on the streets wearing their old plastic overcoats and the new trucker caps that the exchanges across the water had brought: "Alaska Airways," "I Love Anchorage." There was a video store renting *Terminator* and a complete line of Bruce Lee movies. I saw one man wandering in an empty butcher shop wearing the official jacket of the Seattle Seahawks.

Perhaps most alien of all, this Russian city, this museum of brutality, was taking part in a presidential election. On the streets, there was something otherworldly about standing near a building that was once a camp barracks and listening to sidewalk political arguments that in spirit, if not content, sounded like primary-year debates on the street corners of Nashua or Sioux City. It did not take a computer poll to figure out where the votes were. Boris Yeltsin was going to win, and, more important, the Communist Party was doomed. Outside a shoe store, people milled around in the cold and debated the election. A few young men in leather jackets and scarves handed out Yeltsin leaflets printed by the Democratic Russia group in Moscow. Another kid held up the red, white, and blue tricolor, the flag of czarist Russia. "The point is to get rid of the Communists in Russia, once and for all," Tamara Karpova, a housewife who was with the Yeltsin group, told me. "My parents and grandparents lived in the Ukraine until the Communists sent them here to the camps," Karpova said. "Why should I vote for anyone in the Communist Party?"

Bogdanov had been replaced as head of the Magadan Party organization, but his successors were no smarter. Their only cause was survival. They printed one article after another in their newspapers describing Yeltsin as a "wrecker" and his Communist Party rival in the race, Nikolai Ryzhkov, as the voice of "unity" and "justice, honesty and order." Ryzhkov was the man to help the Party men keep their jobs. Without Ryzhkov, they would lose their offices with the baize tables and red runner carpets at Party headquarters. Without Ryzhkov, they would lose their dachas in "Snow Valley" outside of town. Yeltsin represented a new order and, most likely for them, unemployment.

In totalitarian society, habit replaces happiness, and habits were in jeopardy. "My father was a Party member, my husband is a Party member, and that is how I will vote. The rest are all adventurists," said Svetlana Murashkina, a woman who passed out Ryzhkov leaflets on the same street corner.

In the village of Palatka, I spoke to Boris Sulim, who had worked in one of the camps when he was a teenager and was now serving on the local *raikom,* the Party committee. Sulim was a sawed-off shotgun of man with a broad, meaty face. He was a Ryzhkov man—"fast and firm." But the longer we talked, the sadder he got. He seemed exhausted, uncertain. All he had believed in, all he had worked for, was finished, and he knew it. His local Party committee, which had always ruled Palatka, had no influence now, "and I guess I know that."

Under Stalin, Sulim worked in the Omsuchkan camp, about four hundred miles from Magadan. "I was eighteen years old and Magadan seemed a very romantic place to me. I got eight hundred eighty rubles a month and a three-thousand-ruble installation grant, which was a hell of a lot of money for a kid like me. I was able to give my mother some of it. They even gave me membership in the Komsomol. There was a mining and ore-processing plant which sent out parties to dig for tin. I worked at the radio station which kept contact with the parties.

"If the inmates were good and disciplined they had almost the same rights as the free workers. They were trusted and they even went to the movies. As for the reason they were in the camps, well, I never poked my nose into details. We all thought the people were there because they were guilty. Why should I have believed anything else? In 1936, when I was still in the first grade, our teacher made us blot out the pictures in history books of the generals Tukhachevsky, Blucher, and Yegorov, and we had to cover them over with swastikas and write in the margin, 'enemy of the people.' "

Sulim said that after watching a few television documentaries on the Stalin era he would admit there had been "mistakes" and "abuses." I asked him if he had ever seen any of the prisoners executed or any of them die from the cold and the endless work in the mines. "Deaths?" he said. "I don't know. I wasn't interested then. But I think death is a natural phenomenon under any circumstances. Look, I was not part of the gulag system, so I have no intention of repenting."

MOSCOW

Sulim was a man of the old regime: ignorant, angry, unrepentant. But even in his worst moments, Gorbachev held firm to his better self, his ability to change, if only to survive. On April 23, with Yeltsin clearly headed for victory and his own percentage in the popularity polls nearing single digits, Gorbachev had yielded to the obvious. Despite the bad information he was getting, despite the betrayals around him and his own tragic vanity, even he could look out the window and see. He could see that the people were no longer his. They were Yeltsin's, and Landsbergis's, and Nazarbayev's in Kazakhstan

. . . but not his. And so Gorbachev moved once more to the left. He did not announce a favorite candidate—many people assumed he would vote not for Yeltsin or Ryzhkov, but for Vadim Bakatin, the former interior minister—but he did sign a "nine plus one" agreement. The document, drafted jointly by Gorbachev and the republican leaders, was an agreement to agree: republican leaders (so far, the Baltic states, Georgia, Armenia, and Moldavia declined to participate) were announcing their intention to form a new Union Treaty, under which the republics would acquire vastly more political power.

In June, Yeltsin won the election, as Gorbachev and everyone else knew he would. For his inauguration at the Kremlin's Palace of Congresses, Yeltsin planned a ceremony, both moving and pompous, clearly intended to distance the new office from Soviet history and align it with a kind of liberal Russian nationalism. He stripped away all signs of the Bolshevik state in the Kremlin hall. In place of the massive picture of Lenin that had always been the backdrop for ceremonies of state, there was simply a red, blue, and white Russian flag. Priests, rabbis, muftis, and ministers sat in the front row. Patriarch Alexy II, with his flowing robes and Tolstoyan beard, blessed Yeltsin with the sign of the cross and said, "By the will of God and the choice of the Russian people, you are bestowed with the highest office in Russia. . . . We will pray for you." Russia, the patriarch said, "is gravely ill." An actor from Leningrad, Oleg Basilashvili, read a long speech describing the degradation of the country through seventy years of Bolshevik rule.

Introduced by regal trumpeters and a blaring fanfare, Yeltsin swore himself in. At times he seemed overwhelmed by the occasion, and his voice broke once or twice with nervousness. He did not begin with the traditional *tovarishchi,* "comrades." "Citizens of the Russian Federation . . . Great Russia is rising from its knees . . ." he began. "The president is not a god, not a monarch, not a miracle worker. He is a citizen . . . and in Russia, the individual will become the measure of all things."

Gorbachev, for his part, tried to appear gracious at the ceremony, but he did not quite bring it off. He made a clumsy speech and even clumsier attempts at humor about the strangeness of a country with two presidents. At one point he said, "People on all continents are watching with great interest what you and I are doing." The intonation was such that people in the hall understood it to mean that the two men were up to some sort of shenanigans. The hall fairly buzzed with discontent until Gorbachev moved on.

But even as he was trying to assert his power, Yeltsin was hoping that his presidency would help Gorbachev realize that there could be no future in an alliance with Kryuchkov, Yazov, Pugo, and the old guard. He needed to seduce and bully Gorbachev at the same time. And so when Gorbachev was finished with his speech, Boris Yeltsin was the first out of his seat to lead a standing ovation.

But in 1991, nothing was stable. You couldn't relax for a moment, you could never think for an instant that all would be well. As Sobchak had said, the side-by-side existence of a totalitarian regime (no matter how subdued compared to the Stalin era) and a fledgling democracy was impossible. Something would have to give.

In June, there were clues once more that the hard-liners were prepared to act, no matter what sort of marriage—of convenience or conviction—existed between Gorbachev and Yeltsin. The Soviet Prosecutor's Office, backed up by a report by Marshal Yazov, said, "In the course of the examination of the events [in Novocherkassk in 1962], it was established that arms were used by the military in accordance with the law, in order to defend state property from criminal attack and for purposes of self-defense. . . . The shooting started only after the unruly crowd attacked the soldiers and tried to seize their weapons." To most Soviet readers, the report was a justification not only of an event thirty years past, but of the assaults in Tbilisi, Vilnius, and Baku. And perhaps they were a threat, too; a threat of more violence to come.

Yeltsin answered that veiled threat with a veiled warning. He sent a representative to Novocherkassk with a message from the Russian president: "The truth about the tragedy of Novocherkassk is a stern warning to anyone who tries to resolve social problems by means of military force." Like General Shaposhnikov, the people would resist.

Two weeks later, on June 17, the Soviet prime minister, Valentin Pavlov, went before the parliament and asked to be given many of Gorbachev's powers. Pavlov, who clearly had the backing of Supreme Soviet Chairman Anatoly Lukyanov, said he was making the proposal out of consideration for Gorbachev's onerous schedule. "There are just not enough hours in the day," Pavlov suggested sweetly. What he forgot to say was that he was acting without Gorbachev's knowledge.

"I heard about it and told Gorbachev," Aleksandr Yakovlev told me. "Gorbachev was outraged. It was the first he had heard about it." But before Gorbachev had a chance to act, Pugo, Yazov, and Kryuchkov all went before a closed session of the Supreme Soviet and read out speeches accusing the leadership (they would not say "Gorbachev") of selling out the Party and leading the country to ruin. Yazov complained that hundreds of thousands of young men were refusing to obey their draft notices. Pugo railed on about "disorder" and "lawlessness." Kryuchkov was most vicious of all, saying that the reforms of the leadership and the fondest wishes of the CIA seemed to coincide. He was charging treason. That gave the delegates from the Soyuz faction the cue to rise from their chairs and call for resignation.

"Away with Gorbachev! And away with his clique of liberals!" cried Leonid Sukhov, a cabdriver from Kharkov and a deputy in the Soyuz faction.

"A great power has been reduced to the lowly status of a beggar standing by others' doors with outstretched hands instead of working out its problems here where its problems are," charged Yevgeny Kogan, a Russian speaker from Estonia and another member of Soyuz.

Gorbachev was slow to react, but when he finally came to the Supreme Soviet to respond on June 21, he was able to summon for the occasion one of his vintage performances, full of indignation. Still he could not go all the way. Just as he would never admit to any conflict with Yegor Ligachev in 1988, he said he had no differences with Pavlov. The prime minister's proposals, he said, were "not well thought out."

When the session was over, Gorbachev came out of the chamber to meet the press. He was surrounded by none other than Messrs. Yazov, Pugo, and Kryuchkov. The three ministers were stone-faced and silent. "The coup is over," Gorbachev said. He was laughing. He meant it as a joke. And it was.

PART IV

"FIRST AS TRAGEDY, THEN AS FARCE"

Evil has great momentum, but the forces of good are inert. The masses . . . have no fight in them, and will acquiesce in whatever happens.

—Nadezhda Mandelstam, *1970*

Boris Yeltsin was twelve when he had his first run-in with the Communist Party. He'd had a mean childhood. His father was a construction worker who beat him with a belt. The family lived in a hut near a building site in the Urals, and the six of them, and their goat, lived in one room. Everyone slept on the floor. Once, when Yeltsin was six, he woke in the middle of the night to see his father being led out of the hut by strange men. The family was lucky that the arrest did not lead to a long jail term or the camps.

As a boy, Yeltsin was a good student and a troublemaker. "I've always been a bit of a hooligan," he told me. In the fifth grade, he encouraged the entire class to jump out the first-floor window while the teacher was out of the room. He took part in gang fights and got his nose broken when one of his friends took a swing at him with a club. When he was eleven and the war was on, Yeltsin and a few of his friends broke into an arms depot in a local church. They climbed through three layers of barbed wire and stole a couple of hand grenades: "We just wanted to see what they were made of." Yeltsin, of course, decided that he would take charge. Without removing the fuses, he tried to open the grenades with a hammer. The explosion mangled the thumb and forefinger on his left hand, and when gangrene set in, the fingers had to be removed. "Wouldn't you say that was brilliant?"

Yeltsin's troubles with the Communist Party began at his graduation ceremonies from primary school. As one of the best students in the school, he had the honor of being allowed to sit on the stage. When it came his turn to give a short speech, Yeltsin grabbed the microphone and turned his ceremonial moment into an outrageous harangue. He launched into an attack on a certain homeroom teacher, a hated shrew who cursed the children, smacked them with a thick ruler, and made them clean her house. "She was a horror and I had to say what I had to say," Yeltsin said. The parents and the staff in the audience listened for a while in shock. The principal finally jumped out of his chair and snatched away the microphone and sent Yeltsin back to his seat. The day was ruined. And what was more, instead of a diploma, Yeltsin received a "wolf's ticket," a certificate forbidding him from getting a high school education. At home, Yeltsin's father came at him with the strap. It was the usual punishment. But this time, Yeltsin grabbed his old man's arm and fended him off. No more, he said, and then went looking for retribution at the local headquarters of the Communist Party. For weeks, Yeltsin heard nothing from the local bureaucrats but rebuke. Finally, he got one official to listen to his complaints against the teacher, how she had humiliated her students. A board of inquiry was established. The teacher was fired and Yeltsin was reinstated as a student in good standing. He had won his first battle inside the "horror house" of the Soviet system.

By the middle of 1991, Yeltsin was hoping to transform himself from an executioner of the sacred cow, a political figure who made his name by attacking Ligachev, the Party, Gorbachev and all the rest, into a statesman of the "new Russia." As Russia's first elected president, he hoped to rebuild the bridge to Gorbachev and move into a new era in which the sovereignty of the republics would allow for greater wealth and liberty. Yeltsin knew that real power still lay elsewhere: with the army, the KGB, the police. He, like Gorbachev, had heard rumors of a coup, and while the two men negotiated a new Treaty of the Union that would give far greater powers to the republics, Yeltsin warned Gorbachev that he was surrounded by reactionaries who could eventually betray him. Yeltsin had seen what had happened in Lithuania in January and then in the Supreme Soviet when Pavlov and his sponsors made their grab for power. He had no reason to expect that these men would go quietly.

———

It must have been the first coup d'état in world history to have been announced in advance, and in the national press.

The first to plow the rhetorical earth were the military ideologists, the men of the lunatic fringe who saw the army as the sainted institution of the Russian empire, the bulwark of a great world power. With Defense Minister Dmitri Yazov's blessing, Major General Viktor Filatov edited the monthly *Military-Historical Journal,* which featured excerpts from *Mein Kampf,* attacks on Sakharov, and, most prominently of all, the collected works of Karem Rush, a full-throated booster of the Soviet imperial idea. "The military," Rush wrote, "should consider itself the backbone and sacred institution of a thousand years of statehood." By publishing such stuff, Filatov boosted circulation from 27,000 in 1988 to 377,000 in 1990. He was a lovely man, Filatov was. He published the famous anti-Semitic forgery *The Protocols of the Elders of Zion,* and told *The New York Times* that he regarded the document "as a normal piece of literature, like the Bible or the Koran." He was an ardent supporter of Saddam Hussein and wrote pro-Iraqi propaganda during the Gulf War. Perhaps his favorite target was the liberal press. Once, Filatov wrote, "It's a pity we have no Beria now; if he had read today's *Ogonyok,* he would have shot half [the staff] and sent the remaining rubbish to rot in a camp." *Nash Sovremenik,* another journal of the nationalist right wing, seconded that emotion, declaring the army "not only has the right, but also the duty, to become extremely involved in internal affairs."

For a long time, the country's most important reactionaries, ministers like Yazov, Kryuchkov, and Pugo, hid behind figures like Filatov, Rush, and the editors of *Nash Sovremenik.* They did not risk the appearance of outright treason. But, eventually, such niceties faded. On May 9, 1991, Aleksandr Prokhanov's paper, *Dyen* ("The Day"), published a roundtable discussion with some of the most hard-line figures in the military: Valentin Varennikov, the general in charge of all ground forces and the leader of the charge on Vilnius; Igor Rodionov, the general most responsible for the 1989 massacre in Tbilisi; and Oleg Baklanov, the head of the country's military-industrial complex. Only the naive could have read what these men had to say and not come to the conclusion that they wanted nothing less than a coup d'état. Baklanov spoke with touching modesty about the military's ability to rule the country. But rule they could, and would: "The defense industry has much greater organizational experience than, say, the newly appointed politicians who are incapable even of ensuring garbage collection on the streets of Moscow."

———

If Gorbachev needed greater proof that the rhetoric of the hard-liners matched their real intentions, he got it at the end of June.

On June 20, the foreign ministers of the United States and the Soviet Union were holding talks in Berlin in preparation for a Bush-Gorbachev summit a month later in Moscow. Secretary of State James Baker and Foreign Minister Aleksandr Bessmertnykh had already spent a long day with each other in meetings on a wide range of issues. But when Bessmertnykh returned to his embassy in the late afternoon, Baker was on the phone saying they had to meet again.

"Jim, what's the matter? What's happened?" said Bessmertnykh, who spoke English fluently.

"It's something very urgent," Baker said. "I'd like to meet you very much."

Bessmertnykh said that he had a meeting. Couldn't it wait?

Baker tried to find the words to convey the gravity of the matter and yet not give away any detail on a phone line that was probably not secure.

"It's a somewhat delicate matter," he said. "If I go, a lot of cars will follow with guards, and there will be a lot of commotion in town. The press will be on to us. If you can, I'll wait for you at the hotel room where I'm staying, but please let everything be quiet!"

"Is it really that urgent?" Bessmertnykh said. "I have a scheduled meeting."

"If I were you, I would, perhaps, put off all my affairs and come over."

In an unmarked car, Bessmertnykh rode cross town to Baker. He brought with him one of his policy advisers, a specialist from the USA-Canada Institute, but Baker said he would prefer to meet alone with Bessmertnykh.

When they were alone, Baker said, "I've just received a report from Washington. I understand it may come from intelligence sources. It seems that there may be an attempt to depose Gorbachev. It's a highly delicate matter and we need to convey this information somehow. According to our information, Pavlov, Yazov, and Kryuchkov will take part in the ouster. . . . It's urgent. It must be brought to Gorbachev's attention."

The initial report had come from Moscow's Mayor, Gavriil Popov, who told the American ambassador in Moscow, Jack Matlock, that the KGB and the military were preparing a coup.

Baker asked if it was possible to call Gorbachev on a direct line from the Soviet embassy in Berlin. Bessmertnykh said that such lines were under KGB control and, therefore, useless. Baker suggested instead that they set up a direct, private meeting between Gorbachev and the American ambassador in Moscow, Jack Matlock. Bessmertnykh agreed.

On June 22, Gorbachev, Kryuchkov, Yazov, and the rest of the Soviet leadership took part in an annual ceremony in Moscow—laying a wreath at the Tomb of the Unknown Soldier outside the Kremlin gates. In retrospect, it was a tableau out of a Shakespearean tragedy: the monarch surrounded by his men, his deferential advisers, his betrayers.

After the ceremony, Gorbachev held a short private meeting with Bessmertnykh.

How had the session gone with the American ambassador? the minister asked.

It had gone well, Gorbachev said. Once he had the information, he said, he had had a "tough talk" with those concerned. And that was all.

———

In a document dated June 20, 1991, the same day as Baker's secret meeting with Bessmertnykh, the KGB quoted a source in Gorbachev's "inner circle" coolly analyzing how to push Gorbachev out of power or, at least, into an increasingly conservative position. The document, uncovered later by the Russian prosecutors, said that the Bush administration held Yeltsin in disdain and considered the possibility of his ascension to supreme power as "catastrophic" for U.S.-Soviet relations. It also said that the Bush circle was beginning to wonder if Lukyanov was positioning himself as a successor to Gorbachev. The document said that the "most logical and sensible" course would be to force Gorbachev to abandon a radical course in the same way he was "persuaded" to abandon the 500 Days program. The source of the analysis was not named.

———

It was a season of deception. Little by little, the conspirators were undermining the authority of the president. The attempt to grab Gorbachev's powers in parliament in June had failed, but they were still chipping away, humiliating the president in a hundred different ways.

Despite promises to the contrary, the military carried out nuclear tests in Semipalatinsk and Novaya Zemlya without consent of the republics or national authorities. The Ministry of Defense and the general staff came close to scotching the Conventional Forces in Europe treaty that they despised so much by playing games with the rules on the counting of weapons. While Gorbachev was in Oslo to collect the Nobel Prize in June, the General Prosecutor's Office released a report exonerating troops involved in the Vilnius violence; on the same day, troops in Lithuania set up fifteen checkpoints and made two arrests. All this assured that Gorbachev would have to answer some embarrassing questions at what would have otherwise been a triumphant press conference. While Gorbachev was trying to get himself invited to the summit of industrialized nations in London, the commander of Soviet forces in East Germany sent a letter to the German Foreign Ministry threatening to slow down troop withdrawals if Bonn did not move faster to build apartments in the Soviet Union for the returning soldiers.

With every new incident, the leading officials denied any political meaning, and each time they tugged a little on the trigger.

It was easy to look away. Despite all the ominous signals to the contrary, most of the talk in Moscow in the early summer of 1991 was reasonably optimistic. Gorbachev seemed to have shifted course once more, this time making his peace with Yeltsin and the other republican leaders. Negotiations on the Treaty of the Union appeared to be moving along without the usual disasters.

But three days after Yeltsin issued a decree barring Party cells in government institutions, and just one week before George Bush landed in town for a summit with Gorbachev, the leading paper of the reactionaries, *Sovetskaya Rossiya,* published a stunning appeal called "A Word to the People." Signed by leading right-wing generals, politicians, and writers, the appeal, dated July 23, declared that Russia was in the midst of an "unprecedented tragedy":

"Our Motherland, this country, this great state which history, Nature, and our predecessors willed us to save, is dying, breaking apart and plunging into darkness and nothingness. . . . What has become of us, brothers?" The language was apocalyptic, the imagery of a ship of state "sinking into nonexistence," evil forces selling out a great power. "Our home is already burning to the ground . . . the bones of the people are being ground up and the backbone of Russia is snapped in two." It even condemned the Communist Party for giving power to "frivolous and clumsy parliamentarians who have set us against each other and brought into force thousands of stillborn laws, of which only those function that enslave the people and divide the tormented body of the country into portions. . . . How is it that we have let people come to power who do not love their country, who kowtow to foreign patrons and seek advice and blessings abroad?"

The key signatories were General Boris Gromov, the last Soviet commander in Afghanistan and now Pugo's deputy in the Interior Ministry; General Varennikov, again; Vasily Starodubtsev, the head of the conservative agricultural lobby; and Aleksandr Tizyakov, the head of an association of military plants. For months, Tizyakov had been carrying around documents in his briefcase outlining the shape a military coup could take. But the main author of the appeal was Aleksandr Prokhanov, the editor and novelist whose ode to Soviet empire in *A Tree in the Center of Kabul* led him to adopt the sobriquet "the Soviet Kipling." He waited for the coup as if it were Christmas. "Get ready for the next wave, my friend," he once told me. "Get ready." Prokhanov, with likely help from two other writers and signatories, Yuri Bondarev and Valentin Rasputin, managed to capture the tone of apocalypse in every reactionary's heart. As the critic Natalya Ivanova pointed out in a stunning essay in the monthly journal *Znamya,* the July 23 appeal, with its vulgar nationalism and self-pity, matched almost perfectly the language of the doomsday declarations issued on the first morning of the August coup. The conspirators envisioned a new vanguard, not of Communists, but of soldiers, priests, workers, peasants, and, of course, writers. "I also can't help but be reminded," she wrote, "that on the eve of the coup, the military state publishing house issued in the millions a brochure called 'The Black Hundreds and the Red Hundreds' which laid out in detail the program of the national party in 1906." The nationalists of 1906, like the putschists of 1991, wanted to dissolve parliament, declare military, emergency rule, and ban all left-wing newspapers and journals. "A Word to the People" was a blatant call for a coup d'état.

"We were making no secret of what we wanted," Prokhanov told me. "Why keep secrets? We live in a democracy, don't we?"

———

Even if Gorbachev was not paying much attention to the smell of a storm, Yeltsin was. On July 29, Yeltsin went out to Gorbachev's dacha to finish negotiations for a new Treaty of the Union. Gorbachev had already agreed to language that would give the republics far more power and make it possible for the Baltic states to become independent very quickly. Yeltsin wanted more. He wanted the power of the purse, and he made it his goal at this meeting to convince Gorbachev that the republics, and not Moscow, should have the ability to levy taxes and distribute the funds as they saw fit.

The talks went on for hours. Yeltsin, Gorbachev, and the Kazakh president, Nursultan Nazarbayev, went back and forth over the taxation issue so long that they had to break for dinner and then come back at it.

At one point, the two republican leaders could not hold back. Yeltsin told Gorbachev that the right-wingers in the Union leadership were doing everything they could to undercut a transition to genuine democracy and a market economy. Kryuchkov and Yazov were clearly against the Treaty of the Union, he said. Nazarbayev agreed with Yeltsin, and added two more names to the list of "resisters": Prime Minister Valentin Pavlov, and Gorbachev's great friend of forty years, Supreme Soviet Chairman Anatoly Lukyanov.

These people realized that the treaty would rob them of power, Yeltsin said. In a Union led mainly by the republican leaders, Yazov and Kryuchkov must be fired and sixty or seventy Union ministries would have to be liquidated.

Gorbachev said, well, yes, of course. He was not blind, after all. "Everything will have to be reorganized, including the army and the KGB," he said. But let's wait until after the treaty is signed, he said. And, you know, he added, Lukyanov, Kryuchkov, and the rest are "not as bad as you think."

At this point, Yeltsin got out of his chair and stepped out onto the balcony.

Nazarbayev and Gorbachev were dumbfounded. What was Yeltsin looking for?

"To see if anyone is eavesdropping," he said.

Nazarbayev and Gorbachev laughed. What a card Yeltsin was. Imagine. Bugging the president and general secretary of the party. How absurd!

———

After all, how could a man like Anatoly Lukyanov, the chairman of the Supreme Soviet, betray a friend he had known since university days? The man was a lawyer, just like Gorbachev, an amateur poet, just like Andropov, and his friendship was a matter of immortal verse.

> Safeguard your conscience for your friends.
> A friend seeks neither gain nor flattery.
> A friend and conscience are as one
> In tempest, cold, and thunder,
> Safeguard your conscience for your friends!

"I love him," Lukyanov would say of Gorbachev. "I love him, I can't change him, though, speaking openly, I know his weaknesses, his shortcomings. . . . Of all the people who made perestroika, I alone stayed next to Gorbachev, the rest left, from the left and right. . . ."

But that was later, when Lukyanov was in jail charged with treason.

———

As Bush was arriving in the Soviet Union for the summit in the last few days of July, *Moscow News* had asked me to write a short article about the U.S. reaction to what was going on in the Soviet Union. I used the opportunity to say that as long as Gorbachev was surrounded by anti-Western reactionaries, there would be no end to Washington's caution about providing aid and investment. "It's a mystery to the West why Gorbachev's circle is still stocked with so many aides and professionals so seemingly at odds with reform," I wrote. "For every Aleksandr Yakovlev—a figure who has transformed his own vision of the world—there are, it seems, at least a dozen Pavlovs."

I was only repeating what I had heard a thousand times, but who was listening in the Kremlin? I went around with Michael Dobbs and a couple of visiting editors to see some of Gorbachev's closest advisers: the apparatchik-liberals like Andrei Grachev, Yevgeny Primakov, and Georgi Shakhnazarov. We asked about "A Word to the People" and other dark signs, and they explained them away. "Such is the atmosphere," Grachev said, but he didn't seem particularly worried, and neither did the others. In contrast, Yeltsin's top adviser, Gennadi Burbulis, told us that Moscow resembled a "political minefield."

"We tread through it very lightly," he said with a waxen smile.

And, as if to underscore his point and my own, some of Pugo's men slaughtered eight Lithuanian border police during the Bush visit. Pugo denied any knowledge of the incident. He just had no idea.

Gorbachev was humiliated. "It's hard to say what has happened," he told the press, with the American president sitting next to him.

In the meantime, Kryuchkov had tapped Gorbachev's phones and everyone with even the remotest access to the president—even Raisa Gorbacheva's hairdresser. The eavesdropping logs had Gorbachev as "110," Raisa as "111," and dozens of other codes. Kryuchkov could tolerate the president no longer. "Gorbachev is not reacting adequately to events," the KGB chief said repeatedly to his fellow conspirators.

———

Maybe it was the weather that confused everyone, the bright sun and cool wind that duped one into thinking that soon all was going to be just fine. Or maybe it was the news that Lazar Kaganovich, Stalin's last surviving lieutenant, had dropped dead.

For nearly four years I had been trying to meet Kaganovich, all to no avail. "I see no one," he said over the phone in a voice like worn leather. He had been duped once. A Soviet pensioner, pretending friendship, had come by to talk, and the old and lonely man had let him in, answered his questions. He never suspected his remarks would be published in *Sovetskaya Kultura.* In that conversation, Kaganovich made no apologies for his life, and described the reform of the Stalinist state in a tone of wan disgust. He thought it incredible that people could still blame Stalin for the rotten state of the country.

"Stalin died thirty-five years ago!" he said. And besides, how could they attack a man who "saved the country from fascism"?

Kaganovich complained about his health, his heart attacks, his sleepless nights. But one thing, he said, kept him going: "Socialism will be victorious. Of this I am sure." It was outrageous, he said, that we were letting Hungary and Poland and the rest "return to a bourgeois line." Here, in the Soviet Union, such a reversal was impossible.

"I believe in the strength of our party," Kaganovich said. "And socialism will be victorious. This is for sure."

———

Even in death, Lazar Moiseyevich managed to insult his country's dignity. In the 1930s, the secret police used to bring the bodies for cremation to the Donskoi Monastery. At the height of the purges, as many as one thousand victims were cremated there every day. And now Kaganovich, who oversaw much of this industry, was going to be cremated at Donskoi.

While I was off doing summit business, my friend Masha Lipman managed to sneak into Kaganovich's apartment and had a long talk with the old man's nurse. The poor women smelled as if she'd downed at least a bottle of vodka. The apartment was like the library of a ghost, shelves packed with dusty volumes of Communist Party proceedings from long ago.

At Donskoi, Kaganovich's mourners did not seem much interested in the man's victims. They crowded around a dilapidated bus as it pulled onto the grounds, the long, ribbon-covered coffin laid out in the rear end. Kaganovich's daughter, Maya, an old woman herself, led the relatives into the chapel. Before the eulogy, someone opened the coffin lid to reveal the face of Stalin's loyal henchman: black suit, flabby neck, long nose, a fine gray mustache, a huge and withered corpse. The mourners listened as they heard the brief eulogy lauding the great man's construction of the Moscow subway. No one mentioned that he had played a leading role in collectivization. When the eulogy was over, the coffin somehow sank below floor level and automatic doors closed over it. The furnace, I was told, was downstairs. Soon Kaganovich would be a handful of ash.

Outside, afterward, Kaganovich's nephew Leonid told me, "History is still being debated. But what is evil? You must understand the times he lived in." Besides the family, there were about a hundred Stalinists there to bury their last great hero. People were weeping. "He was a man who never changed his mind," said Kira Korniyenkova, one of the Stalinists in town I knew best. "He was a great Marxist-Leninist." Another mourner told me, through his tears, that this was a great man, but "if it were Gorbachev laid out dead here today, I wouldn't lay down a single flower, I can tell you that."

As we left the monastery, Masha and I saw Ales Adamovich. A few years before, Adamovich had been sued by the Stalinist lawyer Ivan Shekhovtsov for slander. It was Adamovich who had warned Gorbachev in the Congress of the generals who would one day commit bloodshed and wipe the evidence on his suit. He could not resist going to the funeral of Lazar Kaganovich. "Stalin and Hitler and Nero: I think Kaganovich fits into the list," he told me. "This represents the fall of Stalinism. So who will be next to die? The Communist Party itself?" I'd never met a man at a funeral in a better mood.

———

Maybe what made the men of the regime seem so vulnerable that summer was that they had long ago lost the Mystery.

The Mystery—the theological notion that the acts and purposes of the deity are unknowable—was always a critical part of the pseudo-theology of the atheist state. Stalin must have gotten the idea during his failed career in the seminary. One of the keys to his own mystery was to stay out of sight; hence, a pockmarked mediocrity becomes a god. For decades, the Thursday-morning meetings of the Politburo were more mysterious than sessions of the College of Cardinals; transfers of power were more difficult to decipher in the Kremlin than in the Vatican. The catechism language of *Vremya,* the iconic posters of the great leaders, all added to the Mystery. And now it was all but gone. Now we learned from the press the details of the Lenin Mausoleum; it turned out that there were other floors beneath the holy of holies, and on one of them there was the gymnasium for the guards and a bathroom and buffet for visiting luminaries; beneath that there was a "control room" which carefully monitored the temperature and deterioration of Vladimir Ilyich. Yeltsin's memoir, *Against the Grain,* became an underground best-seller precisely because it hacked away at the Mystery. He revealed what the mighty talked about in private, their petty greed, their weakness. He described for all Gorbachev's taste for luxury, his marble bathrooms and swimming pools.

One morning, *Komsomolskaya Pravda* ran a story about a woman who had worked for many years as a seamstress in the secret tailor shop the KGB maintained for the use of the country's highest leaders. Klava Lyubeshkina stitched suits for everyone, from the entombed corpse of Lenin ("every eighteen months the cloth begins to lose its original splendor") to Gorbachev. "The tailor dummies of the Politburo members were kept in special closets which nobody except us, the cutters and tailors, dared ever to touch," she told the paper. "We always worked behind closed doors and surrounded by armed guards. . . . Two or three times a year a KGB specialist would go abroad, usually to Scotland or Austria, to buy material for the suits."

The secret police had opened the shop in 1938, the height of the purges. Klava saw her customers only on *Vremya* and referred to them, mysteriously, as "units." She was devoted. She would watch the leaders on television expressly "to see if their suits fit them well or if there were wrinkles." She remembered how she worked night and day for three days to get ready the gold-embroidered laurel leaves and stars in heavy gold thread for the new defense minister, Marshal Ustinov. She remembered Andrei Gromyko's stinginess ("He always sent in for repairs, never a new suit") and Mikhail Suslov's temper tantrums when the fit was not quite right.

Klava's sense of the Mystery ended one day when three men in white smocks attacked her, twisted her arms behind her back, and dragged her off to a psychiatric clinic. The KGB had mistaken her for a dissident. Klava asked to be released, saying that she was making a suit for Yuri Andropov which had been left "unattended" at the studio. The agents let her use the phone and she was able to tell her colleagues where she was. Soon the KGB released her. For the "moral damage" committed, the state awarded Klava a Japanese watch. Just before she retired in 1987, she had the pleasure of making a suit for Gorbachev. The new Soviet leader rewarded her with a box of chocolates.

In her old age, Klava received a poverty-level pension of 100 rubles a month. She wrote the Kremlin for more but got nothing. The Bolsheviks, however, could not be counted as unfeeling men. In 1991, Kryuchkov mailed all the seamstresses cards wishing them well on International Women's Day. Klava, for her part, took her pleasure in revealing her trove of secrets from the Kremlin sweatshop to the twenty-five million readers of *Komsomolskaya Pravda*. "We worked there for so long in silence," she said, "and all along we wanted to reveal the mystery."

———

Most of the apparatchiks who still came to work at the Central Committee that summer were tired and old and deeply worried. They were hanging on, hoping to get another year on the gravy train. The smart ones had all become businessmen.

Arkady Volsky had been a loyal servant to the Party. He was an aide to Andropov, a captain of socialist industry, an adviser to Gorbachev. And he knew what was coming. So Volsky and some of his semiliberal and ultra-clever friends started to take a look around at the new world. They saw how the Young Communist League, once the incubator of rising ideologues, had become the Harvard Business School of the new culture, turning out entrepreneurs who moved quickly into everything from video-game concessions to computer sales to publishing. With access to government connections, extraordinary tax breaks, and hundreds of millions of rubles in Party funds, Komsomol leaders set up huge commercial banks that began to dominate the Soviet financial scene. Some of the older liberals in the Party were cashing in, too. Svyatoslav Fyodorov, an internationally known ophthalmologist and member of the Central Committee until 1990, set up a modern, independent clinic and made a fortune. When Prime Minister Pavlov visited Fyodorov's clinic and demanded 80 percent of the clinic's hard currency earnings, Fyodorov told him, "Fuck off."

"The political fight for power now is the fight for property," Fyodorov told *Komsomolskaya Pravda.* "If people get property, they will have power. If not, they will forever remain hired hands."

Volsky and an experienced factory manager named Aleksandr Vladislavlev started the Scientific Industrial Union. The idea was that they would act as fixers between potential foreign investors and the existing enterprises in the Soviet Union. As if to make sure that everyone understood the kind of connections he had within the Party and the world of Soviet industry, Volsky rented office space for 750,000 rubles a year in a building adjacent to the Central Committee. "We're here for the same reason a bank in New York wants to be on Fifth Avenue," Vladislavlev told me. It was brilliant. The union was the place to go for high-powered access. "We link our resources and cheap labor with your brains and technology," Vladislavlev said. "You come to us because we know where the best deals in privatization are." Thirty-nine Soviet industrial associations, such as the Association of Military Factories, paid 10,000 rubles annually to be members. Another two thousand individual enterprises paid a percentage of their profits as dues.

It was a sweet deal, and I wrote an article for the *Post* about the emerging class of Communists-turned-capitalists in the spring. When a couple of my editors came for the Bush summit, I had to find places for them to go, people for them to see. They mentioned they might like to see Arkady Volsky. Why not?

We arrived, three of us, at Volsky's office for what we thought would be an interview about the economy.

"Pleased to meet you," Volsky greeted one editor.

"Pleased to meet you," he said to the next.

And then to me, "Less pleased to meet you."

He glared and flared his nostrils like a bull. This was not going to be easy, I thought. I had no idea why.

For a few minutes, Volsky complained that my article had been unfair, that it made fun of a "normal" process of creating a market economy. But then his complaints took an ugly turn. Volsky noted that I had written that one of his main "konsooltants" was Rodimir Bogdanov, a well-known KGB officer. Through the late stagnation and early glasnost years, Bogdanov was one of the few people visiting foreigners could come to for an interview. What's more, Volsky pointed out, I had written that Seagram's chairman Edgar Bronfman and the real estate and publishing magnate Mortimer Zuckerman had met with Bogdanov and other people at the union in hopes of completing possible business deals.

"You are the worst kind of anti-Semite!" Volsky barked. Why had I besmirched the reputation of such a good man as Bogdanov, why had I mentioned two such obviously Jewish names as Bronfman and Zuckerman. "Don't you realize what people will do with this?"

I could not quite tell yet whether Volsky, in his fury, knew that I was Jewish. To be frank, a Malawi tribesman could take one look at me and say, "This man is a Jew." But Volsky was off on a flight.

"This is ridiculous," I said finally. "Don't you realize I'm no different from Zuckerman or Bronfman? Just poorer. Where do you get off lecturing me on anti-Semitism?"

I did not understand what it was all about until Volsky finally said, "Don't you realize what those people up the hill can do with this?"

"Up the hill" from us was Lubyanka, the headquarters of the KGB.

———

Volsky, for all his financial cleverness, for all his guile and connections to the military industrialists, was one of the moderates in the upper echelons of the apparat. He helped found in August, with Yakovlev, Shevardnadze, Popov, and Sobchak, the new Movement for Democratic Reforms. And like the others, he had a sixth sense for what was brewing in the minds of the men who would make the coup. Volsky was a nervous wreck, and he had taken a little bit of it out on me.

The liberals who still had some access to Gorbachev were hopeful about the new alliance with Yeltsin, but they saw ominous signs that summer. They had always known, despite their public assurances, that an open counterrevolution was a possibility. The truth was, Shevardnadze told me, "We have always had difficulties since the very first days of the April plenum in 1985 and the beginning of perestroika. If someone thinks that Pavlov, Kryuchkov, and Yazov's predecessors were more progressive, they are mistaken. There were also very strong conservatives back then. It's important to have at least a general idea of the sort of struggle there was in the political leadership for the 'general line' and for perestroika."

Shevardnadze said that after his resignation as foreign minister in December 1990, he still got calls from his conservative rivals in the leadership on matters of practical politics: how to deal with the Afghans, who was who in the various Western governments. But he said he noticed by about June 1991 that he was no longer being consulted as he had been. He got the sense that a vacuum was growing around him and that his phone was bugged. "A shadow power was forming," Shevardnadze said.

Yakovlev, too, said he watched helplessly as Lukyanov, Kryuchkov, and the rest surrounded Gorbachev with deceptive advice. "These are toadies," Yakovlev told me. "They will look at you with these honest blue eyes and say, 'We're with the people, we're your only saviors, the only ones who love and respect you. And these democrats, they criticize and insult you.' Gradually, it affects a person. Lukyanov would pretend to be a democratic cohort, and then at Politburo sessions he would be a bigger hawk than anyone. Lukyanov would say, 'Suppress them totally! Mercilessly!' He would say, 'You know, Mikhail Sergeyevich, they are aiming at you, they are trying to get you, to overthrow you.' "

In July, just before he left Gorbachev's staff for good, Yakovlev told Gorbachev, "The people around you are rotten. Please, finally, understand this."

"You exaggerate," Gorbachev said.

Shevardnadze and Yakovlev, the two men who had been closest to Gorbachev at the peak of perestroika, now watched helplessly as the storm clouds gathered. "Gorbachev is a man of character. A person with no character could not have started perestroika himself," Shevardnadze wrote in his memoir. "Gorbachev will enter history as a great reformer, a great revolutionary. It was not so easy to begin. But he enjoyed maneuvering too much. . . . Of course, a major politician has to know how to maneuver, but there must be limits. There comes a moment when one has to say that tactical considerations are not the most important thing, that this is my strategy, my stake is with democracy and the democratic forces. And in this, he was too late, my dear friend."

The hints of betrayal were everywhere that summer. Gorbachev's press secretary, Vitaly Ignatenko, picked up little clues of impertinence and overconfidence among the conservatives that worried him. He saw how on August 2, before there was any order from Gorbachev, someone cut off Yakovlev's Kremlin phone lines and government communications systems. Meanwhile, the darling of the apparatchiks, Yegor Ligachev, who had been retired for a year, still had Kremlin phone lines . . . in his apartment.

Ignatenko also said that while he was on vacation in Sochi in the days before the coup, he noticed that Politburo member Oleg Shenin moved into dacha No. 4 on the special compound, a separate personal residence. "He was vacationing not according to his rank," Ignatenko said, "but in a huge dacha which had not been occupied in six years or more. . . . Only the president had the right to his own dacha there, or maybe the prime minister."

For those in the know, the clues were unending. Aleksandr Prokhanov told *Nezavisimaya Gazeta* that the time had come for the "patriotic forces" to seize power "by the throat." Prokhanov said that the movement allying

"Marxist-Leninists, Marxist-Stalinists, Russian Communists, social demo-cratic liberals, extremist pro-fascist organizations, writers, artists, the mili-tary industrialists, monarchists, and pagans" was forming fast to prevent the disintegration of the country. "Our nation should have a real leader," he said. "People cannot be left to the mercy of fate at a time like this."

In June, Kryuchkov flew to Havana at the personal invitation of Fidel Castro. According to a report in *Izvestia* months later, Kryuchkov concluded several secret agreements with Castro in which they assured each other that Cuba would remain Communist and in the Soviet sphere of influence—despite the conflicts between the two countries during the Gorbachev era. A few weeks later, Kryuchkov's ally Vice President Gennadi Yanayev sent Castro a letter saying that he should not worry about the situation in Mos-cow: "Soon there will be a change for the better."

———

On August 6, after Gorbachev and his family had flown to the Crimea for their summer vacation, Kryuchkov called two of his top aides and told them to write a detailed memorandum analyzing the situation in the country in terms of instituting an immediate state of emergency. The two KGB officials were joined by General Pavel Grachev of the Ministry of Defense. After two days at the KGB's posh recreation and work complex in the village of Mashkino, the working group told Kryuchkov that a state of emergency would be an extremely complicated affair politically and might even cause further disorder in the country.

"But after the Union Treaty is signed it will be too late to institute a state of emergency," Kryuchkov told them.

On August 14, Kryuchkov called the working group together once more and told them to work out documents for a state of emergency. They had no time to lose. By the 16th, a draft of the first declaration of the State Commit-tee for the State of Emergency was on Kryuchkov's desk. At two o'clock that afternoon, Kryuchkov called in his deputy Genii Ageyev and told him to form a group to go to Foros in the Crimea to plan the disconnection of Gorbachev's communication system with the outside world.

———

In mid-August, Esther and I were preparing to leave Moscow after three and a half years. We were going to miss our friends, our life in Moscow, but there was a vacation to take and a year-old son, Alex, who had not gotten to know his grandparents and countless cousins. It was time. In those first weeks of August, we said good-bye to friends, and during the day I tried to finish up some pieces and interviews that I wanted to do before going home. Aleksandr

Yakovlev, for one, agreed to see me a few days before I left, and I went with Michael Dobbs and Masha Lipman to meet him at his new office at the Moscow City Hall. We talked about many things, especially some of the main events of the previous six years, and at one point we asked if there would be a military coup. He said the reactionary forces were still dangerous, but as for a military coup, well, there was no tradition of it, and besides, the military "can't run anything on its own—including the military."

It was strange, then, that two days later, on the 16th, in his resignation from the Communist Party, Yakovlev issued a statement via the Interfax news wire, saying, "The truth is that the Party leadership, in contradiction to its own declarations, is ridding itself of the democratic wing of the Party and is preparing for social revenge and for a Party and state coup." In view of what was to come, it seemed that Yakovlev had found something out, something specific, on the 15th or 16th. But months later, in a second interview, Yakovlev told me that he knew nothing about the actual planning for the coup. "It's just that there was a certain logic at work, a feeling I had," he said. "It made sense that they would struggle for their power. Without it, they had no future."

On August 17, Shevardnadze told me later, Yakovlev and the other twenty-one leaders of the Movement for Democratic Reforms had met in a closed session and agreed unanimously that a right-wing coup was an imminent threat. "This should have been more than enough warning," Shevardnadze said. "I reprove the president because he could have come to the same conclusion and the coup would have been prevented."

The U.S. government was concerned as well. Intelligence reports only grew more anxious after Baker's meeting with Bessmertnykh in Berlin. In fact, it turned out, according to documents recovered later, that Kryuchkov began holding meetings and drawing up plans for a coup as early as November 1990.

———

On the 17th, Esther and I went on a picnic in the country with a bunch of our friends and everyone's babies. The kids splashed around at the river's edge and smeared themselves with lunch. We watched the Russians sunbathe, marveling at how you could actually see their winter-pale flesh flame up as quickly as a sheet of paper.

After a while, Masha, Seriozha, and I took a long walk along the river and through the woods, past the dilapidated dachas and the old men in dirty T-shirts working on cars that would never run again, past kids chasing their dogs in the dust.

A few weeks before, the three of us had gone to a meeting of Moscow

Tribune and heard Andrei Nuikin, a popular journalist and activist, say that a coup d'état was "not only possible, but inevitable." Nuikin had been saying this for years, and we left the meeting that day thinking he was slightly off his rocker, like someone who has been poring over the Kennedy assassination just a little too long.

Now, as we walked, I asked Seriozha and Masha what they thought. The most important thing, they said, was that they had decided they would never leave, no matter what happened.

"We have this 'last boat out' policy," Masha said. "And that is that if things go really bad, if there are tanks in the streets and people are starving, if the worst happens, then we'll leave to save the kids. But not before that."

"Besides, a coup would never hold," Seriozha said. "I'd be shocked if they were stupid enough to try it, more shocked if it lasted."

———

That same afternoon, at a KGB compound outside Moscow known as ABC, Vladimir Kryuchkov convened a meeting of conspirators. It was another of the KGB's sanatoria, with a swimming pool, saunas, a movie theater, and masseuses. Kryuchkov could feel sure that the meeting would be confidential here. The compound was surrounded by guards and high walls. Gorbachev and his more liberal aides, Anatoly Chernyayev and Georgi Shakhnazarov, were all on vacation in the Crimea. And who listened to Shevardnadze or Yakovlev anymore?

Kryuchkov convened the session outdoors, at a picnic table. Present there were Defense Minister Yazov, Prime Minister Pavlov, Politburo chief Oleg Shenin, military industries chief Oleg Baklanov, and presidential chief of staff Valery Boldin. There were assorted snacks on the table, and everyone drank either Russian vodka or imported whiskey.

"The situation is catastrophic," Pavlov said. "The country is facing famine. It is in total chaos. Nobody wants to carry out orders. The harvest is disorganized. Machines are idle because they have no spare parts, no fuel. The only hope is a state of emergency."

Kryuchkov and the others agreed. "I regularly brief Gorbachev on the difficult situation," Kryuchkov said. "But he is not reacting adequately. He cuts me short and changes the subject. He does not trust my information."

This was not the first such meeting of the hard-liners, and these were the familiar complaints. But now the situation had changed, grown more urgent. Gorbachev was planning to return to Moscow to sign the new Union Treaty with Yeltsin and the other republican leaders on August 20. With Kryuchkov as their leader, the conspirators decided they could not wait. They would notify their other allies: Vice President Gennady Yanayev, Interior Minister

Boris Pugo, and Supreme Soviet Chairman Anatoly Lukyanov. Months later Lukyanov ruefully told *The Washington Post* that Gorbachev had surely adopted "antisocialist positions" and that a state of emergency was required to "save the existing order." But, he admitted, the opportunity to succeed had been "hopelessly missed." Yeltsin and the other republican leaders were now too strong, too popular.

Still, the conspirators pressed on. They decided to send a delegation to the Crimea to confront Gorbachev. They would give him an ultimatum: support the state of emergency or step down. Someone suggested that one member of the delegation ought to be Boldin, Gorbachev's chief of staff, his liegeman for more than a decade.

Yazov turned to Boldin and said, *"Et tu, Brute?"*

On his trip home, Yazov recalled later, he felt a fleeting sense of pity for Gorbachev.

"If he had signed the treaty and then gone on vacation," the marshal thought, "everything would have been fine."

AUGUST 18, 1991

The morning after he'd been arrested, Marshal Dmitri Yazov sat in full-dress uniform and answered the first questions of the Russian prosecutor. Yazov said he felt like "an old idiot." He would spend the rest of his life wondering how he could have been so stupid, how he could do something that would bring such dishonor on him and the armed forces that he had served for a half century. The plot was slipshod from the first, he admitted, the product of occasional emotional discussions and then the sudden impulse to head off Gorbachev and the republican leaders before it was too late.

"We were already meeting earlier at various places. We talked about the situation in the country," Yazov said in his slow, slightly doltish voice. "It was unavoidable that we came to the conclusion that the president was to blame. He had distanced himself from the Party. . . . Gorbachev in recent years had been going abroad and often we had no idea in general what he was discussing there. . . . We were just not ready to become greatly dependent on the U.S.A., politically, economically or militarily. . . ."

QUESTION: In what form did you make a decision?
YAZOV: There was no real plan for a plot. We met on Saturday [August 17].
QUESTION: At whose invitation?
YAZOV: Kryuchkov's.
QUESTION: Where did you meet?

YAZOV: At a point in Moscow at the end of Leninski Prospekt—a left turn near the police post, there is a road there. . . . At the end of the working day, Kryuchkov called and said we had to talk. I came. Then Shenin came, then Baklanov. And then it was said: maybe we should go to Gorbachev and speak with him.

QUESTION: Why was there such a hurry? Was it because the Union Treaty was to be signed [on the 20th]?

YAZOV: Of course. We were not happy with this draft and we knew the state would fall apart. . . .

QUESTION: What brought up the idea of an Emergency Committee?

YAZOV: We were in Pavlov's office. Yanayev was there, and at about nine Lukyanov came. He came by plane. He'd been on vacation. Lukyanov said: "I can't be a member of such a committee, I'm chairman of the Supreme Soviet, a legal organ which is ruled by this and that. Naturally, I can do something—I put out an announcement saying that the result of the Union Treaty would be the destruction of the constitution." After that, he left. Yanayev was already rather drunk. . . .

The last good coup operation had been in Poland, in December 1981. On a freezing night between 2:00 and 3:00 A.M., the military and the secret police rounded up thousands of Solidarity activists and sympathizers and locked them up in "internment camps." The military regime secured the borders and then invaded its own country with tanks and troops, cutting up Warsaw and other key areas into carefully patrolled zones. They took over the radio and television stations. Over and over, they broadcast martial music, the national anthem, and the words of the Leader, the declaration of a "state of war." In case anyone missed the point, the newscasters wore army uniforms. All demonstrations, all unions and student organizations were banned, all mail and telephone traffic censored. There was a curfew from 10:00 P.M. to 6:00 A.M. The Military Council told the population that they were acting to prevent a "reactionary coup." They were acting in the name of "national salvation." It was a perfect operation.

Perfect, but nothing new. In a letter dated September 26–27, 1917, Lenin wrote a letter that later became a widely distributed pamphlet called "Marxism and Rebellion." Just a few months from grabbing power, he was clearly obsessed with the need for absolute ruthlessness and efficiency: "To approach a rebellion in a Marxist way," he wrote, "that is, as one would an art, it is necessary not to lose a minute moving loyal battalions to the most important objects, to arrest the government . . . seize the telegraph and telephone.

. . . One cannot at this critical moment remain true to Marxism and not treat rebellion as an art."

The successors to Lenin and Jaruzelski made feeble attempts to ape the old efficiency. From a factory in Pskov, they ordered a quarter million pairs of handcuffs; they ordered the printing of 300,000 arrest forms. Kryuchkov issued secret orders doubling the pay of all KGB men and called them back from vacation to go on alert. He cleared out two floors of Lefortovo Prison and prepared a secret bunker in Lubyanka in case the leaders of the coup needed to find safe refuge. And to keep pace with the times, they would carry out the coup under legal pretenses: a nation in crisis, a president taken ill. They would fill the stores for a few months, drawing on military stockpiles kept in case of war. The people would acquiesce. Hadn't they always?

———

Gorbachev was resting in splendor. When he came to power in 1985, he built himself a magnificent place to rest, a compound in the Crimean town of Foros that cost the Soviet government an estimated $20 million. He and his family lived in the main house, a three-story structure with a central hall done up in marble and gilt. It was the sort of opulence you see sometimes when a sheik moves into Beverley Hills. There was a hotel for the staff and security guards, a guest house for thirty people, fruit trees, an olive grove, an indoor swimming pool, a movie theater, an elaborate security system, and an escalator to the Black Sea.

It was a wonder that Gorbachev went on his vacation at all. At the worst moments, it was never really safe for him to leave Moscow. The Nina Andreyeva letter in 1988 was published as he was leaving for Yugoslavia. The planning for the Tbilisi massacre of 1989 came when he was in England. The conservatives in the Politburo often made right-wing speeches when Gorbachev was in the Crimea. And now, despite all the warnings and omens, he left Moscow again. He took long walks on the beach with Raisa. He swam, watched movies, read volumes on Russian and Soviet history. His doctors did what they could for his bad back. Gorbachev also took time to write a speech for the Union Treaty signing ceremonies and a long article on the future—an article that even pondered the possibility of a right-wing coup.

Gorbachev has said that he was not naive, he knew well what the conservatives were capable of; but he has also insisted that he had no prior knowledge that there would be a coup, or even a concerted demand for the declaration of a state of emergency. According to phone logs obtained by Cable News Network, Gorbachev talked four times with Kryuchkov on August 18; he also talked with Yanayev, Shenin, Pavlov, and the deputy prime minister,

Vladimir Shcherbakov. Sometime after 2:00 P.M., Yanayev called Gorbachev and asked about meeting him at the airport in Moscow when he returned from vacation the next day. They agreed to see each other then.

Yanayev, who was probably making sure the mark was still in place, was the worst sort of Party nonentity. He was a vain man of small intelligence, a womanizer, and a drunk. I'm not sure it is possible to describe just how hard it is to acquire a reputation as a drunk in Russia. And Yanayev was not merely a drunk, he was a buffoon. On the day he went before the Congress for confirmation as vice president, one of the deputies asked him if he was a healthy man. "My wife has no complaints," Yanayev said and snickered.

At around 4:00 P.M., Georgi Shakhnazarov, one of Gorbachev's last remaining liberal advisers, called to check on details for the trip to Moscow. Then, almost as an afterthought, Shakhnazarov asked Gorbachev about his health. Gorbachev said he was fine except for his chronic back pain.

Gorbachev had worked hard on his speech for the treaty signing, and now he wanted to spend some time with Raisa and their daughter, Irina, son-in-law, Anatoly, and granddaughter, Oksana. But at 4:50, the chief of Gorbachev's security detail told him that they had unexpected visitors, including Yuri Plekhanov, the head of the KGB's Ninth Directorate, the division charged with the security of the leadership.

Gorbachev picked up a phone to find out what this was all about. He had called no meetings and he was not accustomed to unannounced visitors. The line was dead. Then he picked up another, also dead. Gorbachev was stunned. Raisa came in to see what was going on. "Mikhail Sergeyevich has eight or ten telephone operators and all the phones were silent," she said later. "I picked up the receiver and checked it out and all the phones were silent, even that of the commander in chief. We have this phone everywhere— in our country house, in our flat—everywhere. It's under a kind of lid and we do not even remove dust from this phone because we are not supposed to remove the lid. He picked up the receiver on that phone and there was silence there. We knew that was it. There was nothing else we could do."

Before the visitors got inside the house, Gorbachev knew perfectly well something was very wrong. He called his family around him and told them "that anything could follow this." They, in turn, said they were ready to see it through with him "to the end." Later, when she described the scene, Raisa seemed to refer to the murder of the Romanov family after the Bolshevik coup to describe the depths of her own worst fears: "We know our history and its tragic aspects."

"I paced the room and thought," Gorbachev recalled. "Not about myself, but about my family, my granddaughters. I decided: in this situation, it is impossible to value my own skin."

The delegation arrived: Plekhanov, Shenin from the Politburo, Baklanov of the military-industrial complex, Gorbachev's personal assistant, Boldin, and, representing the army, General Varennikov, the head of ground forces. Gorbachev led them to his study.

"Who sent you?" he said.

"The committee," one of them said. "The committee appointed in connection with the emergency."

"Who appointed such a committee? I didn't appoint such a committee, and neither did the Supreme Soviet."

Varennikov told Gorbachev he had little choice. Either go along or resign.

"You are nothing but adventurers and traitors, and you will pay for this. I don't care what happens to you, but you will destroy the country. Only those who want to commit suicide can now suggest a totalitarian regime in the country. You are pushing it to a civil war!"

Gorbachev reminded the delegation that there was to be a signing ceremony of the Union Treaty in Moscow on August 20.

"There will be no signing," Baklanov said, according to Gorbachev. Then Baklanov said, "Yeltsin's been arrested. He'll be arrested. . . . Mikhail Sergeyevich, we demand nothing from you. You'll be here. We'll do all the dirty work for you."

Gorbachev said he would play no part in their "adventure." The delegation continued to press. They gave Gorbachev a list of the members of the State Committee for the State of Emergency (the GKChP). Gorbachev was especially stunned to see the names of Yazov and Kryuchkov. He had plucked Yazov out of obscurity to make him defense minister precisely for the sake of having his own man. And besides, he was not bright enough to be disloyal. Yazov, Aleksandr Yakovlev would say, "is no Spinoza." Kryuchkov, who was perhaps the most forceful and determined of all the plotters, surprised Gorbachev because he had come through the recommendation of their mutual mentor, Yuri Andropov. Gorbachev thought of Kryuchkov as a cultured man, someone who had been abroad, seen something more than the inside of Lubyanka. But as the prosecutor's report on the putsch said, "For Kryuchkov, Gorbachev was a madman. Gorbachev destroyed the system that had given him everything—servile aides, the respect of his foes, and a comfortable, even splendid life-style. Could a person in his right mind get rid of all that?" Time and again, Kryuchkov urged Gorbachev to break up demonstrations, to "show, at last, our strength." And when Gorbachev would refuse, Kryuchkov would tell his friends, "The president is not responding to events."

Boldin was a terrible betrayal, too. He had started working for Gorbachev in 1978 and had his absolute trust. Boldin was the chief of staff. He vetted every appointment, controlled absolutely the flow of paper to the president's desk. Along with Kryuchkov and Boldin, the other chief plotter was Oleg Baklanov, a figure little known to the public, but one with tremendous power. Baklanov's chief interest in a coup was clear: he wanted to prevent any deterioration of military spending or might. In one speech prepared for the April 1991 plenum of the Central Committee, he wrote that current policy had caused the Soviet Union to "fall practically under the dictate of the United States." According to one of the country's leading weapons scientists, Pyotr Korotkevich, Baklanov "froze" a major plan worked out by specialists in the hierarchy to create a smaller, but professional, army, demilitarize the economy, and reduce military spending by half.

The rest of the list was less surprising. Pavlov and Yanayev were obvious enemies of radical reform, though they were too bumptious, too drunk, to have acted alone. The rest were symbols of the conservative interests. Aleksandr Tizyakov, the president of the Association of State Enterprises, had given Gorbachev an ultimatum the previous December to end strikes and impose economic discipline. "You want to frighten me," Gorbachev had said then. "Well, it won't work." And there was Vasily Starodubtsev, the head of the Union of Collective Farm Chairmen, an ardent opponent of private farming and private property.

Gorbachev tried now to persuade the delegation to take up the question of a state of emergency in the parliament. There could be a full debate. Let the Supreme Soviet decide. "If you go to a state of emergency, what are you going to do the next day?" Gorbachev told them. Varennikov said they were carrying out this mission because the "committee" would not allow "separatists" and "extremists" to dictate the future of the country.

"I've heard all this," Gorbachev said. "Do you think the people are so fatigued that they will just follow any dictator?"

But it was no use. "It was a conversation with deaf mutes," Gorbachev said later. "Their cycle was in motion."

As the delegation was preparing to leave at about 7:30 P.M., Baklanov stuck out his hand to shake hands with Raisa Maksimovna. She looked at him, said nothing, and walked away. The delegation rode back to the Belbek airport. In the front seat, Plekhanov spoke on the radiophone to Foros, giving further instructions on the isolation of the president. In the back, the others spoke in short, disgruntled phrases. They had thought Gorbachev would give in to their demands, and he hadn't On the trip back to Moscow, they began to drink.

———

Raisa, the Gorbachevs' daughter, Irina, and Gorbachev's aide, Anatoly Chernyayev, had waited outside the study until the meeting was over. After the plotters left, Gorbachev looked at Chernyayev and said, "Well, have you guessed?"

"Yes."

Gorbachev described the demands and his replies "in terms I cannot repeat with ladies present." He showed Raisa a list of the conspirators he had copied down, and added at the bottom "Lukyanov . . . ?" He still could not see that his great and loyal friend from college days had turned on him, too.

Gorbachev said he would not go along with a state of emergency or a return to dictatorial rule. "I was always an opponent of such measures," he said later, "not only for moral and political reasons, but because in the history of our country they have always led to the deaths of hundreds, thousands, and millions. . . . And we need to get away from that forever."

Raisa said that it would be best now, if there was anything to discuss, to talk out on the balconies and on the beach, the better to avoid the listening devices that were obviously in place and working.

———

When they arrived at the Kremlin that evening, Vice President Yanayev and Prime Minister Pavlov (the twin fools of this low comedy) saw Kryuchkov, Boldin, Shenin, Pugo, Yazov, and the rest sitting at a long conference table. Lukyanov called from his car and said he was on the way. No one sat at the head of the table, the president's chair.

"A catastrophe is taking place," Kryuchkov said. There would soon be an armed uprising against the leadership. They were going to take over key points, the television tower at Ostankino, the rail stations, two hotels. They had heavy arms, missile launchers, everything. They must be stopped and there were only a few hours in which to do it. Then Plekhanov chimed in. He and Boldin had just come back from Foros. Gorbachev was ill. "It's either a heart attack or a stroke or something," Boldin said.

Yanayev hesitated. He said he could not sign the document creating the Emergency Committee and making him the new president. Kryuchkov pressed him. "Can't you see?" he said. "If we don't save the harvest, there will be hunger and in a few months the people will be on the streets. There will be a civil war."

Yanayev was smoking one cigarette after another. He said he wanted to wait to meet with Gorbachev before taking action, and besides, he did not feel morally prepared or otherwise qualified to be the president. But the men around the table kept after him, stressing that Gorbachev was sick, that the situation would be temporary.

INVESTIGATOR: Why did it fall apart?

VALENTIN PAVLOV: Most of those present [at the Kremlin on the 18th] did not understand what the whole thing was about. Emergency measures had been discussed before. They'd been discussed in the spring. So there was nothing unusual about it. But when it came to Gorbachev being sick and no one knowing what was wrong, when it was unclear whether or not he could fulfill his duties, then we hesitated and decided to transfer it to the Supreme Soviet. Yanayev did not want to sign it. He kept saying, "Guys, I do not know what to write. Is he sick or not? It's all hearsay." The rest said, "Take the decision." Whose word did he take? Hard to tell.

Lukyanov arrived late to the meeting carrying a copy of the draft Union Treaty and the Soviet Constitution under his arm. Eventually, after listening to Lukyanov describe how the Supreme Soviet would eventually "legitimize" the state of emergency, Yanayev began to waver.

"Sign, Gennadi Ivanovich," Kryuchkov said.

And finally he did. In his trembling hand, Yanayev signed the documents grabbing power from his president. Then he passed the document around the table. One after the other, Yazov, Pugo, Kryuchkov, Pavlov, and Baklanov put their names to the decree declaring the state of emergency.

Now Aleksandr Bessmertnykh, Shevardnadze's successor as foreign minister, arrived. He had been on vacation and had flown to the meeting having no idea what was going on. Kryuchkov took him into an anteroom.

"Listen, the situation in the country is terrible," Kryuchkov said. "A chaotic situation has emerged. It's a crisis. It's dangerous. People are disappointed. Something should be done, and we decided to do something through emergency measures. We have established a committee, an Emergency Committee, and I would like you to be part of it."

"Is the committee arranged by the instructions of the president?" Bessmertnykh asked.

"No," Kryuchkov said. "He's incapable of functioning now. He's flat on his back at his dacha."

Bessmertnykh asked for a medical report, but Kryuchkov refused. Something was obviously very strange about this, though Bessmertnykh's instincts either were not sharp enough or he saw danger and tried to negotiate a safe course for himself. In the days to come he called in sick and refused to come out publicly against the coup. But at least he turned down Kryuchkov.

"I am not going to be part of this committee and I categorically reject any participation in that," he said.

As they went back to the meeting, Kryuchkov told the others that the foreign minister had refused. Bessmertnykh told the group that their idea would isolate the country, it would bring on sanctions from the West, maybe a grain embargo. The committee seemed glum. They so wanted the appearance of consensus, of legality, before the world and the people.

"We still need a liberal," Kryuchkov said.

———

"Then the so-called committee began to fall apart and to split," Pavlov told the prosecutors months later. "The whole situation was odd. Bessmertnykh fell sick. I was sort of carried out of the room. I did not think it would end this way. If someone had not decided out of foolishness to bring in the military hardware, nothing at all would have happened."

At one point at the Kremlin meeting, Lukyanov asked what sort of plan had been worked out, what the details of the state of emergency were. In fact, was there a plan?

"Why do you say that?" Yazov said. "We have a plan." But as he told the prosecutors later, Yazov knew there was nothing. "I knew we had nothing except the sketch that we had been absorbed in that Saturday at ABC. This was no plan and I knew very clearly that, in any case, we had no real aim at all."

AUGUST 19, 1991

Ol'var Kakuchaya, the director of *Vremya,* was dead asleep when the phone rang at 1:30 A.M. It was his boss on the line, the head of state television and radio, Leonid Kravchenko.

"Ol'var, what's your address?" Kravchenko said urgently.

"Are you sending someone to me?"

"I want to send a car."

"What for?"

"I'll tell you when you get here."

Can't this wait? Kakuchaya asked.

No, it can't, Kravchenko said. We have an emergency.

The morning show had to be changed—changed drastically. He'd explain when they got to the studios at Ostankino. Kravchenko told Kakuchaya that they needed two newscasters to get ready, one man and one women—or whoever could get to the studios fastest.

The car came for Kakuchaya in no time and brought him to work. Kravchenko called again, this time from his car on the special "Kremlin line."

"We're on the way," Kravchenko said. "Go outside and I'll give you the scripts you need."

"How long will you be?"

"I'll be there in seven minutes."

Kravchenko's car pulled up in the parking lot. He was usually a dapper man, an apparatchik for the television age, but now he seemed absolutely pale. He said that he had just gotten into bed when he was called and told to come immediately to the Central Committee. He was given a stack of documents—the appeals and pronouncements of the Emergency Committee that would begin going out over the air at six that morning. He was told to create an atmosphere on television similar to that on the day of a state funeral: somber, classical music, deadpan announcements.

Kakuchaya took a quick look at the documents. They seemed to have been typed in haste on an ordinary typewriter. And there was Yanayev's signature, a hasty scrawl. Kravchenko told him that soon there would be tanks around the TV tower. No one should go outside. Use the underground tunnels connecting the various buildings to get around. And obey orders.

———

Gennadi Yanayev, still buzzed from drink, took power at 4:00 A.M. Thirty minutes later, Marshal Yazov dispatched Coded Telegram 8825 ordering heightened alert status for all military units. Soldiers were ordered back from furlough. The Taman Guards, the Dzerzhinsky and Kantemirovskaya mechanized divisions, and several units of the Ryazan Airborne Division would occupy the city of Moscow.

At the Ministry of Defense, Yazov repeated Kryuchkov's elaborate conspiracy theory about an imminent anti-Soviet coup and the need to take the upper hand. "There will be people in the crowd who will throw themselves in front of tanks or throw Molotov cocktails," Yazov warned his commanders. "I want no bloodshed or carnage."

It was a hellish morning for Prime Minister Pavlov. He had stayed up most of the night drinking with Yanayev, and now Kryuchkov was trying to reach him to organize planning sessions at the Kremlin.

At about 7:00 A.M., one of the Kremlin doctors, Dmitri Sakharov, was summoned to Pavlov's dacha and told only that the prime minister was "very unwell."

"Pavlov was drunk," Sakharov testified later. "But this was no ordinary, simple intoxication. He was at the point of hysteria. I proceeded to give him attention."

———

The barracks of the Kantemirovskaya Mechanized Division in the town of Naro-Fominsk outside Moscow were quiet, and Private Vitaly Chugunov, a young man with wheat-blond hair from the city of Ulyanovsk, was in the middle of a deep, untroubled sleep. These were the last sweet moments before Monday reveille and another week of training. Chugunov had thought he would be among the first generation of Soviet soldiers blessed by the rise of a peaceable kingdom, a country in which a policy of "new thinking" ensured against another Afghanistan, another occupation of Eastern Europe.

Suddenly, an officer burst into Chugunov's barracks, shouting his charges out of bed. There were no complicated explanations, nothing about Gorbachev or a state of emergency. "We all thought it was one of those training alerts, and we quickly got everything ready to go," Chugunov said. Soon he was inside his armored personnel carrier, part of a huge convoy headed for Moscow. Chugunov and his buddies were confused, not quite sure why they were taking the highway north into the city at such a fast clip and churning up the asphalt.

Along the way, Chugunov could see a few people waving at the tanks and the armored personnel carriers; people shouting at them to turn around and go home. Slowly, the young soldiers began to understand, Chugunov fastest of all. His father had been in a tank when the Soviet army invaded Prague in 1968. He'd always told his son how scared he was that day. The commanders had told them that the Czechs would give them boxes of chocolate and the chocolate would have poison inside them. Watch out for poisoned wine, they told them. And then, as his tank rumbled into the city, he heard the insults: "Occupiers!" "Pigs, go home!" Looking out at the road now, Chugunov thought that he was headed for something far worse than his father had ever known.

———

The coup went on the air at six. The announcers, so obviously nervous and confused, began to read the documents that had been delivered to Kravchenko at the Central Committee:

"We are addressing you at a grave, critical hour for the future of the Motherland and our peoples. A mortal danger has come to loom large over our great Motherland.

"The policy of reforms, launched at Mikhail Gorbachev's initiative and designed as means to ensure the country's dynamic development and the democratization of social life, have entered for several reasons into a blind alley.

". . . All democratic institutions created by the popular will are losing weight and effectiveness right in front of our eyes. This is a result of purposeful actions by those who, grossly violating the fundamental law of the USSR, are in fact staging an unconstitutional coup [!] and striving for unbridled personal dictatorial powers. . . .

"The country is sinking into the quagmire of violence and lawlessness.

"Never before in national history has the propaganda of sex and violence assumed such a scale, threatening the health and lives of future generations. Millions of people are demanding measures against the octopus of crime and glaring immorality."

———

Yeltsin was eating breakfast at his dacha in the village of Usovo when the calls started coming in. Gennadi Burbulis, Ruslan Khasbulatov, and all the other Russian officials in the smaller dachas in the woods near Yeltsin's quickly gathered round. Yeltsin had gotten some hints from agents in the Russian republican secret service that a coup was coming. With Gorbachev flirting to the end with his own worst enemies, Yeltsin knew that a coup was possible. But until now he hadn't thought it would actually happen. And now he had to act without hesitation.

The Leningrad mayor, Anatoly Sobchak, heard about the coup by phone at his hotel room in Moscow. Tanks were on their way, he was told. Sobchak called his driver, and together they headed out of town at top speed for Yeltsin's dacha. Along the way, they saw armored personnel carriers and tanks. One tank had fallen into a ditch and was burning. Sobchak, like Yeltsin and around seventy other reform politicians, including Aleksandr Yakovlev and Eduard Shevardnadze, were on KGB arrest lists, but so far the secret police had made only a few arrests of some minor officials. Sobchak made it to Usovo untouched.

Sobchak saw that Yeltsin was already determined to do what he could to shore up resistance to the coup. Yeltsin had called the leaders of the biggest republics and was taken aback by their calm, their lack of resolve. They told him they did not have enough information to act. Yeltsin was on his own. As he strapped on a bulletproof vest and then his shirt and suit, Yeltsin said that he and his aides would head for "the White House," the massive Russian parliament building on the Moscow River. Without saying so, they would follow almost precisely the tactics of the Lithuanians in January: use the parliament building as a barricade, an oasis and symbol of democratic resistance, communicate with the outside world by whatever means possible. Yeltsin told his aides to convene immediately a nonstop session of the Russian parliament.

As Yeltsin got into his car, his daughter said, "Papa, keep calm. Everything depends on you."

After following the convoy part of the way to the city to make sure Yeltsin got past the tanks, Sobchak and his driver peeled off for Sheremetyevo Airport to wait for the first flight home to Leningrad. When he got to the waiting lounge, Sobchak saw three bodyguards coming at him. For a moment, he thought he was finished. To the contrary. They were bodyguards from the Russian KGB there to make sure that the mayor caught his plane.

———

By 9:00 A.M., tanks surrounded Moscow City Hall. Soldiers had taken down the Russian tricolor and replaced it with the red Soviet flag. Tanks were taking positions in all the key points of the city: the TV and radio stations, newspaper offices, Lenin Hills, the White House. A journalist called General Yevgeny Shaposhnikov, the commander of the air force. Shaposhnikov had listened to Yazov's commands and explanations of the coup, but he made no secret to the reporter that he was revolted by what had happened. "Let the sons of bitches comment on what they are going to do with the country," he said.

———

While Yazov worked at the Ministry of Defense and Kryuchkov at Lubyanka, Yanayev sat in his Kremlin office wondering what it was he was supposed to do.

Yuri Golik, the chairman of the Supreme Soviet committee on legislation, got through the gates of the Kremlin without any problem and went immediately to see Yanayev.

"Is it a putsch?" Golik asked.

"It's a putsch," said Yanayev.

Later, Vadim Bakatin, a member of Gorbachev's Defense Council, also came to see Yanayev. Bakatin, like Golik, was loyal to Gorbachev, and he demanded an explanation. Before he could even work up his temper, Bakatin noticed what bad shape Yanayev was in.

"I've been here since four o'clock in the morning," Yanayev said, pacing, smoking, excitable, bags under his eyes. "I don't know myself what is going on. They came and tried to persuade me for two hours. I didn't agree, but they finally persuaded me."

"Who came?"

"They came."

———

The Kazakh leader, Nursultan Nazarbayev, called Yanayev, who seemed to be in a daze, drunken or otherwise. "He didn't seem to know what was going on," Nazarbayev told reporters in Alma-Ata, the Kazakh capital, "or why I was calling or even who I was."

Yanayev's desk was stacked with unread documents, many of them months old. Usually he let his aides do all his serious work for him; among those aides was Sergei Bobkov, the son of Filipp Bobkov, Kryuchkov's trusted deputy at the KGB. But while Yanayev was foggy at times, obsessed with love affairs and the bottle, he kept on his desk one document that made it clear that the coup itself was more serious than he was, that the real powers behind it—Kryuchkov, Baklanov, Boldin, and Yazov—knew their history and the methods of the old regime.

REGARDING CERTAIN AXIOMS
OF THE EXTRAORDINARY SITUATION

1. We must not lose the initiative and enter into any kind of negotiations with the public. We have often ended up doing this in an attempt to preserve a democratic facade. As a result, society gradually becomes accustomed to the idea that they can argue with the authorities—and this is the first step toward the next battle.

2. One must not allow even the first manifestations of disloyalty: meetings, hunger strikes, petitions, and information about them. On the contrary, they become, as it were, a permitted form of opposition, after which even more active forms will follow. If you want to proceed with a minimal amount of bloodshed, suppress contradictions at the very beginning.

3. Do not be ashamed of resorting to clearly expressed populism. This is the law of winning support from the masses. Immediately introduce economic measures that are understandable to all—lowering of prices, easing up on alcohol laws, etc.—and the appearance of even a limited variety of products in popular demand. In this situation do not think of economic integrity, the inflation rate, or other consequences.

4. One must not delay in informing the populace about all the details of the crimes of one's political opponent. At first they will avidly search for information. Exactly at this point one must bring down an information storm of exposure, the revelation of guilty groups and syndicates, corruption, and so forth. On other days the information about one's opponent should be given in an ironically humorous key. . . . The information must be graphic and as simple as possible.

5. One must not crack the whip with direct threats; better to start rumors about the strictness of the regime and the control of discipline in production and life, as if there were systematic raids on stores, places of relaxation, and others.

6. One must not be slow in dealing with personnel decisions and reassignments. The population should know who is being punished and for what evident reasons; who is answering to whom for what; and to whom the population should turn with its problems.

———

Before going to the *Washington Post* bureau on Kutuzovsky Prospekt, where she was working as a translator, Masha Lipman watched the bland declaration of a state of emergency. As she stared at the television her first thoughts were of her children, her six-year-old daughter, Anya, and her sixteen-year-old son, Grisha. She was terrified. Suddenly, these years of promise seemed betrayed. After years of thinking the problem through, Masha and Seriozha had decided against emigration. They'd cast their lot with Moscow. Now all she could think was "Will Anya be indoctrinated as we were? Is it all coming back? Will we emigrate? Should we? Can we?"

———

Nadezhda Kudinova, a seamstress at a parachute factory on the edge of town, arrived at work. On the way, she had heard some vague rumors on the bus that the newscasters were announcing that Gorbachev had resigned for "health reasons" and that Yanayev and some unpronounceable committee— the "GKChP"—had taken power. It all seemed so vague and unreal. The factory director immediately gathered all the workers and insisted that they all stand by the Emergency Committee, that what the country needed now was stability and discipline in the workplace.

Kudinova looked out the window. There was nothing to see, nothing to hear. On the radio, the announcers repeated the decrees of the committee, over and over again. She and her friends began talking about what they could do, whom to support. At the factory, opinion was split down the middle. Half were outraged. Half thought that maybe life would be better now without Gorbachev. Maybe there would be food in the stores for a change.

Kudinova thought to herself that the workers who were taking sides with the committee were counting on a passive country. As the day went on and she heard that Yeltsin had begun organizing the resistance at the White House, Kudinova brightened. "Maybe I should start writing some leaflets," she thought. On her way home, she saw the tanks, she saw how the tanks had chewed up the road, a violation. She saw the crowd beginning to gather at the White House, and she made a decision. She would protect the president she had voted for just two months before. She had no thought of Mikhail Gorbachev. She went to the White House for Yeltsin, for an independent

Russia. It wasn't about Gorbachev, she thought. Gorbachev had gotten what he deserved.

———

Yeltsin arrived at the White House at around 10:00 A.M. He and Ruslan Khasbulatov, the chairman of the parliament, and Ivan Silayev, the Russian prime minister, drafted an appeal, "To the Citizens of Russia," denouncing the putsch as a "reactionary unconstitutional coup d'état" and calling for a nationwide strike. Khasbulatov and Vice President Aleksander Rutskoi, a war hero in Afghanistan, began broadcasts from a makeshift radio station inside the parliament building, the White House. Vladimir Bokser, a young pro-democracy politician, organized a phone network of activists to come to defend the White House. Yeltsin dispatched his foreign minister, Andrei Kozyrev, to Paris to seek Western support and establish a Russian government abroad if the resistance was crushed.

"By eleven the depression in the city was beginning to lift just slightly," said Masha Lipman's husband, Seriozha Ivanov. "People riding in the trolleys were laughing at the tanks, mocking them." Children climbed on the tanks and asked the young soldiers how to drive; pretty young women teased the recruits and said that maybe they should all go home and do something more interesting than sitting around on a tank.

Then, just after noon, Yeltsin walked down the front steps of the White House and clambered up on a T-72—Tank No. 110 of the Taman Guards. It was an indelible image that would set the tone for the next three days. As a small crowd of demonstrators and reporters listened, Yeltsin's voice boomed out. "Citizens of Russia," he began. ". . . The legally elected president of the country has been removed from power. . . . We are dealing with a right-wing, reactionary, anti-constitutional coup d'état. . . . Accordingly, we proclaim all decisions and decrees of this committee to be illegal. . . . We appeal to citizens of Russia to give an appropriate rebuff to the putschists and demand a return of the country to normal constitutional development."

Then Konstantin Kobets, a retired general now appointed Russian defense minister by Yeltsin, climbed aboard and addressed not only the citizens, but the soldiers of Russia. "I am the defense minister of Russia," he said, "and not a hand will be raised against the people or the duly elected president of Russia." Kobets had led a battalion during the Prague invasion in 1968, and he said he was not about to repeat his mistakes. He would organize the military resistance and try to convince the officers and troops that they could not, as soldiers or citizens, follow the commands of a junta.

Yeltsin had been criticized in recent months for flirting too much with the military. He had spent much of his campaign in places like the Tula military bases and, over the objections of many radicals in the parliament, made Rutskoi his vice president. Now he was counting on that relationship to pay dividends. Rutskoi responded instantly and went on the radio: "Comrades! I, an officer of the Soviet armed forces, a colonel, a Hero of the Soviet Union who has walked the battle-torn roads of Afghanistan and knows the horrors of war, call on you, my brother officers, soldiers, and sailors, not to act against your own people, against your fathers, brothers, and sisters."

Outside the White House, the first demonstrators cheered as the gunners in ten tanks of the Taman Guards turned the barrels of their guns away from the parliament. The attackers were now ready to defend the White House.

———

Private Chugunov sat in his tank, parked in the Lenin Hills. At first there was real fear, he said. People shook their fists and shouted, "Don't shoot your own people! Turn against your officers!" He saw women crying, people brought them food to eat, flowers to stick in their guns, leaflets from the White House, Yeltsin's appeal to the military to obey their oath to the people.

The soldiers unloaded their AK-47s and kept them out of sight. "Why don't we make a U-turn and go home?" they began to say to one another. Chugunov and his friends felt ashamed, and they told the crowds around them they would do nothing to disgrace the names of their fathers, they would not shoot at their own people.

———

At noon Yeltsin went on the radio: "Soldiers and officers of the army, the KGB, and the troops of the Interior Ministry! Countrymen! The country is faced with the threat of terror. At this difficult hour of decision remember that you have taken an oath to your people, and your weapons cannot be turned against the people. You can erect a throne of bayonets but you cannot sit on it for long. The days of the conspirators are numbered. . . . Clouds of terror and dictatorship are gathering over Russia, but this night will not be eternal and our long-suffering people will find freedom once again, and for good. Soldiers, I believe at this tragic hour you will make the right decision. The honor of Russian arms will not be covered with the blood of the people."

———

At the White House, a retired lieutenant from the Taman Guards—"Baskakov is my name, here is my tattoo"—took command of Civil Defense Unit No. 34. He was proud to see that it was his boys who were the first to come over to the side of the resistance. Baskakov had quit the Communist Party the year before and he felt that it was his duty "as a Christian" to come to the barricades. He never said a word to his family, just walked out the door and took the metro to the White House. Baskakov's men, a ragtag outfit of Afghan vets, took command of entrance 22 of the parliament, where key figures, like Shevardnadze and Popov, were going in and out.

Baskakov's men spotted snipers in the windows of the Hotel Mir across the street and near the American embassy. For years, American diplomats had assumed that the KGB used the hotel as a lookout point on the embassy. Baskakov's troops were pathetically armed with black-market pistols, knives, billy clubs, an occasional machine gun. If there was an attack, they'd be cannon fodder, and they knew it. Everyone knew it. It was that combined sense of heroism and fatalism, especially among the kids who had joined the resistance units, that moved Baskakov. "I used to be critical of the young," he said. "But there were bikers, the Rockers, going on reconnaissance missions on their motorcycles across the barricades, giving us news about the troop movements. The young girls that people call prostitutes, they were there giving us food and drink."

The defenders of the White House came slowly: first a few thousand, then ten thousand. By the end of the day there would be around twenty-five thousand. With advice from the military men, they began building barricades, gnarled heaps of scrap: construction rods, concrete blocks, rusted bathtubs, bricks, tree trunks, even cobblestones from a small bridge nearby that had been the site of an anti-czarist uprising in 1905. The strike leader, Anatoly Malikhin, showed up wearing a United Mine Workers Union T-shirt ("United We Stand, Divided We Fall"). He went inside and quickly strapped on a machine gun. Somehow, he said, he had had the feeling it would come to this when the first mines went out on strike two years before.

———

At the airport in Leningrad, Sobchak's aides were there to meet him. They told him that the Leningrad regional military commander, Viktor Samsonov, had already been on television to announce that the Emergency Committee had taken power from Gorbachev and that a state of emergency had begun. So far, there were no troops into the city. Sobchak told his driver to take him straight to the city's central military command at top speed. Once he was there, Sobchak left his guards downstairs.

"I saw that they were bewildered and confused, and right away I didn't let them open their mouths," Sobchak recounted. "I told them if they moved one finger they would be tried the way the Nazis were tried at Nuremberg. I scolded Samsonov: 'General, remember Tbilisi? You were the only one there who acted as a reasonable man. You remained in the shadows. What are you doing now? You are involved in this gang. This committee is illegal.'

"Why is it illegal?" Samsonov said. "I have an order. I have this coded cable. I can't show it to you. It's a secret."

Sobchak pressed, telling Samsonov to remember how the generals in Tbilisi in April 1989 had also exceeded orders and turned a peaceful demonstration into a bloodbath.

"Why do you raise your voice?" Boris Gidaspov, the Leningrad Party chief, shouted.

"Shut up!" Sobchak said. "Don't you realize that with your presence you are liquidating your own Party?"

For the rest of the meeting, Gidaspov whimpered in his chair, a beaten dog.

Samsonov faced a choice. Yazov and Kryuchkov had appealed to his commitment to empire and discipline. Sobchak, who had the support of the city, appealed to his conscience, his commitment to history. The choice was what the past six years had been all about. And the general found it almost easy. He backed off and ordered his men to stay out of the city. Leningrad, now St. Petersburg again, was saved.

That evening, Sobchak went on the local television show *Fakt* and referred to the conspirators as "former" ministers and as "citizens," the way a Russian prosecutor would refer to the accused.

Samsonov kept getting calls from the conspirators, but he held fast. Sobchak was pleased. "General," he said, "can't you see how these people are just nothing? They will not hold on to power long even if they are able to seize it!"

———

The leaders of the junta had already failed miserably to follow the prescriptions of Lenin or Jaruzelski. Nearly everyone on their arrest lists was still free and working with the resistance. The editors of a group of liberal papers, including *Moscow News,* had already begun planning a joint underground paper to be called *Obshchaya Gazeta*—"The Common Newspaper"—and the editors at *Nezavisimaya Gazeta* were also putting together a samizdat edition. Opposition radio stations, particularly the Echo of Moscow, would go off the air for a few hours and then return. Telephone, fax, and telex lines at the bureaus of foreign news organizations worked flawlessly. CNN, the BBC, Radio Liberty, and the Voice of America pumped out continuous coverage. Reporters commandeered phone lines inside the White House and called out their reports without a hitch.

At the offices of the key Soviet newspapers, the situation was more complicated. The junta had ordered the shutdown of all the main liberal papers and used the high-circulation Party and government papers to do nothing more than publish their decrees and spurious reports on how normal the situation was, how calm. *Sovetskaya Rossiya* was enthusiastically cooperative, some of the others less so. At *Izvestia,* there was a war.

Izvestia was one of the most paradoxical institutions in the country. On the one hand, its editor, Nikolai Yefimov, was a shameless sycophant. His patron was the parliament's chairman, Anatoly Lukyanov. Yefimov was only too happy to fulfill the demands of his betters: about half the paper's staff of thirty foreign correspondents were KGB operatives. Although official government censors no longer sat in the editorial offices, Yefimov was more than able to handle the job himself. He was always quick to kill stories that he thought might damage or insult precisely the men now leading the coup d'état. On the other hand, the paper was brimming with talent. Mikhail Berger published some of the sharpest economic pieces in the country. Andrei Illesh wrote a series of articles on the shootdown of Korean Airlines 007 that was more revealing and critical of the Soviet leadership than anything published in the West. The better reporters and editors, the honest ones, despised Yefimov. They thought they had the talent and the resources to report the news far better than even the young renegades over at *Nezavisimaya Gazeta.* If they only could.

At around 1:00 P.M., a fight broke out in the composing room at the *Izvestia* plant on Pushkin Square. A few of the reporters had brought back a copy of Yeltsin's appeal to the people for resistance to the coup, and, with the support of the printers, they had already set it in type for the evening edition. But Yefimov's deputy, Dmitri Mamleyev, demanded that Yeltsin's words not appear.

The printers were furious. Pavel Vichenkov, one of the foremen, shouted, "We voted for Yeltsin! You can publish the statements of the committee, but we insist on Yeltsin's statement going into the paper as well."

"It's not your job to decide what goes into the paper," said Yevgeny Gemanov, one of Yefimov's men. "That's the job of the editors. Your job is to print what you are told to print."

"You can shoot us," a worker, Pavel Bushkov, said, "but we're not going to put this paper out without Yeltsin's statement. We live the life of animals, in poverty, and we don't want our children to live the same way."

Yefimov had missed the start of the battle because he was racing back to Moscow from his vacation house. As soon as he walked through the door, a small group of reporters surrounded him and demanded he publish Yeltsin's statement. Yefimov said there was no way and yanked the metal type from the printing press.

Ordinarily, Yefimov would have had his way. But now the printers, like the Siberian miners or the factory hands of Minsk, said they would sooner quit than give in. They would sooner destroy the presses than publish *Izvestia* without the appeal of Boris Yeltsin.

Twenty hours late, *Izvestia* appeared on the streets of Moscow and in every city and village of the Soviet Union. The Emergency Committee's proclamations blared out from page one. Yeltsin's appeal to resist the coup was on page two.

———

It was time for the junta to face the press. An early-evening appearance at the Foreign Ministry press center was part of their strategy to put a face of normalcy on the situation, to create the impression somehow that this was not a putsch but a legal, constitutional transition. This was their chance to compete on the evening news broadcasts of the world, to counter the image of Yeltsin, like Lenin at the Finland Station, rallying the people from the top of a tank.

In the first hours of the coup, Kryuchkov, for one, felt euphoric. There were no strikes, no demonstrations. Radical republican presidents such as Zviad Gamsakhurdia in Georgia made no move to act against the coup. Yanayev, for his part, wandered around his office and the Kremlin hallways. Other men were making the decisions. But this was his moment. At the press conference, he had to convince the people beyond the camera that all was well, that he was in control.

The problem was that Yanayev could not control his own self. He sniffed like a smack addict in need of a fix, and his hands trembled like little wild animals quivering in front of him. He was lost from the start. His answers were transparent lies, his attempt at calm had the brittle ring of hysteria. The reporters, except some of the obvious reactionary plants, showed no fear or respect in their questions. They even laughed at him! Gorbachev had been stripped of his "nuclear football," the case containing the codes. All the codes were now in the hands of the military and the KGB. A junta in control of a vast nuclear power, and they laughed!

About halfway through the disaster, Yanayev called on a twenty-four-year-old reporter from *Nezavisimaya Gazeta,* Tatyana Malkina. Just a year before, Malkina had worked as a low-level researcher at *Moscow News,* rummaging through the clips, doing scut work for the older reporters. Now she was a staffer on the hottest paper in Moscow. She got out of her seat, took the microphone, and fixed her eyes on the half-drunk pretender to power.

"Tell me, please," she said, "do you realize you have carried out a state coup? And which comparison do you find more appropriate—1917 or 1964?" The Bolshevik coup or the overthrow of Nikita Khrushchev?

For an instant, the man who would be king looked at his own wretched hands; he seemed sad, as if he wondered if the shaking would ever stop.

At the Ministry of Defense, Dmitri Yazov watched the press conference with his wife, Emma. She wept as she watched the pathetic spectacle and begged her husband to call Gorbachev and call off the coup.

"Dima, what have you joined?" she said through her tears. "You always laughed at them! Call Gorbachev. . . ."

But the marshal told his wife that was impossible now. The connections had all been severed.

———

Working out of a war room on the third floor, Yeltsin signed a decree creating a backup shadow government and dispatched a team of twenty-three civilian and military leaders in the Russian government to set it up in a secret headquarters thirty-five miles outside Yeltsin's home city of Sverdlovsk in the Urals.

"The idea was to act in the name of the Russian government if the White House was captured," said Aleksei Yablokov, Yeltsin's environment minister and one of those who went to Sverdlovsk. Working in bunkers thirty feet underground that had been built during the cold war, the Russians began sending an unending series of faxes and telexes calling on local organizations and governments around the Soviet Union to resist the decrees of the junta.

The leader of the Urals Military District was one of the most reactionary generals in the country, Albert Makashov. It had been Makashov who had run against Yeltsin for the presidency on a purely Stalinist platform. Now Makashov was telling his charges to round up any suspicious people, including "cosmopolitans," the old Stalinist code word for Jews. But his troops paid little attention. The passions of the city of Sverdlovsk were with Yeltsin. More than 100,000 people staged a demonstration defying the junta in the main city square. There were no arrests.

———

Valentin Pavlov convened a meeting of all the government's ministers at 6:00 P.M. Environment Minister Nikolai Vorontsov, the only non-Communist in the group, took notes on the session and read some of them to Masha and me before they came out in the press days later.

"It was a chorus of agreement," said Vorontsov. Every minister but three expressed absolute support for the coup. After Pavlov repeated the tale of the "counterrevolutionaries" with their Stinger missiles and evil intentions, one minister after another rose to say the committee was their last hope. They made little secret that what they wanted most of all was a chance to stay in power, to hold on to the last sweet scraps of privilege. Vladimir Gusev, the head of the state committee on chemistry and biotechnology, was a typical case, telling his fellow ministers, "If we step back even an iota, we will sacrifice our jobs, our lives. We will not have another chance."

When Pavlov finished the meeting, he spoke with Yazov on the phone. Yazov could tell immediately that the prime minister, whom everyone knew as "Mr. Porky," was drunk again.

"Arrest them all," Pavlov said at one point.

Yazov knew things were going badly. Where was the plan? He was beginning to think that the collapse of the plot would be better than its success. But he pressed on.

———

The junta, of course, had banned the Russian Republic's new television station. The public would have no chance to see the puckish hosts of the news program *Vesti*. There would only be Central Television, and for news, there would be only *Vremya*. Just like the old days.

Even the best directors and reporters at *Vremya* knew they could not be heroes. They could not take to the airwaves with appeals for resistance. Their entire operation was riddled with informers, agents, and officers of the KGB. It was out of the question. Besides, all the really irreverent people had long ago gone to *Vesti* and the more liberal shows.

But a young *Vremya* reporter named Sergei Medvedev watched the CNN feeds and decided he had to do something. His editors gave him an assignment for the 9:00 P.M. broadcast: film a feature on "Moscow today." The idea, he knew, was to show how calm everything was, how "life is going on as normal." In fact, it was true. Much of Moscow, like nearly all of the rest of the country, did seem normal. People went to work. Some watched television and read the papers and tried to figure out what had happened. There were millions of people who thought the coup might even do some good; and there were millions who could not have cared less. But Medvedev also made sure to fill in the rest of the picture. He got some brief footage of the scenes around the White House: the barricades, the protesters. He even included a clip of Yeltsin on the tank. He handed it over to his editors and hoped for the best.

Yelena Pozdniak, a veteran director at *Vremya,* also decided she would do what she could to preserve, at the very least, a marginal sense of honesty. She got the word from Kravchenko and his deputies that if it was technically possible, she should edit out Yanayev's trembling hands at the press conference, the laughter in the hall, the scoffing reactions of the correspondents. Although that was easy enough to do, Pozdniak thought, "Let them see it all!'' She'd had enough of the lies. In the days of Brezhnev, she had cleaned up the stutters and blurts of the leaders on a nightly basis. Brezhnev had the verbal style of a senile crocodile and required special polishing. "He used to have a favored word, *kompetentnost* ["competency"], to which he always added an extra letter: *kompententnost*," Pozdniak recalled. "I had to find another speech where he said it correctly and then dub that in so no one would notice." But not this time.

Valentin Lazutkin, Kravchenko's deputy and a semiliberal man, also made his move. On the air, his rebellion would look slight, if not invisible; the broadcast was filled with the proclamations and approved commentaries of the committee. But he put Medvedev's piece on the air and he let the clips of the press conference run, complete with Yanayev's waggling hands.

"People got to see that Yeltsin was alive, that he was free and working, and that meant there was hope," Lazutkin said. The minute *Vremya* went off the air, the calls started coming in: three Politburo members and, worst of all, Boris Pugo, the interior minister.

Pugo was in a rage. "The story on Moscow was treacherous!" he said. "You have given instructions to the people on where to go and what to do. You will answer for this."

Later, Yanayev called, too. He did not seem to know what to talk about, and so Lazutkin politely asked him how he had liked the newscast. "I saw it," Yanayev said. "It was a good, balanced report. It showed everything from different points of view."

"But they said I would be punished for it," Lazutkin said.

"Who are they?" Yanayev asked. "From the Central Committee? Fuck 'em."

———

Beginning that night, Lazutkin acquired a new friend: a colonel of the KGB. The colonel went wherever Lazutkin went, listened to all his conversations, watched as he made all his decisions.

"Why are you here?" Lazutkin asked.

"For your security," the colonel said.

But soon the KGB man came around. He and Lazutkin exchanged smiles as the coup began to erode. And then they took out the bottle, the eternal equalizer of men.

"Cheers!" the agent said.

"Cheers!" said the man who had shown Big Brother with his pants down.

Lazutkin's son was proud of his father's subtle rebellion, but he could not call him to say so. Sergei Lazutkin was at the White House, on the barricades.

AUGUST 20, 1991

For the three days of the coup, Yeltsin did not sleep. Early on the morning of the 20th, he and his aides looked out the windows and out to the barricades. There were still people outside the White House, about ten thousand or so gathered around portable radios or little campfires. But those inside were nervous. They needed huge crowds. They had to depend on the most undependable thing in the history of Russia: the stubborn, free will of its people.

In the hallways, people milled around, fueled by nerves and rumor. There were middle-aged men armed to the teeth, men who had not held a rifle since the day they left the army. A few hundred young men who worked for new security guard agencies, such as "Bells" and "Aleks," signed up with the Afghan vets. In the corners of offices, under secretaries' desks, there were little mountains of machine guns, grenades, Molotov cocktails. Mstislav Rostropovich, who had played his cello less than two years before in front of the remnants of the Berlin Wall, returned to his homeland now and stood guard near Yeltsin's office for a few hours cradling an AK-47 assault rifle. Some of the best-known "men of the sixties" were coming: Yuri Karyakin, the Dostoevsky scholar; Ales Adamovich. The New Wave politicians were there, too: Sergei Stankevich with his peachy cheeks and leather jacket looking like a student council president trying to be cool; Ilya Zaslavsky, limping urgently from office to office; the constitutional scholar Oleg Rumantsyev and the lawyer Sergei Shakrai hunched over desks, drafting decrees for Yeltsin.

Yeltsin's men seemed to have a pipeline to all the goings-on at the key points of the coup. They had military men calling them with intelligence reports, Russian KGB calling in with information about Kryuchkov. At about the same time, Yazov was at the Ministry of Defense cursing about a lack of active support from the Party, cursing the passive resistance of some of his top generals. One group after another was telling him they were "not prepared" to attack, and he, too, felt that it was all going wrong, that a "lake of blood" would not bring victory but deeper shame.

As traffic picked up out on the streets, Yeltsin's people could see that the crowd around the White House was thickening. With the help of leaflets pasted up in subway stations and bus stops, people heard more about the truth of what was going on and what was needed. Yeltsin called a demonstration for 10:30 A.M.

Standing on the White House balcony above a huge Russian tricolor and behind a bulletproof shield, he showed his combative face and sounded his baritone, warning that the "junta used no restraint in grabbing power and the junta feels itself under no restraint in keeping it."

"Doesn't Yazov have his hands covered in blood from other republics? Hasn't Pugo bloodied his hands in the Baltics and the Caucasus? . . . The [Russian] prosecutors and the Interior Ministry have their orders: whoever fulfills the commands of this illegal committee will be prosecuted!

"The troops have refused to follow these putschists blindly. I believe it is necessary to support these troops and together with them observe a sense of order and discipline. . . . I am convinced that here, in democratic Moscow, aggression of the conservative forces will not win out. Democracy will. And we will stay here as long as it takes for the junta to be brought to justice!"

It was not a brilliant speech, but it gave more than 100,000 people the chance to see the symbol they were risking themselves to protect, whatever his faults and vanities, Yeltsin was now the symbol of democracy, he was the man they had elected—not Gorbachev. Of all the speakers on the White House balcony, it took Yelena Bonner, Sakharov's widow and no friend of Gorbachev, to mention the man who was now languishing in fallen luxury in Foros: "I had my disagreements with Gorbachev," she said, "but he was the president of this country and we cannot allow a bunch of bandits to take over."

Oleg Kalugin, who had eluded arrest by his former colleagues at the KGB, introduced a lieutenant colonel in the secret police who appealed to "Volodya" Kryuchkov to stop the coup which was "about to collapse." The much-loved comic Gennadi Khazanov imitated Gorbachev the way Rich Little used to do Nixon. In his best Gorbachev voice, full of softened *g*'s and grammatical slips, he said, "I feel healthy, but I just can't help thinking that you can't carry off a clean policy with trembling hands."

Then Yevgeny Yevtushenko, the poet of equal parts irreverence and self-promotion, got his chance at the microphone.

No! Russia will not fall again on her knees for interminable years,
With us are Pushkin, Tolstoy.
With us stands the whole awakened people.
And the Russian parliament, like a wounded marble swan of freedom,
defended by the people, swims into immortality.

It was far from Yevtushenko's worst, and the crowd loved it. All the same, I preferred the four-liners that were already spreading around Moscow, including:

> We're told that order's now assured us,
> But the junta's hand can't rest;
> They're a little Pinochetist
> And just slightly Husseinesque.

In a cool drizzle, I walked down Kutuzovsky Prospekt, across the bridge, and to the White House. I saw a group of men in their twenties, well-dressed Soviet business types, carrying stacks of pizzas from the Pizza Hut down the road. Another delegation of ruble millionaires had been dispatched to McDonald's for further provisions.

I stayed all afternoon and into the night. At 4:00 P.M. there was a rumor that plainclothes KGB agents had gotten into the building and had been caught. Then Yeltsin cut short a phone call with John Major, the British prime minister, saying that tanks were on their way to the White House. There was, it turned out, no such raid in progress. The Kremlin was busy with other things. For one thing, Yanayev contacted Saddam Hussein and promised to restore good relations with Iraq. In all, the coup won support from Hussein, Muammar Qaddafi, and Fidel Castro.

By the early evening, support for the resistance was pouring in over the telex and fax machines. The leaders of Kazakhstan, Ukraine, and other regions, after some hesitation, were speaking out against the junta. Even the Ukrainian KGB chief, General Nikolai Golushko, called to say that he did not support the coup. Just as important, there were pathetic signs of weakness, news that Pavlov had been hospitalized for "high blood pressure." There were rumors that Yazov and Kryuchkov had resigned. Lukyanov, oily to the last, told one of Gorbachev's aides, "I had nothing to do with the putsch." The military leaders supporting the Russian government were growing bolder by the hour. Colonel General Pavel Grachev, commander of the airborne units, kept putting off Varennikov, the ground forces commander who wanted him to get in place for a raid on the White House. Shaposhnikov even ordered his men to be prepared to intercept and shoot down assault helicopters on the way to the White House. Later, Shaposhnikov said that he had even considered the possibility of making a retaliatory air raid on the Kremlin if the conspirators managed to storm the White House.

In the war room, Yeltsin, Kobets, and Rutskoi knew that if there was going to be a raid it would have to come soon, that night. The plotters could see that the crowds around the White House were growing. In the West, some commentators were saying that Moscow had not reacted the way Prague had in 1989, when virtually the entire population was on the streets. True enough. But the Czechs could also rest assured that their leaders were not about to launch a full military attack against them. In Moscow, with fifty thousand troops in the city, with the Manezh, Red Square, the Ring Road, Lenin Hills, and other points lined with tanks, there were no such assurances. What assurances could there be after Baku, Tbilisi, Vilnius, Riga, and Osh?

On the barricades outside, as people milled around, their feet sloshing in the puddles, there were new rumors every minute, and every rumor went out over the radio. There were self-appointed leaders with megaphones making pronouncements, few of which made any sense, all of which caused even greater nervousness and confusion. Just to stand still in that crowd took some endurance. For a while there was boredom, and then, with the newest rumor, the skin tingled the way it does before you jump from a high board or head, inexorably, into a car accident. I saw one man, a vet in his old jungle fatigues, holding a stick in one hand for protection and a bottle of vodka in the other for bravery. The most reassuring sight was the way the soldiers in their tanks welcomed kids aboard and flirted with the girls. There was hope in that.

And there was real hope in the grit of these people. Along one barricade on Kutuzovsky Prospekt, I talked with a middle-aged woman, Regina Boga-chova, who said she would sooner be crushed by a tank than move. "I am ready to die right here, right on this spot. I will not move. I am fifty-five years old and for years nothing but obedience and inertia was pounded into my brain. The Young Pioneers, the Young Communist League, the unions, the Communist Party, all of them taught me not to answer back. To be a good Soviet, a screw in the machine. But Monday morning my friend called me and said, 'Turn on the radio.' I didn't need to. I heard a rumbling and went out on my balcony and saw the tanks rumbling down below, on the Moz-haisk Highway. These monsters! They have always thought they could do anything to us! They have thrown out Gorbachev and now they are threaten-ing a government I helped elect. I will ignore the curfew. I'll let a tank roll over me if I have to. I'll die right here if I have to."

————

The dramas at the newspaper offices had only heightened.

At *Izvestia,* Yefimov took a call from Yanayev and was told that he should not publish any more of Yeltsin's decrees or any other material not autho-rized by the junta. Yefimov, of course, wheezed his ready agreement. When one of his deputies told him that he was acting so weakly that "none of us are going to defend you if they put you on trial," Yefimov fired her. He was going to follow the orders of the junta, no matter what.

At *Nezavisimaya Gazeta,* the staff worked day and night gathering mate-rial. Especially after the first day, when the junta showed its wavering hand, they were having a blast. This was their moment. Vladimir Todres, a twenty-five-year-old political reporter, said that he and his friends at the paper saw the coup as the defining event of their generation, the street-level, media-age equivalent of what the Twentieth Party Congress had been for Karpinsky, Gorbachev, and the thaw generation. "For us, the putsch was not a matter of simple politics," Todres said. "Usually we hate politics, to tell you the truth. But this was the Pepsi Generation under threat. Our very existence was in jeopardy. The bikers feared for their motorcycles. The young businessmen worried about their markets. The racketeers even thought about their bottom line and came to defend the White House. Prostitutes, students, scholars, everybody had an interest in this new life, and we were just not willing to give it all up to these old men. And also, it was like being in a great movie. Life and art were all mixed up together. My friends who were abroad were heartbroken, not because they felt fear, but because they felt left out. They couldn't be in the movie."

The journalism part of the movie was splendid. On the first day of the coup, *Nezavisimaya Gazeta*'s editor in chief, Vitaly Tretyakov, had decided not to defy the coup plotters' press ban. His thinking was that a quick, wrong move could endanger the staff and end the paper entirely. Some of the younger reporters were furious, especially when they heard that the printers at *Izvestia* were willing to challenge the ban and work the presses. Tretyakov insisted. But on the 20th, as it became slightly clearer that the coup leaders had neither the will nor the level of organization to mount a full-scale attack on the press as a whole, Tretyakov and the staff put out a photocopied version of *Nezavisimaya Gazeta* with the lead headline "The Feeble Coup: It Is Still Not Over." The edition was filled with news about the putsch from Moscow and the provinces. The few thousand readers in Moscow who managed to find the underground edition learned that the coup was almost completely centered on Moscow. The main problem spots outside Moscow were the Baltic capitals, where troops quickly took up positions at the main television towers and other points, and the region of Tatarstan, where Party leaders calculated that they had a better chance of gaining independence from the Russian Republic if they supported the coup. The attack on Leningrad had stalled, and, despite some early wavering by the republican leaders, Kazakhstan, Ukraine, and other key republics saw almost no visible sign of the coup on the streets. Otherwise, the country was quiet. You could walk for just a few minutes from the very center of Moscow and not know that there was a coup d'état in progress.

But at the center of the coup, the reporters were working the story hard, especially Sergei Parkhomenko and Pavel Felgenhauer, the paper's military correspondent. Felgenhauer stayed in the White House throughout the siege and was in constant contact with the military leaders who planned Yeltsin's strategy of resistance in their makeshift "war room." Felgenhauer, a bearish man who spoke fluent English, had never set out to be a journalist or a military expert. He had a Ph.D. in biology and had won what he called "a measure of international fame" with his thesis, "RNA Synthesis During the Maturation of Frog Oocytes." He told me, "I quit science because you can't do science anymore in this country. We can't even afford test tubes or food for the frogs. So I became a journalist. I always liked to write."

Felgenhauer had followed military affairs the way some American kids follow baseball. It was all a game, a combination of action and statistics. "Pavel is a kid who likes toy soldiers. He's a gigantic forty-year-old kid who is a genius," Parkhomenko said. "He loved the coup because he got to play soldier and war correspondent all at once."

Parkhomenko could not believe the look of supreme contentment in his colleagues' eyes as they sat in the White House. "As for me, I was terrified," he said after the coup. "I thought I was a dead man. They try to say that it was all nothing, that there was never any danger. But that's ridiculous. It was all a war of nerves, a dangerous telephone war. There were orders and counterorders by phones. When the Russian government found out that a contingent of tanks was being sent, they set up rows of gas canisters so that there would be a huge explosion. Their strategy all along was to maximize the threat of bloodshed, to scare the shit out of the KGB and the putschists by essentially using unarmed people as a shield."

———

In Foros, Gorbachev listened to his Sony transistor radio. Several times a day, he passed along his demands to his captors: to be freed, to address the people. Raisa told him not to eat the food he was served; eat some of the food given to the guards instead. She was afraid he would be poisoned, shot. "We tried to keep calm," Raisa would say later. "We tried to go through our normal day." But it was impossible, and she, especially, suffered, losing control of one hand—from sheer fright, apparently. Late at night, Gorbachev's son-in-law, Anatoly, set up a videocamera and taped Gorbachev reading what was essentially his last testament, declaring that he had refused the plotters and saying what he stood for.

". . . I have been deprived of my governmental communications, the plane which was here with me, also the helicopters. . . ."

Gorbachev and his son-in-law made four copies of the film and snipped them up into pieces. They thought they could hide them somehow, sneak them out to Moscow.

". . . I am under arrest, and no one is allowed on the grounds of my dacha. . . ."

Gorbachev's aide Chernyayev said maybe he could swim along the shore to freedom and, from there, reach the Russian government. But it was absurd. There was nothing they could do. The battle, now, was elsewhere.

———

The first shots came just before midnight, the distant popping sounds of tracer bullets. Had the storming of the White House begun?

General Kobets knew that if the KGB and military units got past the barricades, they would lose the White House in "not less than fifteen minutes." There were a number of elements still in the Russians' favor. The barricades, organized by the war room, had been built high and strong by the protesters on the street. They might not stop everything—or anything—but they put an element of doubt and chaos into the plotters' blueprints.

Suddenly, tens of thousands of people who had come from all parts of the city to protect the White House began their defiant chant: *"Pozor! Pozor!"* ("Shame! Shame!") And then, *"Rossiya! Rossiya!"*

Until the next morning, few would learn what had happened. Three protesters were killed when they clashed with a tank near the barricades on the Garden Ring Road. Some of the demonstrators set fire to tanks with Molotov cocktails. The smell of burning gasoline in the air did nothing to ease the nerves of the huge crowds defending the White House.

———

Now the coup had produced three martyrs. How many more were to come?

The factory seamstress, Nadezhda Kudinova, took up her position on the barricades across Kutuzovsky Prospekt. She was soaked from the rain, but someone gave her dry socks and shoes. The usually surly administrators across the street at the Ukraine Hotel opened up their rooms for the women on the barricades to sleep in two- and three-hour shifts. All the while, Nadezhda kept her radio tuned to *Echo of Moscow* and listened to Rutskoi and Khasbulatov, who were urging calm—civil disobedience, but calm. Every few minutes there were bulletins about troop movements, the possibility that reconnaissance planes would signal an attack. "We always felt they were there with us," Kudinova said. "They spoke in a special sort of language, in a heightened tone, like the words a man speaks before his death. They spoke to us very candidly, creating a feeling of unity beyond description. We heard them and they heard us."

The women defenders formed the front line of the southern barricade with a handpainted sign: "Soviet Soldiers: Don't Shoot Your Mothers." They were ready to die as heroes of war. "The people in the White House ordered us to step aside, not to jump on the tanks if they came," Kudinova said. "But we knew that if the tanks came, we would step in front of them. We talked about where we should put the tanks that had defected over to our side, in front of the barricades or behind them. We put them behind the barricades, because if they had been captured, the coup loyalists would have shot their crews dead. They are just young kids, after all."

———

The plan to storm the White House was brutally simple.

On the afternoon of the 20th, the deputy defense minister, Vladislav Achalov, presided over a planning session for "Operation Thunder," a meeting that included such leading generals as Boris Gromov, Pavel Grachev, Aleksandr Lebed, and Sergei Akhromeyev, Gorbachev's lead military adviser, as well as KGB leaders Genii Ageyev and Viktor Karpukhin, the head of the elite Alpha Group. With the help of airborne and KGB troops, the Alpha Group would storm the parliament, blasting through the doors with grenade launchers, and then they would make their way to the fifth floor to arrest, or kill, Yeltsin. The Beta Group would suppress any resistance while the Wave troops, working with other KGB units, would arrest the other Russian leaders. The tanks would fire shells to deafen and stun the defenders of the White House, and helicopter gunships would provide support and storm the roof and balconies.

The Alpha Group already had a reputation for bloody efficiency. In 1979, they burst into the palace of the Afghan dictator Amin and murdered him on the eve of the Soviet invasion. (This was later described in the Soviet press as the "fraternal invitation of the Afghan peoples.") And it was the Alpha Group that had been the lead unit in Vilnius during the January 1991 massacre.

Although Kryuchkov's intentions were clear, the loyalties and intentions of the KGB as a whole were a muddle. KGB sources were the first to alert the Russian government that Yeltsin was to be arrested as the coup began. They provided the Russian government with crucial information about the communications systems of the Defense Ministry and the KGB itself. *Moscow News* reported later that the KGB gave Yeltsin's team a printing press to publish its leaflets, and retired agents now in private business contributed more than a million rubles to a Russian defense fund. Early in the putsch, middle-rank officers in the KGB drafted a statement denouncing the junta.

Yeltsin's sources in the KGB told him that the Alpha Group would move on the 19th at about 6:00 P.M. But there was dissension in the ranks. After the coup, sources in the KGB told me that the middle and "upper-middle" ranks of both the secret police and the army had no faith in their leaders. They saw them as muddled dinosaurs, not to be trusted. They saw how, time and again, the leadership conceived its schemes—the war in Afghanistan, the assaults in Tbilisi, Baku, and Vilnius—and then avoided all blame. Gorbachev's aide Aleksandr Yakovlev told me that even such generals as Gromov and Grachev, decorated veterans of the Afghan war, "were working both sides of the street, keeping in close contact with the White House even as they were sitting in on the planning sessions of the coup. They're no democrats, but they refused to have blood on their hands for the sake of such idiots as Kryuchkov and Yazov."

"There is a huge crowd," General Aleksandr Lebed said at the afternoon meeting with Achalov. "They are building barricades. There will be heavy casualties. There are many armed men around the White House."

Yazov arrived and said, "Well, what have we got?"

Achalov said they simply didn't have the force to storm the White House successfully. Yazov told his subordinates to call in more troops, "we can't lose the initiative." But he seemed to let the matter drop.

At a separate planning meeting of the Alpha Group, a senior officer, Anatoly Salayev, got up and said, "They want to smear us in blood. Each of you is free to act according to his conscience. I for one will not storm the White House." In Tbilisi, Baku, and Vilnius, the military and KGB rank and file had seen how they had been used to shed blood, and each time the leading men in power dodged responsibility. They simply would not let it happen again, especially not when it involved killing their own countrymen.

In the meantime, KGB and undercover police agents continued to take photographs and videos of the scene outside and inside the White House. "We filmed everything," Karpukhin told a reporter from *Literaturnaya Gazeta*. "We had agents both among the defenders and inside the parliament. At night, General Lebed and I toured the barricades. They were toys; we could have smashed them easily."

"What was the battle plan?"

"At three A.M. the OMON police troops would clear the square. They would disperse the crowd with tear gas and water cannons. Our units would follow, from the ground and from the air, by using helicopters, grenade launchers, and other special means. . . . Then we would take the building. . . . My boys are practically invulnerable. The whole thing would be over in fifteen minutes. . . . It was all up to me. Thank God I couldn't bring myself to do it. It would have been a bloodbath. I refused."

There were more mundane considerations, too, for the KGB. Like the difficulty of landing helicopters in rainy weather and on a roof that had deliberately been strewn with broken furniture and other debris. Like the problem of air force commander Shaposhnikov, who refused to allow the use of his helicopters for the raid and even threatened an airborne counterattack against the junta. There was also the threat of an extremely high body count. Anyone on those barricades that night—KGB informers included—knew that there was at the White House a general willingness to die, a refusal to clear the way for an attack. What's more, there was also the possibility of humiliation, even defeat. Yeltsin and some of his aides spent part of the night in an underground bunker sealed by a twenty-inch-thick steel door. The KGB might have wondered what would happen if, at the cost of thousands of lives, they "took" the White House, but could not come away with Yeltsin. According to the prosecutor's report, Generals Grachev and Shaposhnikov agreed that if the Emergency Committee began to storm the White House, they would retaliate and give the order to send bombers over the Kremlin.

———

At 8:00 P.M., the Emergency Committee met at the Kremlin. Yanayev shocked his colleagues, telling them that he had heard "rumors" that the committee was organizing an attack on the White House. He proposed that they announce on television that the rumors were untrue.

There was a silence, witnesses told the Russian prosecutors, and then Yanayev said, "Is there really someone here among us who wants to storm the White House?"

No one answered. When Kryuchkov began to talk about how he was hearing from all over the country that the committee had won massive support, Yanayev said, no, he had been getting telegrams telling him just the opposite. The putschists were hoping to win support by flooding the stores with goods and lowering prices, if only for a few weeks. But it was all a fantasy. The military reserves were not what anyone thought they were. There was just enough to feed the army for a few days.

The coup was unraveling. At 3:00 A.M. on the 21st, Kryuchkov called the White House. He spoke with Yeltsin's closest aide, Gennadi Burbulis.

"It's okay now," the spy chief said. "You can go to sleep."

AUGUST 21, 1991

Thousands of people woke on the barricades that morning happy to be alive. They were still there, and that was something. Most of the talk I heard there was about the death of the three demonstrators on the Garden Ring Road; they pieced together the details of that quick burst of hysteria and gunfire that had killed Dmitri Komar, Ilya Krichevsky, and Vladimir Usov. Most of all, people were exhausted, sore, still nervous, still overstimulated by the stream of rumors. Some people were still passing around bottles of vodka and Armenian cognac. Nadezhda Kudinova headed for home, satisfied she had done what she had to do. "On the barricades," she said, "there was this incredible feeling of fellowship, which you will never get on a queue or on a trolley where men will never give you a seat. In everyday life, I guess you just don't notice it. But these were extreme circumstances, and somehow this week I saw the profound aspects of human nature. I never knew there were so many kind people in my country."

What Kudinova and the others could not have known was that they had won. The coup, insofar as it had ever really taken hold, had collapsed. The combination of confusion, stupidity, drunkenness, lack of will, miscalculation, and happenstance (the blessed rain!) had all conspired against the committee. And just as a change in consciousness in the people had led to this incredible resistance, one could not rule out that even the conspirators had evolved beyond their ancestors. They had the same Stalinist impulses, but not the core of cruelty, the willingness to flood the city in blood, call it a victory for socialism, and then go off to a midnight screening of *Happy Guys*. They could pick up the pistol, but not always shoot it. They were bullies, and bullies could be called on their bluff.

Already the members of the committee were thinking about the future. Oleg Baklanov was still talking about arresting Yeltsin and his aides. "If we don't get them, they will hang us," he told General Gromov.

At three separate meetings—with Kryuchkov at Lubyanka, with Yazov at the Ministry of Defense, with Yanayev at the Kremlin—the Emergency Committee was making plans to shut it all down.

"We must think now what to do," Yazov told his senior commanders. They responded quickly, voting unanimously to send troops back to their barracks and lift the curfew. Yazov knew that some of these officers had defied him, even provided intelligence to Yeltsin, and so he agreed, saying, magnanimously, "I will not be another Pinochet." Then the generals demanded that Yazov quit the committee, but, for all his reservations, he refused.

"I'm not a boy," he said, as he got up to leave. "I can't act in this manner, joining yesterday and resigning today. . . . I'm sorry I ever got mixed up in this business."

———

Yeltsin hung up the phone and knew it was over. Kryuchkov had called, suggesting they fly together to Foros. Yeltsin knew well that it might be a ruse, a way for Kryuchkov to flush him from his nest, capture him, and keep the junta going. But it smacked of desperation. He would stay in Moscow, but he would send Rutskoi, the Russian vice president, and Ivan Silayev, the prime minister.

"We've got the bastards," Yeltsin told Burbulis. "They're on the run."

The retreat began after 11:00 A.M. when the first tanks turned around near Red Square. By 1:00 P.M., huge convoys stormed along the main arteries out of town, endless columns of tanks and personnel carriers chewing up the soft asphalt and heading toward their barracks.

I jumped into a car with Debbie Stewart of the Associated Press, who drove wildly along the tank column. Weaving in and out of the convoy and racing up and down the columns, we saw an amazing display of joy. The armies of Napoleon, Hitler, and other would-be conquerors of Moscow had time and again fled Russia in despair and defeat. These soldiers were retreating in relief and sheer pleasure, as if they had won the victory of an age. The machines made Leninsky Prospekt tremble. I could feel the rumbling at the base of my throat and on the soles of my feet. All along the convoy, the soldiers, most of them eighteen or nineteen years old, smiled and laughed. The worst had not happened. They had not shamed themselves. They had not shot at their brothers and sisters, their mothers and fathers. In gratitude, old women threw bunches of red carnations and white roses at the boys in their tanks. Construction crews stopped work and applauded the parade. The soldiers answered with the thumbs-up and applauded back.

"It's over! We've got our orders!" a commander shouted above the furious din. "Thank God, we're headed home!"

At one point along the retreat, at the huge sign on Leninsky Prospekt declaring "The USSR: Stronghold of Socialism," a man named Sergei Pavlov pulled his Lada over to the side of the road and shouted out his window that he was ready to follow the parade all the way to the barracks. "I'm taking no chances," he said. "I want to make sure the tanks are really leaving."

———

Thus commenced the "race to Foros," with both Yeltsin's representatives, Vice President Rutskoi and Prime Minister Silayev, and the men of the putsch, Yazov, Baklanov, Tizyakov, and Kryuchkov, flying on separate planes. Lukyanov, in a marvelous touch, took yet another plane, as if to distance himself from all but his own peculiar position. He brought along Vladimir Ivashko, the deputy general secretary of the Party.

And while everyone else was migrating south, Yanayev sat in his office, disheveled, as two of Gorbachev's men came in. The aides had been down the hall working during the entire coup d'état.

"Has everyone been arrested?" Yanayev said, his face twitching.

"Yes," said the former steelworker Veniamin Yarin, in a blatant lie.

Yanayev whined about how the plotters had threatened him with jail and a "tribunal" if he didn't cooperate. He had joined only "to avert bloodshed," he said, meaning his own, not Moscow's.

"Yanayev realized why I was there," Yarin said later. "There was fear in his eyes. . . . And, yes, he was very drunk."

Yanayev stayed in the office all night, and when Yarin returned early the next morning, there were empty bottles all over the floor. Yanayev was awake, but he could no longer recognize Yarin. As Jim Hoagland of *The Washington Post* wrote of the putsch, it began like Dostoevsky and was ending like the Marx Brothers.

———

On the flight to the Crimea, Rutskoi's men—around fifty troops from the Ryazan officers' school—sat in their seats cleaning their machine guns. One colonel said that if there was a problem at the dacha, "We'll break through anything." But Vadim Bakatin, the liberal interior minister who had been fired as Gorbachev began his shift to the right, spoke up and said the soldiers should stay out of sight and avoid any sort of provocation. "If there's even a single shot, they'll blame it on us when Gorbachev is found dead," Bakatin said. The soldiers agreed to stay on the plane.

When the delegation of Russians arrived in Foros, they were let through the gates, but they saw snipers in the trees and on balconies. They were anxious until the very moment they made it to the door. There was no attack, no trap. Clearly, the KGB guards had been instructed to stand down.

Gorbachev wanted only to see the Russians. He refused to meet with Kryuchkov or Yazov. As he greeted Rutskoi and the rest, Gorbachev looked weary but relieved. He wore a light gray sweater and khaki trousers and was literally trembling with excitement. He kept repeating that there had been a coup against a legitimate president, a commander in chief, that the briefcase with the secret codes had been taken away from him, that it was all a "blasphemy." "There's one thing I want to say," Gorbachev explained. "I made no deals. I maintained a firm position, demanding the immediate summoning of a session of the Congress or the Supreme Soviet. Only they can decide the issue. Otherwise, after any other step, I would have had to finish myself off. There could be no other way out. . . . I was cut off from any communication. The sea was closed off by ships. There were troops all around. It was complete and total isolation."

Bakatin and Yevgeny Primakov, two Gorbachev loyalists who had supported the resistance, told their man several times what a singular role Yeltsin had played and that when Gorbachev returned to Moscow there could be no more conflicts. Gorbachev promised he would do this. Some of the Russians, none too gently, reminded Gorbachev that the conspirators had all been the president's men. It was true, Gorbachev admitted. "I had complete confidence in the people around me, and I relied on them. My gullibility undermined me. On the one hand, it's probably good to trust people, but not to this extent."

Gorbachev got testy when someone said he had to pass a decree saying that he was reinstated as president. "I never stopped being president!" he said. And as for the charge that he had been critically ill, it was all "nonsense, an absurd pretext." Silayev had brought along two doctors—both heart specialists—but there was clearly no need. Gorbachev, Silayev said, "looked amazingly well." Raisa was quite another story. The Russians were startled as they saw her try to navigate the stairs and come down to greet the Russians. "She was in horrible condition," said one member of the Russian delegation, Vladimir Lysenko. "She wobbled as she walked, but she did make sure to kiss all of us."

"Should we fly home tonight?" Gorbachev finally asked Raisa.

"Yes," she answered softly. "We must fly immediately."

———

Gorbachev did have a brief meeting with Lukyanov, his old friend from Moscow State University and the Komsomol. Right away, Lukyanov tried to explain his position, how difficult it would have been to convene an immediate emergency session of the Union parliament, how he had tried to fend off the coup.

Gorbachev was having none of it.

"We have known each other for forty years!" he said. "Cut the bullshit! Stop hanging noodles on my ears!"

———

At the Belbek military airport, the presidential plane, the Ilyushin 62 marked "Sovietsky Soyuz," idled on the tarmac. A half mile away, near some MiG-29 fighter jets, was the smaller Tupolev 134 which Rutskoi had brought from Moscow. The Zil limousines raced between the two planes, trying to make it seem as if Gorbachev had been dropped off at his usual jet. He hadn't. Finally, Gorbachev boarded the Tu-134.

On the runway, Gorbachev approached the state chief of civil aviation and his personal pilot and said, "Please don't have hurt feelings, but I'll be taking the Russian plane. Understand the situation. I'm doing the right thing."

"Let's go," Raisa said, "but only with the Russians."

_____

With the collapse of the coup, the Russian Republic's own news show, *Vesti,* returned to the air at 8:00 P.M.. The lead announcer, Yuri Rostov, who had been thrown off the air by the head of state television, Leonid Kravchenko, could barely contain his glee. He was grinning and on the edge of tears. "Congratulations!" he told us. "The junta is at an end!"

Rostov did not bother with the niceties of objectivity and did little to control his contempt for the men he wryly called "the saviors of our Motherland"—the plotters who had engineered the coup. He also made sure to warn the viewers that Russia "should not repeat one of Gorbachev's greatest mistakes: forgetting that the KGB is the biggest opponent of reform." After going through the stunning news of the day, Rostov delivered the bulletin that may have delighted him most of all, the dismissal of "that man beloved by us and treasured by you TV viewers, Leonid Petrovich Kravchenko."

_____

In the early hours of the morning, Gorbachev sat in the forward cabin of the plane surrounded by his exhausted family. His granddaughter was wrapped in a plaid blanket, and slept on the floor. Rutskoi and Silayev talked quietly with Gorbachev, the better not to wake the others. They opened a bottle of wine and drank to the end of the coup.

Off in the rear cabin, Kryuchkov sat alone, a captive, his head thrown back, his eyes closed, but he was not asleep. He spoke to no one and no one spoke to him. Armed guards watched his every twitch.

When the plane landed in Moscow at Vnukovo Airport, the escort delegation told Gorbachev to wait a bit before coming down the steps until the guards were sure there would be no surprise attack. A guard with a machine gun came out the door first and scanned the airfield. There was nothing, no last trap. The conspirators had nothing left in them. Finally, Gorbachev appeared in the doorframe. He wore a beige windbreaker. His suntan looked, under the circumstances, ridiculous. His face was a cross of pleasure and fear as if he did not know quite what awaited him even now. Behind him was his daughter in her denim miniskirt, Raisa, and his granddaughter clumping sleepily down the stairs. Raisa was dazed, spent.

From the minute Gorbachev got off the plane, people kept telling him that he had returned to a "different city," even a "different country." The "slave mentality" that had plagued poets from Pushkin on was at an end, and Gorbachev seemed to agree. He could not afford to disagree. At least he understood that much.

Gorbachev paused in front of a television camera. Before anyone could ask a question, Yevgeny Primakov said, "No, Mikhail Sergeyevich is tired. The car is ready. We should go."

"No, wait," Gorbachev said. "I want to breathe the air of freedom in Moscow."

———

Out on the tarmac, the Russian prosecutors arrested Kryuchkov, Yazov, and the industrialist Tizyakov.

"Did the people really see our actions as so terrible?" Kryuchkov said. "Well, now it is the end of the committee."

Sergei Shakhrai, one of Yeltsin's closest legal advisers, said Kryuchkov "lost control of himself when he was detained. He could not control his hands or his facial expressions or recognize his own things. The man could be seen to be in a state of profound depression. . . . Yazov behaved more calmly and was in possession of himself, though he was deathly pale. The first thing he requested was help for his sick wife. . . . Tizyakov was outwardly normal, but you could sense he was bursting with spite. You got the feeling that he was ready simply to bite and tear to pieces anyone who got too close."

The men who had set out to save the empire were now under arrest. An officer of the law took away their shoelaces, belts, and all sharp objects. It was standard procedure.

The conspirators had launched the putsch to save the Soviet empire and their positions in it. Their failure was the finishing blow. No Baltic independence movement, no Russian liberals, had ever done as much to bring it all down. And now Yazov, at least, seemed to know it. "Everything is clear now," he said as they led him into a van with bars on the windows. "I am such an old idiot. I've really fucked up."

PART V

THE TRIAL OF THE
OLD REGIME

For two days after the fall of the coup, the dictators of the proletariat and their assistants at Central Committee headquarters ransacked their desks and emptied their safes. They fed one incriminating document after another into the shredding machines. To destroy everything in the archives would have taken months or years, yet there was a chance, at least, that they could eliminate all evidence of the Party's support of the coup and other recent embarrassments.

There was so little time. Thousands of furious demonstrators were shouting up at the windows of the Central Committee, demanding the destruction of the Party, the confiscation of its properties. The same crowds of students, housewives, workers, and intellectuals who had defended the White House now fanned out across the city, toppling the monuments of the regime and carrying signs reading "Smash the KGB!" "Send the Party to Chernobyl!" "Bring the Party to Trial!" But then the shredders began to jam and break, one after another. In their haste, the men of the Party had failed to remove the paper clips.

With the shouts from the street throbbing in their ears, some panicked officials suggested building a huge bonfire in the courtyards. Their juniors, however, advised them that if the demonstrators saw smoke coming from the

Central Committee, they would know what was happening and would storm the building. What could they do? Party workers were already driving truck-loads of material away through the hidden tunnels and back exits of the Central Committee building, and even that was not enough. There was so much to destroy and hide! And so now these ashen men—men who had ruled an empire with an inimitable blend of insouciance and banality—began tearing apart documents with their bare hands. They would sooner die of paper cuts than leave the evidence to the hordes.

The Party men, of course, were not interested merely in history's judgment. They refused to leave anything to the masses. To the very end, their serene sense of entitlement guided them. They stole telephones, computers, fax machines, television sets, video recorders, stationery. Anatoly Smirnov, an aide in the Party's International Department, said that his superior, Valentin Falin, gave him 600,000 rubles in cash and told him to stash it in his personal safe. Immediately.

And change the nameplate on my door, Falin ordered. Falin was sure that if he identified himself as a "People's Deputy" rather than as Central Com-mittee secretary he would be immune from future prosecution.

Falin had a great deal to answer for. His office was in charge of dispensing millions from the state purse to "brotherly parties" or terrorist organizations in Greece, Portugal, the United States, Angola—nearly one hundred coun-tries in all, according to the Russian government. He ran the secret workshop within the Central Committee that produced fake passports, beards, and mustaches for operatives on the road. Falin eventually took refuge in Ger-many, lecturing to the university students of Hamburg.

"Those were awful days for us," Vladimir Ivashko, the deputy general secretary of the Party, told me. "We were all terrified. We were suffering terribly inside the Central Committee. The Party was in the midst of reform, but no one would listen to that! It was terribly unfair!"

———

Even after he returned from captivity to Moscow following the fall of the August coup, Gorbachev defended the Communist Party. He was its son, its protector, and he would neither abandon nor kill it. At his first press confer-ence after the putsch, Gorbachev spoke earnestly about his allegiance to the "socialist choice" and the Party's "renewal." He told all who would listen that he had returned to a "different country," but he did not seem to know what that meant.

Gorbachev's closest adviser, Aleksandr Yakovlev, grew furious as he watched that mystifying session with the press. For six years, Yakovlev had prodded Gorbachev to abandon the hidebound nomenklatura and join forces with the urban intelligentsia, the pro-independence forces in the Baltic states—with all those who actually sought a transformation of the old order. But Gorbachev refused, insisting that the party had "begun perestroika and would lead it." Even now, after falling victim to a putsch, Gorbachev failed to see what was right and necessary.

"You have given the worst press conference of your career," Yakovlev told Gorbachev privately. "The Party is dead. Why can't you see that? Talk about its 'renewal' is senseless. It's like offering first aid to a corpse!"

Yeltsin catered even less to the sensibilities of Mikhail Gorbachev. Their personal battle had gone on for so long and contained so many seriocomic incidents that they seemed paired in eternal tension and dependence. Yin and Yang. Punch and Judy. On August 23, at a raucous session of the Russian parliament, Yeltsin clearly had the upper hand, and he used it to flay and humiliate his opponent. He forced Gorbachev to read aloud a transcript of the August 19 Council of Ministers meeting at which all but two of the ministers whom Gorbachev himself had nominated pledged their hearty support of the coup.

Gorbachev looked small and weak, but Yeltsin was not finished. "And now on a lighter note," he said with a jack-o'-lantern grin, "shall we now sign a decree suspending the activities of the Russian Communist Party?"

"What are you doing?" Gorbachev stammered. "I . . . haven't we . . . I haven't read this . . ."

But it was too late. Gorbachev was powerless. And on August 24, he resigned as general secretary of the Communist Party, dissolved its Central Committee, and declared, in essence, an end to the Bolshevik era.

———

The people of Moscow did not celebrate Gorbachev for his announcement. He could have done no less. Perhaps one day they would come to recognize and revere Gorbachev's contribution, but not now, not yet. Now they celebrated themselves and the ruin of the System. All around the city, young people smeared statues of Old Bolsheviks with graffiti and uprooted them with crowbars or, when necessary, cranes. The Moscow city government sponsored the removal of the huge statue of "Iron" Feliks Dzerzhinsky from the square outside KGB headquarters, thus creating the ultimate image of the regime's demise: the founder of the secret police dangling from a noose as the crowd cheered. Within a few days, the field next to the Tretyakov Gallery had become a Communist mortuary; children climbed on toppled statues of Sverdlov, Dzerzhinsky, and other fallen revolutionaries. The Museum of the Revolution put up a display honoring the resistance to the coup, and the Lenin Museum simply closed down "pending reconstruction."

For a while, the celebration was mixed with the macabre.

Marshal Akhromeyev, Gorbachev's military adviser, was found dead in his office, his neck in a noose, a series of suicide notes laid out neatly on his desk. The first described how he had botched a first attempt: "I am a poor master of preparing my own suicide. The first attempt (at 9:40) didn't work—the cord broke. I'll try with all my strength to do it again." Another letter was addressed to Gorbachev, and in it Akhromeyev explained why he had rushed home from vacation to support the coup; in closing, he asked forgiveness for having broken military regulations. And in a letter to his family, the marshal wrote, "I cannot live when my Fatherland is dying and all that I have made my life's work is being destroyed. My age and all I have done give me the right to leave this life. I struggled to the end."

Investigators arrived at the apartment of Boris Pugo to arrest him for his role in the coup and instead found a revolting scene of carnage. Pugo, dressed in a blue track suit, was dead, a gaping bullet wound in his head; his wife was also shot, but half alive. Pugo's aged father-in-law, in a late stage of dementia, wandered around the small apartment, as if nothing had happened. Pugo left a suicide note for his children and grandchildren: ". . . Forgive me. It was all a mistake. I lived honestly, all my life."

Nikolai Kruchina, a Communist Party official who had administered the finances of the Central Committee, jumped from his apartment window to his death. The newspapers speculated that Kruchina knew better than anyone else about the Party's foreign bank accounts, its funding of foreign Communist parties, its secret squandering of gold reserves and other resources. According to Russian journalists, the official news wire Tass was aware of at least fifteen other suicides but did not report them.

Under arrest, the chief conspirator, the now former chief of the KGB, was cool and unrepentant. "My heart and soul are full of various feelings," Kryuchkov told a reporter for Russian television. "I recall the entirety of my life, the way I lived it, and if I had the chance, I would take the same course. I believe I've never done anything in my life my Motherland could blame me for. If I could turn back the clock five or six days, I might have chosen a different way and I would not be behind bars. I hope the court will pass a fair decision, an optimal judgment, that will allow me to work in conditions of freedom and serve my Motherland, whose interests mean everything to me."

After his plea of innocence failed in the Supreme Soviet, Anatoly Lukyanov also went to jail—isolation cell No. 4 of Matrosskaya Tishina, "Sailor's Rest," one of the most notorious prisons in Moscow. And as he waited for the prosecutors to prepare their case and begin a trial, he turned once more to poetry. He still believed in "the cause," and that the people of the Soviet Union should trust in him. His new theme was self-pity:

Human gratitude! There will be none of that!
Do not wait for it, do not torment or mourn,
All trust is now in ashes,
And there are glib slanders in all the papers,
But I know that there will be rewards,
There will be an honest trial in our souls,
There will be new shoots, like the gifts of spring.

Andrei Karaulov, the cultural editor for *Nezavisimaya Gazeta,* visited Lukyanov and heard him complain about Gorbachev. "I love him. I can't change him, though. Speaking openly, I know his weaknesses, his shortcomings," Lukyanov said. "Of all the people who made perestroika, I alone stayed next to Gorbachev, the rest left, from the left and right. . . . Time will show I was loyal. . . . I will remain a Communist, maybe without a Party membership card, but all the same. . . . I am to blame before the parliament, because this dealt it a blow. These are my children, my pain, my creation. This is very painful. I feel my blame before my mother, who lost her husband, lost her first son, and now is losing me. She is eighty-five and I love her very much. I am to blame before my wife, a great scholar, a corresponding member of the Academy of Medical Sciences, before my daughter . . . I am to blame before my grandson, my greatest pleasure, but to him and to all people I can say that I lived honestly, worked, without complaining, sixteen hours a day. And maybe they will remember some good poetry I wrote. . . . I don't know if I'll write again, but I . . . well, I'll say that my book closes with these words:

> " 'And yet, and yet,
> I hurried to turn
> The final page . . .
> I believed in our shining destiny . . .'

"No, no, that's not it. Now . . . now I remember . . .

> " 'I believed in our shining destiny,
> I never avoided the hard work,
> I was ashamed to work poorly . . .
> And if . . .' "

But Lukyanov gave up. "I've forgotten it," he said. "I've forgotten. . . ."

———

With time, Gorbachev himself began to admit that he had played a dangerous game with the Party for far too long. In interviews he seemed a kind of
political analysand, rambling on, finding moments of self-discovery among
the ego, the pride, the self-deception: "Do you think I did not know that the
Party's conservative circles, which had united with the military-industrial
complex, would make a strike? I knew, and I kept them beside me," he said.
"But they procrastinated. They, too, were also afraid that the people would
not follow them, and they waited for the people's discontent. . . . I will tell
you: if [the conspirators] had acted twelve or eighteen months earlier the way
they did in August, it would have come off. It is worth realizing this. . . ."

He was right. Had the leaders of the KGB and the Central Committee
wanted in 1988 or 1989 to get rid of Gorbachev and return to an Andropov-
style regime of modest reform and bitter discipline, they could have succeeded. At least for a while. But now they had to deal with an elected leader
of Russia and tens of thousands of people who now felt themselves to be
citizens, empowered. Gorbachev had to admit that he had failed to understand the fury of the hard-line opposition. "I certainly did not think they
would go as far as a putsch," he said. "At some point, I misjudged the
situation. For all the importance of strategy, it is important in politics to
make the right decision at the right moment. It like a battle in war. . . . I
should have forged a strong common front with the democrats. . . . I should
have realized that earlier, in August 1990. I should have looked for some
form of cooperation then, held a roundtable discussion or some other meeting. I missed that opportunity and paid dearly for it."

———

In early September, Gorbachev assembled the Congress of People's Deputies
at the Kremlin for what would be its last session. It would be the last time,
in fact, that the Kremlin would function as "the center."

The session itself was an elaborate ruse, a last bit of political theater
directed by Mikhail Gorbachev. While the Baltic states, Moldavia (now
Moldova), and Georgia already considered themselves independent, the remaining ten republican leaders decided with Gorbachev to dissolve the Congress and create the basis for a new decentralized Union. Gorbachev
envisioned the new Union with Moscow retaining some key functions as a
coordinator of the common defense and foreign policy. Yeltsin differed and
said that the Union presidency would be ceremonial, "something like the
Queen of England." What was most remarkable was the way Gorbachev and
his newfound allies rammed the interim proposals on a new Union through
the Congress, a body, after all, that was packed with Communist Party
apparatchiks. Gorbachev was so eager to get what he wanted and finish the

Congress that he promised the deputies that even after the dissolution of the legislature, they would still get salaries and priority access to plane and railway tickets. That was enough to win their votes.

———

On December 26, 1991, at his dacha in the woods outside Moscow, Mikhail Gorbachev climbed into the backseat of his Zil limousine and headed north toward the Kremlin. Suddenly the Soviet Union was a half-remembered dream and its last general secretary a pensioner. Ukraine's decision to pull out of the negotiations for a new Union finally ended Gorbachev's hopes for a place for himself as its president. Instead, the leaders of Russia, Ukraine, and Byelorussia patched together a sketchy plan for a new commonwealth. There was no role left for "the center." The republican leaders voted on Gorbachev's retirement package.

Now, in Moscow, Gorbachev wanted to take care of some last-minute meetings and clean out his desk before leaving for a few weeks of vacation. The Russian government had promised him a peaceful boxing day before they took up residence. But when Gorbachev arrived at the Kremlin, he saw his nameplate had already been pried off the wall. "Yeltsin, B. N." gleamed brassily in its place. Inside the office, Boris Nikolayevich himself was behind the desk. For days there had been the air of self-pity about Gorbachev, and this petty incident, a gaudy exclamation in the intricate narrative of these revolutionary days, magnified his fury. Never mind Gorbachev's own assaults on Yeltsin over the years. "For me, they have poisoned the air," he complained. "They have humiliated me."

Comeuppance was what it was. In 1987, Gorbachev had dragged Yeltsin from a hospital bed and made him stand before the Moscow city Party organization for hour after hour of denunciations. Yeltsin spent the next several weeks under a doctor's care, suffering from nervous exhaustion. When given the chance to humiliate Gorbachev, Yeltsin grabbed it.

In their last meeting, Gorbachev had promised Yeltsin he would stay away from politics. He would not be an opposition figure. He had, it seemed, no other choice. "Yeltsin had Gorbachev by the balls," said Sergei Grigoriyev, who had been deputy spokesman for Gorbachev. All the KGB, Communist Party, and military archives were now in Yeltsin's hands. KGB officials told me that in the days before and after the coup, secret police workers were dumping crates of documents into underground furnaces, but the few files that did leak after the coup could only have embarrassed Gorbachev. There were documents showing Gorbachev's approval of secret funding of the Polish Communist Party even after Solidarity came to power. Another file showed him maneuvering to prevent the German government from opening the old East German archives. Yeltsin also came into possession of transcripts of his own phone calls from the days when the Gorbachev government and KGB tried desperately to discredit him. Gorbachev's handwritten notes were in the margins.

Moreover, few believed anymore that Gorbachev was merely an innocent bystander during the worst moments of the perestroika years: the military attacks on peaceful demonstrators in Tbilisi, Vilnius, Riga, and Baku. When his popularity was at its height, he escaped blame. He was out of the country or out of the loop. But now even those closest to him admitted otherwise. "I am sure Gorbachev knew all about what was going on in Vilnius and Riga," said Nikolai Petrakov, who had been Gorbachev's chief economist. Other top-ranking officials, sympathetic to Gorbachev, agreed.

But that was all past, and now Russia faced a great historical moment, an elected president occupying the Kremlin for the first time in the thousand-year history of Russia, the hammer and sickle gone from the flagpole, the regime and empire dissolved. And yet it all had the pallid, made-for-television feel of Washington ceremony. History felt like nothing more than a miserable winter day, the sky as empty and wan as the butcher shops. The Western press corps roamed Red Square in desperate search of passion or comment. "You care, we don't," a fist-faced old woman from the provincial city of Tver told a clutch of reporters. With that the woman stormed off in search of potatoes and milk for her family.

In the afternoon, Gorbachev's press secretary, Andrei Grachev, invited a small group of aides, foreign reporters, and Russian editors to a reception at the Oktyabrskaya Hotel. A farewell party, Grachev billed it, and he could not have chosen a more appropriate stage. For years, the hotel across from the French embassy had been a symbol of the Communist Party's opulence, heavy on the marble and mirrors.

At a few minutes before five o'clock, the reporters and editors stood waiting at the top of the marble stairs for the guest of honor to arrive. By chance, I took my place near Len Karpinsky, who was now the editor in chief of *Moscow News,* and Vitaly Tretyakov, whose *Nezavisimaya Gazeta* was now, with *Izvestia,* the most respected paper in the country. Gorbachev's resignation meant a transition from the intellectual idealists of Karpinsky's generation to a breed of younger men and women like Tretyakov—business neophytes, scholars, hustlers, and, in this case, newspaper editors—who would perhaps build a new world not so much out of the jagged ruins of the old experiment, but on a model, faintly perceived, from the West, from Europe and America. As Gorbachev was leaving center stage, so, too, was Karpinsky. *Moscow News,* which had broken one taboo after another in the first years of perestroika, was a tired paper: still interesting at times, still honest, but one that spoke to a generation that now seemed, like Gorbachev, exhausted.

"It's good that Gorbachev's leaving now, but I am moved to the core of me," Karpinsky told me. "How can I deny that I have just finished the most important chapter of my life?"

———

In the spring of 1992, Gorbachev toured the United States in the Forbes corporate jet, *The Capitalist Tool.* He saw nothing odd or ironic in this. The crowds tossed garlands at his feet, plutocrats deposited checks in his name. He spent an afternoon with Ronald Reagan drinking wine and eating chocolate-chip cookies. They reminisced about the cold war, long over. It seemed to all the victory tour of the century's last great man.

But in Russia, Gorbachev was unwanted, hated by the Party men he had betrayed and ignored by the democrats he had abandoned. Many were ready to think the worst of him. *Izvestia,* the most authoritative daily in Russia, published a front-page item in May saying that Gorbachev was getting ready to walk out the very doors he had opened. The first and last president of the Soviet Union, *Izvestia* said, had bought a two-story house in Florida "with a lot of land" for $108,350 in a development called Tropical Golf Acres.

In fact, Gorbachev had not bought land abroad and denied any plans to emigrate. "I repeat, for anyone who is still willing to listen," he said, "I have no dacha in California, nor in Geneva, nor in Tibet with tunnels leading to China." And yet some of Gorbachev's closest friends and confidants admitted to me that he was angry and on edge, harboring both terror and grand illusions about his future. "Gorbachev fears he may have to flee the country one day like some kind of Papa Doc Duvalier," said the playwright Mikhail Shatrov, who was helping Gorbachev write his memoirs. "He knows only too well that eleven of the fourteen coup plotters have testified against him, claiming he somehow encouraged the August putsch. Gorbachev knows the situation is unpredictable. At the same time, Gorbachev has delusions of returning to power. Not right away, but someday. But it won't happen. He cannot return to power."

Gorbachev's new base of operations was now a plush building in northern Moscow once known as "the School with No Name." Foreign Communists from nonsocialist countries once came to this institute to learn their ideological catechism. Under Gorbachev, the institute was intended as half think tank and half nonprofit foundation. But it wasn't much of either. Gorbachev was restless and open for anything, it seemed. For a sequel to Wim Wenders's *The Wings of Desire,* he played himself, wandering around a soundstage improvising a soliloquy on Dostoevsky and the state of the world. For

300,000 pounds, he sold the world television rights to his life story to an independent British company, Directors International, promising interviews, archives, and other access for a four-part series.

Naturally, Gorbachev's enemies in the press were prepared to attack him as a carpetbagger. "Those who are responsible for this country's catastrophe and smeared the word 'Communist' are now making a cozy nest for themselves at the expense of ordinary people," wrote *Sovetskaya Rossiya*.

Gorbachev was furious. " 'Yesterday's men' are a vengeful breed," he said in a long interview with *Komsomolskaya Pravda*. "Before, they tried to steer us away from the democratic path, and now they are after me personally. Well, to hell with them! What am I supposed to be afraid of? The firing squad? The courts? I am not going to tolerate accusations coming from people who have spent too much of their time believing in the slogans of the thirties."

Unfortunately, many commentators in Russia and in the West thought it necessary to choose sides, to be "pro-Gorbachev" or "pro-Yeltsin." They failed to see the beauty of what history had provided. Without Gorbachev, the agony of the system might have gone on indefinitely, not forever, surely—there was no money for that—but another ten, twenty, who knows how many years. What would the world look like in that case? But without Yeltsin, Gorbachev might well have dallied more than he did, the radical democrats might never have found a single, strong leader, the coup might have succeeded. As much as they had come to despise each other, Gorbachev and Yeltsin were linked in history.

Some of the best minds in the urban intelligentsia—the constituency that Gorbachev courted and ultimately lost—now regarded their former leader with a certain air of superiority. "His speech is that of an uncultured man. He whips the air," said Leonid Batkin, one of the leaders of the Democratic Russia movement. "Yet he is an outstanding man in his way, a great apparatchik. After Stalin, Gorbachev was the most skillful of all the apparatchiks. But when the time came for a real politician, Gorbachev did one stupid thing after another. He played his great role by yanking the stopper from the bottle. Now, he is not really interesting."

Natalya Ivanova, a literary critic, compared Gorbachev to "the man who gave the orders to begin the fateful experiment at Chernobyl. He wanted to refine the machine, but the machine went out of control and exploded."

And the novelist Viktor Yerofeyev said that Gorbachev was "like Valentina Tereshkova, the first female cosmonaut. She fainted right away and was dangling in orbit but still managed to press the right buttons at the right time just because she was dangling in the exact right place. She took off, she dangled, and she didn't die. That was her triumph. The same with Gorbachev. Gorbachev pressed the buttons he needed to and the combination of wrong and right buttons turned out to be just right. That created a metaphysical figure—a divine provident for Russia. Gorbachev guided Russia to its historical fate. He has entered the pantheon of Russian history and gradually he'll come to be seen as that great figure. But not soon. Russians are an ungrateful people."

Even Gorbachev's most sincere critics missed the point of what he was and who he was. Gorbachev was not Andrei Sakharov. He was not a moral prophet or an intellectual giant. He was not even a man of exceptional goodness. Gorbachev, above all, was a politician. He combined a rough sense of decency with a preternatural ability to manipulate a system that had seemed, from the outside, unbendable. If, in the language of the Greek fable, Sakharov was the fox, a man with a singular sense of moral and political ideals, then Gorbachev was the hedgehog, a man capable of deceit and cruelty, a man of shifting values and ideas, but a genius at a nasty game. An irreplaceable man in his moment.

From March 1985, when he began, until June 1989, when he presided over the first elected legislature of the Soviet Union, Gorbachev chipped away at the totalitarian monolith. From there, his personal story became tragic. He was dragged along by events and never seemed able to decide how to maneuver from one day to the next without losing himself entirely. "Watershed moments in history are not particularly pleasant to live through," Gorbachev said many times. "Before you stands a man who has been through a lot."

While he was in Palo Alto in 1992, Gorbachev delivered a speech at Stanford University that echoed that moment in November 1987 when perestroika really began in earnest. It was the seventieth anniversary of the Bolshevik Revolution, and Gorbachev used the occasion to declare the crimes of the Stalin era "unforgivable." At the time, he had to speak in euphemisms, he had to celebrate six ugly incidents to denounce one. But, now, in California, with power long gone, Gorbachev wanted us to feel as though he had always been a democrat, a liberal in his heart. Instead of quoting Lenin endlessly, he referred to Tocqueville, Solovyov, Jefferson, and Berdyaev. He even thanked the dissidents for their "contribution to the intelligentsia and even parts of the Party apparatus."

"Politics is the art of the possible," he said. "Any other approach would be voluntarism. . . . There were failures, mistakes and illusions, but the task was to unfetter the democratic process. . . . I tried to use tactical means to gain time, to give the democratic movement a chance to get stronger. As president, I had powers, including emergency powers, that people tried to push me into using more than once. I simply could not betray myself."

———

When I returned to Moscow at the end of 1992, the relics of Soviet Communism were passing quietly into the museums of the world and into the flea markets where kitsch is sold. "The Great Utopia," a vast exhibition of early revolutionary art, drew enormous crowds in Amsterdam, Frankfurt, and New York. On the main pedestrian mall in Moscow, the Arbat, young capitalists were conducting a bankruptcy sale of the fallen regime. They sold jackboots, epaulettes, Warsaw Pact compasses, thick tomes on dialectical materialism and scientific Communism. Maps of the Soviet Union were now sold as arch amusements, like bowling shirts or lava lamps. One student I met on the Arbat was making a killing with his stunning array of silk and velvet Communist Party banners. "I buy them cheap from retired apparatchiks," he said. "They dig them out of the closets, and then I sell them for five times the price."

In the triumphant days following the defeat of the coup in August 1991, the newspapers were filled with speculation over what was to become of the Lenin Mausoleum, that transcendent model of Soviet kitsch. Surely Lenin's waxy remains should be given a decent burial. Surely a better use could be found for the neo-cubist tomb on Red Square. A museum? An office building? A Pizza Hut? Boris Yeltsin hinted broadly that he, too, would just as soon put Lenin's corpse in the ground and get on with the new era.

At first, the leading figures of the Communist Party gave Yeltsin little reason to fear. He could afford a sense of irony. A few old apparatchiks gave interviews voicing muted resentment that Yeltsin had "undemocratically" outlawed the Communist Party and seized its properties in a series of three decrees issued in August and November 1991. But their voices were strained, wan, not quite convincing. Viktor Grishin, a former member of the Politburo who had made a feeble attempt to challenge Mikhail Gorbachev for the top Communist Party post in 1985, created a pathetic and fitting symbol of the old order's sorry fate: he dropped dead while waiting in a long line at his local pension office. He was hoping for a raise.

The Russian earthquake, however, for all its drama and ruthless speed, was far from complete. Much of the old regime survived. The smartest of the Communist Party men had long ago hired themselves out as "*biznesmeny*" and "*konsultanty.*" The average apparatchik hardly left his chair. Although the headquarters of the Communist Party's Central Committee had become the headquarters of the Russian government, the personnel inside were much the same. A few weeks after the fall of the coup, one of Yeltsin's aides visited the commandant of the Central Committee, Aleksandr Sokolov, and asked for a copy of its old phonebook. The Yeltsin government needed experienced bureaucrats. "The result is that most of the same people are sitting in the same offices as they did a year ago," Sokolov told Michael Dobbs of *The Washington Post.* "When we were forming the new structures, we had to hire people from the old structures. Our supporters—the people who came to rallies and street demonstrations—didn't know anything about how to run a country."

In the Russian parliament, the most influential block of deputies was aligned with Civic Union, a band of moderate to conservative collective-farm chairmen, bureaucrats, and provincial bosses. A more reactionary alliance of nationalists and Communist ideologues known as the National Salvation Front controlled another sizable block of votes. The Communists in the Russian legislature never really renounced their allegiance to the Party. Hardliners like Sergei Baburin talked of the "renewal" of the "old ideals," and vengeance for the destruction of the Party. The conservative newspaper *Dyen* ("The Day") wrote openly of seizing power, "by any means." Yeltsin could count on the firm support of no more than 25 percent of the deputies in parliament.

Somewhere to the side of the daily political struggles that dominated post-totalitarian Russia, a historical sideshow had begun—a judicial battle over the life, death, and potential resurrection of the Communist Party. After members of the old regime had recovered from the shock of the coup and its humiliating aftermath, a group of thirty-seven Communist deputies petitioned the newly formed Constitutional Court of the Russian Federation in late 1991 for a hearing, declaring that Yeltsin's decrees outlawing the Party were unconstitutional. Wasn't Yeltsin acting as a dictator while pretending to be a democrat? A group of fifty-two anti-Communists—Yeltsin's supporters in the parliament—filed a counterpetition, claiming that the Communist Party was an unconstitutional organization. They agreed with Yeltsin's November 6, 1991, decree that the Party "was never a party" but rather "a special mechanism for the creation and realization of political power."

On May 26, 1992, Valery Zorkin, the chief justice of the new Constitutional Court, decided to try the suits simultaneously. After all, he declared, the issue was the same: was the Communist Party of the Soviet Union a constitutional political party, or something else?

Since late 1987, with the rise of such historical societies as Memorial and the publication in the press of the atrocities of the Stalin era, scholars and human rights activists had wondered if a time would ever come in the Soviet Union for a legal accounting, a Nuremberg-style trial. The mere mention of a trial was revolutionary, for one of the fundamental principles of the Bolsheviks had been to deny the primacy of civil law. Constitutions were written, celebrated in the pages of *Pravda,* and ignored: the Party was above the law.

Or as Lenin put it in 1918, the dictatorship of the proletariat "is unrestricted by law." Within months of taking power, Lenin liquidated the fragile legal system that had been in place since the czarist reforms of 1864 and commenced a system of state terror that was designed to intimidate the population and ensure the survival of the regime. "We must execute not only the guilty," Lenin's commissar of justice, Nikolai Krylenko, said. "Execution of the innocent will impress the masses even more."

Despite their hunger for historical judgment, even some of the best-known democratic activists in the country worried about the wisdom of a trial centered on the Communist Party. With the economy in collapse, with political structures so unsettled and moral questions of responsibility and repentance so painful and raw, where would such a trial lead? "Finally, the time has come now for this reckoning, and for repentance, but our circumstances are so peculiar in Russia that such trials are bound for failure," Arseny Roginsky, one of the founders of Memorial, told me one evening. "Nuremberg was a trial on war crimes, and the criminals were being judged by the victors, the victims of those crimes. Here we must judge ourselves. We judge each other. And who is unsullied? Who was a pure victim of the Party? Who was not complicit? I realize that is not the stated purpose of the Constitutional Court, but those are essential questions."

Such a trial was certain to be hopelessly confused—a political event in which old rivalries and resentments would be at issue. The Communists wanted the forum to charge Gorbachev with the betrayal of the Party and Yeltsin with the collapse of Soviet power. Yeltsin's team wanted to discredit Gorbachev—to take the shine off his historical reputation—and make sure that the old men of the Party had no easy access to building a conservative opposition. What was more, this was, in essence, a Constitutional Court without a constitution. The post-Communist state was still operating under the old Soviet Constitution while waiting for a new one to be written and approved.

Gorbachev, for his part, had become a bitter, deluded man, unable to understand why his fellow Russians would want to do anything but celebrate him. From the first announcement of the trial, he declared unequivocally that he would refuse to testify in court. It offended his dignity, his stature, his sense of propriety. He would not be questioned. In public, in private meetings, and in an interview with me, he wore his resentment like a pistol. "Look," he said, "I am not going to take part in this shitty trial."

———

The Constitutional Court convened on the morning of July 7, 1992. The courtroom was a remodeled meeting room in a part of the Central Committee complex that was once the offices of the Party membership committee. Thirteen judges, all but one of whom were former members of the Communist Party, sat at a curved dais in front of the Russian tricolor, the czarist-era flag. They wore long black robes, a strangely elegant and ecclesiastical outfit. The court had bought the fabric from the headquarters of the Russian Orthodox Church, and then Slava Zaitsev, the best-known fashion designer in Moscow, shaped it for judicial purposes. The haphazard mixture of symbols underscored the historical jumble prevalent in the court—the looming presence of the past, the fragility of the future.

Instead of brandishing a gavel to preserve order in the court, Chief Justice Valery Zorkin tapped his pen against a golden plate that dangled before him, gonging the lawyers into silence. Zorkin's task was as complicated as any jurist's in modern times. In a country with such a dubious legal history, he had to invent the procedures and decorum of the Constitutional Court just as he was presiding over what would surely be its most sensational trial for years to come. Zorkin himself had been a member of the Communist Party until October 1991—a fact that initially gave the pro-Communist side some relief—but he did not much romanticize the country's regard for law. "We have always swung from the icon to the ax," he said. "Everyone who came to power tried to make himself into an icon, but then they were cut down by the ax, metaphorically speaking. Every ruler liked to wield state power, but no one really tried to build a rule-of-law state. It is too soon to talk of Russia as a democratic state. Only these first few steps have been taken toward the rule of law."

On that first day of the trial, an angry crowd of pro-Communist demonstrators gathered outside the building. They screamed at the police, demanding to be let in. This was largely the same crowd that staged regular weekend protests outside the Lenin Museum near Red Square. They sold hard-line, neo-Stalinist newspapers and carried such placards as "Gorbachev and Yeltsin: To the Gallows!" Inside, the Communists, who had initiated legal proceedings in the first place, argued, in tones of injury and outrage, that they were "on trial" only because they had had the bad luck to lose power after the coup. One of the first speakers for the Communist side was Viktor Zorkaltsev, a Communist deputy in the Russian parliament, who shifted from ornate respect to high indignation within seconds:

"High court!

"Esteemed chairman!

"The Party that is banned here is the Party that consolidated society and rallied it to battle against fascism, thus ensuring the victory in the Great Patriotic War and sustaining, together with the people, irreplaceable human losses. . . . This does not mean that there have been no mistakes or negative moments in the Party's activities. There was the dramatic phase of Stalinism in the thirties; there was suppression of dissent in the seventies; and there was the apostasy of the Party elite during the [Gorbachev] period. All of this happened. At the same time everyone knows that there have always been forces within the Party that rose up against these vices. And so it renewed itself, cleansed itself of this scum—sustaining losses, restoring its ranks, maintaining its ideals. And now, once again, this process is interrupted and it is banned at a turning point.

"Having shackled the party, the [democrats] have destroyed the national economy and the Union itself. They have changed the social system. The carving up of Russia has begun. The country has arrived at a dead end. What Hitler, world fascism, and capitalism were not able to accomplish has now become possible after the banning of the Party. The ban on the CPSU is also a signal to other parties: 'Beware! You are next!' And many parties feel this danger. Therefore only those who pathologically hate democracy and do not accept the socialist idea are gloating on this occasion. Thoughtful politicians do not approve of the president's decrees and do not support them. . . ."

And so on. The Party would be shameless to the end. Its members would argue their case on the basis of civil liberties, political pluralism, and the historical record. The Party men said now that the country had triumphed under their rule and gone to ruin in their absence. Such was history as they were prepared to present it in court.

When that high-minded tactic did not seem convincing to the court, or perhaps to themselves, the Communists' tone shifted from mock-heroic to threatening. At one point, another of the Party's representatives, Dmitri Stepanov, said that if Yeltsin's decrees were declared constitutional in court, then the Communists were prepared to use "the same methods" as the members of the August putsch to grab power.

"Emergency committees are nothing out of the ordinary," he said. "We have them all the time." He also defended the "alleged" brutality of the Party by saying that more people are killed in a couple of years in traffic accidents in Russia than were killed by Stalin. And besides, he added, the Party was never as brutal as the U.S. Army: "The Americans mowed down whole villages in Vietnam, whereas in the Baltic states we just exiled people to Siberia."

Sergei Shakhrai, Yeltsin's lead advocate in the Constitutional Court, was also prepared to argue the historical record. Shakhrai, a celebrated jurist in his mid-thirties, had written nearly all of Yeltsin's legal decrees during the siege of the White House. With the help of two other lawyers, Andrei Makarov and Mikhail Fedotov, Shakhrai set out to establish a case against the

Communist Party based on a historical record of dictatorship, deception, and violence.

"The organization that called itself the CPSU was neither a de facto nor a de jure party," Shakhrai said after a court session one day. "According to every canon of the Marxist-Leninist theory of the state and the law, we had a state that called itself the CPSU. There was a particular group of persons who dealt with the government and had a monopoly on the state: the one and a half million people in the Party nomenklatura, several million civil servants, and, finally, the special apparatus of coersion. The KGB was the armed detachment of this organization that called itself the CPSU and it was even used for the physical destruction of dissidents. Essentially we had a regime in which the basic law of the state and society were the rules of the Communist Party."

Among Shakhrai's first witnesses were three well-known political dissidents and former political prisoners: Lev Razgon, a writer who spent more than a decade in forced labor camps under Stalin; Vladimir Bukovsky, who was in the camps under Brezhnev from 1967 until he was finally traded to the West for the Chilean Communist leader Luis Corvalán in 1976; and Gleb Yakunin, a dissident Russian Orthodox priest who was imprisoned and later banished from practicing in Moscow. All three men provided firsthand testimony to the Party's brutality. To supplement the historical record, Richard Pipes, a historian at Harvard University and the author of *Russia Under the Old Regime* and *The Russian Revolution,* submitted into evidence an eighteen-page essay outlining the Communist Party's assumption of absolute state power within three months of the October coup.

"From the point of view of historical science," Pipes wrote, "the so-called party of the Bolsheviks was, of course, not a party, but an organization of a wholly new type, which had some features of a political party: Its structure was without precedent, an organization which was beyond government, which controlled the government and controlled everything, including the country's wealth. It was beyond any outside control. In no sense of the word was it a political 'party,' nor a voluntary social organization. . . . This political organization of an absolutely new type . . . was a precedent for the Fascist party of Mussolini and the Nazi party of Hitler and the countless so-called political parties of a totalitarian character which, beginning in Europe and then spreading throughout the world, established single-party government. . . . Never, in all its years of activity, did the Communist Party consider itself responsible to the law or constitution. It always considered its will and its goals the decisive factor; it always acted willfully, that is, unconstitutionally."

Although the testimony of former political prisoners, legislators, and Western historians was impressive enough, Shakhrai and his team meant to build an even more specific case. As a bureaucratic machine, the Party and the KGB left behind a paper trail of tens of millions of documents. Shakhrai petitioned the Russian government's new committee on the declassification of Party and KGB archives in order to provide documentary, and not merely anecdotal, proof of the way the Communist Party wielded and abused power. "Every kid in school now knows about the horrors perpetrated by the Communist Party, but we want to prove our case legally, with documents, so it cannot be denied," said Andrei Makarov.

When they first considered using the archives, Shakhrai's team had no idea what would be available to them. There was no telling what was lost—the tradition of destroying documents began early on when Lenin is said to have ordered the archive on the Red Terror cleaned out—but tens of millions of papers are now in government hands.

The Shakhrai team, of course, could not possibly hope to read even a fraction of the available documents, but they were able to obtain files describing in painful detail the purges of the 1930s, the repression of dissidents in the 1960s and 1970s, even transcripts of Politburo meetings at which the invasion of Afghanistan was discussed.

During the court's August recess, Shakhrai, Fedotov, and Makarov read through tens of thousands more pages of documents marked *Soversheno Sekretno,* "Top Secret." They were preparing for the climax of the trial scheduled for late September and early October when some of the biggest names of the Gorbachev era were scheduled to testify, Politburo members and Central Committee secretaries known mainly by their grainy portraits and the rumors of their politics and personalities: Yegor Ligachev, Nikolai Ryzhkov, Vladimir Dolgikh, Valentin Falin, Aleksandr Yakovlev, Ivan Polozkov.

Gorbachev, for his part, was still warning the court that he had no intention of testifying, that he would not appear "even if they dragged me there in handcuffs." (For this latter remark, the puckish daily *Nezavismaya Gazeta* published a front-page cartoon featuring Gorbachev being dragged to the court, hands cuffed.) The lawyers on Yeltsin's side certainly wanted to question Gorbachev, mainly to establish the idea that no one was above or beyond the legal system, but they also felt they could do without testimony from him. Mainly, it was the Communists who wanted the opportunity to put their former general secretary on the stand, to lacerate him for what they said was his betrayal of the Party. "Gorbachev had evil plans," Dolgikh said. "He destroyed the Party in 1989. Sure, the Party made mistakes. But the whole world recognized our power. When there was a Party, this country was not falling apart." Ligachev, who had been the number-two man in the Party from 1985 to 1990, called Gorbachev a "revisionist," the same word Stalin once used like a branding iron on his doomed opponents. "Gorbachev started us on the path of anti-Communism," said Ligachev. "Perestroika lost its way and headed toward bourgeoisism."

After the first few days of the trial in July, most Russian and foreign journalists stayed away. They had more urgent things to do than cover this curious epilogue to the Communist era. There were wars in Abkhazia, Nagorny-Karabakh, and Tajikistan. There were breadlines and no electricity in Armenia. Vast hunks of Russia, from the northern Caucasus to Yakutia, were threatening to break away from Moscow's rule. The crime rate was spiraling almost as quickly as inflation. Shady businessmen were exploiting the new economic chaos and were exporting billions of dollars in capital out of the country. The Russian army was threatening to go to war in Moldova. The West was worried that the republics were still playing politics with the control of nuclear weapons. There were reports of arms deals with Iran and China. In Latvia and Estonia, few of the heroes of the independence movements showed themselves as nasty racists, forcing Russians, Poles, and other non-Balts into the status of second-class citizenship. In anger, Yeltsin put a halt to the withdrawal of troops from the region just weeks after it began.

So, no, the former Soviet Union was not wanting for more urgent issues and tragedies. For most, the trial was an afterthought. But, still, I wanted this last glimpse of the old regime—the last exhausted generation of Communist leaders. I could not resist it. For so many years, Soviets had seen these men as distant antigods, men with rumpled faces and dark fedoras, possessed of immense power, and silent. In the first years of the perestroika era, their unearthly quality faded somewhat as Gorbachev stripped the city of the old ubiquitous portraits and slogans. But they were still accountable to no one, available to no one. By the end of the decade, the press, both foreign and domestic, began to learn more about these elusive shades from their opponents, from rumor, even from actual interviews. But until now, they manipulated interviews the way they did the state. They were perfectly capable of listening to a reporter's question and then reeling off a pompous, hour-long speech, then dismissing the guest, his tea now cold in its china cup. But in court the Party men were nonentities, tired men in bad suits. In the audience, they mumbled angrily during testimony they did not approve of, and, like Baptist parishioners, they barked agreement to urge on their compatriots at the lectern.

On a day when Nikolai Ryzhkov was testifying on his five years as prime minister under Gorbachev, I spent the two-hour afternoon recess with Ivan Polozkov, a Party chieftain from the southern Russian city of Krasnodar who in 1990 had become the leader of the Russian Communist Party and Ligachev's successor as the conservative "dark prince." At Central Committee meetings in 1990 and 1991, Polozkov had been openly critical of Gorbachev, but even then there was something guarded about his speech. A glimmer of traditional Party discipline, to say nothing of simple desire for self-preservation, prevented him from saying the things he was saying now.

"I am free now," he said, "free now to vent my spleen." Like the other Party men who came to court every day, Polozkov operated on the fuel of resentment. He was, in his mind, a great man made small by the deceptions of Gorbachev, Yeltsin, and the Central Intelligence Agency.

I asked him why he thought the Communist Party and the Soviet system had collapsed with such stunning speed after seeming to all the world to be unconquerable, a monolith of power and strength.

Polozkov's eyes widened, more in surprise than in anger. "They had so much and we . . . we had nothing!" he said.

"What do you mean?" I said. "That the Communist Party had nothing and the opposition had everything?"

"Precisely," Polozkov said, with a satisfied little nod. "We know the CIA financed parties here. You gave them Japanese cameras, German copying machines, money, everything! You had your dissidents who worked for you, the liars, the diplomats, the military double agents. Gorbachev, Yakovlev, Shevardnadze, these men were all yours, too. They were yours! Look at the book contracts they've gotten! Millions! One of our secretaries in the Russian Communist Party, Ivan Antonovich, was in the United States and he was invited to speak at a conference. Shevardnadze was on the bill, too. Shevardnadze spoke first, and then he left. Then Antonovich spoke. Afterward they gave him a souvenir: a copper coffee cup. Someone came up to him from our embassy and said how unfair it was, that Antonovich had only gotten a mug and he spoke in English while Shevardnadze spoke in his bad Russian and got five thousand dollars!

"Look, I understand what it was all about. It was a confrontation of two systems. Reagan called us an 'evil empire' and other Western leaders were judged according to how anti-Soviet they could be. The putsch was just a culmination of this struggle. And I will admit this: so far you have been winning this war. But I want to emphasize—'so far.' Remember this: Napoleon was in Moscow, but France did not defeat us. The Nazis were near Moscow, but look what happened. But I must tell you—and listen carefully—the war is still on and, in the end, you will not be able to endure in this competition with Communism."

I asked Polozkov if he thought that Gorbachev was a paid traitor. He began nodding, rapidly, crazily.

"Look," he said, "who do you think is on Gorbachev's level, historically speaking? What sort of stature do you think he has?"

I said that I'd just read an article in the French press comparing Gorbachev to de Gaulle.

"What?" Polozkov barked. "How can you compare Gorbachev to de Gaulle? Pétain is more like it! He lies like Pétain! He betrayed his country like Pétain! De Gaulle did not bend low before Hitler the way Gorbachev did to the West. It's an insult to our people to compare Gorbachev to de Gaulle. Gorbachev fled the Party like a coward. For his first couple of years, Gorbachev did well. But then he began to travel. He was praised abroad. They celebrated him as a great leader, and this tickled his ambition. He lost a sense of who he was, where he came from. He became vain, always out for his own career. And then they gave a Nobel Prize to a man who destroyed his country with wars and collapse. They made a mockery of that prize."

After talking with Polozkov and several other Communist Party chieftains who came to the small courtroom every day to watch the proceedings, I realized that these men had processed the August coup in their own minds, first as tragedy and now as farce. That is, they were so shaken by the way it changed the world that when they recovered from the shock of losing power, they began to excuse the putsch as a mockery, a nonevent. It simply never happened.

Vladimir Ivashko, the former deputy general secretary of the Party, was typical in the way he regarded the coup as "no coup at all." He had served the Party so long, and so well, he had lived by its myths so thoroughly, that he could not, and would not, think of the "August days" as the study in betrayal and incompetence that they were. "I know these men who are in prison," he said. "I know them as well as one man can know another. They are capable men, the top men in the Party. Honest men. Do you think they are fools? Yeltsin was never arrested. There were tanks, yes, but they never fired. People put flowers in the gun barrels. This is a coup? No, I am sorry. This was a drama, designed to crush the Communist Party and create bourgeois power in Russia.

"In the West, even here, they try to say that the Communist Party was reactionary, that it was against change. Those in power—and I knew them all well—none of them were against change. The discussion was always about the pace of change, about the retention of the Union. The members of the so-called putsch acted in the interest of a native power. To say they acted as opponents of reform is groundless. The Party kept this country together. Look at the Balkans, look at Ireland. Why were we able for so many years—until now—to avoid such conflict? Because there was unanimity from the top to the bottom. The tragedy of Gorbachev and of Yeltsin is that they destroyed the Party mechanisms but created nothing in their place. Nothing will take the place of the Party. Nothing. Never."

———

I spent the better part of two days watching both sides question Nikolai Ryzhkov, a politician so emotional and prone to personal slights in his time that he was known in the press as "the weeping Bolshevik." In his days as Gorbachev's prime minister, Ryzhkov would choke up and splutter if members of the Supreme Soviet dared question his economic plans or his role in a weapons scandal. Unlike Ligachev or Polozkov, who affected the steely toughness of a regional Party boss, Ryzhkov had a touching vulnerability and righteousness that was his last selling point before his popularity vanished completely by late 1990. His memoir, *Perestroika: A History of Betrayals,* was filled with venom toward Gorbachev, Yakovlev, and Yeltsin.

Uncommonly slender and spry for a Party leader of his seniority, Ryzhkov stood at the witness stand with a studied casualness, his hip cocked, his left hand thrust in his pocket, as he answered the first easy volleys from the Communist side. Then, as Makaraov and Fedotov began to ask questions based on confidential Party documents, he bristled at what his life had come to. He came to attention.

Makarov picked up one bound set of documents after another and seemed to mock Ryzhkov simply with the manner of his question. Makarov was possessed of an elephantine girth and the voice of a field mouse; somehow this queer combination made him seem skeptical, even sarcastic, with no effort at all. He needed only to open his tiny cupid's mouth.

Respected witness, he would say. Here is a document describing secret arms sales to foreign Communist parties using government monies. Here's another specifically setting out the plan to cover up the nuclear accident at Chernobyl. Here the Politburo allocates money to "education." Do political parties usually have educational systems? Respected witness, respected Nikolai Ivanovich, the CPSU supported left-wing parties in capitalist, developed countries. Does that mean we gave succor to capitalist, developed countries? Toward what end?

For a long time Ryzhkov kept his cool and deflected painful questions about the past by saying "that was then" and "the Party was in the process of reform."

"Why did the Party, even after it relinquished its constitutional guarantee of power in 1990, why did it continue to control the government and virtually run public life?" Makarov asked. "Does that indicate to you constitutional, legal behavior?"

Finally, Ryzhkov lost his temper. "I protest these questions!" he said.

"You are asking me questions as if I were a criminal. . . . You are trying to paint me into a corner!"

Ryzhkov's self-image, that of the reasonable moderate surrounded by reactionaries like Polozkov and unconscionable radicals like Gorbachev and Yakovlev, began to appear ridiculous. When transcripts were read to him describing how he voted for one pernicious measure after another, his explanations were weak and absurd.

"Many times I spoke out against a measure," he said, "but when I found myself alone or in the minority, I voted for it."

Chief Justice Zorkin tried to keep the proceedings above emotion and raw political battle, but the effort was doomed. After Makarov had whispered into his microphone the proceedings of yet another Politburo meeting that the Communist Party never imagined would be read aloud, Ryzhkov snapped.

"Secrets are secrets!" he said. "One day soon we'll realize that. There were always secrets! Try and make an American turn himself inside out for you!"

At one point, Makarov swung his bulk in Ryzhkov's direction and said he "worried" whether the "respected Nikolai Ivanovich" wasn't tired.

"You don't have the figure for worrying," the former prime minister said. "You shouldn't worry."

"Well," the lawyer huffed, "at least I don't cry."

———

One night after a long court session, I accepted an invitation from Shakhrai's team to follow them out to their "work dacha" at a government compound in the village of Arkhangelskoye. The compound was one of the Russian government's many spoils of victory. Although most former members of the Communist Party leadership were still living lives of relative splendor even as they pled poverty in court and on television, most of the booty—the vacation homes, the resorts, the limousines—were now in the hands of the state. Yeltsin made his name by mocking the privileges of the Party powerful, but he was now doing a fairly good imitation of Louis XIV. Gorbachev's old arrangement of a cortege of three Zil limousines did not suffice; Yeltsin traveled in a fleet of three or four Mercedes-Benz sedans.

A high gate, a surveillance camera, and an armed guard marked the entrance to the compound. Shakhrai himself was in Austria that day— "buying himself a dacha in Salzburg, no doubt," one of the Party lawyers had cracked—and Fedotov and Makarov had a long night ahead of them to prepare for the next witness, Yegor Ligachev. They seemed unfazed by their twenty-hour workdays. Fedotov, whose reddish beard and bald pate earned him the nickname "Lenin" among his friends, had grown up in what he called "dissident circles." In the early 1960s, he attended public readings at Pushkin Square and Mayakovsky Square of banned poetry; for his trouble, he was expelled for a while from university. Fedotov was now the Russian government's minister of "intellectual property," presiding over the country's copyright bureaucracy.

If Fedotov was the earnest intellectual of the team, Makarov was its rogue. In 1984, he defended the Soviet president of a Soviet-Swiss bank that went mysteriously bankrupt. "Americans killed the bank, the CIA," Makarov said without malice. "Nine members of the Politburo testified in the case, and so anything I learn now about the Party comes as no surprise." In 1988, Makarov defended Brezhnev's son-in-law Yuri Churbanov. After his marriage to Brezhnev's daughter, Churbanov won a high-ranking post in the Interior Ministry police, a job he rather quickly exploited for its bribe-taking possibilities. On a trip to Uzbekistan, he accepted a suitcase stuffed with a few hundred thousand rubles. Makarov won high marks for his defense, but there was not much he could do for a son-in-law who was on trial as much for his relation to a family in disgrace as for his hunger for gold.

Fedotov led the way into dacha No. 6—the same cabin where Gorbachev's and Yeltsin's advisers had tried to hammer out the abandoned 500 Days economic package in 1990. While dinner was being prepared, Makarov and Fedotov led me to a small study. A desk was stacked high with folders, many of them red and marked "Materials of the Politburo."

"We have to meet for a while," Makarov said. "Why don't you sit down and help yourself."

The hors d'oeuvres he offered were several short stacks of some of the most closely guarded secrets of the 1970s and 1980s in the Soviet Union.

"We've gotten about eighty thousand documents," Fedotov said. "Now there's only around forty million more to go."

"Oh, before we leave you with these things, you might want to hear our performance of the Politburo meeting of August 29, 1985," Makarov said.

The two men began laughing with the anticipation of it, and like an old radio team—Bob and Ray coming to you live from dacha No. 6!—they read their script from one of the documents marked "Top Secret, Sole Copy." Makarov read Gorbachev's lines, giving a fair approximation of Gorbachev's southern accent and grammatical flubs, and Fedotov read the remaining parts. The document was even more fascinating than its bizarre performance.

At that session, the members of the Politburo discussed their strategy options regarding Andrei Sakharov and Yelena Bonner, who were still living in forced internal exile in the closed city of Gorky (its name has since been changed back to the original, Nizhni Novgorod).

Gorbachev says the Politburo has received letters from the Sakharovs and from elsewhere asking that Bonner be allowed to go abroad for medical treatment.

Viktor Chebrikov, chief of the KGB, dominates the discussion and informs the other members of the Politburo that Sakharov "is not in excellent health and now is receiving an oncological exam because he is losing weight." He fails to mention that Sakharov's weight loss was due to a hunger strike which led the KGB to attempt to cram a tube down his throat and feed him.

Another participant, Mikhail Zimyanin, warns that "no decency can be expected of Bonner. She is a beast in a skirt who was appointed by imperialism." They are clearly worried that Bonner, half Jewish and half Armenian, will plead the case for emigration and human rights while in the West. Chebrikov cautions that if they allow Bonner to go to the West for treatment "she may make statements and get awards. . . . But it would look like an act of humanism. . . . Sakharov's behavior is under the huge influence of Bonner and he is always subject to that. . . ."

Gorbachev: "Well, that's what Zionism is!"

Makarov and Fedotov collapsed in laughter.

Later on, over a dinner of broiled chicken and rice, Fedotov said that the two of them had spent hours reading the documents and had been alternately stunned and amused at the banality of the Politburo sessions. Makarov said he hoped that the theaters of Moscow would soon stage the old sessions of the Politburo using the transcripts as scripts.

"When we read these absurd documents we laugh ourselves all the way to the floor," Fedotov said. "But that is only when we are not crushed and despondent. Recently I read a Central Committee document from 1937 that said that the Voronezh secret police, according to the 'regional plan,' repressed in the 'first category' nine thousand people—which means these people were executed. And for no reason, of course. Twenty-nine thousand were repressed in the 'second category'—meaning they were sent to labor camps. The local first secretary, however, writes that there are still more Trotskyites and kulaks who remain 'unrepressed.' He was saying that the plan was fulfilled but the plan was not enough! And so he asked that it be increased by eight thousand. Stalin writes back: 'No, increase by nine thousand!' The sickness of it! It's as if they were playing poker."

"It's true," Makarov said. "Later, we read a document from Marshal Tukhachevsky giving instructions to his men saying if you meet a person on the street and he fails to identify himself immediately . . . shoot him! This is 1921, not the Stalin era. See, the thing to remember about the documents is not the sensations they provide. It's their routineness, their banality, the way these very ordinary directives ordered the life of the country."

After dinner, I sat at the desk once more leafing through documents that recorded those banalities and, until now, were considered "eyes only": KGB analyses of a school of writers in 1970 known as SMOG; a list of Western correspondents and dissidents at a rally at Pushkin Square on December 5, 1975; copies of private letters sent by Aleksandr Solzhenitsyn and intercepted by the KGB; a KGB dossier on the creation in Krasnodar at School No. 3 of an eighth-grade "Club for the Struggle for Democracy"; a September 1986 Politburo meeting at which the KGB chief, Chebrikov, says that while political prisoners are being released, "they will be watched . . . in connection with prophylactic work"; an analysis by Brezhnev's ideologist Mikhail Suslov of Sakharov's first set of underground essays ("To read this is to become nauseated").

The minutes of a July 12, 1984, Politburo session revealed a truly nauseating spectacle: the leaders of the Party still defending Stalin against Khrushchev's revisionism. At the meeting, the members listen to a report on how Vyacheslav Molotov, Stalin's foreign minister, was "overwhelmed with joy" at the Politburo's decision to restore him to the Party ranks. Molotov had been expelled during Khrushchev's "thaw."

"And let me tell you," says Marshal Dmitri Ustinov, the head of the armed forces. "If it hadn't been for Khrushchev, they never would have been expelled and there never would have been these outrageous actions regarding Stalin. . . . Not a single one of our enemies has inflicted so much misfortune on us as Khrushchev did regarding his policies and his attitude toward Stalin."

Gorbachev, who knew well at the time that he would have to get the support of the conservatives to win the top job once Chernenko finally died, plays a marvelous game, saying that he would support the restoration to Party ranks of Molotov's cohorts, Lazar Kaganovich and Georgi Malenkov. ("Yes, these are elderly people," the Leningrad Party boss, Grigori Romanov, chimes in. "They may die.") But Gorbachev also knows the value of discretion. As for the Molotov rehabilitation, he says, "I think we can do without publicity." Ustinov gets so excited by this little neo-Stalinist wave that he says, "And in connection with the fortieth anniversary of our victory in the Great Patriotic War, shouldn't we rename Volgograd back to Stalingrad?"

"Well," Gorbachev says, "there are pluses and minuses to this."

Even after Chernenko's death and his own assumption of power, Gorbachev offered bones for his reactionary colleagues to gnaw on. At a March 20,

1986, Politburo meeting he suggests changing the name of the icebreaker *Arktika* to *Brezhnev*.

"Yes, let's do it," Ryzhkov says, "but don't announce it on television."

———

Finally, I lingered over a document that Sovietologists have been waiting to see for years: the transcript of the March 11, 1985, Politburo meeting at which Gorbachev was made general secretary. For years there had been speculation that it was a close vote, that the chief of the Moscow Party organization, the hard-liner Viktor Grishin, challenged Gorbachev, and had it not been for the absence of one or two conservative voters, Grishin might have won. Former Politburo members Geidar Aliyev, Yegor Ligachev, Aleksandr Yakovlev, and Grishin himself, in a brief phone conversation before his death, told me that it was untrue, that the vote was unanimous. But that was never good enough for Sovietology.

Gorbachev opens the fateful meeting with the announcement of Chernenko's death, and Yevgeny Chazov, the minister of health, gives a detailed description of Chernenko's illnesses and final hours. Then, in a move that stunned some of the conservatives, Andrei Gromyko, a top official under every Soviet leader since Stalin, stands up at his place at the table and nominates Gorbachev. First, he provides some ritual words of praise for Chernenko's "historical optimism" and the general "rightness of our theory and practice." And then, in nominating Gorbachev, the baby of the Politburo, Gromyko pays tribute to his man's "indomitable creative energy" and his "attention to people."

"When we look into the future—and for many of us this is hard—we have no right to let the world see a single fissure in our relations," Gromyko says. "There is more than enough speculation on this abroad."

For his part, Viktor Grishin says, "When we heard yesterday about the death of Konstantin Ustinovich, we predetermined to some extent this issue [of the new leadership] when we arranged to approve Mikhail Sergeyevich chairman of the funeral commission." Clearly, Grishin, who had worked with one party ideologist, Richard Kosolapov, to devise a program for his own election, could not have been thrilled that the behind-the-scenes maneuvering had left him powerless and Gorbachev head of the committee in charge of Chernenko's funeral and, now, general secretary. But he did not challenge Gorbachev, and, instead, sings his praises just as loudly as the rest. During Chernenko's illness, Gorbachev had proved a superior politician and Grishin must now swallow his ambition.

Finally, Gorbachev gets up to speak. His performance, even on the page, is worthy of Machiavelli's demands for a would-be prince. "Our economy needs more dynamism. This dynamism is needed for the development of our foreign policy," he says. "I take all your words with a sense of tremendous excitement and emotion. It is with this sense that I am listening to you, my dear friends.

"We do not need to change policy. It is correct and it is true. It is genuine Leninist politics. We need, however, to speed up, to move forward, to disclose shortcomings and overcome them and realize our shining future. . . . I assure you I will do everything to justify the trust of the Party."

Then he announces a plenum of the Central Committee in a half hour at which the leadership question will be "resolved."

Thus was the last general secretary of the Communist Party elected—with, as the old newspapers would add in parentheses, "prolonged and thunderous applause."

———

The morning after my trip to Arkhangelskoye, I went to court to hear the testimony of Yegor Ligachev, once the second most powerful man in the country. In power, "he was like a locomotive," Ryzhkov recalled, and he certainly looked fit now. Ligachev had just published a memoir titled *Zagadka Gorbacheva* ("The Enigma of Gorbachev"), in which he laid out the conservative case against the last general secretary. Gorbachev, he wrote, "began well" with a gradualist program, but then fell victim to international acclaim, vanity, and the duplicity of the "extremists" in his midst. And instead of reforming the system, Gorbachev started on the road to "antisocialist" thinking. As he had in his memoirs, Ligachev tried in his testimony to portray himself as the last honest man victimized by endless conspiracies to destroy him and the socialist state. He was never an "opponent of perestroika," as he had been portrayed in the press in Russia and abroad, but merely an advocate of gradual change.

The Communist lawyers wanted Ligachev to feel comfortable and lobbed him a few easy leading questions to fuel his soliloquy. The government lawyers were not nearly so accommodating. For their part, they insisted on knowing Ligachev's reaction to a raft of Politburo and Central Committee decisions during his years in power. Once more, Makarov read through the documents:

Respected Yegor Kuzmich, he would say, what of this document dated November 1, 1989, in which the Politburo approves the funding for the construction of a rec room for the Afghan leader and his family? And what of this document that you drew up dictating to the press the rules for the coverage of the war in Afghanistan? "There will be not more than one report of a death or wound per month among Soviet servicemen."

And what of this document in which the Politburo approves of the creation of a news bureau for *Komsomolskaya Pravda* in Canada and stipulates that the resident correspondent be an officer of the KGB?

"What of it?" Ligachev said. "This is a practice broadly implemented by other countries."

And what of the Politburo decision to create a special military unit of the KGB manned by people "infinitely loyal to the Communist Party of the Soviet Union and the socialist Motherland"? Isn't it curious that the Party, which had allegedly relinquished the one-party system, could still dictate such a policy to a government ministry?

"Well, I am sure there was no ill will intended," Ligachev said.

And what of this document, esteemed Yegor Kuzmich, a Politburo session on March 24, 1987, at which the members agree that permissions given for business trips abroad must be tightened up because, as they say, "we regret that only professional competence is being taken into account and not political concerns"?

"What's wrong with that?" he answered. "That just means that we were not indifferent to how people behaved abroad—moral factors included."

Finally, after a long day at the witness's lectern, Ligachev began to show flashes of why he was feared by the hundreds of men and women working in the Central Committee apparatus. For years he had been the one asking the tough questions, not answering them, and now he, like Ryzhkov, snapped.

"Look," he said, "if we'd taken decisive measures at the beginning, this country would not be on fire as it is today! This war is not only close to Russia, it is entering our own homes. It is here! . . . Mikhail Sergeyevich took decisions only when every last citizen in the country knew they were necessary, when every last apple had ripened and fallen from the tree!"

———

After a few days of watching the testimony at the Constitutional Court, I found it remarkable that there was hardly any interest at all among the public. The spectators' gallery was nearly empty. Some days there were no more than five or six journalists around. Nearly all the regulars—the true court buffs—were themselves dinosaurs of the Communist Party.

For nearly everyone else, the struggles and pleasures of the present were of far greater concern, for Moscow now, little more than a year after the coup, had become a phantasmagoria, a post-Communist world as painted by Hieronymus Bosch. Younger Muscovites, especially, seemed determined to rush headlong into some weird, pleasurable, vulgar world of primitive capitalism. In a leap typical of all Russian history, the new economy had bounded from one stage of development to the next, gliding quickly from complete deficit to sensual indulgence, never stopping to solve the mundane problems of subsistence, structure, and property. In the subway stations and the kiosks, you could buy a lace tablecloth, a bottle of Curaçao, Wrigley's spearmint gum, Mars bars, a Public Enemy tape, Swiss chocolate, plastic "marital toys," a Mercedes-Benz hood ornament, American cigarettes, and Estonian pornography.

In the alleyways and restaurants, Moscow was beginning to look like the set of *Once Upon a Time in America.* As the old Communist Party mafia structures withered, more conventional ones took their place. The city was awash with twenty-five-year-old men wearing slick suits and black shirts and announcing their occupation as "a little buying, a little selling." Their molls dressed in spandex and fox. A kiosk owner's failure to pay his weekly protection money usually left him with a kiosk reduced to sticks and broken glass.

As hyperinflation drove the ruble into irrelevance, a system of financial apartheid arrived. The dollar, suffering everywhere else, was supreme in Russia. Every day more foreign business executives arrived at Sheremetyevo Airport, toting their briefcases like pickaxes and pans, hoping to find the new Klondike. In the meantime, they were also the new colonials, hiring servants and snapping up Russian antiques for a song. In the House on the Embankment, the swank home of the nomenklatura a half century ago, the former apartment of Stalin's chief executioner was now occupied by the top executive of McDonald's.

There was no nostalgia or reverence for the old dogma. At the biggest bookstore in the city, the House of Books, I saw a weary sales clerk using a stack of the collected works of V. I. Lenin as a stool while she handed out copies of the latest editions of Agatha Christie and Arthur Hailey. Moscow had become a city of disorientation, so much so that you could easily take a wrong turn into the nineteenth century. A former journalist named Vadim Dormidontov sat in an office at Moscow City Hall and decided which streets and neighborhoods would lose their Soviet-era names and regain their old ones. Lenin Hills was Sparrow Hills once more. The residents of Ustinov Boulevard now lived again on Autumn Boulevard.

While nearly everyone tried to get his bearings in this strange new world, Yeltsin struggled with a hard-line opposition more than willing to exploit the collapse of the economy for its political gain. The coalition of conservatives was often known as the "red and browns," the alliance of former Communist Party bosses and ultranationalists, even neofascists. For Yeltsin, the trial was a critical front in the battle to stave off the reactionaries. "The so-called red and brown forces are advancing," he said on the eve of the trial. "I would say that today Russia's destiny depends on the Constitutional Court rather than on the president. . . . Any support for the Communists may play into their hands and promote their destructive activity, which may push us into a civil war."

In Moscow now, hardly any politician dared refer to himself as a "democrat," for fear of appearing too Western, too liberal, incompetent. Some of the leaders of the radical reform movement tried to broaden their political appeal by playing, however cautiously, the nationalist card. Sergei Stankevich, the young adviser to Yeltsin, had begun his political career in 1989 as a radical democrat and now referred to himself as a "statist democrat." He wanted a little nationalist shading to broaden his political base. Yeltsin, too, had to emphasize his "national feeling," making fast friends with the hierarchy of the Russian Orthodox Church and refusing to make a deal with the Japanese on the Kuril Islands. Yeltsin realized that it was hard for Russians to lose all the time—lose territory, power, influence—and count it as victory.

But the radical right was not impressed with Yeltsin's guile. He was considered the chief culprit in the fracturing of the Soviet state and the fragmentation of Russia itself. The historian Yuri Afanasyev, a deputy now in the Russian parliament, told me he thought the Russian scene was one of dangerous flux. "The old system will never regain its shape, but all kinds of possibilities exist for the future of Russia," he said. "We could look like South Korea, or, say, Latin America with a taint of Sicily. It is a far from sure thing that we will resemble the developed Western democracies. The pull of the state sector, the authoritarian tug, is still a very dangerous thing. Fascism, in the form of national socialism, is a major threat. And it is finding supporters not only in the lunatic fringe, but in the alleged center. The Russian consciousness has always been flawed by a yearning for expansion and a fear of contraction. Unfortunately the history of Russia is the history of growth. This is a powerful image in the Russian soul, the idea of breadth as wealth, the more the better. But the truth is that such expansion has always depleted Russian power and wealth. Berdyaev was right when he said that Russia was always crippled by its expanse."

To some degree, the Communist Party's myth-making machinery had been replaced by Russian nostalgia for a prerevolutionary utopia that never was. Stanislav Govorukhin's 1992 film *The Russia We Lost* portrayed the last czar—previously considered a dolt and a weakling in Communist propaganda—as a man of great learning, military skill, and compassion. Lenin is a "slit-eyed" fanatic with "pathological obsessions" and, naturally, Jewish forebears. Gorvorukhin told the newspaper *Megapolis-Express* that were there to be another putsch he would not rush to the White House to defend the popularly elected government as he had during the August coup. "Following a totalitarian regime," he said, "a sea of democracy and freedom is a safe road to fascism." His credo now was the famous declaration of the czarist reformer Pyotr Stolypin to the Russian Duma: "You want great upheavals, but what we need is a great Russia."

Although there were only a half-dozen people in the Moskva Theater when I went to see *The Russia We Lost,* and while the opinion polls did not indicate a great public longing for an overthrow of the Yeltsin government, Moscow seemed filled with demagogues who would be czar. The first to appear on the scene was Vladimir Zhirinovsky, an unabashed neofascist who won six million votes—almost 8 percent of the electorate—in June 1991 when he ran against Yeltsin and four other candidates for the Russian presidency. Just after the coup, I watched Zhirinovsky at a parliamentary session at the Kremlin deliver two hour-long monologues to clumps of fascinated deputies in the corridors. He rambled on, picking up so much speed as he described his imperial ambitions that he showered his listeners, and the television cameras, with little sprays of spit:

"I'll start by squeezing the Baltics and other small nations. I don't care if they are recognized by the UN. I'm not going to invade them or anything. I'll bury radioactive waste along the Lithuanian border and put up powerful fans and blow the stuff across the border at night. I'll turn the fans off during the day. They'll all get radiation sickness. They'll die of it. When they either die out or get down on their knees, I'll stop it. I'm a dictator. What I'm going to do is bad, but it'll be good for Russia. The Slavs are going to get anything they want if I'm elected.

"I will send troops to Afghanistan again, and this time they'll win. . . . I will restore the foreign policy of the czars. . . . I won't make Russians fight. I'll make Uzbeks and Tajiks do the fighting. Russian officers will just give the orders. Like Napoleon. 'Uzbeks, forward to Kabul!' And when the Uzbeks are all dead, it'll be 'Tajiks, forward to Kabul!' The Bashkirs can go to Mongolia, where there's TB and syphilis. The other republics will be Russia's kitchen garden. Russia will be the brains.

"I say it quite plainly: when I come to power, there will be a dictatorship. I will beat the Americans in space. I will surround the planet with our space stations so that they'll be scared of our space weapons. I don't care if they call me a fascist or a Nazi. Workers in Leningrad told me, 'Even if you wear five swastikas, we'll vote for you all the same. You promise a clear plan.' There's nothing like fear to make people work better. The stick, not the carrot. I'll do it all without tanks on the streets. Those who have to be arrested will be arrested quietly at night. I may have to shoot one hundred thousand people, but the other three hundred million will live peacefully. I have the right to shoot these hundred thousand. I have this right as president."

Despite his surprisingly strong showing in the last Russian presidential race, the vast majority of people believed Zhirinovsky was either mad, an agent of the secret police, or both. But he was not alone in his extremism. Aleksandr Sterligov, a former KGB colonel who promised the "iron hand," was only the latest in a collection of would-be dictators who were hoping the public would grow so disenchanted with the Yeltsin government that it would turn to them.

One afternoon on my trip in the fall of 1992, I visited the grungy editorial offices of *Dyen,* the newspaper that was now one of the leading voices of the hard-right coalition. Just weeks before the August coup, *Dyen* published the infamous "Word to the People," the front-page appeal for a military seizure of power. I met with the author of the appeal and the editor of the paper, Aleksandr Prokhanov, and his deputy, Vladimir Bondarenko. Bondarenko told me he had just returned from the United States, a trip, he said, that was sponsored, in part, by David Duke, the former Nazi and Ku Klux Klansman.

"Perhaps Duke's views are a bit extreme," Bondarenko allowed. "I suppose my views are better compared to those of your Patrick Buchanan."

We talked a long time about the coup, and here, too, the conservatives spoke of the putsch as a shadow play, something that was not what it seemed.

"When people heard about the putsch, most of them said, 'Finally, at last, they are doing what they have to do,' " Bondarenko said. "They did not believe in terror, but they wanted elementary order, the sort of order that states have everywhere. But the leaders of the coup were so stupid. They are to be condemned not because they pulled off a coup, but because they did it so stupidly."

Prokhanov, a performance artist of the right wing, made Bondarenko seem almost rational. "You did it!" he said, pointing at me as the representative American. "You did it! And how do I know? I have friends at Langley, at the State Department, and at the Rand Institute. The general concept was yours—the CIA's. I am sure of it. The process was regulated and designed by your people. The so-called leaders of the coup were pushed forward and then betrayed. They were left to be torn to pieces by the public opinion. They were so stupid to have believed Gorbachev.

"In this whole drama, only the CIA was smart. They alone knew that the Soviet Union would fall apart under the concept of republican sovereignty— an idea they planted in the Baltics and then elsewhere. Do you think East

Germany fell apart on its own? Do you think Poland, Bulgaria, Yugoslavia, and finally the Soviet Union fell apart on their own? The plan of struggle against the Soviet Union has existed ever since World War II."

Prokhanov said he was "elated" on the first morning of the coup and "disgusted" when it collapsed three days later. But he said he was sure that his time would come again. "After a year in which the government has lost trust and the democrats are in a state of collapse, the patriots from the left and the right will come together and the war will continue. And it will be, I assure you, an anti-American movement. There are three ways we can come to power—and we will use any means to do it. First, we can do it in parliament. Second, there can be a split within the government and the liberals lose the support of the army, the new KGB, and there is a gradual drift to the right. Or we can do it through extra-governmental means: strikes, demonstrations, general chaos. In any case, the Yeltsin people should not relax."

———

The trial shoved ahead. Interest dwindled even further. "Society is sick of history," Arseny Roginsky, of the Memorial historical society, told me. "It is too much with us. For people trying to cope with crazy inflation and adjusting to a new economy in which the rich get richer and the poor get poorer, it's a natural psychological situation. People do have some sense that their current troubles are tied to the history of the Party, but it is not always easy to step back and see that."

The only aspect of the trial of the Communist Party that was grabbing any space in the newspapers and on the evening news was the question of Mikhail Gorbachev's refusal to testify. Chief Justice Zorkin insisted from the start that Gorbachev's testimony, as general secretary of the party from March 1985 until August 1991, was essential. In Zorkin's summons, however, Gorbachev saw only the invisible hand of Boris Yeltsin and another attempt to humiliate him. The two men had been playing out their opera of rivalry and unconscious cooperation for so long that Muscovites had wearied of it. As part of his "retirement package," Gorbachev got from Yeltsin a dacha, bodyguards, a pension, and a fine piece of real estate—the former Party institute on Leningrad Prospekt. Gorbachev, for his part, said he would use the institute as a base for research, not political opposition. But détente, such as it was, collapsed quickly. Gorbachev began accusing Yeltsin of running a government not dissimilar to "an insane asylum," and Yeltsin's aides began chipping away at Gorbachev's retirement deal, first taking away his limousine and replacing it with a more modest sedan, then threatening worse. "Soon," one newspaper cracked, "Mikhail Sergeyevich will be going to work on a bicycle."

During the trial, I went to see Gorbachev at his institute, hoping to talk about many things besides the furor over his refusal to testify. There was no chance of that. He had already been fined 100 rubles by the court—around 30 cents at the time—and he knew well that more sanctions were on the way. After he greeted me, he plopped himself down into an armchair, saying with false cheer, "They are running around like mad. They all got into this shit and they don't know what to do now."

Gorbachev was furious, obsessed. I asked a question and he finished his answer forty minutes later, an answer that was part set piece, part harangue. I had spent many hours while living in Moscow listening to Gorbachev at press conferences, summits, interviews, meetings, and he was never one for concision. But now, he seemed at times like Lear raging about plots against his underappreciated self. He truly believed that the court's summons amounted to political persecution of the most heinous sort.

"Even Stalin's sick mind could not have dreamed up anything like this!" Gorbachev said. "To rule that eighteen million Communists be deprived of their citizenship and swept away! Not just simply to deprive them, but sweep them away with a broom. And with their families, we are talking about fifty to seventy million people. Only a lunatic would do this. If you call yourselves democrats, prove it with your deeds. Gorbachev had enough courage always to tell the truth to everyone and endure the pressure. I've got plenty of courage and even now I will not yield.

"What is this, a Constitutional Court? There is no court in the world that can judge history! It is up to history proper to judge history. Historians, scholars, and so on. . . . Will the court go all the way back to the October Revolution, to the Bolsheviks, or even earlier? Will they anathematize it all? Is this the business of the Constitutional Court? Let's analyze what Lenin did to take power. Does this mean that all the countries that cooperated with Soviet Russia, and all the agreements that were made, do they all go . . . pffffft? . . . Is it all rubbish? Unconstitutional? God knows what this all is! You don't have to be too bright to understand what this process is likely to lead to."

Somewhere along the way I managed to ask Gorbachev if he kept in contact with Yeltsin any longer. Gorbachev frowned. He was being ignored. This seemed to him worse than any sanction of the court.

"He never calls me," Gorbachev said. "I called him several times at first, but from his side there has never been a call. Boris Nikolayevich knows everything! We have no relations. What kind of personal relations can there be when his press secretary publishes a statement saying that they will take measures against Gorbachev, that they will put him in his place? What relations can there be? This is ruled out.

"The democrats have failed to use their power. Look at how they struggled for power and how much they promised. There were even statements that the Russian president would lay himself down across the railroad tracks if living standards went down. Well, now they've gone down fifty percent! The tracks must be occupied.

"They have to tell the people how they are going to get through the winter, what there will be to eat, whether there will be any heat, and what will happen to reforms. And they have no answer. They don't know what to say. They need to play for time and they need to find a lightning rod. It's amazing—Yeltsin's team, the Constitutional Court, and the fundamentalists who defended against the August coup are all in this struggle together against Gorbachev. This is phenomenal!"

———

I left Gorbachev's office thinking that everything about him was outsize: his achievements, his mistakes, and, now, his vanity and bitterness. At one point in his monologue he even passed on a rumor that at the tensest moments of the coup, Yeltsin had been making plans to hide in the American embassy. This was hard, if not impossible, to believe. For all of Yeltsin's shortcomings, it was his courage that won the day in August of 1991. Gorbachev, in suggesting otherwise—especially in such a dark and clumsy way—revealed the depths of his bitterness. He had loved his place in the world—a place he had earned despite all the mistakes—and now, it seemed, it was slipping away, almost gone. He was despised in his own country.

Feeling a little stunned, I left Gorbachev and headed down a flight of stairs to visit the man who had been his closest friend and ally in the leadership, Aleksandr Yakovlev. I told Yakovlev what I had just heard, and he rolled his eyes in amusement and frustration. Yakovlev had always betrayed a certain intellectual condescension for Gorbachev, but he also appreciated his political gifts, his complexity.

I told Yakovlev I had finally seen the transcript of the historic March 11, 1985, Politburo meeting and I was a little surprised that things had gone so easily for Gorbachev. Why had there been no opposition? And had Gorbachev been deceiving the conservatives? Why had they made him general secretary if they knew he would try to change the system?

"There was a preliminary agreement," Yakovlev said. "Everything was agreed on beforehand. Everything was clear. Grishin's entourage prepared a speech, a program for him. Richard Kosolapov, the editor of *Kommunist,* was very active on Grishin's behalf. But that was just in case. In fact, there were no other candidates for this position. Once Gorbachev was made chairman of the funeral commission for Chernenko's funeral on March 10, everything was clear.

"But about deception. This was really a question of the inertia of the Communist Party. Every new general secretary got carte blanche at the beginning. A new man would come to the fore and he was supported. You know, let him talk about innovations, about something new, it has to be tolerated, and then he will calm down and everything will go back to normal. Let him talk about democracy and pluralism, but sooner or later we'll all be back together harnessed to the same horsecart. That happened with every newcomer: Khrushchev, Brezhnev, Andropov. And the same destiny was expected of Gorbachev.

"Gorbachev played politics, but he also realized that things had to change. It was impossible to go on living as we were. But when he started changing things, the system resisted those reforms. These changes were hindered by the simple logic of the state. And whether he wanted to or not, Gorbachev had to deal with these contradictions. Like Gorbachev, at the beginning, I believed that in our country, only a revolution from above was possible.

"Even now Gorbachev talks about our 'socialist choice.' . . . But we cannot speak of a socialist choice in this country. Our experience, our 'choice,' is not socialist and never was. We had a slave system here. Who can talk about a socialist choice? Maybe Germany, or Israel, or Spain. But not us. . . . But Gorbachev could not overcome his mentality. In general, this power, the concept of power, acts like a poison on a person."

———

During my talk with Gorbachev, his press aide, Aleksandr Likhotal, had slipped him a note. Gorbachev went silent, read the note quickly, darkened with what seemed to be anger, composed himself, and then picked up the long string of his monologue. I didn't think much of it then. But later that evening, as I watched the evening news show *Vesti,* I realized what the note must have said: for his refusal to appear in court, he was being deprived of his right to travel abroad. He had a trip planned to South Korea and there were more on the schedule. That was a cruel and clever blow. Gorbachev was endlessly applauded abroad; he was treated as one of the great figures of the century. In Moscow, he was punished, mocked, and ignored.

Three days later, the Russian government announced it would take back most of the building it had given Gorbachev as part of his resignation package. On a cool, gray morning, three buses filled with Moscow police officers pulled up to the institute. The police chief, Arkady Murashev, ordered his men to surround the building.

Just minutes later, Gorbachev arrived, in a rage. The press gathered around him on the front steps of the building. "You don't know the pressure that my family and I have endured in the past seven years!" he told the reporters. "But personal matters are not the thing. They are trying to put Gorbachev in his place! The Russian press speculates that Gorbachev is traveling the world looking for a vacation house! There's the rumor that my daughter is in Germany and her husband is to join her there. Or America. And now that he has a daughter settled, Gorbachev is looking for a warm place for himself. Well, they'd be very happy if Gorbachev left the country. They'd probably pay a million for it. But I'm not leaving. . . ."

A few miles away, the Constitutional Court heard its next witness. The tired men of the Communist Party protested their innocence. How could we have been what you charge? they seemed to say. Just look at us. We are plain. We are ordinary. We are nobody now.

A few weeks later, the Constitutional Court of Russia ruled that Communists were free to meet on a local level but the Communist Party, as a national entity, was illegal. The Party's assets and properties remained under the control of the elected government of the Russian Federation. The era that had begun in 1917 with the Bolshevik coup had now ended—in a court of law.

AFTERWORD
TO THE VINTAGE EDITION

"THE HEART IS
NOT YET JOYFUL"

From the first moment that Mikhail Gorbachev began his frenetic tinkering with the Soviet system, time, and the perception of time, lost its normal rhythm. Every year seems like an entire era. So many triumphs, agonies, and bitter surprises register on the landscape of the old empire that it is hard to focus on anything more distant than the previous week much less on that Christmas night, in 1991, when Gorbachev signed his resignation papers and the red flag over the Kremlin was lowered for the last time. But even now I cannot forget that time. As Gorbachev was preparing his departure, I went to the Kremlin to see one of his most loyal aides, Giorgi Shakhnazarov. Like Gorbachev, Shakhnazarov had hoped to reform communism, to rescue the system and drag it into the modern world. That project, the last lingering dream of socialism, turned out to be folly. Now the regime was in ruins and the empire in dissolution. All the talk was of a democracy and a free market; Gorbachev had passed into history and the movers were coming to cart away the boxes.

"How will all these republics survive without Moscow?" Shakhnazarov said. He was a gnomish man—half scholar, half apparatchik—and now he looked resigned, withered. "What will become of them? What will a republic like Georgia do? Do you think they'll get any oil selling mandarin oranges to Saudi Arabia? And Armenia and Azerbaijan: don't you think they will be at each other's throats?"

Shakhnazarov's desk was bare but for one single-spaced letter he was leaving behind for the next occupant, "whoever that might turn out to be."

"I'm just letting him know I wish them all luck," Shakhnazarov said. "They're going to need it."

In the more than two years since, Russia and the former Soviet republics have surely not been blessed with anywhere near the amount of luck they have needed. Nor have they always had the wisdom or the means to avoid economic and political disaster. One can only begin to count up the mounting catastrophes in the old Soviet Union: the collapsed economies; the troubling diaspora of twenty-five million Russians in "foreign" lands; the threat of nuclear accidents and ecological ruin; the rise of a hard-line Russian nationalist and the astonishing persistence of various Communist parties. In retrospect, Boris Yeltsin wishes that he had acted even more quickly and decisively in the wake of the August coup. While he still had the political support, he should have dissolved parliament and called for elections, thereby avoiding the disastrous two-year-long confrontation with parliament that led to the bloody storming of the White House in October, 1993. But history is unforgiving; it does not accommodate the words "if only."

On my last trip to Moscow, toward the end of 1993, everywhere I went, from the central market to the villages outside of town, from newspaper offices to Kremlin anterooms where aides sat dully around, watching music videos, there was a sense of drift, even hopelessness, about political life. "The October events" and then the dispiriting December elections, which brought into the new parliament dozens of ultra-nationalists and Communists, obliterated any shred of triumphalism left over from the defeat of the August coup of 1991. The relatively easy verities of the old political struggle—good versus bad, reformers versus reactionaries, democrats versus Communists—had dissolved into a bitter soup of uncertainty. The December elections confirmed the despair among Russians, as nearly 25 percent voted for the ultra-nationalist Vladimir Zhirinovsky, more as a protest against the squalid status quo than as an endorsement of his mad program of aggression abroad and the iron fist at home. Nearly half the electorate did not bother voting.

Much of the opposition to Yeltsin is rooted in one form or another of mythic nostalgia: the Communist nostalgia for the order of Stalin and the supposedly dependable standard of living under Brezhnev; the military nostalgia for the fear the Soviet arsenal once struck in the heart of the Western enemy; the nationalist nostalgia for empire and higher spiritual purpose. It is natural—all too human—that nostalgia should be such a powerful force of politics now in Russia, just as it was for the Ottomans and the British as they lost their hold on the earth. Empires are not lost happily. Enoch Powell was driven to fits of poetry over the loss of India and even today "neo-Ottomanism" is a powerful force in Turkish politics.

For tens of millions of Russians, the story of their country since Gorbachev's advent in 1985 has been one of unremitting loss and wounded pride. What took decades for the citizens of Constantinople and London to absorb struck the Russians in an instant. The empire has vanished. That the economy has been dying is obvious to any Western visitor. Less obvious is the Russian's anxiety about his place in the world. The jewels of empire are lost: the beaches of the Crimea, the vineyards of Moldova, the oil fields of Kazakhstan, the ports of Odessa—to say nothing of Prague, Budapest, and Warsaw—are all within foreign lands now. The army is fraught with draft dodging and erosion. Foreign policy is a road map of retreat. A leading sociologist in Moscow, Yuri Levada, recently published a poll in the daily newspaper *Izvestia* showing that only 11 percent of the population believe that Russia is still a great power while two-thirds of the respondents said that the country should regain its lost prestige on the world stage. Between those two statistics is a great longing, a feeling of national loss and anxiety. And that longing, as much as the failing economy, is a lethal weapon in the hands of Yeltsin's political opponents. While Yeltsin and his supporters are trying to create, all at once, a market economy, a democratic political system, and a civil society, his hard-line opponents, more often than not, indulge in a politics of loss, a new sort of populism.

Many influential liberals in politics, such as Yeltsin's former adviser Galina Staravoitova, feel that Russia's economic failure and wounded self-esteem are so profound and combustible that the rise of a charismatic authoritarian movement in Russia cannot be ruled out. "One cannot exclude the possibility of a fascist period in Russia," Staravoitova said on the radio station Echo of Moscow. "We can see too many parallels between Russia's current situation and that of Germany after the Versailles Treaty. A great nation is humiliated, and many of its nationals live outside the country's borders. The disintegration of an empire has taken place at a time when many people still have an imperialist mentality. . . . All this is happening at a time of economic crisis."

In his campaign for parliament, Vladimir Zhirinovsky played on the feelings of humiliation in the post–Great Power era and spoke in a rhetoric of stark simplicity and darkest comedy. Jews, Central Asians, Armenians, and Azerbaijanis should be driven from positions of power; only people with "kind Russian faces" should appear on Russian television. He declared himself willing "to blow up a few Kuwaiti ports and aircraft plus a few American ships" to defend the old Soviet ally Iraq. And should the Japanese press their demands for the Kurile Islands, "I would bomb the Japanese. I would sail our large navy around their small island and if they so much as cheeped I would nuke them." As if this were not enough, he promised everything from a magical end to the economic crisis to "love and romance" for the lonely. The pro-reform democrats, for their part, gave Zhirinovsky his opening. They were smug and divided, nearly oblivious to the fact that they were doing nothing to build support for radical economic reforms that have proved painful to millions of people. Zhirinovsky's triumph was a warning. Russia and the world cannot afford a President Zhirinovsky.

———

If Russia was ever under any illusions about its being a democratic country, it is no longer. In conversations with Yeltsin's aides, all of them admitted that the illusion of a smooth and swift transfer from a communist dictatorship to a free-market democracy is gone. It turns out that the fall of the old regime, which had been so morally satisfying, has left the new regime in an impossible moral position. The choice is stark: Behave with the manners of a western democrat and allow the current anarchy to overwhelm Russia, or take "decisive measures" and risk flouting any semblance of civil society. Now the talk is of a transitional regime of "enlightened authoritarianism" or "guided democracy" or some such hybrid that makes no secret of the need for a prolonged concentration of power in the presidency. "The hand of power cannot be totally weak," Yeltsin's legal adviser, Yuri Baturin, told me one afternoon at the Kremlin. "When the use of power was necessary during the October events, it was impossible to use it right away because the so-called power ministries—defense, security, police—were hesitating. Had they used their force more quickly, it would have been accomplished sooner, with less blood."

But Yeltsin's advisers also admit that in trying to restore some degree of order in Russia, there is a constant danger of an imperceptible drift into the traditional habit of iron rule. "Like Gorbachev's perestroika, everything now in the development of democracy is being guided only from above," said Giorgi Satarov, a member of the presidential council. "It is very easy to slip into dictatorship. There are no checks. Monopolistic rule is responsible for checking itself, and this self-restriction has to hold somehow before there are real checks and balances. There can be little steps toward dictatorship, each one seeming small in and of itself, but the trend can drag us into dictatorship. This can happen. But so far as I know the president and his motives, I do not think he has any intention of becoming a dictator."

There are more than enough people who have called on Yeltsin to become an unabashed autocrat. A poll published recently in *Izvestia* showed that three-quarters of all Muscovites welcomed the brief state of emergency that followed the October events and wanted to see it prolonged indefinitely. But even if Yeltsin were inclined to become the leader of a full-scale authoritarian regime—and he is not—he wouldn't be able to manage it. Although some of his advisers point to South Korea and parts of Latin America as places that built potential democracies under authoritarian rule, the analogy falls flat before Russian realities. Despite the military's decisive role in October 1993, the army has no Latin-American-style ambitions for junta-dom; the generals would much rather win higher wages and other social guarantees than take the upper hand in politics. Nor can Russia rely on an Asian work ethic or efficiency, to say nothing of a democratic political culture—a feature of life in Chile before Pinochet. Russia has to make democracy with Russians.

The truth is that Yeltsin, or any other leader who emerges as his potential successor, has the near impossible task of trying to build a democracy in conditions of social and economic anarchy. Aleksandr Rutskoi and Ruslan Khasbulatov may be in jail after their failed grab for power in October 1993, but theirs is not likely to be the last episode of rebellion or violence. Even those who accept or, at least, are resigned to Yeltsin's notion of transition understand that the anger and disillusionment throughout Russian society is growing ever worse. The dulling realities of Soviet society—equality in poverty, the stability of repression—have come unwound, and now Russia is a scene of radical polarization. The fondest wish of the Russian reformers in 1991 was that out of economic change would emerge a huge middle class and a business elite that would become the main constituencies for further change. There are no signs of this happening. Instead, Russians have watched with fury and envy as a handful of people have grown rich—gaudily rich— amid growing chaos and criminality. Capitalism in Russia has spawned far more Al Capones than Henry Fords. Reform is not a period of retreat.

There is not a single field of activity, not a single institution, free of the most brutal sort of corruption. Russia has bred a world-class mafia. According to Luciano Violante, chairman of Italy's parliamentary committee of inquiry into the mafia, Russia is now "a kind of strategic capital of organized crime from where all the major operations are launched." He said that Russian mob leaders have held summits with the three main Italian crime organizations from Sicily, Calabria, and Naples to discuss drug-money laundering, narcotics trade, and even the sale of nuclear material. Russia, he added, "has become a warehouse and clearing house for the drug market."

The new Russian mobsters, who are into everything from arms sales to banking, have learned to work with former officials in the highest ranks of the Communist Party and the KGB as well mob bosses abroad. There is also little doubt that the ministries of Yeltsin's government—especially in areas like foreign trade, customs, tax collection, and law enforcement—are thoroughly corrupt. According to Yuri Boldyrev, until recently the government's chief investigator, the corruption in state and public institutions now "goes beyond the limits of the imagination." A ten-page report drafted by the police and security ministries and submitted to Yeltsin in 1993 described how senior military officers based for years in the former East Germany have been involved in huge embezzlement schemes. The officers set up their own companies to buy food and liquor, had them transported as military supplies, and then sold them on the free market in Poland and Russia. Sales were estimated at a hundred million Deutsche marks—fifty-eight million dollars. In another case, Air Force Major General Vladimir Rodionov and his deputy, Colonel Giorgi Iskrov, were charged with using military aircraft for commercial flights and keeping the proceeds.

Yeltsin has not been averse to admitting what is before the eyes of everyone. According to a report by Victor Yasmann of Radio Liberty, Yeltsin told the heads of the central and regional law enforcement agencies that two-thirds of all commercial and financial enterprises in Russia—and 40 percent of individual businessmen—were engaged in some form of corruption. He said in 1992 that two billion dollars had simply "disappeared" from the budget of the Ministry of Foreign Economic Relations. Even the anti-Mafia investigators are suspect. One of the chiefs of the Interior Ministry was arrested in 1993 for taking a one-million-ruble bribe. A subsequent search of his home found another 805,000 rubles in cash.

Foreigners trying to do business in Russia have become easy targets. A friend told me about a Westerner who was caught in traffic in Moscow and, as he inched along, lightly touched the bumper of the car ahead of him. A man dressed mainly in jewelry and leather leaped from the car, ran up to the foreigner's window, stuck a revolver in, and said, "Buy my car now or I will kill you!" The foreigner, an experienced resident of Moscow, knew well that this mafioso was not joking. He went home, gathered up all the cash he could find, and bought the car. The following week, the same unfortunate man was traveling to St. Petersburg on the midnight train. Someone drugged him, and when he woke up in the morning all his valuables were gone. Such crimes shock no one in the West, but they are an ominous novelty in Russia.

Law enforcement, too, is a bitter joke. Mobsters at every level have more troops and more powerful weapons than the police. Army officers and recruits, desperate for cash, are only too glad to sell guns, rocket launchers, and grenades to the highest bidder. It is not unknown for members of mafia gangs in southern Russia to use a tank to settle an especially stubborn account. And at a time when nearly everyone is impoverished—including police, jailers, and judges—the likelihood of successful prosecution is minuscule. Vladimir

Rushailo, chief of the Moscow police department, said, "Even if we manage to jail an influential member of the mafia, his fellow bandits immediately unleash a campaign pressuring the victims, witnesses, judges, public accessors. And they do this quite freely. Clearly, the criminals are more inventive than the law makers."

———

Perhaps the constituency that has been most stunned by the course of Russia since the collapse of the old regime is the liberal intelligentsia—the array of writers, artists, academics, and journalists who were at the forefront of the perestroika era. For centuries, Russian intellectuals had been a kind of shadow government, a moral prod to the tsars and, later, the Communist Party. When Pushkin stood up to the tsar, or Sakharov to the General Secretary, they were asserting a belief in the power of truth and the individual against a brutal system. For years, American writers like Philip Roth would return from the Soviet Union and Eastern Europe marveling at the importance of literature there. Roth once remarked that in the West everything is permitted and nothing matters, and in the East nothing is permitted and everything matters. Now in the East everything goes—and the intelligentsia matters less than it ever has.

One afternoon I went to the ramshackle offices of *Znamya (The Banner)*, which was one of the leading literary and political monthlies in the Gorbachev years, to see the deputy editor Natalya Ivanova. I had been visiting Ivanova as a reporter on and off for six years and had never known her to be so pessimistic. At first I thought it might be the fate of *Znamya* and the other literary magazines. Where once they sold over a million or more copies in the late 1980s, none now sells more than eighty thousand or so. Where once the best-seller lists were filled with titles from Solzhenitsyn, Orwell, and Brodsky, they are now litanies of mass-lit: Dale Carnegie, John Grisham, Latvian sex manuals. Larissa Vasilieva, a Russian pop-historian, has made a fortune with *Kremlin Wives,* a look at the seamy world of political boudoirs in the Communist era. Rex Stout may now be the most popular novelist in the country. "People want a little pleasure," one writer told me. "If they have to read about one more concentration camp, they'll die."

But Ivanova was worried about more than the statistics of culture. It was inevitable, she realized, that once the regime fell, the importance (and outsized popularity) of serious literature would fade. "We can all accept the idea that the only people reading now are the ones who read for non-political reasons," Ivanova said. "Now you see the rise of advice columns, personal ads, Harlequin romances. Well, that's OK. What is unexpected is the general degradation of culture and of the intelligentsia itself. Its dominant position is now held by this new class of so-called businessmen and they have no class at all. This new bourgeoisie is mostly made up of speculators stealing from the country." Ivanova showed me the galley proofs for an article of hers called "Double Suicide." It is an angry piece in which she accuses her fellow artists and thinkers of being more interested in "the course of the dollar than in moral problems," of bowing humbly before a new and vulgar image of what the Leninists once called the "shining future."

Where once the Russian landscape was littered with one kind of propaganda—"We Are Marching Toward Leninism!" etc.—television, radio, and the newspapers are now filled with a propaganda of a different sort: advertisements for unaffordable luxuries, fantastic commercials geared toward lives that hardly exist. One minute you are Homo Sovieticus surrounded by the aggressive blandness of communism, the next minute you are watching a Slavic vixen sucking on a maraschino cherry and telling you which casino to visit. There is something profoundly irritating (and American) about ads for investment funds or "premium" cat food in a country where the vast majority live in poverty. A year or two of exposure to American-style commercials has produced what decades of Communist propaganda could not: genuine indignation on the part of honest people against the excesses of capitalism. But the intelligentsia is bewildered by it all and incapable of providing moral guidance. "They struggled for a new life and it turned out that this life deceived them," Ivanova said sadly.

For the young, there is just no sense, no prestige, in pursuing intellectual life. At Moscow State University, it is suddenly a cinch to gain admission to the humanities department; everyone wants to learn finance. The endless ethereal conversations around the kitchen table, the wonderful no-show jobs at academic institutes, the huge audiences for poetry readings—that world is dwindling. "What we had under Gorbachev and for the years before was like the ecological system in Australia before the English brought their dogs and rabbits," another friend, the political scientist Andrei Kortunov, said. "We had this weird, authentic, original kind of culture. The intellectuals were even a privileged class. But when the English came with their dogs and rabbits, the ecological system decayed. I suppose we need to go through this period of consumerism and pop culture, just as they are in Poland and Czechoslovakia. The question is whether Russia will ever be able to preserve even part of the old ecology, its distinctive intellectual character."

One night I took Leonid Radzikhovsky, the journalist, to dinner at the plush Italian restaurant in the Kempinski, a new, German-owned hotel across from the Kremlin. When I asked him about the lost world of the Russian intelligentsia, he betrayed no wistfulness. "I am a cynic maybe, a realist," he said, "but there is no more moral authority in Russia. Russia is a country in the stage of primitive accumulation of capital. Look around you, at this restaurant. What will dinner cost? At least one hundred dollars, right? An average Moscow salary for a month. In the nineteenth century there were landlords and peasants and no thought of mixing them. But now everyone thinks he has a right to have dinner at the Kempinski. And everyone wants it. This is *all* anyone thinks about. They don't think about novels or plays or poetry. If it is true that everything in America is about dollars, it is even more true now in Russia. This is a hungry country and it wants to be fed."

————

A while after returning from Moscow, I traveled up to Cavendish, the small town in Vermont where Aleksandr Solzhenitsyn has lived in exile for eighteen years. When I visited him, he had just finished his life's work, the massive historical novel *The Red Wheel,* and was preparing to return at last, in May 1994, to Russia. The house was filled with packing crates. His wife, Natalia, was frantically trying to find a mover that could ship all their books and papers to Moscow without losing anything. A fax came from Moscow with more troubling news: the roof on their new house on the outskirts of the city was damaged and would have to be repaired at great expense.

"All the same, we can't wait to go home," Natalia Solzhenitsyn said over lunch in the kitchen. "Our minds are already back in Russia. It's as if we are no longer here in this house we have lived in for so long."

There are two adjacent houses on the property, and Natalia led me to the smaller one, where Solzhenitsyn has worked, fourteen and sixteen hours a day, without a day off since the family moved to Cavendish in 1976. He sat at a small table in his study, his face a kind of living photograph of a nineteenth-century man. But while his beard and Asiatic eyes are reminiscent of Dostoevsky, Solzhenitsyn is a man of the Russian twentieth century. He, more than anyone, more even than Sakharov, made it impossible for the West to ignore any longer the true nature of the Soviet regime. If literature has ever changed the world, his books surely have. *One Day in the Life of Ivan Denisovich* opened the world of the camps up to the people of the Soviet Union in the early sixties, and the three volumes of *The Gulag Archipelago* erased all lingering doubts in the seventies.

We talked for the better part of the day, and Solzhenitsyn spent much of the time criticizing Gorbachev, whom he dismisses, for "running in place year after year," and Yeltsin, whom he admires, for letting so many millions of Russians fall far below the poverty line. What was strange to me was that Solzhenitsyn never betrayed a moment's pleasure in the victory that he, after all, had done so much to bring on: the fall of the Communist regime. "In August 1991, my wife and I were incredibly excited to watch on television as

Dzerzhinsky's statue was taken down in front of the KGB. That, of course, was a great moment for us," he said. "But I knew inside that this was not yet true victory. I knew how deeply Communism had penetrated into the fabric of life. And what were we doing? What was Yeltsin doing? We forgot everything and just fought each other. The same even now. All is decay. It's too early to celebrate. Why was I silent for so long about Gorbachev? Well, thank God something did begin, but everything was begun so badly. So what do you do, celebrate or weep? It is too early to celebrate. I just could not have gone over to Moscow in August '91 and had a glass of champagne in front of the White House with Yeltsin. The heart is not yet joyful."

What he hopes for now, he said, was not a new empire, not the resuscitation of a great power, but simply the development of "a normal country." It was time to join in that process. After a life that had reflected the agonies of the old regime—a communist youth, the war, prison, the camps, the battle with the Kremlin, forced exile—now, at the age of seventy-five, he was completing the circle. He had tickets to return home. "Even at the worst times, I knew I would be coming home," he said. "It was crazy. No one believed it. But I knew I would come home to die in Russia."

—David Remnick
January 1994

ACKNOWLEDGMENTS

The last generation of foreign reporters in the Soviet Union was the luckiest. We were witnesses to a singular triumphant moment in a tragic century. What's more, we could describe it, we could talk to the players, major and minor, with relatively little fear of jeopardizing anyone's freedom. In the past, journalists, historians, and diplomats writing about Russia and the Soviet Union were always wary about acknowledging their friends and sources. It is with a great sense of relief and promise that I feel freed of that constriction.

During my time in the twilight of the Soviet Union, I had occasion to interview hundreds of people, some repeatedly and for many hours, some for just a little while in a Kremlin corridor or on a park bench. At first there were the old risks. I remember meeting the Ukrainian human rights defender Bogdan Horyn in a park in Lvov, the better not to be overheard or arrested. By the time I was preparing to leave for New York, I was interviewing Bogdan in the independent Ukrainian parliament, of which he was a prominent member. In my source notes, I've listed the interviews that were especially important to this book.

The greatest source of my education in Moscow was the friendship of those who let me and my wife, Esther Fein, and our son, Alex, into their homes and lives. They were much more than sources of information. Masha Lipman, a superb translator and reporter, worked tirelessly for *The Washington Post* and on behalf of this book. I was lucky to count her as a friend and to have her wise counsel, her sharp eye for the fatuous and the absurd. Masha's husband, Seriozha Ivanov, is a friend and guide through the academic and historical forests. The other members of the "gang of four," Masha Volkenshtein and Igor Primakov, were good friends and teachers. Thanks also to Grisha Kosazsky and Lyola Kantor, Judith and Emmanuel Lurye, Eduard Gladkov, Misha and Flora Litvinov, and many others.

The press corps in Moscow was superb, and I want to thank some my friends among them: Frank Clines, Bill Keller and Ann Cooper, Jeff and Gretchen Trimble, Xan and Jane Smiley, Eileen O'Conner and John Bilotta, Jonathan Sanders, Laurie Hays and Fen Montaigne, Marco Politi, and, at the *Post,* Eleanor Randolph, Gary Lee, Fred Hiatt, and Margaret Shapiro. My main running mate and bureau chief at the *Post,* Michael Dobbs, was indispensable, both as a friend and as a colleague. Lisa Dobbs showed my own family constant friendship just as surely as she showed Moscow the meaning of free enterprise.

A number of scholars, both in the United States and in Russia, were of great help, among them Richard Pipes, Stephen Cohen, Arseny Roginsky, Leonid Batkin, and Natalya Ivanova.

At *The Washington Post,* a raft of editors supported my work in Moscow, and I am especially grateful to Michael Getler, David Ignatius, and the wizard, Jeffrey Frank, for their advice and editing as the copy flowed in. Thanks also to Ben Bradlee, Leonard Downie, Robert Kaiser, Don Graham, and Katharine Graham for giving me one of the best jobs in journalism the century could offer.

At my new home, *The New Yorker,* I am grateful first to Robert Gottlieb and Pat Crow for publishing an early piece of the book, and then to Tina Brown and Rick Hertzberg for making the arrangement permanent.

Barbara Epstein invited me to write for *The New York Review of Books* while I was still in Moscow and has showered me with kindness, superb editing, and Federal Express packages ever since. Barbara, Jeff Frank, Masha Lipman, and Seriozha Ivanov read the manuscript with great care and insight.

I am also grateful to the Council on Foreign Relations for making me its Edward R. Murrow Fellow in 1991–92, which gave me the time, the room, and the quiet in which to work.

At Random House, Jason Epstein's intelligence, wit, and skillet are all matchless. My agent, Kathy Robbins, is the source of endless patience and wise counsel. Early on, Linda Healey also gave me some very good editorial advice.

I received great support from family and friends before, during, and after my time in Moscow. My parents gave me the go-ahead to move to the Motherland. I am in awe of their strength and forever grateful for their unquestioning love and support. My brother, Richard, and sister-in-law, Lisa Fernandez, as well as my grandmother, Miriam Seigel, were just as helpful, and to them much thanks and love. Esther's parents, Miriam and Hyman Fein, let me take their daughter off to a terrifying place for them, and then they visited us there. They are a joy. Steve Fisher helped in the mysteries of the computer.

Eric Lewis and Elise Hoffmann, Richard Brody and Maja Nikolic, Marc Fisher and Jody Goodman, Michael Specter and Alessandra Stanley, and Henry Allen were all friends in deed, even at such a great distance.

My son Alexander Benjamin, named for great-grandfathers born in the last empire, was a little late getting to the show—he was born smack in the middle of the Twenty-eighth (and final) Congress of the Communist Party—but when he did arrive, he took Moscow by storm. Our second son, Noah Samuel, came later still. I only hope that one day both Alex and Noah will visit a democratic and prosperous Russia.

My greatest thanks are to Esther, who ran off to Russia with me—a strange and wonderful way to begin a marriage. In Moscow, she wrote a string of elegant features and news stories for *The New York Times,* visited some of the stranger corners of the empire, and delighted the competition all the while. Back in New York, she was the manuscript's keenest editor, and its author's sustenance. This book is not only for Esther, it is also very much hers.

NOTES ON SOURCES

My main source of information for this book was personal interviews. Because many of those interviewed speak for themselves in the text, I have not noted them formally here. I also picked over many of my own dispatches in *The Washington Post* from January 1988 to January 1992, as well as longer pieces in *The New York Review of Books* and *The New Yorker*.

While in Moscow, I also gained a great deal from reading, among others, Bill Keller, Francis X. Clines, Esther B. Fein, and Serge Schmemann in *The New York Times* and, especially, Michael Dobbs in the *Post*. Dobbs's reports on Chernobyl, the assault on Lithuania in January 1991, and the August coup, including the battle for control of *Izvestia*, were particularly useful. The following notes mention some supplementary material and sources not self-evident from the text.

PART I

1. THE FOREST COUP

Allen Paul's book on the Katyn massacre is the best so far in English. As the archives open there has been more material than ever coming from Moscow, including evidence that the Gorbachev leadership knew far more than it ever let on to the Polish government. Interviews with Colonel Aleksandr Tretetsky, Yuri Afanasyev, Yegor Ligachev, and Aleksandr Yakovlev were important, as was Tretetsky's interview with the executioner Vladimir Tokaryev, first published in the *Observer*, October 6, 1991, p. 1.

2. A STALINIST CHILDHOOD

Natalya Gorbanevskaya's account of the Red Square demonstration and Pavel Litvinov's speeches, essays, and letters were helpful, but the Litvinov family members were the key sources here.

3. TO BE PRESERVED, FOREVER

Yerofeyev's *Moskva-Petushki,* available in English as *Moscow Circles* (with the author's name transliterated Benedikt Erofeev), is a seminal novel of the Brezhnev, or stagnation, era. The Brodsky trial transcript is available in a number of dissident anthologies. Brodsky's letter to Brezhnev is quoted in *The Washington Post,* July 25, 1972. I interviewed Yurasov several times, and he also gave frequent interviews in the Soviet press. The best article on him in Russian is Viktoriya Chalikova's essay "Arkhivni Yunosha" ("The Young Archivist") in the St. Petersburg–based journal *Neva,* No. 10, 1988.

4. THE RETURN OF HISTORY

Gorbachev's history speech of November 2, 1987, was published in *Pravda, Izvestia,* etc., in Russian on November 3, 1987, and in *The New York Times* the next day in English. Both *The Short Course* and *The History of the Communist Party of the Soviet Union* are available in English editions. Yeltsin's *Against the Grain* contains a colorful version of the negotiations over the language of Gorbachev's speech, and his retelling agrees for the most part with accounts given me by Yakovlev, Ligachev, and others.

5. WIDOWS OF REVOLUTION

Stephen F. Cohen's *Bukharin and the Bolshevik Revolution* is still the definitive work on Bukharin. However, there are more negative assessments in Adam Ulam's *The Bolsheviks* and Nekrich and Heller's *Utopia in Power.* Anna Larina Bukharina's memoir will be available in an English edition from Norton in 1993.

6. NINOTCHKA

I've tried to piece together the Nina Andreyeva intrigue through interviews with the main players in the drama, including Nina Andreyeva, Mikhail Shatrov, Yegor Yakovlev, Aleksandr Yakovlev, Viktor Afanasyev, Yevgeny Yevtushenko, Aleksandr Gelman, Len Karpinsky, and Yegor Ligachev. Her article originally appeared in *Sovetskaya Rossiya,* March 13, 1988. Among the more useful articles on the affair are Robert Kaiser's "Red Intrigue: How Gorbachev Outfoxed His Kremlin Rivals" in *The Washington Post,* June 12, 1988; Dev Muraka's "The Foes of Perestroika Sound Off" in *The Nation,* May 21, 1988; and Vladimir Denisov's " 'Krestni Otets' Nini Andreyevoi" ("The Godfather of Nina Andreyeva") in *Rodina,* No. 1, 1991. Ligachev's description of the Andreyeva affair in his memoir is an attempt to paint himself as a victim of an intrigue by Yakovlev and Gorbachev. The BBC documentary series *The Second Russian Revolution* was an excellent source of information on the Andreyeva affair, as well as on other secret deliberations of the Communist Party, including the Politburo's control over information surrounding the Chernobyl nuclear disaster.

7. THE DOCTORS' PLOT AND BEYOND

The Rapoport family was the key source here, as well as Yakov and Natalya Rapoport's memoirs. There are good descriptions of the Doctors' Plot in Salo Baron's history of the Jews in Russia as well as in the Ulam and Volkogonov Stalin biographies and Khrushchev's memoirs.

8. MEMORIAL

I interviewed many of the original and eventual leaders of Memorial. Arseny Roginsky, Yuri Afanasyev, Andrei Sakharov, Leonid Batkin, Nikita Okhotin, and Lev Ponomarev were especially helpful. Roy Medvedev in Moscow and Zhores Medvedev in London both spent many hours describing their early years.

9. WRITTEN ON THE WATER

Aleksandr Milchakov's articles in *Vechernaya Moskva* describe in great detail his search for the remains of gulag victims in Moscow and elsewhere. Among the more useful articles appeared in that paper on June 9, 1990, July 12, 1990, September 28, 1990, October 20, 1990, April 14, 1990, May 17, 1991, August 10, 1990.

PART II

10. MASQUERADE

Jay Leyda's classic *Kino* is by far the best history of the Soviet cinema. So far the literature on Soviet television is relatively thin. Ellen Mickiewicz's book contains useful information on *Vremya* and other early glasnost programs but was a bit early to include the real wave of liberation. Leonid Parfyonov, Eduard Sagalayev, Bella Kurkova, Igor Kirillov, and many other executives and journalists at the main glasnost-era programs were the best sources of information.

Mikhail Gorbachev, understandably, still awaits his biographer, a wait that could take years while scholars gather all the necessary documents, interviews, and material accumulated over his incredible career as the Soviet Union's last leader. In the meantime, he is at work on what his aides say is a serious memoir. So far the memoirs that have appeared, including Gorbachev's *The August Coup,* are thin justifications of policy written in the heat of the political moment. Zhores Medvedev and Michel Tatu wrote early, useful biographies, and journalists such as Christian Schmidt-Haeur, Gerd Ruge, Dusko Doder and Louise Branson, Robert Kaiser and Angus Roxburgh have gathered useful information in their various books. Gail Sheehy's biography contains some interesting information from her own trips to the Stavropol region, but the book is too weighted down by inaccuracies and misunderstandings of Soviet history and politics. Raisa Gorbacheva's memoir, *I Hope,* is sentimental and almost entirely useless, but it does contain some interesting letters and other glances at life in Stavropol and in the Kremlin. Ligachev and Yeltsin, while ideological opposites, have written the most engaging (if not always truthful) memoirs, while Shevardnadze and Yakovlev have, so far, been hesitant and dry.

11. THE DOUBLE THINKERS

Sakharov's two volumes of memoirs are remarkable, especially the first half of the first volume, in which Andrei Dmitriyevich describes his transformation from a man of science and the system into a dissident.

Len Karpinsky described his strange career to me in a series of interviews. I am also grateful to Stephen Cohen for bringing Karpinsky to the attention of the West by publishing the essay "Words Are Also Deeds" in *An End to Silence* and then an interview with Karpinsky in a book edited by Cohen and Katrina vanden Heuvel, *Voices of Glasnost.*

I interviewed many of the most prominent of the men and women of the Gorbachev generation, including Fyodor Burlatsky, Andrei Sakharov, Lev Timofeyev, Giorgi Shakhnazarov, Vitaly Korotich, Tatyana Zaslavskaya, Abel Aganbegyan, Oleg Bogomolov, Nikolai Shmelyov, Aleksandr Bovin, Mikhail Ulyanov, Giorgi Arbatov, Yegor Yakovlev, Yuri Karyakin, Andrei Bitov, and Sergei Khrushchev.

12. PARTY MEN

Leonard Schapiro's *The Communist Party of the Soviet Union* remains the classic history of the Party, but I also found useful Michael Voslensky's *Nomenklatura,* Konstantin Simis's *USSR: The Corrupt Society,* and, especially, Arkady Vaksberg's *The Soviet Mafia.* Geidar Aliyev, Dinmukhamed Kunayev, Arkady Vaksberg, Lev Timofeyev, Andrei Fyodorov, Yuri Shchekochikin, Dmitri Likhanov, Andrei Karaulov, Arkady Volsky, Telman Gdlyan, Boris Yeltsin, and Yegor Ligachev all provided me with their own versions of what was the Communist Party.

13. POOR FOLK

All the material, except where noted in the text, is based on reporting trips to Turkmenia, the Vologda region of northern Russia, the steel town of Magnitogorsk in the Urals, and the Moscow netherworld. I am grateful to Murray Feshbach at Georgetown University for his work on the question of poverty. Stephen Kotkin's book on Magnitogorsk and John Scott's *Behind the Urals* are complementary portraits of that city and industrialization. Robert Conquest's *The Harvest of Sorrow* is the key—even heroic—work on collectivization. Esther B. Fein's articles on poverty in *The New York Times* (January 29 and August 14, 1989) and *Komsomolskaya Pravda*'s reports on infant mortality in Central Asia (April 25, 1990) and poverty in general (April 19, 1990) were very helpful.

14. THE REVOLUTION UNDERGROUND

Officials at the Red Proletariat machine-tools factory in my neighborhood in Moscow kindly gave me access to the election process there. I received even greater hospitality and access in western Siberia at the Yagunovsko mines and in other mining villages surrounding the city of Kemerovo. Anatoly Shcheglov and Anatoly Malikhin were just a couple of the miners who gave me long interviews and tours of the mining region. I had similar help from miners in Donetsk, Ukraine, in Karaganda, Kazakhstan, and on Sakhalin Island, Russia.

15. POSTCARDS FROM THE EMPIRE

Bogdan Nahaylo and Victor Swoboda's *Soviet Disunion* is a useful primer on the nationalities issue. The works by Hélène Carrère d'Encausse anticipating the ethnic crises in the Soviet Union remain invaluable.

16. THE ISLAND

Chekhov's book is available in an excellent English edition, *The Island: A Journey to Sakhalin.* Nikolai Batyukov, Anatoly Kapustin, Vitaly Guly, and Ivan Zhdakayev, a bulldozer driver and deputy in the Supreme Soviet and friend, arranged my trip to Sakhalin and were extraordinarily helpful in describing life and the political transformation on the island. I am also grateful to Bruce Grant, an anthropologist at Rice University, who spent six months working in a fishing collective farm, for his tales of Sakhalin.

17. BREAD AND CIRCUSES

Anatoly Kashpirovsky and Alan Chumak both gave me a series of interviews and I attended their healing sessions. The Byzantine scholar Sergei Ivanov provided the quotation from Agathias.

18. THE LAST GULAG

Elena Chukovskaya, Vadim Borisov, Sergei Zalygin, Natalya Solzhenitsyn, Yegor Ligachev, Aleksandr Yakovlev, Lev Timofeyev, Tatyana Tolstaya, and Viktor Yerofeyev helped me piece together the Solzhenitsyn drama. John Dunlop's *Radio Liberty* report (#407, 1989) was also helpful.

Solzhenitsyn's article "Kak nam obustroit' Rossiya?" first appeared in *Komsomolskaya Pravda,* October 2, 1990. Michael Scammell's biography of Solzhenitsyn is a superb work, and Charles Truehart provides some additional details on Solzhenitsyn's current working life in *The Washington Post,* November 24, 1987.

Before going to Perm-35, I interviewed a number of former political prisoners, including Bogdan Horyn, Vyacheslav Chernovil, Sergei Kovalev, Levon Ter-Petrossian, Sergei Grigoryants, and Lev Timofeyev. Natan Shcharansky's memoir *Fear No Evil* has a fine description of the Perm camps. The researchers at

Helsinki Watch also provided useful details on political prisoners and Perm-35. All the prisoners with whom I spoke at Perm were released in the wake of the fall of the August coup.

PART III

19. "TOMORROW THERE WILL BE A BATTLE"

After his return from Gorky, Sakharov was not quite as available to journalists as he had been in the 1970s. I had one formal interview with him at his apartment and numerous short interviews with him at meetings of Memorial, Moscow Tribune, the Congress of People's Deputies, and other public venues. There are helpful glimpses of Sakharov in many books by dissidents and Western journalists, but Sakharov's own books are the best source: *Memoirs, Moscow and Beyond, Alarm and Hope, My Country and the World, Sakharov Speaks,* and *Reflections on Progress, Peaceful Coexistence, and Intellectual Freedom.*

Yelena Bonner's *Mothers and Daughters* and, especially, *Alone Together* are extremely moving accounts of her life.

Of all the tributes to Sakharov published after his death, the best was a special edition of *Moscow News,* December 17, 1989.

20. LOST ILLUSIONS

Aleksandr Yakovlev's books include *Predisloviye. Obval. Poslesloviye.* ("Preface. Collapse. Afterword."), *Muki Prochiteniya Bitiya* ("The Pain of Perceiving Life"), and *On the Edge of an Abyss: From Truman to Reagan.* The two recent books in Russian include the major speeches and an especially valuable interview first printed in *Komsomolskaya Pravda,* June 5, 1990. Yakovlev's article "Protiv antiistorizma" ("Against Anti-historicism") appeared in *Literaturnaya Gazeta,* October 15, 1972.

My own interviews for this chapter that were the most helpful were with Yakovlev, Vitaly Korotich, Yegor Ligachev, Stanislav Shatalin, Nikolai Petrakov, Arkady Volsky, Eduard Shevardnadze, Anatoly Sobchak, Giorgi Shakhnazarov, Sergei Grigoriyev, Fyodor Burlatsky, Vyacheslav Shostokovsky, and Yuri Afanasyev.

Bill Keller's profile in *The New York Times Magazine,* February 19, 1989, was also helpful.

21. THE OCTOBER REVOLUTION

Ilya Zaslavski gave me free run of the October District, and I was able to sit in on meetings and private planning sessions as well as conduct interviews with his allies and enemies. The mayor of Moscow, Gavriil Popov, was also helpful with an interview on the difficulties of building a municipal government.

Alex Kahn helped guide me through the world of the trade mafia in Leningrad and was able to arrange my meeting with "the Charity Society." I also had useful meetings with young businessmen, legitimate and not, in the Baltic states, Tbilisi, Yerevan, Baku, Leningrad, Perm, and Magnitogorsk.

22. MAY DAY! MAY DAY!

Gavriil Popov, Aleksandr Yakovlev, Yegor Ligachev, and numerous demonstrators gave me their versions of what happened on May Day 1990. I was also able to read the Politburo's anxious analysis of the event in the Party archives during my trip to Moscow in September 1992. Masha Lipman, Masha Volkenshtein, Seriozha Ivanov, Igor Primakov, Alex Kahn, and Kolya Vasyn were especially helpful on the theme of generations.

23. THE MINISTRY OF LOVE

I am grateful to Jeff Trimble of *U.S. News & World Report* for his help on many subjects, and he was especially insightful about the KGB.

24. BLACK SEPTEMBER

Members of Aleksandr Men's family as well as his parishioners were helpful in providing me with interviews and copies of his lectures, sermons, and writings. Andrei Yeryemin, Men's assistant and follower, was especially generous with his time, as were Pavel Men, Gleb Yakunin, Aleksandr Ogorodnikov, Lev Timofeyev, Andrei Bessmertni, Aleksandr Minkin, Maria Tepnina, and Tatyana Sagalayeva. Also useful were *Twentieth Century and Peace,* No. 1, 1991; Andrei Eremin's "In Memory of Aleksandr Men," *Znamya,* No. 9, 1991; Tamara Zhirmunskaya in *Smena,* No. 11, March 1991; and Mikhail Aksyonov-Myerson in *Russkaya Misl,* September 21, 1990.

25. THE TOWER

In reporting on the crackdown and eventual independence in the Baltic states, I am grateful to the staff of the newspaper *Diena* in Riga and a range of politicians and activists in Vilnius, including Vytautas Landsbergis, Arvydas Juozaitis, Romouldas Ozolas, Kazimiera Prunskiene, Algimantis Cekoulis, Justas Paleskis, Vladislav Shved, and Algirdas Brazauskas.

Vitaly Tretyakov, the editor of *Nezavisimaya Gazeta,* gave me free run of the editorial offices there, and the staff, especially Sergei Parkhomenko, Pavel Felgenhauer, and Tatyana Malkina, described the short and brilliant history of the paper.

In Moscow, both sides of the crackdown were available for interviews, if not always completely forthcoming. Eduard Shevardnadze, Stanislav Shatalin, Grigori Yavlinsky, Vitaly Korotich, Ales Adamovich, Aleksandr Yakovlev, Len Karpinsky, Andrei Grachev, and Giorgi Shakhnazarov—all, in their own way, defenders of reform—talked with me about the tense months leading up to the coup. Nikolai Petrushenko, Viktor Alksnis, Aleksandr Nevzorov, Sergei Akhromeyev, Aleksandr Prokhanov, and other conservatives were, strangely enough, just as helpful.

26. THE GENERAL LINE

Volkogonov's main work so far is *Stalin: Triumph and Tragedy*. The Trotsky biography is available only in Russian; Volkogonov is also at work on a biography of Lenin and a memoir.

Walter Laqueur's *Stalin: The Glasnost Revelations* is a helpful compendium of the recent discoveries about Stalin that have supplemented the standard biographies by Robert Tucker, Adam Ulam, Isaac Deutscher, Roy Medvedev, and Boris Souveraine.

The transcript of the meeting denouncing Volkogonov was published in *Nezavisimaya Gazeta,* June 18, 1991. Nina Tumarkin's "The Great Patriotic War and Myth and Memory," *Atlantic,* June 1991, describes the role of the war as a legitimizing myth in the minds of the older generation.

27. CITIZENS

In Rostov, General Matvei Shaposhnikov described for me his experience at Novocherkassk. Olga Nikitina's "Novocherkassk: Chronicle of a Tragedy," *Don,* Nos. 8 and 9, 1990, is an excellent oral history of the massacre. At the Communist Party archives, I was able to read KGB documents on the Novocherkassk affair made available only in 1992. Solzhenitsyn's account in the third volume of *The Gulag Archipelago* has stood up well despite the appearance of new materials.

Robert Conquest's *Kolyma: The Arctic Death Camps* is the best historical compendium so far on the camps of the Soviet far east, but I was told that a number of scholars are now beginning work in the Kolyma region on more complete histories.

PART IV

For this account of the August coup, I depended largely on my own experience and the reports from the *Post* by Fred Hiatt, Margaret Shapiro, and, especially, Michael Dobbs.

I am also grateful for having had the chance to read the reports by *The New York Times, The Wall Street Journal, The Boston Globe,* the *Los Angeles Times, Nezavisimaya Gazeta, Komsomolskaya Pravda, Literaturnaya Gazeta, Izvestia, Argumenti i Fakti, Ogonyok,* and *Stolitsa.* A useful compendium of press reports from Russia and the other republics on the coup is *Korichnyevii Putsch Krasnikh*

Avgust '91, published in 1991 by Tekst. The Russian, Moscow, and "main" television channels also carried helpful interviews, especially in the three or four days after the fall of the coup.

Eventually, the best history of the August coup will come out of the dozens of volumes of testimony assembled by the Russian prosecutors. As I write, a year and a half after the coup, there has been no trial though one is scheduled for Spring 1993. The testimony and "inside" workings of the coup in my account come from the prosecutors' attempt to select the highlights from the still-closed investigation; in most cases, these details checked out with other published reports in the Western and Russian press.

Stuart Loory and Ann Imse's CNN album of photographs and reports, *Seven Days That Shook the World,* is based largely on the network's excellent coverage. The BBC series *The Second Russian Revolution* also has excellent interviews with Gorbachev, Yeltsin, and other key players.

Sobchak, Yakovlev, Gorbachev, Shevardnadze, Ryzhkov, and Bakatin were useful in their books, since each had his own angle of vision in this Roshomon tale.

Karaulov's interviews with Yanayev, Lukyanov, and other players in the coup for *Nezavisimaya Gazeta* will soon be published as part of a book. But perhaps the most revealing interview was Yuri Shchekochikin's talk in the October 2, 1991, issue of *Literaturnaya Gazeta* with Pyotr Korotkevich, a top missile scientist in the military industry, who described Baklanov as a conspirator of dark genius.

P A R T   V

THE TRIAL OF THE OLD REGIME

This section came out of an article on the trial of the Communist Party I wrote for *The New Yorker*'s November 30, 1991, issue and an article on Gorbachev's trip across America for *Vanity Fair*'s August 1991 issue.

I N T E R V I E W S

In one way or another, hundreds of interviews, long and short, helped me with this book. The "ordinary people" I spoke with for this book are usually cited by name in the text only. What follows is a list of those interviews with public or semipublic figures who were especially helpful. The list seems chockablock with "legislators," "historians," "activists," and, God help us, "journalists." But such were the times. In Moscow, Leningrad, and the Baltic states, especially, these people were at the center of public life. There were times when the Congress of

People's Deputies seemed, in part, like a joint convention of political hacks and the faculty club. That is changing now as a class of professional politicians evolves. Rather than list just the names, I have given some short indication of who these people were during the perestroika period and the immediate aftermath of the failed August coup of 1991. My thanks to all of them.

Tengiz Abuladze (filmmaker)
Ales Adamovich (writer, legislator)
Viktor Afanasyev (editor, *Pravda*)
Yuri Afanasyev (historian, legislator)
Abel Aganbegyan (economist, adviser to Gorbachev)
Marshal Sergei Akhromeyev (military adviser to Gorbachev)
Vasily Aksyonov (novelist)
Yuz Aleshkovsky (novelist)
Abdulfaz Aliyev (Uzbek nationalist)
Geidar Aliyev (former Politburo member)
Colonel Viktor Alksnis (leader of Soyuz faction)
Anatoly Anayev (editor, *Oktyabr*)
Nina Andreyeva (neo-Stalinist, chemistry teacher)
Anton Antonov-Ovsenko (historian)
Giorgi Arbatov (government adviser, Americanist)
Tatyana Baeva (participant Red Square demonstration, 1968)
Grigori Baklanov (editor, *Znamya*)
Dmitri Barshevsky (filmmaker)
Leonid Batkin (historian, legislator)
Zoya Belayeva (television journalist)
Valentin Berezhkov (Stalin's translator)
Andrei Bessmertni (Christian activist)
Andrei Bitov (novelist)
Mikhail Bocharov (economic adviser to Yeltsin, legislator)
Oleg Bogomolov (sociologist, legislator)
Larisa Bogoraz (human rights activist)
Aleksei Boiko (legislator)
Yuri Boldyrev (legislator)
Vadim Borisov (subeditor, *Novy Mir*)
Artyom Borovik (journalist, *Ogonyok, Top Secret*)
Aleksandr Bovin (commentator, *Izvestia*)
Algirdas Brazauskas (former Lithuanian Party chief)
Joseph Brodsky (poet)
Gennadi Burbulis (adviser to Yeltsin)
Aleksandr Burdansky (Stalin's grandson)
Fyodor Burlatsky (journalist, playwright)
Shaun Burns (U.S. diplomat)
Algimantis Cekoulis (Lithuanian journalist, legislator)

Giorgi Chanturia (Georgian nationalist)
Yelena Chekalova (student, Memorial activist)
Yuri Chernichenko (writer, agriculture expert)
Vyacheslav Chernovil (former political prisoner, mayor of Lvov)
Micah Chlenov (Jewish activist)
Lydia Chukovskaya (writer, human rights activist)
Yelena Chukovskaya (writer, human rights activist)
Alan Chumak (faith healer)
Ivan Drach (leader of Rukh, Ukrainian activist)
Major Nikolai Dronin (military investigator)
Yevgeny Dzugashvili (Stalin's grandson)
Nikolai Efimov (former editor, *Izvestia*)
Yakov Ettinger (Memorial leader)
Mikhail Fedotov (lawyer)
Pavel Felgenhauer (journalist, *Nezavisimaya Gazeta*)
Vladimir Fromin (editor, *Komsomolskaya Pravda*)
Thomas Gamkhrelidze (literary scholar, Georgia)
Zviad Gamsakhurdia (former Georgian president)
Mikhail Gefter (historian)
Aleksandr Gelman (playwright, former member Central Committee)
Boris Gidaspov (former Leningrad Party chief)
Lev Ginzburg (music critic)
Lydia Ginzburg (literary critic)
Eduard Gladkov (photographer)
Vitaly Goldansky (physicist)
Vitaly Goldovitch (prisoner, Perm-35)
Andrei Golitsyn (monarchist)
Mikhail Gorbachev (president, general secretary of CPSU)
Anatoly Gorbunovs (Latvian government leader)
Andrei Grachev (former Gorbachev aide)
Daniil Granin (novelist)
Sergei Grigoriyev (former Gorbachev aide)
Sergei Grigoryants (journalist, activist)
Boris Grushin (sociologist)
Igor Gryazin (Estonian activist, legislator)
Nikolai Gubenko (actor, director, former minister of culture)
Vitaly Guly (journalist, Sakhalin Island)
Father Ivan Hel (priest, Lvov)
John Hewko (American-Ukrainian, government legal adviser)
Bogdan Horyn (former political prisoner, Ukrainian legislator)
Mikhail Horyn (former political prisoner, Ukrainian legislator)
Edward Lee Howard (former CIA; alleged defector to KGB)
Sergei Ivanov (police official, Interior Ministry)
Sergei Ivanov (historian)

Natalya Ivanova (literary critic)
Dainas Ivans (Latvian nationalist and leader)
Vladimir Ivashko (deputy general secretary, CPSU)
Arvydas Juozaitis (Lithuanian legislator)
Janis Jurkens (Latvian activist and foreign minister)
Genrikh Joffe (historian)
Nadezhda Joffe (camp survivor)
Boris Kagarlitsky (Moscow Popular Front)
Alex Kahn (music critic)
Sandra Kalniete (Latvian government leader)
Oleg Kalugin (former KGB general)
Anatoly Kapustin (legislator, Sakhalin Island)
Andrei Karaulov (journalist, *Nezavisimaya Gazeta*)
Len Karpinsky (journalist, *Moscow News*)
Yuri Karyakin (literary historian, legislator)
Anatoly Kashpirovsky (faith healer)
Tikhon Khrennikov (head of composers' union)
Igor Kirillov (former news anchor, *Vremya*)
Yuri Kiselyov (activist for the disabled)
Vladimir Klushin (husband of Nina Andreyeva)
Rudolf Kolchanov (Gorbachev college friend; journalist, *Trud*)
Igor Kon (sociologist; sexologist)
Kira Korniyenkova (neo-Stalinist)
Vitaly Korotich (journalist, *Ogonyok;* poet)
Andrei Kortunov (academic, foreign policy expert)
Sergei Kovalev (human rights activist, legislator)
Andrei Kozyrev (Russian foreign minister)
Dmitri Krupnikov (Latvian nationalist)
Gregory Krupnikov (Latvian nationalist)
Mikhail Kubrin (October District politician)
Yuri Kukushkin (historian, Moscow State University)
Dinmukhamed Kunayev (Communist Party chief, Kazakhstan)
Stanislav Kunayev (editor, *Nash Sovremenik*)
Bella Kurkova (television journalist, legislator)
Vytautas Landsbergis (Lithuanian president)
Anna Larina (widow of Nikolai Bukharin)
Yuri Laryonov (October District politician)
Mikhail Leontyev (journalist, *Nezavisimaya Gazeta*)
Yuri Levada (sociologist, pollster; Gorbachev college friend)
Yegor Ligachev (former Politburo member)
Dmitri Likhachev (literary scholar; camp survivor, legislator)
Dmitri Likhanov (journalist, *Ogonyok, Top Secret*)
Masha Lipman (translator)
Endel Lippmaa (Estonian nationalist)

Vladislav Listyev (television journalist, game-show host)
Mikhail Litvinov (Pavel Litvinov's father)
Pavel Litvinov (human rights activist, teacher)
Flora Litvinova (Pavel Litvinov's mother)
Judith Lurye (Jewish activist, now in Israel)
Vladimir Lysenko (Russian legislator)
Aleksandr Lyubimov (television journalist)
Igor Malashenko (Central Committee staff, adviser to Gorbachev)
Anatoly Malikhin (coal miner, strike leader)
Tatyana Malkina (journalist, *Nezavisimaya Gazeta*)
Sergei Matayev (journalist, Alma-Ata)
Roy Medvedev (historian, legislator)
Zhores Medvedev (biologist, historian)
Pavel Men (brother of Father Aleksandr Men)
Lennart Meri (Estonian activist, former foreign minister)
Andrannik Migranyan (political scientist)
Aleksandr Milchakov (historian, Memorial activist)
Aleksandr Minkin (journalist)
Viktor Morozov (actor, director, Lvov)
Arkady Murashev (legislator, Moscow police chief)
Aleksandr Nevzorov (television journalist)
Olga Nikitina (journalist, Rostov)
Nodar Notadze (Georgian nationalist)
Andrei Nuikin (journalist)
Aleksandr Ogorodnikov (Christian activist)
Nikita Okhotin (Memorial activist)
Lieutenant Colonel Nikolai Osin (commandant, Perm-35 camp)
Anya Ostapchuk (journalist)
Romouldas Ozolas (legislator, Lithuania)
Justas Paleckis (legislator, Lithuania)
Leonid Parfyonov (television journalist)
Sergei Parkhomenko (journalist, *Nezavisimaya Gazeta*)
Dmitro Pavlichko (legislator, Ukraine)
Janis Peters (poet, legislator, Latvia)
Nikolai Petrakov (economist, adviser to Gorbachev)
Colonel Nikolai Petrushenko (Soyuz faction leader)
Aleksandr Podrabinek (human rights activist, editor, *Express-Khronika*)
Ivan Polozkov (chairman, Russian Communist Party)
Mikhail Poltaranin (adviser to Yeltsin)
Grigori Pomerants (philosopher)
Lev Ponomarev (Memorial activist, legislator)
Gavriil Popov (economist, mayor of Moscow)
Igor Primakov (seismologist)
Yevgeny Primakov (adviser to Gorbachev)

Aleksandr Prokhanov (editor, *Dyen*)
Kazimiera Prunskiene (prime minister of Lithuania)
Andres Raid (television journalist, Estonia)
Yakov Rapoport (survivor of the Doctors' Plot)
Natalya Rapoport (biologist)
Vika Rapoport (set designer, now in Israel)
Lev Razgon (camp survivor, writer, Memorial activist)
Oleg Rumyantsyev (author of Russian constitution, legislator)
Anatoly Rybakov (novelist)
Yuri Rybakov (writer, Russian nationalist)
Nikolai Ryzhkov (Politburo member, prime minister)
Yuri Ryzhov (legislator, Russian ambassador to France)
Eduard Sagalayev (television executive)
Roald Sagdeyev (physicist)
Andrei Sakharov (physicist, human rights campaigner)
Mohammad Sali (Uzbek activist)
Yuri Samodurov (Memorial activist)
Vasily Selyunin (economist)
Julian Semyonov (detective writer, editor)
Igor Shafarevich (mathematician, Russian nationalist)
Giorgi Shakhnazarov (adviser to Gorbachev)
Tofik Shakhverdiyev (filmmaker)
General Matvei Shaposhnikov (retired army general)
Stanislav Shatalin (economist, adviser to Gorbachev)
Mikhail Shatrov (playwright)
Anatoly Shcheglov (miner)
Yuri Shchekochikin (journalist, *Literaturnaya Gazeta*)
Yuri Shcherbak (environmentalist, doctor, legislator, Ukraine)
Ivan Shekhovtsov (neo-Stalinist, lawyer)
Eldar Shengalaya (filmmaker, legislator, Georgia)
Eduard Shevardnadze (former Soviet foreign minister)
Nikolai Shishlin (Central Committe staff)
Nikolai Shmelyov (novelist, economist)
Vyacheslav Shostokovsky (former rector, Higher Party School)
Vladislav Shved (hard-liner, Lithuanian Communist Party)
Yuri Sigov (journalist, *Argumenti i Fakti*)
Olga Sliozberg-Adamova (camp survivor)
Anatoly Sobchak (mayor of Leningrad)
Natalya Solzhenitsyn (wife of Aleksandr Isayevich)
Sergei Stankevich (legislator, deputy mayor, Moscow)
Galina Starovoitova (legislator)
Vladislav Starkov (editor, *Argumenti i Fakti*)
Olzhas Suliemenov (legislator, poet, Kazakhstan)
Boris Sulim (Magadan Party activist)

Maria Tepnina (friend of Father Aleksandr Men)
Levon Ter-Petrossian (president of Armenia)
Lev Timofeyev (former political prisoner, journalist)
Tatyana Tolstaya (short-story writer)
Nikita Tolstoi (physicist, legislator)
Yelena Tregubova (Memorial activist)
Colonel Aleksandr Tretetsky (military investigator)
Vitaly Tretyakov (editor, founder, *Nezavisimaya Gazeta*)
Artyom Troitsky (rock critic)
Aleksandr Tsipko (Central Committee staff, historian)
Mikhail Ulyanov (actor, director)
Arkady Vaksberg (journalist, *Literaturnaya Gazeta*)
Kolya Vasyn (rock and roll pioneer, Leningrad)
Trivimi Velliste (Estonian nationalist)
Akhmuhammed Vilsaparov (journalist, activist, Ashkhabad)
Masha Volkenshtein (sociologist, pollster)
Colonel General Dmitri Volkogonov (historian, adviser to Yeltsin)
Arkady Volsky (adviser to Andropov, Gorbachev; industrialist)
Ulo Vooglaid (legislator, Estonia)
Andrei Voznesensky (poet)
Aleksei Yablokov (environmentalist, adviser to Yeltsin)
Aleksandr Yakovlev (chief adviser to Gorbachev)
Vladimir Yakovlev (editor, *Commersant*)
Yegor Yakovlev (editor, *Moscow News*)
Father Gleb Yakunin (former political prisoner, legislator)
Grigori Yavlinsky (economist, adviser to Gorbachev and Yeltsin)
Boris Yeltsin (president of Russia)
Viktor Yerofeyev (novelist)
Andrei Yeryemin (former aide to Father Aleksandr Men)
Arnold Yeryomenko (human rights activist, Magadan)
Yevgeny Yevtushenko (poet, legislator)
Dmitri Yurasov (archivist, Memorial activist)
Igor Zakharov (journalist, *Nezavisimaya Gazeta*)
Sergei Zalygin (editor, *Novy Mir*)
Tatyana Zaslavskaya (sociologist)
Ilya Zaslavsky (leader of October Region, Moscow)
Ivan Zhdakayev (legislator, Sakhalin Island)
Tatyana Ziman (refusenik)
Samuel Zivs (deputy head of the Soviet Anti-Zionist Committee)

BIBLIOGRAPHY

Afanasyev, Yuri, ed. *Inogo ne dano* (There Is No Alternative). Moscow: Progress, 1988.

Arbatov, Georgi. *The System: An Insider's Life in Soviet Politics.* New York: Times Books, 1992.

Arendt, Hannah. *The Origins of Totalitarianism.* New York: Harcourt Brace Jovanovich, 1951.

Aslund, Anders. *Gorbachev's Struggle for Economic Reform.* Ithaca: Cornell University Press, 1989.

Babyonyshev, Alexander, ed. *On Sakharov.* New York: Knopf, 1982.

Bakatin, Vadim. *Izbavleniye ot KGB* (Deliverance from the KGB). Moscow: Progress, 1992.

Baron, Salo. *The Russian Jew Under Tsars and Soviets.* New York: Macmillan, 1976.

Berlin, Isaiah. *Russian Thinkers.* New York: Viking, 1978.

Beschloss, Michael, and Strobe Talbott. *At the Highest Levels.* Boston: Little, Brown, 1993.

Bialer, Seweryn. *The Soviet Paradox.* New York: Knopf, 1986.

Billington, James. *Russia Transformed: Breakthrough to Hope.* New York: Free Press, 1992.

Bonner, Yelena. *Alone Together.* New York: Knopf, 1986.

———. *Mothers and Daughters.* New York: Knopf, 1992.

Brodsky, Joseph. *Less Than One.* New York: Farrar Straus Giroux, 1986.

Brumberg, Abraham, ed. *Chronicle of a Revolution.* New York: Pantheon, 1990.

———. *In Quest of Justice.* New York: Praeger, 1970.

Bukharina, Anna Larina. *Nezabivayemoe* (Unforgettable). Moscow: Novosti, 1990.

Carrère d'Encausse, Helène. *L'empire éclate.* Paris: Flammarion, 1978.

———. *The End of the Soviet Empire.* New York: Basic Books, 1993.

Carswell, John. *The Exile: A Life of Ivy Litvinov.* London: Faber & Faber, 1983.

Chekhov, Anton. *The Island: A Journey to Sakhalin.* London: Century, 1987.

Cohen, Stephen F. *Bukharin and the Bolshevik Revolution.* New York: Knopf, 1974.

————, ed. *An End to Silence: Uncensored Opinion in the Soviet Union.* New York: W. W. Norton, 1982.

————, and Katrina vanden Heuvel. *Voices of Glasnost.* New York: W. W. Norton, 1989.

Conquest, Robert. *The Great Terror.* New York: Macmillan, 1968.

————. *The Harvest of Sorrow.* New York: Oxford University Press, 1986.

————. *Kolyma: The Arctic Death Camps.* New York: Viking, 1978.

Davies, R. W. *Soviet History in the Gorbachev Revolution.* Bloomington: Indiana University Press, 1989.

Erofeev, Benedikt. *Moscow Circles.* New York and London: Writers and Readers Cooperative.

Garton Ash, Timothy. *The Uses of Adversity.* New York: Random House, 1989.

Ginzburg, Eugenia. *Journey into the Whirlwind.* New York: Harcourt Brace Jovanovich, 1967.

————. *The Magic Lantern.* New York: Random House, 1990.

Gorbachev, Mikhail. *Perestroika.* New York: Harper & Row, 1987.

————. *The August Coup: The Truth and the Lesson.* New York: HarperCollins, 1991.

————. *Dekabr'-'91: Moya Pozitsiya* (December '91: My position). Moscow: Novosti, 1991.

Gorbachev, Raisa. *I Hope.* New York: HarperCollins, 1991.

Gorbanevskaya, Natalya. *Red Square at Noon.* New York: Penguin, 1970.

Havel, Vaclav. *Letters to Olga.* New York: Knopf, 1989.

Heller, Mikhail. *Cogs in the Wheel: The Formation of Soviet Man.* New York: Knopf, 1988.

————, and Aleksandr Nekrich. *Utopia in Power.* New York: Summit, 1986.

Hosking, Geoffrey. *The Awakening of the Soviet Union.* Cambridge, Mass.: Harvard University Press, 1990.

Kaiser, Robert. *Why Gorbachev Happened.* New York: Simon & Schuster, 1991.

Karaulov, Andrei. *Vokrug Kremlya* (Around the Kremlin). Moscow: Novosti, 1990.

Khrushchev, Nikita. *Khrushchev Remembers.* Boston: Little, Brown, 1970.

Korotich, Vitaly. *Zal Ozhidaniya* (The waiting room). New York: Liberty, 1991.

Kotkin, Stephen. *Steeltown, USSR.* Berkeley: University of California Press, 1991.

Laqueur, Walter. *The Long Road to Freedom: Russia and Glasnost.* New York: Scribner's, 1989.

————. *Stalin: The Glasnost Revelations.* New York: Scribner's, 1991.

Lewin, Moshe. *The Gorbachev Phenomenon.* Berkeley: University of California Press, 1988.

Leyda, Jay. *Kino: A History of the Russian and Soviet Film.* New York: Macmillan, 1960.

Ligachev, Yegor. *Inside Gorbachev's Kremlin.* New York: Pantheon, 1993.

———. *Izbranniye, rechi i stat'i* (Works, speeches, and articles). Moscow: Political Literature Publishers, 1989.

Likhachev, Dmitri. *Reflections on Russia.* Boulder, Colo.: Westview, 1991.

Litvinov, Pavel. *The Demonstration in Pushkin Square.* London: Harvill Press, 1969.

Mandelstam, Nadezhda. *Hope Against Hope.* New York: Atheneum, 1970.

———. *Hope Abandoned.* New York: Atheneum, 1972.

Medvedev, Grigori. *The Truth About Chernobyl.* New York: Basic Books, 1991.

Medvedev, Roy. *Let History Judge.* Rev. ed. New York: Columbia University Press, 1989.

———. *All Stalin's Men.* Garden City, N.Y.: Anchor Books, 1985.

———, and Giulietto Chiesa. *Time of Change.* New York: Pantheon, 1989.

Medvedev, Zhores. *Gorbachev.* New York: W. W. Norton, 1987.

Mickiewicz, Ellen. *Split Signals: Television and Politics in the Soviet Union.* New York: Oxford University Press, 1988.

Nahaylo, Bogdan, and Victor Swoboda. *Soviet Disunion: A History of the Nationalities Problem in the USSR.* New York: Free Press, 1990.

Nove, Alec. *Glasnost in Action: Cultural Renaissance in Russia.* Boston: Unwin Hyman, 1989.

Okhotin, Nikita, Arseny Roginsky, et al., ed. *Zven'ya* (Links). Moscow: Feniks, 1990.

Paul, Allen. *Katyn: The Untold Story of Stalin's Polish Massacre.* New York: Scribner's, 1991.

Pipes, Richard. *The Russian Revolution.* New York: Knopf, 1991.

———. *Russia Under the Old Regime.* New York: Scribner's, 1974.

Rapoport, Yakov. *Na Rubezhe Dvukh Epokh: Delo Vrachei 1953 Goda.* (On the edge of two epochs: The Doctors' Plot of 1953). Moscow: Kniga, 1988.

Reddaway, Peter, ed. *Uncensored Russia: Protest and Dissent in the Soviet Union.* New York: American Heritage Press, 1972.

Reed, John. *Ten Days That Shook the World.* London: Boni & Liveright, 1919.

Roxburgh, Angus. *The Second Russian Revolution.* London: BBC Books, 1991.

Ryzhkov, Nikolai. *Perestroika: Istoriya Predatelstv* (Perestroika: A history of betrayals). Moscow: Novosti, 1992.

Sakharov, Andrei. *Memoirs.* New York: Knopf, 1990.

Scammell, Michael. *Solzhenitsyn.* New York: W. W. Norton, 1984.

Schapiro, Leonard. *The Communist Party of the Soviet Union.* New York: Knopf, 1960.

———. *Russian Studies.* New York: Viking, 1986.

Scott, John. *Behind the Urals: An American Worker in Russia's City of Steel.* London: Martin, Secher and Wanburg, 1943.

Shalamov, Varlam. *Kolyma Tales.* New York: W. W. Norton, 1982.

Sharansky, Natan. *Fear No Evil.* New York: Random House, 1988.

Shcherbak, Yuri. *Chernobyl.* London: Macmillan, 1989.

Shenis, Zinovy. *Maxim Litvinov*. Moscow: Progress, 1990.

Shevardnadze, Eduard. *The Future Belongs to Freedom*. New York: Free Press, 1991.

Shlapentokh, Vladimir. *Soviet Intellectuals and Political Power: The Post-Stalin Era*. Princeton: Princeton University Press, 1990.

Shtepps, Konstantin. *Russian Historians and the State*. New Brunswick, N.J.: Rutgers University Press, 1962.

Simis, Konstantin. *USSR: The Corrupt Society*. New York: Simon & Schuster, 1982.

Smith, Hedrick. *The New Russians*. New York: Random House, 1990.

Sobchak, Anatoly. *For a New Russia*. New York: Free Press, 1991.

Solzhenitsyn, Aleksandr. *The Gulag Archipelago*. 3 vols. New York: Harper & Row.

Stepankov, Valentin, and Yevgeny Lisov. *Kremlyevski Zagovor* (The Kremlin Plot). Moscow: Ogonyok, 1992.

Tarasulo, Isaac, ed. *Gorbachev and Glasnost: Viewpoints from the Soviet Press*. Wilmington, Del.: SR Books, 1989.

Timofeyev, Lev, ed. *The Anti-Communist Manifesto*. Bellevue, Wash.: Free Enterprise Press, 1990.

Tsipko, Aleksandr. *Is Stalinism Really Dead?* New York: HarperCollins, 1990.

Tucker, Robert C. *Stalin in Power*. New York: W. W. Norton, 1990.

Vaksberg, Arkady. *The Soviet Mafia*. New York: St. Martin's Press, 1991.

Volkogonov, Dmitri. *Stalin: Triumph and Tragedy*. Edited and translated by Harold Shukman. New York: Grove Weidenfeld, 1991.

———. *Trotskii*. 2 vols. Moscow: Novosti, 1992.

Voslensky, Michael. *Nomenklatura*. Garden City, N.Y.: Doubleday, 1984.

Yakovlev, Aleksandr. *Muki Prochteniya Bitiya* (The pain of perceiving life). Moscow: Novosti, 1991.

———. *Predisloviye. Obval. Poslevsloviye*. (Preface. Collapse. Afterword). Moscow: Novosti, 1992.

———. *On the Edge of an Abyss: From Truman to Reagan: The Doctrines and Realities of the Nuclear Age*. Translated by Yuri Samsovov. Moscow: Progress, 1985.

Yeltsin, Boris. *Against the Grain*. New York: Summit, 1990.

Yerofeyev, Venedikt. See Erofeev, Benedikt.

Zaslavskaya, Tatyana. *The Second Socialist Revolution*. Bloomington: Indiana University Press, 1990.

INDEX